Paisley

Paisley

FROM DEMAGOGUE
TO DEMOCRAT?

ED MOLONEY

POOLBEG

Published 2008
by Poolbeg Press Ltd
123 Grange Hill, Baldoyle
Dublin 13, Ireland
E-mail: poolbeg@poolbeg.com
www.poolbeg.com

© Ed Moloney 2008

Incorporates material from *Paisley* (Poolbeg Press, 1986),
© Ed Moloney and Andy Pollak 1986

Copyright for typesetting, layout, design
© Poolbeg Press Ltd

1 3 5 7 9 10 8 6 4 2

A catalogue record for this book is available from the British Library.

ISBN 978-1-84223-324-5

Typeset by Patricia Hope in Sabon 10.5/14.5
Printed by Litographia Rosés, S.A., Spain

CONTENTS

PART ONE
War

PART TWO
Peace

ACKNOWLEDGEMENTS

This book is an attempt to update Ian Paisley's story and to explain its remarkable ending. Ian Paisley was there at the beginning of the Troubles – many would say he lit the first fuse – and his accession as First Minister of Northern Ireland marked the ending of the Troubles. When the original edition of this book was published in 1986, one would have been thought disordered to believe that he would end up wielding power at Stormont. But to predict that Paisley's partner in office would be Martin McGuinness, that the DUP and Sinn Féin would be the dominant forces in Northern Ireland's electoral politics and that they would all be happily sharing power together, would be to risk a diagnosis of incurable insanity.

But that is how the story has concluded and it is necessary and important to try to describe and understand how and why this, one of the most astonishing episodes in modern Irish history, happened.

It has fallen to me alone to undertake this task. My partner for the first edition, Andy Pollak, was unable to participate in this venture for reasons that neither concern nor affect this narrative but it is important to place on record his invaluable contribution to the first part of the book. I alone bear responsibility for the additional material and analysis.

In 1986 we listed all those we wished to thank then for their assistance and I do the same again. Once again Ian Paisley refused all co-operation, as did his son, Ian Paisley Junior, although Ian Senior at least had the courtesy to respond to my request. However, there was this time, as before, no shortage of DUP and Free Presbyterian Church members who happily spoke to me to share their memories and understanding of events. They must remain unnamed for their own good and safety, as must the various government sources who also gave so generously of their time and insights. I can, though, thank some who were happy to be named and they included David, now Lord, Trimble, Sir Reg Empey, Bob McCartney, Cedric Wilson, Clifford Smyth and Sydney Elliott of QUB Politics Department. Once again Yvonne Murphy and her tireless assistants in the Linenhall Library's Political Collection gave enormous help and for that they have my gratitude.

I also want to thank my editor at Poolbeg, Brian Langan, for his great assistance and, once again, my agent, Jonathan Williams, for his experience and wisdom. My wife, Joan McKiernan, deserves special mention for carrying the burden imposed by my absence from home and afterwards the long hours chained to my word processor. Her support and love sustained me through it all.

Finally, a particular word of gratitude must go to the Keenan family in Holywood, County Down and Dublin – Francis, Colette and Giselle – without whose generous hospitality this book, quite literally, could not have been written.

Ed Moloney
New York
December 2007

INTRODUCTION

If their American trip was, as one government official put it, the final act in the peace process, then this was its climactic scene. First Minister Ian Paisley and Deputy First Minister Martin McGuinness seated on either side of President George W. Bush in the White House on a bitterly cold and snowy December afternoon in Washington, one day shy of seven months since the power-sharing government in Northern Ireland had taken office.

The official reason for their trip was to drum up advance publicity for an investment conference scheduled for the following May in Belfast, but it was difficult not to see another purpose in their visit to the US capital: a mission to secure America's benediction for their partnership, to have the mantle of approval from the world's only superpower draped over their enterprise.

It must have been a strange week for the 81-year-old Ian Paisley, who brought his wife, Eileen ("Mammy") and Ian Junior with him, the Paisley dynasty on parade alongside America's finest, for all the folks back home to see. Sharp, if cynical, eyes noticed the prominence at various events accorded to Ian Junior, the family's preferred heir-apparent, and the absence of the senior Paisley's complex deputy, Peter Robinson, the professional DUP politicians' favourite to succeed him as party leader, who had been left behind in Belfast.

Their trip began in New York with a journey of homage to American capitalism's Temple Mount, the Wall Street stock exchange, and for breakfast there with business leaders. A photograph was taken showing the pair with their encircled hands jointly bringing down the ceremonial gavel on the elegant podium overlooking the usually frantic trading floor, which is used to signal the opening and closing of business. The photo, which appeared on the front page of the following morning's *Irish Times*, might have suggested to those unschooled in Wall Street's ways that they had something to do with that day's trading session – a losing one, as it turned out. But in fact the photo was staged and had been taken 90 minutes before the stock exchange opened for business.

The two men did, however, get to open another New York financial market two days later when they rang the bell to trigger trading on the smaller NASDAQ exchange, which specialises in technology stocks. But that was a much more mundane affair, although just as contrived. Staged in a Times Square TV studio in front of a camera and a studio populated only by technicians, to the untutored eye it seemed as if an audience of eager brokers stood just yards away, watching and itching for the signal to start another day of moneymaking. In fact the NASDAQ has no trading floor and deals are done via anonymous computers. DUP and IRA dissidents could be forgiven for seeing in both events a metaphor for all the political artfulness and sleight of hand that had made the two men's partnership possible.

Ian Paisley's excursion to New York and then to Washington was his first journey into Irish-America, albeit the respectable Irish-America of political power and corporate wealth which Sinn Féin had befriended in recent years and not the working-class Irish-America of the Bronx which had sustained the IRA when the war was raging. Nonetheless, Irish-America of any stripe had in the past been foreign, alien territory to Paisley, which he had shunned in preference for the more familiar surroundings of the Bible Belt in places like Greenville, South Carolina, the home of Bob Jones University, his *alma mater* in a manner of speaking or at least the institution that had awarded him an honorary doctorate.

In New York it was breakfast and a reception organised by the American-Ireland Fund, an all-Ireland charity patronised by Irish-America's power elite. Dinner that night was with Bill Flynn, the chairman *emeritus* of insurance giant Mutual of America, one of Irish-America's corporate leaders, who had eased Sinn Féin's entree to Congress and the White House in the early days of the peace process.

The first time the two men had interacted, way back in December 1994, the circumstances could not have been more different. Flynn was appearing at a session of the New Ireland Forum in Dublin and went out of his way to condemn recent remarks by Paisley alleging that Britain, the Republic and the Vatican were in league with the IRA. "This is the language of the seventeenth century and we have such voices still in the North and in that voice we heard the voice of fear and suspicion," he said, adding that Americans found such views "shocking and frightening".[1]

In Washington there were meetings with more Irish-Americans, people who for decades had been hate figures for Paisley and his DUP followers – until now. There was lunch with the unashamedly pro-Sinn Féin Friends of Ireland in Congress whose leading spokesman, Peter King, was a long-time supporter of the IRA, a personal friend of Gerry Adams and others in the IRA leadership, who had helped the organisation's American wing, Noraid, raise money to send to Ireland.[2]

It was Congressional figures not unlike King who had successfully lobbied to bar Paisley, in 1981 and again in 1983, from entering the US following his "Third Force" demonstrations in Ireland in protest at Margaret Thatcher's dialogue with Charles Haughey and later in the wake of the IRA's murder of Unionist MP the Rev Robert Bradford. At the time a State Department spokesperson had outlined the then White House view of the DUP leader: "We consider [Paisley's] rhetoric and actions were contrary to the public interest in achieving a peaceful settlement to the problems of Northern Ireland."[3]

The lunch was followed by a meeting with Senator Ted Kennedy and a session with the then Democratic presidential frontrunner, Hillary Clinton. Kennedy was one of the "Four Horsemen" – along with New York Governor Hugh Carey, Senator Daniel Moynihan and Speaker "Tip" O'Neill – who had pressed for the hated Anglo-Irish Agreement back in 1985 and had been an ally and friend first of John Hume and then Gerry Adams. Hillary Clinton's husband, Bill, Paisley had called "the Whitewater crook" when as President he had lent his weight to support the peace process by granting Adams an entry visa to America.[4] When it was suggested that Bill Clinton should travel to Ireland in the autumn of 1998 to help get the power-sharing Executive up and running, memories of the Monica Lewinsky scandal were still fresh and Paisley issued a warning: "If he [came] we'd have to lock up all the women!" As recently as 2005 he had dismissed the former President as "a fellow traveller with Sinn Féin/IRA".[5]

But in the Washington of December 2007 all this was forgotten. America's long support for Irish Nationalism, the sympathy shown by some of its citizens and politicians for the IRA, was left unrecalled and uncondemned. The Ian Paisley of yesteryear, the political ogre, dinosaur and hate-monger, the voice of the seventeenth century, had morphed into the smiling, avuncular devotee of peace and harmony, an Ian Paisley who could break bread with Bill Flynn, laugh and joke with Hillary Clinton, shake hands with Ted Kennedy, and keep a straight face when saying to

George Bush, "Thank you to the American people for all they have done for us in the past."

The only figure on his trip with whom the Ian Paisley of old had much in common was George Bush and that link, like Paisley's politics, was not the same as once it had been. In early 2000, after losing the New Hampshire primary to John McCain, Bush prepared for the contest in South Carolina with a trip to Bob Jones University, or BJU as locals call it, to show the evangelicals of that state he shared with them their political prejudices and their literal belief in the words of the Bible. BJU banned Black students in those days, was fiercely anti-Catholic and holds that Darwinism is a dangerous fraud. The visit sparked a huge controversy but it did the trick. Bush easily won the South Carolina primary, one of the dirtiest contests of the Republican presidential primary season, destroyed McCain's candidacy, and went on to capture the White House, a victory that, like his re-election in 2004, was attributed to votes from America's Christian Right, people with whom the Free Presbyterians of Ulster would have much in common. As with Paisley, fundamentalist religion played a huge part in Bush's political success.

Ian Paisley had been visiting Bob Jones University since 1964 and became a close friend, first, of Bob Jones Junior, the son and namesake of the fiercely anti-Catholic and deeply racist founder of America's premier Christian university and then, in turn, his son, Bob Jones III. Jones Junior performed the ceremony at the opening of the Martyrs' Memorial church in Belfast and Paisley's first American Free Presbyterian congregation was founded near the BJU campus in Greenville. From Bob Jones Junior, Paisley learned the tricks of telemarketing his sermons and the skill of modulating his grating Ballymena accent to better suit the preacher's pulpit. Ian Paisley still preaches at the campus during BJU's spring break and these days is sometimes joined by his son Kyle.

But BJU is not the place it once was. For the first time since its founding in 1927, BJU is not headed by a Bob Jones but by 37-year-old Stephen Jones, who became president of the university when his older brother, Bob IV, turned down the job. A mild-mannered man by all accounts who describes himself as "laid-back", he confesses to being embarrassed by some of the more extreme remarks made in the past by one or other of the Bob Joneses. "I don't want to get specific," he told one reporter, "but there were things said back then that I wouldn't say today."[6]

The ban on Black students has been lifted, Stephen Jones has admitted that past Christian hostility to homosexuals may have been wrong and BJU has applied for and received official accreditation as a university from the federal authorities, something the early Bob Joneses resisted for fear that "atheistic" outsiders would weaken its fundamentalist curriculum. And when a BJU graduate, Dwight Longenecker, stunned his family and friends in 2006 by becoming a Catholic priest, BJU spokesman Jonathan Pait declared that the university "probably wouldn't use . . . terms today" like Antichrist, to describe the Pope.[7]

In a world where even Bob Jones University can be accused of "going soft", Ian Paisley's journey from demagogue to democrat becomes a metaphor for the change that overcomes everybody and everything. Even so, Paisley's journey was special and extraordinary for the sheer distance it spanned, a journey unequalled in Irish history. For Paisley's often bewildered followers and for the rest of Irish society, one question above all others demands an answer. Why did Ian Paisley do it? Why did he put aside years of animus to all things Irish, Nationalist and Catholic to go into government with the IRA's political wing? This book is an attempt to answer that question but, having done so, one is left with the nagging thought that maybe the wrong question is being asked. Perhaps the more appropriate question is this: Was Ian Paisley possibly the only member of his flock who never really or fully believed his own gospel?

PART ONE

War

"Come out from among them and be ye separate, saith the Lord, and touch not the unclean thing."

II CORINTHIANS, CHAPTER 6, VERSE 17

CHAPTER ONE

A Separate Youth

Northern Ireland in 1926 was drawing its breath. Five years earlier, in the middle of a bloody twenty-four months which left over 400 people dead and nearly 1,800 wounded, Ireland's six north-eastern counties had been partitioned from the rest of the country. Unionist resistance in those counties had thwarted the age-old Nationalist goal of complete independence and brought into being the truncated, but still British, state of Northern Ireland. It was a state dominated by its Protestant majority. Its Catholic minority accepted it sullenly and unwillingly.

The new creation was the result of over four centuries of struggle between British and Irish, Protestants and Catholics, Unionists and Nationalists. It was the latest and most concrete manifestation of the siege mentality of the Protestant "planters" who had arrived from England and Scotland in the sixteenth and seventeenth centuries. Unionists did not emerge from the violent years surrounding its birth as a confident majority, prepared to be generous to their Nationalist fellow-citizens, but as beleaguered and obsessed with their history as ever.

They still looked back to the first great slaughter of their forefathers by the native Irish in 1641. Their celebrations of the victories against Catholicism represented by the 1689 Siege of Londonderry and the 1690 Battle of the Boyne were still the high point of the official year. Their heroes were Oliver Cromwell and King William of Orange, the seventeenth-century scourges of the Catholic Irish, and the Protestant Apprentice Boys who closed the gates of Derry to prevent the traitorous Governor Lundy from dealing with the enemy. Most recently, and potently, tens of thousands of them remembered how a decade earlier they had banded together in the manner of their ancestors into the Ulster Volunteer Force, and under Sir Edward Carson's leadership had defied an attempt by the British parliament and government to impose Home Rule on Ireland. This, rather than the establishment of Northern Ireland, they regarded as their finest hour.

Meanwhile the new state struggled into existence and its people back to some kind of normality. By the end of 1922 the violence was over. Its first prime minister, Carson's lieutenant Sir James Craig, later Lord Craigavon, lifted internment at the end of 1924. In 1925 the first and last Stormont election held under proportional representation returned twenty opposition MPs, the biggest number that parliament would ever see. Nationalist MPs dropped their boycott and started to take their seats, encouraged by a Catholic hierarchy who were worried about the Unionist regime's only attempt at non-sectarian legislation, the 1923 Education Bill.

The year 1925 also saw the securing of Unionism's new frontier. After the Boundary Commission's report was leaked, the London, Dublin and Belfast governments hastily agreed that partition would remain in place exactly as it was. The new state was protected by the draconian measures of the Special Powers Act and a formidable array of overwhelmingly Protestant security forces, including the Royal Ulster Constabulary and the part-time "B Specials" of the Ulster Special Constabulary.

Ian Richard Kyle Paisley became the youngest citizen of this new state on 6 April 1926 in a modest two-storey terraced house opposite the railway station in the little cathedral city of Armagh. He was born into a town which illustrated the Northern Ireland problem in miniature. Just over half its population was Catholic, and the Paisley house was in a largely Catholic area. Armagh's classic colonial layout meant that Protestants ran the town's commercial centre in English and Scotch Street, while its southern and western districts, in Irish Street and around their recently completed cathedral, were overwhelmingly Catholic. The countryside to the south and west was mixed but mainly Catholic, and to the north and east strongly Protestant. Seven miles north-east of the town was the Diamond, where in 1796 Catholic Defenders and Protestant Peep o'Day Boys fought a battle which resulted in the formation of the Orange Order. Over the following century this Protestant secret society, bringing together in hundreds of "lodges" men of all classes, social backgrounds and denominations, would become one of Unionism's most important weapons in the struggle against Irish Catholicism and Nationalism.

The city of Armagh's one unusual feature was that in the 1920s, before the gerrymandering designs of the Unionists were put into effect, it was run by a Catholic council.[1] The year before Paisley was born its Nationalist councillors had petitioned the Boundary Commissioners to be included in the Irish Free State, if necessary by a narrow corridor to link it to the predominantly Catholic areas of south Armagh and north Monaghan.

The experience of being surrounded by the ancient Nationalist enemy was nothing new to the child's father, James Kyle Paisley, the local Baptist pastor. Known as Kyle, his mother's family name, he was then 34. He came from a long line of staunch Orangemen from the hill country around the County Tyrone village of Sixmilecross, an area of poor land with a long history of conflict between the native Irish and the descendants of Protestant "planters" from lowland Scotland and northern England. The Paisleys and the Kyles had arrived in the townland of Brackey, just outside Sixmilecross, with the first wave of Scottish settlers in the early seventeenth century.

Members of both families had marched with the Brackey Orange lodge through the neighbouring village of Beragh in the 1830s, in defiance of a British government ban on Orange parades. An ancestor of Kyle's mother, John "Belt" Kyle, a leading member of the Brackey lodge, had died from injuries received in a violent brawl between the Orangemen and local Catholics after one such march.

In 1916, on the eve of the Easter Rising, Kyle Paisley's uncle, David, for 51 years Master of the Brackey lodge, was tipped off by the local police inspector that an attempt would be made by Republicans from nearby Carrickmore, reinforced by a force from Belfast, to seize the military barracks at Omagh. According to local loyalist legend, he rallied his old Ulster Volunteer Force unit and laid an ambush for the Republicans, successfully scaring them off.[2]

David Paisley was something of an expert at instilling fear into local Catholics, a talent his great-nephew was to inherit. When Catholic children in the area saw the big Brackey farmer approaching them along a country lane, they would take to the fields rather than risk coming face to face with such a dangerous Orangeman.

The young Kyle Paisley had himself served in Carson's Ulster Volunteer Force during the Home Rule crisis of 1912–13. It was a service which his son Ian, conscious of his own lack of experience in the violent front line of Protestant Ulster's defences, would frequently recall in order to boost his credentials as a loyalist leader. Long after his father's death he would proudly show visitors the bandolier his father carried in those days and the wooden rifle he trained with.

Kyle's father, Richard, was a farmer, shoemaker and member of the Church of Ireland. Like many Ulster members of the established church in the late nineteenth century, he was an "evangelical": meaning that, like his Presbyterian neighbours, he was suspicious of ritual and dogma and held to a simple faith in the teachings of Christ as laid down in the New Testament. So it was not totally surprising when in 1908 his son, a big quiet-spoken boy, was converted to "born again" evangelical Christianity while working behind the counter of a drapery store in Omagh. Kyle went home to the family farm at Kilcam, outside Sixmilecross, cleaned out an old barn, put seats in it and started to preach to his family and neighbours. He had found his vocation.

A short time later he took his conversion one step further when he was baptised in the River Strule outside Omagh by the Baptist pastor, a famous local character who played the fiddle and doubled as a farmer, creamery manager and postmaster. Baptists were looked upon as strange people in those days, and were sometimes socially ostracised because of their belief that only people who were re-baptised by total immersion in water could be "saved". But Kyle Paisley did not worry that he might be cutting himself off from family and friends by this new departure. He was "absolutely uncompromising" when he believed something to be right, his son boasted later, and "the more he was persecuted the more he excelled in evangelism". He became an itinerant preacher, a "fire and brimstone" hot gospeller trying to save souls in the prayer meetings held in the farm kitchens, tent missions and open-air pulpits of Protestant mid-Ulster.

In 1915 he moved to Armagh to work in a big drapery store run by a family of strict Plymouth Brethren, an evangelical sect considered ultra-Protestant even by the rigid standards of the north of Ireland. His new employers, the Lennoxes, refused to take on anyone who was not a "born again" Christian.

Here, in October 1918, he was invited to become the first pastor of Armagh's twelve-strong Baptist congregation. They held their services in a tin hut rented from a local Presbyterian minister, who had opened it as a teetotal gathering place for local drunks. Kyle Paisley was a well-liked and hard-working pastor, who did a correspondence course with the Irish Baptist College in Dublin at night while working behind the drapery counter during the day.

He soon became well-known in the countryside around Armagh for the fieriness of his preaching. On one celebrated occasion he was returning to the town after a rural mission on his bicycle when he was stopped by an IRA unit. They put him up against the hedge but let him go when they found out that he was only an evangelist. By 1923 he had succeeded in building up his tiny church's membership to 54 souls, with a Sunday morning attendance of twice or even three times that number. In August of that year he married Isabella Turnbull, a 24-year-old railway worker's daughter from Kilsyth, near Stirling in Scotland. He had met her while preaching in the neighbouring town of Lurgan, where she was working as governess to the children of a local doctor. His new wife had been brought up as a strict Bible-reading Presbyterian in a town famous for its associations with the seventeenth-century Presbyterian "Covenanters" and their struggles against successive English monarchs.

At the age of 15 she was converted to "born again" Christianity when she heard a coal-heaver preaching in a gospel hall in Edinburgh, and started going to Baptist services. She had come to Northern Ireland some years earlier following the death of her mother in an influenza epidemic in the Scottish capital. The new Mrs Paisley was as assertive and abrasive as her husband – outside the pulpit – was gentle and unassuming. At Lurgan Baptist Church she had occasionally preached the sermon, almost unheard-of behaviour for a woman at that time.

She held strong views on everything from the leading role a pastor's wife should play to the unseemly behaviour and dress of the younger generation. "Ian got most of his fire and fury from Scotland", someone who knew her in Lurgan once remarked.

In 1924, while the Paisleys were living just outside Armagh in the village of Killylea, their first son was born, and was named Harold Spurgeon after the famous nineteenth-century English Baptist preacher. Shortly afterwards they moved from the Killylea house, noted for the huge Biblical text painted on its roof for the enlightenment of passing train passengers, back into Armagh. A member of the Armagh Baptist congregation had donated to the church the redbrick house opposite the station to be used as a residence for its pastor. It was here that the Paisleys' second son first saw the light of day, half a mile away from the splendid new seat of the Irish Catholic Church he was to come to hate with such venom.

◄○►

But the new addition to the family was to know little of Ireland's ancient religious capital, the place where St Patrick had built his first cathedral. For in May 1928, when he was two years old, his father answered a "call" from the considerably larger Baptist congregation at Hill Street in Ballymena, County Antrim. For the next five years Ian and Harold lived and played in the pastor's spacious house and garden which adjoined the rear of the church, while their father ministered to the spiritual needs of his new 200-strong congregation.

Ballymena in the 1920s was a staunchly Presbyterian town, proud of the puritan traditions it had inherited from its Scots settler founders. In the late eighteenth century it had briefly been a centre of Presbyterian dissent and even rebellion against the British and their established church. It boasted five Presbyterian churches, including one that had celebrated its 300th anniversary the year before the Paisleys arrived. It had two reputations, both traceable to its founders: its tight-fisted attitude to money and its extremely strait-laced views on everything else.

Its more devout citizens viewed most of the pastimes and styles of the contemporary Western world as sinful. Their list of vices was endless: smoking, drinking and gambling, of course, but also all forms of dancing, from the waltz to the Charleston. Girls who wore lipstick, make-up and their hair short in the "bobbed" fashion of the day were regarded as the next worst thing to prostitutes.

Going to the cinema, even when, as in Ballymena, films were shown in the local Protestant hall, was frowned upon. Even attending local soccer matches was discouraged on the grounds that the language of the spectators might be offensive to devout Protestant ears. There was a ditty that parents in the town used to teach teenagers:

> There is one thing I will not do, I will not stand in a cinema queue. There are two things I do detest, a painted face and a low-backed dress. There are three things I will not do, I will not gamble, smoke or chew.

The religious expression of this puritanism was an old-fashioned evangelical doctrine which emphasised the absolute authority of the Bible and the need for everyone, even those who were already practising Protestants, to be converted to "born again" Christianity and thus be "saved" from the hellfire of eternal damnation. The climax of the evangelical movement in Irish Protestantism had come with the "Great

Revival" of 1859 – an explosion of religious enthusiasm in which it was claimed that more than 100,000 people had been converted. That revival had started in the Ballymena area and the Hill Street church was a product of it.

The 1920s saw the emergence of a powerful "hellfire" preacher in the 1859 mould, an ex-seaman and reformed alcoholic called W.P. Nicholson who had turned his back on his evil ways to become a Presbyterian evangelist. During the years of sectarian violence which followed the birth of the state, the Northern Ireland Prime Minister, Sir James Craig, had persuaded Nicholson, in the interests of community harmony, not to preach against Catholicism.

He turned instead to exposing the sins of mainstream Presbyterianism. He became notorious for the aggression of his attacks on loose morals, lifeless religious observance and the "bastard theology" of that church's leadership. Although ordinary church members may have found his language shocking, they loved his revivalist message – a lesson Paisley was to take to heart in later years. And once again Ballymena, the most devoutly Presbyterian town in the North, was at the centre of things: during a five-week mission by Nicholson in the town in the spring of 1923 over 2,500 people were "saved", more than a quarter of its total Protestant population.[3]

In stark contrast to Nicholson's revivalist tirades was a new spirit of liberal enquiry among a small group of Presbyterian intellectuals, led by Ernest Davey, a young professor at Assembly's Theological College, the church's training college for ministers in Belfast. Davey set out to re-examine a number of key Presbyterian beliefs in the light of contemporary theology. He studied Christ's virgin birth, and the riddle of how He could have been a divine and a human being at the same time. And he asked what Christ's crucifixion signified for twentieth-century people seeking Christian "salvation".

His attempt to demystify the birth and death of Christ proved particularly offensive to many of the church's more old-fashioned evangelicals, and sparked off a Nicholson-supported campaign against him. This in turn led to a group of conservative churchmen taking the almost unprecedented step of laying charges of heresy against him. After a brilliant defence he was acquitted, and an appeal to that year's General Assembly, the church's highest authority, was dismissed. A small group of hardliners quit the church in protest, leaving behind a sizable rump of conservatives, particularly in rural congregations, who were still deeply suspicious of the "modernist" ideas of Davey and his friends. They were to provide Ian Paisley with some of his first followers a quarter of a century later.

It was against this background of evangelical fervour and heresy-hunting that tensions started to develop between Kyle Paisley and some senior members of his new Ballymena congregation. Mrs Paisley was at the centre of most of the storms. Her rigid puritan beliefs, quick temper and fondness for bringing disagreements to a head with a sharp word, seemed to make for discord. In later years she was also to divide the Ballymena St John's Ambulance Brigade, in which she was a superintendent, over her strict interpretation of Sunday observance.

In the Hill Street church Mrs Paisley insisted on rudely displacing the much-loved former pastor's widow at the organ. She got rid of the choir after a row over what kind of hymns should be sung. She had complained that the girls in the choir were wearing their hair short in the current "bobbed" fashion, in contravention of St Paul's admonition that women should never be "shorn or shaven". She also claimed that some of the leading men at Hill Street had liberal or "modernist" tendencies.

Although fellow pastors more experienced in dealing with the sensitivities of congregations warned him not to make an issue of such internal disputes, the quiet-spoken Kyle was totally unable to curb his wife's tempestuous nature. "She threw a tantrum if she didn't get her way", recalled one member of the church. "Pastor Forbes, who took over from Kyle Paisley, said they should have thrown a bucket of water over her."

According to Ian Paisley's version, matters came to a head in 1933 when his father preached two sermons denouncing the sale of alcoholic drink and sexual immorality. According to his son, these were aimed at two leading church members: one who owned a plot of land on which there was a pub; the other, the church's treasurer, who was allegedly paying women "large sums of money to keep their mouths closed" about his immorality. Not surprisingly, the church's deacons as well as the Baptist Union headquarters in Belfast asked him to withdraw his accusations.[4]

It was not for nothing, however, that Paisley had boasted that his father was "absolutely uncompromising". Kyle Paisley's response was to break away from the Hill Street church together with nearly 80 followers, many of them younger men and women whom he had brought into the church by his tent and gospel hall missions in the countryside around Ballymena. In the autumn of 1933 he started to hold meetings in a room at a local iron foundry.

Within a year the foundation stone for a new "gospel tabernacle" had been laid in Waveney Road on a plot beside the main Ballymena to Belfast railway line. The ceremony was carried out by a Canadian friend of Kyle Paisley's, Dr T.T. Shields, himself the breakaway pastor of a large independent Baptist congregation in Toronto, and a man prominently identified with the fundamentalist movement in North America. Fundamentalism had been a fast-growing movement in America until the 1920s. It emphasised the literal truth of every word in the Bible about the birth and development of man, in opposition to Darwin's Theory of Evolution and the "modernist" Protestant theology which followed it. In the US, fundamentalists had fought bitter court battles against the teaching of evolution in schools. They became increasingly "separatist", both from other Protestant churches and wider American society, which they denounced as sinful and ungodly for its indulgence in drinking, dancing and sexual licence. In the late 1990s and the early years of the new millennium, American evangelists, the Christian Right as they became known, abandoned their hostility to politics and became a powerful force in the Republican Party, assisting George W. Bush's election to the White House in 2000 and launching, among other things, a new bid to challenge Darwinism, this time by sponsoring the Creationist theory to explain the development of mankind.[5]

Separatist fundamentalists followed to the letter St Paul's warning not to have any dealings with "unbelievers", however Christian they might claim to be. Their most sacred text was his message to the early Christians of Corinth: "Come out from among them and be ye separate, saith the Lord, and touch not the unclean thing." It was to become the guiding slogan of Ian Paisley's life.

Kyle Paisley's new congregation was both fundamentalist and separatist: it believed in "the whole Word of God, the Bible, verbally inspired by the Holy Ghost, as the final authority on all matters of Doctrine, Faith, Practice". It aimed to be "a faithful remnant . . . free from compromise", supporting "the supernaturalism of Christianity against the anti-supernaturalism of modernity".[6]

Many of the breakaway Baptists were young farmers from the surrounding countryside, and it was their contributions, together with some help from evangelical circles in Canada, which raised the £1,200 needed to build the little tabernacle. They also provided the unpaid labour to construct the plain single-storey structure, an example that his son's congregations were to follow in their more ambitious church-building projects in later years.

Times were hard for the Paisleys. It was the middle of the Depression. Mrs Paisley wanted a daughter, so they adopted the youngest daughter of a cousin of Kyle Paisley's in Tyrone, a small farmer with seven children, all of them girls. They moved into a three-storey redbrick house a few doors down from the new church, but Kyle Paisley never took a regular salary from his congregation, relying for survival instead on the Sunday collection and the generosity of individual members. They were often left with a bare larder and literally praying for enough food to get them through the week.

Once again the farmers came to their aid in the shape of families like the Beatties, dissident Presbyterians looking for "old-style" gospel preaching and the values that went with it. Their son William was later to become a Free Presbyterian minister and Ian Paisley's deputy in the Democratic Unionist Party, while two daughters were to marry leading Free Presbyterian ministers. The Beatties had a farm above Broughshane, north-east of Ballymena towards the Antrim hills, and regularly brought them in eggs, milk, potatoes and vegetables.

Contemporaries of the Paisley brothers at the Ballymena Model School in the 1930s remember them as big ungainly boys, always dressed very neatly in dark suits, collars and ties. Ian had become a "born again" Christian at the extraordinarily young age of six during a children's service conducted by his mother in the Hill Street church the year before the split. He told later how he had been affected by her sermon about the good shepherd and "the little lost sheep". After the service he remained behind and told her: "I don't want to be a lost sheep. I want to be a saved lamb." They knelt down in a pew in the church "and at that spot I found Jesus Christ as my Saviour and Lord".[7] Nearly 50 years later, when the church was being renovated, Paisley asked for and was given that pew: it now adorns the front hall of his home in East Belfast.

Both Ian and Harold were taught that as children of a family and a congregation that had "separated" themselves from the sinful ways of ordinary religious and social life, they had to be very careful whom they mixed with. This meant that they usually played by themselves, never went to the cinema (even for a school-organised educational film) and on Sundays stayed indoors praying and reading the Bible while other children were outside playing. As a result of this upbringing Ian was not a boy who mixed well at school: he did not take part in football matches in the school yard, stammered nervously when asked questions by teachers and went off home by himself as soon as the school bell sounded at the end of the day. But as the years passed he started to follow the example of his more confident older brother, and by the time he reached his teens he had a reputation as something of a bully.

One former Model School boy, now a clergyman, remembers Ian, then around 12 years old, punching his 12-year-old brother, knocking his ice-cream out of his hand, and getting a bloody nose for his trouble. However, most boys of their age were afraid of the size and belligerence of the Paisley boys and kept out of their way. Other contemporaries remember Ian as a very pious boy. His mother used to claim that at eight years of age he was already reading books of Calvinist theology like the seventeenth-century classic on damnation and salvation, *Death of Deaths*. In his early teens he used to get up at three or four in the morning to pray and read the Bible. Above his bed hung a picture of one of his earliest heroes, the founder of the Salvation Army, General William Booth, and the text "Salvation to the Uttermost". It was a phrase Paisley the preacher would use in later years to glorify the ascent from deepest depravity to transformation through "born again" Christianity – "from the guttermost to the uttermost".

Both Harold and Ian were quite able at school, though not clever enough to pass the scholarship exam at age 12 or the pupil teachership exam the following year, which in those days were the only routes by which poor bright boys could get to the local grammar school and on to university or teacher training college.

On the eve of the Second World War, Harold, already the "black sheep" of the family, left home, lied about his age and joined the Royal Air Force. He would go on to spend time in both the Merchant Navy and the RUC, which he left after waving around a gun while under the influence of drink. It was a brief rebellion. By the mid-1940s he had returned to the fundamentalist fold as a Plymouth Brethren evangelist. His views were by now even more extreme than his family's: he refused to allow his mother, as a woman, to join in when he said prayers, and attacked his brother for wearing a priestly dog collar on entering the ministry.

Meanwhile 14-year-old Ian had moved to the local technical college, intending eventually to go to the Greenmount Agricultural

College near Antrim. After being told that he would first need a year of practical farming experience, his father arranged to send the boy back to his home village of Sixmilecross in County Tyrone to serve his time with a former neighbour called George Watson. Watson was a member of the local "tin hut" mission hall, built by members of the village's three Protestant congregations. It was here, in April 1942, that the tall, skinny 16-year-old with the thick Ballymena accent preached his first sermon, on the subject of the good Samaritan, to a congregation of eight people. Even he admitted in later years that this first effort was a disaster, lasting less than four minutes. His second attempt, after a month spent working by himself in the outlying fields of the Watson farm, was more successful. It was shortly after this, again while out in the fields harrowing corn, that he says he received his "call" to follow in his father's footsteps and become a minister of religion.

—◄○►—

In the autumn of 1942 Paisley travelled to South Wales to enrol in the Barry School of Evangelism, ten miles south of Cardiff. Although only 16 years old, Ian was allowed into the school as a personal favour to his father, a close friend of the principal, Rev S.B. Fidler, who, like Kyle Paisley, was a fundamentalist Baptist. Fidler had broken with the mainstream Baptist Union because of its heretical "modernist" leanings. Under him, Barry was known for its fundamentalist theology, but even more for its emphasis on practical evangelism and the art of preaching.

Paisley shared a room there with an Englishman called Dennis Parry, a conscientious objector who had spent three months in Cardiff jail because of his pacifist convictions. Parry later became a missionary and was killed by Simba tribesmen in the Congo. His bust is one of those – alongside Luther, Calvin, Knox and Wyclif – which now line the inner walls of Paisley's Martyrs' Memorial Church, giving it its name.

Paisley too had thoughts about being a missionary after the war. A short time afterwards he became friendly with one of the pioneers of the Acre Gospel Mission, a Belfast-based evangelical mission which sent people to that most desolate corner of Brazil's Amazonian jungle. He always took a keen interest in its work, and Brazil would become one of the favourite destinations of Free Presbyterian missionaries in later years.

Although enrolled in Barry for a year's course in preparatory Hebrew, Paisley also acquired there a valuable training in the art of preaching to difficult and often hostile audiences: the tough dockers and navvies of

Cardiff and Barry ports; the seamen who sailed into them; and the highly critical chapel congregations of the Welsh valleys. The latter were often less than happy when their preacher turned out to be a gangling teenager with an unfamiliar Ulster accent.

But many of the preachers were away at the war, and the less than a dozen students at Barry had to fill in. Despite his extreme youth, Ian Paisley was soon in great demand for his flamboyant style, his swingeing attacks on the heresies of the mainstream Baptist Union and his already impressive knowledge of the Bible. One of his most effective mentors was a former boxer called Teddy Sherwood, who would gather a large crowd around his soapbox, preach until he was hoarse and then call the young Ulsterman "into the ring".

It was in such situations that Paisley developed the aggressive preaching style that was to serve him so well in later political arenas. When confronted by hostility, he soon learned to turn it to his advantage by the age-old orator's trick of challenging a hostile questioner with a question of his own. In later years he told the story of how, during one sermon to an unruly Welsh crowd, a woman called out, "How do you know there is a Jesus Christ?" Paisley recalled what happened next:

> There was a great shout of derision that went up from the crowd. And there I was, a mere stripling . . . and faced with a hostile crowd. I said to the Lord, "Lord, give me a weapon that will turn as a boomerang in the face of the Devil." And God gave me the answer. I said, "Young woman, I come from Ireland, and an Irishman always answers a question by asking another . . ." "What's your question?" she said. I asked, "What day is it?" And then the crowd laughed. She said "It's Sunday." I then asked, "Could you tell me what month it is?" She said it was the month of August. I said, "I have only one more question. Can you tell me what year it is?" Then the crowd knew what I was getting at. They started to laugh and sneer at her. She said, "It is 1942." I said, "How could you get that number – 1942 years from where? From where?" And she mumbled and stuttered. I said, "I'll help you out. It's A.D.; the year of our Lord. There is a Christ! And, young woman, when you take your diary out and you look at the year, the year stands as a living testimony that there is a Christ!"[8]

The Second World War reached Barry in 1943, and Ian Paisley, like all the students at the school, was out on fire-watching duty during that year's massive wave of German bombing raids on the docks and arms factories of nearby Cardiff. But the young evangelist, unlike his rebellious brother, was more interested in serving his God than his country – leaving himself open to charges in later years that he had dodged the war.

That autumn found Paisley, aged 17, back in Belfast as a guest student at the tiny seminary, or "theological hall", of the Reformed Presbyterian Church of Ireland. Once again his father had interceded for him with a friend who was a Reformed Presbyterian minister and professor at the theological hall, Rev T.C. McFarlane.

The Reformed Presbyterians were known as Covenanters because of their uncompromising adherence to the Scottish Covenants of the 1640s, which bound the puritan parliaments of England and Scotland "to rule in accordance with God's will". In Ireland they were a small sect with fewer than 40 congregations of God-fearing puritan people who held to an old-fashioned gospel as taught by Calvin and John Knox, with a particular emphasis on the latter's doctrine that kings and governments who trample on the religious liberties of their people forfeit their right to rule.

Their theocratic views led them to reject all twentieth-century politics. They did not vote, refused to take any oath of allegiance to the British monarchy, and condemned secret societies like the Freemasons and the Orange Order. They were the most conservative of the various strains in Scottish Presbyterianism, and had gone their own way after the rebellion by militant Scottish Covenanters against the Catholic James II in the 1680s. Theirs was a creed with which the strict young evangelical Baptist from Ballymena could easily feel comfortable.

The three-year part-time course in the Reformed Presbyterian meeting house on Belfast's Grosvenor Road was not an arduous one. In his final two years Paisley was one of only two students attending classes in Greek, Hebrew, elocution, theology and church history. As the only non-graduate and non-member of the Reformed Presbyterian Church, he was not entitled to receive any of its usual bursaries and prizes. But since he did reasonably well in all his exams, the committee of ministers who ran the theological hall, only too conscious of the potential embarrassment when it came to the annual distribution of awards to the minute student body, gave Paisley a special prize for each of his three years there.

Paisley's real interest, however, continued to be in preaching. Long before he left the Covenanters' seminary he was starting to become a regular fixture in mission halls and on open-air pulpits around Belfast. He was befriended by Rev W.J. Grier, a leading figure in the small Irish Evangelical Church, which grouped together a couple of hundred hardline evangelicals who had broken away from the Irish Presbyterian Church after the Davey heresy trial of 1927. Grier helped the impecunious theological student financially, and introduced his protégé, already becoming known as "the boy preacher", to the Evangelical Church's half a dozen congregations around Belfast.

Belfast in 1946 was already the "city of religious nightclubs" that the English Methodist leader Donald Soper was to be so scathing about many years later. Every Saturday the *Belfast Telegraph* carried advertisements for services the next day at over 200 places of Protestant worship, three-fifths of them held by denominations and sects outside the three main Protestant churches: the Presbyterians, Methodists and Church of Ireland.

Audiences of 6,000 people attended revival campaign meetings run by the Irish Evangelization Society at the Kings Hall. In High Street, where German bombs had left a wide open space known as "Blitz Square", evangelical preachers of all sects and sizes rubbed shoulders uneasily with the occasional socialist orator promising a new beginning in the wake of the British Labour Party's overwhelming victory in the 1945 general election.

There was precious little chance of any new beginning in postwar Northern Ireland. Churchill's reflection after the First World War still held as true as ever: the unchanging integrity of the Unionist-Nationalist quarrel and the dreary steeples of religious controversy still dominated the political landscape.

A new Nationalist assault on partition was heralded by the formation in Dungannon in November 1945 of the Anti-Partition League. Two months later the Northern Ireland government refused to follow Britain's example and introduce "one man, one vote" in local elections. The Unionist chief whip, Major L.E. Curran, was brutally frank about the reason for this: it was to prevent "Nationalists getting control of the three border counties and Derry City". Such people, he went on, did not have "the welfare of the people of Ulster at heart", and the best way to prevent them overthrowing the government was to disenfranchise them.[9]

The other burning issue of the next few years would be the bitter campaign by Protestant churchmen against the 1947 Education Act, which for the first time since 1930 allowed teachers in state schools to opt out of giving Bible instruction. A second source of Protestant grievance was the old sectarian bogey of financial aid to Catholic schools, and in particular a proposed increase, from 50 per cent to 65 per cent, in government capital grants.

This was the atmosphere in which Ian Paisley, aged 20, made his first small entry into Northern Ireland's ecclesiastical and political life. He had been preaching regularly at Irish Evangelical churches in East and North Belfast since his return from Wales, and at gospel hall and tent missions in and around his native Ballymena. In December 1945 he was invited to take a service at the Ravenhill Evangelical Mission Church by an elder, a senior lay member there, who had heard him preach and had been impressed.

The Ravenhill church was a small independent evangelical congregation which met in a tin-roofed hall on a rather grimy working-class street within shouting distance of both the Belfast shipyard and East Belfast's only Catholic district, the tiny enclave of Short Strand. Paisley preached there a number of times over the next eight months and so impressed the church's elders that they invited him to become their pastor the following summer.

It was a congenial appointment for him. The 60-strong congregation, much influenced by W.P. Nicholson's sermons against sins of dress, adornment and hairstyle, had broken away from the Ravenhill Presbyterian Church in 1935 over the issue of girls in the choir – including the daughter of the deeply conservative minister – wearing their hair short and "bobbed" in the style of the "flappers". It was the same issue which had played a minor part in the split in Paisley's father's church two years previously. Three of the Ravenhill elders who broke away had been among those who signed the heresy charges against Professor Ernest Davey in 1927.

Despite some opposition from an extreme puritan element in the congregation who said they wanted no pastor of theirs to wear what they called the "Roman collar", Paisley declared his intention of being ordained as a minister. Oddly enough, even five weeks before his ordination on 1 August 1946, he was already being billed as the Reverend Ian Paisley at an Irish Evangelical Church in North Belfast.[10]

His actual ordination was to be the subject of heated debate in Presbyterian circles for the next quarter of a century. Some theologians argued that, despite Paisley's claims that the ceremony was firmly in the tradition of evangelical Presbyterianism, it was never valid under Presbyterian rules – although it might be recognised by smaller more congregationally oriented sects like the Baptists and the Plymouth Brethren.

Only one recognised clergyman, his father Kyle Paisley, an independent Baptist pastor, actually "laid hands" on him in the traditional Presbyterian manner of ordination, as well as a number of the church's leading lay members, the elders. However, three clergymen took part in the service who were all recognised Presbyterian ministers of some kind – Rev W.J. Grier of the breakaway Irish Evangelical Church; Professor T.B. McFarlane of the Reformed Presbyterian Church, who had brought Paisley into his church's theological hall; and Rev Thomas Rowan, an old ultra-evangelical Presbyterian minister who had worked with visiting American revivalist preachers at the turn of the century.

Paisley himself has dismissed the later controversy over his ordination, claiming that he had no great commitment to a specifically Presbyterian ritual, despite his attempt five years later to set up a direct rival to mainstream Presbyterianism. He claims to set more store by the imprimatur he says was given him by the legendary Presbyterian evangelist Rev W.P. Nicholson at the first service after his ordination.

He has repeatedly told his congregations that Nicholson walked up to him after that service and asked him if he had ever seen a cow's tongue. When he said he had, Nicholson asked him what it was like. Paisley replied that it was like a file, and Nicholson lifted his hand and prayed "Lord, give this young man a tongue like an old cow".[11] However, a former Free Presbyterian who was at this service as a child claims that Paisley, always prone to exaggerate stories to his own benefit, turned a passing conversation during Nicholson's only visit to the Ravenhill church into a clinching piece of evidence of his own legitimacy as the inheritor of the true Presbyterian preaching tradition.

—◄○►—

It took Paisley little more than a month to translate his new religious status into political involvement. In late August and September he helped to organise an inaugural series of meetings in Northern Ireland for the National Union of Protestants (NUP), a group of evangelical extremists set up in England in 1942 to combat "Romanist" and high church tendencies in the Church of England, and whose principal activity appeared to be disrupting Anglican services. Its general director was Paisley's maternal uncle, a fundamentalist Baptist called Rev W. St Clair Taylor.

At the organisation's inaugural meeting at Belfast's "Blitz Square", St Clair Taylor was the main speaker and Paisley said that they were looking for 50,000 Protestants from Northern Ireland to join up. At a private meeting earlier Paisley had become treasurer of the NUP's local branch, with a young East Belfast Baptist called Norman Porter as secretary. However, they soon found that high church practice in the Church of England was not an issue guaranteed to raise the ire of Protestants locally. So Paisley and Porter travelled to London and obtained the NUP's agreement to start their own autonomous organisation, the NUP (Ireland).

This was an altogether more red-blooded body. An early circular made it clear that politics and discrimination in employment, as well as religion, would be its business:

> Roman Catholics in Ireland are demanding a United Irish Roman Catholic Republic. Roman Catholics in Northern Ireland are buying up Protestant farms, houses, land and property in their efforts to establish the Papacy in Ulster. The NUP has helped Protestant employers to obtain Protestant employees. . . .
> The NUP has pledged its determination to maintain its allegiance to the Protestant Throne and Constitution of England . . . and has opened the door to a Protestant way of life for every true loyalist who wants to see in Northern Ireland a Protestant country for a Protestant people.[12]

Over the next two years Paisley built up a minor reputation as one of the NUP's most colourful speakers. He accompanied travelling fundamentalist evangelists from America and converted Irish and Italian priests on tours of the North. He himself spoke at open-air meetings and in Orange and church halls on such topics as "Popish Tyranny versus Protestant Tolerance", Sunday observance, the buying up of property by Roman Catholics, the evils of mixed marriage and the dangers of allowing Catholic teachers to be appointed to state (i.e. Protestant) schools.

The atmosphere at such meetings was one of strong and occasionally hysterical anti-Catholicism, sometimes accompanied by a dose of the anti-Communism of the early Cold War years (although Communism was usually seen as the lesser evil and often the result of

Catholicism). The speakers were not all extreme Loyalists. For example, at a meeting of the supposedly extremist Ulster Protestant League in April 1948, the chairman was Alderman Kennedy Leacock of Belfast City Council and the vote of thanks was by Senator Joseph Cunningham, the County Grand Master of the Orange Order. The speaker on this occasion – on the subject "Rome or Moscow? A study in dictatorships" – was the Grand Master of the Orange Order in England, Alderman H.D. Longbottom from Liverpool.

Catholic property and Catholic teachers were particularly sensitive issues to those determined to defend the Protestant ascendancy in Northern Ireland. In several speeches in 1948, including a Twelfth of July address to Ballymena Orangemen, Paisley warned against Catholics buying up Protestant property, and supported the Derry Unionist MP, Rev J.G. McManaway, in his scheme to ensure that Protestants were provided with capital to buy houses, farms and businesses in border areas. Later that year he was prominently involved in an agitation mounted in Ballymena against the appointment of a Catholic art teacher to the town's newly opened intermediate school.

The year 1948 was a particularly busy one for the 22-year-old agitator. He was in constant demand as a speaker at NUP meetings: on waste ground in the fiercely loyalist Shankill Road, in Orange halls and Presbyterian churches in Antrim and Down, and at Belfast's big Wellington and Grosvenor Halls. One evening in May he even found himself at Crossgar Presbyterian Church in east Down, to which he would return three years later in order to divide it and form the first congregation of his Free Presbyterian Church of Ulster.

Paisley was also one of the leading protagonists in the controversy that raged that year (and every year until the early 1950s), sparked off by the decision of the Redemptorist priests at the Clonard Monastery in the Falls Road to hold an annual "mission for non-Catholics". This provoked a howl of outrage among Belfast's evangelical Protestants, led by the NUP. An audience of more than 2,000 people turned up to hear Paisley and others attack the Clonard priests at one of the first of the NUP's counter-meetings to Clonard at the Ulster Hall in March 1948. Hundreds more who could not get in were addressed by separate speakers in the street outside.

In May 1948 he was one of the speakers at an NUP double protest meeting: against a Corporation proposal (later thrown out) to open Belfast Museum and Art Gallery on Sunday afternoons; and against the heir to the throne, Princess Elizabeth, going racing and dancing on a Sunday during a visit to Paris. The chairman of this meeting, Senator William Wilton, said the Border was a minor matter compared with "the preserving of the Sabbath day".[13]

The young Paisley, however, had already started to take a strong interest in the politics of that Border, and the state on the other side of it. The Protestants of Monaghan, the vast majority of whom were still Unionist in politics, had organised themselves into the Monaghan Protestant Association in order to ensure a voice for themselves on the county council. Three years earlier they had been furious because they suspected two of the three candidates in the 1945 presidential election, Seán MacEoin of Fine Gael and an independent Republican called Patrick McCartan, of having been involved in attacks on Monaghan Protestants during the war of independence in the early 1920s. In 1948 they put up their own candidate for the Dáil. Hearing of this, Paisley wrote a letter to the secretary of the Protestant Defence Association, a Clones solicitor, offering to come down and lend his support to their election campaign. On the advice of a local Presbyterian minister, they wrote back declining his services.

In the event Paisley's first visit to the South as a Protestant controversialist had to wait until the following October when, in the more peaceful surroundings of the Dublin YMCA, he led an "evangelistic service" as part of an NUP initiative to try to set up a branch in the Irish capital. It proved to be his last visit to the Irish capital for 30 years.

The NUP was obsessively interested in the South. In the 1930s Roman Catholic triumphalism in the Irish Free State had reached new heights following the 1932 Eucharistic Congress and the pro-Franco agitation during the Spanish Civil War. The Catholic primate, Cardinal MacRory, had said that Protestants had no right to take part in the fifteenth centenary celebrations of St Patrick's coming to Ireland, pointing out that their churches were "not even a part of the Church of Christ". Anticipating a fine distinction Paisley would adopt two decades later, he later added that he had no ill-feeling towards individual non-Catholics – it was their churches he was opposed to.

In 1937 the Irish Free State's territorial claim to Northern Ireland and the Catholic Church's teaching on the family, education and property were enshrined in de Valera's new Irish Constitution. This appeared to confirm every Northern Protestant's fear that in a united

Ireland their own religion would be totally subordinate to Roman Catholicism.

By the late 1940s the Catholic ethos across the border seemed, if anything, to be growing even stronger. A group calling itself Maria Duce, which attracted large crowds to its rallies in Dublin's O'Connell Street, demanded that the Constitution be changed so that the Roman Catholic Church was recognised as the only true Church. In 1947 the hierarchy backed Galway farmers who were refusing to let a local hunt pass over their lands because its joint master was a divorced Protestant woman.

In 1950 came the Tilson case, when the President of the High Court in Dublin ordered three children of a mixed marriage to be taken from their Protestant father and returned to their Catholic mother, thus apparently giving legal recognition to the Catholic Church's contentious rule that Protestant partners had to sign away their rights to bring up their children in their faith. The Catholic Protection and Rescue Society was active in preventing the adoption of Catholic children by Protestants. And finally, of course, there was the long drawn-out "Mother and Child" controversy between Irish Health Minister Noel Browne and the Catholic hierarchy in 1951.[14] That was greeted with predictable glee by Unionists. The Unionist Party published the Dáil debate in book form, and the NUP used it to make their case against a united Ireland throughout England and America.

In this atmosphere of cold war between Irish Protestantism and Catholicism, the NUP was only one of a plethora of politico-religious pressure groups making up the Northern battle line. There was the Protestant Action Society, in which Norman Porter had been involved, formed to combat the rash of Catholic propaganda organisations which had sprung up in Belfast during the previous two decades, and to make sure that Protestant property was not bought by Catholics. There was the more respectable Ulster Protestant Defence and Propaganda Society, whose meetings were chaired by establishment figures like the former Presbyterian moderator, Rev William Corkey, who had led the rearguard action to keep Protestant influence and Bible instruction in state schools; and Orange leader and NUP president Rev Henry O'Connor.

Then there was the once very disreputable Ulster Protestant League (UPL), formed in 1931 to "safeguard the employment of Protestants" during the Depression, and deeply involved in fomenting the sectarian riots of 1935. One of the UPL's supporters was J.W. Nixon, a notorious former RUC district inspector who had led police squads to assassinate Catholics in the Shankill Road area in 1922, and been dismissed for making an inflammatory speech from an Orange platform two years later. Nixon was elected to Stormont as an independent Unionist in 1929. He used to terrify MPs by producing what he called his "black book", which he alleged contained details of their connivance in sectarian attacks during his RUC days.

Paisley, already a fascinated follower of the Unionist-dominated politics of the Northern state, was a friend and admirer of Nixon's. He used to visit Stormont once a week, usually on a Tuesday, driving there with Nixon in his car. He thought him "the most able and effective politician" of those days. Later, in the 1970s and 1980s, when the SDLP was boycotting Stormont and Jim Prior's new Assembly, Paisley remembered Nixon and the independent Unionists who followed him, and declared that Stormont could carry on its business even more effectively when there were no Nationalists present.[15]

Another Ulster Protestant League platform speaker and close friend of both Nixon and Paisley was Senator William Wilton. He was to provide a link to the new generation of Paisleyite extremists. A prosperous undertaker and well-known figure in the Shankill Road, he made his funeral parlours available for meetings of the political groups Paisley would lead in the 1950s and 1960s, Ulster Protestant Action and the Protestant Unionist Party.

—◄o►—

Nixon and Wilton were not the only contacts the young Ravenhill minister had in politics. He had joined the Orange Order, first in North Belfast, later moving to the Mountpottinger Temperance Lodge near his church in East Belfast. This automatically made him a chaplain of both the lodge and the No. 6 East Belfast District which, with 55 lodges, was the largest in Ireland. He shared Orange platforms with the Belfast Grand Master, Senator Joseph Cunningham, and – in July 1949 – with an up-and-coming young Unionist politician called Brian Faulkner. That month he also led 2,000 Belfast Orangemen on a demonstration in Motherwell in Scotland.

He was on friendly terms with a wide range of Unionist political figures who had chaired NUP meetings: people like the Westminster MP for Down, Rev James Little; the Mayor of Londonderry, Sir Frederick Simmons; William Morgan, a prominent Presbyterian lay preacher, businessman, Stormont MP and later a cabinet minister under Terence O'Neill; and Dinah McNabb, the hardline Unionist MP for North Armagh.

NUP Secretary Norman Porter had also introduced him to the Westminster MP for East Belfast, Tommy Cole, yet another speaker on Ulster Protestant League platforms, who would bring Paisley for the first time into the electoral arena. Cole, originally from Cavan, one of the "lost" Ulster counties, was a colourless but extremely wealthy chemist, estate agent and property developer. He had already been defeated twice in Stormont elections but, largely through his generosity to Unionist Party funds, had managed to gain the nomination for the East Belfast seat in 1945. In such an overwhelmingly Protestant area, this meant automatic election.

In January 1949 the Northern Ireland Prime Minister, Sir Basil Brooke, called a snap election for the following month to hammer home Unionist antipathy to the South in the wake of the Dublin government's declaration of a republic outside the Commonwealth the previous September. It was clearly a single-issue election: Norman Porter, who had been planning to stand as an independent against Education Minister Major Hall-Thompson on the Protestant education issue, was persuaded to stand down in the general Unionist interest.

Cole asked Paisley to work in his campaign in the marginal Dock ward, a poor working-class area, the scene of sectarian rioting and killing in both the 1920s and 1930s, which by the 1940s had become the nearest thing in Northern Ireland to a Labour stronghold. In the 1945 Stormont election it had returned Hugh Downey, a Catholic barman from West Belfast, who defeated Sir George Clark, a wealthy farmer and company director, later to become head of the Orange Order. In the municipal elections the following year, it sent four more Labour men to Belfast Corporation.

In the event Paisley took over and virtually ran Cole's campaign single-handed. He organised canvassing, speakers, processions and postering with an energy rarely seen before by a local Unionist organisation more used to fleeting visits by Unionist and Orange bigwigs. He worked closely with Unionist party secretary Billy Douglas, who had a notorious reputation for organising personation and vote-stuffing in marginal constituencies. He paid young men like "Buck Alec", the famous Protestant street fighter, to fly-poster even the toughest nationalist streets. The posters were aimed at Downey's ambivalence on the Border: one showed the Labour man as a goalkeeper with the question "Which way will he kick?" and two arrows, one pointing to "Northern Ireland and prosperity", the other to "The Republic and poverty".[16]

Cole was a small insignificant-looking man and a poor public speaker. He looked even less impressive beside the strapping young clergyman from Ballymena, 6 feet 3 inches tall and with a voice to match, who had little problem in identifying with the election's only issue. The late Gerry Fitt, who was to become Stormont MP for the area 13 years later, remembered Paisley "roaring like a bull" on a street corner between the Catholic New Lodge and the Protestant Duncairn districts: "Pulling at his clerical collar he shouted, 'This is what you're voting for, you're voting for your Protestantism'."

It was a black and white election even by Northern Ireland's standards, and there was no room for socialist interlopers who might be weak on the Union. The tone had been set by the Southern political parties, who, blatantly ignoring Northern political sensitivities, had organised a church gate collection in the South to raise money for anti-partitionist candidates. This outraged Northern Unionists, confirmed all their worst fears about the new Republic's Catholic ethos, and led to the poll being dubbed the "chapel gates election".

It was also the most violent election campaign since 1921, with Labour and anti-partitionist candidates being beaten up and stoned off platforms, and widespread intimidation. In the small Catholic New Lodge area, Paisley was involved in his first sectarian skirmish when Cole's procession came under fire from stones and bottles in Spamount Street on the eve of polling.[17] Two future cabinet ministers, Robert "Beezer" Porter and William Craig, shared the platform with him that day. At the end of it Cole was presented with a lucky black cat by the Loyalists of East Belfast and a Bible by the workers in Gallahers tobacco factory.

The result the next day was a triumph for the all-class alliance of Unionism and the politics of sectarianism. The Unionists gained three seats, including Downey's in Dock by a margin of 284 votes. The Labour vote was decimated. For the first time since 1925 Stormont consisted entirely of a Protestant government and a Catholic opposition. Cole told friends there was no way he would have won if it had not been for Paisley's organising flair. Although barely 23 years of age, the young extremist from Ballymena had already played his first small part in the movement towards the final violent polarisation of Northern Ireland society more than two decades later.

To the working-class Unionists of Dock, Paisley was a revelation. He spoke their language and understood their concerns: one observer remembers him roaring at a street meeting that disloyal Catholics, by breeding large families, were deliberately exploiting the new family allowance system. This had been recently and reluctantly introduced by the Unionists into Northern Ireland as part of the Labour government's Welfare State provisions, largely because the British Treasury was underwriting it.

Before one election meeting in the Unionist Labour Hall in York Street, a group of constituency workers asked Paisley why he did not think about standing as a Unionist candidate himself in the next election. He replied that he would go away and give it "prayerful consideration". A few days later he came back and said that he saw his future in the church and not in politics. However, he thought he had seen an easier way to get into politics: by being elected to the Northern Ireland Senate. This body – largely made up of ageing landlords, businessmen and Unionist retainers – was chosen by the newly elected members of the Stormont House of Commons. Tommy Cole lobbied among his fellow Unionists and independents like Nixon to get his young protégé the four votes required for a Senate seat, but in the end without success. Ironically Nixon was doing the same thing for Paisley's colleague in the NUP, Norman Porter, again in vain.

Porter had to wait only another four years, until 1953, to get into Stormont, when he stood as an independent Unionist, once again largely on the issue of Protestant education. Paisley, meanwhile, turned his attention after 1951 to building up his new church. It was to be another 20 years before he ran for Stormont, although he would be deeply involved in politics again long before that.

In any case he already had his eye on another more spectacular road to prominence. One day in the late 1940s he told a colleague as they walked along Belfast's Great Victoria Street after a National Union of Protestants meeting that the only way to get anywhere in Northern Ireland was to go to jail. When this remark was retold to other NUP committee members they treated it as a joke. But it stuck in that colleague's mind for years afterwards: "I said to myself – this guy will go to jail. He'll make it seem that he's been persecuted. That's where his road to success in politics lies. And what happened? He tried for years to get to jail before he got there. And he got there eventually."

The year 1950 saw Paisley's first clash with the Unionist establishment in Northern Ireland, in the shape of the Orange Order, of which until then he had been such an ambitious member. It was over the issue of temperance, always a sensitive one among strait-laced Northern Protestants. The temperance movement had been a feature of Unionist politics since the 1859 Revival. A "local optionist" group, led mainly by Presbyterian clergymen, had gone as far as putting up three candidates in the 1929 Stormont election, on a ticket demanding the right of local authorities to prevent the sale of alcohol in their areas.

In January 1950 the National Union of Protestants called on the "Protestant representatives in the Belfast City Council" to oppose the advertising of alcoholic drink on Belfast Corporation buses and trams. The transport committee, headed by its chairman, the Orange Order's County Grand Master, Senator Joseph Cunningham, ignored this call and recommended that advertising on the buses go to the highest bidder. A heated if intermittent debate on the issue continued throughout the spring and summer of that year. On 31 August, at an NUP protest meeting on the eve of a crucial city council vote on the issue, both Norman Porter and Paisley bitterly attacked Cunningham for voting "in the company of the Irish Labour Party, a Republican party, for liquor advertisements". The *Irish News* report described the scene:

> Raising his eyes ceiling-wards and with outstretched hands, the Rev. Paisley, in a loud voice, declared: "The liquor traffic is a liar. It promises men health but gives only disease; it promises strength but gives weakness; it promises prosperity but brings only adversity. I'm telling you it's a liar. We don't want to see trams and buses used as a signpost to hell. Lord Craigavon coined a slogan, 'Not an inch' and we say to the Corporation: 'Not an inch of space on the trams for advertising liquor'."

The accusations against Cunningham, which Paisley and Porter had incorporated in a handbill published by "a group of loyal Orangemen", caused a furore inside the Order. The Belfast Grand Master tried to have the two men expelled. However, Porter got his own lodge to pass a similar resolution against Cunningham, and the Grand Master retreated. But it was the first sign that Paisley was prepared to make enemies in the high places of Unionism.

In the summer of 1950 he had struck the first tiny blow against a Unionist politician he would spend a good part of the next 20 years reviling. Five years earlier Captain Terence O'Neill, a young Irish Guards officer brought up in England, had been returned unopposed as the Stormont member for Bannside, which included Paisley's home town of Ballymena. On the last Sunday of July 1950 the Catholics of Rasharkin, a mixed village north-west of Ballymena, planned to march with their bands to a local field for their annual parochial sports day. To the outrage of local Orangemen, the route agreed with the RUC took them past a local Orange hall on the townland of Ballymaconnolly, where Protestant Sunday school classes were usually held.

A protest deputation was sent to O'Neill's house in the neighbouring village of Ahoghill, and another, from the County Grand Lodge of the Orange Order, to Home Affairs Minister Brian Maginess, who was something of a liberal in Unionist terms. It might have been a storm in a teacup, but the teacup was an Orange one, and a County Antrim Orange one at that, and both delegations were received and listened to respectfully at the highest level. They even obtained an audience with the Prime Minister, Sir Basil Brooke, himself. On this occasion, however, neither the police nor the politicians believed that the Catholic procession threatened civil order in Rasharkin, and it went ahead without incident.

Two weeks later, at a protest meeting in the Ballymaconnolly Orange hall addressed by Paisley and leading local Orange luminaries, a resolution was passed calling for the resignation of both O'Neill and Maginess. There was loud applause when the Sunday school superintendent warned that by their attitude on this issue the authorities had "started something in Ballymaconnolly that would go to the ends of Ulster".

Paisley said they were determined, come what may, that never again would a Hibernian procession pass along that road, destroy their Sabbath school meeting, and throw defiance in their faces. This was a Protestant area, he declared, and what they had they were determined to hold. They wanted a leader who could grace their platform by standing up for their principles, but no such leader had come forward. He said that such a man would arise from among themselves, a man who would stand with them in defence of their heritage.[18]

If the 24-year-old Paisley yet saw himself as that leader, circumstances, at least in the immediate future, would dictate that he spent more time on church affairs than on becoming a Protestant political champion. For in June 1949 an event had taken place that radically changed the whole direction of his career. Worried about his Ravenhill congregation's small size and lack of enthusiasm, he had asked four men to join him in an all-night and all-day 36-hour prayer meeting to ask God for guidance. On the second evening of this marathon session, Paisley told his congregation later, he was "anointed with power" by God. He said he had been given a vision that thousands of souls were going to be saved and that the Ravenhill church would prove far too small for his ministry. God had told him to finish with politics, because his calling was to preach the gospel and help bring about a spiritual revival in Northern Ireland, he went on. If anyone objected to this they should do it now, because he was quite prepared to leave and proclaim his new message elsewhere: "the canopy of heaven is my roof", one man who was there remembers him declaring.[19]

It quickly became clear that this new divinely inspired Paisley intended to be the boss in his own church. Suddenly the place became a hive of activity: there were prayer meetings nearly every night; open-air and street meetings in Ormeau Park, the shipyard and Belfast city centre; drunks were brought in to fill the church on Friday nights and were preached to outside the pubs on Saturday nights.

However, their minister's vehement new mixture of hellfire evangelism and intolerance of those who failed to match his fervour did not suit everyone in the church. Particularly unhappy were those respectable former Presbyterian folk who had already been irritated by the amount of time he spent away from it because he was involved in political and NUP affairs.

Over the next few years there were several ugly rows. Following his father's example, he sacked the choir. He forced out a leading woman member who had complained to the elders over a sermon about hell which Paisley had preached when her elderly unconverted father was in the congregation. "When you meet a devil wearing trousers it's bad, but a devil wearing a skirt is ten times worse," Paisley would tell his congregations in later years when recounting this tale.

Throughout his career Paisley felt uncomfortable with strong-minded women. The first significant split in the church was to come when a woman stood up to him. There had been discontent with his high-handed ways and growing attacks on other churches for several years after the marathon prayer meeting. It reached a breaking point in the early summer of 1953 when Paisley barred the dissidents from the communion table. Finally, Paisley announced during one Sunday morning service in July that there were people in the church with "sin in their lives", and the congregation would sing the hymn "Would you be free from your burden of sin" while they left.

A woman from one prominent dissident family rose to her feet and called out "What's the sin in my life, Mr Paisley?" "Let your women keep silence in the church" was his only response before he started into the hymn in his usual loud, tuneless singing voice.

On the way out after the service the woman's husband, normally the mildest of men, seized Paisley by his lapels. "If it wasn't for the grace of God, I'd wring your neck," he barked at him. Around 25 people had left the church before that drawn-out dispute was over.

Around this time the Ravenhill minister was also having worries over women in his personal life. In 1951 he had met Eileen Cassells, the 17-year-old daughter of a devout East Belfast Baptist family, in the house of Norman Porter's parents, where he was lodging. Eileen, whose father was a prosperous Baptist shopkeeper, was working as a secretary and Paisley asked her to take a shorthand note of his speeches for a magazine he was planning to start.

Eileen was a shy and retiring girl, but she took an immediate fancy to the big brash clergyman and they became unofficially engaged on their third evening out together.[20] It would not be the easiest of courtships: Ian Paisley has never been noted for his sensitivity to human feelings, and acquaintances remember Eileen being reduced to tears on several occasions when he stood her up to go to some church meeting or speaking engagement.

The problem arose because, until a short time before, Paisley had been engaged to another girl in Ballymena, whom he had known when they were teenagers together at his father's church. The Paisley children had been regular visitors to her family's farm on the edge of the Antrim Hills. She had first started going out with Harold Paisley, and then with Ian. After he had been in Belfast for several years he broke off the relationship. But she had held on to the engagement ring and friends remember Ian living in mortal fear right up to his wedding day that she would reappear and threaten to sue him for "breach of promise".

Ian Paisley and Eileen Cassells were eventually married in October 1956 at the Ravenhill Church. John Wylie, Paisley's number two in the Free Presbyterian Church, was best man.

◄○►

Until 1951 Paisley's minor – but growing – reputation as an anti-Catholic evangelical preacher and National Union of Protestants speaker had made him a welcome guest in many conservative Presbyterian congregations. But in February and March of that year a series of events took place in the Presbyterian Church in the small town of Crossgar in County Down which would change all that. They would turn Paisley into an outcast from, and an angry rebel against, the religious establishment of Northern Ireland.

Crossgar was a typically quiet one-street Ulster Protestant town in the prosperous east Down countryside five miles outside the market town of Downpatrick. The local Lissara Presbyterian Church was just as typical. But there were also undercurrents of tension in the congregation which were symptomatic of the strains between liberal "modernists" and conservative "evangelicals" in Northern Irish Presbyterianism. The minister's job at Lissara was vacant, the previous incumbent having retired in the summer of 1950.

One of those who had applied for the vacancy was Rev Geoffrey Chart, a strong conservative with whom Paisley had shared NUP platforms. However, he had narrowly failed to get the necessary two-thirds majority in a vote of the church's members. There followed a row over the voting list used in the election, with objections coming from a vociferous group of evangelicals led by an elder called George Gibson, an architect who came from one of the area's most prominent and devout Presbyterian families.

Gibson also ran his own mission hall, inherited from his uncle, a cattle-dealer and lay preacher nicknamed "Hallelujah Gibson" who had shared pulpits with the legendary W.P. Nicholson. His group of evangelicals were much influenced by itinerant "Faith Mission" preachers, who made a fetish of holy living and were fanatically opposed to people who smoked, drank and engaged in other "ungodly" and worldly pleasures.

The previous year Gibson invited Paisley to lead a gospel campaign in Crossgar in February 1951. Since his little hall was too small, Gibson requested and was given permission to use the larger Lissara church hall. However, at the last moment the Down Presbytery, the governing Presbyterian body in the area, ruled that Paisley could not use the hall as long as the church had no minister. The decision outraged the church's evangelicals. They alleged that the local Presbyterian bigwigs were unhappy about Paisley's mission, not because of any particular fear of Paisley, but because it might boost the campaign of the conservative Chart and get him the votes he needed in a fresh election for the minister's job.

The Presbytery's decision was communicated to Gibson and his friends on the Saturday that Paisley's mission was due to open. Paisley acted immediately. The next morning, as the moderator of the Down Presbytery, Rev William Boland, arrived to read out suspension notices on Gibson and another Lissara elder who had refused to accept its ruling, he was greeted by a noisy and abusive picket led by Paisley and around 30 supporters. The protesters invaded the service with their placards, and afterwards the RUC had to escort Boland to his car, which they discovered had been put out of action when water was poured into its petrol tank. That night the gospel mission went ahead in Hallelujah Gibson's hall down the road, with Paisley as the preacher.

However, Paisley was now not merely interested in running a gospel campaign. This squabble within Crossgar's Presbyterian community offered an opportunity to launch his own separate denomination and he was determined to seize it. Over the next five weeks there were a number of lengthy meetings between Paisley and the Lissara dissidents at Ravenhill. Paisley claimed later that they were also attended by two conservative Presbyterian ministers, Geoffrey Chart, the candidate at Crossgar, and Ivor Lewis, another Presbyterian minister and NUP stalwart. On 11 March five Lissara elders announced that they were breaking away, with Paisley's backing, to form the Free Presbyterian Church of Ulster.

Their "manifesto" was a mixture of Paisley's recently found revival enthusiasm, Gibson's obsession with holy living, and their common belief in separation from "the unclean thing" of mainstream Presbyterianism. It was contemptuous of "the dead and stagnant, powerless and fruitless religion of our day". It accused ministers of preferring financial security, material comforts and worldly pleasures, like smoking tobacco, to saving the souls of their congregations (the last was a reference to the previous minister at Lissara, who liked his pipe). And it concluded that "clear-thinking people are beginning to realise that the only course to pursue is to save that which is worth saving, and like Sodom and Gomorrah, leave the rest to God's wrath and judgement".[21]

By the following Saturday, 17 March – St Patrick's Day – Hallelujah Gibson's little hall in Killyleagh Street had been transformed into a temporary church building complete with a new stained-glass window bearing the emblem of the new denomination, a burning bush and the motto "Christ for Ulster". The name "Free Presbyterian" was at least partly dictated by the terms of Gibson's will, which stipulated that the hall had to be used in conjunction with a Presbyterian church. Paisley's first task that day was to induct the new church's temporary minister, a returned missionary called Rev George Stears from the unheard of and unrecognised "Presbyterian Church of South America". In his sermon Paisley accused the Irish Presbyterian Church of having "sold the past". "We in Crossgar are going back to the old standards," he declared, "and to preach the faith of our fathers."

The breakaway church may not have been planned by Paisley. "It came out of the blue, an overnight decision," recalled one former associate in the National Union of Protestants. "Ivor Lewis said to him jokingly, 'Why don't you start the Free Presbyterian Church?'" Paisley had spent the Saturday night before the first protest at Crossgar desperately trying to find someone to stand in for him the next morning at Ravenhill. It would be late April, five weeks after the breakaway, before he could overcome opposition within his own Ravenhill congregation and persuade it, on a split vote, to join the new denomination.

Then, using the same skilful pragmatism that was to govern his later political career, he moved quickly to consolidate the Free Presbyterian Church as a real alternative to established Irish Presbyterianism. Its manifesto not only attacked lifeless religion and godless tobacco-smoking ministers, but also the "modernism" of the Presbyterian Assembly's Theological College and its principal, Ernest Davey, and the mainstream church's "betrayal of the Reformation" through its membership of the ecumenical World Council of Churches, formed in 1948. Its doctrinal statement, which allowed it to carry out adult baptism, was aimed at making it more attractive to those of the Baptist faith Paisley had grown up in.

The reaction of the Irish Presbyterian Church was to express "great sorrow" at the break, and to claim that the breakaway group's St Patrick's Day service was "completely invalid in Presbyterian history, practice and tradition". However, Northern Ireland's largest church, despite its long history of schism, was protected by an astonishing smugness about its own well-being. The same meeting of Belfast churches which discussed the Crossgar split also heard a report that: ". . . people in district after district are simply crowding to church and then spending their entire time during the rest of the week in embodying in their work all the fine

Christian exhortations they hear on the Sunday; and in many, many areas not the slightest suspicion of a social blemish is showing itself above the horizon." [22]

The Irish Presbyterian Church was out of touch with its own grassroots. For in congregations as far apart as south Tyrone and north Antrim there were ugly stirrings and social blemishes that would play right into the hands of Ian Paisley and his little group of fundamentalist troublemakers.

"We know the hells declared
For such as serve not Rome."
"ULSTER" BY RUDYARD KIPLING, WRITTEN IN 1912

⁓⁓⁓

"They were determined that Free Presbyterianism would
never get recognition anywhere."
ORANGEMAN SPEAKING ABOUT REACTION TO THE GROWTH
OF PAISLEY'S CHURCH IN THE 1950S

⁓⁓⁓

"To maintain a Testimony to the truth of Christ against the
Roman anti-Christ, the supernaturalism of Christianity against
the anti-supernaturalism of modernism so-called, the divine unity
of the Church against the delusive uniformity of the ecumenical
movement headed up by the World Council of Churches, the
doctrine of the Holy Spirit's infilling against the deceptions of
charismatic fanaticism and the fervour of true Christian zeal
against the formality of dead and defunct orthodoxy."
THE FREE PRESBYTERIAN CHURCH OF ULSTER COVENANT,
28 FEBRUARY 1988

CHAPTER TWO

Building a Church

The village of Pomeroy in County Tyrone is, in all the important ways, Northern Ireland writ small. Set in rolling countryside in the foothills of the Sperrin mountains, it is a place where the native Catholic and the planter Protestant populations have lived uneasily together for over three centuries – the peace process of the 1990s notwithstanding. Although open conflict is rare, the village displays its divisions for all to see.

Like so many of Northern Ireland's rural towns and villages, Pomeroy is separated into ghettoes. The western end of the village's one and only main street is Catholic and Republican, as the IRA slogans and graffiti that adorned the walls for most of the Troubles amply testified. At the eastern end of the town during all those years squatted an ugly British Army and RUC post, its walls and roof protected from mortar attack by wire mesh. A few yards away the pavement kerbs are painted red, white and blue, and straddling the road is a spindly wooden arch. It is here, every Twelfth of July, that the local Orangemen assemble, ready to parade their politics, their Protestantism and the claim that this part of Pomeroy is forever theirs.

Pomeroy occupies a special place in Nationalist mythology. It was here in 1951, only nine months after Paisley had founded the Free Presbyterian Church, that Saor Uladh (Free Ulster), a violent splinter from the IRA, was born. In 1953 Catholics fought the RUC hand to hand in the village when they welcomed home from jail their local MP, Liam Kelly, who had been imprisoned for making seditious election speeches. Two years later Saor Uladh, which was Kelly's brainchild,

37

began a series of bomb and gun attacks that prompted the IRA's own ill-fated 1956 campaign, a campaign that was to have a considerable impact on the course of Unionist politics and the career of Ian Paisley.

Paisley himself was no stranger to Pomeroy. Just as the village was a fertile ground for militant Republicanism, so it was for Loyalists and fundamentalist Protestants. In the late 1940s and early 1950s the National Union of Protestants was in the vanguard of that ideology. The NUP's favourite tactic was to parade converted Catholics at its meetings as living proof of the superiority of the Reformation and – by implication – Unionism also. In October 1950 the NUP and Paisley came to Pomeroy to stage one such show.

The star of the NUP rallies in those days was an Australian woman who had been born a southern Irish Catholic. Monica Farrell had, to judge from the advertisements for her meetings in Ireland, made a career out of describing her conversion and the perfidies of Rome. "Thousands attend her meetings in all parts of Australia" trumpeted one newspaper ad, which went on to describe how she would address the subject of "Women in chains – Rome's convent laundries" to the faithful in Lurgan, County Armagh. Although her message outraged Catholics at the time, revelations in the 1990s about Ireland's Magdalene laundries showed that her complaints had substance. From the mid-nineteenth century onwards, some 30,000 so-called "fallen" women, many just girls, were detained in Church-run institutions for many years, forced to work in laundries, kept in isolation and often subjected to sexual, physical and mental abuse. Named after St Mary Magdalene, a prostitute who became a follower of Christ, the last Magdalene laundry closed in 1996.

Monica Farrell and the NUP were given a warm welcome by Pomeroy's fundamentalists in 1950 but Catholics were outraged. The meeting had been arranged by Richard Reid, a local farmer and evangelical Presbyterian who had become friendly with the NUP secretary, Norman Porter. Eager to hear Miss Farrell's testimony, he arranged to hire the local courthouse for the evening but before long local Catholics got to hear of the plans and objected. The RUC sergeant, a Catholic, was worried that the meeting would cause conflict and even violence in the village and he persuaded Reid to move the meeting elsewhere. The local Presbyterian minister duly obliged and his church hall was made available instead.

Monica Farrell's meeting was a big success and passed off peacefully but Reid was surprised to see arriving with the NUP entourage the tall, gangly figure of Ian Paisley. He hadn't been listed to appear and had turned up apparently in anticipation of trouble. "He said he'd come because he'd heard about the objections from Catholics," recalled Reid, who has an abiding memory of Paisley and Norman Porter prowling Pomeroy's main street after the meeting looking, in vain, for hostile Catholic crowds.

Monica Farrell was a big hit with the village's Protestants, so much so that Porter asked Reid to arrange a return meeting in early April 1951, with the young Paisley also billed as a speaker. When the time came for the meeting, however, Reid discovered that it wasn't just local Catholics who had objections to it.

Just two weeks before, the traumatic split in the Presbyterian congregation of Crossgar had given birth to the Free Presbyterian Church of Ulster, and the event had received wide coverage in the Unionist newspapers. The scandalous tales of Paisleyites interrupting the service in Crossgar, the images of strident placards and of the RUC having to protect a senior minister from howling pickets had spread throughout the network of Presbyterian churches. Irritated by the unseemly publicity, Presbyterian ministers began closing ranks against Paisley.

The news of Crossgar had also made its way to Pomeroy and there Paisley discovered, for the first time, what the Lissara split would cost him. Presbyterian doors in Pomeroy were barred to him, as they soon would be elsewhere. Reid remembers the reaction of the Pomeroy Presbyterians: "I had hired the church hall again but I hadn't told them that Paisley's name was to be on the handbill. When they found out, two elders came to me after Sunday service and said that we'd either have to remove his name or they wouldn't give permission to hold the meeting in the church hall."

Outraged, Reid left the Presbyterian church and sought out a more fundamentalist gospel elsewhere. He had found Paisley's message and style attractive, however, and when the opportunity arose in later years he became one of Paisley's most ardent supporters. He was a founder member and elder of the Dungannon Free Presbyterian Church and stood successfully as a DUP candidate for Mid-Ulster in the 1975 Northern Ireland Convention until his own acrimonious parting of the ways with Paisley in 1979.

It was discontented, conservative Presbyterians like Reid who were, in its early years, to form the basis for the growth of the fledgling Free

Presbyterian church, as Paisley, transformed by Crossgar into the leader of a new denomination, sought out splits in other congregations to exploit.

Only two months after Crossgar, he found his first dissident congregation in north Antrim, only fifteen miles from his Ballymena home. In 1951 the minister of Drumreagh Presbyterian church, a parish on the southern outskirts of Ballymoney, was the Rev Billy Hyndman, a liberal cleric with no liking for the evangelicals of Presbyterianism and a man who, as a former colleague recalled, "was fond of a glass of whiskey on a Saturday night".

The Drumreagh congregation had had a recent history of dissension. The minister before Hyndman was John Barkley, a prominent liberal cleric who went on to become Principal of the Assembly's Theological College in Belfast. Barkley had found himself in constant argument with a group of evangelicals in the church led by a local farmer called Sandy McAuley and when Hyndman replaced him, the disputes continued. McAuley had been "saved" by W.P. Nicholson in the 1920s and he and his family shared the same rigid, uncompromising faith.

McAuley's arguments with Hyndman, though, were not just theological. In the spring of 1951 he levelled an accusation against him which was to cause scandal in the area. Hyndman, he alleged, had fathered an illegitimate child by a woman who already had four illegitimate children. She had relatives in the congregation and McAuley made the issue church business. The matter soon deteriorated into violence: Hyndman heard of the accusation, confronted McAuley and floored him with his fists. The congregation soon split into warring factions and the story came to the ears of Ian Paisley's newest disciple, John Wylie. An electrician from Dundonald in East Belfast, Wylie, already a conservative Presbyterian dissident, had heard the young Paisley preaching at gospel missions. He was immediately attracted by his anti-Catholic, anti-liberal message and decided to join the Ravenhill congregation. That summer, he was tent-preaching in the Cabra area, near Ballymoney, preparing to enter the Free Presbyterian ministry when the Drumreagh congregation divided.

"Wylie held counter meetings outside the Drumreagh church every Sunday denouncing Hyndman and the Presbyterian church," recollected another local Presbyterian minister. "He also canvassed the district urging people from the congregation and their sympathisers to leave, going to their homes for private chats and generally putting anti-Hyndman propaganda around." Wylie also brought Paisley down to

Drumreagh and the two of them intensified the effort to divide the congregation.

Eventually the allegation against Hyndman – which he had always denied and for which there was never a shred of proof – was brought to the Route Presbytery, the governing body of the local Presbyterian church. Hyndman was cleared of the charge, but to save his wife and family further distress he left Drumreagh and emigrated to Canada. That June, between 20 and 30 of the congregation left as well, some to go to other Presbyterian churches nearby, but a handful, led by McAuley and his family, joined the Free Presbyterian Church. It initially met for worship in the upstairs room of a barn until a more permanent building was erected in Cabra a year later, with Wylie as the first minister.

Nearby Rasharkin, on the border of Counties Derry and Antrim, was the scene later that summer of the next Presbyterian split and again Paisley's infant church was quick to exploit it. Once more a suggestion of scandal and sexual innuendo was at the centre of the divisions. The minister of Rasharkin was the Rev Ernest Stronge, a very strict evangelical who was married to a local woman, a member of a large family called Wallace, who were both wealthy and influential in the Orange Order. The marriage had never been happy. Although they had children, the Stronges had been incompatible for some years and there were stories of violence and ill-treatment in the home. Early in 1951 they separated. The children left with their mother, and so bitter were relations between husband and wife that the children were forbidden to acknowledge their father when they met him in the street.

Predictably this marital argument spilled over into the congregation. Many Rasharkin Presbyterians took the side of their local friends, Mrs Stronge and her family, against their minister. Eventually in the winter of 1951 the couple were divorced, an almost unheard of event in those days. When the case came to court, there were so many ministers in the courtroom eager to hear the scandalous detail unfold that the presiding judge, Lord Chief Justice McDermott, himself a pillar of the Presbyterian establishment, rebuked them for neglecting their spiritual duties.

The divisions in Rasharkin came to the ears of Paisley via the ever alert John Wylie and again the Free Presbyterians moved in, in force, to take advantage. The tactics were the same as in Drumreagh; noisy meetings were held outside the Rasharkin church during the summer months attacking Ernest Stronge, and dissidents hosted private meetings with Wylie. That August some of the congregation split off – Paisley claimed between 200 and 300 – and led by Mrs Stronge's father, Daniel Wallace, the family formed the core of the third new Free Presbyterian church which, to begin with, worshipped in a barn donated by the Wallaces; local Presbyterian loyalists immediately dubbed them "barnrats".

Only eight months after the Crossgar split, Ian Paisley had brought two new churches into his Free Presbyterian fold – one other church, Mount Merrion in East Belfast, had been started in 1951 but this was a poorly attended extension of the original Ravenhill congregation which didn't properly get off the ground until the next year. Only Crossgar, however, could be properly classified as a product of the battle for theological principle.

The significance of both the Cabra and Rasharkin splits was that Paisley's assaults on Presbyterianism there were not centred on his theological criticisms. In each case he seized the opportunities presented by sexual scandal and marital division to woo away dissidents. One of the casualties also happened to be an ally in his battle against liberal Presbyterianism – Ernest Stronge, the Rasharkin minister, was a conservative evangelical and a member of the National Union of Protestants along with Paisley.

An NUP colleague offered this insight into the Rasharkin split and the then widely held interpretation of Paisley's behaviour:

> Old Stronge was a doting old fool of a man but sound as a bell theologically. Paisley could have found no fault there. Stronge and I would sit on the same NUP platform and he would have grunted amen to what I would say and I would do the same with him. Stronge was on our street, in every way he was on our side but he still had a go at him. Paisley would find an issue in those days, it didn't matter what the issue was, if it gave him an opening he was in. He was shrewd enough.

If Crossgar had irritated the Presbyterian church, Cabra and Rasharkin set alarm bells ringing. The message from Paisley and his Free Presbyterians was clear – he had meant what he said about splitting the church from top to bottom and it seemed that it wasn't going to matter how he did it.

The first reverberations from Cabra and Rasharkin were felt in the interdenominational ranks of the National Union of Protestants. Many in the NUP were already envious of Paisley's impressive preaching style, his popularity with crowds and his phenomenal, photographic memory. "He could read Churchill or he could read Spurgeon, it didn't matter, he could stand on a platform and it would come out of him like water from a tap," recalled an NUP colleague – but his behaviour at NUP meetings had made him an unpopular and resented figure.

"I would go on to the platform of the Ulster Hall like everyone else at the start of the meeting, but no Paisley. Then just after the opening prayer or hymn, on he would stride to get his own round of applause," complained one NUP official.

Others accused him of over-ambition and egotism:

> The day after a meeting he would come into my office and say, "*The Belfast Telegraph*'s report is not bad. I see you got 39 lines. I got 54." He would actually count the number of lines he got in reports of our meetings. Then he would say, "Let's attack the Archbishop of Canterbury, pass a resolution and send it to the press." I'd say, "You can't pass a resolution, you can't say anything until we call a committee meeting." But it was no use, he couldn't see the need.

Annoying as these traits were, the Cabra and Rasharkin episodes caused much more concern among Paisley's NUP colleagues, particularly the Presbyterians. It seemed to them that if he was declaring open war on Presbyterian churches all around the country and was ready to take advantage even of Ernest Stronge's difficulties, then none of them could rest easy. The NUP executive member most disturbed about things was the Rev Eric Borland, a Presbyterian minister from Bangor, County Down, who was vice-president of the NUP and a high-ranking Orangeman. His concern was shared by other Bangor Presbyterians; after the Crossgar split, Paisley had been banned from preaching in one church there.

That winter at an NUP executive committee meeting Borland brought matters to a head. A fellow Presbyterian minister, the Rev Martin Smyth, later the Official Unionist MP for South Belfast and Grand Master of the Orange Order in Ireland, was a regular speaker on NUP platforms. He remembered what happened next:

> At the committee meeting they were discussing these things and Borland challenged Paisley: "Am I hearing you right, Ian? You're saying that if any of us would have any trouble you

would come down to try to capitalise on that trouble to build up your cause?" And Paisley said he would. Then says Eric: "Any of us in the ministry can have differences of opinion with our congregations at any time and for any reason, but I have to say I can no longer work with you if that's your attitude to brother ministers."

Other Presbyterians in the NUP shared Borland's concern. Norman Porter intervened to try to avoid the inevitable parting of the ways, but to no avail. One of them recalled:

Norman went to Paisley and said, "Look, I'm not worried about you splitting Presbyterian churches, provided you go for modernist churches and if the truth be told neither would anyone else. But if you're making an attack on all Presbyterian churches how can you sit on the same platform as Borland and his people?" He just laughed. I don't know what his motive was but it looked as if he wanted to build up a congregation and it didn't matter what price or what issue.

In February 1952 at the annual general meeting of the National Union of Protestants in Belfast, Borland took his challenge to Paisley a stage further. Addressing the 100 or so delegates, Borland gave the membership a simple choice: they could either keep him in the NUP or have Paisley, but he was not prepared to stay in the same organisation as Paisley. The NUP rank and file chose Borland, and Paisley was voted off the executive committee.

Paisley stepped up his feud with the NUP. He won the support of the head of the English National Union of Protestants, Arnold Perkins, and with his help staged rival meetings advertised under the label of NUP (England). At some meetings he would launch bitter attacks on former colleagues, particularly Norman Porter, who, unusually for a Baptist, was becoming increasingly involved in politics as a hardline Independent Unionist.

"Paisley wasn't interested in politics in those days and when Porter got elected to Stormont, he attacked him at a big rally in the Ulster Hall, saying that was no place for a Christian to be. He would also criticise Porter for sharing a platform with Tommy Henderson (the Independent Unionist MP for Shankill) because Tommy was known to take a drink," remembered one NUP member. Criticism like this conveniently ignored his own flirtation with politics in 1949 and was totally forgotten when Paisley later immersed himself in political activity.

Having alienated mainstream liberal Presbyterianism, Paisley now grasped every opportunity to divide and attack his former conservative allies. He was determined to portray himself as the only principled voice of fundamentalist Protestantism and in the spring of 1954 he showed that he was ready to go to some lengths to do it.

Earlier that year a woman supporter of the National Union of Protestants had died, leaving a sum of money to be divided amongst various evangelical organisations. Among the bequests was £400 for the NUP – a considerable sum for those days – and eventually the money was handed over to Porter. Paisley got to hear about it, contacted Perkins in England and together they decided to challenge the will, on the grounds that the woman had not stipulated which branch of the NUP – English or Irish – was to get the money.

Since the English branch of NUP was the parent organisation, they reckoned they had a good claim and Paisley and Perkins pursued it to court. On the day of the hearing, however, lawyers for Porter and Paisley got together and persuaded the two men to divide the money between them and to drop the action to protect "the good name of Protestantism".

Paisley was delighted with the outcome of the case. "He went to his church and said the NUP is finished, the NUP is gone; he'd wiped it out," recalled a witness. Paisley's victory was sealed at the next NUP committee meeting. The name of the Irish branch of the NUP was changed to the Evangelical Protestant Society, leaving Paisley in sole possession of the title. Right up until the early 1960s, he would use the name National Union of Protestants for many of his protest meetings. He had beaten his old allies.

Despite an encouraging start, the Free Presbyterian Church grew only slowly. There were many other fundamentalist sects around to compete with and by 1959 Paisley had managed to add only four tiny congregations to the Crossgar, Cabra and Rasharkin churches. More importantly, the reaction against him inside the NUP was repeated on a much more significant level. The Orange Order, the most powerful of all Protestant and Unionist organisations, turned against him. This, more than anything else, ensured that Paisley would never quite repeat the aggressive church-building tactics of the summer and autumn of 1951.

In the late 1940s and early 1950s Paisley's powerful oratory and his strongly anti-Catholic message had made him a popular speaker on the Orange Order's circuit of arch-opening and marching each summer. Paisley himself was a member of an Orange Lodge, first in North Belfast and then in a Lodge near his Ravenhill church where he became Chaplain. In 1949, after a year in the post, he automatically became one of the Orange Order's Chaplains for No. 6 District, the administrative body for private Lodges throughout the entire East Belfast area, the largest in the Order.

To become a District Chaplain, at least for a Protestant cleric, is an important step on the road to power and influence in the Orange Order and, for many years, in Official Unionist party politics as well. It confers automatic eligibility for election to one of the seven County Grand Lodges, which govern the Order in each of Northern Ireland's six counties and in Belfast. The membership of the Order's overall ruling body, the Grand Lodge of Ireland, is in turn drawn from the officer boards of the County Grand Lodges.

In those days the Orange Order was dominated by the Official Unionists and nearly all the Grand Lodge's members were members of the party. But the party became a shadow of its former self, challenged for Unionist supremacy by Paisley and, for the years of the Troubles, deprived of considerable power and patronage by British direct rule. In the 1950s and right up until the suspension of the Stormont parliament in 1972, however, the Grand Lodge and County Lodges were peppered with cabinet ministers, Unionist MPs and party officials. Political power, patronage and influence were synonymous with the Orange Order and the higher one could rise in the organisation the nearer one came to the source of all that power and influence. The Rev Martin Smyth MP, who became a contender for the leadership of the Official Unionist Party on more than one occasion, rose to power by such a route.

After the Crossgar, Cabra and Rasharkin splits, the hierarchy of the Orange Order, moved decisively to block off this route to Paisley and his Free Presbyterian ministers. NUP officials like Eric Borland, who knew Paisley well, sat on the Grand Lodge, as did the Rev Jack Finch of the Church of Ireland, another NUP man and a Chaplain in the senior Orange body, the Royal Black Preceptory. They were worried at the divisive impact Paisley and his ministers could have on the Order. That worry was shared by senior Orangemen of all denominations.

In December 1951, only months after Paisley had stirred up ructions in County Antrim Presbyterianism, the Grand Lodge formalised its rules for the eligibility of Orange Order Chaplains. Prior to that, there had been an understanding that any Protestant minister who was a member of an Orange Lodge would automatically become its Chaplain. As a chaplain, the way was then open to becoming influential and gaining promotion to the County Grand Lodges. Paisley's ministers could thus rise in the Order in the same fashion as other Protestant clerics. But the Grand Lodge drew up a list of Protestant denominations and ordered that only ministers of those denominations could be made chaplains. The Free Presbyterians were deliberately excluded from the list.

The list included the main Protestant denominations – Presbyterian, Church of Ireland, Methodist, Baptist, Congregationalist, the Reformed Presbyterians and the non-subscribing Presbyterians. Even the tiny Moravian sect, which in the 1981 census was outnumbered by Northern Ireland's Muslims, was included – but not Paisley's Free Presbyterians. Only in those few Lodges that didn't have a Protestant cleric as a member could the Free Presbyterians have a chance of gaining office as chaplains. The Grand Lodge rules allowed for the election of lay chaplains in such cases but even then the Free Presbyterians could be frustrated by the simple expedient of ensuring that any Lodge which contained a Free Presbyterian minister also included a minister from one of the recognised denominations. The Orange Order's refusal to recognise Free Presbyterianism as a Protestant denomination was a major snub to Paisley. "Their opposition to the Free Presbyterians was desperate," recalled an Orange colleague of Paisley's. "They were determined that Free Presbyterianism would never get recognition anywhere."

The move against Paisley in the Loyalist establishment wasn't confined to the Orange Order. Paisley had also risen through the ranks of the Apprentice Boys of Derry, the smallest of the three Loyal Orders, but symbolically the most evocative to Protestants. He had impressed the Belfast Apprentice Boys with his oratory and Loyalist convictions in the same way as he had the grassroots Orangemen. They had elected him to the Chaplaincy of the Belfast and District Amalgamated Committee, the ruling body for Apprentice Boys' clubs in the city. But again the Presbyterians in the Apprentice Boys mobilised against him.

The vice-chairman of the Committee at that time was James Smyth, father of the Rev Martin Smyth. In 1952, largely at his urging, Eric Borland was persuaded to stand against Paisley in the annual election for the Chaplaincy. Borland was successful and Paisley was deposed. He was to leave the Apprentice Boys after that but rejoined in 1971 when the hardline Dromara Apprentice Boys Club in County Down invited him back in. After that, Free Presbyterians flocked to the Apprentice Boys, a much smaller organisation than the Orange Order, where they have been able to exercise much greater influence.

During the 1950s Paisley's relationship with the Orange Order deteriorated even further. In 1958 a prominent member of his own Mountpottinger Lodge threatened to bring a disciplinary complaint against him under one of the more serious charges possible in the Orange Order – that of "unbrotherly conduct". The complainant was the Rev Warren Porter, who had succeeded Paisley as Chaplain at Mountpottinger. A Presbyterian minister based in Baillieboro, County Cavan, Warren Porter had, until his return to the orthodox fold, been a member of the Irish Evangelical Church, the product of the last division in the Presbyterian church in the 1920s. He had also been a member of the National Union of Protestants and strongly sympathised with its conservative brand of evangelism. But when he left the Irish Evangelical Church to join Presbyterianism, Paisley rounded on him in his magazine *The Revivalist*, calling him a treacherous and compromising "time-server", a "very bitter enemy of the Free Presbyterian Church" who "Like Lot . . . began pitching his tent towards Sodom before he went to reside in the Sodom of Irish Presbyterian apostasy".

According to a member of the Lodge, Paisley had long avoided attending meetings of the Lodge if he thought Warren Porter might show up – he wanted to avoid open confrontation. But one night Porter happened to be in Belfast for a Lodge meeting and so by chance was Paisley. He immediately challenged Paisley over his attacks on him but what followed showed that, in this case at least, Paisley was not eager for a fight.

Paisley had no answer for him that night but said he would come back the next week to answer Porter's complaints. But in fact he didn't come back. Porter came up from Baillieboro, but Brother Ian wasn't there; instead there was this letter from him requesting a transfer to another Lodge. Porter had threatened to charge him with unbrotherly conduct, it would have been debated on the floor of the Lodge but the most that could have happened to him was a reprimand. I don't think he wanted to face criticism and the possibility that Warren would have won.[1]

Paisley's request for a transfer was granted and he moved over to a Lodge on the Shankill Road led by a political friend called Charlie McCullough. By all accounts he was an infrequent attender there but several times over the intervening years he was to try, without success, to persuade the Grand Orange Lodge to include the Free Presbyterian Church on its list of Orange chaplains.

In September 1962 he finally quit the Order, citing as the reason the attendance of the Lord Mayor of Belfast, Sir Robin Kinahan, a Unionist and Orangeman, at the funeral Mass of a Catholic Alderman. Kinahan was not expelled, as others had been, for breaking this cardinal rule of Orangeism, which forbids attendance at a Catholic Mass. Paisley accused the Grand Lodge of ignoring the offence because of Kinahan's political influence in the Unionist Party. He was later to tell his supporters that what angered him most was that Kinahan had brought his mayoral mace-bearer, a lifelong staunch Orangeman, to the Mass and that the man had later died of a broken heart.

Whatever he told his supporters, this was not, however, the reason Paisley gave when he handed in his resignation to the Orange authorities. "He resigned because he objected to certain chaplains in the Order, whom he named, having what he called 'a Romeward trend' in their philosophy," recalled a leading Orangeman of the day.

> At that particular time he was denouncing anyone who as much as showed friendship towards Roman Catholics. He had his spies out everywhere reporting back to him and then he would have stood up at a ceremony, perhaps the opening of some Orange arch, hold up a slip of paper and roar, "I have proof! I have proof!" But we always suspected that he really resigned because he finally realised that he was not going to get anywhere inside the Order. Being outside also gave him the freedom to attack us as much as he wanted to.

Paisley's quarrels with the Orange Order in the 1950s automatically deprived him of access to political influence within mainstream Unionism – the leadership of both overlapped – and compounded his enmity of Presbyterianism. Almost at the very start of his career he had the three pillars of the Protestant establishment lined up against him and he against them. The rest of his career would be dominated by the battle between them but, in that apparently unequal struggle, Paisley would always have important allies.

While the leaders of Orangeism, Unionism and Presbyterianism were united in their hostility towards Paisley, their rank and file would find his anti-Catholic message and his warnings of compromise and sell-outs by their leaders increasingly appealing. Nowhere was this more apparent than in the Orange Order, the body which united all three.

Despite his break with the Order, Paisley was to remain a regular speaker at Orange ceremonies in Belfast and around the country; his popularity with ordinary Orangemen gave him an invaluable platform from which to mount attacks and foment dissension. He was to be a sharp thorn in the Protestant establishment's flesh for years to come.

But in the early and mid-1950s Paisley's chief targets were still the main Protestant churches. During his days with the National Union of Protestants he had established, beyond any shadow of doubt, his anti-Catholic credentials. After Crossgar, however, he directed his hostility as much towards Protestant sects that showed any sign of friendship towards Catholicism or any flexibility in their own theologies.

Membership of the World Council of Churches (WCC), an international ecumenical body set up in 1948 to promote Christian dialogue and unity, or its smaller affiliate, the British Council of Churches, automatically made a church the target for Paisley's invective. The WCC's membership was almost entirely Protestant – the Catholic Church had declined an invitation to the inaugural meeting in Amsterdam but the WCC included the Greek Orthodox Church and sects like the Unitarian Hickside Quakers whom Protestant fundamentalists regarded as heretical. The WCC – "the Antichrist's bride" – became the focus for Paisley's increasingly aggressive and divisive campaigns.

In April 1952, barely a year after the formation of the Free Presbyterian Church, the British Council of Churches met in Belfast and Paisley seized the opportunity to mount his first large-scale protest. Free Presbyterian pickets were placed outside the meeting and Paisley called a rally to explain his opposition.

The annual meeting of the Presbyterian General Assembly the following June saw Paisley lead his flock from Ravenhill into the centre of Belfast where, on the blitz ground in High Street, in conscious imitation of Martin Luther burning Papal Bulls nearly 450 years earlier, they burned books and articles written by the hated liberal theologian Professor Ernest Davey, who had just been installed as Moderator.

During that year and the next, Paisley toured Northern Ireland, sometimes conducting gospel missions to recruit Free Presbyterians from disgruntled rival congregations, sometimes at NUP (England) rallies with his ally, Arnold Perkins.

In April 1955 he published the first regular issue of his monthly church magazine, *The Revivalist,* which was produced with the help of his church secretary, Bob Cleland, who worked in a Belfast printworks. That issue set the tone of the magazine: "Antichrist's Bride Prepares Herself" screamed the headline above a story attacking Presbyterians in Ballymoney who had celebrated the second assembly of the World Council of Churches in the United States by holding an interdenominational Protestant service.

On the inside pages of that inaugural issue Paisley, who edited the magazine and stamped it with his own shrill style, castigated the BBC – always a favourite target – as being under the control "partly of Romanists and partly by modernists and infidels", and launched attacks on two other arch-enemies: "the near Communist", Donald Soper, then President of the Methodist Church, and the "blasphemous" Professor Davey, both of whom were suspect on the doctrine of the Virgin birth of Christ.[2]

From then on *The Revivalist* was Paisley's main vehicle for launching assaults on theological liberalism in other Protestant churches, and as the years went on, for lambasting the slightest sign of moderation by Unionist politicians. For although Paisley had promised in 1949 to stay out of politics, he always saw theological and political liberalism as the major, twin threats to traditional Protestant values.

The fourth issue of *The Revivalist* showed that clearly. The entire issue was devoted to a thunderous exposure of "the betrayal of Ulster Protestantism – Bible-believing, Bible-defending, Bible-practising Protestantism". The Protestantism which Carson and Craigavon had stood for – the Protestantism which had resisted every conspiracy by Rome from 1641 to 1916 – was being undermined by sinister forces, he cried. It was being undermined by "unfaithful and unregenerate clergy" in the World Council of Churches, some of them Orangemen, who had invited the "Roman Antichrist" to join their ranks, and also by compromising Unionist politicians.

There was betrayal in the home where liberal ideas were destroying morals; betrayal in the schools where, thanks to the Unionist government's Education Act, Bible Protestantism had been replaced by the heresy of evolution; betrayal of the Christian Sabbath, desecrated by "Rome's Continental Sunday", and finally political betrayal by Unionists. They, he warned, were "subsidising the enemies of Ulster" by giving grants to Catholic schools and they were planning to spend £300,000 on "a Roman Catholic Boy's Training school built by the Ministry of Home Affairs" in Belfast, complete with an attached Catholic church.

Paisley's advice to his faithful was that it was better "to face the stern facts now than to realise too late our peril when hopelessly wrecked on the reefs of disaster. If we cannot regain what is lost, then we can, alarmed at what is lost forever, make doubly sure that those things which remain are not lost in the same treacherous and subtle manner".[3]

That, simply, was to be Paisley's manifesto for the next fifteen years, a manifesto that was to become increasingly attractive to Northern Ireland Unionists as the movement towards religious and political ecumenism slowly gathered speed.

Subsequent issues of *The Revivalist* continued the assault on all forms of "backsliding compromise" by all denominations. The Presbyterians remained the major target for his criticism – their pews after all were the richest ground for recruits – but they weren't alone. The Church of Ireland was attacked on a variety of fronts, some of them absurd. Selling vacant churches to Rome, entertaining "Romish" High Anglicans like Trevor Huddleston, and the Church's commemoration of the centenary of Guinness's brewery were typical of his assaults.

The conservative and evangelical Irish Baptists, who theologically were on Paisley's side, were also a target. Although not members themselves of the WCC, they were guilty by association because the English Baptists were members – a clever exploitation of the half-truth that was to be Paisley's hallmark later in politics. The Methodists were beyond redemption not just because they too were in the WCC but because they favoured the opening of parks and playgrounds on Sundays or because they nursed in their bosom the viperous Donald Soper.

Individual ministers were also singled out for attack – sometimes *The Revivalist* carried paragraph after paragraph naming them and detailing their offences – usually over some tenuous association with the WCC. The Church of Ireland Dean of Belfast, Bishop R.C. Elliot, a senior Orangeman, was a constant target because of his suspected sympathy with the WCC – Free Presbyterians capitalised on the initials of his Christian names by chanting "RC Elliot" whenever he spoke on Orange platforms. The slightest gesture of friendship towards Roman Catholics was rank blasphemy – like the Presbyterian Moderator in 1958, the Rev R.J. Wilson, who was visited by a Catholic priest during a tour of Donegal: "the massing priest and the modernistic presbyter . . . under the ecumenical umbrella" shrieked *The Revivalist*.

If Protestant liberalism and ecumenism were *The Revivalist's* foes, hatred of Roman Catholicism remained the staple fare for his church services on the Ravenhill Road. There the credulous faithful were treated to a simple message of superstition, Popish plots and distortions.

In July 1959, shortly after a frost-melting visit to Pope John XXIII in Rome by the British Queen Mother and her daughter Princess Margaret – the first contact between British royalty and Rome since the Reformation – the Protestant monthly review *Focus* sent an anonymous writer to report on one of Paisley's services, a service that was typical of the 1950s' genre. The article described a semi-fictional service conducted by "a Rev John McIlhagga", a thinly disguised Paisley as *The Revivalist* acknowledged, when it reprinted the piece the following month. The church was packed out and the writer was half-forced, half-carried by the pressure of people into the small Ravenhill hall. He described the scene that followed:

> The Rev Mr McIlhagga appeared and shouted informally down the hall: "Come on up, friends – there's a couple of seats up here!" He was a burly, fairly youthful figure, with heavy full face and cold grey eyes.

> The first hymn almost stunned me with the exultant joyous roar of voices concentrated behind me. Rhythmic, with almost rollicking refrains, it released a kind of heart-catching uplift into the air; gaily, yet fervently, indeed almost fiercely, they shouted their happiness in being washed in the Blood of the Lamb. Then the minister prayed. In the plain voice of the people he prayed against Romanism; and in particular, in a tone of sad solemnity, for members of Royalty "now flirting with the Anti-Christ".

> The perils of "Popery" were expounded and exposed in a thundering invective which rose from height to height of

vehemence to finally come down in crushing denunciation. With hand outflung in furious gesticulation, he hurled his scorn of Rome down the hall. On all sides the murmur of "Hallelujah!" and "God save us!"

The thesis was simple, England was being slowly recaptured by Rome. "Every time an English ruler moved towards the Pope", he cried, plunging into history, "England decayed; every time the English King stood out against the Pope, England prospered. Take William the Conqueror; he resisted the Pope and in his time England ruled more land in France than the French did".

The present Royalty were committing spiritual fornication and adultery with the Anti-Christ, he thundered, and "God will be displeased, and God's curse will fall on England! And look at the tutors appointed for Prince Charles and Princess Anne," he said darkly. "I wouldn't be surprised if they were Jesuits in disguise and paid by the Pope!"

He could quote them hundreds of examples, he went on, of where disaster followed anything to do with the Pope, but here were just a few: The Queen of Brazil was going to have a baby. She sent for the Pope's blessing; the baby was born deformed. The Emperor of Mexico had the Papal blessing; he was shot. The ship *San Spirito* set sail for Naples in 1888, having been blessed by the Pope; it sank with terrible loss of life. "And now that Princess Margaret is after seeing the Pope", he added, "I hear she's got a cold." He smiled grimly at the joke upon his own thesis. Laughter stirred through the church.

In the Belfast of the 1950s Paisley found a natural constituency for that sort of message among the working and lower middle classes, reared in a city where "No Pope Here!" was to be found chalked on many a red-brick gable end and where regular outbreaks of conflict between Protestants and Catholics were part of growing up.

Attendance at his Ravenhill church steadily grew: by the end of the decade he had plans to install an upstairs gallery to accommodate the crowds, and had opened an American-style gospel telephone service, an early sign of the growing influence on him of that continent. His NUP services in the Ulster Hall – Unionism's cathedral, where Carson had ended his anti-Home Rule campaign with a huge eve of Covenant rally – regularly attracted crowds of up to 2,000.

At an institutional level, relations between the Catholic Church and Protestantism in the 1950s by and large mirrored those between East and West at the time. There was very little dialogue between leaders, and on the extreme fringes between the two – as in Ireland – there were occasional outbursts of cold warfare. Paisley's anti-Catholic, anti-ecumenical rhetoric, although bizarre and strident, found a distinct echo in the mainstream.

The Church of England for one still distrusted Rome, as the Archbishop of Canterbury, Dr Geoffrey Fisher, demonstrated in October 1953 when he denounced "the oppressions and denials of just liberties which lie at the door of the Roman Catholic Church". He later commended "as a brief but effective reply" to Catholic propaganda a Church booklet which accused Rome of "duplicity, reckless and impertinent propaganda and the wholesale exploitation of simple people's credulity".[4]

Even the faltering moves towards reconciliation between Protestant denominations, as represented by the work of the British and World Councils of Churches, were viewed with some anxiety by conventional Irish clerics. "It is sometimes felt that our ecumenical friends exaggerated a little the harm that was done by the fact that the churches were not united" warned the Presbyterian Moderator, the Rev Hugh McIlroy, when the Belfast Council of Churches affiliated to the British Council.[5]

Abroad, the persecution of small Protestant communities in Franco's Spain and South America caused concern to Northern Protestants. They saw there warnings of their own possible fate in an all-Ireland Republic – a warning that was amplified when, in 1952, the Republic's census results revealed a half per cent rise in the Catholic population and a 13 per cent drop in Protestant numbers between 1936, the year before de Valera's Constitution gave the Catholic church a special position in the State, and 1946.

The June 1954 Presbyterian General Assembly heard that Spain's 20,000 Protestants encountered "the utmost difficulty and frustration" in practising their faith, thanks to Franco's pact with the Vatican. Protestants were not allowed to run their own schools and their churches were forbidden to advertise services or publish literature. In some areas they were not allowed to hold religious services when burying their dead and only close family members were permitted to attend the last rites. They were barred from the armed services and from practising law. Worst of all, "only in rare instances can people be legally married, [and only] if one of the two should happen to have been baptised a Roman Catholic".[6]

The plight of Spanish Protestants was raised at Westminster by a Unionist MP in an effort to get the Foreign Office to act. In 1953 the Unionist Party published a pamphlet linking the Spanish Protestant experience with their own argument against Irish unity. During these years many of Paisley's Sunday services featured missionaries returned from Catholic South America with blood-curdling stories to tell of similar persecution. In Belfast the Catholic church and Protestant evangelicals fought guerrilla warfare trying to out-proselytise each other.

Norman Porter had organised an Evangelical Catholic Fellowship group partly as an escape route for converted Catholics "saved" by Protestant missioners at factory and workplace gospel meetings. The Legion of Mary aggressively sold Catholic literature from stalls in the centre of Belfast and on the Falls Road; the Redemptorist priests of the Clonard monastery were still running their missions aimed specifically at converting Protestants. Paisley was an occasional attender, loudly disputing theology with Catholic clerics.

Some in the Catholic hierarchy regularly warned their flock of the dangers of mixing with Protestants. Bishop Farren of Derry was one who was particularly concerned about the effects on young Catholics of their "seeking amusement" in non-Catholic dance halls. "If you allow your children to be contaminated by those who are not of the fold," he told Catholic parents in 1951, "then you can expect nothing but disaster."[7]

Protestant intolerance was, however, backed up by political power. In Enniskillen the local Unionist-controlled borough council sacked thirteen Catholic relief workers when they attended Mass without permission on New Year's Day 1953. A local Catholic priest protested that the incident "gives us just one more proof that freedom of worship is not recognised by the Protestant bigots who control the jobs in North-East Ulster".[8]

Evangelical Protestants and working-class Loyalists, on the other hand, firmly believed that the Catholic Church, through an organisation called "Catholic Action", was conspiring everywhere to take jobs away from them and to prevent them preaching the gospel. In fact "Catholic Action" was a figment of their imagination; it was a handy name for all those Catholic groups which, in one way or another, seemed to threaten them just by their very existence. But it was a sign of the times. Paisley's anti-Catholicism was an integral part of a tradition that stretched way back into the nineteenth century.

—◁○▷—

Protestant–Catholic relations in the religious world were mirrored in politics. The Unionist government showed no signs of relaxing its unchallenged grip on the levers of power. Catholics were either Nationalists or Republicans and, by definition, enemies. They had deeply held grievances over discrimination in jobs and housing and were deprived of political power in local councils by the Unionist gerrymandering of electoral boundaries.

In addition, draconian legislation like the Special Powers Act was regularly used to suppress even normal political activity. After the war, Nationalists had tried to improve their lot by contriving to work the system and by participating in Unionist institutions like the Stormont parliament, but when Unionists refused to respond, they moved back to abstentionism. When attempts to highlight their grievances or assert their identity by flying the Irish Tricolour at marches and parades in the early 1950s were met with RUC baton charges, they drifted towards violence.

The split in the County Tyrone IRA in 1954, which gave birth to Saor Uladh, galvanised the IRA into action and, partly to forestall any more defections and partly in response to the growing impatience of Catholics, plans were laid for another campaign – the first stage was to collect weapons and a spectacular raid was mounted on Ebrington barracks in Derry which netted machine guns, rifles and ammunition.

The mood of Nationalists was reflected during the Unionist celebrations for the Coronation of the young Queen Elizabeth II in the summer of 1953. While Nationalist MPs publicly repudiated her right to reign over Northern Ireland, the IRA let off bombs in Kilkeel, County Down, and in Belfast. In Newry, a Border town controlled by Nationalists, the council forbade the use of council property for the flying of patriotic bunting.

In contrast, Protestant areas of Belfast vied with each other to display the largest Union Jacks or the biggest street arches and held street parties and religious services. Catholic Belfast shunned the celebrations.

The flying of bunting in divided areas soon became a political issue. In Cookstown, County Tyrone, Catholics tore down flags and streamers erected by the Unionist council, which promptly replaced them under police guard. Union Jacks were burned in Dungannon and other villages in County Tyrone, while in the townland of Derrymacash outside Lurgan, County Armagh, the police had to intervene to prevent sectarian fighting when Catholics erected Tricolours in reply to two Union Jacks raised by their Protestant neighbours. Peace was restored only when the police persuaded everyone to lower their flags.

In the Nationalist town of Dungiven, County Derry, Loyalist plans for a children's parade on Coronation day were disrupted when a crowd of Catholics gathered with hurley sticks to prevent a notoriously bigoted Orange band, the Boveva flute band, from joining it. Catholics allowed the parade to go ahead only when the Loyalists removed a large Union Jack from one of the floats.

The Unionist government of Lord Brookeborough – he was made a Viscount in 1952 – was largely undisturbed by these signs of growing Nationalist aggression. In July 1953, to underline Unionism's sense of security, the new Queen paid her first visit to Northern Ireland and was greeted everywhere by crowds of cheering Protestants. Catholic sensitivities were largely ignored. In the predominantly Catholic city of Derry, 1,300 police, nearly a third of the entire force, were drafted in to make sure the natives gave no trouble when the royal visitor made a fleeting visit. At Hillsborough Castle, the Governor's residence, she was entertained after dinner to a display of Lambeg drumming, the huge Orange war drums beaten feverishly with cane sticks strapped to the drummer's wrists until they bleed.

But trouble was brewing for Brookeborough and not just from the Catholics. His own right-wing extremists were stirring. In June 1952, the Minister of Home Affairs, Brian Maginess, had banned Orangemen from parading on the Longstone Road, a Nationalist enclave at the foot of the Mourne mountains near Annalong, County Down. They hadn't marched there for 25 years and their plan was clearly an attempt to parade Protestant triumphalism and was a potentially violent one at that.

The ban was rescinded a month later in the face of Orange protests, but hardline Loyalists had been angered at Maginess's "appeasement" of Catholic sensitivities and they decided to try to unseat him at the next available opportunity. That came in a Stormont general election in October 1953.

Another group of Loyalists, Independent Unionists, whose base until then had been confined to the tough Shankill Road area of Belfast, also decided to mount challenges to the Unionists' monopoly of power elsewhere. They had been angered at the government's inability or unwillingness to stamp out Catholic disaffection during the Coronation and they also accused the government of "appeasing" the Catholic Church over a decision to increase building grants to Catholic schools. They sensed a betrayal of traditional Unionism by their leaders.

There was also unconscious class antagonism in their opposition – resentment at "Big House Unionists", the landowners and businessmen who controlled the Unionist Party and dominated Orangeism – and they demanded more jobs, better conditions and more housing for Protestants. The Unionist Party's influence in the Orange Order was a particular grievance – they felt that the Order, like the Unionist Party, was falling out of the hands of rank-and-file Loyalists and into the control of a privileged and increasingly liberal élite.

Seven Independent Unionists stood in the election on a platform of ultra-Loyalism, anti-Catholicism and social and economic populism. Exactly the same ingredients were to make up Paisley's political manifesto over a decade later. They got mixed results. Norman Porter, Paisley's old rival from their NUP days, won comfortably in Clifton in North Belfast, but Tommy Henderson lost the Shankill seat he had represented since the 1920s.

Maginess's Iveagh constituency, in south-west County Down, was the scene of the most bitter contest. There he was opposed by Willie John McCracken, a poor farmer and a member of the youth branch of the Unionist Party. McCracken's manifesto included demands for jobs and better conditions for farm-workers, but he campaigned mostly on Maginess's "appeasing" record as Minister of Home Affairs.

During the campaign, McCracken attacked Maginess for banning the Longstone march, for allowing the RUC to take down Union Jacks at Derrymacash and for "weakness" towards the Catholic enemy – a plan by Catholics to build a church in a town in his constituency was blamed on Maginess. The affair in Dungiven during the Coronation celebrations, when Catholics had stopped the Boveva flute band from parading, quickly became a *cause célèbre*. McCracken's supporters, who included prominent local Orangemen, claimed that the IRA had actually stopped the band and had taken over the town while the RUC stood idly by. That charge, the gravest that could be directed at Unionism, implicated the entire government.

A worried Brookeborough was forced to come to Maginess's rescue and he addressed election meetings for him. At one, in an Orange hall, he was constantly heckled by 30 to 40 McCracken supporters who threw firecrackers at the platform; one singed Lady Brookeborough's fur coat. Brookeborough defended the Longstone ban, saying that violence could have spread to areas where Protestants were outnumbered, but he shifted the blame for the Union Jack incidents on to the RUC and pledged: "I can promise you that the Union Jack will fly in any part of this country in future."

Maginess survived the challenge but was badly bruised. His vote dropped by over 3,000 and his majority was cut from 7,500 to 1,500. Brookeborough got the message and moved him into the Finance Ministry, away from controversy.

The Independent Unionists pressed home their advantage after the election. In December they formed an Ulster Protestant and Orange Committee and called a huge anti-government rally in the Ulster Hall for the next month. Their manifesto was simple: "We believe the time has come for the Loyalists of Ulster to awake and to consider their position before it is too late. Ulster is the heritage of our forefathers; Ulster is ours and we mean to hold it come what may. Our motto is still 'No Surrender!'"

At the rally the government was fiercely attacked over the Coronation incidents. The RUC was bitterly criticised for removing Union Jacks in Derrymacash and the Boveva bandmaster, William Douglas, gave a lurid account of the IRA's "takeover" of Dungiven. A vote of no confidence in the government was unanimously passed and, to cheers, Porter called for Brookeborough's resignation.

Faced with this challenge, the Unionist establishment retreated. The Orange Order ordered an enquiry into the Dungiven affair and Unionist MPs from Stormont and Westminster met in emergency session to discuss the crisis. Despite an RUC report which had dismissed the Dungiven allegations as nonsense, the new Home Affairs Minister, G.B. Hanna, also ordered a government enquiry.

Eight days after the Ulster Hall rally, on 12 January 1954, the government – as its predecessors had done in earlier decades –

surrendered to the pressure from extremists. In the 1960s Paisley would apply the same pressure with the same success. Hanna announced that new legislation to protect the Union Jack would be introduced. The law, called the Flags and Emblems Act, would make it an offence to interfere with the Union Jack, and the police were empowered to remove any other flag whose display might provoke a breach of the peace. This section was aimed at the Irish Tricolour – announcing the new law, Hanna apologised that he couldn't ban the Tricolour outright since this was a matter of foreign policy reserved to Westminster.

Encouraged by their victory, the Orange and Protestant Committee formed a new political party called the Ulster Loyalist and Democratic Unionist Association, with Independent Unionists as the leaders. Their aim was to extend the electoral challenge to the official Unionists – "every appeaser would be contested" at the next poll, declared McCracken.

These early precursors of Paisley's own Democratic Unionists never really got off the ground. The IRA campaign two years later reunited Unionism and some prominent Independent Unionists were bought off with the promise of official Unionist nominations.

Another serious weakness was their lack of a coherent organisation and grassroots followers, as Willie John McCracken explained thirty years later: "We never had what Paisley had when he started, churches all over the place to give him people to work with."

During all this Loyalist ferment, Paisley was nowhere to be seen – he was still honouring his promise to stay out of the worldly life of politics. He was to keep that promise for another three years, until late 1956, when a bizarre religious controversy involving the disappearance of a young Catholic girl brought him notoriety throughout Ireland and with it an entrée to the world of Loyalist politics.

—◦—

In the mid-1950s, Protestant gospel meetings in factories and other workplaces were commonplace; the practice had started in the Belfast shipyard in the 1920s and had spread. Sometimes the workers from two or three factories gathered together in one canteen to hear preaching and to sing hymns as they ate their sandwiches.

The Star Clothing Company on Belfast's Donegall Road, a Protestant area near the fiercely Loyalist Sandy Row and on the fringes of Catholic West Belfast, was the regular scene of such evangelising efforts. Although the workforce was predominantly Protestant, it did include some

Catholic women who worked as stitchers. One of them was a 15-year-old girl called Maura Lyons, the eldest of a family of five. The family, all devout Catholics, lived in Iris Drive in the heart of the Falls Road.

In the early autumn of 1956, the Star Clothing Company was visited by missionaries from the Elim Pentecostal church and, according to her later, much-publicised testimony, Maura was deeply struck by their message: "There was something about them which impressed me. My own religion was a religion of fear and dread, while their religion was so simple and so free from fear".[9]

There were a number of "saved" Protestants in the Star workforce; one of them was a Free Presbyterian, Joe Walker, and Maura discussed her doubts about Catholicism with him. Walker put her in contact with the Rev David Leatham of the Dunmurry Free Presbyterian Church and through him she met Paisley. She was a guest at Paisley's wedding to Eileen Cassells in the Ravenhill church in mid-October.

On 18 October she joined the Free Presbyterian Church, renouncing her Catholicism and, three days later, on the Sunday, she told her parents. Her father was so outraged that he beat her: "He would rather have a traitor than one who was giving up her religion," she said. The next day she returned from work to find two priests in the tiny house. One was her parish priest, a Father Madden, the other a stranger. They pleaded with her to change her mind, to tell God how sorry she was, but as they knelt to say the family rosary, she stubbornly remained on her feet.

Two days later there were three priests in the house when she came home. They demanded to know if she had repented and returned to her faith. "They seemed determined to force me into convent life," she said. Her father had already packed her suitcase, but on a pretence she slipped upstairs, opened her bedroom window and climbed out, making good her escape through the backyard door.

She made straight for Joe Walker's house near the Star Clothing factory and from there was taken by car to Leatham's house. Leatham immediately got in touch with Bob Cleland, the secretary of Paisley's Ravenhill presbytery, and together they decided to approach Norman Porter for help. His Catholic Evangelical Fellowship could provide her with an escape route to a quiet life in England and away from the convent she so feared.

Paisley was in Scotland on honeymoon with his new bride, Eileen, when Maura had made her getaway. But on the night Porter had agreed to handle her case, he returned and intervened to prevent his old rival reaping the kudos. A member of Porter's group recalled: "Cleland told him what had happened but he said, 'Porter will have nothing to do with this. I'll handle it'." Maura Lyons's case, after all, encompassed all the Romish perfidies he had been preaching about – intimidating priests, convent imprisonment and a Church conspiring to deny a young girl the true word of God.

The Maura Lyons case was handed over to Paisley's trusted deputy, John Wylie. Together with another Belfast Free Presbyterian, Emma Munn, they took Maura to Belfast docks and, posing as her parents, boarded the ferry to Liverpool. From there they travelled first to stay in the homes of sympathisers in England and then to Scotland, where she was deposited in the care of a retired Protestant missionary, Jock Purvis.

The news of her disappearance didn't break until early November but when it did the Belfast newspapers made it a front-page story. Soon the whole of Northern Ireland was either fascinated or outraged by this bizarre manifestation of its own religious conflict. Her parents made a public appeal on 5 November, saying they were convinced that she was being held against her will. The RUC started investigations and traced her to Leatham, who at first denied any involvement. He later admitted helping the girl, but elsewhere the police came up against a brick wall of silence.

Paisley issued a statement when it emerged that his church was involved:

> The missing girl, an RC, attended a lunch hour meeting at her work which was not conducted by my church. She became friendly with a member of my congregation and requested to be taken to see one of my ministers, the Rev David Leatham. While with him she professed salvation and later attended a prayer meeting and two church services. This was before she left home. On the night she did leave she arrived at Mr Leatham's house and he sat praying with her and talking to her. He does not know where she is at present and neither do I.

That version of events, noticeably incomplete as it was, appeared, however, to be accurate in one revealing aspect, as a former church member could testify:

Although, when the police came to see Ian, he could honestly say that he didn't know where she was – and that was true in that he didn't know exactly where she was at that moment – he knew who had her and what was happening. There were some things that happened in the Church that people didn't tell Ian about deliberately. He knew that things were going on, he didn't inquire and they protected him so that he could honestly say that he didn't know.

Those responsible for spiriting Maura Lyons away were guilty of a criminal offence – the law forbade the removal of any child under 16 from the control of her parents, even if done voluntarily – but despite the risk, or perhaps because of it, Paisley was unapologetic for the "militant Protestant activities" of his church members, as he called them, and showed himself ready to make as much mileage as possible out of the teenager's conversion.

His ten years of preaching anti-Catholicism at NUP rallies and at his own services throughout the North had given Paisley a fine sense of what appealed to his audiences and theatre was always an essential ingredient. On 21 December at an Ulster Hall rally, two months after Maura Lyons's disappearance, he staged his most dramatic spectacle yet.

The adverts for the rally hinted at a personal appearance by the missing girl and the crowds flocked to the Ulster Hall, as did the police, who mingled in plain clothes with the audience. But that was not to be. Instead a tape recording of her voice, recounting her conversion to Free Presbyterianism and the wickedness of the priests, was played. It had been made by John Wylie, who had travelled to Scotland to record her. Paisley's explanation for the tape was ingenious: "I got it when my wife went out for the milk a few mornings ago. It was there with the bottles."

The crowds were not disappointed, though. The *Belfast Telegraph* reported that "several hundred people chanting religious songs queued five deep outside the Ulster Hall", and they gave his performance, albeit minus Maura Lyons in person, a tremendous reception.

Paisley began the rally, the report went on, with a frontal attack on the old enemy: "'There are certain members of the Roman Catholic community who have threatened to create trouble at this meeting tonight,' he shouted. 'I can say we are not going to tolerate . . .' At this point his remarks were drowned in a roar of applause from the body of the Hall."[10]

Nine days earlier, the IRA had launched bomb and gun attacks against the police and "B" Specials along the Border and in rural Catholic areas, and Paisley brought this new threat to Protestantism into the performance. He claimed that "he had received two communications saying that the building would be blasted with explosives and that the meeting would be wrecked". It was the first of many claims to be on an IRA hit list. He went on to issue a challenge to the authorities to prosecute him, but it was a subtly worded challenge which placed his own innocence firmly on the record:

It was suggested to me by a policeman that I was responsible for Miss Lyons going away. I went to the police station and protested against this allegation. They said that they believed I knew where the girl was. I told them I did not know and I tell you the same. If I did know the girl's address tonight, I would never divulge it to any man. Do you think that I, as a Protestant minister, would hand over any girl to a convent of Rome? If I knew where the girl was I would not take her to the police. I am happy that I don't know where she is but if I did know all the policemen in Ireland would not get it out of me. The police say, "You are committing an offence". Very well, I am committing an offence. I will do time for it. I would be proud to do time for Protestant liberty.[11]

To hushed quiet, Maura Lyons's tape was played. Among the audience, listening to her account of her escape from a convent life, were her brother and her father. Hugh Lyons later told the press that he was sure that the voice in the tape recording was not his daughter's, but he was the only one not to be convinced.

Maura Lyons was fast making Paisley a household name. Most people in Northern Ireland date the first time they heard of Paisley to the affair and many Catholics trace their fear and dislike of him back to it also.

The Maura Lyons affair, while upsetting Catholics' religious sensibilities, also took on a political flavour. One Nationalist MP complained in Stormont that while the RUC was able to round up IRA suspects daily for internment, the force couldn't manage to trace one young girl.

The RUC had appointed their most senior policewoman, District Inspector Marion McMillan, to handle the case, and she had travelled to England in her search. Other British police forces were helping, as were the Garda Síochána across the Border. But despite renewed appeals from her parents and from newspapers like the *Belfast Telegraph*, the police got nowhere. The affair was also exacerbating sectarian tensions. The Republican Labour MP for Falls, Harry Diamond, had named Joe Walker in a Stormont debate, and later Norman Porter alleged that Walker had been intimidated out of his job and had been manhandled by Catholics who had threatened to kidnap his son. He had been forced to leave Northern Ireland a frightened man, Porter said. The government meanwhile insisted that there was "no letting up" in the search and that if evidence came to hand of criminal activity, then those responsible would be prosecuted. Nationalists greeted that with scepticism.

Nothing more was heard of Maura Lyons until the following February when her parents received a letter from a Mrs Standage, of the Sentinel Union in Sussex, a refuge for converted Catholics, offering to return the girl if they agreed to allow her to practise her new religion. The same month an interview with Maura was published in the *News Chronicle* – Paisley denied all knowledge of it – and that was followed by another flurry of police activity as they hurriedly interviewed the reporter responsible.

The RUC were never to find Maura Lyons. On 10 May 1957 she turned up at 423 Beersbridge Road in East Belfast, the Manse of the Ravenhill Free Presbyterian Church. It was her sixteenth birthday and now she was legally free to go where she pleased. Paisley explained her dramatic reappearance in a statement to the press: "A knock came to the door of my home yesterday. It was Maura Lyons. I did what any public-spirited citizen should do. I got in touch with my solicitor and then with the police. I did not delay."[12] His new-found public spiritedness contrasted sharply with his Ulster Hall defiance, but no-one seemed to notice.

Maura was reunited with her parents at the RUC City Commissioners' office but didn't go home with them. The police detained her under the Young Persons Act and took her that night to a welfare home until the Attorney General had decided her fate.

She didn't want to return home anyway; by all accounts the brief reunion with her parents was traumatic. Her aunt sprinkled her with holy water, as if to disinfect her of Free Presbyterianism, and tried to embrace her, but Maura objected. Her father tried to hug her as well but Maura shrieked and pulled away; he then knocked Paisley's solicitor to the ground, mistaking him for one of her abductors. Then Maura and her parents shouted names at each other and when her father again pleaded with her to come home, she became hysterical and ran out of the room screaming.

Her real fear, it seemed, was of being locked away in a convent, the fate fundamentalist Protestants believed awaited all converted Catholics who fell back into the clutches of the priests. Her parents denied all along making this threat or intimidating her with priests; the fear of a convent, they said, had been put into her imagination by Free Presbyterians. Induced or not, Maura Lyons's fear was real enough.

Paisley appeared to be apprehensive as well about what would happen when Maura Lyons returned to Belfast. Three days before her reappearance he made an effort to show that when it came to converting teenage girls he could be even-handed. An 18-year-old girl from a Church of Ireland home, Kathleen Kelly, who had worked with Maura Lyons in the Star Clothing Company, had also disappeared and had been converted to Free Presbyterianism. On 7 May, three days before Maura Lyons turned up on his doorstep, Paisley took Kathleen Kelly around newspaper offices in Belfast, trying to stimulate interest in an interview, but with no success. Protestants converting Protestants, like dogs biting men, made poor copy.

The Maura Lyons case came to the Belfast High Court on 20 May 1957 before the Lord Chief Justice, Lord MacDermott, on an application from her father to have her made a ward of court. Paisley meanwhile had been working hard to keep her out of her parents' grasp. He approached the Belfast Bible College and asked them to admit her as a missionary trainee, but he had often attacked the College for "ecumenism" and they refused. Finally he persuaded Mr and Mrs George Gibson, veterans of the Crossgar split, to offer Maura a home and he brought them to court with him on the day of the hearing.

But it was no use. Lord MacDermott granted Mr Lyons's application and made him her guardian. She was to return to Iris Drive, he ruled, but she was not to be taken out of Northern Ireland. Furthermore, she was to be free to practice her Protestantism if she desired and was to be kept out of a convent. Even marriage could only take place with the court's permission.

As he deprived Paisley of his prize, Lord MacDermott took a sideswipe at him. The reports of the Ulster Hall rally, he said, were evidence that "Mr Paisley was in touch with the girl when prima facie she was abducted". Paisley was asked if he was prepared to assist the court by throwing some light on the matter but after consulting his solicitor he refused. Even Lord MacDermott's promise that he wouldn't incriminate himself couldn't budge him.

Maura Lyons returned to her parents and, eventually, to Catholicism. Two years later she got married in a Catholic Church. When he was presented with this proof that her conversion to Free Presbyterianism had been short-lived, Paisley claimed that the wedding was an elaborate fraud. But the young woman never spoke of the events that followed her dramatic escape from Iris Drive in October 1956. She kept silent to the police when she returned to Belfast and she stayed silent.

By the mid-1980s Maura Lyons had moved to a beleaguered Catholic ghetto in Belfast, the scene of some of the bloodiest sectarian killings carried out by Loyalist paramilitaries during the Troubles. In those days a reporter who visited her home would be closely questioned at the door by one of her three daughters; at the first mention of Paisley's name, it would be hurriedly slammed shut.

—◦—

Paisley's handling of the Maura Lyons affair had embarrassed many Protestants. Sincere evangelicals with experience "handling" converted Catholics quietly and with the aim of keeping them converted were disturbed at the way he had shamelessly milked publicity out of the affair with little regard for Maura Lyons's own interests. The Presbyterians had been irritated at the way English journalists easily confused their church with Paisley's and, not for the last time, publicly repudiated the Free Presbyterian Church.

But among hardline Loyalists, Paisley's activities had struck a chord. The summer of 1957 saw an outbreak of anti-Protestantism in the Republic for which the Maura Lyons affair seemed an appropriate response. In the tiny County Wexford village of Fethard-on-Sea, local Catholics started a boycott of Protestants, and Northern Unionists soon saw in it vindication for their own anti-Catholicism. In many Loyalist eyes, the boycott also justified Paisley's handling of the Maura Lyons affair, but more significantly it was to bring Paisley together with a man who was to have a significant influence on his career.

The cause of the Fethard boycott was the break-up of a mixed marriage between a local farmer, Seán Cloney, and his Church of Ireland wife, Sheila. On their marriage, Mrs Cloney had agreed to abide by Catholic doctrine, which stipulated that the children of a mixed marriage should be brought up as Catholics. But when the eldest of their two daughters reached school age, Mrs Cloney changed her mind, the couple quarrelled and on 27 April 1957 she left home with the children and fled to Belfast. Fethard Catholics blamed local Protestants for aiding her and, with clerical approval, started their protest. Protestant shops were boycotted and Protestant teachers lost nearly all their pupils.

Three days after Sheila Cloney's disappearance, Seán Cloney had a surprise visitor. A car drew up in his farmyard and out stepped a young Belfast barrister called Desmond Boal who asked to speak to him. Boal was then in his fifth year at the Northern Ireland Bar, where he had already established a reputation as a gifted and articulate advocate. He also had a name for uncompromising Loyalism. Born and bred in the tough, working-class Protestant Fountain area of Derry, a small enclave on the Catholic side of the city, Boal had brought his politics with him to Trinity College, Dublin where he had helped to start an Orange Lodge. Like Mrs Cloney, Boal was a member of the Church of Ireland.

According to Cloney's later court testimony, Boal told him that he had been in touch with his wife in Belfast and that he had come to offer terms for a settlement which would allow the couple to reunite. Cloney could have his wife and daughters back, Boal said, if he agreed to sell their Fethard farm, emigrate to Australia or Canada, consent to the children being brought up as Protestants and if he himself agreed to consider abandoning Catholicism. Cloney refused and Boal left.

The next day Cloney changed his mind and travelled up to Belfast where he met Boal at his home. He told Boal that he wanted to discuss emigration with his wife and Boal went to fetch her. But he never returned. The following morning Cloney again went to Boal's home where the two men argued. Boal accused Cloney of dishonesty and said that he had closed the door on negotiations with his wife. She wouldn't see him but she might contact him by letter later.

Cloney then applied for a writ of habeas corpus seeking the return of his daughters, and named his wife and Boal as the people who knew their whereabouts. It was conditionally granted but a month later, when an application was made to make it absolute, the High Court adjourned it in the hope that the couple might be reconciled. They were, and the Fethard boycott ended.

The Fethard incident had, though, stirred Loyalist emotions. It was mentioned on virtually every Orange platform that Twelfth of July as evidence of Romish perfidy, and Boal's involvement brought him an invitation to address Orangemen in County Donegal. He told them that the boycott weapon "must surely have been forged for the Roman Catholic Church, so enthusiastically had it been used by her to her political advantage in other countries".[13] Other Loyalists singled out for criticism marriages between Protestants and Catholics.

Boal had become involved in the Fethard affair through his friendship with the Rev George Thompson, a Church of Ireland minister who ran the Church's mission in the Republic. Thompson helped to raise funds to alleviate Protestant distress in Fethard and had enlisted the aid of Norman Porter and his Evangelical Protestant Society. Through Thompson, Boal met Porter and soon he was a regular visitor to Porter's Howard Street office in Belfast.

Paisley was also an occasional caller at the office. Although he had broken with Porter during their quarrels in the National Union of Protestants, he still visited him now and then. Porter was on the executive of the right-wing International Council of Christian Churches and Paisley would borrow its literature from him to use in his services. On one such visit Boal was in the office, and Porter introduced them.

It was the start of a strange but productive relationship between the worldly barrister and the hellfire-preaching Free Presbyterian Moderator. The two had little in common except their hardline Loyalism and a dislike of the Unionist establishment and the Catholic Church.

In religious matters the two could hardly have been more different. Boal had an apparently open-minded attitude to religion and a compelling interest in the bizarre and offbeat – he had been known to spend summer holidays wandering alone in the Himalayas, the Far East or Africa and once lived for weeks in a Buddhist monastery. Although he neither drank nor smoked, he loved fast cars and the excitement of the roulette wheel. (Now retired from the Bar, these days his health has deteriorated and he winters on the Gulf coast of Florida.)

The relationship prospered nevertheless, and Boal was to be always on hand with legal and political advice for Paisley. Eventually the two formed the Democratic Unionist Party together, but it was to be an unequal relationship; apparently spellbound by Boal's intellect, Paisley invariably deferred to his judgement.

The two stayed together as political allies until 1973 when Boal became a convert to the cause of Irish Federalism. But it was an affable separation. For years afterwards, until Paisley went into government with Sinn Féin and their breach became irreparable, Paisley would at the end of what was always a day of arduous meetings and speaking engagements, often order his RUC driver to go to Boal's house where, sometimes until the early hours of the next morning, the two men would sit discussing politics.

"We can never relax and if we do, Ulster is doomed."

LORD BROOKEBOROUGH, PRIME MINISTER OF NORTHERN IRELAND,
ADDRESSING COUNTY FERMANAGH ORANGEWOMEN, 25 APRIL 1958

CHAPTER THREE

God, Guns and Politics

At the time that Paisley was hitting the headlines with the Maura Lyons affair, there were ominous stirrings in Belfast's Protestant underworld, among those whom a decade later would be dubbed Loyalists to denote their association with extremism or violence and to distinguish them from respectable Unionists. They would soon provide Paisley with a platform for increasingly turbulent protests and present him with a route into electoral politics. Out of that would spring his lengthy and ultimately successful battle with the Unionist establishment, during which he would become, for many rank and file Loyalists, one of the most charismatic Protestant leaders since Carson and Craig. But with all that would also come contact with the fanatical and violent side of Protestantism, an association that would dog him throughout his career.

Loyalists were stirring because in 1956 Northern Ireland was expecting a renewed IRA campaign to break out at any moment, and Protestants feared that it would be the fiercest onslaught against the State since the early 1920s. All the signs were there. Aside from the Derry raid, the IRA had mounted a well-executed sortie against the British Army's barracks in Armagh in June 1955, netting another large haul of rifles and machine guns. A raid on Omagh barracks the following October had been a fiasco, but nevertheless the IRA was arming itself with the weapons of war. In July 1955, a Dublin-based jeweller blew himself to pieces with his own bomb in East Belfast on his way to put government phones out of action in the Stormont parliament. He was a member of a violent IRA splinter group; the other

73

splinter, Saor Uladh, launched a bomb and gun attack on Rosslea RUC barracks in County Fermanagh four months later.

Furthermore, in May 1955, the IRA's violent remedy for their ills was apparently endorsed by the Nationalist population. Its political wing, Sinn Féin, outmanoeuvred the Nationalist Party by running candidates in all 12 Westminster seats at the general election and unopposed, except by Unionists, won 152,000 votes and the Mid-Ulster and Fermanagh-South Tyrone seats. It was the biggest anti-Partition vote since 1921. Northern Unionists braced themselves for a violent campaign which they imagined would be directed at every conceivable target, Belfast included.

In the autumn of 1956 some Loyalists in Belfast decided that they too would have to prepare for the coming violence. One of them was Ernie Lusty, a lamplighter from the lower Shankill Road who had been a member of the militant Ulster Protestant League in the 1930s and had a name as a gunman. The other was a shipyard worker called Albert Thoburn. Both men were members of the Unionist Party.

They contacted other sympathetic Loyalists and in December called a meeting in the Unionist Party's headquarters in Glengall Street near the city centre. Their idea was to organise a semi-paramilitary group, partly to defend Protestant areas, partly to retaliate as the old Ulster Protestant Action had done in the 1920s. That group had been deeply involved in an assassination campaign aimed at Catholics. Their imitators in 1956 wanted to be ready to react to the IRA's violence.

As one of the founder members of the group remembered: "We were half-convinced that the war was going to be waged against the Protestant community. We felt it necessary to be in a position to take on and destroy the IRA. We would have gone out looking for them, you know, take them on. I think a considerable number of us would have been quite happy to have done that."[1]

Among those invited to the inaugural meeting were some who were to make their mark later, more conventionally, in Unionist and Loyalist politics, and others whose contribution would be violent. A former British Army Chindit from the Shankill Road, Johnny McQuade, was one who straddled both. Charlie McCullough, also from the Shankill and a future Unionist Senator, was in the former category as was Frank Millar, a prominent Independent Unionist whose son went on to become Secretary of the Official Unionist Party and then one of Ireland's top journalists. Another leading Shankill Loyalist who worked in Belfast Corporation's Transport department as a timekeeper was also invited.

His name was Billy Spence. His brother Gusty, then serving in the British Army as an NCO in the Royal Ulster Rifles, was to make his own bloody imprint in Northern Ireland ten years later.

The Maura Lyons affair had earned Paisley an invitation too, and had brought him to the attention of Loyalists who were rarely to be found in church. "He was looked upon as one of the more forthright Protestant clergymen because of Maura Lyons," recalled one of those at that first meeting. Norman Porter, by then an MP at Stormont, also received an invitation but left when he saw Paisley arriving; his NUP experiences had warned him off too close an association with Paisley.

A name for the organisation was chosen at that meeting. Ulster Protestant Action (UPA) was decided upon, the initials suitably evocative of its bloody 1920s' forerunner.

On the nights of 11 and 12 December 1956, just after that meeting, the IRA launched its much-awaited campaign, Operation Harvest, the brainchild of its new Chief of Staff, a young Dublin journalist and ex-Irish Army officer called Seán Cronin. As Border RUC stations were bombed and machine-gunned and bridges mined, UPA's members congratulated themselves that they had acted just in time.

For the first nine months or so of its life, UPA meetings were full of discussion of vigilante patrols, barricades, emergency medical services, transport and communications as its members waited for the IRA to strike in Belfast. A smaller group within UPA made its own plans. They drew up a list of suspected IRA members in Belfast and rural areas, and collected a small cache of handguns left over from the 1920s and 1930s, in preparation for a campaign of assassinations.

> If it had got to the stage where ordinary Protestants had been murdered by the IRA, there would have been retaliations, there would have been murders committed.

> We had a number of volunteers who were prepared to do that sort of thing; they weren't really interested in the discussions we were having, they just sort of sat there at meetings and didn't say much, but they had it in their minds to do that sort of thing and would have spoken about how things had been handled in the twenties and thirties.[2]

But the talk of violence didn't last for more than a year. The IRA threat to Belfast never materialised and its campaign was confined almost entirely to the remote Border areas of Fermanagh, Tyrone and Derry. Even then, swift government reaction on both sides of the Border, primarily through the introduction of internment, had cut swathes into the IRA's personnel and logistical capacity. By the beginning of 1958 incidents were fewer and further between.

Another major factor, not acknowledged publicly by Unionists until 1959, was the lack of Catholic support for the IRA. Although Catholics had voted in huge numbers for the IRA's political wing, a vote repeated on a smaller scale in the Republic in June 1957, the benefits of the Welfare State – grudgingly introduced by the Unionists in the post-war years – and a growing social services gap between North and South, led some Nationalists, particularly those in the middle class, to re-question their political ideals. The Sinn Féin vote was as much, if not more, a protest against Unionist intransigence as a vote for violence. When it came to the bit, Catholics were reluctant to openly assist the IRA.

With Belfast untouched by the IRA, there were small signs of a defrosting in community antagonisms as the 1950s wore on. UPA members noticed it and were alarmed at the implications:

> There were Prods who were drinking in bars, not many bars, but in one or two bars on the Lower Falls and RCs who were drinking in the Shankill area with people they worked alongside.

> Despite our involvement, despite the IRA's performance, there were people who were just living together and mixing together. The Twelfth of July came and passed without a care. Loyalists cared but there was never any annoyance taken to Orange demonstrations. In fact the vast majority of RCs in our area, you could have seen them right along the route of the Orangemen on the Twelfth morning. They waved at them. Whenever the bonfires were lit on the Eleventh night, a considerable number of RCs were there and mixed. Protestants really didn't want to know about UPA, they didn't want to become involved. If the IRA had opened its campaign in Belfast there would have been a far greater response but they weren't feeling threatened.[3]

Despite this, UPA soldiered on and by the beginning of 1958 had set themselves new goals: the strengthening of Protestantism in factories and the backstreets of Belfast, and resistance to any attempt to dilute or weaken Bible Protestantism. Desmond Boal was asked by UPA to draft a constitution and prominently featured in it was a pledge to work only by "lawful means". All Paisley's subsequent organisations would contain a similar commitment – something he could always point to as a defence when accused of inspiring violence. Boal's constitution described UPA as:

- ULSTER: Its field of activity is Ulster. Its great objectives are the solving of Protestant problems, the strengthening of Protestant bulwarks and the stabilising of new Protestant safeguards in order that our glorious Reformation Heritage may be preserved and our Province delivered from the slavery of a Roman Catholic Republic.

- PROTESTANT: Its basis and bond of union is Protestantism, the Protestantism of the Bible. It unflinchingly maintains the cardinal doctrines of Christianity as set forth in the Apostles' Creed and uncompromisingly denounces and resists all forms of Popery.

- ACTION: It is Ulster's Protestantism in Action. It operates by efficient organisation, effective propaganda and eternal vigilance. It resists by all lawful means every activity which would jeopardise our Protestant faith and heritage. Its purpose is to permeate all activities, social and cultural with Protestant ideas and in the accomplishment of this end it is primarily dedicated to immediate action in the sphere of employment.

As the last of its aims implied, UPA's base was to be found in the Protestant workplaces of Belfast where, as the 1960s arrived, rising unemployment was beginning to affect Protestants, and where the imaginary "Catholic Action" was thought to be at work ceaselessly striving to take away Protestant jobs and to place them in Catholic hands.

Branches of UPA were formed in various factories and workplaces, or in Protestant areas of Belfast. Paisley had his own branch formed around his Ravenhill congregation and called, appropriately, the Premier branch. There was also a women's branch, which excelled at collecting funds, and a branch in Coleraine, County Derry, the only one outside Belfast, led by John Wylie.

But the bulk of UPA's sixteen or so branches, claiming a membership of some 2,000, were workforce-oriented. There were branches in the shipyard, in the aircraft factory Shorts, in Mackies engineering works, the docks, Belfast Corporation and the City's gasworks. They were given names like Steadfast, Bulwark, Bible and Crown, Lutheran and Protestant Link. Sixteen years later, in 1974, other Loyalist workers were to unconsciously imitate the UPA. Calling themselves the Ulster Workers' Council, they launched a general strike which brought a British government to its knees.

A ruling Executive body was formed, with each branch sending along two delegates. Paisley was an ex-officio member and others on the committee were McQuade, Billy Spence, who was chairman, Charlie McCullough, Richard Fenton, Frank Millar Snr, Sammy Verner, later a Major in the Shankill Road UDA, Herbert Ditty, who became Belfast's High Sheriff in 1986, Bob Newman, later Belfast's deputy mayor. From Paisley's Premier branch in East Belfast came a 16-year-old apprentice printer called Noel Doherty.

Branches met in Orange halls or in Unionist Party rooms across the city. The Executive at first met above a butcher's shop in Woodvale in the upper Shankill area but then moved down the Shankill Road to a room above a pub called the Berlin Arms, which two decades later became a regular haunt of members of the Ulster Defence Association. A member of the UPA can recall the teetotal, fiercely anti-alcohol Paisley sitting down to meetings as other Executive members filed up the stairs with pints of foaming Guinness in their hands.

UPA members sold tin badges around the shipyard and other factories to raise money. That activity alerted the police, who suspected a more sinister use for the money; the Special Branch on the Shankill took an increasing interest in UPA's activities and occasionally raided UPA homes looking for hidden guns.

Some branches, like Protestant Link in the tough and violent York Street area of North Belfast, raised money to keep Catholics out of their areas, an obsession with Unionists even of Lord Brookeborough's social class – he had encouraged similarly motivated organisations in Fermanagh and Derry in the late 1940s. If a house went up for sale and no Protestant family could afford the deposit, Protestant Link would offer them an interest-free loan.

UPA's abiding concern, however, was to keep jobs in Protestant hands. That concern intensified in the late 1950s as unemployment in the shipyard and Shorts grew. It attempted to infiltrate the trade union movement and scored a notable success when a UPA member, John

Gregg, was elected as a full-time official in the Boilermakers Union in the shipyard. In the docks, where workers were employed on a daily casual basis, UPA persuaded foremen to hire only Protestants. Elsewhere, as *The Irish Times* reported: "The purpose, in any given context, was simply to have a Protestant employed or given overtime or not sacked, rather than a Catholic."

UPA also continued the agitation over flags started in 1953 by the Independent Unionists. Rallies were held at the Ulster Hall demanding that the Union Jack be flown over every public building. After one rally in 1958, Paisley led a large crowd to Henry Street in the mixed Catholic/Protestant Docks area where, with a large force of nervous RUC men looking on, they hoisted a Union Jack over a children's play centre and burned the Irish Tricolour. The agitation paid off in the following year when Belfast Corporation ordered all schools in the city to fly the Union flag.

Paisley soon came to dominate UPA. A former member recalled: "We found we were more and more dependent on Ian Paisley to address rallies and things of that nature. Most of us were working-class people who never had to get up and make a speech or anything like that and we left that to Paisley, who was a born preacher." He also had the branch most active and keen on protests, and he pushed UPA into confrontational religious protests and, ultimately, into electoral politics. He was swift to exploit even the smallest situation.

Typical of UPA's religious protests was a takeover of a Legion of Mary bookstall in Belfast's Royal Avenue in April 1959. The Legion of Mary had been selling Catholic literature there for years but one Saturday they arrived to find UPA people in their place selling gospel tracts and religious magazines. A crowd gathered and the police hastily moved in to prevent a confrontation. The Legion of Mary never came back.

In August 1957, Paisley's confrontational tactics brought his first brush with the law and his first, but by no means his last, appearance in a courtroom. In Donaghadee, a pleasant seaside town on the north County Down coast, householders on the seafront had objected to the noise made by "beach" preachers – itinerant evangelists who blasted out their gospel message with loudhailers. One Monday they called the RUC in to ask the preachers to turn down the volume. Paisley got to hear about it from John Wylie and the next night the pair travelled to Donaghadee, set up their own loudspeakers, and turned the volume on full blast.

It was a clear invitation to the police to take action against them and it worked. This tactic of defying the authorities, inviting them to take action and then denouncing them as traitors to traditional Protestantism if they did, was further refined by Paisley in the 1960s. It was to be an important element in his appeal to hardline Loyalists for it echoed past Orange heroes who had similarly defied "appeasement".

An RUC sergeant moved in to ask Paisley and Wylie to turn down their loudspeakers. Predictably they refused. Their names were taken and later they were summonsed under a council bye-law for making a public disturbance. Paisley extracted considerable publicity out of the incident in the Belfast papers. Donaghadee councillors were called Romanists and Iscariots, the RUC were taken to task for harassing Protestant ministers when they should have been out fighting the IRA, and Donaghadee Catholics were blamed for making the original objections to the preachers.

The case came to Donaghadee petty sessions on 6 September, with Paisley and Wylie defending themselves. Some 150 UPA supporters packed the courtroom an hour before proceedings started and cheered and clapped when the Magistrate dismissed the charge on a technicality – the summons had been issued before the council had authorised prosecution and no-one could find the relevant minute.

Paisley and Wylie were surrounded by jubilant supporters on the steps of the courthouse, where Paisley reminded them who was really responsible for their success: "We thank God for the victory which He gave and for the many Donaghadee people who stood with us in our stand for civil and religious liberty." Not for the last time, God was invoked as Paisley's personal ally.

◄○►

Seven months later, in the March 1958 Stormont general election, Ulster Protestant Action decided, at Paisley's urging, to extend its campaign against Protestant "appeasers" to the hustings. It was Paisley's first foray into electoral politics since 1949 and signalled the start of his long campaign against the Unionist Party. The first target was the Independent Unionists' old enemy, Brian Maginess, now the Attorney General.

Perhaps because his 1949 pledge to stay out of politics was still fresh in some memories, or because some in his church disapproved of his links with the "toughs" of UPA, Paisley resisted all efforts to persuade him to stand. Instead, another evangelical called Albert "Da" Duff, a lay preacher who ran a gospel mission in Aughrim Street in Sandy Row, was chosen under the party label "Protestant Unionist", the name Paisley later chose for his own party.

Maginess's Unionist credentials had long been suspect and he had been opposed in Iveagh by ultra-Loyalists at four general elections – he was married to a Catholic and "leaned too much to the other side" was how it was put. Duff, with Paisley as his election agent, campaigned on almost the same issues as the Independent Unionists had five years before, and the campaign was as bitter.

Once again the ban on the Longstone Orange march was raised and Maginess was blamed for a government decision to build a training school for juvenile delinquents in West Belfast which would be run by the Catholic De La Salle order. State finance for Catholic schools, in the form of a 65 per cent building grant, was once again an issue – Duff alleged that the 1947 Education Act, which had made this obligatory, had destroyed Protestant schools.

Maginess became a focus for all Loyalist grievances against Brookeborough's government and Duff got the support of the County Down Orangemen who had backed McCracken in 1953. A decision to withdraw the Family Allowances Bill, an extraordinary Act which would have penalised Catholics by depriving large families of increased financial aid, was an example, Duff said, of the "appeasement" of the Catholic Church. So was the fact that citizens of the Republic were allowed to work in Northern Ireland.

Paisley and Duff, who ran their campaign from Paisley's car, planning their next moves at the roadside, also made unemployment and the cost of living an issue. Billy Belshaw, a long-time Paisley disciple and subsequently the DUP mayor of Lisburn, County Antrim, can remember these issues being raised: "Paisley was speaking to a large crowd when someone shouted at him 'Vote Maginess!' He was quick with his reply – for Maginess in parliament had tried to get the bus fares put up and he had voted for dearer coal. So Paisley shouted back, as quick as a flash, 'Yes, vote Maginess and dearer bus fares and dearer coal.'"

Once again Brookeborough was forced to come to Maginess's aid – just as he had in 1953 – and spoke for him at election meetings. At one meeting in Gilford Orange Hall, Brookeborough said that he had been disturbed to hear that Maginess's opponents had labelled him a "Lundy", the worst sort of Protestant traitor, and he invoked his own impeccable Loyalist credentials in his defence.

The *Belfast Telegraph* reported Brookeborough as saying that as County Grand Master of the Orange Order in County Fermanagh and the honorary commandant of the "B Special" Constabulary, he could vouch for Maginess's loyalty: "Do you think for one minute," asked the Prime Minister, "that the County Fermanagh Grand Orange Lodge would have elected me to the high office of County Grand Master and would continue to have me as their honorary County Commandant if they thought I was nursing in my bosom a Lundy? Never!"

Another feature of the 1953 campaign was repeated – Maginess was again the target for violent protest. A week after that speech from Brookeborough, Maginess was surrounded by a hostile mob of 200 Loyalists as he left Dromore Orange Hall, booing and jeering as the police struggled to make a passage for him. When he got to his car, he found the tyres had been let down, and then some of the crowd tried to overturn the car with Maginess, his wife and brother in it. He eventually made his getaway but the next morning in Belfast, as he left home to go canvassing, he found that his car tyres had once again been punctured.

Maginess survived the challenge but with almost the same result as in 1953: 6,600 votes to Duff's 4,700. At the same time, Norman Porter lost his seat in Belfast, leaving the leadership of ultra-Loyalism free for Paisley to grab. In his car on their way home from the count, Paisley, encouraged by the Protestant Unionist performance, suggested to Duff and Charlie McCullough that the time was opportune for UPA to take its electoral challenge to Belfast Corporation where elections were due to take place in May.

Duff and McCullough agreed. Duff had been an Official Unionist councillor in the late 1940s, but had resigned over a sexual scandal in the party. McCullough, a travelling salesman, wore a clean suit, was articulate and was thought a suitable choice to represent UPA in the City Hall, where the middle-class Unionist establishment still reigned supreme. Duff chose the St George's ward in Sandy Row, while McCullough stood in Woodvale in the upper Shankill.

They weren't the only Protestant Unionist candidates. John Wylie stood in Ballymoney where, a few weeks before the poll, a lurid series of anti-Catholic spectacles organised and stage-managed by Paisley had given him a platform.

In January 1958 Paisley brought over to Northern Ireland a converted Spanish priest, Juan Juarte Arrien and his wife, the daughter of an American Methodist minister, and toured them around 14 different locations to address crowds on the evils of Roman Catholicism – "The inside workings of Rome" or the more titillating "Life behind convent walls". His wife's subject was always "I married an RC priest", an unashamed appeal to the sexual curiosity of the strait-laced Northern fundamentalists. In early newspaper ads Arrien was described as "the priest who said 8,000 Masses and heard 50,000 confessions", although the latter were increased to one million by the end of his tour.

Arrien was a professional anti-Catholic, earning his living by taking his roadshow to any audience that would listen and afterwards contribute to his living and travelling expenses. Paisley had been told about Arrien by his NUP friend in England, Arnold Perkins, and realised that he would be a big draw.

Part of Arrien's attraction was that he was from Spain, where Protestants were still persecuted by Franco's fascist rule. His main drawing power, however, were the mock Masses that he staged, complete with Catholic vestments, a chalice and the communion wafer, which Catholics believe is miraculously transformed during the ceremony into the body and blood of Christ. Paisley had staged similar shows in the early 1950s throughout Northern Ireland, but to have a converted priest performing was, in the strange world of ultra-Protestantism, an enormous coup.

The Arriens' tour in January and February was, by all accounts, a big success, drawing large crowds everywhere. Paisley had to apologise to "the many hundreds of people" who couldn't get into the Ulster Hall for the tour's grand finale, but he announced that because of the response, he was bringing Arrien back in April for a repeat visit.

In mid-April, he duly returned and Paisley arranged an exhausting schedule for him. Arrien was to speak in Belfast, Coleraine, Derry, Lisburn, Rasharkin, Donaghadee, Newtownards, Downpatrick, Ballymoney and scattered Orange halls throughout County Down. Some of those towns had substantial Catholic communities and, deeply offended by Arrien's mock Masses, they strenuously objected.

Only in Ballymoney, though, did anyone pay heed to their protests. There the local Catholic priest, supported by some Protestant ministers, wrote to the council objecting to the use of the town hall by Arrien and Paisley. The council listened sympathetically and cancelled Arrien's booking, as they had a similar anti-Catholic meeting by Paisley in 1954.

Paisley reacted immediately, turning the issue into a threat to Protestant and Unionist values by the Ballymoney councillors. *The Revivalist* thundered against the Catholic priest who had objected:

> Priest Murphy speak for your own bloodthirsty, persecuting, intolerant, blaspheming, political-religious papacy but do not dare to pretend to be the spokesman of free Ulster men. You are not in the South of Ireland, Ballymoney is not Fethard and the flag of this land is not the tricolour but the glorious red, white and blue of the Union Jack. Go back to your priestly intolerance, back to your blasphemous masses, back to your beads, holy water, holy smoke and stinks and remember we are the sons of the martyrs whom your church butchered and we know your church to be the mother of harlots and the abominations of the earth.

A busload of UPA supporters was quickly organised to travel to the town two days after the council ban and, with Wylie and Arrien at his side, Paisley held a protest rally on the steps of the town hall. The councillors were denounced as "traitors" bent on stifling "the message of Protestantism" and there were scuffles between police and some in the UPA crowd.

Once more in imitation of a Reformation hero, Paisley nailed a protest to the door of the town hall, as Luther had his 95 Theses in Wittenberg almost 450 years before. Then he announced that John Wylie would take up the council's challenge at the polls and stand for a seat on the issue of the ban.

Wylie's election manifesto linked the council ban with the IRA's campaign – both were attempts to undermine and destroy Ulster's liberty and freedom to practise the Queen's religion. The voters of Ballymoney agreed. Wylie was elected with just over 600 votes, while in Belfast, Duff and McCullough, who were both popular in their own right, topped the polls.

◄○►

Forcing confrontation was now an essential ingredient in Paisley's politics and in 1959 he helped to provoke one in Belfast which led to an outbreak of some of the worst anti-Catholic violence seen in the city for years. On the night of 17 June, Ulster Protestant Action called a rally at the corner of Percy Street in the lower Shankill Road and Paisley and McCullough addressed it. A large crowd of mostly young people had gathered, attracted by the music from an Orange band. A witness recalled what was said at the rally:

> Paisley was speaking and he said, "You people of the Shankill Road, what's wrong with you? Number 425 Shankill Road – do you know who lives there? Pope's men, that's who! Forte's ice-cream shop, Italian Papists on the Shankill Road! How about 56 Aden Street? For 97 years a Protestant lived in that house and now there's a Papisher in it. Crimea Street, number 38! Twenty-five years that house has been up, 24 years a Protestant lived there but there's a Papisher there now."

Incited by the rhetoric, and stirred up by the Orange music, the crowd marched up the Shankill Road and headed straight for suspected Catholic homes, breaking windows, throwing stones and daubing "Taigs out" with paint on the doors. Shops thought to be Catholic-owned were attacked and one, which had a display of crucifixes in the window, was looted. It was coming up to the "Twelfth", a traditional high point for Loyalist emotion, and tensions were already high following attacks on Protestant businessmen in the Shankill suspected of having Catholic partners. Two youths were arrested and later fined. The pair, Clifford McComish and David McConnell, share the distinction of being the first people in Northern Ireland to suffer in court the consequences of Paisley's invective.

Paisley himself was unapologetically pleased at the night's events, as a contemporary recalled: "Paisley rang me up to tell me about the great meeting. 'Did you read the paper this morning?' says he. Says I: 'You're responsible for that shop being broken into.' 'Not me,' he said, 'I was in the car on the way home.'" It wouldn't be the last time that Paisley would disclaim responsibility for sectarian violence caused by his anti-Catholic tirades.

—◦—

History was repeating itself in the late 1950s in more than one way; in 1959 another issue that had stirred up Loyalists in 1953 surfaced again for Paisley to exploit. Orangemen had forced Brookeborough's Government to concede their right to march over the Catholic Longstone Road in 1955, when Norman Porter and several hundred Orangemen had defied a Ministry of Home Affairs ban on their parade. The government surrendered after that and in succeeding years drafted in large numbers of RUC men to escort the Orangemen through.

In Dungiven, where in 1953 Catholics had forcibly stopped the Boveva flute band from parading through their streets, the Orangemen had made no further attempts to assert their supremacy. Content with having forced the Flags and Emblems Act out of the government, the Orangemen had left the village in peace. In 1958, however, Orangemen marched through the town with a heavy escort of police, catching the local Catholics by surprise; the march had gone ahead thanks to a private agreement between the Orangemen and the Minister of Home Affairs, William Topping, and there had been no advance publicity.

There was little chance of Catholics being caught unawares again. When the Orangemen announced plans for a parade to be led by the Boveva flute band in June 1959 to mark the visit to Northern Ireland of Princess Margaret, the government reckoned that Catholics would use violence to stop it and Topping stepped in to impose a ban. Three days later another planned march by the Boveva band was also banned. Behind the Unionist action was the fear, later admitted by Brookeborough, that sectarian violence could give Catholics a reason to support the IRA's weakening campaign.

Paisley immediately saw the hand of Unionist "appeasers" at work, capitulating to Rome and Irish Republicanism. On 10 July, two days before the Twelfth parades, he called a UPA rally and march in the Belfast shipyard to condemn the government's action. Nearly 2,000 shipyard men, tough Loyalists, took part and the atmosphere in the yard, as *The Irish Times* reported, was tense: "More than one Roman Catholic avoided, as far as possible, speaking to Protestants – even Protestants they knew and liked. Some stayed away from work . . . for it was known that Ulster Protestant Action was holding a mass meeting."

Paisley rounded fiercely on the government: "There are no Nationalist areas in Northern Ireland! Ulster is Ulster and the flag should be allowed to fly anywhere. Let us tell them that if necessary, the Protestants in the Queen's Island [part of the shipyard] will go to

Dungiven and march behind the Union Jack," he roared. A vote of no confidence in Topping was passed, as was a motion recognising "that Rome is the great enemy of Protestantism and Ulster".

At that time UPA was a small organisation – at most it could muster 2,000 members in the whole of Northern Ireland and had only three councillors in elected office. Despite this, Brookeborough's government felt that it couldn't ignore this pressure from an extremist fringe and Topping was authorised to issue a statement justifying the Dungiven ban. He did so almost apologetically, claiming that he had not banned the Boveva band parade, only rerouted it, and he maintained that he had Protestant support in Dungiven, even in the Orange Order, for his action.

Two days after the shipyard meeting, catcalls, boos and jeers greeted Topping from a crowd of 120 hecklers when he addressed Orangemen at the field at Finaghy, where the Belfast Orangemen assembled after their Twelfth parade through the city. Topping was prevented from speaking when the crowd struck up the Orange hymn "The Sash", and UPA supporters mingled with the crowd distributing leaflets which read: "The plain truth is that the Minister capitulated to the threats of the rebels." At Coleraine there were similar disturbances.

Paisley's pressure had worked, as it would repeatedly with future governments, and as similar pressure from other extreme Loyalists, like the Independent Unionists, had in the past. The Unionist Party's habit of answering its own extremists with appeasement was by then well established.

A few months later, Brookeborough gave them a sop and removed Topping from the Home Affairs Ministry – just as he had removed Maginess six years earlier. Shortly after that, Topping retired from politics to take up a judicial post in Belfast. Paisley could justifiably claim to have collected his first Unionist scalp; it certainly wasn't to be his last.

Topping's successor was Brian Faulkner, the young ambitious son of a shirt manufacturer. He had impressed Unionists with his anti-Nationalist rhetoric and had also established hardline credentials when he joined Norman Porter in leading Orangemen over the Longstone Road in 1955 in defiance of the government ban. In July 1960, a year after Paisley had challenged the government over the Dungiven ban,

Faulkner took care not to repeat Topping's mistake and allowed the Orangemen to march through the village. The result was two nights of rioting between the RUC and local Catholics and a boycott of Protestant shops. Paisley's pressure had established the right of Loyalists to parade their triumphalism through Catholic districts – it was an important concession which Orangemen, often led by Paisley, would always resist surrendering.

The Dungiven saga had an interesting sequel. In July 1960 Nationalist MPs and Senators, despairing of getting satisfaction from the Unionists, asked for a meeting with a British Home Office Minister to complain about the Orangemen's march. Dennis Vosper, a Parliamentary Secretary in the Home Office, unexpectedly agreed, the first time a British Minister had ever listened to Nationalist complaints.

It was not, from the Nationalist viewpoint, a productive meeting – Vosper said he thought Brookeborough's government had made every effort to give the Catholic point of view a fair deal – but it marked a watershed in Nationalist tactics. From then on they would look increasingly to British politicians, not to Dublin, for a remedy to their grievances. Paisley's protest ironically began a process that would see the Nationalist case receive a growing sympathetic hearing in Britain.

—◁○▷—

Within two weeks of the shipyard rally, Paisley was in the headlines again. This time, however, it was because of a religious protest, not politics, although the affair, which brought him more notoriety, very soon took on a political colour.

Among the many British Protestant clerics who had attracted Paisley's ire over the years, it is probable that the Rev Dr Donald Soper, a former President of the Methodist Church in England and, at that time, a noted public speaker, was at the very top of the list. In theological matters Soper was a liberal; he did not believe that the Bible should be interpreted literally but rather as a collection of metaphorical tales which Christians should be free to explain rationally. This had led him to question and then to reject a central tenet in Free Presbyterian and general Protestant theology – the idea that Christ's mother, Mary, was a virgin when she conceived.

Soper was also, by the standards of the 1950s, a political radical. He was sympathetic to Communism and believed that the Russian leader, Nikita Khrushchev, should be the first president of a world government. He was also opposed to the nuclear arms race and was a strong British Labour Party supporter. In addition, he had supported the Northern Ireland Labour Party in the 1953 Stormont election and had spoken at campaign meetings in Belfast, an offence in Loyalist eyes graver than his rejection of the Virgin birth.

Paisley despised Soper for his politics and theology but he also had a more personal reason for disliking him. In 1954, on his own home base of Belfast, Soper had made a public fool of Paisley and the Northerner had neither forgotten nor forgiven him. In April that year Soper came to Belfast to hold a meeting at the blitz ground in High Street. In London, Soper regularly preached at Speakers' Corner in Hyde Park and had developed razor sharp reactions to hecklers. Despite warnings from friends that he could be mauled, Paisley decided to take on Soper.

Paisley brought supporters along carrying placards and as soon as the meeting began they heckled and interrupted him, but Soper very quickly had the upper hand. "Jeers of people supporting a questioner," reported the *Belfast News Letter*, "were drowned many times by the applause that greeted Dr Soper's withering replies. So effectively did he deal with the most persistent hecklers that at the end of half an hour he had succeeded in getting comparative quietness for his speech.

"His most persistent heckler was the Rev I.R.K. Paisley, Minister of Ravenhill Free Presbyterian Church and general secretary of the Free Presbyterian Church of Ulster. Mr Paisley stood beneath a banner proclaiming 'Dr Soper denies the Virgin birth of Christ' and he frequently interrupted to ask Dr Soper about his attitude to the Virgin birth. When Dr Paisley took off his hat halfway through the meeting Dr Soper commented, 'Keep your hat on, the woodpeckers are about.'" The crowd broke out in laughter. Paisley had been humiliated and the next day, all Belfast would read about it.

In July 1959 Soper paid a return visit to Northern Ireland for preaching engagements. On 1 August he was due to preach at Fair Hill, Ballymena, Paisley's home town. Paisley, Wylie and a recently converted Church of Ireland curate, Harold Magowan, travelled there, armed with placards and pamphlets, determined to silence him this time.

Soper never really had the chance to start his sermon. Paisley and his Free Presbyterians started heckling as soon as he stood up on the platform and kept it up for the best part of an hour. Each time Soper started to speak, the Free Presbyterians shouted him down. Insults were traded; Paisley called Soper a Communist and Soper retorted that the Free Presbyterians were behaving like Fascists and intellectual rabbits. A Bible was thrown, apparently at Soper, by a Paisley supporter. The police moved in to keep order and eventually Soper was forced to leave the platform, which was immediately occupied by the victorious Free Presbyterians, who then held their own service. Soper later called the meeting "the most animal-like of any I have spoken at".

The following day Soper was pursued by Wylie and a group of UPA members to a Methodist church in Belfast where Wylie attempted to drape rosary beads over his neck. A large force of plainclothes police, alerted by the trouble in Ballymena, surrounded Wylie and escorted him away.

A week later Paisley, Wylie, Magowan and two other Free Presbyterian supporters were summonsed for disorderly behaviour and for the second time in as many years Paisley appeared in court. The case came before Ballymena magistrates on 2 September with Paisley's friend Boal appearing for him and the other accused. The case lasted five hours and at the end of it Paisley and his co-accused were found guilty and each was fined £5. Paisley immediately stood up and told the magistrate that he would not pay the fine and would go to jail for two months instead. Outside the court hundreds of people had gathered and they hoisted Paisley shoulder high, cheering him wildly.

Four days later Paisley held what he called a "farewell" service at his Ravenhill church and once again announced his determination to go to jail. So many people tried to jam into the church that 400 were left standing outside and Paisley himself had to use the side door to get in. Support for Paisley and his noisy protests was clearly growing.

The next day, only hours before the deadline for paying the fine expired, Paisley was suddenly deprived of his prison martyrdom. The British Prime Minister, Harold Macmillan, announced a general election to be held in October and the owner of a magazine called *The Unionist*, George Allport, quickly moved to save Brookeborough's government the embarrassment of having three Protestant ministers in jail during the election campaign. He walked into the Crown offices in central Belfast and handed over £15 in the names of Paisley, Wylie and Magowan.

He later admitted that the imminent general election had caused him to act. The imprisonment of Protestant ministers, he explained, could cause repercussions far and wide, especially in marginal seats held by the Unionists. "We cannot have three Protestant ministers in prison in a Protestant state," he declared.

Paisley was angry at Allport's action and accused the Unionist government of putting him up to it. Then he announced that "certain influential people" had approached him to stand for the East Belfast seat but that he had not yet made a decision.

He withdrew that threat just before nomination day without explaining why, but at an Ulster Protestant Action Rally in the Ulster Hall a week before polling he gave a clue. UPA, he announced, had written to every Unionist Party candidate asking them two questions. Did they believe that the Union Jack should be flown without hindrance anywhere in Northern Ireland and, if elected, would they be prepared to sponsor legislation at Westminster proscribing Sinn Féin in Great Britain?

Only one candidate, the sitting member for East Belfast, Stanley McMaster, a barrister, had replied and had answered both questions in the affirmative. Paisley told the cheering crowd: "You may remember that many people in East Belfast have asked me to stand there. I am not going to do so, but I am glad to say that we have one man who is not ashamed to nail his colours to the mast. As an elector in East Belfast I will be proud to cast my vote on polling day for Mr McMaster. I trust you Protestants in East Belfast will take notice and support him."

East Belfast was normally a safe Unionist seat but in the previous 1955 Westminster election, the Northern Ireland Labour Party had done surprisingly well. By 1955 the NILP had split over the Border with more Republican-minded members leaving to form the Irish Labour Party. The NILP loyalists stressed their allegiance to the Union in an effort to attract Protestant support. It paid off in the 1958 Stormont election when the party had won four seats, and its support in Protestant working-class areas like East Belfast was rising with unemployment.

A Paisley challenge in the constituency could have split the Unionist vote, conceivably giving Labour a chance of stealing it – but McMaster had, by his deal with Paisley, ensured his re-election. Twice, within the space of weeks, Paisley had shown that some Unionists were beginning to run scared of him. Now it was clear that one Unionist MP owed him a favour.

─◄○►─

Unionists had made the 1959 general election a plebiscite against Sinn Féin – that "snake which must never be allowed to crawl along the roads of Ulster", as Brookeborough put it – but some Nationalists were viewing it that way too. The IRA's campaign was getting nowhere, the jails were full of internees and the benefits of the Welfare State, particularly in education, were beginning to reconcile some more prosperous Nationalists to the idea of working within the State to reform it. Some Nationalist MPs openly urged Catholics not to vote for Sinn Féin, the first time this had ever happened.

Once again Sinn Féin were unopposed on the Nationalist side, but this time their vote dropped dramatically from the 152,000 votes won in 1955, to just over 63,000 votes. As the *Belfast News Letter* commented: "The bulk of those to whom they appealed have stood aloof and by so doing have shown convincingly that they do not want a campaign of violence waged on their behalf."[4]

Other Unionists agreed and interpreted the results even more positively. On 2 November, at a Young Unionist conference in Portstewart, County Derry, the chairman of the Unionist Council, Sir Clarence Graham, suggested the possibility of Catholics being allowed to join the Unionist Party and even being selected as Parliamentary candidates. At the same meeting Brian Maginess made an appeal for an end to tribal politics. The Border was secure and accepted as a permanent fact, he declared, and now "greater toleration and co-operation between all sections of the community – whether of politics, class or creed – was desirable".

The rest of the Unionist Party were aghast at their remarks and there was an immediate and violent reaction against them. They had dared to publicly question the central characteristic of the Unionist Party – its virtually exclusive Protestantism – and such was the controversy that there was talk of a split in party ranks if the matter wasn't settled.

On 7 November the Unionist executive moved to defuse the crisis. It issued a statement reaffirming the principles of Carson's and Craig's Unionism, which included the defence of "civil and religious liberty" – code language for Protestantism – and said that only those prepared to give unconditional support to those aims would be welcomed within the party. Faulkner went further, attacking the Catholic Church and declaring that talk of co-operation with Nationalists was "co-operation to achieve a united Ireland".

Three days later the Orange Order came out in complete opposition to Graham and Maginess. The Grand Master, Sir George Clark, declared that it was "difficult to see how a Roman Catholic, with the vast differences in our religious outlooks, could be either acceptable within the Unionist Party as a member or, for that matter, bring himself unconditionally to support its ideals".

On 21 November, Brookeborough put the issue beyond doubt and dismissed Sinn Féin's poor performance as insignificant. "There is no use blinking the fact that political differences in Northern Ireland closely follow religious differences," he told Fermanagh Unionists. "If that is called intolerance I say at once it is not the fault of the Unionist Party. If it is called inflexible then that shows that our principles are not elastic."

Two weeks later the Minister of Finance, a rising star in the Unionist Party called Captain Terence O'Neill, appealed for party unity – in effect an end to the debate – by recalling Carson's warning that if divisions within Unionism "became wide and deep, Ulster would fall".

The Unionist Party, prisoners of their extreme past and their modern-day extremists, had thrown away an opportunity to reconcile a significant number of Catholics to the Northern Ireland state. By their re-assertion of Protestant exclusivity and Catholic inferiority, they had once again sown the seeds of violent rebellion.

Although Brookeborough had rapped Maginess and Graham over the knuckles and killed off the debate before it had really started, Paisley and Ulster Protestant Action were furious with him. They demanded nothing less than the expulsion of the two men from the Unionist Party.

When that didn't happen, they organised a double-decker bus, filled it with placard-carrying UPA supporters and, led by Boal, drove up to

Stormont Castle and held a protest meeting. One of Brookeborough's cabinet ministers can recall the protesters standing in the cold outside the cabinet offices, chanting "Brookeborough Out!" When Paisley was later to contrast the good old days of Unionism under Brookeborough with the treachery of his successor, O'Neill, this incident was always conveniently forgotten.

By this stage Boal was deeply involved with Ulster Protestant Action as its legal/political adviser and was developing political ambitions. In early 1960 he won the Unionist nomination for a by-election in the Shankill constituency – one Nationalist MP later alleged that UPA had infiltrated the Shankill Unionist Association to help him secure it – and in February 1960 he was returned to Stormont.

In an interview in the DUP newspaper, *The Voice of Ulster*, in December 1982, Paisley revealed that UPA had indeed been to the fore in securing Boal's nomination:

> I remember the resignation of Harry Holmes and the vacancy in the Shankill seat. I took a leading hand in that movement, and, of course, it came to the contention for Shankill and a lot of the Protestant Action people were associated with Shankill and they suggested that Desmond Boal should go and run for the nomination which, of course, he did and got the nomination.
>
> Then the Protestant Action decided that they would let the Unionist Party run their own campaign and we would run a parallel campaign backing Boal. So we had our own election machinery all running for him and we had our own election meetings as well. It was a most interesting election and Mr Boal had a tremendous victory.

Paisley and UPA were active throughout the campaign and Boal needed their help. That February was bitterly cold. Most of the Shankill area was covered in heavy snow and Boal succumbed to influenza and was out of action for most of the campaign. On the eve of polling, Paisley and UPA were out on the wintry streets urging Protestants to turn out for their campaign. "Some men suddenly become Protestants and Orangemen when they are looking for the nomination of a particular party but Mr Boal has proved himself in the past to be 100 per cent Protestant," Paisley told them. With Boal's election, Paisley and UPA now had a friend and ally in the corridors of power.

By this stage, Paisley was dominating UPA's activities and was beginning to cause friction between himself and other equally tough-minded members. One UPA member can remember Paisley regularly over-riding Executive decisions to get his own way, much to the annoyance of other members. Some of his ideas were opposed by UPA's working-class membership – like his opposition to Northern Ireland playing in the 1958 World Cup soccer finals in Sweden because they would have to play on Sundays; or the proposal to stand against a woman Unionist councillor in Belfast because it was rumoured that she was sexually involved with another councillor.

Things came to a head in the May 1961 elections for Belfast Corporation when UPA stood five candidates in Belfast, this time under the UPA, not the Protestant Unionist, label. In the meantime McCullough had left UPA to join the Official Unionists but Duff had stayed and once again stood in St George's ward, Sandy Row. Another UPA candidate in the ward was James McCarroll, one of Paisley's closest Free Presbyterian allies. McCarroll was a building contractor who was later to erect Paisley's huge Martyrs' Memorial Church on the Ravenhill Road. In Woodvale, a shipyard worker called Jackie Bickerstaff stood for an alderman's seat and trying for council seats were Billy Elliot, another shipyard worker, and a Shankill Road butcher, called William Spence, who was unrelated to the UPA chairman, Billy Spence. Another Free Presbyterian stood in Clifton in North Belfast.

Paisley threw his weight behind Duff and McCarroll and they were the only ones to win, but the method of their victory caused dissension in UPA ranks in Sandy Row and West Belfast. Their Official Unionist opponents in St George's were Herbert Henry, whose family owned a glazier's shop in Sandy Row, and John Armstrong and his wife Elsie, who ran a pub and bookmakers shop. Duff and McCarroll put a leaflet around the ward alleging that Henry and the Armstrongs employed Catholics and this at a time when "good Protestants" from Sandy Row were unemployed.

The tactic worked and only John Armstrong of the Official Unionists was elected. After the election Paisley and McCarroll were confronted by UPA supporters in Sandy Row, who were friends of the

Henrys and Armstrongs. "They were criticised at a meeting for their smearing tactics, for it wasn't true, Henry and Armstrong didn't employ RCs," recalled an old Unionist party worker. "In fact it was found out that McCarroll himself employed five Catholics but he replied that he couldn't get Protestant bricklayers. Then he was challenged to sack them and the next day there would be five Protestants round to take their place but at that, McCarroll and Paisley just walked out." Some of the UPA Executive wanted to take action against Duff and McCarroll anyway, for it had also emerged that they had gone into the voting lobbies with Nationalist councillors in the City Hall. They were summonsed to an Executive meeting to explain themselves but never turned up and were expelled. Paisley's Premier branch objected and quit UPA. Paisley himself wrote a resignation letter to the Executive explaining that he wanted to leave politics to concentrate on his church-building and religious work.

But there were also ideological differences behind the split. The core of UPA members on the Shankill Road and North Belfast had become disillusioned fighting the Unionist Party from the outside, and the growth in Labour Party support had left them open to the charge that they were splitting the Unionist vote. They were getting nowhere and by 1961 they decided to infiltrate the Unionist Party in an effort to make it more responsive to the demands of working-class Loyalists from within.

In early 1962 the bulk of UPA's leadership on the Shankill – McQuade, Bickerstaff, Billy Spence and Billy Elliot – joined the Unionist Party in Court ward, an area taking in the staunchly Loyalist lower Shankill and Crumlin Roads. They came with a recommendation from Boal. Millar later joined the Unionists in Dock to oppose a new threat, a Republican Labour councillor called Gerry Fitt, who was making his mark as an aggressive exponent of the Nationalist cause, while Ernie Lusty had joined the Unionist Labour Association, the Unionist Party's "working-class" wing.

To Paisley, the separatist and bitter enemy of the Unionist establishment, this was anathema. Although he remained friendly with UPA, and continued to develop his relationship with Boal, he remained true to the promise in his resignation letter that he would stay out of politics. The promise, however, lasted only two years.

Ulster Protestant Action continued without Paisley until 1966, sometimes supporting him in protests, sometimes mounting its own efforts. During the O'Neill years its leadership drifted towards violence in response to his liberalising efforts and one member, the UPA chairman, Billy Spence, was responsible for the creation of the Ulster Volunteer Force, an organisation that was to become one of the most violent in Protestant history. Unlike UPA, the UVF carried out the threat to kill, and UPA itself finally disintegrated in the bloody summer of 1966 when it was blamed for the death of an elderly Protestant woman, burned to death in a petrol bomb attack meant for a Catholic pub.

The first three years of the 1960s were reasonably quiet for Unionism, settled by comparison with 1958 and 1959. In February 1962, the IRA formally abandoned its campaign and admitted that lack of Nationalist support had made it a failure. In June 1962, a Stormont general election saw no Loyalist challenge to the Unionist Party, although the Labour Party did increase its vote, a reflection of growing unemployment and some relaxation in community tensions, particularly in Belfast.

There was no sign, however, of any relaxation in the Unionist policies which had produced the 1955 Sinn Féin vote. Catholic grievances over discrimination, voting rights, housing and gerrymandering went unremedied and Faulkner allowed the Orangemen to parade their coat tails through Dungiven each year. There was no Catholic backlash, however, and, on the surface, it seemed that nearly everywhere Nationalists had accepted their lot.

The Brookeborough era finally came to an end in March 1963 and it was, ironically, Paisley's friend Desmond Boal who helped to instigate it and pave the way for the premiership of Terence O'Neill.

In February that year, Boal had collected the signatures of ten Unionist MPs calling for Brookeborough's resignation. Brookeborough was 75 and had been Prime Minister for 20 years – the natural desire for change was reinforced by discontent on the Unionist backbenches about rising unemployment. Boal had had the party whip removed when he voted along with the Labour Party on a motion censuring the government over its economic policies, and other MPs were openly criticising the government on the same issue.

Brookeborough survived the challenge but, in February, a scandal broke over a directorship in an insurance company held by Lord Glentoran, the leader of the Senate. Unionist MPs claimed there was a conflict of interest and the issue was turned against Brookeborough, who immediately developed a "diplomatic" duodenal ulcer. On 25 March, after a decent interval, Brookeborough retired for health reasons.

There were two candidates for the succession; O'Neill – Brookeborough's Finance Minister, a member of the Protestant landed gentry who could trace his aristocratic lineage back to the Plantation squires – and the hardline Minister of Home Affairs, Brian Faulkner, a representative of Unionist commercial interests. Social class made O'Neill the favourite.

Unionist MPs had no choice in the matter, for in those days Unionist leaders, like British Tories, "emerged" after a mysterious round of consultations. Had they been given one, it is almost certain that they would have chosen Faulkner, for O'Neill was suspected of dangerous liberalism. Once he had been the victim of a "whispering" campaign in the Unionist Party, alleging that he was encouraging Catholic recruitment to the civil service. O'Neill's Unionism, furthermore, was not rooted in anti-Catholic bigotry or hardline Loyalism; he always stressed more the economic and social benefits which derived from the British link. Significantly, Brookeborough declined to make any recommendation when asked whom he wanted as his successor.

At 6 p.m. on 25 March, over a whiskey and soda in the drawing room of Hillsborough Castle, the British monarch's representative in Northern Ireland, the Governor, Lord Wakehurst, informed O'Neill that he was Northern Ireland's new Prime Minister, the successor to Craigavon and the inheritor of Carson's mantle.

Dublin politicians welcomed O'Neill's appointment. The end of the Brookeborough era seemed to mark a watershed in Irish history. The new Unionist leader was a technocrat with little of the bitterness and overt bigotry of his predecessor. The Republic was furthermore entering a period of economic modernisation and prosperity. Talks to negotiate a new trade treaty with Britain were under way and old Republican attitudes to the North were accordingly being questioned for the first time. The new man in the North symbolised the hope that all of Ireland might be modernising and changing for the better.

Comparisons were immediately made with Seán Lemass, Taoiseach in the Republic since de Valera's retirement in 1959 and another technocratic politician. The *Belfast Telegraph*'s Dublin correspondent, quoting political sources in Dublin, wrote:

> He speaks like Lemass, only using Northern Ireland instead of Ireland and he makes the very same demands on his people – and with the same dynamic approach as the Dublin Prime Minister. Surely between these two there should be a common interest.

"He [O'Neill] is a bridge builder, he tells us. A traitor and a bridge are very much alike for they both go over to the other side."

IAN PAISLEY, JANUARY 1966

CHAPTER FOUR

The Traitor on the Bridge

If there was one reason for Dublin politicians to be optimistic about the political climate when O'Neill took power at Stormont, it was to be found primarily in the world of religion. By 1963, international Protestant and Catholic church leaders had, for the first time since the Reformation, started a constructive, healing dialogue. In Ireland there was hope that this new spirit of friendliness would spill over into political life and help reconcile divisions within and between North and South.

After a faltering start, O'Neill did indeed start to talk to the Republic in the mid-1960s and to make conciliatory gestures towards Catholics inside Northern Ireland. They weren't sufficient to satisfy most Nationalists but were enough to enrage Paisley and other militant Loyalists. O'Neill's efforts at reconciliation convinced Paisley that all the traditional values of Unionism and Protestantism – summed up in those unyielding Orange slogans "No Surrender!" and "Not an inch!" – were being sold out.

The principal accusation Paisley hurled at O'Neill deeply impressed many Protestants – the Prime Minister was "a dictator" who was betraying Unionists behind their backs, a modern Lundy scheming to open the castle gates to a hostile Catholic army. Paisley played the role of the brave Apprentice Boys and slammed it shut again.

He accelerated the noisy protests he had started against Unionism in the 1950s and, in paramilitary-style organisations and on the streets, mobilised hundreds of Protestants behind his campaign to unseat O'Neill. Paisley himself, like Orange heroes of the past, was imprisoned for his defiance. It was an astonishingly successful campaign, tapping a nerve centre in Unionism, but it exposed Loyalism's deep insecurity and intransigence and brought to the surface violent and bloody opposition.

The first danger signals for Paisley had come with the emergence of the ecumenical movement in the late 1950s and 1960s, with its emphasis on conciliation between Catholicism and Protestantism.

This effectively began with the death, in October 1958, of the arch-conservative Pope Pius XII, a pontiff notable for his hostility towards the Protestant faith. His successor, John XXIII, a much more liberal thinker, moved quickly to defrost relations between the Church of Rome and Canterbury. Five months after his accession he invited the British Queen Mother and Princess Margaret to Rome; in November 1960 the Archbishop of Canterbury, Dr Geoffrey Fisher, travelled to the Vatican to heal a centuries-old hostility; the following May, Queen Elizabeth II, the head of the Church of England, cemented the new cordiality during a private audience in John XXIII's study.

Anglican leaders were not the only ones taking ecumenical initiatives. In 1962 the Moderator of the Presbyterian Church of Scotland, Dr Archibald Craig, travelled to Rome to meet the Pope, and in Ireland the Presbyterian Moderator, Dr William Clark, publicly welcomed the new and growing dialogue. John XXIII also moved to improve relations with the World Council of Churches (WCC) and in 1961 the Catholic Church sent observers along to the WCC's New Delhi conference. Within Northern Ireland, the Protestant churches moved more slowly. In a few places Methodists and the Church of Ireland shared church buildings, reflecting the moves in Britain towards theological unity between the Methodists and the Anglicans. And there were increasing contacts between individual Catholic and Protestant clerics in organisations like the Irish Association for Cultural, Economic and Social Relations.

Paisley and other fundamentalists in Northern Ireland viewed even these limited developments with alarm. Reconciliation with Rome, they believed, could be achieved only at the expense of Protestant principles and, in Northern Ireland, that meant a dilution of Unionist principles as well. Inevitably, the logic of ecumenism pointed in the direction of Irish unity.

In the early 1960s, Paisley and his Free Presbyterians stepped up their protests against "compromising" Protestant religious leaders in response to this movement. The language of their protests became ever more vituperative. The Queen Mother was accused of condoning the murders of South American Protestants; Dr Craig, who had travelled to

Rome, was "drunk with the wine of the Roman whore's fornication"; the WCC was so eager "to court the great whore" that at their New Delhi conference special privileges were to be given to "the black-coated agents of the Romish See"; Irish Presbyterians were "scarlet" partners in a Romish plot and Orange ministers had huge "yellow streaks" down their backs.

Every opportunity was seized to confront liberal Protestant clerics. Free Presbyterian pickets outside the annual meetings of the Presbyterian General Assembly grew in size, boisterousness and hostility and even the BBC began to take notice and feature Paisley protests in news programmes.

October 1960 saw Paisley and the then Presbyterian Moderator, Dr Austin Fulton, trading public insults following a noisy Free Presbyterian protest during a lecture in Ballymoney by Dr George McCleod, a liberal former Scottish Moderator who had founded an inter-denominational community on the island of Iona.

Fulton, referring to Paisley, warned of the development of a "Fascist-type" movement in Northern Ireland led by "manipulators whose interest is power, and who are skilled in rousing passion and inculcating hatred in the name of religion". Paisley replied, saying that there were three Fascist-type movements in Ulster and that Free Presbyterianism was not one of them; they were the Roman Catholic Church, the World Council of Churches and the IRA. He challenged Fulton to go to court to substantiate his allegations.

Paisley's was by no means a lone voice. To many ordinary Protestant churchgoers, reared on a diet of anti-Catholicism and anti-Nationalism, ecumenism was foreign and something to be viewed with deep suspicion.

This was reflected in Orangeism. In 1960, the Orange Order's Grand Lodge had set up a committee to investigate the implications of the Protestant churches remaining in the WCC. In the ministry of the Presbyterian Church, as well, there were growing public signs of concern about this and about the general spread of ecumenism.

In 1962, right-wing Presbyterians attempted to persuade the General Assembly to refer the issue of WCC membership to the more conservative, individual church Presbyteries, where it was likely to be strongly objected to, but the liberals won the day. Two years earlier, McCleod's visit had been opposed by many in the church and he was banned from speaking from pulpits in the Coleraine area. In 1964, 69 Presbyterian ministers, three of whom became Moderators in the more conservative 1970s, issued a public statement expressing their concern at WCC membership.

Liberals still controlled the Presbyterian leadership, however, and the concerns of grassroots church members largely went unheeded. The ecumenical trend, like O'Neill's liberalism a few years later, was led by a small social elite who, to the fury of traditionalists, ignored the will of the grassroots. To Paisley and his supporters the "dictatorship" of Presbyterian liberalism was to be mirrored in the political world.

The inability of Protestant fundamentalists to reverse the liberal trend in their churches gave Paisley a perfect stick with which to beat those who believed in "fighting from within". His philosophy was separatist – "those within are easily shouted down, those without cannot be shouted down" became the recruiting slogan for Free Presbyterianism.

The louder he could shout, the more he earned a name among ordinary Protestants for forthright and unyielding opposition to the strange, unwelcome changes that were happening in their Churches and the quicker his own congregations grew. His appeal led him into bigger and more audacious protests. One of John XXIII's first actions on becoming Pope was to summon a General Council of the Church's Bishops, called Vatican II but popularly known as the Ecumenical Council, to review and modernise Catholic teaching. He hoped the Council would have relevance for Protestants and might accelerate ecumenical trends towards Christian unity. It was to be held in the Vatican in October 1962, and the WCC had accepted an invitation to send observers. It was an ideal opportunity for Paisley to take his campaign right into the beast's lair. That August he was at the Amsterdam conference of the International Council of Christian Churches (ICCC), a deeply conservative amalgam of fundamentalists. There he met for the first time Bob Jones Junior, an American Southern Baptist who would become one of his closest friends and who shared his flair for gimmickry and the marketing of religion.

Paisley was trying to join the ICCC at the time and, perhaps to impress them but also in the knowledge that he would reap enormous publicity for his cause, he announced on his return to Belfast that he and two other ministers, John Wylie and John Douglas, would be going to Rome to protest against the WCC's presence at the Vatican Council.

In the days before their departure, he orchestrated a series of publicity-grabbing stunts which kept his name in the headlines. Austin

Fulton was picketed and interrupted in Coleraine during an address on the WCC. In a BBC interview Paisley called the Pope "the Roman Antichrist" and the Catholic Church "the harlot of Babylon"; the BBC was flooded with complaints and apologised. The next day he brought one hundred supporters to Broadcasting House and stuck posters on the walls calling the BBC "the voice of Popery". Then he announced that a group of Catholic priests had asked to meet him in Rome to discuss their leaving the Church – but they never materialised.

The three Free Presbyterians left for Rome on 8 October. Every twist and turn of their week-long trip was chronicled by the Belfast newspapers which received regular lengthy statements from Paisley. Even the Italian and British media, fascinated by this throwback to the seventeenth century, showed interest. They brought a home movie camera with them and produced a jerkily shot little film called "In the hands of the Pope's Gestapo" to show later to the faithful in halls around the country. The plot, reproduced in detail in *The Revivalist*, was full of Romish machinations and courageous Protestant defiance, interspersed with examples of Catholic absurdities like the priest in one Rome church who granted confessions by tipping the heads of penitents "with a fishing rod".

According to *The Revivalist*, everywhere the three went in Rome, "eager hands" had stretched out to grasp their pamphlets but this was too much for the "Anti-Christ". First a Vatican official confronted them and tried to get them arrested, and then a policeman attempted to confiscate "the word of God", but they made their getaway distributing gospel tracts to nuns, priests and bishops on the way to their *pensione*.

More harassment came on their second day. The police called at their hotel and they were taken, singing "I'm not ashamed to own my Lord", to the station. There "aggressive" *carabineri* refused them access to the British consul and threatened Douglas. Their passports were taken away and they were asked to sign a commitment that they would hold no more protests, but "as Protestant ministers we absolutely refused to sign".

After three hours they were released but the Vatican was clearly alarmed at their presence, for they were to be shadowed everywhere by policemen. The Pope himself, claimed *The Revivalist*, was worried enough to order them barred from the Vatican. "Ever since we have been shadowed, police even sleeping in our hotel. All who visit us are requested to produce identity documents. Special doubling of the guard takes place when we approach the Vatican."

The Italian police denied all their allegations but that did not matter. Back in Belfast, where he called an Ulster Hall rally to recount the ordeal, they loved it and Paisley was a hero.

—◄○►—

On the political front in those years there were also some signs of an easing of sectarian antagonisms. In 1962, for the first time ever, the Catholic Bishop representing the Belfast area was a guest of the Unionist Lord Mayor at City Hall. During the same year the Orange Order had accepted an invitation from its Catholic counterpart, the Ancient Order of Hibernians, to start the so-called "Orange and Green" talks. The Nationalist leader, Eddie McAteer, had addressed Young Unionists at Queen's University, and after O'Neill's accession a party of Young Unionists had travelled to Dublin for talks with one of the branches of the main opposition party, Fine Gael. So when on 3 June 1963, Pope John XXIII finally succumbed to cancer, it was not surprising that Protestant leaders joined in the sympathy. The Presbyterian Moderator, whose General Assembly had just started when the news came through, paid tribute to him, as did the Church of Ireland primate. The Governor of Northern Ireland, Lord Wakehurst, sent condolences to the Catholic Church, and O'Neill, in his message to Cardinal Conway in Armagh, said of the late Pontiff: "He had won widespread acclaim throughout the world because of his qualities of kindness and humanity."

The Lord Mayor of Belfast, William Jenkins, also sent a message to Bishop Philbin conveying his deepest sympathy "on the grievous loss of a good and saintly man who worked unceasingly for peace". The next day the Union Jack on the dome of the City Hall was lowered to half-mast, an unheard-of tribute from Unionism's capital city.

That night, outraged by all this, Paisley hurriedly called an Ulster Hall rally under the auspices of the old National Union of Protestants. For the best part of an hour he fulminated against "the Iscariots of Ulster" who had sent condolences to the Catholic church. "This Romish man of sin is now in hell", he roared to cries of "Hallelujah!" and "Amen" from the audience.

He then led over 500 men, women and children on a 200-yard march to the City Hall where an impromptu protest at the lowering of the Union Jack was held. It was an illegal march, for strictly speaking 48 hours' notice should have been given, but very few people imagined any action would be taken. After all, Paisley had staged impromptu marches and protests before and nothing had been done.

But then a week later something happened which seemed to indicate that the authorities were, at long last, ready to act against Paisley-style public rabble-rousing. In Smithfield, on the edge of Catholic West Belfast, a street preacher notorious for his bigotry was stopped by the police in the midst of haranguing the Unionists who had sent messages of sympathy to the Catholic Church – they, he said, were stooping "so low as to kiss the Pope's backside". When he resisted, he was arrested and charged with disorderly behaviour. Nationalists welcomed the police action. On 8 July Paisley and three others, including his Protestant Unionist colleague Councillor McCarroll, were summonsed for holding an illegal march (Paisley at first refused to accept his summons because it omitted his title of "Reverend"). In the meantime temperatures had been raised elsewhere by Wylie who went to the Catholic town of Dunloy in County Antrim to hold a religious service on the edge of a Gaelic football field where he proceeded to denounce Popery. The results were predictable – Wylie was attacked by a crowd wielding hurley sticks and they fractured his nose, destroyed his loudspeaker equipment and wrecked his car.

Paisley now had three parallel issues to exploit – his own impending prosecution, the police harassment of the Smithfield street preacher and "the Dunloy outrage". And they all pointed to the same thing – an accelerating betrayal of Protestant values by compromising Unionist and religious leaders. It would never have happened in Brookeborough or Craigavon's day.

The incidents had stirred up Loyalist militants. Boal raised the street preacher's arrest in Parliament, the letter columns of the Unionist dailies were full of letters denouncing the attack on Wylie, and there had been some public protests from Presbyterian ministers at their Moderator's show of sympathy with the Vatican. Paisley accelerated his protests. On 9 July he and 500 supporters staged another illegal march from his church to a city centre police station, demanding that others be prosecuted with him. Two weeks later, on the eve of the court case, he told a packed Ulster Hall that, once more, he would go to jail rather than pay a fine.

On the day of the hearing, 25 July, he marched several hundred supporters over from his church to the courthouse where so many tried to get in that the police had to close the doors of the building.

Defending himself, Paisley accused the policeman who had arrested him, a Catholic, of bias, and tried to subpoena the Lord Mayor. He was fined £10 and given a week to pay or go to jail for two months; the other defendants were fined £5 or one month's jail.

The much hoped-for prison martyrdom loomed once more. He warned the large crowd outside the courthouse that anyone who paid the fine for him would be denounced as "a Lundy and a traitor" and he gave notice that the Lord Mayor would be challenged at the hustings over his treachery. From the courthouse he went to an Orange demonstration at Lisburn, attracting a crowd of 2,000. His prosecution, he told them, was part of the same Popish plot which had produced the World Council of Churches and the talks between Orangemen and Hibernians. "The question was not Orange and Green but Orange or Green," he declared. (Two years later the Orange–Green dialogue broke down when the Orange Order insisted that the Hibernians recognise Northern Ireland's constitution.) Paisley lodged an appeal against his conviction but abandoned it on 10 September. The next day someone paid his fine, denying him his prison wish for a second time, and he immediately accused the government. In a telegram to O'Neill he said: "Congratulations to you, the Minister of Home Affairs, the Crown solicitor, the police and the Unionist Lord Mayor on not permitting your law to take its course and on arranging for my fine to be paid. No Surrender!"

But he was wrong. Six years later an English businessman, Peter Courtney, then based in County Antrim, admitted that he was the anonymous donor. In a lengthy attack on Paisley written in September 1969, he wrote: "You had filled me with your own hate which was destroying me too. Each time you were in the headlines I pondered coming over, buying a gun, and shooting you down at one of your meetings in the Ulster Hall."

◄○►

By the autumn of 1964, O'Neill had been in office for eighteen months and while Catholics still regarded him positively, there was little concrete evidence to show that things were changing for Nationalists. The Irish Congress of Trade Unions, an all-Ireland body, had been given official recognition despite strong opposition from the likes of Faulkner, and a fresh economic strategy to attract modern industry had been adopted. There were plans for a new city to be called Craigavon, new motorways and a new university in Coleraine, but Catholic complaints went unanswered. O'Neill's technocratic modernisation was being implemented, but Northern Ireland's sectarian institutions went untouched.

In 1963 a Dungannon, County Tyrone doctor and his wife, Con and Patricia McCloskey, decided that more direct action was needed. They organised Catholic women in Dungannon to protest outside the council offices against discrimination in housing allocation, and then they started to build up a dossier of other examples of Unionist bias in council employment, calling their project the Campaign for Social Justice. It was the start of what became the civil rights movement.

Interest in the Nationalist cause was also rising in Britain. A group of backbench Labour MPs formed themselves into the Campaign for Democracy in Ulster and called for an enquiry into Northern Ireland. The National Council of Civil Liberties was also pressing for a probe into the Special Powers Act, which gave the Unionist government a free hand, without recourse to parliament, to flog, intern and to ban newspapers and meetings, among other powers.

In September 1964, the British Prime Minister, Sir Alec Douglas-Home, called a general election for the following month. His predecessor, Harold Macmillan, had been badly battered by a sex and espionage scandal involving his War Minister, John Profumo, and there were signs that Britons were tired of 13 years of uninterrupted Tory rule. The Labour Party, under Harold Wilson, looked set to win.

It was going to be a difficult election for the Unionists as well. Support for the Northern Ireland Labour Party was growing and attracting Protestant votes. With only Republicans again standing in most Nationalist areas, and their vote unlikely to reach the heights of 1955, it was possible that enough Catholics and Protestants could desert their traditional camps to give Labour or other anti-Unionists a chance in some places.

Two seats were thought to be in danger: Mid-Ulster and the sectarian cockpit of West Belfast, where close contests were the norm. Harry Diamond of the Republican Labour Party was the favourite in the latter. Opposing him for the Unionist Party was Jim Kilfedder, a barrister who had studied law with Boal at Trinity College, Dublin. Billy McMillen, later the Official IRA's Belfast commander, stood for the Republicans and Billy Boyd for the NILP. Unionists were worried that Billy Boyd could take enough Protestant votes to give the seat to Diamond.

The Unionists had good reasons not to want any anti-Unionists at Westminster. At the beginning of the campaign Harold Wilson had written to the NILP candidates promising "new economic vigour and social justice" in Northern Ireland if the Tories were defeated. He followed that up with a letter to the McCloskeys, which they published, promising that a Labour government would outlaw religious discrimination and legislate against biased housing allocation.

Wilson's pledges cut right across the Government of Ireland Act, which had reserved certain powers to Stormont, and the Unionists, alarmed by this, moved to solidify their support. O'Neill made the "Republican anarchists" the main issue, while Faulkner, speaking on Kilfedder's platform, said a vote for Boyd was a wasted vote: West Belfast was a straight fight between Unionism and Republicanism. They were tactics Brookeborough would have been proud of.

To press home the message, the Unionist newspapers, quoting official sources, carried stories saying that the IRA was using the election to recruit members in preparation for a new campaign and were raising money for it in the United States. In part this was true. The Republicans were recruiting – one of the 1964 intake was a sixteen-year-old called Gerry Adams – but under the influence of a Marxist called Roy Johnston they were moving towards left-wing political agitation and away from military conspiracies.

Up to then, 1964 had been a busy year for Ian Paisley. Two new churches had been built, his wife Eileen had stood unsuccessfully in the Corporation elections against the Lord Mayor on the issue of her husband's prosecution – Paisley was still unwilling to incur disapproval in the church by standing himself – and he announced plans for a "Protestant" weekly paper.

But in late September, just as the campaign intensified, Paisley abandoned his pledge given to the UPA leaders two years earlier and re-entered the worldly arena of politics in order to ensure a Unionist victory in West Belfast.

The issue which excited him and other Loyalists was, as it had been in 1954 and 1959, about a flag. At the start of the election campaign, the Republicans established their election headquarters in an abandoned shop at the bottom of Divis Street, where Catholic West Belfast meets the city centre. In the window they displayed a Starry Plough, the flag of James Connolly's Citizens' Army, and a small Irish Tricolour. The latter's display, though not illegal, could be banned under the Flags and Emblems Act. That gave the police power to remove a Tricolour if its display might cause a breach of the peace; in practice this meant if there were complaints from Unionists. The flag, half-concealed behind a grimy window front, had been on show for some time but the local police, judging that discretion was the better part of valour, had decided to do nothing about it. By Sunday, 27 September, however, Paisley had heard about it and at an Ulster Hall rally he threatened to march his supporters to Divis Street to remove it if the authorities didn't act. It was a repeat of the threats made by the Independent Unionists in 1954 and by himself in 1959.

The previous day the *Belfast Telegraph*, quoting RUC sources, had reported that "anonymous telephone complaints" had been received about the flag and, the next morning, Sunday, a conference was held in the RUC City Commissioner's office to decide what to do. There had also been threats that armed "B" Specials would take their own action and the Ministry of Home Affairs was consulted. Paisley's threat, later that day, to cause mayhem in West Belfast settled the matter. The police would act.

The question of how Paisley was alerted to the Tricolour has never been satisfactorily settled. At the time he said that he had heard about it from local Protestants and had complained personally to the RUC City Commissioner as early as the Friday before his Ulster Hall threat. Seven years later, during his testimony to the Scarman Tribunal of Inquiry into the riots of 1969, he said the *Belfast Telegraph* had written about the flag "before I ever mentioned it". Senior RUC officers then based in West Belfast, when interviewed for this book, agreed that the controversy broke only after the *Belfast Telegraph* article appeared. Their suspicion is that the Unionist Party manufactured the crisis for its own benefit.

Whatever the truth, the effect of Paisley's threat was instant. On 28 September the RUC removed the Tricolour peacefully. Paisley called off his march and held a rally outside the City Hall instead. But Catholics gathered in Divis Street expecting him and there were clashes with the police.

There was more rioting the next night and buses were burned. By 1 October, the Tricolour was back in the Republican HQ window and this time the RUC, led by a Catholic Head Constable, Frank Lagan, smashed the window with pickaxes to remove it. More rioting broke out and the police brought in water cannon; petrol bombs were thrown by the rioters and the IRA sent out some of its men with handguns.

The riots, the worst Belfast had seen since the 1930s, had reverberations elsewhere. In Enniskillen, the RUC used their batons at a Republican election meeting when the Tricolour was flown; in Coleraine there were clashes between rival crowds when a policeman tried to remove a Tricolour, and in Dungannon a crowd of Loyalists disrupted a Republican rally with shouts of "We want Paisley".

The effect of it all was to solidify Unionist support in West Belfast, and Kilfedder, who had joined in the demands for the flag's removal, easily won, pushing Billy Boyd into third place.

During the campaign he had courted Paisley's support and at one rally in the lower Shankill, Paisley was pulled from the crowd to speak from his platform. On the night of the count Kilfedder publicly thanked Paisley for his victory – "without whom it would not have been possible" – and, as his jubilant supporters carried him off for a victory parade, they chanted, "We want Paisley".

As the dust settled, O'Neill, the liberal *Belfast Telegraph* and the Presbyterian Moderator combined to rebuke Paisley's "brainless" intervention but there was little doubt in NILP and Nationalist minds that he had done the Unionist Party a great service. The affair, though, had also enhanced his outspoken reputation among rank-and-file Loyalists. As one Nationalist Senator pointed out during a Stormont debate on the riots: "The Unionists thought that they had used the Reverend Ian Paisley but Mr Paisley in turn was convinced that he had trounced the Unionists".

For Paisley himself, the cheek of the Republicans in flying the Tricolour was a sign of much more trouble on the way. The real nature of Romanism had been revealed, he told a packed Ulster Hall, and the people who had kicked policemen in Divis Street would kick Protestants tomorrow. "Protestantism has faced many serious crises in its history. We are facing a crisis now and the province is heading for even greater crises." Thanks in no small part to himself, that was to be a prophetic statement.

◄○►

The first of those "crises" began just after one o'clock on a cold January afternoon in 1965, four months after the Divis Street riots. A car carrying the Taoiseach of the Irish Republic, Seán Lemass, drew up to the entrance of Stormont House and Captain Terence O'Neill walked out to greet his visitor with four words: "Welcome to the North."

The historic act of inviting the Republic's Prime Minister for talks about economic co-operation was a calculated gamble by O'Neill. None of his predecessors had dared do it for fear of angering extremists and O'Neill admitted the dangers by keeping the visit a closely guarded secret from the Unionist Party and the Orange Order. His cabinet ministers were not consulted. Only one, William Craig, was informed of the visit and then only the night before. A small group of civil servants – Cecil Bateman, the Cabinet Secretary; his assistant, a rising young technocrat called Ken Bloomfield, and O'Neill's private secretary, Jim Malley – had organised the whole thing out of sight of O'Neill's colleagues.

Despite the political risks, there were good reasons why, in 1965, the two Prime Ministers should meet. For both the North and the South, there could be considerable savings from increased trade between them and other forms of economic co-operation. Both had growing numbers of jobless and both were trying to attract foreign investment; the economics of scale made co-operation sensible.

But O'Neill had breached an important tenet of Unionist faith, one which every Prime Minister from Craigavon onwards had accepted: there could be no contact between Dublin and Belfast until the Republic recognised Northern Ireland's constitutional position within the United Kingdom. Nothing less than the Republic dropping its constitutional claim to the North would satisfy traditional Unionists.

Calls from Dublin for talks with the Belfast government had started as soon as Lemass took over from de Valera but each time, in 1959, 1961, 1962 and 1963, he got the same response from Brookeborough: "If he accepts Northern Ireland's constitution then I am quite prepared to meet him." Each time Lemass's reply was the same: the aspiration to Irish unity was inviolable. Unionist suspicions about the Republic's motives, furthermore, had been hardened by de Valera, who in 1957 had said that the best way to end partition was "to have as close relations as they could with those in the six counties and try to get them to combine on matters and interests common to them both".

O'Neill also had a few of his own hostages to fortune. A few days before he replaced Brookeborough, he had publicly supported a Unionist backbench motion at Stormont which ruled out cross-Border contact until the Republic formally accepted the North's British link. A month later, as Premier, O'Neill declared: "I very much regret that the Government of the Republic has never seen its way to recognise the constitutional position of Northern Ireland. This attitude must continue to be regarded as an obstacle to meetings between the Heads of the two governments." On the "Twelfth" in 1964 he told Orangemen the same thing. Those statements would hang like an albatross around his neck for years to come.

Lemass made some efforts to overcome these obstacles but without success. In July 1963, in a speech at Tralee in County Kerry, he came close to accepting the existence of Northern Ireland but followed that up with a diplomatic offensive against partition in Britain and the USA. Each time O'Neill counter-attacked. When the two men met on 14 January 1965 it came like a bolt out of the blue to most Unionists.

Paisley was the quickest to react. The following afternoon he and his two Protestant Unionist councillors, McCarroll and Duff, drove to the Stormont estate in a car trailing a huge Ulster flag. They staged a quick protest for the benefit of television cameras, showing placards which read: "No Mass, no Lemass", "Down with the Lundies" and "IRA murderer welcomed at Stormont".

Then they went into the lobby of Stormont Castle to deliver a protest letter to O'Neill. A civil servant accepted it on his behalf. The letter homed in on O'Neill's tactical errors: "By breaking your word and by acting without consulting the elected representatives of the Protestants of our country, you have adopted the tactics of a dictator and forfeited your right to be Prime Minister. We challenge you to go to the country on this issue. Surely the people have a right to a say in this grave departure from the stand of your predecessors in office."

Reaction elsewhere in Unionism was more muted. Only one cabinet member, the right-wing Harry West, the Minister of Agriculture from the backwoods of Fermanagh, had protested by staying away from a tea and biscuits session with Lemass. On the backbenches only two MPs – Boal and the former Attorney General, Edmund Warnock – had complained, the former with his usual dazzling rhetoric, about O'Neill's secrecy and his broken pledges.

Elsewhere, O'Neill's assurances that politics had not entered his talks, and that Lemass had, by coming to Belfast, given de facto recognition to Northern Ireland, appeared to have been accepted. The media on both sides of the Border had welcomed the new era of cordiality which was dawning. RUC chiefs, hopeful of better relations with Nationalists, had privately welcomed the meeting and even Brookeborough issued a supportive statement, albeit cautiously and carefully worded. The Orange Order's Grand Master, Sir George Clark, had also praised the meeting, stressing the potential economic benefits, and saying that he was sure that the general feeling among Orangemen was that it would be regarded as a "non-political" issue.

Paisley knew otherwise. There was a gulf between the middle-class leadership of the Order and its rural and urban rank-and-file. The leadership may have become more moderate over the years, but at grassroots level, the bulk of Orangemen were still deeply conservative and hostile to Catholicism. Many of them instinctively saw the O'Neill-Lemass meeting not only as "political", but as potentially dangerous to the Union – a mechanism maintained only by perpetual domination of Catholics. Their resentment at the actions of their distant leadership could be easily roused, and Paisley was quick to realise that the ordinary Orangeman could be a ready convert to his cause.

Within a week of the meeting, he announced that signatures of Orangemen were being sought for a petition against O'Neill. At an enthusiastic Ulster Hall rally in front of 1,000 foot-stamping supporters, he once more denounced "the O'Neill–Lemass conspiracy" and announced that "Protestant" candidates would stand against every O'Neill supporter at the next election: "He is a bridge builder, he tells us. A traitor and a bridge are very much alike for they both go over to the other side."

His increasingly useful aide, Noel Doherty, organised an "Orange Defence Committee" to garner Orange discontent – Paisley couldn't be a member because he had severed his links with the Orange Order three years before. Doherty distributed leaflets at Orange meetings, pointing out that O'Neill had not consulted the Orange Order before meeting Lemass. "Are you going to sit by and allow this insult to be hurled at you?" the leaflet asked.

In February, when O'Neill paid a return visit to Lemass in Dublin, Doherty and McCarroll accused Sir George Clark of "treachery" to Orangeism and threatened to bring a complaint against both him and O'Neill to the Grand Lodge. When the Grand Lodge countered with a move to expel them, they accused the Unionist Party of "manipulating the Grand Lodge in order to stifle the voice of Protestantism". The same sort of accusation had been made by the Independent Unionists a decade earlier.

Later that month O'Neill encountered the first of what were to be regular Paisleyite pickets, organised by John Wylie and some Free

Presbyterians in Coleraine. Then on 25 February he narrowly escaped being besieged in the Unionist Party headquarters in Belfast where he was a guest speaker. Only some alert police work saved him from being mauled by a mob of 2,000 that had been marched over by Paisley behind Orange bands from Sandy Row, the Shankill and East Belfast.

Paisley told the crowd that O'Neill, aided by the *Belfast Telegraph*, had declared war on Loyalists. "They may control the police force, they may control the judiciary, they may control the powers that be, but we are determined to remain free. They can spill as much printers' ink as they like but we are prepared, if necessary, to spill our blood." As the crowd dispersed, someone shouted: "Up the Falls and burn them out."

But O'Neill looked as if he was going to survive. The Grand Lodge gave him a vote of confidence, as did the Ulster Unionist Council. Only two other MPs, Kilfedder and Sir Knox Cunningham, who also sat at Westminster, had joined the ranks of the critics. In October, a Stormont general election saw no sign of the threatened "Protestant" candidates. Encouraged by a good result, O'Neill began to make overtures to Catholics, visiting their schools, drinking tea with nuns and priests and even entertaining Cardinal Conway, the Catholic Primate of Ireland.

It seemed as though O'Neill was going to get his own way, unchallenged within his own party. To unrepentant and now thoroughly alarmed Loyalists, it seemed, as 1965 turned into 1966, that the only voice of effective protest was coming from Ian Paisley.

After the Lemass–O'Neill meeting, Paisley, in a call for Protestant resistance, neatly summarised his political philosophy in an article in *The Revivalist*: "It is quite evident," he wrote, "that the Ecumenists, both political and ecclesiastical, are selling us. Every Ulster Protestant must unflinchingly resist these leaders and let it be known in no uncertain manner that they will not sit idly by as these modern Lundies pursue their policy of treachery. Ulster expects every Protestant in this hour of crisis to do his duty."

In 1966, the fiftieth anniversary of the Easter Rising in Dublin and of the slaughter of Carson's Ulster Volunteer Force on the battlefield of the Somme, some Loyalists were to answer that clarion call to action with devastating results for Northern Ireland.

―◇―

It was, however, God's work which preoccupied Ian Paisley in the first weeks of 1966. In January it was announced that a Catholic priest would, for the first time, preach a sermon at Westminster Abbey, and Paisley, announcing plans for a protest in London, telegrammed the Queen to demand that the sermon be cancelled. On 21 January, accompanied by 30 of his ministers and lay church members and a delegation from the British section of the ICCC led by Pastor Jack Glass from Scotland and the Rev Brian Green from London, Paisley picketed Westminster Abbey. He attracted only bewildered stares from Londoners, the brief attention of a policeman but valuable headlines back home.

In Belfast, however, things were happening which were to show that he was nursing political ambitions as well. The O'Neill-Lemass meeting, O'Neill's overtures to Catholics, and a growing pressure to admit Catholics to the Unionist Party were combining to unsettle more and more Loyalists. Some were ready to move into more militant forms of political opposition. In the next three months, Paisley was to create vehicles that would both give them that opportunity and promote his own cause.

Their inspiration was the faithful printer, Noel Doherty, who had followed Paisley from the inception of Ulster Protestant Action. Born and bred on the lower Newtownards Road in East Belfast, under the shadow of the shipyard cranes, Doherty's printing skills had already helped make *The Revivalist* a more professional product. In early 1966 he formed an idea that would allow Paisley to harness the political discontent that was all around him.

It was the coming Republican celebrations of the fiftieth anniversary of the 1916 Dublin Easter Rising that sparked Doherty's imagination. The air was already thick with stories of thousands of Southerners planning to pour across the Border to mark the anniversary and there was talk also that the IRA would use the event as a springboard for another campaign. Yet in Belfast, O'Neill's government was full of compromise and weakness; once more, as so often in Ulster Protestantism's history, Loyalists would have to look to themselves.

The result was the Ulster Constitution Defence Committee (UCDC), an idea which Paisley, seeing its potential, immediately endorsed. It was soon to be invested, at least in the eyes of its members, with Biblical meaning. At the head of the committee, Christ-like, was Paisley as chairman, and underneath him were 12 committee members – "apostles" – called together by him, pledged as a body of "Protestant patriots" to defend the union, the Protestant monarchy and the Williamite Settlement. Its first meeting continued the Biblical parallels. Like the

Last Supper, it was held in a room above a restaurant. O'Neill was the "Judas" and Paisley would soon become the martyred saviour.

Doherty's idea caught on, and Loyalists showed so much interest that the UCDC was snowed under with applications for membership. Paisley had the idea of forming the putative recruits into divisions of Ulster Protestant Volunteers (UPV), a name he thought up himself, as he later explained to the Scarman Tribunal: "it had an historic connection with the formation of the state, with Carson's Ulster Volunteer Force and we were Protestants and Ulstermen." To underline the continuity, the UPV adopted the old UVF's motto, "For God and Ulster".

Assisted by a Free Presbyterian Sunday school teacher called Billy Mitchell, who was later to gain notoriety as a modern UVF gunman, Doherty was made UCDC Secretary and given the task of touring Northern Ireland helping Loyalists to form UPV branches. His new responsibilities brought him into contact with people whose opposition to O'Neill did not stop at politics.

The UPV, who were at all times subservient to the UCDC, were organised in branches and divisions within counties, as was the Orange Order and other Loyalist institutions. Membership was open only to born Protestants – Catholics and RUC members were disqualified. Paisley always distrusted the police because they accepted Catholic recruits but members of the exclusively Protestant and often extremist "B" Specials were welcomed into the UPV. The UCDC was empowered by its constitution and rules to take "whatever steps it thinks fit" to expose unconstitutional acts by the government but there was a safeguard against accusations of lawlessness.

Rule 15 stated: "Any member associated with, or giving support to, any subversive or lawless activities whatsoever shall be expelled from the body." Paisley was given full authority to act in such cases. It would prove to be an extremely useful rule.

During the next few years the UPV acted primarily as a magnet for Orangemen and Unionist Party members disillusioned with their leaderships – just as the Free Presbyterian Church attracted religious malcontents. Increasingly the UPV modelled itself on the Orange Order. Some branches had chaplains and, like Orange Lodges, began their meetings with prayers or a reading from the Bible. A sash, white with red and blue fringes, was worn and UPV marchers lined up three abreast led by "Kick the Pope" bands. In later years the UPV proved to be invaluable in the development of Paisley's career. With 17 divisions throughout the North, and hundreds of members, it provided Paisley with a vote-collecting machine which he was able to transform into the Democratic Unionist Party.

"It was almost like a new Orange Order or Apprentice Boys," recalled an original member: "a body of like-minded people who felt that Ian Paisley was articulating on behalf of the Ulster people and for whom the Orange Order was too pro-establishment. It filled a gap."

Doherty also filled another gap, a communications gap. Aside from *The Revivalist,* which primarily serviced the Free Presbyterian Church, Paisley had no outlet for his political message. The local media were hostile to him and he had long lambasted them as his enemies. The BBC was "infested with Papists" and the *Belfast News Letter* was "cowardly"; but he reserved his strongest language for the "lying and treacherous" *Belfast Telegraph,* which, under the ownership of the Thompson organisation and the editorship of Jack Sayers, had enthusiastically supported O'Neill's liberal policies. In 1966 the *Telegraph* refused to carry adverts for Paisley's political or religious events and later, when it sponsored a campaign to back O'Neill, Paisley began a Protestant boycott of the North's most popular daily.

Journalists too were his enemies. They were "the whirring multitudes of pestiferous scribbling rodents commonly known as Press reporters, newsmen and journalists. . . . They usually sport thick-lensed glasses, wear six pairs of ropey sandals, are homosexuals, kiss holy medals or carry secret membership cards of the Communist Party. Most of them are communistoids without the guts of a red-blooded Communist, or Roman Catholics without the effrontery of a Pope Pius XII. Sometimes these anonymous editorial writers are a mixture of the two. Spineless, brainless mongoloids. But, because of it, as maliciously perilous as vipers."

As he prospered later in political life, Paisley soon learned that it was wiser to woo and charm the "pestiferous scribbling rodents" than to alienate them – something he would do with great aplomb throughout his career. While some of his more sophisticated followers learned to do the same, many would not and continued to treat newsmen with suspicion and hostility, as Paisley's rhetoric had urged them to do.

Doherty's scheme, which he had been planning since 1964, was to start a "Protestant" publishing company to produce a regular paper, leaflets and pamphlets so as to by-pass the hostile media and get

Paisley's thoughts directly to the Loyalist masses. Paisley was keen on the plan and not just because of its political potential – the more pious members of his church had been complaining for some time that there was too much politics in *The Revivalist*.

In 1965 Doherty acquired a large second-hand typesetter and flat-bed press and set up shop in a basement on the Ravenhill Road opposite Paisley's church, forming a company, The Puritan Printing Company, with himself and Paisley as directors. In April 1966 the first issue of the *Protestant Telegraph,* with the slogan "The Truth shall set you Free" beneath its masthead, hit the streets of Belfast.

Its twelve broadsheet pages, at first produced fortnightly and then weekly, provided its Loyalist readership with a regular and often bizarre diet of anti-Catholicism – sometimes heavily laced with sexual innuendo. It became an outlet for bigotry, insecurity, ignorance, frustration and latent violence.

Typical of the paper's contents was the serialisation of the works of Joseph Hocking, an American writer who specialised in lurid tales of Vatican plots – one epic, called "The Jesuit", told the story of a Protestant politician who rescues a young heiress from the clutches of priests just as they are about to steal her millions.

There were also articles on the "Hidden wealth of the Roman Catholic Church" and the scheming Pope Joan, "the female Pope who sat on the Throne of Peter". "The Love Affairs of the Vatican", disappointingly short in detail, won a whole page in the paper to satisfy some inexpressible sexual yearning on the part of its readers. Homosexuality occasionally featured, like the story of two Dutchmen who were married in a Catholic church. "Only in the Harlot Church of Rome would such a ceremony be conceived" thundered the paper.

Another series of articles dealt with one priest who had "destroyed or scandalised at least 1,000 married and unmarried females". Nuns, those female celibates whose mysterious convent life had excited Paisley's audiences in the days of the National Union of Protestants, featured too. "Any resident of or visitor to Belfast or Dublin may have noticed of late a rise in the number of nuns parading the streets. Their habit or costume is not the typical nun's garb. These modern nuns are novices, or in lay terms, apprentice nuns. One cannot help but admire their physical beauty, but their furtive smiles and glances show that they are not completely instituted nuns. It would appear that the statement made by some local wit is true: 'The older nuns are raving, while the younger ones are craving'."

The paper dwelt at length on Catholic plots like the formation of the ubiquitous "Catholic Action" in the RUC, in reality a harmless guild of Catholic policemen: "The cassock directs the constabulary" screamed the headline. "It could happen in Ulster!" warned one advertisement. "If the RC bigots have their way. The suppression of civil liberties . . . the arrest of Protestant clergymen . . . the closing down and burning of Protestant churches . . . Roman Catholic padres as commanders of Protestant churches . . . long-term imprisonment without trial . . . the execution of Protestant individuals and groups and more horrors! Impossible . . . Incredible . . . Unbelievable? Then my answer to the Roman Catholic extremists is . . . read *Catholic Terror Today* by Avro Manhattan. These things happened – not long ago – in a country with the same religious and political problems as Ulster. It is the most sensational, the most dramatic, the most revealing book ever!"

Together with these titillations, Paisley used the *Protestant Telegraph* to transmit his world view of the state of Northern Protestantism and Unionism to an audience far wider than the Ulster Hall or his rural gospel missions could ever reach. One early *Protestant Telegraph* reprinted in full a sermon Paisley had given to mark the fiftieth anniversary in 1964 of the UVF gun-running expedition to Larne, County Antrim when Carson's volunteers were supplied with thousands of German rifles to resist Home Rule and if necessary the British parliament. It neatly encapsulated his philosophy and his view of himself.

His text was Daniel, chapter 3, verse 18: "Be it known unto thee, O King, that we will not serve thy gods" – or as Paisley translated it: "in the language of Ulster that means simply, 'No Surrender!'" The context was Biblical Babylon, a country subverted by an all-pervasive idolatry. Only three men could be found to resist it and there were, Paisley implied, parallels in Ulster in the growth of ecumenism and liberal Unionism – "surely this is the type of men which Ulster needs today, men who will really stand in this evil day," he thundered.

The modern Babylon, of course, was Roman Catholicism which all down the centuries had been the implacable foe of Ulster's Protestants. Quoting from popes, priests and historians, he gave examples. The massacre of Protestants in 1641 "when Rome sought to exterminate the Protestant planters of this Province"; the Williamite Revolution in 1690, when Protestantism successfully fought back; and the 1798 United Irishmen rebellion, a clever plot by Rome because gullible Protestants were inveigled to join Catholics to resist English rule.

The threat had returned in 1914, when a British government, blackmailed by 80 Irish Nationalist MPs, promised to give Ireland Home Rule but Carson and his UVF gunrunners, roared Paisley, knew who the real enemy was – Home Rule was Rome Rule. The proof was there, Paisley cried, pointing to an illuminated address fixed to the ceiling of the Ulster Hall which read: "Ulster would not only arm but if need be fight to the death against being robbed of her religious and civil liberties."

There were striking similarities between those early Unionist heroes and Paisley's campaigns against ecumenism and O'Neillism, the sermon implied. Like Paisley now, Colonel Crawford, who had organised the gun-running, faced danger, imprisonment, and the fatal weakness and cowardice of others. Paisley claimed that Crawford had recognised himself in the Free Presbyterian Moderator – he gave him a "treasured" copy of his account of the gun-running expedition.

The Orange Order and many in the Unionist Party had opposed Crawford's plan out of fear, just as now they were too frightened to resist O'Neill. But Crawford was inspired by God and Carson. God had actually whispered encouragement in Crawford's ear, just as he had told Paisley to work for a great revival in Ulster in 1949. Crawford had ignored the peril of prison and defied a British government to save Ulster, as Paisley would do again. What Ulster needed now, Paisley shouted, was "a revival of the spirit of Carson" and the defiance of the three Babylonians who resisted the spread of idolatry. Paisley was clearly the man to provide it.

In one sermon Paisley linked his own campaign firmly into the traditional mainstream of Unionism and himself, inspired by God, risking imprisonment and surrounded by compromise, equally firmly into the tradition of Crawford and Carson. He was beginning to capture Unionism's talismans and, as he stepped up his campaign against O'Neill, his invocation of Unionism's past heroes would be a powerful weapon in his armoury.

◄○►

His next battle against O'Neill over, of all things, a bridge, gave Paisley his first opportunity to demonstrate a continuity with Unionism's heroic and defiant past.

In mid-February 1966, Belfast Corporation met to decide the name of a new bridge across the River Lagan. The previous year the new city in County Armagh promised by O'Neill had been christened Craigavon in honour of Northern Ireland's first Prime Minister. The Unionists of Belfast now thought it appropriate to honour Carson, the other founder of the State, by naming the bridge after him.

The choice of Craigavon, coming after that of Protestant Coleraine instead of Catholic Derry as the site of the new university, had irritated Nationalists. This time the new Governor, Lord Erskine, anxious not to cause more annoyance, stepped into the bridge issue. Since Queen Elizabeth II was due to visit Northern Ireland in July, he suggested naming it after her and she could open it. The Unionists on the Corporation reluctantly agreed.

Hardline Unionists, however, were angry at this interference by Erskine, an ally of O'Neill's – Carson ranked much higher in the Loyalist pantheon than did the British monarch. Paisley's councillors, together with Brookeborough, Kilfedder and Cunningham, all objected. Then Carson's son, the Honourable Edward Carson, a rather dim former Tory MP turned law student, wrote to the Belfast papers objecting to this "slight" on his father's name.

It was Eileen Paisley who, on reading Carson's letter, had the idea of inviting him over from England to join her husband's protest rallies. Paisley contacted Carson, who immediately agreed. Carson remembered them meeting in a pub in Ascot near his home to discuss the arrangements.

He duly arrived on 28 February and that night at a Paisley-organised rally in the Ulster Hall he called for Erskine's resignation and threatened "trouble" if the Corporation did not reconsider its decision. Exultant at his new prize, living proof of the historic continuity and righteousness of his cause, Paisley challenged O'Neill to repudiate Ulster's hero: "Let the Prime Minister speak. Let him tell Ulster if he is for Carson or against Carson."

Paisley paraded Carson around in the following days. On 1 March, he and Carson reviewed the first rally of the Ulster Protestant Volunteers in Lisburn and Carson said that there was a "rot" in Unionism which had begun when O'Neill became Prime Minister.

That same day Harold Wilson called a general election in the hope of bolstering a slim Westminster majority, and Paisley seized this opportunity. Four "Protestant" candidates would stand in the Belfast seats opposing O'Neillism, he announced, and one of them would be Carson's son.

The announcement was the signal for a bitter backroom struggle between Paisley and O'Neill. The public was told that Carson would probably stand in North Belfast, but in reality Paisley was trying to force the Unionist Party to nominate him in West Belfast instead of Kilfedder.

Two emissaries, one of them a Baptist preacher friend of Paisley called Willie Mullan, met the Unionist Party secretary, Jim Baillie, in an attempt to get agreement. Paisley meanwhile had learned that while at Trinity College Dublin, Kilfedder had attended meetings of the university's branch of the Fine Gael party. If Kilfedder didn't stand down, he threatened, the Shankill voters would be told of this Republican treachery. But O'Neill outmanoeuvred Paisley. According to Carson, the Prime Minister had managed to lay his hands on a letter written by Carson some years before in which he had made a remark about widespread gerrymandering in Northern Ireland. The circulation of this letter would cause Carson and Paisley untold embarrassment and it led to Carson's last-minute withdrawal. O'Neill and Paisley carried on their squabble for the allegiance of Carson during the rest of the year and O'Neill finally won.

When Carson's mother died some months later, it was O'Neill who stood beside the grieving son at the funeral, not Paisley. Carson later bitterly regretted his brief liaison with Paisley: "I think you could accuse me of having preached a gospel of dissension instead of a gospel of reconciliation. That must have been the wrong thing to do and therefore I'm culpable."

Paisley carried through his threat against Kilfedder. During the campaign, leaflets appeared on the Shankill naming him as a Fine Gael sympathiser. The NILP was responsible for circulating some but others came from Loyalist sources and Paisley was held responsible. Kilfedder lost the election by 2,000 votes to Gerry Fitt of the Republican Labour Party, who also represented Dock in the Stormont Parliament. Fitt was able to use his influence at Westminster to win considerable sympathy for the Nationalist struggle for civil rights and was detested for that by Loyalists. Ironically he would eventually turn against Nationalism, lose his West Belfast seat to Gerry Adams of Sinn Féin and be elevated to the House of Lords as a life peer.

Thanks to a fall in the number of Protestant voters in West Belfast, Fitt would probably have won despite Paisley's assistance. But Shankill Loyalists, some of them former allies, believed Paisley had lost Kilfedder vital votes and they never forgave him. Their bitterness towards him would later that year provide Paisley with a perfect alibi.

However, by the next month, April, it was Paisley who had O'Neill on the retreat. The celebrations for the fiftieth anniversary of the Easter Rising had caused something near hysteria among Unionists. O'Neill and his Home Affairs Minister, Brian McConnell, warned that the IRA could use them to foment trouble or even to re-start a military campaign. So 10,500 "B" Specials were mobilised for the Easter weekend, British army helicopters were sent to the Border and a special hot line was set up between the RUC and the Garda Síochána in preparation for the dozens of parades and demonstrations to be held in Nationalist areas.

The largest Republican parade was to be held in Belfast the Sunday after the Easter weekend, on 17 April, when contingents from the Republic would join Northerners in a march from near the city centre to Andersonstown. Condemning the government for not banning it, Paisley announced a UCDC protest march to the Ulster Hall to take place at the same time and along a route which would pass the Republican assembly point.

Both parades were illegal, since the RUC had not been notified of them. Faced with the real possibility of ugly clashes, O'Neill's cabinet had to choose which one to confront. Dealing with Paisley's parade would risk antagonising a wide band of Unionism and not just militants, for the Easter celebrations had alarmed even moderates. O'Neill chose to deal with the Republicans.

A special cabinet meeting toyed with banning their march but that idea was dropped and, instead, stringent security measures aimed at curbing the Republicans were announced. All train services from Dublin on the day of the march were cancelled and extra police, armed with machine guns and given authority under the Special Powers Act to stop and question all traffic, were sent to the Border. It was the first example of Paisley's counter-march tactic, a tactic refined to an art two years later. It had its first outing that weekend and exposed, to the fury of Nationalists, the government's weakness in the face of extremist threats.

Six weeks later Paisley announced another march, this time to the Presbyterian General Assembly on 6 June to protest at the Church's "Romanising tendencies". This one would pass right by the Catholic Markets area near the city centre but the Home Affairs Minister, McConnell, who had recently shared an Orange platform with Paisley, did nothing to stop it – even though no Loyalist march had been allowed near the area since 1935, when Orangemen and Catholics had fought a fierce hand-to-hand battle there.

The consequences were utterly predictable, as Paisley and the authorities must have guessed. His parade – several hundred supporters with placards attacking the Catholic Church and singing "Onward Christian Soldiers" – marched from his Ravenhill church across the Albert Bridge to find 200 Markets' Catholics blocking the road at Cromac Square. The police moved in to force them off the road and a hail of bricks and broken guttering showered on to the Paisleyites; one youth, armed with an iron bar, got within a few feet of Paisley before he was pinned to the ground.

After a few violent minutes, the Paisley parade was past Cromac Square and into the city centre, but the fighting between Markets' Catholics and the police continued for several hours. There were repeated baton charges and an armoured car was brought in. By midnight eight people had been arrested and four policemen hospitalised. One of those arrested, and radicalised by the riot, was a seventeen-year-old seaman called Seán Flynn. Within a decade he was a leader of the Official IRA and when its more violent splinter, the Irish National Liberation Army, was formed, he became a Belfast councillor representing its political wing. Paisley's protests recruited militants not just to Loyalism.

Unionists were less upset at the battle of Cromac Square – O'Neill firmly blamed the IRA for organising it and Faulkner laid the blame on a Catholic mob "lying in wait" – than they were at the scenes in Howard Street, outside the Presbyterian Assembly, which followed it. From Cromac Square, Paisley led his parade three times around the City Hall, apparently waiting for Presbyterian dignitaries and their guests, including the Governor Lord Erskine and his wife, to file across Howard Street from the Assembly buildings for a reception in the Presbyterian hostel.

As they emerged from a side door, a sea of angry faces and waving fists greeted them. The police hastily called in reinforcements to push the crowd back and with ropes they blocked off the road to make a passageway for the dignitaries. As they walked across, insults, jeers and shouts of "Popehead", "Romanist" and "Lundy" were hurled. The new Moderator, Alfie Martin, a liberal cleric, was a favourite target but the crowd reserved its strongest abuse for Erskine because of his role in the Carson bridge affair. Lady Erskine was so upset that two days later she had to receive medical treatment for an aggravated heart complaint.

Grateful at the chance for once to strike back at this troublesome cleric, the Unionist establishment rounded on Paisley for insulting the Queen's representative and marring the Presbyterian Assembly.

McConnell was sent to the Assembly to give a grovelling apology, the RUC collected evidence with a view to prosecuting Paisley, and moderate Unionists vied to insult him with names like "the bloated bullfrog". But the condemnation was almost entirely reserved for the fracas at Howard Street – Catholics were blamed for the riot at Cromac Square.

In a Stormont debate, O'Neill compared Paisleyism to Fascism: "To those of us who remember the Thirties, the pattern is horribly familiar. The contempt for established authority; the crude and unthinking intolerance; the emphasis upon monster processions and rallies; the appeal to a perverted form of patriotism: each and every one of these things has its parallel in the rise of the Nazis to power."

O'Neill's verbal onslaught backfired. The comparisons with Fascism made by him and others, notably Presbyterian leaders, served only to further strengthen Paisley's claim on traditional Unionism. All the famous Unionist leaders, from Craigavon through to Brookeborough, had been similarly condemned as Fascists by Republicans. By calling Paisley a Fascist, O'Neill placed himself in the Republican camp and Paisley among the Loyalist immortals.

A few weeks later, the Howard Street fracas finally gave Paisley the prison martyrdom he had been seeking since his days in the National Union of Protestants. But the strength of the Unionist reaction to it undoubtedly forced him to pull in his horns. When he later appealed for votes to the wider Protestant electorate for votes, he realised that his violent picketing of General Assemblies could alienate Presbyterian voters – the largest section of the Protestant community – and he all but abandoned them. The political price of his pickets was further highlighted when he attempted to persuade right-wing Presbyterian ministers to join his fledgling DUP in 1971. The memory of that aggressive demonstration was a large obstacle to their co-operation.

In other Unionist circles, however, the reason for Paisley's march on the General Assembly had struck a chord. For the best part of six years the Orange Order had been wrestling with the vexed question of Protestant membership of the World Council of Churches but had shelved it because of the controversy it would undoubtedly cause. But grassroots pressure was growing and in May 1966 the committee responsible for drawing up the resolutions to be passed at each Twelfth of July demonstration finally decided to face the issue.

The resolution they formulated reflected widespread Orange unease at ecumenism, an unease which Paisley – still a regular and popular speaker at Orange demonstrations despite his break with the Order – had helped to foment. It condemned the visits to Rome by the Archbishop of Canterbury and the influence of the World Council of Churches on the trend towards "one united Church". It also called for a return to Protestantism based on sixteenth-century Reformation principles.

By framing the resolution, the Orange Order had given Paisley another victory. But some senior Orangemen also believe that it led directly to his aggressive march on the General Assembly. They suspect he got wind of it and decided to pre-empt the Orange demonstrations. Usually he mounted small pickets on the Presbyterian Assembly but that year, five weeks before the "Twelfth", he had organised a large and noisy march. Said one: "He had his spies who would tell him things like that and it was my view that he held his protest to get in before us and to show Orangemen that he was forcing the pace."

The resolution was introduced almost apologetically on the "Twelfth" by the Grand Master, Sir George Clark, but he linked it with an appeal to Orangemen to bar Paisley from their platforms. The Order could be split, he warned, if brethren gave solace to a man who so viciously attacked a fellow Orangeman, Captain O'Neill. Paisley was now threatening the inner bastion of Unionism.

Six days before Sir George Clark's appeal was to fall on deaf ears, Paisley and six others, including two of his ministers, John Wylie and Ivan Foster, were charged with unlawful assembly in Howard Street. On 18 July, after another protest march from his church, they appeared in court, defending themselves, with Eileen Paisley taking copious notes.

An attempt by Paisley to call Lord and Lady Erskine, O'Neill, McConnell, Alfie Martin and the editor of the *Belfast Telegraph*, Jack Sayers – all his ecumenical enemies – as witnesses failed, and he abandoned the defence case. After a two-day hearing all seven were convicted, fined £30 and given 24 hours to enter into a bail bond of £30 to keep the peace for two years or go to jail for three months.

That day Paisley told an Ulster Hall rally that once again he, together with Wylie and Foster, would choose jail before they would pay their fines or abide by the bail bond. And he went on to make a prediction: "With the help of God and the Protestants of Ulster, the day is coming when I will be in the House of Commons. The only way the Protestant people are going to be able to answer the ruling junta of Lundies in Stormont is to have someone there."

This time Paisley was going to go to jail. As in 1959 and 1963 someone eventually paid his fine but the anonymous donor couldn't sign his bail bond for him. On 20 July he was arrested at his Beersbridge Road home and taken off to Crumlin Road jail where, as Prisoner No. 1271, he was joined the next day by Wylie and Foster.

The next day a thousand-strong crowd, chanting "We want Paisley", blocked the road outside Crumlin Road jail. The following night, a Saturday, a crowd of 2,000 gathered when the Shankill pubs emptied and was soon fighting the police. Catholic-owned pubs were looted and the police came under a hail of bottles. When baton charges failed to restore order, the police brought in water cannon to turn on the rioters. The cabinet met in emergency session and in desperation announced a three-month ban on all but traditional (i.e. Orange) parades and meetings in the city. An uneasy peace returned to Belfast.

Paisley had his martyrdom at last. Although he denied in the *Protestant Telegraph* that he had chosen prison for political advantage, the truth was that, among his followers, it would elevate him to a hero of Biblical proportions. As for O'Neill, Paisley now had his "proof" that by imprisoning a Protestant minister in a Protestant state he was a traitor to all that Unionism had ever stood for. The Loyalist unrest would also be used against O'Neill by conspirators within his own cabinet.

—◦—

As much as Paisley savoured his martyr's cell, the experience must have been tempered by the knowledge that he had just escaped being charged with a much more serious offence: conspiracy to provide explosives for the purpose of endangering life or causing damage to property.

The complex web of events which were to lead to that had their origin in the bitter loss of the West Belfast seat to Gerry Fitt in March. With Fitt's victory coinciding with the emotive 1916 commemorations, enflamed Loyalists, blaming O'Neill's liberal policies, decided that extreme measures were needed to counter what they saw as a burgeoning Republican conspiracy. Under the leadership of former Ulster Protestant Action chairman, Billy Spence, who had graduated inside the Unionist Party to become Kilfedder's election agent, Loyalist militants, many of them old UPA hands, began meeting in a Shankill Road public house, the Standard Bar. They decided to form themselves into a Loyalist "army" to resist O'Neill and the IRA.

With the fiftieth anniversary of the Somme looming in June, they decided to call their group the Ulster Volunteer Force, in memory of Carson's men. Paisley's appeal for "a renewal of the spirit of Carson" had been answered.

The UPA had travelled the full Loyalist circuit. At first they had tried to change Unionism by agitation and electoral competition with the establishment party but that had failed. Then they decided to change Unionism from within and infiltrated the Unionist Party, but that too came to nought. Now they looked to violence and conspiracy to achieve their goals.

The military commander of the UVF was Spence's brother Gusty, then a shipyard worker, but a man with some useful military experience – he had served with the British Army in Cyprus fighting against Colonel Grivas's pro-Greek guerrillas. He was the UVF's front-man but there was little doubt in the minds of the RUC Special Branch that Billy Spence was the brains behind the organisation.

Three years later the Special Branch were to conclude that Billy Spence had formulated the UVF's strategy for 1966 – a clever plan which was designed to mislead the authorities into thinking that bombings and gun attacks carried out by the UVF were really the IRA's work. The idea was to halt O'Neill's "bridge-building" policies and maybe even cause a reaction against him within the Unionist Party which would force his resignation.

For that, the Spences needed explosives and their search led them to the countryside, to the people who had access to dynamite – to quarrymen in County Armagh and particularly County Down where for decades Mourne granite had been cut out of hillsides to construct Belfast's solid buildings. That brought the UVF into contact with rural Loyalists. Some were in the Free Presbyterian Church, such as Tommy McDowell, a Kilkeel, County Down quarryman who was to imitate Spence's 1966 plan of deception three years later with devastating results. The UVF soon began to construct small rural units and by the summer of 1966 there were cells in south Antrim, Portadown, County Armagh, and Pomeroy, County Tyrone.

Some efforts to implement the plan of deception were made in Belfast. There was a bomb attack on the Unionist Party headquarters and two shots were fired through the door of the Shankill home of Unionist MP Johnny McQuade in April – that attack was carried out with his connivance, for he had links with the Spences. They had been in Ulster Protestant Action together, had joined the Unionist Party together and were members of the same Orange Lodge, "The Prince Albert Temperance".

The Belfast UVF, perhaps fifteen to twenty strong, were tough characters, some with criminal records stretching back twenty years, and they were nearly all violently anti-Catholic. Almost inevitably they succumbed to old temptations and turned their guns on the traditional enemy: Catholics and Republicans. It was to be their undoing. The UVF's original plan of deception, as a senior RUC officer put it, "was destroyed by Belfast drunks".

On 7 May, a UVF member – an Ulster Protestant Action veteran who was subsequently jailed for arms offences – threw a petrol bomb at a Catholic-owned pub on the Shankill. It missed and crashed through the window of the house next door. An elderly Protestant woman, Martha Gould, was burned to death in the blaze. On 27 May, Spence and three other UVF members, George McCullough, William Millar and Hugh McClean, drove to the Falls Road with plans to shoot a prominent Republican called Leo Martin, but when they couldn't find him they instead shot a Catholic drunk, John Scullion, who had the misfortune to cross their path singing Irish rebel songs. Two weeks later he died. At first the police thought Scullion had been stabbed but his body was exhumed and a post-mortem discovered evidence of a bullet wound.

The climax to their campaign came at two o'clock in the morning on Sunday 26 June outside a pub called the Malvern Arms in Malvern Street, off the lower Shankill Road. Four young Catholic barmen who had stopped off at the bar for a late-night drinking session stepped out on the street and into a fusillade of gunfire. Three were hit and one, Peter Ward, a barman in a city centre hotel, was shot through the heart and died instantly.

Rumours about the UVF's existence had been rife for weeks. In May it had threatened, in a statement phoned to the press, to declare war on the IRA, and at Stormont Nationalist and Labour MPs had asked questions about UVF recruitment of "B" Specials. The Home Affairs Minister, Brian McConnell, told them that there was no evidence that the UVF had anything but peaceful protest in mind.

The Malvern Street killing destroyed that complacency and the government had no option but to respond swiftly and strongly. Ironically, O'Neill had been in France at the time of the shooting, commemorating the part played in the battle of the Somme by Carson's UVF, and he hurriedly returned to Belfast to proscribe the organisation.

Within a matter of days Spence, McClean and another man, Bobby Williamson, were arrested and charged with the Ward murder. They had been drinking in the Malvern Arms earlier on the night of the killing and, assuming the unfortunate Catholics were IRA members (the distinction is often a fine one in militant Loyalist eyes), had decided to shoot them. They were ultimately convicted and sentenced to minimum terms of twenty years.

Paisley was embroiled in the sordid affair when his name featured both at their trial and at two other related UVF trials. He knew two of the accused, Gusty Spence and Williamson, as he later told the Scarman Tribunal. He had met Gusty through Billy Spence – in 1959 he and Boal had advised Gusty Spence during a protest he held at Belfast City Hall. The protest was against Gerry Fitt, who in a council debate had described Spence's regiment, the Royal Ulster Rifles, as the "murderers" of innocent Cypriot civilians.

A much more serious link with the killing came from the third accused, McClean. When charged with the Malvern Street murders, McClean told the police: "I am terribly sorry I ever heard of that man Paisley or decided to follow him. I am definitely ashamed of myself to be in such a position." Later, during the trial, it emerged that when detectives had asked him why he had joined the UVF, McClean had replied: "I was asked did I agree with Paisley and was I prepared to follow him. I said that I was."

During the trial a senior police witness gave evidence of more tangible links with Paisley. He had seen McClean carrying a placard on the Shankill Road in a Paisley-led march to the Ulster Hall on 16 June, a week after the Cromac Square riot and Howard Street fracas. At another UVF trial in 1966, that of three south Antrim men, Leslie Porter, George Bigger and William Blakely, on arms offences, evidence was given by police that McClean had accompanied the three, who were armed, all the way to the Ulster Hall where they went to have a drink in a city centre pub before rejoining the Paisley parade back to the Shankill.

Paisley and the UVF have always denied McClean's statements. Two days after the Malvern Street murder, Paisley, somewhat ambivalently, condemned the killing as a deplorable incident but "not as deplorable as those in which policemen like Norman Anderson (killed in 1961) were brutally butchered by the IRA." Of McClean he denied all knowledge : "I don't know Mr McClean. He is not a Free Presbyterian. Mr McClean was never a member of the UCDC, never was a member of the Ulster Protestant Volunteer Divisions and he has never been associated with me at all."

The UVF maintain that Spence questioned McClean in jail about his statement and the latter gave an entirely different version. According to a senior UVF source: "He said that it was through Paisley's agitation that he had become interested and involved, the general Paisley agitation. There was never a hint of a link between Paisley and us." McClean, who died before finishing his sentence, attempted without success to have his statement rejected as inadmissible at his trial.

Paisley had much more compelling evidence to distance himself from the Malvern Street killers, however – evidence provided by some of those convicted of the crime. It had come out of the bitter row between himself and Shankill Loyalists the previous March when he had undermined Kilfedder's election campaign in West Belfast with the story of Kilfedder's links with Fine Gael.

The person most angered by Paisley's behaviour was Billy Spence, Kilfedder's election agent. When Fitt won the West Belfast seat, he wrote an angry letter to Paisley on UPA notepaper accusing him of "treachery". Spence got thirteen signatures to the letter in imitation of the thirteen young Derry apprentice boys who had slammed shut the gates of the city in the face of Catholic King James's army in 1689. Among those who signed it were his brother Gusty and Hugh McClean, two of the Malvern Street killers.

When detectives came to question Paisley about the UVF, he handed over the letter to them as proof of his innocence. It cleared him but earned him even more animosity on the Shankill. All those who signed the letter were interrogated by the RUC and their homes searched for weapons.

Amid the tangled network of UVF plots and personnel uncovered by the RUC in the wake of Malvern Street there was, however, a much more direct link between Paisley's UCDC, the Ulster Protestant Volunteers and the UVF. The link was Noel Doherty, Paisley's closest lieutenant at the time.

Through his organising work for the UPV, Doherty had met Robert Murdock, a Free Presbyterian from Loughgall, near Portadown, County Armagh, who had expressed interest in forming a local branch of the UPV. On 21 April, Paisley drove him and Billy Mitchell to Murdock's house, from where Paisley went on to another meeting. At Murdock's house Doherty met a quarryman called James Marshall and other men whose names, he later told police, he couldn't remember.

The conversation soon turned to violence. Doherty had been considering moving the UPV in a more "militant" direction and he had toyed with the idea of blowing up IRA monuments and, as his subsequent confession to the police recorded, his new friends were in a position to help him: "I learned that gelignite could be obtained through Marshall. It was also learned at the meeting that arms could be supplied. These men were of the opinion that IRA monuments [could be blown up] and IRA leaders could be shot."

According to Doherty's statement, Paisley arrived later that night at around eleven o'clock and after a cup of tea he drove Doherty and Mitchell back to Belfast. On 21 May, Doherty brought George Bigger of the Belfast UVF to Murdock's house, introduced him to Marshall and left some UCDC leaflets. A week later Bigger collected 27 sticks of gelignite, fuse wire and detonators from Marshall and hid them in a derelict house in the northern suburbs of Belfast. Two days after that Doherty went to Bigger's home and was shown some of the gelignite and a revolver, and the two men again talked of shooting IRA men and blowing up monuments.

On the strength of all this, Doherty was charged with conspiracy to provide explosives and was ultimately convicted along with Marshall and sentenced to two years. When Doherty admitted his part in the conspiracy and told of the journey to Loughgall in Paisley's car, RUC detectives questioned Paisley. Afterwards they decided that he too could be charged with the same offence. However, the office of the Attorney General, Teddy Jones, advised against it – their view was that Paisley's connection with the enterprise was too tenuous to support a charge for any length of time. Possibly at the first bail application and certainly by the stage of a preliminary hearing, the charge would have to be dropped – all that could be gained was embarrassment for Paisley. That would leave the government open to the charge that it was persecuting a political opponent, a charge that might well redound to Paisley's advantage. Thus Paisley escaped facing one of the most serious charges in the criminal book.

Paisley has always denied knowing anything of Doherty's plans. In evidence to the Scarman Tribunal he maintained that on the way home from Murdock's home he never once asked Doherty or Mitchell what had been discussed: "I took it for granted that this was UPV business. I have so many commitments . . . that I cannot look into every detail." As soon as Doherty's involvement in explosives was known to him, he claimed, Doherty was expelled from the UCDC under Rule 15. According to other founder members of the UCDC, another charge was levelled at Doherty, perhaps more serious in Loyalist eyes: this was that pornographic books had been found in the Puritan Press printing works.

Doherty's confession revealed two things. Firstly, that the UCDC/UPV had helped to provide the UVF with explosives; and secondly that, through Doherty and Bigger, the link between the UCDC/UPV and the UVF stretched to McClean and Spence. The UVF denied any more substantial connection and the two UCDC members who were at that crucial meeting in Loughgall either would not or could not add to the picture. Doherty emigrated to South Africa where he ran a successful publishing business but he always refused to talk about the affair, while Mitchell went on to become a senior UVF figure in the east Antrim area and was convicted and sentenced to life for a double murder. After his release he became a strong supporter of the peace process and helped steer the UVF into a ceasefire. He died in 2006.

In all legal senses, Paisley had no connection with the UVF and the bloody events of the summer of 1966, but in one important way his violent rhetoric and stormy Ulster Hall protests undoubtedly helped to create the atmosphere in which they thrived, as a former Free Presbyterian can attest: "Ian had that gift for inflaming people to boiling point. A man I knew, not a Christian – I needn't say that because Christians do get inflamed too listening to him – used to say that he would go to meetings Ian held in the Ulster Hall and that when he came out he could have killed the first Catholic he saw."

O'Neill attempted to blacken Paisley by listing the Ulster Hall speeches he had made before the Malvern Street killings in which he had thanked "the Ulster Volunteer Force" for their support. Paisley always insisted that he was referring only to Carson's force and O'Neill's efforts to link him in with Spence did him little damage. There was more evidence during the remaining months of 1966 that it was O'Neill who was under the greater pressure.

In August, apparently on cabinet advice to make a conciliatory gesture, he met a Free Presbyterian delegation, led by Paisley's temporary replacement as Moderator, the Rev Bert Cooke, to discuss

Paisley's imprisonment. The same month O'Neill sent a special message of reassurance to the Unionist Party, telling them that the Border and traditional Protestantism were safe under his government.

The message had been prompted, he said, by the worries of "one of those decent, sensible Orangemen who have long been the backbone of Ulster" who had said to him: "We had the Unionist Party to defend the Constitution, and the Orange Order to defend our Protestant religion. Are these things still safe in Ulster today?" O'Neill assured Unionism that they were.

In September it became clear that not everyone in the Unionist Party believed him. Boal circulated a petition critical of O'Neill's policies and for a few crucial days it looked as if O'Neill could be ousted. The real force behind the conspiracy was the ambitious Brian Faulkner, but the attempted putsch – based partly on the discontent whipped up by Paisley, and partly on O'Neill's personal and political unpopularity – failed, thanks to a spy in the rebel camp who reported back to O'Neill after the rebels' clandestine meetings in Faulkner's home.

O'Neill was "quite hysterical", according to his Home Affairs Minister, Bill Craig. By the time Paisley was released from jail in October, O'Neill persuaded Craig to ban all the homecoming celebrations planned for him in Belfast.

O'Neill had good reason to be worried. The violence of 1966 was ugly and disturbing – three people had been killed and there had also been petrol bombings and intimidation aimed at Catholics throughout the year. That, and the political turmoil, had combined to cause the British to put their Irish neighbours under closer scrutiny.

A highly critical ITV documentary on Northern Ireland's sectarianism, the first ever made, had been shown in Britain – but banned in Northern Ireland – and the *Sunday Times* had published its seminal article "John Bull's political slum". Political pressure for change was also growing. Gerry Fitt and the Labour Party's Campaign for Democracy in Ulster intensified their demands to discuss Northern Ireland affairs at Westminster – parliamentary convention forbade it – and Harold Wilson had summoned O'Neill to London to urge a speeding-up of reforms. They were signs of things to come.

As for Paisley, the fruits of 1966 were at first in the Free Presbyterian Church. At the time of the Maura Lyons affair he had told his congregation that if he was ever jailed he would follow St Paul's example and write epistles from his cell to the faithful. In between his duties in the prison kitchen, he fulfilled that promise, writing "an exposition" of St Paul's epistle to the Romans – once described as "the product of a powerful if confined intellect". His new friend, Bob Jones Junior, awarded him an honorary doctorate from the Bob Jones University in Greenville, South Carolina in recognition of his prison martyrdom. It was Paisley's first legitimate academic award.

More importantly his imprisonment had won hundreds of new converts, attracted by his political message as much as by his fundamentalism. Over the next two years the number of Free Presbyterian churches virtually doubled, and in Belfast he made plans to build a huge new church farther up the Ravenhill Road, to accommodate the growing crowds.

Politically, though, he was still some way from the breakthrough. A week before his release, Eileen Paisley stood in a council by-election against an O'Neill supporter and was roundly beaten. It was a dirty campaign. Her opponent, Harold Smith, was Jewish and her election literature made an appeal to an older, more deep-seated bigotry: "The Unionist Party are boasting that he is a Jew. As a Jew he rejects our Lord Jesus Christ, the New Testament, Protestant principles, the Glorious Reformation and the sanctity of the Lord's day. Mr Smith is not, and cannot be, a traditional Unionist. The Protestant Throne and Protestant Constitution are nothing to him."

Nevertheless, in July, in the midst of the UVF bloodshed and Paisley's court appearance, there had been a sign that political approval could be on its way. An opinion poll conducted by Lancaster University revealed that one in five Protestants, some 200,000 people, were opposed to O'Neill's policies. Half were opposed to ecumenism and a quarter said they didn't approve of the O'Neill–Lemass meeting.

As Paisley addressed a large crowd of people who had gathered in Dundonald on the eastern outskirts of Belfast to welcome him home from jail, he made a significant change in the slogan, coined that Easter, "O'Neill must go!" From then on Free Presbyterian placards would read: "O'Neill must go – O'Neill will go!"

"Captain O'Neill has sown the wind, now he is reaping the whirlwind."

EILEEN PAISLEY, APRIL 1969

CHAPTER FIVE

The Whirlwind

The year 1967 was barely a month old when Paisley forced another retreat by O'Neill and demonstrated that the Prime Minister was fast losing any enthusiasm for confronting him and the Loyalist militants stirred up by his rhetoric.

The occasion was the proposed visit to Belfast by the Bishop of Ripon, Dr John Moorman, a controversial ecumenist who was the Church of England's observer to the Vatican Council and the leader of an Anglican delegation which was conducting unity talks with Catholic theologians in Italy. Moorman believed in one, united Christian church with the Pope, the leader of the largest constituent member, as head.

Concern in the Church of Ireland about his views on the Papacy had led to an invitation to come to Belfast in January to explain them. Such was the interest that St Anne's Cathedral in the city centre had been booked and a large audience was expected.

Moorman's visit was like a red rag to a bull for Paisley, who immediately announced plans for a "monster" march and rally outside the Cathedral. Once again he appealed directly to Orangemen to join him, and thousands of leaflets were pushed through letterboxes in Protestant districts of the city calling for 100,000 Orangemen to join in protest "against the Romanising Bishop of Ripon".

The Orange Order, again under pressure from Paisley, joined the controversy. An extraordinary meeting of the Belfast Grand Lodge was called to decide on protest action and officially the Order was said to feel "real concern" at the visit. Even the pro-O'Neill Grand Master, Sir George Clark, was described as "perturbed".

The Church of Ireland authorities wanted the visit to go ahead. An important principle, their freedom of speech, was at stake. O'Neill, however, was worried at the prospect of ugly street scenes outside the Cathedral and intervened to prevent it. At a dinner party hosted by the Dean of the Cathedral, Dr Cuthbert Peacocke, he persuaded him to cancel Moorman's booking.

A guest at that dinner described what happened: "Peacocke wanted Moorman to come, saying that if someone didn't stand up to Paisley sometime, the thing would just keep on escalating but O'Neill, I think, was looking for the easy way out. Finally he managed to talk Peacocke into cancelling the visit, that there would be trouble if he didn't and that was that. But I've often wondered what would have happened had we taken a firmer line with Paisley earlier on."

If O'Neill felt under pressure the Orange Order was increasingly facing open defiance. After Paisley's imprisonment and before his own, Noel Doherty moved to capitalise on Orange discontent and set up a new organisation called the "Orange Voice of Freedom" to highlight the Order's "lack of leadership".

In August 1966, it announced plans for a march from the Shankill to the Ulster Hall, and in newspaper ads called on Orangemen joining the parade to wear their Orange collarettes. Both were challenges to authority – the government had banned all marches and meetings in the Belfast area and the Orange Order frowned on their members wearing regalia on any but officially sanctioned occasions.

Home Affairs Minister Brian McConnell banned the march, once again using the Special Powers Act against Protestants, and earned himself heckles at the Black Preceptory's annual parade at the end of August. The Orange authorities threatened to take disciplinary action against the rebels but never followed through. During the rest of the year and in the early months of 1967, meanwhile, the number of individual Orange Lodges which passed motions deploring Paisley's imprisonment or attacking O'Neill's policies steadily grew.

Grassroots Orange disgruntlement finally came to the surface on the "Twelfth" in 1967 in one of the most violent and unruly commemorations of King William's Boyne victory ever seen in twentieth-century Orangeism.

In those days Orangemen who gathered at their "fields" throughout Northern Ireland each 12 July invariably passed three resolutions put to them by Unionist leaders before they lined up behind flute bands for the weary trek home. Traditionally, one reaffirmed loyalty to the Crown, one to the Protestant faith and the other paid a routine tribute to the Prime Minister and government of the day. The resolution honouring O'Neill in July 1967 was, at many Orange venues, either openly scorned or ignored. At the County Tyrone gathering in Coagh, the bitterness towards O'Neill spilled into violence when the pro-O'Neill Westminster MP for Mid-Ulster, George Forrest, was hauled down from the platform and kicked unconscious when he argued with a heckling crowd as the resolution backing O'Neill was being read out.

In Belfast, hundreds of people shouted down the platform speaker when the resolution was introduced and so confusing was the scene that nobody could be sure that it had been carried. In Tandragee, County Armagh the speaker could not be heard above the shouting and cries of "Up Paisley", "O'Neill must go" and "What about Lemass?" In Lisburn, County Antrim the hecklers used loudhailers, and in Fintona, County Tyrone the resolution paid tribute to the government but deliberately omitted the name of the Prime Minister.

In Enniskillen, County Fermanagh there was a much more serious and deliberate snub to O'Neill from the Orange and Unionist establishment in the county. It was partly a reflection of unease with his policies but more a result of O'Neill's sacking of the Minister of Agriculture, Harry West, over a controversial land deal which O'Neill said conflicted with his Ministerial duties.

There, no resolutions were put to the Orangemen but O'Neill's predecessor, Lord Brookeborough, referred in his speech to the first two while deliberately making no reference to the pro-O'Neill resolution. It was a calculated insult by the former premier. West also spoke and indirectly criticised O'Neill's liberalism. Echoing Paisley, he declared: "The type of Unionism being advocated today would not be acceptable to our forefathers." West's dismissal had created influential enemies for O'Neill.

During this period the Orange Order was also being pressurised over the question of Orangemen attending Roman Catholic religious ceremonies, a favourite complaint of Paisley's. Under the Order's rules this was an offence meriting expulsion but gradually, in the early 1960s, a blind eye had been turned to offenders.

In June 1967, thanks to the climate Paisley had created, the Order's attitude hardened. Two Unionist MPs, one of them Phelim O'Neill, a cousin of the Prime Minister's, were summoned to appear before their County Grand Lodges to explain their attendance at a Catholic service during a community week in Ballymena. Phelim O'Neill ignored the summons and was expelled a year later.

Elsewhere, the Worshipful Master of a Lodge in Larne was thrown out for attending a Catholic wedding and, in Belfast, an Orangewoman who wanted to go to Rome to witness the ordination of a man whose father had saved her brother's life during the war was forced to cancel the trip. Soon other prominent Unionist liberals were under attack and there was talk of a split in the Order. The "Orange Voice of Freedom" meanwhile congratulated the Orange authorities on "the improvement" in their policies.

The strain was beginning to tell in the Order's higher echelons. In October, the Grand Master, Sir George Clark, resigned. Officially the reason given was pressure of work on his County Down farm but the choice of his successor revealed otherwise. He was John Bryans, an elderly Orange veteran who, unlike Clark, had no overt connections with the leadership of the Unionist Party. He was a non-controversial, little-known figure and would not be an easy target for the Paisleyites. But his appointment was an admission that the Order could not control its extremists in the face of Paisleyite assaults.

Inside O'Neill's cabinet meanwhile another contender for the throne was emerging. Following Faulkner's failed putsch in September 1966, the Home Affairs Minister, Bill Craig, previously an O'Neill ally, threw his hat into the ring in a bid to lead the dissident right wingers. One former civil servant recalled Craig telling James Chichester-Clark, then the Unionist Party Chief Whip, at the time "that he was going to outdo Faulkner and get to the right of him".

Craig signalled his rightward move in November 1966 when, in response to Nationalist complaints that Catholics were under-represented in top legal positions, he claimed that Catholics suffered from "educational and social deficiencies". The next month he dismissed a joint NILP/Trade Union delegation seeking the introduction of one man, one vote in local government with the remark that in this respect Britain was "out of step" with Northern Ireland.

In March 1967, to placate Loyalists, Craig prohibited celebrations to mark the centenary of the Fenian Rising and banned the Republican Clubs, a recently adopted guise for Sinn Féin which had been proscribed ten years earlier. The latter in particular was a clear concession to Loyalist extremists, for Craig had acted against RUC Special Branch advice – the police had accurate intelligence that the IRA's move towards left-wing politics, of which the formation of Republican Clubs was part, was causing dissension in the military-minded Northern units and a split was possible.

The ban once again gave Paisley an opportunity in the autumn to demonstrate the effectiveness of his countermarch tactic. At Queen's University, students had formed a Republican Club in October 1967, but the university authorities refused to recognise it and the RUC began an investigation. At meetings and debates the students condemned the ban and decided to organise a protest march in mid-November to Unionist Party headquarters in the city centre.

Paisley immediately demanded that Craig ban the march and when he didn't, he called a rally to block the students' route. Five hundred Paisleyites waving Union Jacks gathered for the expected clash but at the last minute the RUC rerouted the students in the opposite direction. Carrying a coffin symbolising the "death of democracy", they marched to Craig's South Belfast home instead to hand in a protest note. Violence had been averted but Paisley had shown that he could almost dictate the authorities' response to his protests; it was a small but significant victory, a repeat of his success against the Republicans in Easter 1966.

The year 1967 brought encouraging signs of growing political support for Paisley. In May, his wife won a seat in the Belfast Corporation elections in a straight fight against O'Neill supporters while in Lisburn, County Antrim, two Protestant Unionists won seats.

An opinion poll in the *Belfast Telegraph* in December also showed significant Protestant backing for his anti-O'Neill protests: 34 per cent of all Unionists said they agreed with what he said, while 44 per cent didn't think that he had tried to stir up bad feelings between Catholics and Protestants. A clear majority, 55 per cent, were opposed to the Unionist Party curbing the influence of the Orange Order.

Paisley's largest following, according to the poll, was among middle-aged and older skilled and semi-skilled male Presbyterian workers in Belfast; those who felt most threatened by the changing climate around them and most nostalgic for the certitudes of traditional Unionism.

However, there was a far more alarming symptom of the gathering opposition to O'Neill. Earlier that year the RUC Special Branch had uncovered a plot to kill him. Loyalist extremists, probably in the UVF, had acquired a rifle with a telescopic sight and the RUC feared that they would try to carry out a Kennedy-style assassination. From then on a car carrying two armed policemen followed O'Neill wherever he went.

During 1967 and 1968 Paisley stepped up his anti-O'Neill protests to match the mood of growing Protestant anxiety. Whenever he or his supporters had advance knowledge of O'Neill's movements, a crowd carrying placards and jeering "O'Neill must go!" would be hastily assembled to meet him.

Some protests were comical, like the scenes at a troop review at Ballynahinch, County Down in May 1967 when O'Neill was followed by a placard-carrying Free Presbyterian who bobbed up and down in step with the Prime Minister behind lines of soldiers. Paisley won adulation from his supporters, and even the grudging grins of opponents, for the cheek of some of his protests, like that in December 1967 when he, Eileen, Ivan Foster and a new ministerial recruit, William McCrea, threw snowballs at the car carrying Lemass's successor, Jack Lynch, as he left Stormont after a meeting with O'Neill, the first North–South contact since 1965.

Other protests were not so amusing, revealing instead the violence that always lurked not so far beneath the surface of Paisley's protests. In May 1968, O'Neill was pelted with eggs and was hit beneath the eye with a coin as he left a Unionist Party meeting in Woodvale in the upper Shankill. Some 500 Loyalists had gathered when they heard he was there. Paisley addressed them on their right to protest and burned a photograph of O'Neill visiting a Catholic convent the week before. Once again, O'Neill escaped the fury of the incited crowd only thanks to nimble police work.

The spring and summer of 1968 saw a renewal of the frenetic campaign launched by his Free Presbyterian ministers during Paisley's imprisonment. Ulster Protestant Volunteer rallies were held, as one veteran remembers, "nearly every weekend", spreading the message and winning new converts. Between publicity-grabbing anti-O'Neill stunts and a concerted campaign in Loyalist heartlands, Paisley was gradually organising and building up a loyal political constituency.

By February 1968 he felt confident enough about his growing support to announce that the UCDC would contest Westminster seats at the next election and that a Protestant Unionist candidate would oppose O'Neill in his Bannside seat: "Captain O'Neill wants to change the Unionist Party into a party of half-breeds, half for Protestant Britain and half for the Roman Catholic Republic. Now is the time for the Loyalists of Ulster to stop the sellout and let the world know that this province is going to remain uncompromisingly loyal to the principles of the Glorious Reformation and Revolution."

At Easter, threats by the UPV to hold a countermarch in Armagh led to the government banning a Republican parade. Although the ban was defied, once again the countermarch threat had achieved its purpose, forcing the government into confrontation with Catholics and establishing a pattern which was to dominate the next twelve months.

Paisley aimed his protests not just at the figurehead but at his supporters as well. Many pro-O'Neill MPs found that by 1968 there were pockets of Paisleyites in every constituency, harassing and pursuing them, while moderate, middle-class Protestants opted out, as they had done even in Brookeborough's day.

As time went on this was to prove a crucial factor in the fall of O'Neill. One of his supporters at Stormont recalled the fearsome pressure he and other moderates were put under:

> The great thing about fanatics is that they don't go to the pub at night, they pack meetings instead. Every constituency meeting I had was a battle, a sheer struggle, the energy involved in trying to get decisions through and keep going was unbelievable.

> They were there in the front rows at each meeting; they would be booing, stamping, and heckling abuse. If you were walking around the town they'd even be abusive to you, you'd get abusive phone calls in the middle of the night and at Glengall Street [Unionist headquarters] you'd have the police holding them back from spitting at you and trying to hit you. You're eventually broken because you think you're the only one who's saying anything because everyone else is against you. I think, looking back, that physically they completely undermined us and drove us out of politics by pure physical exhaustion.

The pressure told in some revealing ways. One MP can remember being taken to task by the Unionist Party Secretary, J.O. Baillie, because he had declared his support for O'Neill at a constituency selection meeting early in 1968. "He told me: 'You shouldn't have made your stance quite so clear because you could have lost the nomination', but he himself was supposed to be an O'Neill supporter."

Inside the Unionist Party, O'Neill's most effective critic was Paisley's friend, Desmond Boal, whose verbal brilliance inspired the other dissidents. The two men had stood by each other during the turbulence of 1966. Boal defended Paisley's rowdy march to the Presbyterian General Assembly and was promptly sacked from the post of assistant to the Attorney General, Teddy Jones. Paisley meanwhile stood by Boal when shortly afterwards he was named as co-respondent in a divorce case – "Dessie's reading the Gospel of St John", he would assure worried Free Presbyterians.

Boal's anti-O'Neillism was based, like the Independent Unionists of the early 1950s, on his working-class antagonism towards the aristocratic and middle-class Unionist leadership. Although not a religious fundamentalist, he, like Paisley, accused the Orange and Unionist hierarchy of "dictatorship" by ignoring the interests and wishes of the Protestant rank and file.

"He was anti-establishment and the word arrogance comes back to mind," recalled a Stormont colleague. "No one has been able to satisfactorily explain his motivation to me but I think he regarded O'Neill as the Big House still in charge and he resented that and O'Neill's arrogance bitterly. He resented any form of patronage or patronising by anyone, and to him the Unionist Party was full of both. But without his ability to express and put into words others' feelings I don't think the campaign would have been nearly as successful." With Paisley on the streets and Boal in his party ranks, O'Neill faced a formidable double act.

Paisley had, by this stage, probably won the allegiance of most Protestant fundamentalists – a vociferous but limited section of Loyalist opinion – and had stirred up opposition to O'Neill throughout the Unionist Party. But he hadn't managed to persuade mainstream dissidents to join his separatist cause. The majority of them still believed that they could change the Unionist Party from inside and they looked to other leaders within the party to oppose and ultimately replace O'Neill.

Faulkner, spurred on by his ambitious father, a textile millionaire who had long coveted the premiership for his son, had, at least for the time being, shot his bolt with the failed putsch of September 1966. Craig was only beginning to emerge as a rival candidate and had not yet gathered enough support to seriously undermine O'Neill, while Harry West was somewhat isolated in Fermanagh.

Other cabinet ministers and MPs grumbled in the background, susceptible to Boal's rhetoric and constituency pressure, but not yet ready to rebel openly. O'Neill had put a brake on his dialogue with the Republic's government and, although this didn't satisfy his opponents, it deprived them of an issue on which to challenge him.

That was all to change – for Paisley and the anti-O'Neill Unionists – when Nationalist frustration at the slow pace of promised reform spilled into civil rights street protest in the summer and autumn of 1968.

—◁◦▷—

It had taken some time for it all to gestate. The Campaign for Social Justice, the Northern Ireland Labour Party and the British Campaign for Democracy in Ulster, in alliance with Gerry Fitt, had been patiently lobbying for change from 1963 onwards. These movements were a reflection of the new demands of an emerging Catholic middle class and of the impact of the British Welfare State on Northern Catholic attitudes. For the first time since the 1920s, they were aiming not to overthrow the State, but to reform it. It was proving to be a painfully slow process.

The transition from pressure to protest was inevitable and in February 1967 the Northern Ireland Civil Rights Association was formed in Belfast. It was a coalition of Republicans, the Campaign for Social Justice, left-wing activists, the Communist Party and middle-class Catholics. Initially, NICRA attempted to be broad-based and moderate in its methods and demands. It even included on its executive a member of the Unionist Party.

But eventually, NICRA, which at first was uneasy about mounting street protests and worried about a Protestant backlash, succumbed to Catholic pressure for action. A strategy of non-violent protest marches around a series of political demands was formulated: one man, one vote in local government elections; an end to the gerrymandering of electoral districts; anti-discrimination machinery; fair allocation of housing; an end to the Special Powers Act; and the disbandment of the "B" Special constabulary.

Although most in NICRA and other civil rights groups attempted to direct their protests in a non-sectarian fashion and made overtures to Protestants, especially in the working class, each of their demands was a threat to collective or sectional Unionist interests.

The demands for electoral reform and anti-discrimination measures particularly alarmed Unionists west of the River Bann, which divides Northern Ireland into the predominantly Protestant east and the Catholic west. Unionists kept power in local councils there only through rigging the electoral system and by the sectarian allocation of housing; NICRA's demand, if granted, would take away that power and hand it to their traditional enemies. Outlawing discrimination east of the Bann meant, in Northern Ireland's high unemployment economy, giving jobs to Catholics at the expense of Protestants, especially the Protestant working class.

In both areas, Unionists were either alarmed at the demand for the repeal of the Special Powers Act and the disbandment of the "B" men – their two major lines of defence against absorption into an all-Ireland Republic – or were instinctively disposed, with the encouragement of Stormont Ministers, the RUC and Paisley, to view Catholic street protest as another clever ploy by the IRA to foment a rebellion which force of arms had earlier failed to achieve.

No one was better able to articulate all those threats to Protestantism than Ian Paisley. His warnings that the civil rights movement would be used by Republicans to stir up trouble would, as the trouble inevitably came, be seen even by non-fundamentalist Protestants as evidence of special prophetic powers. And his tactic of confronting the civil rights protests, while O'Neill and his ministers appeared to appease them, earned him new Loyalist converts. Thanks to all this, Paisley bridged the gulf between his limited fundamentalist religious support and the much larger Loyalist mainstream.

Inside the Unionist Party, the civil rights campaign gave the anti-O'Neillite Unionists the issue that they had previously lacked, as O'Neill desperately struggled to balance pressure from Catholics and the British government against immovable elements inside his own party.

This tension helped to create a coalition of differing interests inside the Unionist Party. Ambitious dissidents like Faulkner and Craig joined hands with the west of the Bann Unionists, the fundamentalist right-wing and the Protestant working and lower middle classes, all of whom felt under political threat.

By the summer of 1968, Catholic pressure on NICRA to raise the level of its campaign was intense. In Derry, for instance, a Housing Action Committee had been formed by left-wing Republicans and Socialists and was holding protests against the biased allocation of houses by the Unionist-controlled Corporation. In Caledon in east Tyrone, the local Republican Club, supported by the local Nationalist MP, Austin Currie, organised Catholics to squat in a house which the Unionist Council had given to the unmarried secretary of a Unionist parliamentary candidate.

When they were evicted by the RUC, the Campaign for Social Justice decided to hold a protest march from Coalisland to the centre of Dungannon on 24 August and NICRA agreed to support it. No Nationalist parade had ever been allowed into Dungannon's Market Square and the march was seen as Nationalist. The area was regarded by Loyalists as a Protestant redoubt and, when plans for the march were announced, they moved to stop it.

The initiative came not directly from Paisley but from two units of his rural Ulster Protestant Volunteers – in east Tyrone where the march was to be held, and its counterpart from south Derry, the first and largest of all the UPV branches. They met and decided to call a counter rally in Dungannon Market Square to coincide with the civil rights march in the hope of provoking a government ban. The government, for once, didn't rise to the bait. Undeterred, the UPV approached the local Unionist MP, John Taylor, and threatened trouble if the march was not diverted. Paisley later claimed that Taylor had also come to see him to ask him to call off the rally but he, Paisley, had refused.

The report of the Cameron commission, appointed by O'Neill in January 1969 to examine the violence that followed the civil rights campaign, recorded that Taylor brought this warning to the local RUC, who immediately rerouted the march through the town's Catholic areas and away from the centre. Paisley had scored another victory.

Despite this, the UPV followed through with its promised counter-rally. When the civil rights marchers arrived at Dungannon, they found a cordon of police facing them, blocking their original route. Behind them was a crowd of Loyalists, 500 strong, singing "God Save the Queen". The civil rights demonstrators, who included six Nationalist MPs, two Senators and the Sinn Féin leader, Tomás MacGiolla, replied with the Republican hymn "A Nation Once Again" and "We Shall Overcome" – borrowed from the American Black civil rights movement – and placards were tossed at the police.

Austin Currie compared the police cordon to the Berlin Wall and Gerry Fitt angrily shouted from the back of a lorry: "My blood is boiling – only that there is a danger to women and children I would lead the men past that barricade." A young girl speaker exhorted the crowd: "If you want to fight join the IRA!"

The *Protestant Telegraph,* never one for understatement, compared the march to the 1572 St Bartholomew's Day massacre, whose anniversary fell on 24 August, when thousands of French Huguenots were butchered by Catholics: "This year it was celebrated in Dungannon by a Civil Rights march that almost ended in the rebel marchers attacking the police and the Protestants who had turned out to voice their disapproval." The RUC was praised and a warning issued to others who might emulate the civil rights marchers: "The policy of the UCDC, through the UPV, has been and will continue to be to confront the enemy at every opportunity."

The Coalisland-Dungannon march set a pattern for all other civil rights marches. The protestors, despite their claims to be non-sectarian, would be seen by increasing numbers of Protestants as a coalition of Nationalists and Republicans who, by flouting the law and attempting to "invade" Protestant territory under the cover of "civil rights", were in reality working to achieve the old goal of Irish unity and Catholic domination.

Paisleyite threats of counter-protests would invariably force the government to curb, reroute or ban civil rights demonstrations from areas regarded as traditionally Protestant. Nationalist anger at this would be compounded by the RUC's habit of treating them as the potential troublemakers at demonstrations; the police would invariably turn to face civil rights marchers and ignore the crowds of screaming Paisleyites behind them.

To Unionists, the state itself was under threat from civil rights demands; to Nationalists, the attempt to achieve equality of citizenship by peaceful, non-sectarian means was being resisted by the whole Unionist apparatus dancing to Paisley's tune.

After the Coalisland-Dungannon march, Paisley intensified his protest activity. A fortnight later, he led the South Derry UPV through the town of Maghera to denounce the activities of Kevin Agnew, a local solicitor and leading Republican who had helped organise the Dungannon civil rights march.

To Paisley's fury, Craig rerouted the UPV parade away from the town's Catholic area to avoid confrontation. Craig had met Paisley to discuss the march and told him that local Unionists had objected on the grounds that there might be trouble. Paisley rounded on Craig, challenging him to imprison Agnew, chairman of the local outlawed

Republican Club: "I speak as one who was behind prison bars and as one O'Neill and his Lundies tried to silence, but so long as we have a breath we will not be silenced," he cried.

Craig needed no urging to do his Unionist duty when the civil rights protesters again took to the streets, for their target this time alarmed virtually every section of Unionism. It was the Maiden City of Derry, sacred ground to Protestants for nearly three centuries since it withstood King James's siege. Every 12 August, the Apprentice Boys commemorated the siege by parading to the ancient city's hallowed walls, from where they could see stretched out below them, like King James's encamped army, the hostile slums of the Catholic Bogside.

In Nationalist eyes Derry – Protestants call it Londonderry to emphasise its Britishness – was "the capital city of discrimination" and a symbol of their second-class citizenship. Although the city had a clear Catholic majority, the electoral wards were gerrymandered to produce a Unionist majority on the Corporation. Housing conditions in Catholic areas had been deliberately neglected by successive Unionist administrations and Derry's unemployment rate for Catholics and Protestants alike was well above the Northern Ireland average.

In September, local Republicans and left-wing activists announced plans for a civil rights march in the city to take place on 5 October and, reluctantly, NICRA agreed to support it. It was to be "non-sectarian" and, to support this claim, the march would start at Duke Street on the Protestant east bank of the River Foyle and end at the Diamond inside the city's sacred walls.

Paisley didn't need to announce a countermarch. Local Unionists called on Craig to ban the march, while the Apprentice Boys announced plans for an initiation ceremony, which they claimed to be a traditional annual event, along the same route on the same day. No one had ever heard of it before but it gave Craig the perfect pretext to ban the civil rights march. He also claimed that IRA leaders were planning to join the civil rights demonstrators.

A large force of police was sent to Derry to enforce the ban. They blocked off Duke Street at both ends as several hundred civil rights protesters gathered. The marchers moved off but within two hundred yards they met a solid wall of police who first batoned the leaders, including Gerry Fitt, and then baton-charged the crowd. Water cannon were used to hose the crowd, by now trapped between two lines of police.

The fighting spread to the Bogside and petrol bombs were thrown at the police. By the end of the day 77 civilians had been treated for injuries in hospital. The riots in Derry had reverberations much farther afield than Northern Ireland. The police violence, condemned later by the Cameron Commission as "indiscriminate", had been captured by a cameraman from Irish television, RTÉ, and the pictures horrified audiences in Britain. Paisley blamed O'Neill and "the folly of his appeasement policy" for the Derry riots. In the *Protestant Telegraph,* he thundered:

> There is no doubt we have been betrayed by his policies. He takes every opportunity to smear the Protestants and to eulogise and to condone the actions of the Roman Catholic Church and her puppet politicians and her puppet priests, cardinals, monseigneurs [sic] and canons.

> Rome, when she is on the plane of equality, is like a fox. Rome has come to believe that she is on the plane of equality in Ulster, and this has been brought to pass by the encouragement of those hireling prophets occupying professed Protestant pulpits, the ecumenists – the World Council fifth column in our midst. These men have helped to swell the bloated head of the monster of Romanism. The bared teeth of the fox of Romanism have been seen at the weekend in the city of Londonderry, and remember this, that when Rome comes from a place of minority to equality and then to a place of majority, she is like a tiger ready to tear her prey to pieces.

The Roman tiger was on the loose and Paisley set out to cage it. His two latest lieutenants in this struggle were a bizarre former British Army officer and a more sinister figure from the darker side of Loyalism. Each in their own way was to leave an indelible mark on the career of Ian Paisley and on wider Loyalist politics.

The latter was John McKeague, a fiercely anti-Catholic fanatic from Bushmills, County Antrim, who had been converted to Free Presbyterianism in 1966. A greying 38-year-old, McKeague moved with his mother to East Belfast in 1968 where he joined the Willowfield branch of the UPV and immersed himself in Paisleyite activity.

McKeague had a dark secret which was ultimately to prove embarrassing for Paisley. He was a paederast and before he had moved to Belfast, the RUC had questioned him about sexual assaults on two young boys; only the intervention of influential friends saved him from being charged. In the early 1970s he founded a Loyalist paramilitary group, the Red Hand Commandos, which consisted largely of young teenagers. McKeague himself was rarely seen in public without a youthful male escort.

McKeague was later to become a significant figure in Northern Ireland's Loyalist underworld. In 1969 he led the Shankill Defence Association, which was active in the sectarian riots of August that year and was the precursor of the much larger and more violent Ulster Defence Association, of which he was briefly chairman. He broke with the UDA in a dispute over money and, in the resulting feud, his home was petrol-bombed by the UDA and his mother killed. The Red Hand Commandos, which he then formed, was responsible for one of the very first sectarian assassinations when a Catholic pedestrian was gunned down in North Belfast in 1971.

McKeague had the dubious distinction of becoming the only person ever prosecuted under the Incitement to Hatred Act. The charge arose from a Loyalist songbook which he had published, one of whose ballads went: "You've never seen a better Taig than with a bullet in his back." He was acquitted.

The eccentric was Major Ronald Bunting, a 44-year-old mathematics teacher who had quit the British Army in 1950 after service in Korea and Malaya. He was also a member of Willowfield UPV, the same branch as McKeague. He'd had a strange political career before ending up in Paisley's arms. At one stage he had worked for the election of the Republican Labour MP Gerry Fitt and then had moved on to the Clean Air Society and the Ratepayers Association, on whose ticket he was elected a councillor in East Belfast.

Bunting had also founded the Democratic Party, with himself as the only visible member, with the aim of creating "an all-Ireland union of minds" to stamp out prejudice. Bunting had joined in the chorus of condemnation when Paisley had staged his illegal march in 1963 to protest at the lowering of the Belfast City Hall's Union Jack when Pope John XXIII had died.

By 1966 Bunting's political views had swung through a 180-degree arc. That Easter he went to St Patrick's cathedral in Dublin to lay a wreath in memory of British soldiers killed in the 1916 Rising. His action was a protest against Protestant churches joining the state-sponsored 1916 commemorations. The protest brought him to Paisley's attention, the two men met and Bunting was "saved" for the cause.

By early 1970 Paisley had discarded both men, as he had close aides in the past who became either rivals or an embarrassment. Bunting was ditched when his views became more and more heretical – he eventually advocated unity centres where Protestants and Catholics could meet and talk, and his son, Ronnie, had become embarrassingly prominent in the civil rights movement. (Later Bunting Junior joined the Official IRA and helped to found the INLA. UDA gunmen shot him dead in 1980.) In a final bitter letter to Paisley, Major Bunting wrote: "Dear Ian, you are my spiritual father . . . but politically you stink."

McKeague was discarded in late 1969 at a time when rumours of his homosexuality had become rife in Loyalist areas – his boyfriend was arrested during the August riots and McKeague became so distraught it attracted comment. All that McKeague would ever say about his break with Paisley was that Paisley had summoned him to say that he had become "an embarrassment" and would have to leave the Free Presbyterian Church. Both Paisley's erstwhile lieutenants died in the 1980s – Bunting peacefully of a heart attack and McKeague violently at the hands of an INLA gunman.

McKeague's contribution to Paisley's campaign would come in early 1969, while Bunting's was more immediate. His principal "gift" was a wild imagination and a penchant for inventing fictional Protestant organisations like the "Knights of Tubal Cain", "Apprentices and Fellowcraft (Masters and Purplemen)" and the "Menatzchim" as covers for his anti-civil rights protests. Only one of his creations, the Loyal Citizens of Ulster, appeared to have any foothold in reality. It was a small group of UPV and UVF members whom he could call on for protests.

Their first foray came only four days after the Derry civil rights march when angry students at Queen's University organised a protest march to Belfast City Hall. Paisley got to hear of it and blocked their way with 200 followers. The students were re-routed but near the City Hall their way was blocked again by six Paisleyite women. The RUC stopped the march and the students held a three-hour sit-down protest on the street. They then marched back to the university where, after hours of emotional debate, they set up a civil rights group, calling it People's Democracy.

A month later Paisley and Bunting, with several thousand followers, marched to the Diamond in the centre of Derry to lay a wreath of poppies at the war memorial. Paisley warned that the civil rights march four weeks earlier was "but the prelude to an IRA upsurge. The day when Ulster Protestants will have to face the worst IRA campaign in our history has been brought forward."

Events were now fast running out of the Unionists' control. The Nationalist Party quit as the official Stormont opposition, in protest at events in Derry, and Jack Lynch flew to London to urge Harold Wilson to speed up reforms. The *Protestant Telegraph* warned: "Our fathers had to arm themselves in defence of previous traitors in Westminster and it seems as if history is going to repeat itself. Wilson and Lynch will not be dealing with weaklings like O'Neill when they come to deal with the hard core of Ulster Protestants."

On 3 November Wilson summoned O'Neill, Craig and Faulkner to Downing Street and pressed them to implement reforms. On their return to Belfast, the cabinet wrangled over the package and it soon became evident that Craig was emerging as the hard man of the resistance to it. He had banned all civil rights marches from the walled centre of Derry after Paisley and Bunting's wreath-laying ceremony, although it had been repeatedly defied by moderate Catholics in a Citizens' Action Committee led by a young schoolteacher called John Hume. A few weeks before, Craig had been a villain in Paisley's eyes but now he was becoming one of the last lines of resistance and he won plaudits in the *Protestant Telegraph*.

On 22 November O'Neill announced a limited package of reforms. There would be an Ombudsman, a points system for allocating council housing, the multiple business vote was abolished, Derry Corporation was to be replaced by a non-elected commission, and the government would consider suspending parts of the Special Powers Act.

The package satisfied no-one. Hardline Unionists saw it as the thin end of a large wedge while Nationalists complained that their central demand – one man, one vote – had not been conceded. Both sides resumed their contest on the streets. The UPV issued a virtual call to arms: "In face of these present awful and terrible events, when one by one the lights of freedom are going out, we, the members of the UPV, beseech you, our loyal brethren, for the sake of God, our country and our children, to forget all petty quarrels and jealousies and defend our constitution and liberty. He that would be free must strike the first blow."

◄○►

The next NICRA march was scheduled for the centre of Armagh on 30 November. Paisley had a personal interest in "striking a blow" to stop it. "He was furious when he heard about it," recalled a Free Presbyterian.

"He was roaring 'No-one is going to march there. That's my city, that's where I was born. They're not going to desecrate my birthplace!'"

Paisley and a local Free Presbyterian, Douglas Hutchinson, met the Armagh police on 19 November to tell them that the UCDC had made plans for "appropriate action" if the march was not banned. Their attitude, the RUC later told the Cameron Commission, was "aggressive and threatening".

A clue to what that "appropriate action" was likely to be came in the following days. A handbill warning people to "Board up your windows. Remove all women and children from the city on Saturday 30 November" was stuffed through letterboxes. Two days before the march, UCDC posters appeared in the town centre: "For God and Ulster. S.O.S. To all Protestant religions. Don't let the Republicans, IRA and CRA make Armagh another Londonderry. Assemble in Armagh on Saturday 30 November."

On the eve of the march Paisley asked for a meeting with O'Neill, who turned him down, but he secretly met Craig who assured him that his counter-demonstration would be permitted. But the police made their own plans to stop Paisley mounting a protest – 350 policemen were to be drafted in by 9.30 am on the day of the march to seal off the route and there were to be roadblocks by 8.00 am on all roads leading into Armagh.

The RUC's plans were leaked to Hutchinson, who immediately contacted Paisley. He was in the middle of a Church Presbytery meeting when Hutchinson's phone call came through. The meeting broke up with an excited Paisley issuing instructions to the church elders and ministers to round up their congregations and alert UPV divisions to make their way to the centre of Armagh before the police roadblocks went up.

Paisley arrived with Bunting and a convoy of 30 cars at about 1.00 am and they spent the night talking in small groups or sitting in their cars. Paisley told a police inspector that he planned to hold a religious meeting and did not intend to interfere with anyone.

The RUC roadblocks were needed. As hundreds of Paisleyites converged on the city, searches of cars uncovered two revolvers and 220 other weapons, including bill hooks, scythes and pipes hammered into sharp points. In the city centre, meanwhile, the Paisley crowd had swollen to several hundred and many were armed with sticks taken from a building site; Paisley himself was armed with a blackthorn stick and Bunting carried a large black walking stick. By midday the

Paisleyite crowd had grown to 2,000; hundreds more had breached the police cordon around the city centre by knocking down a wall in an alleyway.

Paisley was told by the police that he was now holding an unlawful assembly – by no stretch of the imagination could his menacing gathering be described as a religious service – but he refused to disperse. The RUC had little option but to stop the 5,000-strong civil rights march before it collided with the Paisleyites with what could only be disastrous results.

Fortunately the marchers were well stewarded by Republicans and they agreed. Major violence was averted but there were one or two ugly scenes. An ITN cameraman was knocked unconscious by a Paisleyite wielding a lead-filled sock and an RUC man destroyed a BBC camera with his baton. As the crowds made their way home late that evening, the streets in the city centre were littered with cudgels, bottles and rocks discarded by the Paisley mob.

To distinguish themselves from their civil rights foes in Armagh, many of the Paisleyites had worn little blue badges on their lapels bearing the words "Save the *Clydevalley*". They were evidence of yet another effort by Paisley to link his own campaign to the Unionist heroes of old and to contrast the timeless values of traditional Unionism with the "appeasement" of O'Neillism. The *Clydevalley* was the re-named *Mountjoy II*, a 470-ton steamboat which had smuggled 35,000 rifles and three million rounds of ammunition from Germany to the County Antrim port of Larne in April 1914 to arm Carson's UVF for the expected fight against Home Rule. After that the old boat, one of the few iron-clad ships still afloat, had gone into trans-Atlantic commercial service. In 1966 she was discovered in Sydney, Nova Scotia, and the South Antrim Westminster MP, Sir Knox Cunningham, a regular contributor to the columns of the *Protestant Telegraph*, appealed to Paisley for help in saving her from the scrapyard. He and the man who had discovered her, Sam Campbell, from Whitehead, County Antrim, set up a fundraising committee to cover the cost of making the *Clydevalley* seaworthy and bringing her back to Northern Ireland where she would be a floating Loyalist museum.

Paisley enthusiastically agreed. The *Protestant Telegraph* declared:

We must in these "Ecumenical Days" remind our readers that but for the arming of the UVF the British Government of the day would have forced on us the tragic and unspeakable doom of a Dublin Home Rule parliament. Now we Ulstermen, whether at home or abroad, feel that this tangible reminder of Northern Ireland's formation should be returned to her native land. The Southern Irish government bought out of public funds, for $30,000, the Irish Volunteer *Asgard* and have preserved her for their history. On the other hand our timid and unimaginative Ulster government, who, but for the *Clydevalley*'s cargo wouldn't exist, are frightened to support this project. So finally it is left to us straightforward Ulster Protestants to ensure that our history is not forgotten.

The venture was a disaster. It was two years before enough money was raised to finance repairs and a crew. Finally, on 5 October 1968, as the RUC and civil rights marchers were fighting it out in Derry, the *Clydevalley* set sail from Canada under Captain William Agnew, a retired master mariner from Kilkeel, County Down. Six days out of port the ship developed engine trouble and had to return for expensive repairs. Two weeks later the *Clydevalley* developed a list and more repairs were needed. Paisley's welcome home ceremony, complete with an honour guard of UVF veterans, Orange bands and an expected 25,000 crowd, had to be put off again and again. The cost was rising alarmingly. Between emergency repairs and the original refit, the *Clydevalley* expedition ran up debts of £16,000.

Creaking and belching plumes of black smoke and with Paisley and some UCDC colleagues on board, she finally limped into Larne on 14 December, nearly two months behind schedule. Only 4,000 turned up to welcome her and, while Paisley put a brave face on it, there was little doubt that the affair had been little short of a fiasco.

The *Clydevalley* never became a floating museum. She rusted away for years in Carrickfergus harbour while the local council and Sam Campbell's committee squabbled over who was responsible for her. Finally in August 1974 she was towed across the Irish Sea to a scrapyard in Lancaster to be broken up. There were recriminations over the debts as well. Captain Agnew was left responsible for some of it and he died penniless, some say of a broken heart, not long after docking the ship in Larne. Sam Campbell also died an early death. He had been left with all the *Clydevalley*'s debts to clear and was, say those who knew him, a bitter man.

After his break with Paisley, John McKeague taunted him about the *Clydevalley*'s debts in his newspaper, *Loyalist News*. Money for the *Clydevalley* fund had been raised at UPV rallies but no-one had ever seen the accounts. When Paisley was elected to Stormont a year later, McKeague acidly commented: "If Mr Paisley upholds his promises to the people of Bannside as he has upheld his promises regarding the *Clydevalley*, we will have another O'Neill on our hands."

As the *Clydevalley* made her troubled journey across the Atlantic to commemorate Unionism's last rebellion against Westminster, history was repeating itself in a remarkable way in Northern Ireland. O'Neill, who had contemplated resignation after the Derry riots, was finding Craig increasingly rebellious and ready to exploit Unionist resentment at Harold Wilson's interference.

On 9 December, O'Neill decided to appeal over the heads of the civil rights movement and his own truculent colleagues in a television broadcast which became famous for the opening lines: "Ulster stands at the Crossroads". He appealed to the civil rights leaders to end their protests, promising that the reform package would be implemented but omitting any mention of one man, one vote.

He also took a swipe at William Craig.

> There are, I know, today some so-called Loyalists who talk of independence from Britain – who seem to want a kind of Protestant Sinn Féin. . . .They are lunatics who would set a course along a road which could only lead at the end into an all-Ireland Republic. They are not Loyalists but dis-Loyalists; disloyal to Britain, disloyal to the Constitution, disloyal to the Crown, disloyal – if they are in public life – to the solemn oaths they have sworn to Her Majesty the Queen.

Forty-eight hours later he sacked Craig when Craig insisted that Unionists did have the right "to resist" Westminster if it attempted to reduce Stormont's powers.

Craig was immediately transformed into a Paisleyite hero and, at a rapturous Shankill Road rally hosted by Boal, he responded by declaring that there was room inside the Unionist Party for Paisley's "vocal and virile movement".

For a few heady days, though, it looked as if O'Neill had pulled it off. Moderate Protestants rallied to him and the *Belfast Telegraph* reprinted "I back O'Neill" coupons for thousands of their readers to fill in and post to him. Nationalist politicians welcomed his speech and NICRA and Hume's Citizens Action Committee in Derry called off all protests for a month. The peace was broken when the student People's Democracy movement announced plans for a march from Belfast to Derry to start on New Year's Day 1969.

—◄o►—

Paisley and Bunting once again moved to stop the student march although there was one important difference in this effort to frustrate the civil rights movement. In all the previous protests, Paisley had played a prominent role. But in the days leading up to the infamous Burntollet ambush, it was Major Bunting who played the leading part. When the ambush took place – the most violent incident since 1966 – Paisley would be safely distant – politically as well as physically.

It was Bunting, not Paisley, who promised to "hinder and harass" the PD marchers with his "Loyal Citizens of Ulster", and it was Bunting, marshalling his taunting, Union Jack-waving followers, who was at Belfast City Hall when the small group of no more than 30 students set off on their 90-mile trek on New Year's morning. He was there at the fore again at Antrim town in the afternoon when he and other Loyalists persuaded the RUC to block the students by threatening violence and in some instances meting it out to the marchers.

The next morning, it was Bunting who mustered 400 Loyalists to block the bridge at Randalstown to the marchers and who led a cavalcade of cars in pursuit of the re-routed students to Toome. Again it was Bunting who met the students that afternoon outside Bellaghy in County Derry with another roadblock. Paisley didn't properly enter the story until the third day when he and Bunting had what was officially described as "a courteous and congenial" afternoon meeting with the acting Home Affairs Minister, Captain William Long, during which they asked him to ban the remainder of the PD march.

That night when Paisley and Bunting addressed a Loyalist rally in Derry's Guildhall, it was Bunting's call to Loyalists "who wish to play a manly role" to "arm themselves with whatever protective measures they feel to be suitable", which really laid the basis for the next day's horrifying violence, not Paisley's invective about the IRA and Civil Rights. It was also Bunting who, with military precision, later that night organised the next day's violence from an Orange Hall at Killaloo on the eastern outskirts of Derry.

And when the students walked into the well-organised ambush at Burntollet bridge, some ten miles from Derry, the following morning, to be showered with boulders, rocks, bottles and bits of iron and to be beaten with batons, spiked clubs and cudgels by 400 Loyalists, it was Bunting whom the ambushers looked to for leadership. Of Paisley there was no sign at all.

An Orange ballad published in John McKeague's *Loyalist News* two years later celebrated the real hero of Burntollet:

On the 4th of January in the year '69,
The rebels left St Patrick's Hall thinking all was fine,
To get to Londonderry was all they had to do,
They little knew what was in store for them at Killaloo.
At a place that's called Burntollet, Major Bunting took his stand,
And said "Men, do your utmost to smash this rebel band
They're coming down in hundreds and you are 72",
They answered "No Surrender! We're from Killaloo".

Burntollet has gone down in extreme Loyalist mythology as a famous victory over Catholic rebels, but very few who celebrate it as such ponder the unusually forbearing role of the man they would unhesitatingly view as Ulster's most forthright Protestant leader. Few have ever been tempted to ask what would have happened had there been deaths at Burntollet, as there might well have been, or serious injury. Who would have taken most responsibility and perhaps even the legal consequences – Paisley or Bunting?

The PD march and the Burntollet ambush had a devastating impact on Nationalist attitudes to O'Neill and the RUC. The day after Burntollet, O'Neill issued a statement, 90 per cent of which was taken up with an attack on the "foolhardy, irresponsible and hooligan" civil rights marchers. Bunting's ambushers, on the other hand, had, he said, merely played "into the hands of those who are encouraging the current agitation".

O'Neill's mild rebuke to the Loyalists, coupled with his strongly worded criticism of the students, lost him virtually all the Catholic sympathy generated by his television broadcast in December. To make matters worse, his cousin, James Chichester-Clark, the Minister of Agriculture, had consorted with Bunting's men in Maghera during the march and had interceded on their behalf in an effort to get the march banned. It was further evidence to many Nationalists of respectable Unionism and extreme Loyalism acting in cahoots.

161

O'Neill had also threatened to mobilise more "B" Specials if the civil rights marches and Loyalist counter-protests continued and this outraged Catholics – many of those who had ambushed the students at Burntollet were "B" men. One well-researched estimate put their number at nearly 100, a quarter of Bunting's entire force. Putting more "B" men on the streets was a threat to Catholics and was precisely what the Loyalists wanted.

The greatest damage, though, was done to RUC-Catholic relations. During the march the police had re-routed the students several times and on two occasions the new routes led directly into Bunting's path. Suspicions that the RUC were on the Loyalist side were fuelled by the sight of them mingling amicably with Bunting's men at roadblocks and occasionally joining in the Loyalist taunts.

The Burntollet ambush led to allegations of active collusion between the police and the Loyalists. Afterwards they were accused of knowingly leading the marchers into the attack and of doing little to stop it when it started. Some police were even accused of joining in the attack on the marchers with Bunting's force.

In Derry city antagonism between the police and Bogside Catholics reached new heights. On the night that Paisley and Bunting had addressed Loyalists in the Guildhall, sectarian fighting had been followed by repeated RUC baton charges into the Bogside. The next night, after the stragglers from Burntollet had made it into the city, policemen, many of them apparently drunk, went on the rampage in the Bogside, breaking windows and doors and beating up people. The Bogsiders hastily constructed barricades to keep the police out and "Free Derry" was born.

Although the Cameron report exonerated the RUC of most of the marchers' accusations of bias, it had harsh words to say about the force's behaviour in Derry: "A number of policemen were guilty of misconduct which involved assault and battery, malicious damage to property . . . and the use of provocative, sectarian and political slogans." Burntollet and its aftermath created a level of Catholic hostility to the police from which, arguably, the RUC never fully recovered.

The student march also polarised opinion, squeezing out moderate voices on both sides of the community. Along the route Catholic-Protestant hostility sharpened to a dangerous degree, leading, for instance, to rioting not just in Derry but also in Maghera where hundreds of Loyalists had gone on the rampage against Catholic property. The stage for the slide into a bloody summer had been set.

It was Paisley who chose the next battlefield for a confrontation and it was a more safely familiar one than the fields of County Derry. After his Armagh demonstration, he and Bunting had been charged with taking part in an unlawful assembly. They spurned the chance to postpone their trial for five months, an offer made to all alleged miscreants by the Attorney General, Basil Kelly, in the wake of O'Neill's "Crossroads" broadcast, and elected for an early hearing.

On 27 January their case came before magistrates in Armagh and Paisley soon had the courtroom in turmoil. He accused the magistrates of having already made up their minds and refused to apologise for contempt of court. When Bunting tried to make a speech, he was ordered out of the court. Paisley, together with his followers, tried to follow but were stopped by the police. Amid scuffling and cheering, Paisley could be heard bellowing from the back of the courtroom: "If I was a Roman Catholic I would be allowed to leave."

Eventually he and Bunting were allowed to leave and the case went on in their absence. As they were each found guilty and sentenced to three months' imprisonment, Paisley addressed a crowd outside the courthouse. To shouts of "No Surrender" and "No Popery" he claimed he had been bullied, insulted and kicked inside the court. He was once more the peaceful but defiantly resolute Protestant leader persecuted by brutal police and victimised by O'Neill's "appeasing" government.

The next day brought an opportunity to polish the martyr's image. When the police called at his Beersbridge Road home to arrest him, Paisley was in conference with John McKeague. There was an argument at the door, a glass panel was smashed and Paisley cut his little finger – later he claimed that a policeman had put a foot through the door and that his finger had been almost severed. The police allowed him to have medical treatment but the next morning as he was leaving hospital they arrested him and took him off to jail. Newspaper photographs showed a heavily bandaged and righteously indignant Paisley between two police officers loudly protesting that the police had broken their word.

He served less than 24 hours in jail. The ruling Presbytery of the Free Presbyterian Church had urged him to lodge an appeal – "they said he was much too important to the Church and must never go to jail again," recalled one Free Presbyterian. He signed a bail bond and was released, abandoning Bunting to serve out his sentence alone.

In the next week, however, a political crisis inside the Unionist Party gave Paisley the first real opportunity to demonstrate his growing political support. The crisis had been precipitated by the Burntollet ambush, after which, in response to British pressure, O'Neill set up the Cameron Commission, headed by a Scottish judge, to enquire into the causes of the violence since 5 October 1968.

Three days later, on 23 January, Brian Faulkner resigned from the government in protest at what he called "the political manoeuvre" of appointing Cameron. The next day his ally, the Minister of Health, Billy Morgan, also quit and a week later twelve dissident MPs, led by Boal, Craig and West, publicly called for O'Neill's resignation and demanded a party meeting to decide the issue. Significantly their complaints about O'Neill echoed Paisley's – the rot, said Craig, had set in when O'Neill had invited Lemass to Belfast without consulting the Unionist Party. "Some people would put it this way," he went on. "We have moved too far towards a form of presidential government and not cabinet government."

When the rebels congregated in a hotel in Portadown on 3 February, a meeting which became known as "the Portadown Parliament", O'Neill decided to appeal to the electorate above the heads of his party's extremists and called a general election for 24 February.

No-one was to know that it would be the last general election ever to the old, Unionist-dominated Stormont parliament. Perhaps appropriately, it was also the most confused election in the history of Northern Ireland. Pro-O'Neill Official Unionist MPs were opposed by hardline unofficial Unionists, while anti-O'Neill MPs faced unofficial pro-O'Neill Unionists.

Altogether some 60 Unionist candidates stood, each laying claim to reflect the legitimate voice of Unionism. It was the beginning of the break up of Unionism, the rending of the umbrella under which in the past so many different social, economic and political interests had sheltered. Things were no less complex on the Nationalist side, where the old Nationalist Party found itself opposed by civil rights leaders and left-wingers from the Peoples' Democracy.

Sensing the coming election, or perhaps armed with advance knowledge of the impending meeting of the "Portadown Parliament", Paisley had earlier set about organising his biggest ever march and rally in Belfast. He staged it on 1 February and let it be known that he was going to make an important announcement.

The march's starting point was the Shankill Road and there, for an hour before it moved off, the streets were black with thousands of people, and traffic was brought to a standstill. Mothers had dressed their babies in red, white and blue, the Shankill was in a Twelfth-like festive mood and the hero of the day was Paisley – six hundred "I'm backing Paisley" badges were sold out within half an hour.

When it did move off, led by three Lambeg drummers, the "Young Conquerors" flute band and a sea of Union Jacks and Ulster flags, women pushed forward in an attempt to touch Paisley. In Royal Avenue, as the chant "O'Neill must go!" developed into an enormous roar, Paisley was hoisted shoulder-high and, grinning broadly, was carried into the Ulster Hall. Inside, the scene was like an American political convention. The back of the hall was draped in a huge Orange banner and Union Jacks hung down from the balconies. On the platform more Union Jacks and Ulster flags were waved in tune to the crowd's chant of "O'Neill out!" So excited and aroused were the crowd that Paisley had to appeal for calm three times.

He brought them cheering to their feet with his first words, an appeal to back the twelve rebel MPs. There was uproar when he declared that Ulster Protestants would "fight and die" if necessary to defend the Union, and pandemonium when he made his "important announcement": he would fight O'Neill in Bannside at the next election.

Despite the excitement, Paisley had in fact chosen his words carefully, mindful of his past pledges to stay out of politics. He would enter the political arena, he said, only "if a crisis arose and he was needed to support the Protestant people". The crisis had now arrived. The crisis, of course, was to last for the next four decades, enabling Paisley's move into the worldly arena of politics to become permanent.

Five other Paisleyite candidates were chosen to contest seats when O'Neill announced the poll. The Prime Minister, using words he later regretted bitterly, welcomed their entry: "It could be a healthy thing to have the real strength or weakness of this movement tested at the polls," he said.

Two of the candidates were Free Presbyterian ministers and two others were members of the church. The fifth, Bunting, had stayed loyal to Methodism. The ministers, John Wylie and Billy Beattie, stood in North and South Antrim respectively; Charlie Poots chose Iveagh and William Spence fought in Bloomfield in East Belfast. Bunting stood for the Victoria seat, also in East Belfast.

The Protestant Unionist label, which Paisley had first used back in 1958 against Brian Maginess, was resurrected but this time there was an enlarged Free Presbyterian church and the UPV divisions to help gather in the votes. Its manifesto was also redolent of those far-off days and of the Independent Unionists before them.

It was a mixture of uncompromising, traditional Unionism and social and economic populism. A call for strong law and order and the mobilisation of the "B" Specials to deal with civil rights protests was coupled with demands for a halving of the unemployment rate, a crash housing programme and a rise in household incomes "by 25 per cent".

In Bannside, Paisley didn't confine his attacks on O'Neill to his bridge-building policies. He borrowed an issue from Michael Farrell, the People's Democracy candidate, and complained bitterly about the plethora in Ahoghill of dry closets – outside lavatories which cannot be flushed – as an example of O'Neill's neglect of his home town.

His electioneering style was also traditional, awakening memories among older voters of the uncompromising campaigns of Craigavon and Brookeborough. He would parade – a towering figure, sporting a UPV sash, a white raincoat and a Russian cossack hat – through villages and towns behind a forest of Union Jacks.

Following him would be dozens of his supporters in the UPV's red, white and blue regalia. Accompanying them would be Orange bands beating out familiar and rousing Loyalist ballads – "The Sash", "Dollies Brae" and "The Green, Grassy Slopes of the Boyne" – or Lambeg drummers clattering out incessant warlike rhythms. It was colourful, exciting stuff, luring young and old alike to hear Paisley speak. With minor variations it would become his signature, successful formula.

The world's media was drawn to Northern Ireland by the Bannside contest and it was Paisley's campaign which gave them the exciting pictures and stories. O'Neill's campaign, by contrast, was dull and creaking – Bannside had not been contested since the formation of the State and O'Neill had difficulty getting an election machine together.

The two men never met during the contest, neither on nomination day nor at the count – drawing the telling barb from Paisley that O'Neill was "a superior creature". O'Neill contented himself with long-distance attacks on Paisley. Paisleyites, he declared, were dinosaurs suitable for relegation to "the natural history museum of politics". The Paisleyite riposte was inevitable: if they were dinosaurs, then so too were Carson, Craigavon and Brookeborough.

The result shouldn't have surprised anyone but it did. O'Neill won the seat with 7,745 votes, but it was a pyrrhic victory. For hard on his heels, only 1,414 votes behind, came Paisley; in third place was the PD leader, Michael Farrell, whose 2,300 votes were evidence that substantial numbers of Catholics still distrusted O'Neill.

The other Protestant Unionists polled a total of 19,000 votes, a creditable performance but completely overshadowed by their leader's humiliation of the Prime Minister. From then on, Unionist politicians who had dismissed Paisley as a noisy and troublesome nuisance began to see him as a real political force. No-one could see O'Neill surviving another challenge.

When the Unionist Party reassembled at Stormont, O'Neill found most of his opponents back on the benches. The election had solved nothing, while in the constituencies party organisations had been divided and embittered.

The greatest change, though, had taken place within Nationalism where the Nationalist Party leader, Eddie McAteer, was beaten by John Hume in Derry and other civil rights leaders like Ivan Cooper, Paddy O'Hanlon and Paddy Devlin defeated traditional Nationalist opponents. People's Democracy candidates had also done well – in April one of their leaders, Bernadette Devlin, was elected to Westminster to represent the former Republican stronghold of Mid-Ulster. A sea-change in Nationalist thinking was taking place.

In alliance with Gerry Fitt and Austin Currie, the new Stormont MPs combined to form an articulate and initially a moderate opposition. In August 1970 the coalition was formalised when they founded the Social Democratic and Labour Party; within another year, however, under pressure of violent events, they were to abandon Stormont as a forum for reform.

Paisley's supporters meanwhile were jubilant and saw the hand of the Almighty at work in Bannside. A crude ballad celebrating his achievement was quickly penned:

> God has raised a leader
> To fight for Protestant truth
> His name is Ian Paisley
> You've heard of him I'm sure
> He's slandered by the pressmen
> By adults and by youths

But God is with our leader
To help to fight for truth.
Following Jesus, that's what Paisley does
Nothing will harm him, no matter where he goes.
Pray for him dear people, pray with all your might
That God will over rule in Ulster here tonight.

It was the civil rights movement, more than any religious or political protest campaign he himself had created, which gave Paisley legitimacy among Protestants. The civil rights movement made demands for reform which, even without Paisley, Unionism would have been hard-pressed to grant, but with Paisley crying "Lundy!" at every sign of moderation, it was impossible. But to traditional Unionists, he was their saviour – more and more of them saw him as the only obstacle in the way of victory for the civil rights movement and, by extension, their own defeat.

One of those who became a Paisley follower during those days was Wallace Thompson, then a teenager in Ballymoney, County Antrim. He joined the UPV and later, after graduating from Queen's University, Belfast, became a senior official in the DUP.

I had been brought up to believe that Northern Ireland was a Protestant, British state. I had loved the trappings of Orangeism and very many of my reactions were a basic gut feeling that we had this portion of land and we had to guard it; it was my homeland and any giving in at all to the forces of Nationalism was a disaster.

I can recall going through a fleeting pro-O'Neill phase, a belief that his attempts at reconciliation were reasonable. But as events developed and the CRA took off my first reaction was like a red rag to a bull – here we have the old Nationalism rearing its ugly head and I rejoiced at the hammering the Nationalists received in Londonderry on October 5th, 1968. This was the stuff they deserved.

So Paisley seemed to articulate basically the way I felt. I can recall discussing things with friends at school and them agreeing with me. Here was a man who was speaking out, who was seen to be doing something in the middle of all this changing situation.

Paisley

Paisley's name for "speaking out" – saying publicly and loudly what many Protestants thought privately was, and still is, one of the key reasons for his political success.

—◦—

O'Neill's days were now numbered. His opponents mobilised the larger Unionist bodies against him – the 400-strong Standing Committee and the 900-strong Unionist Council – in an effort to get the grassroots to eject him. But other forces conspired to bring him down as well.

On 25 March, Paisley and Bunting were returned to Crumlin Road jail after they dropped their appeals against their conviction for the illegal Armagh demonstration. Five days later at 3.55 in the morning a large explosion wrecked an electricity sub-station at Castlereagh, six miles from the centre of Belfast. Everyone, the RUC included, assumed the bomb was the work of the IRA.

During April there were four more explosions. On 20 April a bomb damaged an electricity pylon at Kilmore, County Armagh and at the Silent Valley reservoir in the Mourne mountains in County Down a large bomb fractured pipes feeding supplies to Belfast and north Down. Four days later another device fractured a water pipe at Templepatrick, County Antrim which fed supplies from Lough Neagh to Belfast. Between them the two bombs cut off three-quarters of Belfast's water supplies and for the next ten days there was water rationing in the city. The last bomb damaged another pipeline near Annalong, some four miles from Silent Valley.

O'Neill announced the mobilisation of 1,000 "B" Specials and the formation of a special cabinet security committee, while the RUC ordered all officers, bar those on traffic duty, to carry guns. British Army helicopters were used to keep a watch on electricity and water pipe lines and eventually troops supplemented "B" Specials guarding power installations.

If they were intended as gestures to appease his right wing, they failed. The bombings, widely thought to be the IRA's work, had hardened Unionist opinion and there were signs that three or four of his erstwhile supporters were about to join the dissidents. To forestall a humiliating rejection, O'Neill resigned on 28 April, three days after the last explosion.

O'Neill left Northern Ireland two years later, selling up his house in Ahoghill to settle in England. In the New Year's honours list in 1969 he was made a life peer and chose the title Lord O'Neill of the Maine. In Britain and abroad he was lauded as a brave statesman, overwhelmed by irrational bigotry.

To Paisleyites, O'Neill was a Lundy; to many civil rights leaders he was a phoney liberal. The most trenchant assessments of his premiership came, however, from his former political allies in Northern Ireland.

One recalled:

> Terence was a decent man but very difficult to work for. First of all we regarded him as an Englishman, not an Ulsterman. He didn't understand the Catholics and he certainly didn't understand Paisley – both were foreign to him in every way.

> He was also "Big House", with servants and all that goes with it. That put him out of touch with ordinary people. I remember talking to a journalist who went to Ahoghill to see what people there thought of him. The local grocer told him that the nearest sight he ever had of O'Neill was of his wife riding down the main street on her horse. It didn't help that he was a lofty person and a bit haughty. He was also shy and awkward and not very good with people and that cost him. While Faulkner was busy chatting people up, O'Neill was nowhere to be seen and I can remember Jim Mailey (his private secretary) forcing him to go down to the members' room to have a few drinks with his backbenchers.

> His worst mistake was failing to sell his policies to the party and to root out the extremists. The best example of that was the Lemass meeting. Paisley and Boal jumped on that as an example of his dictatorship but even after that he should have been out pumping hands and twisting arms, the sort of thing any political leader should do. But I don't think he had the strength of will.

> Was he a liberal? I suppose everyone remembers that awful patronising comment of his about how frightfully hard it was to explain to Protestants that Catholics could live like decent Prods if they had a good job and a television set. I don't think he was ever conscious of what he was – he was more a symbol created by people around him like Bloomfield, who wrote his speeches, Sayers, Malley and Harold Black, the Cabinet Secretary. They injected him with liberalism.

During April, Eileen Paisley had taken over the reins from her husband and led protest rallies demanding his release in Cookstown, County Tyrone, in Armagh and elsewhere, which attracted thousands of supporters. Her husband's imprisonment had affected her deeply. "Before she was never interested in politics but when Ian went to jail that time she became hard and bitter," recalled a church member.

When the bombs started to explode, it seemed all her husband's terrible prophesies had come true – "Captain O'Neill has sown the wind, now he is reaping the whirlwind," she said. When O'Neill resigned, she thanked God for his intervention. Free Presbyterians everywhere were euphoric. Their leader had said "O'Neill must go!", then "O'Neill will go!" – and now he had gone. An ex-Free Presbyterian remembered how Paisley's flock reacted: "The disappearance of O'Neill was God's work and now all their problems were going to be solved." On the Shankill, meanwhile, less pious Loyalists lit bonfires and danced in the street.

Paisley himself didn't have long to wait to join in his flock's celebrations. O'Neill's successor, James Chichester-Clark, declared an amnesty on 6 May, five days after he narrowly defeated Faulkner for the Unionist leadership, and Paisley was freed from jail. At a victory rally on the Shankill Road, Paisley pledged his support for the new Prime Minister provided he did not stray from traditional Unionism. "We don't think he will," he added.

"I wanted to know if Dr Paisley knew who was doing these jobs and asked Mallon. He said, 'Certainly he does. You have to tell him, and you haven't to tell him. He knows and he doesn't know.'"

STATEMENT OF CONVICTED BOMBER SAMMY STEVENSON,
12 NOVEMBER 1969

CHAPTER SIX

A Cat on a Hot Brick

Terence O'Neill left the premiership blaming the explosions of March and April 1969 for forcing him out of Unionist politics – "they literally blew me out of office," he wrote later – and for some time the authorities encouraged the idea that the IRA or some other extreme Republican group was responsible.

After the Silent Valley explosion, for example, the RUC claimed that the bombings were following an IRA "blueprint". The purpose of the Silent Valley explosion, a police spokesman said, was to cause a diversion of police resources to enable civil rights supporters in Derry to occupy a local police station. Allegations like this helped enormously to substantiate, in Protestant minds, the central theme of Paisley's campaign – that the civil rights movement and the IRA were indistinguishable.

Claims by Nationalist MPs that Loyalist extremists were responsible brought official denials and on one occasion a hint from the Minister of Home Affairs, Robert Porter, that if the IRA was not involved, then it was almost certainly the work of one of the IRA's splinter groups. That was the nearest the government came to publicly admitting that its original suspicions were wide of the mark.

The truth did not emerge until 19 October that year, five months after the last explosion, when the charred but still living body of a man was found inside the perimeter of a power station at Ballyshannon in County Donegal in the Irish Republic. Scattered around him were 180 sticks of gelignite, wiring and fuses; in the lining of the man's coat were inscribed the initials "UVF". He was rushed to hospital but died within 24 hours.

The dead man was Tommy McDowell, a quarry foreman from near Kilkeel, County Down. He was also a Free Presbyterian who had

173

helped to build the Kilkeel church in 1967; a fierce Loyalist, he played the drum in an Orange band and was a member of the South Down UPV, with a long association with violent Loyalism. The RUC eventually discovered that he was part of the network which had helped supply Gusty Spence's UVF with explosives back in 1966 – in 1972 Spence paid tribute to his "hallowed" memory.

McDowell was a principal figure in all the 1969 bombings. He had supplied the explosives from quarries he worked in, he had planted three of the bombs himself and had given others tuition for the remaining explosions. He had escaped the net when the RUC rounded up the UVF in 1966 and it had taken his death to alert the RUC to his activities. The explosions were the culmination of Billy Spence's strategy of deception which he had devised back in 1966 and three years later it worked with devastating effect, earning the 1969 bombs an interesting footnote in Northern Ireland's recent violent history as the only known example of a paramilitary group fooling the authorities into believing that its violence was the work of an opposing group.

The police enquiry that followed his death not only established that McDowell had helped to organise and carry out the spring bombing campaign but also led directly to senior members of Paisley's Ulster Constitution Defence Committee and the UPV.

Once again Paisley was to be plunged into association with violence and conspiracy.

It had taken the RUC some time to conclude that Loyalists were really responsible and much longer to admit it, even amongst the force's higher echelons. The prevailing ethos in the RUC at the time mirrored that of the Unionist government. Republicans and Nationalists were seen as the only threat to the State, and despite the killings carried out by Gusty Spence and the UVF in 1966, the idea that Protestants could use violence against institutions in Northern Ireland was plainly unacceptable. One senior officer, interviewed for this book, described the reaction of his colleagues when, after the first bomb, he raised the possibility of Loyalist involvement at a conference of high-ranking detectives: "They looked at me in amazement and some even laughed."

Terence O'Neill got a similar response when he suggested the same thing. Just before his resignation he and his principal aide, Jim Malley, had come to the conclusion that the bombs were the work of extreme Protestants and O'Neill, as he recorded in his autobiography, raised this with the then head of CID, Bill Meharg: "He looked aghast and his reply was to the effect that Loyalists would never destroy their own country." Inside the force Special Branch surveillance of Loyalist extremists was, with the exception of the Shankill Road, virtually non-existent – all their energies were spent pursuing the IRA.

The RUC did have some important clues indicating that responsibility for the bombs might not be as clearcut as their public statements suggested. Earlier in 1969 militant Protestants had demonstrated that they had both the wherewithal and the will to bomb; in January a Republican monument had been blown up in Toome, County Derry and in March and April bombs had been left outside Catholic churches in County Down and County Antrim. In May the Nationalist MP Austin Currie handed over to the Minister of Home Affairs the names of two men he alleged had been involved in the anti-O'Neill bombs – one of them was subsequently charged – but Currie's information was not pursued at the time. "We thought he had a political axe to grind," recalled a senior Special Branch man.

McDowell ought also to have come under police attention at an early stage – he was well known to the police and Mourne Catholics as an extremist who didn't bother to hide his support for Paisley's anti-O'Neill campaign. He was a regular visitor to the UCDC headquarters in Belfast, which was under Special Branch surveillance after the riots of August 1969, and inside the Free Presbyterian Church, according to one former member, suspicions that he was involved in the bombings was a topic of speculative comment.

Forensic tests at the scene of each explosion had established that quarry dynamite had been used and that the devices were crude affairs which were possibly the work of someone with experience of quarry work. McDowell not only had access to explosives and the necessary skills but he lived only 800 yards from the scene of the Silent Valley explosion and near the site of another bombing which had clearly been carried out by Loyalists in February.

That was at the Longstone Road, the scene of bitter disputes in the 1950s over Orange parades, when the "Long Stone", a huge phallic-shaped boulder which Catholics painted green, white and gold to mark the edge of their territory, was blown up. Unused sticks of quarry dynamite were found at the scene afterwards. Local Catholics clearly suspected McDowell's hand in this and the other bombings; in May the Nationalist MP for Mourne, James O'Reilly, came close to naming him during a Stormont debate as the man who blew O'Neill out of politics. Despite all this, McDowell was never once questioned by the RUC.

The RUC also had another important clue which was never disclosed. According to a high-level government source, a member of the Free Presbyterian church contacted a senior CID officer two weeks after the first explosion in March and told him that unnamed members of Paisley's UPV were responsible. The cabinet was informed and were appraised that the police now had a definite line of enquiry to follow.

Although the RUC were by this stage virtually convinced that supporters of Paisley had carried out the bombings, they lacked evidence. The story of how they came by that evidence has been pieced together from RUC and former UCDC/UPV sources.

The story started at Sunday morning service in Kilkeel Free Presbyterian church on 19 October, a service attended by McDowell, a female relative and two other men who were to be his accomplices on a bombing mission to the Irish Republic. After the service, which ironically included a sermon on the evils of violence, McDowell and the other three packed a van with sticks of gelignite and, pretending to be tourists on a Sunday outing, set out for County Donegal. As night fell they made their way to the power station outside the town. Their plan was to blow up the station and cut off electricity supplies to most of the county; it was to be the Loyalist reply to what they saw as the growing interference in Northern Ireland's affairs by the Fianna Fáil government of Jack Lynch.

The plan badly misfired. McDowell climbed over the perimeter fence and his accomplices started passing the bomb-making material through to him. But it was a tight squeeze and McDowell had to lean over; as he did so, he touched a live connector, there was a blinding blue flash and McDowell screamed and fell to the ground, unconscious and badly burned. The others panicked and fled, believing him to be dead.

McDowell was found by gardaí within the hour and taken to hospital in Ballyshannon. Before he died, he was visited by a senior Free Presbyterian Minister, a close confidant of Paisley's, but he apparently never regained consciousness. The story was circulated that McDowell had been kidnapped by Republicans, taken over the Border and killed and then his body planted inside the power station to convince the authorities that Loyalists had attempted to blow it up. It was Billy Spence's deception plan in reverse and it was Paisley's explanation when questioned about McDowell's death at the Scarman Tribunal.

McDowell was buried in his native Kilkeel. The local minister conducted the service and Free Presbyterians from far and wide turned up. McDowell was a widely known and popular figure, but one prominent Free Presbyterian, Ian Paisley, was absent. McDowell's colleagues in the UPV and senior figures from the UCDC did turn up, though, and were photographed by Special Branch detectives hidden in the hills above the graveyard. When some of them were arrested, the first sight that greeted them in the RUC's interrogation rooms were blown-up photographs of themselves standing at McDowell's graveside.

Within a week the RUC had arrested one of those UPV colleagues, a man called Sammy Stevenson, a 46-year-old former "B" Special who lived off Donegall Pass in central Belfast. A full-time worker in the UCDC's HQ in nearby Shaftesbury Square and a member of the UPV's Cromac branch, he had been on the RUC's list of suspects for the bombings for around three months and had been questioned about them a number of times.

In early October, he had helped McDowell to "scout" the Ballyshannon power station and had been in on the planning of the attack. In August he had been badly wounded during sectarian rioting on the Shankill and Falls Roads and earlier in the year he had been arrested a number of times and questioned about rioting offences – he played such a prominent role at Paisleyite protests that he was known to the police as "the man in the white raincoat". On one occasion the police had searched his home and discovered a revolver holster but couldn't find the accompanying gun and he was released. A Sergeant in the Special Branch from Donegall Pass RUC station had been detailed to keep an eye on him and had befriended him in a casual sort of way, visiting him for chats in the UCDC HQ.

To the surprise of detectives, Stevenson talked freely about his and McDowell's role in the bombings and, impressively, he placed himself in a central role, thus convincing the police of the truth of his confession. The shock of McDowell's death had loosened his tongue.

In a series of statements made from October through to December, Stevenson confessed to his own part in the explosions and his links with the UVF – of which he claimed to be "Chief of Staff" – and named ten other men, all members of the UCDC and the UPV, whom he alleged had also been involved.

Stevenson himself was convicted on 5 December and sentenced to twelve years' imprisonment. His links with the UPV were detailed in court and the prosecuting counsel commented that Stevenson "was prepared to create disorder with the object of bringing about the release of the Rev Ian Paisley, who was at that time in prison, and of bringing the downfall of the then Prime Minister."

Stevenson offered to turn Queen's Evidence against the men he had named in his statements – he was Northern Ireland's first ever "supergrass" – and in February 1970 the first of three trials began, each with Stevenson, by now confined to a secure area of Crumlin Road jail, as the Crown's major witness.

Those accused of conspiracy to carry out the various bombings were: John McKeague; William Owens, a Ballymoney, County Antrim teenager who was staying with McKeague in Belfast; Frank Mallon, the UCDC's treasurer, whose brother Hercules had taken over as UCDC secretary from Noel Doherty; Derek Elwood, a "B" Special and Belfast UPV member; Trevor Gracey, circulation manager of the *Protestant Telegraph*; William Gracey and three UPV members from County Armagh – John Love, a Sergeant in the "B" Specials, David McNally and Robert Murdock, who had been acquitted of explosives charges in 1966 when Doherty was convicted. The tenth man was Robert Campbell from Kilkeel.

They were variously charged with conspiracy to carry out all the bombings except Silent Valley – the RUC had concluded that that was a solo effort by McDowell. All bar McKeague, who had parted with Paisley by this stage, had registered as Free Presbyterians when they were remanded to prison. During their confinement they were regularly visited by Free Presbyterian Ministers.

Stevenson alleged that Mallon had played a central role in the bombings, initiating them and providing him with UCDC money to pay McDowell for explosives and for the hire of cars used to transport the bombing teams. The others, he claimed, had played various supporting roles in planting the bombs. In the event he proved to be unimpressive in the witness box and was easily discredited by the defending barristers – he had been in jail twice for larceny and was portrayed as an unreliable witness, with a score to settle with Mallon over the alleged theft of money from UCDC headquarters.

The Crown furthermore had no corroborating evidence to support Stevenson's word, and nearly all the defendants had remained silent during police questioning. Someone, though, was clearly worried that the jury might nevertheless believe Stevenson. During the first trial a small bomb exploded in the hallway of the Crown Court building – it had been planted by a Shankill Road UPV member to intimidate the jury. Whether that clinched it or not remained a jury room secret. Either way the jury decided to acquit all ten defendants – they were hoisted shoulder high and carried out of the Crown Court building by jubilant Loyalists.

A second trial of Mallon and two of the other defendants came to the same conclusion and the third and final trial wound up in early March with the acquittal of Mallon, who had been rearrested and charged with another conspiracy charge. Stevenson was transferred within a year to Wakefield prison in England, safely out of the reach of vengeful Loyalists, to serve out the remainder of his sentence. He later complained that the police had welched on an agreement on an early release in return for his testimony.

One of those acquitted was certainly guilty and that was John McKeague. Years later, long after his break with Paisley, he would, according to colleagues in his Red Hand Commando organisation, boast that he was the one who really masterminded the bombings, not Stevenson.

The first trial had caused a sensation in Northern Ireland. Stevenson's statement to the police had dragged Paisley's name into the sordid conspiracy and what he had to say about Paisley was made public in the courtroom. Although there was never a question of Paisley being charged with involvement in the bombings, the whole affair was acutely embarrassing, coming at a time when the church's expansion and the prospect of election to Stormont had emphasised his need for respectability.

During the trial Stevenson described an incident he alleged had happened inside Donegall Pass police station the previous August when he was being questioned about the explosions. It brought Paisley uncomfortably close to events.

During a break in police questioning, he was visited in his cell, Stevenson said, by Paisley and Mallon. Paisley asked a District Inspector if Stevenson would be subjected to any more questioning that day and the officer assured him that he wouldn't be. The District Inspector started to leave the room and was followed by Mallon and another policeman. Stevenson went on: "I was last. The Rev Paisley went to go out the room and then stopped, came back and bent down and whispered in my ear: 'Did you talk?'"

At that time Stevenson had been a close aide of Paisley's for some six months. Their association dated back to O'Neill's "Crossroads" election in February 1969 when Stevenson had volunteered to work in Major

Bunting's election campaign. Stevenson was interviewed by the author in 1980 and, according to his account, Paisley asked him after the election campaign to take on the full-time job of looking after the UCDC offices, dealing with housing and welfare queries from the public.

In that capacity Stevenson occasionally acted as Paisley's bodyguard, travelling with him to meetings in the country; he accompanied Paisley to Armagh in March for Paisley's appeal against his prison sentence. He was also asked to organise the guarding of Paisley's new church, the Martyrs' Memorial on the Ravenhill Road, then in the process of being built. Stevenson marshalled a squad of about 30 Free Presbyterians, some of them "B" Specials armed with .303 rifles, to stand watch over the church in rotation 24 hours a day.

Stevenson also had another role in the UCDC HQ with which Paisley apparently did not concern himself. He was the UCDC's "security officer" and, as such, organised guards on the building in case of Republican attack. For that eventuality the UCDC had a modest stock of shotguns and handguns, the former legally held, the latter of more dubious status.

Occasionally there would be as many as six or seven guns on the premises, according to Stevenson. His claim has been independently supported by four people who were either UCDC/UPV members or Free Presbyterians at the time. Two revolvers were normally kept in the main office, another was held by a guard on the first floor, two were held by guards at the door and there were a number of shotguns on the top floor. There, one guard would keep an eye on adjoining rooftops from the skylight in the attic. The Northern Ireland Office, according to a reliable British government source, has a photograph of this armed guard taken by the Special Branch.

Other parts of Stevenson's statements, just as embarrassing as the alleged incident in Donegall Pass RUC station, were not disclosed at any of the trials but some time later, protected by privilege, they were revealed at the Scarman Tribunal.

One of these described an alleged meeting which Stevenson said he had with Paisley at the home of a man called Hubert Nesbitt in Belfast on the night Paisley was released from jail in May: "Mrs Nesbitt brought me into the living room where I saw Dr Paisley, Mrs Paisley and Hubert Nesbitt. The Doctor came across to me, put his arms around my shoulder and said, 'You're a boy and a half; well done, but you will have to lie low now for a while.'"

Questioned at the Scarman hearings, Paisley strongly denied that this conversation had taken place, as he also denied any knowledge of the explosions before or after they happened. He had met Stevenson once in Nesbitt's home, he admitted, but that was to talk to him "about his wife and spiritual problems". This was, however, the first time that Paisley's relationship with the Nesbitts, a couple who had had considerable influence on his career, had ever been publicly aired.

Hubert Nesbitt was a well-known lay Baptist preacher in Belfast and a senior foreman in Mackies engineering factory. He was a good friend of Paisley's father and had known Ian Paisley since he was a baby – "I used to sit him on my knee," he told the author in 1980. He had preached in Belfast in the 1940s with the original Bob Jones, the founder of the now large evangelical empire, and claimed that he had paved the way for Paisley in the United States by introducing him to Bob Jones Junior and other influential and wealthy American fundamentalists.

Late in life, Nesbitt married Elizabeth McRoberts, a former matron of the Samaritan and City hospitals in Belfast. She had become a fan of Paisley's as early as 1947, just after Paisley received his "call" to the Ravenhill Evangelical Mission, and was a regular attender at his services from then on. Nicknamed "the Duchess", she doted on Paisley and during the early, often impecunious days of his ministry had lavished her generosity on him. The smart suits he always wore when preaching were often bought by Elizabeth.

When the couple married, Hubert Nesbitt retired from Mackies to help his wife run a private nursing home on the Ravenhill Road. In 1966 when Paisley was looking for a site on which to build the Martyrs' Memorial church, Mrs Nesbitt sold him the nursing home and the couple moved to nearby Hampton Park and opened a second home. It was here, according to Stevenson's allegation, that Paisley and he met.

In a remarkably frank interview with the author, Nesbitt boasted of the important contacts he had made for Paisley over the years, particularly in the police. Every Sunday night without fail he and his wife would host a dinner party after Paisley's church service for twenty or thirty guests, Unionist politicians and evangelical lawyers and policemen, with Paisley in the seat of honour. The guests would sit down under the gaze of a large oil painting of Paisley.

He counted, he claimed, senior English and Scottish evangelical policemen among his friends and in the RUC he was on excellent terms with high-ranking Christian CID officers. On one occasion, in 1975, he had arranged a secret meeting at his home between Paisley and a very senior RUC officer who had come to Nesbitt saying that he had important information to pass on to the DUP leader. At that time ceasefire talks had started between the British government and the Provisional IRA and the British had agreed to set up incident centres which would be manned by Sinn Féin members to monitor the truce while talks between the IRA and the Northern Ireland Office went on. The exercise was code-named "Operation Rampart" after the tower at Stormont Castle which housed the civil servants who liaised with the Provisionals.

The Northern Ireland Office wanted those manning the Sinn Féin incident centres to be issued with legal handguns – this was partly for protection and partly as a gesture of good faith. The RUC had strongly objected, Nesbitt said, and there was a row between the NIO and police chiefs. The policeman who contacted him wanted to tell Paisley in case the NIO got away with its plan and in due course the meeting took place.

Another Stevenson statement read out at the Scarman hearings included this damaging allegation: "During my meetings with Mallon at my home and in his car outside my home Mallon was always telling me to be very careful, that nothing must leak out that Dr Paisley had anything to do with any of the explosions or had any previous knowledge of them. I wanted to know if Dr Paisley knew who was doing these jobs and asked Mallon. He said 'Certainly he does. You have to tell him, and you haven't to tell him. He knows and he doesn't know.'"

That statement was made to the police on 12 November, about three weeks after his arrest, but a month later on 11 December, after his own trial and his agreement to turn Queen's Evidence, Stevenson hardened up this allegation considerably and, in a significant fashion, apparently altered its context.

The new allegation was made in Stevenson's deposition at a hearing at Newtownards Magistrates court in front of all ten accused. A transcript of the proceedings reads: "McDowell was killed blowing up the Ballyshannon power station. His death had a very great effect on me. I realised that it was time to call a halt to these things in view of the danger to life. I approached Mallon on the subject of the explosions, the reason being to find out if Dr Paisley was aware of these things. He said he was fully aware of them and the persons who were responsible for doing them."

In the intervening month Stevenson had seemingly switched the conversation with Mallon from after McDowell's death to the middle of the first bombings. More importantly, Paisley's alleged knowledge was promoted from "he knows and he doesn't know" to being "fully aware" of both the explosions and those responsible.

At the time that Stevenson's allegations first became public knowledge, in December 1969, Paisley claimed that the government was conspiring to "tie him in" with the bombings and that at one stage the police had even set out to arrest him. He coupled this with an allegation that the government was trying to get him certified as being mentally ill.

It looked as if Stevenson's embellishment of his first statement was indeed an effort to "tie" Paisley closer to the conspiracy but not, apparently, by the authorities. The police never officially questioned Paisley about the bombs. He had, as he pointed out in the *Protestant Telegraph,* the "perfect alibi" – he was in jail when they exploded.

The full story of the 1969 bombings, as related by some of those involved, cannot, for legal reasons, be told nor can the part played by those who suggested the targets and the timing. At least a dozen people know the entire story – most of them escaped the RUC's attention at the time – and some of them fear swift retribution if it were ever told.

Although Paisley was never shown to be culpable, a long thread, stretching back nearly 15 years, associated him and his campaigns with the climate within which Loyalist violence flourished.

Out of Ulster Protestant Action, which he had helped to found, sprang Gusty Spence's UVF. Through the UVF came the ties with other Paisley creations and followers – the UCDC, the UPV, Noel Doherty, Tommy McDowell and Sammy Stevenson. From them came intrigue, murder, violence and finally a conspiracy that successfully subverted a government and destroyed Terence O'Neill, the Prime Minister Paisley had demanded "Must Go!" No evidence was ever produced to associate Paisley with any of those violent events but all those who carried them out were, in one way or another, inspired by him.

"I remember the night the first trial ended," recalled a veteran Free Presbyterian. "There was a Sunday school party going on in the church and we were all expecting the jury's verdict to be announced at any minute. We were very busy but there was somebody up the road who had a television set and Ian, who was like a cat on a hot brick, had us up and down the road to that TV all night. He was worried that night, I can tell you."

"This victory is a victory of true evangelical Protestantism against the apostasy of ecumenism. . . . I believe we have come to the kingdom for such a time as this."

IAN PAISLEY ADDRESSING THE SESSION AND PRESBYTERY OF THE FREE PRESBYTERIAN CHURCH AFTER HIS ELECTION VICTORY IN NORTH ANTRIM, JUNE 1970

CHAPTER SEVEN

The Bog of Bitterness

After O'Neill's resignation in April 1969, and Paisley's release from jail, Northern Ireland quickly and inexorably slipped towards disaster. While the civil rights movement intensified the demands for reforms from the new administration, Chichester-Clark, who was much more a prisoner of his right-wing than was O'Neill, vacillated and pleased no-one.

And in the background there were increasingly ominous signs of the violence to come. Just before O'Neill quit, Derry had seen its worst violence to date when Paisleyites and Bogsiders battled it out in the city centre after the government had banned Nationalists from holding the commemoration march from Burntollet bridge. During the riot a 56-year-old man, Samuel Devenney, was badly beaten by police in his home and died three months later.

In mid-May there was more evidence of the growing hostility between the RUC and Nationalists when the police clashed with Catholics in the Ardoyne district of North Belfast and petrol bombs were thrown. A month later the Shankill Defence Association (SDA) emerged onto the streets for the first time, under the leadership of John McKeague, and forced the government to ban a Republican march to the City Hall. The SDA had been founded by UVF leader Billy Spence in May, ostensibly to agitate against housing redevelopment in the area but Spence had turned the organisation over to McKeague and two leading Free Presbyterians, the Rev William McCrea, Paisley's assistant minister, and a Protestant Unionist called Alan Campbell.

In early July there was sectarian rioting in Armagh and in Lurgan and on the "Twelfth" in Dungiven, County Derry a march by the Boveva flute band, whose activities had so stirred Paisley and the Independent Unionists in the 1950s, led to fighting between Catholics and the police. Later that month there was more rioting in the town and a Catholic man was killed and the Orange Hall badly burned. In Belfast there was trouble at the bottom of the Shankill Road when Orangemen passed the grossly misnamed Unity Flats, a Catholic ghetto.

Paisley meanwhile began to show signs of turning against Chichester-Clark. At a UPV rally in Bessbrook, called to protest against a civil rights march in nearby Newry, he warned Chichester-Clark that he would have to expunge O'Neillites in his party: "It was a long hard struggle to get rid of O'Neill. If necessary there will be another long hard struggle to get rid of O'Neillism and the Lundies in the Unionist party at Stormont." Other more mainstream Unionists echoed Paisley: Harry West accused Chichester-Clark of being panicked into promising civil rights reforms.

On 2 August there was more trouble at Unity Flats after rumours spread on the Shankill that junior Orangemen had been attacked by Catholics. McKeague's SDA attempted to invade the flats but were repulsed. Three days of rioting followed between Catholics and police on one hand, and Protestants and the police on the other. The Shankill was looted by frustrated Loyalists, a Catholic was killed when he was hit on the head with a police baton, and trouble spread again to Ardoyne where the SDA and Catholic vigilantes intimidated each other's co-religionists out of their homes.

Despite Nationalist warnings of major violence, Chichester-Clark refused to ban the upcoming Apprentice Boys parade in Derry on 12 August, an event which nearly everyone thought would end in disaster. Banning it would undoubtedly anger Unionist extremists and, as he had shown during the Burntollet march, Chichester-Clark was not the man to defy the extremists in his party.

The predictions all came true. In the afternoon the Bogsiders and the Apprentice Boys clashed, and within minutes barricades had been erected and petrol bombs were raining down on the police as they tried to demolish them. By nightfall the police were firing cartridges of CS gas into the Bogside and Catholic Derry and the Northern Ireland State were at war.

The next day, as the Bogside rioting continued, civil rights supporters staged demonstrations elsewhere in Northern Ireland, to draw off police manpower from Derry. Trouble spread to Coalisland, Strabane, Newry, Dungannon, Lurgan and West Belfast where police stations were attacked and barricades erected. That night the Fianna Fáil Taoiseach, Jack Lynch, intervened: in a TV broadcast he said that the Stormont government had lost control and he called for a United Nations peace-keeping force to be sent in. The government in Dublin, he said, would not "stand idly by" while innocent people were injured and he announced that Irish Army field hospitals would be dispatched to the Border.

An angry Chichester-Clark replied the next day with a verbal rebuke and the announcement that 8,000 "B" Specials were to be mobilised to help the police. But it was no use. The RUC were undermanned and exhausted and the British Prime Minister, Harold Wilson, alarmed at what might follow the mobilisation of the "B" men, authorised his Home Secretary, James Callaghan, to deploy British troops in Derry. That evening a company of the Prince of Wales Regiment marched into the centre of Derry, set up barbed wire barricades and the RUC withdrew. Peace returned to the Bogside where jubilant Catholics celebrated what they saw as a victory. For the first time in the North's troubled history, Catholics had welcomed the sight of British soldiers marching into their streets.

In Belfast, though, the violence intensified. That night there were sectarian clashes in four areas of the city – at interfaces between the Shankill and Falls and between the Shankill and Ardoyne. In a confused situation Catholic homes were burned out by McKeague's SDA men, the RUC fired Browning machine guns in the lower Falls and there was sniping across sectarian boundaries.

By the end of the night, five people had been killed, four Catholics and a Protestant, dozens of houses had been firebombed and in Armagh a Catholic man was shot dead by a party of "B" Specials. On the next afternoon, 15 August, 600 British troops were sent into Belfast, establishing "peace lines" between the Shankill and the Falls and, the next day, in Ardoyne. They arrived too late to stop a row of Catholic homes in Bombay Street, off the Falls Road, from being gutted.

Britain was now directly involved and at Downing Street meetings later in the month Chichester-Clark was forced by Wilson's diktat to accept measures that would ultimately strip his government of the "B" Specials, control of the RUC and many local government powers.

The agitation which Paisley had orchestrated against O'Neill's mild attempts at change, the civil rights protests generated by O'Neill's subsequent caution, and the aggressive and violent counter-demonstrations organised by Paisley had led Northern Ireland to its gravest crisis. Only three years later the last vestiges of Unionism's once unchallenged authority would be confiscated by Westminster when Stormont was suspended and Direct Rule from London imposed. Paisley's campaign to re-establish "traditional Unionism" would result instead in its final dissolution.

The Cameron Report, although confined to events before the dreadful summer of 1969, laid considerable blame at Paisley's door for the violence which preceded it. Its comments on both Paisley and Bunting's performance at Armagh and Burntollet, could, some would think, equally apply to July and August 1969: "Both these gentlemen," intoned Cameron, "and the organisations with which they are so closely and authoritatively concerned must, in our opinion, bear a heavy share of direct responsibility for the disorders."

As at Burntollet, Paisley kept a low profile during the August riots. Another disciple, John McKeague, played the part of Major Bunting, marshalling the troops of the Shankill Defence Association in petrol bomb attacks and intimidation. On 2 August Paisley made a brief appearance on the Shankill to appeal for peace – at the Scarman Tribunal he claimed he had led a crowd in the singing of the 23rd Psalm in an unsuccessful attempt to cool them off – but during the height of the rioting he was rarely seen.

His next appearance was on 15 August on the upper Shankill "to do welfare work and to see parishioners of mine that live up in that area", he told Scarman, while Protestants and Catholics fought fierce battles in streets only yards away. He presented himself at the Scarman hearings as a public-spirited cleric trying to stop disorder and violence, while at the same time bravely catering to the spiritual and physical needs of his parishioners.

Paisley's fleeting appearances on the Shankill during the August riots were to do him a lot of damage among Loyalists, who expected more from a leader who claimed to embody a renewal of the spirit of Carson. His disowning of Gusty Spence had already done him considerable harm three years earlier – especially since Spence developed into a living Loyalist legend – but, as one Loyalist paramilitant remembers, his forbearance during the violent days of August 1969 did him more.

On the Friday night that the troops came in I saw Paisley at the top of Percy Street. There was still fighting going on at the bottom of it around Andrews flour mill. There was a bus across the street and people were ferrying in petrol bombs from both sides and flat-topped lorries were moving families out. Suddenly there was a flare-up and people surged towards it. Paisley appeared standing at the corner of Northumberland Street and was surrounded by five or six old women who were holding on to him. "I have to get down there to help my people," he was saying but the women were holding on to him: "You can't go down there, Dr Paisley, it's dangerous." There he was, a big hulk of a man being held back by these old women; if he'd wanted to he could have got free of them. It would have been like bursting out of a paper bag.

He was active in other less direct ways, however. On 13 August, the night after the Bogside riot started, Paisley and a group of other Loyalists, some of them UCDC members, some of them Unionist Party members, met Chichester-Clark to demand the immediate mobilisation of the "B" Specials. The Prime Minister told them that that might lead to British soldiers being sent in. Once that happened, Westminster would have control and the result might even be the suspension of Stormont.

The "B" Specials occupied a special place in Paisley's view of Unionism. They were the descendants of Carson's UVF, an entirely Protestant force well represented in the UPV and a body of men Paisley could trust unlike other agencies of law and order. Like other Loyalists, Paisley also claimed that the "B" men's local knowledge had been a vital factor in defeating the IRA in the past. "The 'B' Specials were always Ian's favourite. He felt they were the only people who could be trusted. The RUC were a mixture, they had Catholic members, and there were always questions in his mind about their loyalty, but the 'B' Specials could always be relied upon to do what was necessary for the defence of the Protestant heritage," recalled a Free Presbyterian colleague.

Paisley then had an idea which he suggested to Chichester-Clark. He could raise a "People's Militia", a force of thousands of dedicated Loyalists, which he would put at the government's disposal to defend Northern Ireland alongside the RUC against the IRA conspiracy then unfolding in the Bogside. The Prime Minister gave an encouraging answer: "It might come to that," he said. Enthused, Paisley set about recruiting his Loyalist force. The idea of a "Third Force" – loyal,

Protestant, determined and, most importantly, officially sanctioned – was born. The idea was to recur time and again in his later political life – Paisley once more imitating Carson.

An ad was placed in the *Belfast News Letter* two days after the meeting with Chichester-Clark calling on Protestants to enrol, and a special recruiting form was printed. The recruiting effort lasted for weeks: "Ian quite often interviewed volunteers himself. They signed on at the Martyrs' Memorial and then they enlisted at Shaftesbury Square (UCDC HQ). People came from all over, hundreds of them. They were asked questions, valid questions like could they handle firearms. I remember Ian saying to one man, 'Can you get some of the hard stuff if you need it?' and I don't think he meant whiskey. Ian liked to use that sort of language, it sounded funny sometimes to hear him using gangster-like language." The scheme was finally abandoned in November when Stevenson confessed to the spring bombings. The police raided Frank Mallon's office in Shaftesbury Square and took away hundreds of completed forms, containing the names and addresses of a potential private army.

During the August riots, and indeed for nearly two years afterwards, many militant Loyalists looked to the UCDC headquarters for material assistance in their fight against the Catholic/Republican menace. Many of those who subsequently rose to prominence in the UDA and UVF got their first taste of action with UPV men from Shaftesbury Square. They include Andy Tyrie, who in the late 1970s went on to become Supreme Commander of the UDA, the largest Loyalist paramilitary group: "In those days if we wanted help we went to the UCDC. They were the first to help us out when Glencairn Protestants were intimidated out by the Ballymurphy Catholics in 1970 and it was a place where weapons, men and transport were always available."

The first clumsy Loyalist attempts to smuggle guns into Northern Ireland from Scotland and England were mounted by men who frequented the UCDC headquarters. One notable gunrunner, whose experience was subsequently utilised by the UDA, was later jailed for life for murder. Another, Raymond Pavis, a UPV man who once swore "to kill every Catholic on the Falls" if Paisley was ever harmed, met a more tragic end. He was shot dead by the UDA on the doorstep of his Castlereagh home in 1972, when it was discovered that he was selling guns to Republicans as well. The UPV and the UCDC had, at least in Belfast, a seminal influence on the development of Loyalist paramilitarism.

Although not noticeably active on the streets himself during the violent events of August 1969, Paisley kept his East Belfast congregation up to date with events with lurid versions of what was happening in West Belfast. At the Ulster Hall on the Sunday after the first killings and burnings, he told his flock that he had evidence that the Falls Road Catholics had set fire to their own homes. The story that Protestants had been responsible was a lie – all the Catholic homes were stocked with petrol bombs so when one was set on fire by Catholics, they all went up in flames. Furthermore he had evidence that a Catholic church in Ardoyne had been used as an arsenal and that its priests had been handing out sub-machine guns for use against Protestants. Later he said he had first-hand information that IRA units had taken part in the shootings: on the Falls Road "men were sitting on sandbags with machine guns in their laps" while the police did nothing.

His own Beersbridge Road house, he claimed, had been "sprayed with automatic fire" by the IRA and the RUC had fired after their fleeing car; it later transpired that a car had backfired in the street.

He also had versions of Protestant casualties suitably embroidered to highlight Catholic barbarity. Like the fate of James Todd, a Protestant vigilante shot dead some days after the August riots:

> The young man and two of his friends were doing Peace Corps duty, trying to keep the peace and help the situation – a hopeless situation – in this district; and the Roman Catholics said, "Come down and talk to us. We want to make a treaty of peace with you so that we can control our districts and there will be no trouble." These three Protestants went down into the Roman Catholic district to talk with the Roman Catholics; and as they turned their backs to return to the Protestant area, young Todd was shot dead.

In the United States, which he visited in early September to counter a fund-raising tour by Bernadette Devlin, he tailored his message to suit the political prejudices of his audience. At Bob Jones University in deeply conservative, anti-Communist South Carolina he told a gathering of fundamentalist students, in an address called "Northern Ireland – What is the real situation?": "Listen, my friends. What is happening in Ulster today will happen in America tomorrow. Make no mistake about it. O may God open our eyes to see the conspiracy, the international conspiracy, that is amongst us! May He help us to see that there is a deliberate association of attacks against law and order and for revolution and anarchy and Marxism in the land!"

Loyalists now saw the British as being on the Catholics' side. By intervening to help the Catholics, the British Army had not only done the unthinkable but had made the problem worse. Quite a few Loyalists believed that, left alone, they would have solved the problem of civil rights agitation: "If only the bloody British Army hadn't come in," the *Sunday Times* reported an unnamed Unionist Senator as saying, "we'd have shot ten thousand of them by dawn."

The presence of barricades in West Belfast and Derry, built to repulse Loyalist attacks, became the immediate focus of Loyalist agitation. The RUC had, in many areas, effectively been expelled while the Army stood by and apparently co-operated. Behind the barricades, Loyalists liked to imagine, were hordes of IRA men arming themselves and planning attacks on Protestant areas while the British Army did nothing.

Delicate negotiations to restore normality by dismantling the Belfast barricades were in fact going on between the British Army and the Central Citizens Defence Committee, a group encompassing church leaders, Catholic businessmen and IRA leaders but Loyalists were impatient. There were clashes on the Shankill with the Army, and Chichester-Clark, as sensitive as ever to right-wing pressure, publicly demanded that the barricades come down. His intervention nearly scuttled the British Army's delicate talks.

Political events were also unsettling Loyalists. In September the Cameron Report was published and, as expected, slated the Unionist government for lack of leadership and vindicated Nationalist complaints of sectarian discrimination in jobs, housing and electoral arrangements. Cameron's lavish praise for the moderation of John Hume infuriated Paisley, who had been harshly admonished in the report. "I remember the way he used to snarl about 'Saint Hume'," recalled a former Free Presbyterian.

The British, who exercised influence if not entire control in Northern Ireland through the Home Secretary, James Callaghan, had furthermore insisted that Chichester-Clark undertake a series of reforms. Housing provision was to be taken away from local councils and given to a central body; local government was to be reorganised and stripped of many of its functions; the ombudsman promised by O'Neill was to be appointed and measures to outlaw job discrimination in the public sector and to curb sectarian incitement were announced. On a wider, and much more disturbing front, Callaghan announced a government enquiry into the RUC and the "B" Specials to be led by Lord Hunt, who had led the team that conquered Everest and was reputedly a descendant of one of the 13 Apprentice Boys of Derry.

On Friday 10 October 1969 the Hunt report was published. Although Loyalists had anticipated its recommendations, seeing them in black and white was a nasty shock – the RUC was to be disarmed, the hallowed "B" Specials were to be scrapped and replaced by a new part-time "non-sectarian" force, which would attempt to recruit Catholics, and the British Army General Officer Commanding, Lt-Gen Sir Ian Freeland, was placed in charge of all security operations.

Although Chichester-Clark and the Minister of Home Affairs were to be included in a new security committee, to hardline Loyalists this was a thin film of sugar coating on a bitter pill. To add to their discomfort, the RUC was to be led by an Englishman, Sir Arthur Young, who replaced the pro-Unionist Anthony Peacocke as RUC Inspector-General. Chichester-Clark accepted the report. To outraged Loyalists it seemed that he was meekly acquiescing in the removal of all the safeguards which had kept Northern Ireland out of an all-Ireland Republic.

During the weekend of 10/11 October the Shankill erupted. Fierce rioting broke out and soon deteriorated into a shooting war between Loyalist gunmen and British troops – the first serious gun-battle of the "Troubles". By 2 a.m. on the Sunday, two Protestants had been killed by the Army and a policeman shot dead by Loyalists, the first civilian fatalities caused by the British Army since the Aden campaign and the first RUC fatality since the IRA's 1956-62 campaign. Ironically the policeman was shot dead by people protesting against his disarming. Another 66 people were injured, 37 of them by gunshot. Paisley accused the Army of showing "SS-style brutality".

–◄○►–

During these turbulent weeks Paisley turned against Chichester-Clark's "pussy-footing, fence-straddling" government with increasing venom and made the restoration of law and order – a demand which other Loyalists understood to mean the subjugation of Catholics – the main issue in Unionist politics.

At the end of August, at a press conference in UCDC headquarters which was guarded by young men carrying clubs, he declared war on the Irish Republic and called for a boycott of Irish trade and currency. In September he threatened to call a general strike if the government did not restore law and order by sending the police back into the Falls Road. He warned Chichester-Clark that if the government continued "its policy of selling out Protestants, there would be an affair in Ulster that all the restraining voice I might raise will no longer be heeded".

He predicted that the government in the Republic would stage an incident on the Border and use it as a pretext to get the United Nations involved – "if that happens it will be the end of our province" – and he organised a 100,000-strong petition to oppose the disarming of the "B" Specials. He told Callaghan during a brief interview that, as far as Catholic complaints and the British reforms were concerned, "the incidence of unemployment and the shortage of houses can be attributed exclusively to the Papist population. These people breed like rabbits and multiply like vermin."

Paisley's increasingly violent invective was being echoed elsewhere in more mainstream Loyalism. The principal voice – and Paisley's major competitor for hardline Unionist support – was that of Bill Craig, the aggressive former Home Affairs Minister sacked by O'Neill. To the dismay of many right-wingers, Craig had not been included in Chichester-Clark's cabinet. In September, in an effort to mobilise non-Paisleyite Loyalism, he relaunched the Ulster Loyalist Association (ULA), an umbrella for right-wing Official Unionists, which had been started back in 1962 by former members of Ulster Protestant Action to protect Protestant jobs from Catholic encroachment. Paisley was not invited to join – much to the disappointment of many at its first rally – but his old rival from NUP days, Norman Porter, was.

Like Paisley, Craig's language became increasingly violent as Loyalists got more agitated over the reform programme and the RUC's expulsion from areas like the Falls Road. Craig attacked Chichester-Clark's administration, calling it a "rubber stamp" government. He warned, not for the last time, that Northern Ireland was on the brink of civil war. He also took a leaf from Paisley's book and urged Loyalists to raise a force like Carson's UVF. In October he told a ULA rally that he wouldn't rule out the use of arms if Westminster suspended Stormont. Craig was to be a formidable rival to Paisley for years to come.

As 1969 turned into 1970 the Loyalist backlash began to take on a more violent shape when the UVF – by now a mixture of hardline UPV men, the remnants of Spence's UVF and other Loyalists grouped around a well-known criminal family on the Shankill – started a bombing campaign aimed at Catholic targets and moderate Unionists and Protestants. The moderate New Ulster Movement, a ginger group of liberal Protestants who later formed the Alliance Party, was a particular target.

The traumatic and turbulent events of August 1969 had, at the same time, thrown militant Republicanism into turmoil. In December 1969 the IRA split into two factions when hardliners in Belfast and Dublin broke off to form a rival organisation committed to the use of the gun. They had long been opposed to the left-wing policies of the Republican leadership – despite the success achieved by the part they played in the civil rights movement – but it was the leadership's growing interest in electoral politics which caused the final break. That, they felt, would lead to the ultimate Republican heresy: the formal recognition of the two parliaments in Ireland and thus the recognition of partition itself. The lack of IRA weaponry to protect Catholic areas in Belfast during August was the final straw.

The new group took on the name Provisional IRA, after the 1916 declaration of a provisional Irish Republican government, while those who remained loyal to the political faction were renamed the Official IRA. At first it was the Officials who outnumbered and outgunned the Provisionals – but all that was to change when the Loyalist backlash intensified with the election to Stormont in April 1970 of Ian Paisley.

There were two by-elections held that month, both on 16 April. O'Neill's departure to the House of Lords made the Bannside seat vacant and Paisley immediately announced he was standing. In South Antrim, meanwhile, an O'Neill supporter, barrister Richard Ferguson, had resigned after a series of violent threats against him by Paisley supporters had made life intolerable for his family.

Paisley's minister in Dunmurry, William Beattie, was put forward without much hope of doing well, for he faced a strong opponent, Billy Morgan, an anti-O'Neillite former Health Minister and evangelical lay preacher who had resigned from O'Neill's cabinet in sympathy with Faulkner. In Bannside, on the other hand, a Paisley victory, despite Captain O'Neill's 1,400-vote majority, seemed a distinct possibility.

Paisley had made the restoration of law and order, the disarming of the RUC and the disbandment of the "B" Specials the main planks of his campaign: "I want to see the gun back on the belts of Ulster policemen and I want the Specials back on our streets. No more Republican enclaves! No more Republican pockets through the country! We're going to hold this province for our children and the Union Jack is going to fly through every part of it!" he roared.

Chichester-Clark was soon alarmed by Paisley's campaign. Reports came back from the constituency that the Official Unionist, Bolton Minford, was getting crowds of less than 100 at his meetings – and many of them were there to heckle – while at his colourful rallies and marches Paisley was attracting up to 5,000.

He decided to try to turn the prospect of a Paisley victory to the Unionists' advantage by stressing the horrors that might follow it. Virtually the whole cabinet was mobilised to work for Minford. Finance Minister, Herbie Kirk, spoke for them all when he predicted that a Protestant Unionist government would cause Westminster to impose direct rule or to abandon Northern Ireland altogether to a future of poverty and interminable dole queues, and others soon joined in.

Other levers of traditional Unionism were pulled. Minford's cousin, Nat, the leader of the Stormont Commons, declared that Unionism still stood for "a Protestant parliament for a Protestant people", an effort to out-Paisley Paisley which probably lost the party any hope of attracting Catholic support.

The ageing 82-year-old former Premier, Brookeborough, whose golden era was constantly invoked by Paisley as the benchmark against which modern Unionist treachery should be measured, was brought up from his Fermanagh farm to help out: "I speak to you as a man who came through some of Ulster's most trying days, who was proud to fight for my flag and country and who was privileged to lead this province for two decades. Do you think I would mislead you now?" The reports from Bannside showed no sign of optimism, though – Paisley was still getting the crowds while Minford was getting a tough time on doorsteps.

In a last desperate effort to stave off defeat, the Orange card was played. The Imperial Grand Master of the Orange Order – the world leader of Orangeism – Captain Laurence Orr, who was also a Unionist MP at Westminster, appealed to Orangemen to vote for Minford "both for the protection of the Union and for the furtherance of the just society".

Chichester-Clark issued his own eve-of-poll message spelling out the stark options: "The results of these by-elections will be taken by the world at large as an indication of the road which Ulster now chooses to follow. I have explained the choice as I see it – to go forward on honest, progressive and acceptable democratic principles or to stagnate in a sterile and ultimately destructive bog of bitterness."

The voters of Bannside preferred the bog of bitterness. Paisley romped home with 7,980 votes, 1,200 ahead of Minford. "This is the dawn of a new day for Ulster. Good night Chichester-Clark," quipped Paisley to his delirious followers at the count in Ballymena Town Hall. On a more serious note Paisley paid tribute to the real architect of his victory – "God has done a great thing for us, whereof we are glad," he prayed.

If the government was shocked by the Bannside vote, it was stunned by the result in South Antrim. Confounding all the predictions, Beattie came nearly a thousand votes ahead of Morgan to win the seat. It was a humiliating double blow for Chichester-Clark.

The government's post-mortem was an uncomfortable affair and the lessons were clear. The whole weight of the cabinet had been thrown behind the Bannside campaign but to no avail. In the face of Paisley's powerful appeal to Protestant fears, the Orange ace had been turned into a deuce and Brookeborough was just ignored. Unionist voters clearly regarded Chichester-Clark's government as weak on law and order and too responsive to Westminster pressure for reform.

The first to publicly spell it out was Craig. "What has happened in Bannside and South Antrim could happen in many other constituencies," he warned. "Traditional Unionist supporters throughout the length and breadth of the country are disturbed about the policies the government has committed itself to without the support of the party."

Paisley, sponsored by Craig and Boal, made his victorious entry into Stormont a few days later to deliver his maiden speech – an attack on Faulkner's successor in the Ministry of Commerce, a liberal former television producer called Roy Bradford. The speech was widely regarded as a flop but Paisley could nevertheless find considerable cause for comfort – the worm was turning inside the Unionist Party and soon its gyrations would be visible to all.

Only a week after Bannside and South Antrim, Chichester-Clark came under siege at the Unionist Party's annual conference. His local government reforms were rejected and he only narrowly survived a motion criticising his "weakness" in the face of Westminster pressure. He was attacked for "betraying the 'B' Specials and the RUC", and his own speech was interrupted by cries of "No Popery!" and "Keep Ulster Protestant!"

In the midst of this gathering backlash Harold Wilson called a Westminster general election for 18 June. Paisley, who had said after

Bannside that he already had his eye on better representation of Northern Ireland at Westminster, immediately announced that Protestant Unionists would stand in eleven of the twelve constituencies.

The threat set alarm bells ringing in the Unionist Party, for three normally safe Unionist seats were in danger of being lost to Nationalists if Paisley's Protestant Unionists managed to repeat their Bannside and South Antrim performances. They were South Down, held by Captain Orr; Armagh, held since 1959 by Jack Maginnis; and Londonderry, held by the Prime Minister's brother, Robin Chichester-Clark, ostensibly a liberal Unionist, who had been parliamentary private secretary to the Conservative Prime Minister, Sir Alec Douglas-Home. All had substantial Nationalist populations and a Protestant Unionist vote of around 5,000 could be sufficient to split the vote and hand the seats to the traditional enemy.

The Unionists quickly acted to save their seats and evidence of deals with Paisley soon emerged. Politicians, who only two months before were fiercely denouncing Paisleyism, now energetically courted it. In South Down, Orr boasted unashamedly: "I am a Protestant Unionist. But I am Official Unionist. Here in South Down I am glad to say we are united and my nomination papers have been signed by members of Paisley's Free Presbyterian Church and by Unionists."

In Armagh, Maginnis humbly thanked Paisley for not standing a candidate. "I wish to acknowledge my appreciation of the decision of the Protestant Unionist Party not to oppose me. I fully realise they had and still have valid reasons for doing so and it is only their extreme loyalty and patriotic love for our province that has stayed their hand at this particular time when the common enemy is uniting behind a Unity candidate. I pledge myself, if elected, to defend the Constitution and the good name of this province and County Armagh in particular with much greater zeal than ever before."

In Derry, the local Protestant Unionist Association claimed that they had struck a deal with the Prime Minister's brother, and a detailed account of private meetings between officers of Robin Chichester-Clark's constituency party and their officers was made public. Harold Wilson seized on this and challenged the Conservative leader, Edward Heath, to say whether Chichester-Clark would get the Tory whip. At the British Liberal Party conference, the Unionists were accused of "surrendering to Paisleyism in the biggest display of collective funk in British politics since Munich".

Paisley proudly boasted about the deal, saying that talks had taken place "at the highest level" and that the Prime Minister had been fully aware of them. That drew a denial from Chichester-Clark which did little to convince anyone. He himself had not been party to any deal, he said, although there had, he admitted, been a meeting between Paisley and the Unionist Party Secretary, J.O. Baillie. This, he went on to claim, had only been to impress on the Protestant Unionist leader the risks of splitting the vote.

There had never been a suggestion that the government "would be willing to compromise their policies if Protestant Unionists were not to stand", he maintained. Few Nationalists and only the most credulous Unionist Party supporters believed him. But the toadying to Paisley worked. Only two Protestant Unionists stood – Paisley in North Antrim and Beattie in North Belfast – and the threatened Unionist seats were saved.

Against this background Paisley easily won the North Antrim seat, some 2,700 votes ahead of the sitting member, Henry Clark. "This victory," he declared, "is a victory of true evangelical Protestantism against the apostasy of ecumenism. . . . I believe we have come to the kingdom for such a time as this." Whatever role God had played, the truth was that in the space of two months the Protestant backlash, partly led and mostly directed by him, had propelled Paisley first into Stormont and now into the Mother of Parliaments.

–◄○►–

The backlash soon evidenced itself in another more violent way and with disastrous results. The summer's Orange marching season was getting into full swing during the election campaign and Chichester-Clark was in danger of losing the Orange Order's backing. The Order had already published its resolutions for the Twelfth and had deliberately omitted the routine pledge of loyalty to the government. Instead it called for strong law and order.

Although the previous Orange marching season had propelled Chichester-Clark into the crisis he now faced, the Unionist backlash, dramatically given a new form by the three Paisleyite election victories, meant that there was little chance that he would take a firm line with Orangemen in 1970, whatever the cost.

One Orange march had already provided evidence that relations between Catholics and the British Army were under strain and that the reform programme, whatever its merits, was having little impact in the ghettoes. In early April an Orange march in the upper Springfield Road sparked off a night of clashes between Ballymurphy Catholics and British troops. When the Unionist newspapers complained the next day that there hadn't been enough soldiers to quell the trouble, 600 soldiers were sent in and there was a full-scale riot complete with petrol bombs and CS gas – an indiscriminate weapon which alienated entire streets at a time.

In early June another Orange march paraded up the Crumlin Road towards Ardoyne and a horrified local Army commander tried to re-route it at the last moment. Two nights of Protestant rioting, complete with sniper attacks, followed. Any attempt to interfere with the hallowed right of Orangemen to march where they pleased was, it was evident, going to run into fierce opposition.

During the build-up towards the climax of the Orange marches, Britain was preoccupied with the general election and the changeover to Heath's Conservative government which followed it. So when Orangemen proposed another march on 27 June past Ardoyne and also through West Belfast past the scenes of the previous August's fighting, there was little motivation for the British to intervene, and even less inside Chichester-Clark's cabinet.

The RUC Chief Constable, Sir Arthur Young, and the Foreign Office's representative in Belfast, Ronald Burroughs, saw the danger and urged that the marches be banned. Their advice was ignored. "Chichester-Clark maintained, exactly as he had the previous year, that his followers would destroy him if the marches were banned," reported the *Sunday Times*. He was even opposed to rerouting the marches. The right-wing backlash had paralysed the cabinet. Chichester-Clark had first-hand experience of troublesome extremists and had learned that the easiest way to deal with them was to give in. At the time of O'Neill's "Crossroads" election he had found to his horror that his South Derry nomination, regarded almost as a family heirloom, was being challenged by a right-winger. The rival was William Douglas, the Boveva bandmaster whose Dungiven parades in 1959 had given Paisley his first victory over a Unionist government. Chichester-Clark only narrowly survived this challenge and from then on went out of his way to appease extremists.

When he succeeded O'Neill as Premier, one of his first acts was to draft a letter to the Free Presbyterian Church giving them "unqualified" assurances that "traditional" Unionist attitudes on the Border would be upheld and that no North-South dialogue would take place without full cabinet permission. The unmistakable message was that he was no O'Neillite; his obeisance to Paisleyism was almost total.

The June 1970 Orange marches, as everyone feared, brought Northern Ireland closer to the abyss, particularly the North Belfast parade on 27 June. The first trouble broke out in West Belfast between Catholics and Protestants but this soon developed into a pitched battle between British soldiers and Ballymurphy Catholics.

Rioting spread to other sensitive areas but that evening it got much worse. In Ardoyne there was a confrontation between Orangemen and Catholics, and stones, bottles and petrol bombs were thrown across the Crumlin Road by rival crowds. A gun-battle followed which left three Protestants dead.

In East Belfast there had been tension all day after an Orange parade passed the small Short Strand area, an enclave of some 5,000 Catholics surrounded on three sides by Protestants and penned in by the River Lagan. That night Loyalists made an attempt to petrol bomb the area's Catholic church, St Matthew's, but a small group of Provisional IRA gunmen, led by the Belfast commander Billy McKee, opened fire on them from inside the church grounds. The Loyalists returned fire but the night ended with two Protestants and one Catholic killed and a number seriously wounded.

The British Army, too overstretched elsewhere in the city to intervene in the Short Strand gun-battle, had sealed off the bridges over the Lagan to stop West Belfast Loyalists from joining the fray – but in Catholic minds it looked as if they had opted out in order to give the Loyalists a free hand.

That weekend saw the real birth of the Provisional IRA and laid the basis for its growth. Provisional leaders could now argue in Catholic areas that they, not the British Army, were the only people who could be trusted to defend their areas from Loyalist attack. That was reinforced by messages from other sources that weekend. The indulgence shown to the Orangemen was, in Catholic eyes, evidence that Unionist bigotry prevailed even over the impartial British, while the defeat of the Labour government promised worse to come. That weekend the Catholics began to turn against the British.

The third achievement came in the long term. Small, isolated Catholic areas like Short Strand had in the past been regarded as hostages for the good behaviour of other Catholic districts of Belfast – the fear that Loyalists might wreak revenge on such areas had, for instance, been one of the factors which persuaded the IRA to confine its 1956–62 campaign to rural areas. Having, in 1970, proved its capacity to defend areas like the Short Strand, the Provisional IRA's hand was freed to intensify its assault on the Northern Ireland State – one result of that was the fierce bombing campaign launched in Belfast some six months later.

If the Orange marches marked the beginning of the end of the honeymoon between Catholics and the British, the Falls Road curfew a week later sealed it. On the urging of Chichester-Clark, the British Army was ordered by Heath's government to take a firm hand with the next outbreak of trouble. An arms search in the lower Falls Road on 3 July provided that opportunity.

The confrontation that followed developed into a riot and gun-battles, and the area was saturated with CS gas. By nightfall the British GOC, Freeland, had ordered a curfew of the entire area which lasted for thirty-five hours, during which there were wholesale searches of homes, beatings and some looting by troops. By the end of it four people had been shot dead and an entire community embittered. In the next six months the Provisional IRA grew from a few dozen activists to over 800.

From there Northern Ireland sank deeper into the abyss. The Provisionals stepped up their bombings and shootings and, as Loyalists bayed for tougher and tougher security measures, Chichester-Clark was forced to resign in March 1971. The new hostility between the British Army and Catholics, fuelled by tough anti-riot tactics and a policy of wholesale arrests, wrecked attempts by his successor, Brian Faulkner, to woo the SDLP with political concessions – following the deaths of two Catholics in Derry, the SDLP walked out of Stormont.

In August 1971 Faulkner tried the Unionists' ultimate weapon – the internment of Republicans in an attempt to crush the IRA. Inevitably it made a bad situation worse. IRA recruitment and violence increased in pace with Catholic resentment and anger and the death toll leaped into the hundreds. Just as ominously, Loyalist paramilitaries emerged and multiplied – the largest of them, the Ulster Defence Association, was to account for most of the 600 assassinations of Catholics in the next five years. The violence that followed made other conflicts in Irish history appear tame.

Finally, in January 1972, the killing of 13 Catholics in Derry by British paratroopers on what quickly became known as "Bloody Sunday" exposed the bankruptcy of Faulkner's security policy and an indifferent British government was forced to act. Stormont was suspended by Prime Minister Edward Heath and Direct Rule imposed.

The train of events which led to the prorogation of Stormont had started with Paisley's election victories in Bannside and North Antrim. They gave an aggressive and, to establishment Unionists, a frightening shape to the Loyalist backlash. Faced with it, Chichester-Clark quailed from interfering with the 1970 Orange marches and, from the violence which followed them, the Provisional IRA gained credibility and support.

Throughout the history of Northern Ireland, the response of most Unionists at all levels of government to Loyalist extremist pressure was invariably to placate them with concessions that drove Catholics further and further away from any accommodation. During his own political career Paisley had amply demonstrated the vulnerability of Unionist governments to such pressure. From the Orange marches in Dungiven in 1959 through to the fall of O'Neill and the violent response he orchestrated to the civil rights movement, Paisley had virtually made Unionism his prisoner.

Following his two election victories Paisley received a congratulatory letter from Willie John McCracken, the Independent Unionist whose 1953 election campaign against the liberal Brian Maginess marked the beginning of a campaign against liberal Unionism.

Paisley replied saying that "the battle is only beginning", and asking for McCracken's prayers for divine wisdom and guidance "in the new and heavy responsibility which is now resting upon us". A handwritten note at the end of the letter urged McCracken to pick up his Bible and turn to St Paul's Epistle to the Ephesians, chapter six, verses 19 and 20: "And for me, that utterance may be given unto me, that I may open my mouth boldly, to make known the mystery of the gospel. For which I am an ambassador in bonds: that therein I may speak boldly, as I ought to speak." Thirty-seven years later Paisley would pen the same reference to an autographed photograph of his handshake with Irish Taoiseach, Bertie Ahern, just days before becoming First Minister of Northern Ireland.

By "speaking boldly", Paisley had helped to destroy the slim chances of reconciliation between Northern Ireland's bitterly divided communities and had set it on a violent and bloody course. "Speaking boldly" would help to ensure that the battle, which Paisley prophesied in 1970 was only beginning, would last for the best part of the next four decades.

"The only effective answer to encroaching Romanism is a revived and revitalised Protestantism, believing the Bible, proclaiming the Bible and practising the Bible."

Ian Paisley in his book *The Fifty Nine Revival*

CHAPTER EIGHT

The Fearful Fundamentalists

The Free Presbyterian Church of Ulster, founded, led and dominated by Rev Dr Ian Paisley – until 2007, when his seemingly perpetual moderatorship was ended – has exerted an influence out of all proportion to its size. In the half century and more since the Church was founded, its membership has never exceeded 12,000. With some 60 congregations, nearly all in Northern Ireland, the Free Presbyterians are a small fraction of the mainstream Irish Presbyterian Church, which has 560 congregations and nearly 350,000 members and is much smaller than the Church of Ireland and the Methodists. Yet it was often to the Free Presbyterians, and to Ian Paisley, that conservative and evangelical Protestants would flock in times of political or physical crisis in Northern Ireland, and not to the conventional churches.

The early Free Presbyterian Church mushroomed in size, tripling in its first decade as Bible-believing Protestants, anxious about liberal trends in their own churches and worried by an increasingly assertive Catholic community in their midst, converged on Paisley's church like stranded ships seeking a safe port. Why did such a small and, compared to other sects, young church have such an impact? Part of the answer is that its leader was for most of his life the most powerful and charismatic politico-religious figure the North had seen in the twentieth century. For years, many who declared themselves as Presbyterians, Baptists or even just Protestants on census forms would go to their own churches in the morning and to the local Free Presbyterian church in the evening. *A la carte* Protestantism is by no means unknown in Northern Ireland but, even so, no other church or clerical leader could exert such influence.

Fear was the real key to the church's success. Paisley's religious appeal, like his political appeal, catered to the traditional angst of Northern Protestants: a history and culture rooted in their place as an embattled but dominating religious minority in Ireland. All Free Presbyterianism's elements can be traced to that history: it took its puritanism, its conditional loyalty to the Crown and unconditional loyalty to Protestantism from the rigid beliefs of the covenanting, seventeenth-century Scottish planter; its separatism and elitism, common to all colonising peoples, came from the fear of being overwhelmed by the superstitious hordes of barbarian Irish; its distrust, fear and abhorrence of Catholicism went back to 1641, the year the Catholic dispossessed rose up to massacre the Protestant settlers; its religious enthusiasm was derived from the "Great Revival" of fundamental and evangelical Protestantism that took place in 1859.

It is this last episode, a huge phenomenon in the North of Ireland but little known about elsewhere, that for so long provided Paisley with his favourite answer for all Northern Ireland's problems: the need for another "heaven-sent, sky-blue, Holy Ghost revival" of evangelical religion just like the extraordinary events of 1859. The first book he wrote was about the extraordinary explosion of religious enthusiasm of that year, an eruption that began in the village of Kells, near his home town of Ballymena.[1]

It was a bizarre outburst of religious excess, so out of place where it occurred most often, in the North's most pious and strait-laced communities: church after church, the majority of them Presbyterian, witnessed scenes of uncontrollable religious hysteria. Whole congregations fell prostrate on the ground moaning, weeping and beseeching God for forgiveness and salvation. People went into trances, fell into fits of kicking and screaming, or dropped to their knees sobbing and crying aloud in prayer in the middle of crowded streets.

Ordinary farmers and labourers, claiming to have the power to impart the Holy Spirit to converted sinners, harangued huge crowds on village squares and city streets. By the end of 1859 it was claimed that 100,000 people throughout Protestant Ulster had been converted to "born again" Christianity.

In his 1958 commemorative account of the 1859 Revival, Paisley, welding together religion and politics as only he could, wrote that it had "strengthened Ulster in her stand against Roman Catholic agitation and without doubt laid the foundation which enabled Ulster under the leadership of Lord Carson to preserve her Protestant position". The lessons for contemporary Northern Ireland were grim and clear, he warned:

> Only a revival on a parallel scale can save Ulster from the engulfing tides of evil with which she is encompassed. The dark sinister shadow of our neighbouring Roman Catholic state, where religious liberty is slowly but surely being taken away, lies across our province. . . . Not only have we this enemy without but we have a strong fifth column of sympathisers and compromisers within. The only effective answer to encroaching Romanism is a revived and revitalised Protestantism, believing the Bible, proclaiming the Bible and practising the Bible.

The people to whom he addressed that warning, his target audience as it were, were local members of the Presbyterian Church in Ireland, the largest Protestant denomination in Northern Ireland and the most susceptible to allegations of theological compromise. Many ordinary Presbyterians were "evangelicals", deeply conservative in their God-fearing ways and especially vulnerable to Paisley's powerful gospel. They held to the simple unchanging doctrines taught by Calvin and the Scottish puritan John Knox: that the only route to salvation and heaven was through faith in Jesus Christ alone and through unquestioning, literal belief in an infallible Bible.

They harked back to the kind of Presbyterian orthodoxy which became dominant in the Irish church after 1830. In that year Henry Cooke, conservative in religion and Tory in politics, had triumphed against a liberal, anti-establishment faction in the church which was refusing to subscribe to one of its central, defining deeds, the seventeenth-century Westminster Confession of Faith. This Calvinist declaration, drawn up in the middle of the English Civil War, stated that the Bible was the sole doctrinal authority and designated the Pope – "that man of sin and son of perdition" – as the "Antichrist". To many Northern Irish Presbyterians, even in the late twentieth century, it was an anti-Catholic document that struck a deep and powerful chord.

The Westminster Confession of Faith was a weapon that Paisley would use again and again against a Presbyterian leadership which in those days was attempting to play down the church's anti-Catholic past. Not that there was any real possibility of Northern Ireland's largest Protestant church ever discarding it completely: in June 1986, for instance, the General Assembly in Belfast voted against following the example of its Scottish counterpart and scrapping a description of the Pope that so many Catholics found offensive.

However, there was a twentieth-century skeleton in Irish Presbyterianism's cupboard which Paisley was able to rattle with even more effect: the heresy trial in 1927 of the church's most influential thinker of his day, Professor Ernest Davey. Davey was a liberal, a sympathetic student of radical new ideas, and a re-interpreter of Presbyterian theology: a "modernist", in the language of his conservative opponents. As such, he was blamed by "modernism's" most stringent critics for most of the church's ills, particularly its lack of old-time revival enthusiasm and a dangerous sympathy for ecumenism. To such people Davey was the leader of what Paisley called the "fifth column" of Catholic sympathisers and theological compromisers inside the church.

Many of Davey's contemporary critics, while retaining nominal membership of the church of their forefathers, started to look elsewhere for the old doctrines that had gone missing from Presbyterian pulpits. They found them in the sermons of itinerant evangelists who preached the need to deny such sinful pleasures as drinking, smoking, dancing and cavorting with the opposite sex, and instead to devote one's life to the glorification of God.

Or they went to hear the hellfire sermons of preachers from the Christian Workers Union, founded by the fiercest Presbyterian evangelist of the 1920s, W.P. Nicholson, whose earthy language, aggressive pulpit style and denunciations of loose morals had brought revivalism to thousands of working-class Belfast Protestants. This was the face of Ulster Presbyterianism which came closest to the stereotyped image of American-style fundamentalism: close-minded, belligerent and separatist.

This was also the Presbyterian constituency at which Paisley was aiming when he set up the Free Presbyterian Church of Ulster on 17 March 1951. The new denomination was fundamentalist, believing in the absolute authority and literal truth of every word in the Bible. It was unashamedly opposed to Roman Catholicism, swearing every minister and elder to uphold the Westminster Confession's condemnation of the Pope as the Antichrist. It was "separatist", pledged to keep itself apart from and undefiled by the slightest contact with any church which had World Council of Churches connections or other ecumenical tendencies; and it was "evangelistic", a "soul-winning" church that believed in the need for a new 1859 Revival as the best answer to Northern Ireland's baneful brew of religious and political problems.

This combination produced a brand of Protestantism that was singularly suited to Northern Ireland. Its appeal was to "born-again" Christians, saved in the way their fathers and grandfathers had been saved during the 1859 Revival or by preachers in the mould of W.P. Nicholson. In the countryside they were the hardworking puritan farmers, shopkeepers and self-employed tradesmen and their wives, the sort of people who had crowded the pews at his father's church in Ballymena or who had helped Ian Paisley found his own church in Crossgar in 1951. In the church's ranks in Belfast could be found more tradesmen and the odd small businessman, as well as shipyard and factory workers who, like Paisley, had been reared on a diet of mission hall preaching and preferred to spend their evenings and weekends evangelising at street corners than patronising the local pubs and betting shops.

They were "born again" Christians, living in the "light" of true Protestantism, free men who communed with God without the interference of priests or man-made rituals. Catholics, on the other hand, were benighted and ignorant souls who were enslaved by the "darkness" of Roman superstition, the idolatry of the Mass, and the rule of the papal Antichrist.

Such a view provided a theological framework for a set of political attitudes within which the differences between Unionism and Nationalism became easily and comfortably explicable. These cast themselves as the descendants of people who had "civilised" Ulster and had saved it from savagery and the Catholics as priest-ridden, work-shy, Sabbath-defiling ne'er-do-wells who gambled and drank to excess. When the civil rights movement burst on to the scene, the complaints of discrimination made by Catholics were not the product of social injustice or prejudice but rather living proof of God's righteous judgement in rewarding those who followed the true religion and lived productive, worthwhile lives and punishing those who hadn't.

-◁o▷-

Paisley made it clear from the beginning that his Church's major target for recruits would be the same Irish Presbyterian Church whose congregation in Crossgar had unwittingly brought Free Presbyterianism into being. And to persuade unhappy Presbyterians to transfer to his church, he made a hate figure out of Ernest Davey, by this stage rehabilitated after his heresy trial and now principal of the Presbyterian Assembly's Theological College. Describing Davey as a "vomit-eating dog"[2] who had "poisoned Assembly's college"[3] with his teachings, Paisley labelled him the leader of the school of "God dishonouring, Christ blaspheming, Bible defaming, soul damning modernism"[4] and in that way tried to condemn the mainstream church.

If Davey was the most identifiable prophet of "modernism", then Irish Presbyterianism as a whole was guilty of the related and equally heinous sin of compromise with Roman Catholicism. When an East Belfast Presbyterian congregation invited a Catholic priest to speak to it, for example, Paisley pilloried its clergy as "a lot of milk-and-water, spineless, soft-tongued, velvet-gloved pussyfoots . . . whose peace-at-any-price policy nauseates both God and man."[5]

If Paisley paused from his weekly tirades against the Presbyterians, it was only to attack other Protestant denominations. It did not seem to matter whether they were ecumenical Methodists and Anglicans or fiercely evangelical Pentecostalists and fundamentalist Baptists: the message was the same. Anywhere there was error and enmity to the true path of Free Presbyterianism, Paisley warned his little flock, they must be ever-vigilant in their determination to remain separate from such faith-weakening "apostasies".[6]

But the real enemy, under whose widening umbrella sheltered all the modernists, heretics and "apostates", was the ecumenical World Council of Churches (WCC). Formed in 1948, this brought together nearly 150 Protestant churches from 44 countries, among them the Irish Presbyterian Church, to explore the causes of disunity in world Christianity and to clear the way towards closer cooperation and ultimate reunion. The Roman Catholic Church declined an invitation to its founding conference in Amsterdam in 1948, but by the late 1960s was starting to send observers to its meetings.

To Free Presbyterians, the new body marked a huge step towards reversing the Reformation by moving towards unity with Rome. Paisley denounced the Archbishop of Canterbury of being ready "to barter our British heritage to the Blaspheming Bachelor of the Tiber".[7] He accused the Irish Presbyterian Church of wanting "to play their full part in the marriage of an emasculated Protestantism to the scarlet-robed hag of the seven hills."[8]

However, sermons on the excesses of the Roman church – if possible spiced with sarcasm and sexual innuendo – were the favourite

The Paisley family in the early 1940s. *From left:* Father, Kyle; Ian; brother, Harold; mother, Isabella and sister, Margaret.

At the opening of the Cabra church, 1952.

Maura Lyons

© Belfast Telegraph

An early rival: Norman Porter.

© Belfast Telegraph

A Christmas pageant at the Ravenhill mission, 1953.

Ian and Eileen on their wedding day, October 1956.

© Belfast Telegraph

The aftermath of Pope John XXIII's death; Paisley and John Wylie appear at Belfast magistrates' court on illegal asssembly charges, July 1963. © *Stanley Matchett*

Terence O'Neill and Sean Lemass on the steps of Stormont, January 1965.
© Pacemaker

The hero of the hour; Jim Kilfedder's West Belfast election victory on October 1964 brings congratulations from Loyalists. *© Irish Times*

Opening a Shankill Road Orange arch, 1966.

© *Belfast Telegraph*

With William McCrea and Billy Beattie on a Free Presbyterian picket, 1966.

© *Belfast Telegraph*

Leaving Crumlin Road Jail, October 1966.
© *Irish Times*

Leading a UCDC march through Ahoghill, Terence O'Neill's home village.
© *Irish Times*

A Stormont protest against Jack Lynch's talks with O'Neill, 1967.

Sammy Stevenson, wearing a trilby, accompanies Ian and Eileen to Armagh courthouse, March 1969. Behind him is John McKeague, his co-conspirator in the bombings which ousted O'Neill. *© Pacemaker*

Brookeborough meets a friend on his way to a meeting proposing a no-confidence vote in O'Neill. *© Pacemaker*

His master's voice: Major Bunting
at an anti-civil rights protest.

© *Pacemaker*

Desmond Boal

© *Belfast Telegraph*

Bob Jones Junior at the opening of the Martyrs' Memorial, October 1969.

© *Belfast Telegraph*

In victorious mood after the Bannside and South Antrim by-elections, 1970.
© Belfast Telegraph

Supporters carry John McKeague out of Crumlin Road courthouse after his acquittal of the 1969 bombings. *© Belfast Telegraph*

Paisley outside the UDA headquarters in East Belfast in 1977.
© Crispin Rodwell

Paisley, William Craig and Clifford Smyth canvassing against the Sunningdale deal in February 1974. © *Belfast Telegraph*

Paisley with Loyalist paramilitaries in Larne during the UWC strike in May 1974. © *Associated Newspapers*

Paisley at home in his study in the 1980s.

© Pacenaker

Peter Robinson posing with automatic rifle during a visit to Israel.
© *Pacemaker*

Rev William McCrea
© *Pacemaker*

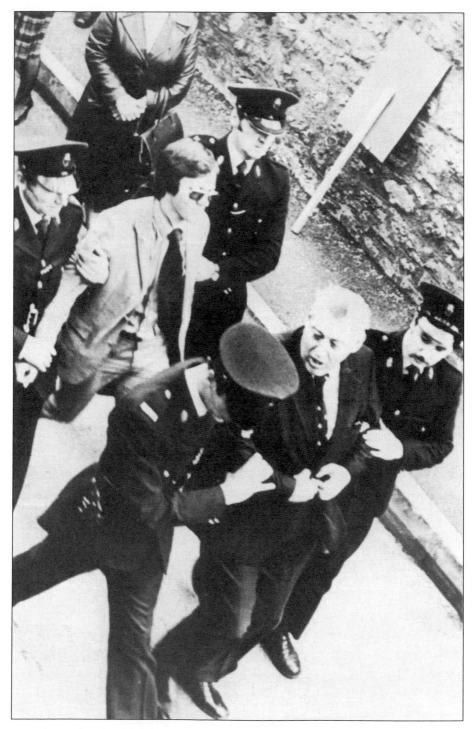

Paisley and Robinson being led away after their arrest outside Armagh Cathedral in May 1980. © *Belfast Telegraph*

fare of most Free Presbyterian congregations in those days. Paisley was particularly skilful at portraying the horror Protestants would feel at the spectacle of a priest, a mere man, hearing confessions:

> I would go into the dark and damnable confessional, where my poor Roman Catholic countrymen entrust their wives and daughters to him, and while the tyrant was pressing his odious and obscene investigation, putting the poor creatures on a moral rack till they sink with shame at his feet, I would drag the victims forth from his grasp and ring in the monster's ear – No Popery![9]

The language of his first lieutenant, John Wylie, a former electrician from Dundonald on the outskirts of East Belfast, often verged on the pornographic: he once described a Church of Scotland moderator who had the audacity to visit Pope John as "this slimy toad, with his sewer-like mind, 'sniffing around' for an opportunity to feed his lustful appetite on the impurities of popish paganism".[10] In a 1961 article Wylie claimed that Pius XII was behind Nazism, that all Popes were "sensual, unholy, unclean and as bloodthirsty as a bloodhound", and that "the extermination of six million Jews is a mere drip in the bucket when compared to the wholesale murder of both Jews and Gentiles by the murderous popes in the Vatican".

One of the church's early problems following its formation in 1951 was that, apart from Paisley and Wylie, they had no preachers of any real calibre. In order to fill his early pulpits Paisley was forced to take on men who had little to offer except an ill-defined sympathy with his sect's theological position.

The ministers at the denomination's founding church in Crossgar were a case in point. The first incumbent, George Stears, was a returned missionary from South America who took on the job, after pressure from Paisley, only because he was in poor health and had nothing better to do. He lasted three months.

His successor, Sidney Lince, was an English butcher from a Plymouth Brethren background. He lasted longer than Stears and even served briefly as the church's moderator – until 2008, the only Free Presbyterian minister other than Paisley to have done so – before stepping down in the face of Paisley's dominating style. He left in the late 1950s, sick of living in a damp, rat-infested farm outhouse, and exhausted by groundless allegations of immoral conduct and rows over theology which at times even spilled onto the street outside the little church – to the great amusement of passing members of the Lissara Presbyterian Church from which it had broken away.

Recognising the need for the church to provide a regular supply of home-grown ministers, in October 1952 Paisley opened his own "theological hall" in a back room in the Ravenhill church. There he tutored the three men who would be his faithful understudies for many years to come: John Wylie, John Douglas and Bert Cooke. The theological hall had its teething problems. Its first two "professors" were a wandering Scotsman who had seen service in three churches and held an unrecognised American doctorate, and a less than competent Ballymena-born Texas-based fundamentalist.

Bad experiences with such men of letters apparently did not deter the ambitious young moderator, only too aware of his own lack of formal education, from acquiring a few equally dubious credentials. From the early 1950s, following the custom of other evangelical preachers, Paisley started to add letters to his name.

Firstly he joined learned societies open to the public, and the initials FRGS (Fellow of the Royal Geographical Society), FRPhS (Fellow of the Royal Philosophical Society) and MRSL (Member of the Royal Society of Literature) appeared after his name.

In 1954 he moved into more questionable territory. He received a bachelorhood in divinity from the Pioneer Theological Seminary in Rockford, Illinois, and seven months later an honorary doctorate in divinity from the same institution.[11]

Six years later, following the death of its founder, Rev Robert Hansen, the Pioneer seminary, run as a correspondence college from Hansen's former home and offering degrees for as little as 25 dollars, was indicted by the US Federal Trade Commission for misrepresenting Bible theology and home study courses in philosophy. Before his death Hansen had been charged by federal authorities with sending obscene literature and photographs through the mail.

By that time Paisley had sent off for another American degree, this time an MA awarded on submission of a thesis from the Burton College and Seminary in Manitou Springs in Colorado. *The Revivalist* claimed he was working on a PhD thesis for the same college on the subject of the 1859 Revival.

Unfortunately Burton College, like Pioneer, was listed by the US Department of Education as a "degree mill", defined by that authority as an organisation, often without even a campus or a teaching staff, which awards degrees, usually by mail, without requiring students to meet the standards "established and traditionally followed by reputable educational institutions". In other words, both Paisley's degrees had come from bogus and disreputable correspondence colleges.[12]

The lack of trained Free Presbyterian ministers continued to be a problem into the 1960s, despite a trickle of faithful graduates from the theological hall. David Leathem, the minister involved in the Maura Lyons case, for instance, had to be dropped when he began preaching the heretical doctrine that some Christians could reach a state of "sinless perfection".

In 1959 Paisley pulled off a seemingly spectacular coup when a Church of Ireland curate based in Antrim, Harold MaGowan, converted and became a Free Presbyterian minister – Paisley's first and only clerical recruit from the mainstream church's ranks. MaGowan had quarrelled with his local rector over a number of issues, including his own belief in the imminent "Second Coming" of Christ, and when he had objected to the use of the parochial hall for mixed Protestant-Catholic dances.

The new recruit turned out to have an unwelcome independent turn of mind: he criticised the annual, unopposed election of Paisley as moderator and complained about his paltry salary, eventually breaking the church's rules by taking a job in an insurance office in Belfast. He lasted until 1963 when he, his family and a couple of friends he had brought with him from the Church of Ireland formed a short-lived "Independent Free Presbyterian Church" of his own.

Finance was less of a problem than personnel for the young Free Presbyterian Church. From the beginning a number of more affluent members contracted or "tithed" a proportion of their income to the church in line with the Biblical exhortation that Christians should give 10 per cent of their wealth to God's work. At Crossgar and Ballymoney a few farmers went further, selling land, machinery and livestock to help their churches get started. At Ravenhill, Paisley could rely on the advice of a number of men who were successful small businessmen.

One of these, an office-bearer in the church in the 1950s and early 1960s, used considerable amounts of his own money to help purchase the churches at Antrim, Whiteabbey and Dunmurry. He was also able to act as a front man when someone selling property did not want it known that he had done business with Free Presbyterians for fear of losing business from customers loyal to other churches.

This manner of buying up property lasted well into the 1970s. In 1972 the Presbyterian Church itself sold an empty church in the Cliftonville area of North Belfast to a well-known evangelical property developer, Ted Burns. Unknown to the Presbyterians, Burns was an ardent Paisleyite who went on to become a DUP Assembly and Convention member. Several months later it reopened as the John Knox Free Presbyterian Church.

Such ways of doing business sometimes led to feuds, which were exacerbated by Paisley's aggressive temperament. The same man who had helped Paisley purchase buildings for use as churches broke with him in 1963, after a bitter row over unpaid debts. The quarrel began when an elderly woman church member left Paisley £800 in her will, a sizeable sum in those days, for his own use – money which the businessman insisted should have gone to the church.

The dispute smouldered for several years and eventually flared into an ugly war of words. Despite the wall of secrecy erected around the affair by Paisley and his elders, several Sunday school teachers took the businessman's part when he accused Paisley, in the sort of Biblical language so favoured by Free Presbyterians, of being "earthly, sensual and devilish". He and around 30 other members resigned shortly afterwards.

There was a nasty little epilogue. Shortly after he left the church, the businessman opened his front door one evening to two young men who began threatening and abusing him. He swung at them with a golf club and slammed the door. Several years later he ran into one of them again. This time the young man was in a mood to talk, and told the businessman that after he had left the Church, Paisley had complained so bitterly about him that he and a friend had decided to teach him a lesson. "We'll do it for the Doc," they told each other.

One thing the Ravenhill church did not lack in the early 1960s was crowded pews. While other Free Presbyterian churches remained small, and the denomination as a whole could barely muster a thousand followers by 1961, Paisley was building a name as the most incendiary anti-Catholic preacher since Thomas Drew and "Roaring" Hugh Hanna a century before. He was also developing his famous "altar call" technique, borrowed from turn-of-the-century American evangelists, in which he appealed for people to come forward and be "born again" into Christianity.

Over the years he refined this to a fine art, a perfected exercise in psychological manipulation. An American researcher, David Taylor, who regularly attended Paisley's church during a two-year period while working on a PhD thesis in the 1980s, recorded the technique in operation:

> Paisley often ends his sermon by warning the congregation in the most graphic and apocalyptic language that they are just "a gasp of breath" away from eternal damnation. Having delivered himself of this dire message, he then asks them to stay behind for a short meeting after the service in order to find out how they can avoid such a fate.

> Those who do will hear Paisley at his most powerful and persuasive, as he delivers an impassioned plea for "sinners to come to Christ". The congregation sing the haunting refrain of a familiar hymn: "Just as I am, without one plea. But that Thy Blood was shed for me. And that Thou bids me come to thee. Oh Lamb of God, I come."

> Paisley steps down from the pulpit and paces up and down in front of the congregation, urging the unsaved few to put up their hands and come forward: "That's right, just lift your hand, anywhere in the meeting. Just lift your hand and say, 'Yes preacher. Here is my hand. I'm going to come.'"

> Suddenly the temperature is turned up. He tells those who are already converted to rise to their feet, leaving only a few lonely "sinners" still sitting. Again and again he urges those who want to "close with Christ" to stand and come forward. He searches the pews in front of him for the handful of people still in their seats. Stewards pace the aisles ready to escort anyone ripe for conversion down to where Paisley is standing in the altar area. The pressure is tremendous. One former steward recalls one man sitting frozen in his seat and muttering desperately to him – "Get me out of this place".

But it worked. In the 1960s and 1970s, hundreds, even thousands, of people were "saved" through such high-pressure appeals, although in later years the numbers declined – blamed by church insiders on fewer fresh faces each Sunday and a greater emphasis on politics rather than God. Most of his followers endorse Paisley's manipulative methods: "Some of those people are under the heavy burden of sin. They need to be prodded to get them to come in," one Martyrs' Memorial member told Taylor.

However, it is an aspect of Paisley's ministry that some ministers and elders have criticised him for, to the extent that he was forced for a period to drop its most high-pressure element – the isolation of the sitting sinners.

—◄○►—

"The walls of Zion are breached and its doors are burned with fire. The enemy has most certainly come in with overwhelming power." That was Paisley's message in the first issue of *The Revivalist* in 1966. "We believe that God has called the Free Presbyterian Church of Ulster to the Kingdom for such a time as this." With the shrewdness of the supreme opportunist, portrayed as the foresight of the prophet, he saw that the heightened sectarian atmosphere of that year could be turned to the advantage of his militant little sect.

Paisley's imprisonment that summer following the Free Presbyterians' protest outside the Presbyterian General Assembly could have robbed it of that advantage. In the event his temporary removal forced his younger ministers, as yet relatively untouched by political controversy, into taking up the torch. And the Stormont government's ban on all open-air rallies within 15 miles of Belfast compelled them to campaign in areas as yet uncanvassed by the church.

The young East Belfast triumvirate of Bert Cooke, John Douglas and Alan Cairns found it easy enough to adapt the anti-ecumenical rhetoric they had learned at their master's knee in the back room at Ravenhill to tirades against ecumenism's political face, Terence O'Neill.

They discovered little groups of sleeping Paisley supporters, many of them still church-going Presbyterians, who had heard his powerful preaching on the gospel hall circuit over the previous 15 years. One of these was Richard Reid, later to become a DUP Convention member and Free Presbyterian elder, who until then had no Free Presbyterian congregation near his home at Pomeroy in south Tyrone.

In common with many rural evangelicals, Reid sincerely believed Paisley when he said he was being persecuted for his Protestantism, because he had seen him being treated as a leper by the Presbyterian establishment as long ago as 1951. Reid travelled all over Northern Ireland attending protest rallies in 1966 while Paisley, Wylie and Foster were in prison.

"The best thing that ever happened for the Free Presbyterian Church was the day that we were put in prison," declared Paisley at the Ulster Hall on his release from Crumlin Road jail. "For God has let these things happen unto us for the furtherance of the Gospel." For him it was the fulfilment of a 20-year-old ambition.

His jail term made him famous. Both disgruntled evangelicals and people with no strong church affiliation flooded to Free Presbyterian services, recalls one trainee minister in Armagh. It had taken the best part of 15 years to form the dozen churches that were in existence at the beginning of 1966. Now 12 new churches were started in barely two years: two in South Down, three in North Armagh, two in the Lagan Valley, and one each in Ballymena (with the affiliation of his father's church), Tyrone, Fermanagh, south Derry and Derry city.

This big push set the pattern for new churches in the future. The usual procedure was that a small group of people who already attended a Free Presbyterian church in a neighbouring town would ask that church to organise a mission, usually lasting five weeks, in their own vicinity.

Advertisements would be placed in the paper read by local Protestants for an "Old Time Gospel Campaign" to be led by Ian Paisley ("Come and Hear this Mighty Man of God preach the grand old Gospel with Power") and exhorting people not to miss the services "or you may miss Christ forever". These appeals could be guaranteed to produce a big turn-out. The services would take place in a local hall, often an Orange hall, a tent pitched on ground provided by a local sympathiser or occasionally, weather permitting, even in the open air.

Thus the tent mission at Dungannon in August and September 1967 was organised by the Armagh church and its new minister, Bert Cooke. Paisley preached on Sunday evenings to congregations of a thousand people and more than 90 people were "saved" during the five-week campaign. William McCrea, then a diffident 19-year-old only a few months out of school, made a big impact when he led the hymn singing. McCrea came from Stewartstown, north of Dungannon, and had joined the Armagh congregation after hearing Mrs Paisley address a protest rally in the town during her husband's imprisonment the previous year.

On the Friday night before the mission ended Paisley asked those who wanted a Free Presbyterian Church in Dungannon to raise their hands. The following Sunday the first meeting of the twenty-first congregation of the Free Presbyterian Church of Ulster took place in the mission tent, and local leaders claimed that 150 applications for membership were requested. Shortly afterwards a portable hall was erected near the site where the mission had taken place. Five years later

Paisley returned to Dungannon to open a new 300-seat church, built and furnished in just over a year, largely by voluntary labour.

Now he planned a big new church in a more middle-class area farther up the Ravenhill Road, in the grounds of a nursing home he had bought from a well-heeled Baptist couple, the Nesbitts. On 4 October 1969, as Protestant mobs gathered in the Shankill Road and East Belfast to attack the Catholic enclaves of Unity Flats and Short Strand, the American fundamentalist Bob Jones Junior opened Paisley's new Martyrs' Memorial Church opposite the Ormeau golf course.

Paisley claimed it was the largest Protestant church built in the United Kingdom since the Second World War, excepting cathedrals. It had pews for 1,450 people, but was capable of seating 2,300 if extra chairs were brought in. It had cost over £170,000, £120,000 of which had already been raised: £20,000 from two American fund-raising trips by Paisley and the rest by collections and individual donations from church members.

Six thousand people attended the opening. It was the most triumphant moment of Paisley's clerical career. He taunted his opponents in the established churches with the splendour of his new shrine, and "the prosperity of God's people" in comparison with their falling memberships and paltry fund-raising efforts: "They have to have daffodil teas and pea-soup suppers and jumble sales and domino dinners and pyjama picnics. It's the way they raise their money, the poor old ministers pleading – 'If you've any dirty old coats and any torn pants you don't want, God'll take them from you.'"

The 1971 census showed that the membership of the Free Presbyterian Church had risen more than sevenfold since 1961, to over 7,300. The vast majority had joined it in the previous five years. In 1970 Paisley was claiming congregations at Martyrs' Memorial of 1,400 every Sunday morning and nearly 3,000 in the evening. Fear was the emotion that had made it all possible: fear of Catholicism, fear of Catholics, fear of weakness and treachery in their own camp, fear of religious and political apostates, fear of losing all they had, fear of being slaughtered in their own beds.

In the summer of 1971, as Northern Ireland was entering the most violent 12 months of the Troubles, Free Presbyterians were celebrating the opening of their thirty-second congregation, and those fears had never been greater or more pressing. As IRA car bombs devastated the centre of Belfast and other Northern towns and gun battles raged nightly, the Free Presbyterian faithful thanked God for sending Ian Paisley to redeem their souls, to rescue Ulster from the Republican scourge and save themselves from their fear. In the midst of carnage and chaos, Paisley's church had finally arrived and so had Ian Paisley. Free Presbyterianism had helped make Ian Paisley a household name throughout Ireland and 1971 would mark the high point in his church's fortunes. But from there on it would be politics that would play the greater part in Ian Paisley's life.

—◄○►—

In 1984 the British Post Office issued a commemorative stamp to mark the second direct election to the European Community's parliament at Strasbourg. The stamp used figures from ancient Greek mythology to celebrate the birth of European culture: it showed Europa, the daughter of the king of Tyre, being carried off by Zeus, in the shape of a bull, to the island of Crete. Here, according to the Greeks, Zeus resumed his human form and they conceived a son, Minos, the founder of Minoan, and thus European, civilisation.

In East Belfast the figures on the stamp took on a startlingly different significance. On the Sunday before the election Ian Paisley delivered a sermon at his Martyrs' Memorial church entitled "The Woman rides the Beast: a remarkable prophetic fulfilment". Europe was not the woman on the stamp, he insisted to the congregation in his usual thunderous crescendo, but the animal on which she was riding. The woman was meant to represent something far more sinister to devout Bible-believing Protestants, like those in the Free Presbyterian Church: she was none other than "the woman of Babylon – the bride of the Antichrist, the Church of Rome herself".

He went on: "The woman is an unclean women. The woman is a brazen woman, because her garments are 'see through' garments showing her naked breasts and naked legs. It is a whore that is upon the beast. The key to the stamp is the child, for this is the Madonna that is riding upon the beast."

The stamp's designer might protest that the baby represented Cupid, and the fish under them the Mediterranean sea between Lebanon and Crete. In the Martyrs' Memorial they knew better. The Pope had made the Virgin Mary the Madonna of the Common Market, declared Paisley, and the fish represented the "trend of Paganism and Popery" which was "polluting the people of the world".

It was a message that found a ready echo in the minds of his listeners, weaned on a diet of Catholic conspiracies against Northern Ireland but this sermon was about a subject that was a favourite for evangelical Protestants around the world – the imminence of Armageddon, the end of the world, or the "end times" as such Protestants call it, and the "Second Coming" of Jesus Christ to earth.

When Paisley preached this type of sermon in the 1980s one could be sure that it would provoke in most people derision and astonishment that adult Westerners in the second half of the twentieth century could believe such stuff. But in 2000 and again in 2004, millions of people living in the United States who held exactly the same beliefs would propel George W. Bush into the White House as the forty-third President of the United States and the single most powerful political leader in the world. Their influence would extend to key Bush foreign policy issues in the Middle East, such as supporting war against Iraq's Saddam Hussein, hostility to Iran and for uncritical financial and military support to Israel. In this type of preaching, taken from the prophecies contained in the Book of Revelations, the last book in the New Testament, the creation of the state of Israel would be seen as the precursor of the end of days battle at Armageddon between the forces of good and evil, the latter represented by the anti-Christ, a one-world ruler. Victory for the forces of good would usher in the second coming before which saved, born-again Christians would be "raptured" into heaven and the victory of the returned Christ over the Antichrist would usher in a new millennium.

Paisley had taught his followers that the European Common Market, as the European Community was known back in those days, was the final antechamber before the appearance of the Antichrist, a terrible amalgam of Catholic pontiff and world dictator. To them, the Biblical evidence for the imminent arrival of the "end time" was unanswerable – it was all contained in prophecies which spoke of ten-horned, seven-headed beasts and the like. So where did the Catholic Church come into all this? For that, said Paisley, turning the pages of the big black Bible in the Martyrs' Memorial pulpit, one had to go to the last book of the New Testament, the Book of Revelation and here could be found a reference to a woman seated on the beast. This brought the story back to those postage stamps depicting Europa bestriding a bull.

The woman "riding upon the beast, who has spread herself and her influence and her control and her domination over the beast" was the

Catholic Church, he said, the whore of Babylon. And the EC was the beast which she rode and controlled. "She's riding on the beast today," he shouted at his now spellbound congregation. "We're in the Common Market and there's a hundred million more Roman Catholics in the Common Market than Protestants, so we're in a tiny minority."

He forecast a merger between countries from the EC, the non-EC Western European countries and the Eastern Bloc Comecon countries. And of course the Catholic Church was intimately involved in this process: "Anybody who has been studying the tactics of Rome recently will see that Rome is moving away from close affiliation with the Western democracies, and especially with the USA, and is moving towards a greater alignment and affiliation with the Communist countries." He cited the visit of the Polish Pope to his home country, conveniently omitting to tell his followers that Pope John Paul II was the most anti-Communist pontiff since the 1950s.

Behind the Pope was the Devil. "What holds the Common Market together?" Paisley asked his congregation rhetorically in 1984. "Satanic power." That was how so many "diverse nations with so many problems, so many difficulties, so many political, economic and military strains upon them can suddenly come together".

Paisley's problem with all this was that the first election to the European parliament in 1979 offered an unprecedented opportunity for electoral triumph. Northern Ireland was allocated three seats and the demographics suggested that one would go to a Nationalist and the other two to Unionists. Paisley knew that he could be one of those two and might even top the poll, confirming his claim to speak for most Protestants in Northern Ireland. But ever since the 1960s, when Britain and Ireland began to express an interest in joining the EEC, he had been issuing dire warnings against becoming involved in the "greatest Roman Catholic super-state the world has ever known". Two leading Free Presbyterian ministers, John Douglas and Bert Cooke, who were the church's experts in prophecy, had confirmed after careful study that the Common Market was a fulfilment of the visions of Daniel and the Book of Revelation.

So it was not surprising that when Paisley first indicated his desire to run in the forthcoming European election, there was a fierce row in the church's governing body, the Presbytery. Paisley's three most senior lieutenants – Douglas, Cooke and John Wylie – spoke strongly against becoming involved in what the Bible had told them was a political expression of anti-Christianity and Popery.

The issue touched on the central, defining characteristic of Free Presbyterianism: its belief in the doctrine of "separation" which taught Free Presbyterians to have absolutely no dealings with any church or religious body, or to have business dealings with anything tainted by contact with Roman Catholicism. Now suddenly Paisley was proposing to become part of an institution, the European Parliament, the creation of an anti-Christian confederacy which was totally dominated by Catholic nations. Such a *volte-face* was difficult for many in his church to stomach.

But Paisley got his way. At a meeting of the church's ruling Presbytery in early 1977, he used all his formidable powers of oratory and exhortation to bring his for once doubting disciples round to his point of view. "In the end," commented a former minister, "they would have said, 'Paisley's a man of God, God has been with him, God has blessed him, God has used him. We can't understand it but we wouldn't want to hinder the work of God, we wouldn't want to stand in the servant of the Lord's way.'"

The argument Paisley used at that meeting he would later repeat to the wider flock. Like Daniel in the lion's den, he, Ian Paisley from the Ravenhill Road, would be God's voice in the anti-Christian assembly in Strasbourg, "a firm, strong, unbending Protestant voice to raise the standard". He would be in Strasbourg fighting the cause of true Christianity, of Bible Protestantism.

It was a perfect example of those traits in Ian Paisley that would make possible his partnership with the Provos in 2007. It demonstrated his great ambition to achieve office and a willingness to sacrifice theological, and presumably political, principle in its pursuit, to bend the rules, and the will of those around him, to get his own way.

In June 1979 Paisley realised his goal. Some 170,000 Unionists voted for him, a staggering total and the largest vote won by any candidate for the European Parliament. At every succeeding election until ill-health forced his retirement in 2004, he would top the Euro poll and be able to boast that he was the most popular Unionist politician in Northern Ireland. And his successes revealed something very interesting about the Unionist electorate, not least those living in the leafy, affluent suburbs of Belfast. In the secrecy of the voting booth they were quite happy to forget all those negative and even frightening aspects of Ian Paisley – his antediluvian religious views, his bullying ways, the embarrassment he brought to the Unionist cause abroad –

and use the opportunity of the European election to send a warning message to the British and their Nationalist neighbours by giving Paisley their first preference votes.

True to form, he made the fighting, protesting start at Strasbourg his followers expected of him. When the Parliament opened in July 1979 he was straightaway embroiled in three noisy public confrontations which earned him headlines and notoriety all over Europe. His was the very first voice heard in the new session. Even before its opening ceremony had got underway, he was on his feet, insisting that the Union Jack outside the Parliament building was flying upside down, and to demand an assurance that this would never happen again.

The opening speech was given by the assembly's oldest member, an 86-year-old French Gaullist called Madame Weiss, who referred to the presence in the chamber of the grand-daughter of the "illustrious de Valera", praised Pope Urban II and Karl Marx and failed to mention the Protestant Reformation. This was too much for Paisley. As she finished, he walked out and handed her a note protesting that Ulster Protestants associated the name of de Valera with "murder and blood which is still going on by the IRA".

The following day brought more showmanship. As the Taoiseach, Jack Lynch, opened his address as the incoming President of the EEC Council of Ministers with a few words in Irish, Paisley started heckling him: "In the name of Ulster's dead I indict you as harbouring their murderers," he shouted before being drowned out by the boos and jeers of his fellow MEPs. He stalked defiantly out of the chamber. Outside he told journalists that it had been the first opportunity ever for a Unionist politician to attack Lynch in person for allowing his country's territory "to be used to launch IRA attacks upon my people".

The leader of the French Gaullist group, Jacques Chirac, later to become his country's Prime Minister and President, said that Paisley should be suspended from the parliament if he continued to interrupt its proceedings. Paisley challenged the authorities to try to silence him – there was nothing he would like better, he said, keenly aware of how he could portray such a move in Belfast as the persecution of Ulster Protestantism's champion. Paisley's antics in his first days at Strasbourg did immeasurable harm to Unionism's image in Europe and farther afield but in Ballymena they just loved it.

"I believe that Ian Paisley was raised for this day."

DUP DEPUTY LEADER PETER ROBINSON ADDRESSING DUP ANNUAL CONFERENCE, APRIL 1986

⌒≈⌒

"The Democratic Unionist Party was born in conflict, and unlike others, will never surrender to Ulster's enemies. When I say that, I say what we mean and we mean what we say. There can be no compromise, because compromise on the vital issue of democracy is surrender. Surrender? Never to the IRA/Sinn Féin murderers!"

IAN PAISLEY AT DUP CONFERENCE, 4 FEBRUARY 2006

⌒≈⌒

"No one, Protestant or Roman Catholic, who respects the law and embraces democracy has anything to fear from the DUP."

PETER ROBINSON, ADDRESSING POLITICAL CONFERENCE IN KILLARNEY, 24 APRIL 2006

CHAPTER NINE

For God and Ulster

The year 2007 was without doubt the culmination of a momentous period in the history of the Democratic Unionist Party. During the previous six years, the party grew at every election in a fashion its founder and leader, Ian Paisley, could never have imagined possible when he and Desmond Boal had founded the party way back in 1971. For decades it had been the other Unionist party, seemingly condemned to live in the shadow of the larger and more respectable Ulster Unionists, just as Paisley's Free Presbyterian Church lived in the shadow of the larger and more respectable mainstream Presbyterian Church. Both, it seemed, were fated to remain the junior versions and to play the barometer of Unionist and Protestant angst, occasionally rising in votes or numbers if the mood demanded it. But in 2001 things began to change in a substantive fashion for the DUP when it won five of Northern Ireland's 18 seats at Westminster in that year's general election, more than doubling its support. All three gains were achieved at the expense of its main rival, the Ulster Unionists. Two years later, at the Stormont Assembly elections, the DUP overtook the Ulster Unionists to become the largest Unionist party in Northern Ireland, an accomplishment that for years had been only a pipe dream for the party's strategists. At the 2005 general election, the DUP domination of Unionism was completed and confirmed when the party won nine seats in the House of Commons, leaving their once mighty Ulster Unionist opponents with a single seat and in a state of demoralised defeat unprecedented in recent Irish politics.

All these election triumphs paid off in 2007 when the DUP became the senior party in a new, coalition government at Stormont and the party's leader, Ian Paisley, was elevated to the position of First Minister of Northern Ireland. It had taken 35 years but finally the DUP and Paisley had taken what its most fervent adherents had long yearned for, its rightful place at the helm of Northern Protestant politics. In any other party such a triumphant year would have been rounded off with a festive, celebratory annual conference – and DUP annual gatherings were fairly passionate affairs as it was. What better occasion could there be to give Ian Paisley the hero's welcome he deserved and share the plaudits with those around him who had crafted, plotted and planned the triumph? But the 2007 annual conference was cancelled for the first time in the DUP's history. No one in the party hierarchy was eager to explain why but it was not difficult to work out the reason. The DUP had got into driver's seat of Northern Ireland's government to be sure, but seated beside it, holding the maps and helping to plot the route forward, was Sinn Féin, still the political wing of the Provisional IRA and, with the exception of other Unionists who had advocated partnership with Sinn Féin in the past or showed signs of getting soft on the question, the one party Paisley and the DUP had reviled the most over the decades.

It is difficult not to conclude that the annual conference was cancelled because the DUP's managers had no idea how they were going to explain to the faithful why they had done the one thing Ian Paisley and his colleagues had always promised they would never do, most recently just ten months before Ian Paisley posed for photographs on the staircase of the Stormont parliament building alongside Sinn Féin's Martin McGuinness, his new deputy. The DUP had successfully presented a united face to the world since going into government with Sinn Féin. Only one major figure had resigned along with a smattering of councillors, and party apparatchiks claimed, with little evidence to disprove them, that a canvass of grassroots feeling had discovered rates of approval for the move in the region of 90 per cent or more. But underneath that façade of unity, the picture was of a DUP grassroots reeling in shock at Paisley's *volte face,* of branches that had ceased to meet or which met only fitfully, and full of anger at this or that party figure, but most of all furious at Ian Paisley himself and incensed that he appeared to be revelling so happily in his new partnership with his deputy First Minister, Martin McGuinness.

Calling a party conference against this sort of background would risk unprecedented scenes of contempt and acrimony directed at the party leadership, and the consequences of that, for remaining party unity and for the stability and integrity of the new power-sharing coalition, would be unpredictable. It remains to be seen when the DUP next holds its annual conference and what sort of conference that will look like, but it is clear that, like everything else in Northern Ireland post-2007, the DUP is in a state of flux. Once the refuge of the more religious Unionists and those who believed that Ian Paisley was some sort of modern-day Moses called by God to lead his people, the DUP now represents all of Unionism, most of which is secular and less unquestioning of their political leaders. The party has grown in part because it has absorbed swathes of Ulster Unionist activists who now sit uncomfortably beside the Free Presbyterian core of the DUP. As this has happened and also in consequence, Unionism itself is undergoing what may be a fundamental realignment. The Ulster Unionist Party has shrunk to a shadow of its former self and it is quite possible that either it will go out of business altogether or its remnants will be absorbed into the DUP. A new DUP is on the horizon, of necessity more secular, broad-minded, less Free Presbyterian and less sectarian – a more Ulster Unionist version of the old party. Ian Paisley was the glue that held the old DUP together but in this developing, new DUP he would be like a solvent applied to nail polish; the new DUP will need a new leader, one more fitting to the new times. When that happens the annual DUP conference will again become a regular, non-traumatic event and one largely indistinguishable from those hosted by other parties.

It was all so different when it began all those years ago.

--◄○►--

The party which Paisley leads in 2007 started from humble origins. It began with the tiny Ulster Protestant Action group and the roadside election campaign of Albert Duff in 1958, but gradually it grew with Paisley's protests against the modernisation of Unionism. First there were the Ulster Protestant Volunteers, then the Protestant Unionists – all the time Paisley tapped a growing Protestant following until his own election to Stormont and Westminster brought the impulse to broaden into the DUP.

The transition from Duff's 4,700 votes to the staggering 207,721 votes won in the 2007 Assembly election took a year shy of four decades to happen. In between, Paisley collected a belt-full of Unionist scalps, of enemies or Loyalist rivals. Some fell directly to him, others due largely to his efforts – O'Neill, Chichester-Clark, Faulkner, West, Craig, Ernest Baird, Jim Molyneaux, David Trimble and Bob McCartney. Slowly but surely he undermined the Unionist establishment and removed competitors, one by one, from the scene. With each departure his party grew, absorbing other politicians' lost support like a sponge.

To begin with, the party contested only a few constituencies – the original UPV and Protestant Unionist heartlands in the main – but gradually its horizons expanded. That expansion brought the DUP into more and more contests with other Unionist parties and each time the DUP grew at the expense of their Protestant competitors. An iron rule determined how well the DUP fared against its Ulster Unionist rivals. When Protestants felt threatened or insecure, then the party's vote rose and that of the UUP fell. During the 1981 hunger strikes, for instance, the DUP actually managed to outpoll the Ulster Unionists by a few hundred votes but when Mrs Thatcher consolidated her premiership and the threat posed by dying IRA hunger strikers had receded, the DUP's vote fell and the UUP's rose, to the extent that eight years after the hunger strike crisis Ulster Unionists won two votes for every one of the DUP's in the 1989 council elections. The next time the DUP's support rose in such a dramatic fashion was during the post-1998 phase of the peace process, except on this occasion the DUP's supremacy over its rivals appears to be final and absolute.

The roots of the DUP lie in the introduction of internment without trial in August 1971, a measure demanded by Unionist right-wingers and regarded by Faulkner as the panacea for the IRA's accelerating campaign. Internment was an abject failure, alienating almost the entire Catholic population, including its moderate middle class. It was a failure too in security terms – in the four months before August four British soldiers and four civilians had been killed but in the four subsequent months 30 soldiers, 11 policemen and 73 civilians died violently. The ranks of the Provisional IRA meanwhile were swelled almost to bursting point.

Internment also exacerbated sectarian tensions, especially in Belfast, to a feverish pitch. Rioting, burnings and intimidation, aimed mostly at Catholics, reached unprecedented levels and hardline Loyalists demanded tougher and tougher action against the IRA. Paisley was again to the fore demanding the reformation of the "B" Specials and the creation of a "Third Force" of Protestants to assist the British Army and RUC. He linked up with Craig and the pair addressed a huge rally in East Belfast demanding stiffer security measures.

The failure of internment, however, quickly brought pressure on the British Conservative government for a new political initiative – from the opposition Labour Party and from Jack Lynch's government in Dublin. Before internment the SDLP had walked out of Stormont and they had pledged never to return to normal politics until internment was ended. Someone needed to throw them a lifeline.

Recognising, almost too late, how desperate the situation was, the British Prime Minister, Edward Heath, invited Faulkner and Lynch to tripartite talks at Chequers, his country home, in September 1971. It was the start of a process that would ultimately produce proposals for a power-sharing Assembly at Stormont and a Council of Ireland. Loyalists were immediately alarmed, despite Faulkner's assurances that no constitutional matter was on the agenda, and they sensed another O'Neill-type betrayal. Paisley's friend Desmond Boal and Johnny McQuade, another veteran of Ulster Protestant Action, immediately resigned from the Unionist Party and were soon joined by others.

No one can now remember quite who, but someone proposed that the various dissident right-wing Loyalist elements, both inside and outside the Unionist Party, should get together to discuss ways of frustrating Faulkner. Those involved were Paisley, Craig, Boal, the Rev Martin Smyth, then head of the Belfast Orange Order, and another right-wing Presbyterian, the Rev Bertie Dickinson from County Derry, who was to go on to become Presbyterian Moderator in the 1980s. A couple of dozen other less well-known Unionists joined and they met regularly from mid-September onwards in a hotel in central Belfast. They called their group the Unionist Alliance.

Inevitably the idea of forming a new right-wing Unionist party combining all the anti-Faulkner elements was floated. There is now intense disagreement among those involved about what was agreed. Some say there was never any real discussion of a new party; others say that agreement in principle to form it had been reached. It scarcely matters who is telling the truth, for Paisley pre-empted the matter.

On the night of 29 September 1971, a bomb planted by the Ardoyne unit of the Provisional IRA exploded in a Shankill Road pub called the Four Step Inn, killing two people and injuring 20, several of whom had to have limbs amputated. It was a frightening escalation of the sectarian warfare that had followed internment.

As news of the bombing came in, a Unionist Alliance meeting in the Grand Central Hotel in Royal Avenue was just breaking up. Paisley and

Boal rushed straight to the scene and, as the bodies were being carried out and angry Loyalists began gathering on the streets, Paisley announced that they would soon have a channel for their anger – he was forming a new party to be called the Democratic Unionist Party.

That effectively killed off any chance that people like Craig and Smyth would join. To do so would look as if they were following Paisley's initiative and would give him the first claim to leadership. Smyth had another reason – his Presbyterian colleagues had never forgiven Paisley for the decades of insults meted out by the Free Presbyterian Church.

In the next few weeks a smattering of Official Unionists left to join the new party but the parliamentary leadership was confined to a small and familiar core – Paisley, Beattie, Boal, McQuade and Charlie McCullough, a Unionist Senator. All but Beattie had been together in the days of Ulster Protestant Action. The name of the new party was redolent of the years before UPA when the Independent Unionists had attempted to start a party called the Ulster Loyalist and Democratic Unionist Association. But it was Boal who thought up the name and persuaded Paisley to abandon the Protestant Unionist tag.

His reasoning was simple. The Protestant Unionists were the Free Presbyterians under a flag of political convenience. As such, other Loyalists would be deterred from joining because of its religious exclusivity or would be reluctant because its leader and members had such a bitter history of attacking their religious denominations.

The choice was straightforward. Either the Protestant Unionists could stay as they were, the political wing of Free Presbyterianism – with little prospect of growing beyond the narrow confines of a fundamentalist, evangelical constituency – or the party could broaden its base and appeal to the wider Loyalist community.

Paisley chose the latter course and assiduously excised many of the old Protestant Unionist characteristics. It was evidence of a deep pragmatic streak in Paisley's nature and strong evidence that, for him, political ambition invariably came before religious principle. When the party's draft constitution was drawn up, for instance, it included as one of its aims the maintenance "of a Protestant monarch under the terms of the [Williamite] Revolution Settlement [of 1688]". This smacked of Protestant Unionism and Paisley rejected it. Others disagreed, notably John Wylie who felt that the new party should be open only to "saved" Protestants. When Paisley launched the DUP, Wylie kept his Protestant

Unionist branch in Armagh going but it soon folded up – even the most zealous Free Presbyterians preferred to be in the Loyalist mainstream.

Boal, who became the DUP's first chairman, also wanted the party to be socially radical and to have no links with the Orange Order. Boal felt that Orangeism should be a purely Protestant religious organisation, free from the control of any party, especially the Official Unionists. Like other Loyalists he believed that the Official Unionists' control of the Order had weakened and compromised its Protestant principles. These were Boal's own political roots in the Protestant working class asserting themselves.

He had also become convinced during the O'Neill period that the Official Unionist Party was undemocratic in its structures and unresponsive to the demands of rank-and-file Unionists. The important decision-making bodies in the Unionist Party, like the Unionist Council and the Standing Committee, were full of the leadership's nominees – even MPs' wives were empowered to vote at meetings. His main charge against O'Neill, echoing Paisley's cry of "Dictator!", was that he was snobbishly autocratic.

Wallace Thompson, a founder member of the DUP, can remember Boal touring the country like an evangelist, explaining his hopes and ambitions for the DUP:

> He explained that it would be a party which would continue to be right-wing on law and order but that there was a need in Northern Ireland for a party with radical social and economic policies which could embrace all people, whether they were RC or Protestant. I think the man did genuinely believe that this was an opportunity to broaden it out to produce a sort of radical alternative to the Official Unionist Party which was seen by Boal as the pro-establishment conservative party which was right-wing on all things and ironically soft on violence and terrorism. In some ways he was reviving the old Independent Unionist tradition and trying to secularise it as much as he could.

Of those lofty aims only one survived – the social and economic populism which already had its place in the Protestant Unionist make-up. The DUP soon established a loose Orange link – not with the official Order but with the small Independent Orange Order which had broken off in 1903 over a row caused when a Loyalist shipyard worker had defeated an Official Unionist candidate in an election. Its roots in

Loyalist populism were the same as the Independent Unionists and ultimately Paisleyism. Paisley, although never a member of the Independent Orange Order, addresses their "Twelfth" gathering in County Antrim each year, the 2007 deal with Sinn Féin notwithstanding.

Boal's hope that Catholics might be attracted to the DUP was hopelessly naive, and there is no evidence that any conscious effort was made by him or anyone else to foster it. Within a few short years the DUP had reasserted its old Protestant Unionist/Free Presbyterian identity. The aspiration to "democracy" in the DUP also died a quick death – after Boal's eventual departure the DUP became more monolithic under Paisley's control than any other party in the history of Unionism.

Boal was partly to blame. He was reluctant to take time off from his increasingly busy life at the Bar to devote the energy needed to build the DUP beyond its Free Presbyterian kernel. He was also intolerant of grassroots Loyalists who were too narrow-minded or stupid to understand his message, as Wallace Thompson recalled: "I can remember Boal trying to explain to a stubborn wee woman what the DUP was all about but he lost his temper and walked out in disgust. 'I don't have the time to explain to people who don't have the brains to understand,' he said."

◄○►

Nonetheless, Paisley's relationship with Desmond Boal was to produce compelling evidence that, behind the façade of Biblical immovability, there was another pragmatic, malleable and implicitly ambitious Paisley. And it was precisely these qualities that would make his 2007 deal with Sinn Féin possible.

Boal was generally recognised to be the most brilliant mind in the old Official Unionist Party. In other ways he was a contradictory figure: he was a hardline right-winger on law and order (although he was against the death penalty); but on social issues he reflected the left-of-centre, populist politics of his working-class constituents in the Shankill Road.

Boal was one of only two contemporaries Paisley ever really admired – the other was Bob Jones Junior. He was also the only man who could ever control Paisley's huge ego and violent rages. "I've seen Paisley in one of his ranting, raving moods standing on the staircase in the City Hall, surrounded by a crowd of his supporters. That's Paisley at his worst, with his own crowd round him, sycophantically chanting 'Yes, Dr Paisley' and 'No, Dr Paisley' – he feeds on that. And Boal went into the middle of that tantrum and put his head down and wagged his finger and lectured Paisley and completely deflated him," recalled one former Unionist politician.

Paisley recognised that Boal had the sharpest brain in Northern Ireland politics, and over the years had come to rely on his political as well as his legal advice. On the rare occasions Boal spoke at Stormont the chamber filled in the expectation of seeing some hapless Unionist minister being savaged by his brilliant and destructive logic.

He spoke for a huge Paisleyite constituency when he condemned the chaos and street violence caused by the civil rights movement, and the inability of "a supine, cowardly and fumbling government" to do anything about a situation where "lawlessness has been made respectable and sedition profitable".[1]

In March 1970, Boal, along with William Craig, Harry West, Johnny McQuade and Norman Laird, lost the Unionist whip at Stormont for refusing to support a confidence motion in Chichester-Clark's leadership. Boal spent the next 18 months contemplating his own and Northern Ireland's future – he even thought of moving to New Zealand at one point.

In September 1971 he left the Unionist Party and the following month joined Paisley in launching the Democratic Unionist Party. "Up to then Boal felt himself to be the guy who pulled the strings," said a former Unionist colleague at Stormont. "I remember him literally lurking in the shadows – coming out of doorways in the city centre as a Paisley parade passed by. He got his kicks through Paisley fronting for him. Now that phase was over and he felt that rather than orchestrating Paisley from a distance, together they would take on the whole establishment."

Boal's value to Paisley was obvious. By the summer of 1971 Paisley was starting to think of himself as a possible future prime minister of Northern Ireland[2] and Boal could help him broaden his appeal beyond the limited allure of Protestant Unionism. But Boal could also fashion and mould Paisley to his liking, as one early episode demonstrated. Like most Unionist politicians, Paisley had always regarded internment without trial as the panacea for IRA violence – after all it had helped to suppress the IRA's 1956–62 campaign. As early as August 1970, long before the Provisional IRA violence reached a peak, Paisley had called for its introduction. Boal, though, was opposed to the measure, believing it to be both unjust and ineffective against a Catholic community containing a large number of people who were opposed to the very existence of the state. As early as March 1971, Boal had denounced internment as "the kind of policy that a panic-stricken hysterical government is likely to bluster into".[3] By August 1971, when Faulkner persuaded British premier Ted Heath to use the weapon, Boal had convinced Paisley to come round to his way of thinking. Paisley had first opposed internment for selfish reasons; the Unionist government would intern Protestants and Catholics on a 50–50 basis and he predicted he would be the first Protestant jailed. Now he came out against it in principle.

This was an incomprehensible stand to most Unionists and damaged Paisley, as one former Stormont MP remembered: "Faulkner had tapped into a vein right across the Unionist spectrum. The country was up against the wall, the smoke was rising from the cities and he was doing his best, while this lout was standing at the gates shouting 'traitor'. It was one argument Faulkner won hand over fist. It was a very low point for Paisley."

That autumn Boal would lead Paisley into even more dangerous territory. But first Paisley made another switch which also landed him in trouble, one prompted partly by Boal and partly by intelligence Paisley had come across on the Westminster grapevine. Like traditional Unionists at large Paisley had always supported the Stormont parliament and regarded it as Unionism's ultimate bulwark against its Nationalist enemies. But when he heard in London that the British were thinking seriously about bringing in Direct Rule, he gave the move a cautious welcome, one that stunned his followers at an Ulster Hall rally: "Those who favour the British connection will at least see in this that we will be more integrated than ever in the United Kingdom," he told them.

The reason for Paisley's about-turn was twofold: firstly, Boal had decided that if Northern Ireland was to be disenfranchised by the abolition of its separate parliament, the logical Unionist response should be for complete integration with Britain. Secondly, Paisley knew that his fledgling DUP would fare better in a political context which the deeply entrenched Official Unionist Party could not dominate in the way it dominated Stormont. Official Unionists had always sent their second division players to Westminster, where Northern Ireland still had only 12 MPs, and kept their most talented politicians for Stormont. But if Stormont was suspended, leaving Westminster as the only remaining arena, then Paisley was well positioned to outshine his rivals.

But Direct Rule was still nearly five months away. In the meantime Boal was crafting a strategy of broad-based opposition to Faulkner's government. In mid-November he and Paisley had talks in his home on the County Down coast with John Hume, Austin Currie and Paddy Devlin of the Social Democratic and Labour Party, formed the previous year by a group of Nationalist, Labour and ex-Civil Rights Association politicians.

They found broad areas of agreement in their opposition to internment, support for state investment to deal with unemployment, and belief in better cross-border relations. "Wolfe Tone is alive and well and leading the Democratic Unionist Party," commented a jubilant Paddy Devlin afterwards.

Already confused by Paisley's political gyrations, his supporters were about to be entirely bewildered by his next move, a recalibration again scripted by Boal. On the evening of Thursday, 25 November 1971, Paisley and Boal met three Dublin journalists, Liam Hourican of Radio Telefís Éireann, Henry Kelly of *The Irish Times*, and Vincent Browne of *The Irish Press*, in Belfast's Europa Hotel. They talked late into the night and at one point Browne said there would be no solution to the Northern problem until a majority of people there supported a united Ireland. Boal agreed. Paisley, always reluctant to take Boal head-on in argument, would not commit himself one way or the other, but started instead to talk about the need to change the 1937 Irish Constitution.

At around three o'clock in the morning Boal persuaded Paisley to give Hourican an interview. After Hourican had recorded an hour-long interview, both Browne and Kelly asked their own questions. Although it was close to six o'clock in the morning by the time they had finished, the journalists remember Paisley being in great humour throughout – "it was an extremely genial atmosphere," recalls Hourican.

In his RTÉ interview, broadcast three days later, Hourican asked Paisley if he would consider the prospect of being part of a united Ireland if the South scrapped its constitution and changed certain of its laws. Paisley astounded everyone by replying that in such a situation there would be "an entirely different set of circumstances". "That would be the greatest guarantee to Protestants that they really meant business," he said.

In the newspaper interviews he was even more specific. "The cancer is not the 1920 Act and not the partition of the country," he told *The Irish Times*, "but the cancer is the 1937 Constitution and the domination of the Catholic Church through it."[4]

To *The Irish Press* he said:

> If the people in the South really want the Protestants of the
> North to join them in a united Ireland, then they should scrap
> entirely the 1937 Constitution and ensure that the Roman
> Catholic hierarchy could no longer exercise an improper
> influence in politics. If this were done, then the Protestant
> people would take a different view – there would be an entirely
> different set of circumstances. We are not saying that the
> majority of the South should cease to be Roman Catholic. All
> we are saying is that they should ensure that rule from Dublin
> would not be rule from Maynooth.[5]

Paisley stressed again and again in the interviews that he was a
"realist", pointing out that the 1937 Constitution had not been scrapped
and was not about to be scrapped. He went on:

> If you ask me whether I can see at some time, some way,
> somewhere in the future a united Ireland, that is a question I
> cannot answer because I cannot say now what will happen in
> the future, and anyway, I cannot answer the question because I
> am too much of a realist and such a question is really not even
> worthy of consideration now.[6]

Boal, sensing the first signs of British fatigue with the whole
Northern Ireland imbroglio, might have thought it was time to discuss
the full range of options open to Unionism. But to most traditional
Unionists, Paisley had scored an astonishing own goal.

The line-up of people welcoming his comments served only to confirm
this: Provisional IRA leader Daithi O'Conaill said that Republicans and
Paisleyites were "allies in the cause of a new Ireland", and praised his
social conscience and the equal treatment of his Catholic and Protestant
constituents.[7] Fianna Fáil Finance Minister George Colley invited him to
Dublin to help draft a new constitution. *The Irish Times* made the
extraordinary prophecy that one day Paisley would sit in Dáil Éireann,
the Irish parliament.

A memory of that extraordinary episode prompted David Trimble a
quarter of a century later to suggest that it was this that persuaded Sinn
Féin to go into government with the DUP. "Sinn Féin went for a Paisley
deal," he said, "because he is the only Unionist leader to ever seriously

consider a united Ireland. Boal made the running on that and Paisley didn't slap him down. I remember at the December 1973 Portrush conference [to co-ordinate opposition to Sunningdale] Paisley was surrounded by his acolytes and he was asked why he didn't go down the road with Boal and his answer was the social power of the Catholic church, not because he wanted to stay British. It all has to do with the conditional nature of the sort of Unionism and Loyalism that Paisley represents."[8]

At the time Paisley was fortunate that his comments were overshadowed by the reaction to Harold Wilson's 15-year plan for Irish unity, announced the previous week. However, a delighted Brian Faulkner dubbed him "the new darling of the Republican press". The bulletin of the paramilitary Ulster Defence Association, noting that "at one time we would have followed Paisley anywhere", now dissociated the organisation from him.[9]

His own followers were totally confused: first opposition to internment, then indifference to Stormont's possible abolition, and now flirting with Irish unity. "The reaction was one of hostility and astonishment," according to a leading DUP man at the time, Clifford Smyth. "People didn't understand it; it was far too radical and advanced for their thinking. One minute they were out kicking the Pope, 'Old Redsocks', and the next they're into this 'entirely different set of circumstances'."

These were mistakes that Paisley would never repeat. In the days following the interviews about the 1937 Constitution he changed tack, returning to the more traditional Unionist view, telling a BBC interviewer that he was "opposed absolutely" to any kind of united Ireland. "That's the thing about him – he's much more the representative of the people than their leader," commented Smyth. "He's not going to lead them through the wilderness like Moses. He's too responsive to the feelings of the people in the wee Protestant hall in Ballymena and simply will not go too far ahead of his supporters."

It also marked the end of his political liaison with Boal, although not their personal friendship. For Boal the interviews with the Southern journalists were to be just the first step in a more ambitious journey. William Craig remembered Paisley taking Harry West and him to see Boal in his suite in the Europa Hotel one morning in 1973. Boal told them that the time had come to consider a federal settlement in order to protect the interests of Northern Protestants within Ireland. Paisley said nothing. West was dumbfounded and Craig told Boal, "Even if there was merit in it, it could never be sold." Boal then lost his temper and the meeting came to an abrupt end.

In January 1974, Boal proposed an "amalgamated Ireland" under a federal parliament, with a Stormont-style provincial parliament in Belfast. He argued that the connection between Britain and Northern Ireland was in the process of being broken anyway, whatever Unionists thought, and "much of the former sentimental attachment to Britain has recently evaporated, even to be replaced sometimes by bitterness and hostility".

Boal gave up active politics – which even at the best of times he treated with the irreverence of the gifted dilettante – and dropped out of sight, at least as far as politics were concerned, when he was made a QC in January 1973.

—◦—

Notwithstanding the efforts of Desmond Boal to broaden the new DUP's base, the reality was that the Protestant Unionists, effectively Paisley's Ulster Protestant Volunteer divisions, had changed only their name, nothing else. They dominated the new party – at the party's inaugural meeting in the Ulster Hall on 30 October 1971, the DUP adopted the same county-wide organisational structure as the UPV. UPV veterans and Protestant Unionists were elected to 13 of the 15 positions on the DUP organising committee. One founder member estimated that 70 per cent of the audience were UPV/Protestant Unionist members.

Most of them, of course, were also Free Presbyterians and it wasn't long before it became apparent that Free Presbyterianism was to dominate the DUP. From the very start DUP meetings opened with a Bible reading and a prayer while early executive meetings were held in a gospel hall in Aughrim Street in Sandy Row – the hall had been Albert Duff's and after his death it had been absorbed into the Free Presbyterian church.

The Free Presbyterian influence was symbolised by Paisley himself who, despite his early history of critical attacks on politically active evangelists, refused to resign his church positions. The perpetual moderator of the Free Presbyterian church, at least until 2007, became the unchallenged leader of the DUP.

At grassroots level the overwhelming majority of DUP members were, from the very beginning, Free Presbyterians. The rise of Craig's Vanguard in protest at the suspension of Stormont coincided with Paisley's conversion to integrationism, a strange and unpopular cause for Loyalists. Militant non-Free Presbyterian Loyalists preferred the familiarity of Craig's campaign and flocked to him, not to the DUP.

The dominance of the Free Presbyterians soon became apparent when the DUP began returning elected representatives. In the 1973 power-sharing Assembly and the 1975 Constitutional Convention all but one of the party's team was in the church. Of the 74 councillors elected in 1977, 85 per cent of those whose religions were ascertainable were, according to one reliable study, Free Presbyterians. In 1981 this rose to 89 per cent. In the 1982–86 Assembly, 18 of the 21 DUP Assembly members were Free Presbyterians and four of them were ministers.

The Free Presbyterian influence in the DUP underlined a major difference between its brand of Unionism and others, a difference that has its roots in the plantation of Ireland by seventeenth-century evangelical Protestants surrounded by displaced and hostile Catholic natives. This also helps to explain why so many church members get so fanatically involved in DUP politics.

While a significant number of Official Unionists, especially in the middle class, regard the Union with Britain as intrinsically worthwhile for social and economic reasons and identify with Britain in cultural ways, the DUP view of the Union is subtly different. While they do share many of the Official Unionist values, principally they see the union as a mechanism through which they can best avoid absorption into a Roman Catholic Irish Republic and destruction of the Bible Protestantism that they believe will follow. It produces a view of their relationship with Britain which is akin to a legal contract and fully consistent with the Scottish Covenanting tradition from which they spring – "We will remain loyal to Britain as long as Britain remains loyal to us." Their loyalty is to the British Crown – as long as it remains Protestant – and to Westminster, as long as it protects traditional Protestantism in Northern Ireland.

The readiness of Protestants to rebel against Westminster, as well as the occasional manifestations of an independent Ulster sentiment, has its roots here. It is a deep strain in Northern Ireland Protestantism and Paisley was able to tap into it. His Free Presbyterian followers' first allegiance is to Protestantism, not to the Union. Their official slogan is: "For God and Ulster." As Paisley often told his supporters: "The Alliance Party is the political wing of ecumenism but the DUP is the political wing of evangelical Protestantism." For Free Presbyterian DUP members, political activity becomes an extension of their religious convictions – they are in fact "doing God's work" in the DUP, or as one former DUP member put it, "working out their own salvation" inside the party. This phenomenon can be seen at election times when virtually the entire energies and membership of the church are thrown behind the DUP, a feature of the party which took other rival Unionist parties entirely by surprise at the start. Whether or not this survives Paisley's loss of the Free Presbyterian Moderatorship and the huge level of disillusion caused by the 2007 deal with Sinn Féin, will be one of the fascinating questions awaiting an answer in the coming years.

This dependence on Free Presbyterianism had its drawbacks, most notably in matters of finance. The obvious wealth of the church, the history of Paisley's famous "plastic bucket" collections, makes many assume that the DUP must be rich. For many years this produced considerable apathy about fund-raising and one consequence was a state of permanent financial crisis which membership subscriptions alone could not solve. It often had to be rescued by generous interest-free loans from sympathetic businessmen or affluent members.

There were also restrictions on the type of permissible fund-raising imposed by the Church which added to the party's difficulties. Any method of raising money that smacked of gambling or games of chance was automatically ruled out. Raffles and ballots, the basis for many another political party's finance, were forbidden, as are, of course, social evenings where alcohol may be consumed.

Eventually, the financial crisis became so acute that Paisley was persuaded that a new and professional approach to party finance was needed and so Wallace Thompson, who had joined the UPV as a teenager but went on to graduate from Queen's University, Belfast, was hired as the DUP's full-time finance officer, with the task of solving the DUP's financial crisis.

He was, as he says, "continually walking a tightrope" between what was and was not a scripturally acceptable way of raising money. Eventually he hit upon an idea which seemed perfect – gospel concert evenings featuring evangelical, country and western-style groups playing music and songs which would not only raise money but would bring young people into contact with the DUP. But he soon ran into trouble.

There were problems because anything that was slightly rock and roll was considered "of the Devil". If a group came along, and one member was in a church which was a member of the World Council of Churches there was a problem because he was apostate and Free Presbyterians weren't allowed to mix with people like that.

My aim was to bring in young people and therefore I wanted the music to appeal to them but some ministers opposed us. For example I advertised a concert with the Rev William McCrea which used the phrase "In Concert" and I was condemned as that was an expression used by the worldly entertainment scene, pop groups, the Beatles or whatever. "In Concert" was regarded as taking away from what it really was, which was an evening of praise for the Lord.

If the Church of England could once be described as the Tory party at prayer, then in these days the DUP was the Free Presbyterian Church at the hustings. And if there were problems about a Methodist being a member of a gospel group playing to a DUP function, just imagine the Free Presbyterian reaction to Ian Paisley sharing the government of Northern Ireland with Martin McGuinness.

—◁○▷—

To understand how Ian Paisley was able to persuade so many inside the DUP, if not the Free Presbyterian Church, to go along with a strategy of joining Sinn Féin in government, it is necessary to appreciate how complete and absolute Paisley's authority over the DUP has been – at least until recently. Paisley's authority has been total, his word final and his freedom of action in policy formation, selection of election candidates and treatment of dissent unique among Western political leaders.

"From my experience," recalled Wallace Thompson, "Paisley's word was the last word and when Paisley spoke, it was regarded as being the ultimate. I know that in executive meetings when Ian wasn't there, we would take decisions by ourselves. But if he came in late or turned up to the next meeting and disagreed with what had been decided, even over minor things like party functions, there would never be any attempt to contradict him. You got much more freedom of debate when he wasn't there but even so it was very often a case of 'Wait till we see what the Doc says'."

That accords with the experience of another former executive member, Clifford Smyth:

> Policy-making in my day was very difficult because the executive would arrive at a policy and then Paisley would jet in from Westminster and say, "Listen, Brother, you can't do that because I've just been to Westminster and if you knew what I knew you'd do it differently." And the policy would be all changed. They were totally dependent on this man and things always went to him for final approval.

Paisley's authority was so absolute because his followers believed he was God's agent or "man for the hour", sent by divine intervention to protect what both they and he believe is the last bastion of Bible Protestantism in Europe. Like Old Testament prophets, Paisley defied authority and was persecuted. Accordingly he has, in the eyes of his flock, special God-given powers which set him above all other party members.

"In the Old Testament, God sent prophets at times of spiritual and political decline in Israel's history and Ian Paisley is seen as one such man sent from the Kingdom to lead Ulster in her own troubles," observed Thompson. "He's referred to as God's man, a prophet among us who therefore speaks with extra authority."

It is Paisley's power of political prophecy which, for his supporters, validates this claim and gives him semi-Biblical status, a status which Paisley does little to contest and which also reaches out into the wider Protestant community outside the DUP/Free Presbyterian fold. Typical of those who held this view of Paisley is Fred Proctor, for many years a Shankill Road businessman and one of the first Protestant Unionist councillors in Belfast. Speaking in the 1980s, he observed:

> He prophesied the birth of the IRA; he said that they would come into being. During the civil rights movement he said that eventually the country would be in chaos. He said that there were people involved in those days who were Communists who would be thrown aside when the time came and would be overtaken by Republicans, which eventually did happen. He

prophesied Direct Rule in 1971 and a few months later that happened as well. To me he's never been proved wrong in any of the predictions he has made – they have always come into being.

David Trimble's handling of the peace process in the 1990s produced more evidence to the faithful of Paisley's prophetic powers. He had said the IRA and Sinn Féin would use gullible leaders like Trimble to advance their agenda and Sinn Féin's ability to get into government without decommissioning was the proof. The idea that some of Paisley's prophecies, such as the birth of the IRA, may be self-fulfilling never occurs to his most devoted supporters. Equally, the realisation that some self-fulfilling prophecies, such as Trimble's downfall, may also be to his own political advantage also passed most by.

Because Paisley had this Old Testament prophet status, his followers rarely questioned his actions and forgave him for all transgressions. Thus the mother of a man imprisoned for serious offences committed in the furtherance of Paisley's cause could invoke the Bible to forgive Paisley for his part in her son's downfall. "Well, maybe he did wrong," she told the author. "But then King David did bad things as well and was responsible for a man's death but God had chosen him too."

Paisley's embroilment in the Kincora scandal was another example. The allegation that he failed to act when warned about the paedophile inclinations of the home's warden, William McGrath, cut little ice with the vast majority of DUP members. "A few asked themselves questions but most accepted his explanation and dismissed the allegations as another perfidious plot against him. There's always hostility towards people who doubt Paisley," recalled a party member. The incidental fact that McGrath was a fellow fundamentalist and head of a bizarre Loyalist paramilitary group, Tara, with which some DUP figures were associated, was conveniently overlooked.

Automatic hostility to his enemies went hand-in-hand with unquestioning obedience, even if on occasion this could produce the most astonishing political gymnastics. "I remember a party meeting back in 1979 before Mrs Thatcher was elected and Sammy Wilson, who has a name for being a bit of a radical, was speaking," recalled Thompson, who described the scene:

Paisley was due to speak but he was late, so Sammy went ahead without him. He warned the audience of the dangers of a Conservative government coming in and praised the Labour government's policy in Northern Ireland in terms of economic growth. He felt that a Conservative government would lead to widespread unemployment and would adopt measures which would cause social deprivation. The audience cheered wildly at this and obviously agreed with him wholeheartedly.

Then Ian came along and in Ian's speech he said that he trusted that God would deliver Ulster from the curse of Socialism which was against the scriptural teachings and he prayed that soon in Britain we might see the return of a Conservative government. Again the audience cheered wildly. They had forgotten entirely what Sammy had said; it's whatever Ian would say that would carry them. I'll never forget the look of disbelief on Sammy's face.

As Wallace Thompson soon discovered in his work raising money for the DUP, Paisley's appeal was unique and astonishingly effective. "I don't know whether they fell under the awe of having Ian Paisley at their home or what but whenever I would arrive with him they just wrote the cheques out. I would have tried and tried by myself but it never worked, but with Paisley it worked straight away. He'd just say, 'Brother, we're in severe difficulties' and they would say 'Yes, Yes, Yes', as they were reaching for their chequebooks."

Paisley also had absolute control over who would represent him at election time. "In all my experience in the DUP," commented an old DUP hand, "Paisley would never allow anyone he felt held conflicting views to himself to get selected. It just never happened and it didn't matter that the local branch wanted that person. If 'the Doc' said no, that was it."

One person with personal experience of this is Clifford Smyth, a former DUP Assembly and Convention member: "Paisley was free to go into a constituency and say this brother or another should stand. I remember he came to me in the vestry in the Martyrs' Memorial and said, 'Would you stand in North Antrim?' There was no question of the party in North Antrim having a say. They didn't even know me. It was self-selecting – I simply went there and they accepted his decision and endorsed me." Smyth was eventually thrown out of the DUP, tried and convicted by a Paisley-led kangaroo court, on suspicion of links to British military intelligence via the strange Loyalist group Tara and its sexually aberrant leader, William McGrath.

One consequence is that dissent from or rivalry to Paisley is rare. When it does occur, God and Paisley together take care of the offender. "He just freezes it out. He won't accept it and tells people 'I won't have it!'," observed one DUP member who was once on the receiving end.

> . . . If the trouble persists, the person is made to feel less than loyal because they've spoken against an authority which derives its power from the idea that Paisley is "God's man for the hour". Most people think they're doing wrong if they speak against him. They think they're challenging the will of God. So if you speak out against Ian Paisley, you're made to feel that you're going against God. You know that old joke about Paisley being the Protestant Pope? Well, it's not a joke. His authority *is* semi-Papal.

—◁○▷—

Paisley's vigilance had seen off a number of putative rivals in the various organisations he has been associated with over the years. Some like Noel Doherty went to jail and then disappeared into obscurity; others, like Bunting and McKeague, were ditched when they became embarrassments; some like Norman Porter he broke with, while there were those like Billy Beattie, a victim of his own political miscalculations, whom he broke.

One man has survived longer than any. Long regarded as the heir-apparent, few people have had as turbulent a relationship with Ian Paisley as has Peter Robinson, the 59-year-old MP for East Belfast, DUP deputy leader and the man widely seen as the person responsible for strategising the DUP's path to government.

Born and raised in the Castlereagh hills on the eastern outskirts of Belfast, Robinson became a Paisleyite when he was a 17-year-old grammar school boy preparing to sit his O-level exams. During the turbulent and violent year of 1966, he attended Paisley's meetings in the Ulster Hall and was converted to the cause. Those who remember him from those days recall a crude anti-Catholicism: "I remember him on his holidays in Portrush with a mate following two nuns down the street yelling 'Popehead! Popehead!'" recalled a schoolmate.

When Paisley founded the Ulster Protestant Volunteers, Robinson enrolled and became chairman of the Lagan Valley branch. When Paisley formed the DUP, Robinson joined as a founder member. On leaving school, Robinson worked for a spell in an estate agent's office but his devotion to Paisleyite politics was to make that a short stay.

In 1968 he wrote a pamphlet called *The North Answers Back* giving the Paisleyite answer to the civil rights campaign. That brought him to Paisley's attention. Paisley recognised an articulate talent in Robinson, and when he was elected to Westminster in 1970 he made Robinson his secretary. Under Paisley's patronage he forged through the DUP ranks to a position of unprecedented influence. Paisley's promotion of Robinson was the first sign of his own leadership talents, an ability to recognise the value of an able lieutenant by his side – in contrast, some previous seconds-in-command were noted for their intellectual poverty as well as their unquestioning awe of Paisley.

Robinson made his name among the rank-and-file as a forceful advocate of tough measures against the IRA, always a popular cause in the DUP. He also won favour with the DUP's Free Presbyterian element when he organised the "Save Ulster from Sodomy" campaign in 1976 against the decriminalisation of homosexual acts in Northern Ireland. None of these, however, are by themselves sufficient to explain his rise.

The key to Robinson's success does not lie in his natural political ambition or frequent declarations of undying loyalty to his leader but in administrative and organisational skills which have made him indispensable to Paisley, particularly as Paisley's political and religious workloads in Britain, Europe, and the United States grew. No-one was more responsible for transforming the DUP into a coherent, well-organised political party with a ruthless commitment to winning votes.

Robinson was one of the few who learned how to deal with Paisley's violent outbursts of bad temper and to profit from them. Former DUP finance officer Wallace Thompson recalled: "He [Paisley] was very easily made angry if things weren't going right. He used to eat the face off the wee secretary girl over at Martyrs' Memorial. I used to feel very sorry for her. If there was a crossed line or a wrong number, it was her fault, not the system's. Everyone took it from him."

Everyone took it from him, that is, except Peter Robinson. "Peter tells the story how he challenged him," remembers Thompson. "Ian could get very angry with you, very gruff and aggressive, demanding that you give in to him. But if you fought back, he would become as soft as a youngster and would become very apologetic and apologise to you for days afterwards. Peter was prepared to push – that's what got him where he is now. Jim Allister took him [Paisley] on as well. The result was that Paisley respected and admired them. I remember Peter telling me, 'You go forward with your own ideas and don't just meekly stand and accept what he says, you'll stand in higher esteem with him.'"

For the first two years of its life the DUP was, in the words of a founder member, "chaotic and directionless". Boal was then chairman and his view was that the DUP would, because of its democratic appeal, virtually rise up from the Loyalist grassroots by its own momentum. That of course didn't happen. Party meetings were infrequent and growth was negligible. By 1973 the DUP had the same number of branches as when it started and all of those were inherited from the UPV/Protestant Unionists.

In that year Boal left and Robinson became party secretary and then two years later full-time general secretary. During those two years he helped to transform the party. Straightaway the DUP moved out of the old Shaftesbury Square UCDC headquarters – "an awful place, full of bird droppings from the holes in the roof," recalled one old hand – into new party headquarters in South Belfast. A full-time secretary/typist was also hired.

Ensconced in his new office, Robinson set about regularising and centralising the DUP's affairs. Party branches were for the first time levied on a regular basis and revenue started to flow in. Communication with the branches was improved, and a set of rules for their meetings and procedures for selecting candidates was issued. Branches also started to receive well-written briefs on election techniques, and meetings of important party bodies like the Executive and the Delegates Assembly – an internal sounding board – were held on a more regular basis.

More importantly, a party constitution creating new party structures which would help to co-ordinate the DUP's membership and election efforts was drafted and got Paisley's imprimatur. Party branches, previously based on the North's six counties, were also re-organised to parallel the twelve Westminster constituencies, the basis for elections both to a Stormont Assembly and the House of Commons.

From there on the DUP expanded in virtually every important Protestant area of Northern Ireland, creating new branches and expanding others. The credit was nearly all Robinson's, as the rank and file recognised: "Whatever else he is, Ian is not a great man for the details of organisation. It was Peter who was really responsible for making the DUP into what it is now. He was very dedicated and effective, working all the hours of the day."

Robinson's work had also placed him in a perfect place to launch his own political career, something which he proceeded to do with all the determination he had shown in building up the DUP.

His power base was in East Belfast, and not long after he became a full-time DUP functionary he set about learning the tricks of the constituency. At the 1974 general election, when the DUP, Vanguard and the Official Unionists were in the anti-Sunningdale alliance, the United Ulster Unionist Coalition, he acted as Bill Craig's very efficient election agent and Craig easily won the seat.

The following year Robinson stood unsuccessfully in the Convention elections for East Belfast but two years later he was elected to Castlereagh council and there discovered the route that would take him to Westminster and to the DUP succession.

It was a traditional path for any ambitious politician – hard work, endless meetings with government bureaucrats and patient lobbying for his constituents. "Peter always used to tell us that the only way to get the support of the people was to go out and work for them," recalled an East Belfast contemporary. In 1978, Robinson persuaded Paisley to move DUP headquarters from South Belfast to the Albertbridge Road in East Belfast, a move which more than one party member suspected was engineered to benefit his political ambitions. "Break-ins were given as the reason," recalled one, "but it was as bad on the Albertbridge Road. It was really to get him a base to fight for the Westminster seat, all geared to building up his own empire."

To win the seat Robinson would have to beat Craig and he set about it with his customary single-mindedness. In the mid-1970s, Bill Craig, once the icon of hardline secular Unionism, proposed a non-mandatory form of power-sharing with Nationalists, called Voluntary

Coalition. In those days sharing power with Catholics was still a heresy for many Unionists and Craig's party, appropriately called Vanguard and which included figures like David Trimble and Reg Empey, split asunder as members took sides for and against Craig. That gave the DUP, Vanguard's chief rival for Loyalist votes, a great opportunity to soak up its support and Robinson crafted the strategy. "Peter had this idea when Craig fell over Voluntary Coalition," recalled a former senior party member. "He got someone to dig out an old photograph of Craig standing with O'Neill when they met Jack Lynch back in 1967. Harry West was in the same photograph but he was still in favour, so he was neatly sliced off the photograph. Then they made it up into a leaflet to hand out round East Belfast with the slogan 'Craig – once with Lynch, now with Cosgrave' [Irish Taoiseach at the time]'"

In early 1978, with a Westminster general election looming on the horizon, Robinson set up a small committee of trusted allies to plan the coming campaign. "They were tireless in their work and dedication to the battle against Craig," remembered one who saw them in action. "They researched Craig completely, digging up all sorts of stuff against him and even making up little jingles. But there was an atmosphere of dirtiness about it all that I didn't like, such as misrepresenting what Craig had said and done. Some of it was clever admittedly, like their election slogan 'Craig can't win'. The vote was going to be split three ways and that persuaded some people that they could only vote for Robinson. But I didn't like it."

Robinson also had help in the election campaign from the largest Loyalist paramilitary organisation, the UDA. He has always had more freedom to consort with shadier elements of Northern Protestantism than Paisley, who finds himself constrained by his more pious Church members. The UDA liked Robinson and would for years to come, thinking him tougher than Paisley, as well as sympathetic to their proposal for an independent Ulster. During the campaign their members canvassed for him, the UDA's Newtownards Road headquarters was plastered with his posters and they provided cars and workers on election day. Robinson returned the favour in various ways, notably by backing a UDA campaign to achieve segregation for its prisoners from Republicans in the North's jails. He was one of the few Unionist politicians willing to be publicly associated with the "hard men".

Some of his supporters employed even stranger election practices, much to the horror of rural DUP members. A few months after Robinson's own election campaign, volunteers from East Belfast went to Ballymena to help out in a council by-election and their methods astounded the local activists, most of them Free Presbyterians. "The East Belfast lot came complete with their various costumes for personation and the Ballymena people were amazed and disgusted. It showed up the gap between them," remembered a DUP man.

Robinson's careful planning worked a treat. In the May 1979 general election he defeated Craig – who was admittedly an ill and tired man by this stage – by 64 votes, overturning a huge 17,000 majority. At the same election Paisley's old ally from UPA days, Johnny McQuade, won the North Belfast seat for the DUP. With North Antrim once again safely Paisley's, it was a remarkable triple triumph for the DUP.

Peter Robinson's election to Westminster and his parallel domination of the DUP machine in Castlereagh enabled him to carve out a base that became remarkably independent of Ian Paisley. In a party whose other two MPs were Paisley himself and the less than cerebral Johnny McQuade, Robinson would also shine intellectually and become the architect of DUP strategy and the party's modernisation. The DUP's growth, he realised, would depend on its ability to reach out beyond the narrow confines of its Free Presbyterian core to the large and mostly secular Protestant. His own East Belfast constituency was a case in point. Largely working class, the Protestants of the area by and large found the dogmatism of Free Presbyterianism less acceptable than rural Protestants in the Church heartlands. They like to drink, gamble and have a more relaxed attitude towards sexual behaviour which would scandalise Free Presbyterians.

"When he [Robinson] looked at East Belfast," recalled a colleague, "and the votes he needed to win and sized up the hard core DUP in it – which basically boiled down to the Free Presbyterian Church – he hadn't a hope of winning it. So he had to broaden the base to bring in people whose loyalty was to the party not the Church and to give him credit he worked incredibly hard to do it," recalled a colleague. Robinson loosened the ties between Church and party, firstly by physically separating them – by holding party meetings in non-Church property so as not to alienate non-Free Presbyterian Loyalists. He then made a concerted drive to recruit non-Free Presbyterians by stressing the DUP's Loyalist and populist social and economic credentials.

He himself stopped attending the Free Presbyterian Church and joined first the Elim Pentecostal Church and then the Assemblies of God, another pentecostal sect. This was all symbolically very important. Free Presbyterians are virtually alone among Northern fundamentalists in their belief that they have the right to impose their theology on the rest of society. Other evangelicals tend more to internalise their beliefs – they believe their theology is right for themselves but shirk foisting it on the world at large. Many of those who gathered around Robinson politically were members of similar sects.

Whereas the Free Presbyterians in the DUP thought it right and proper to impose their rigid Sabbatarianism on the rest of the community, sects like the Pentecostalists did not, and politically that translated into supporting the "local option" policy to closing or opening swimming pools, parks and leisure centres on Sundays. That was the policy Robinson pursued in Castlereagh where such facilities were opened on Sundays and eventually Paisley accepted this as party policy, recognising that not to do so would inhibit the DUP's growth.

Robinson transformed the DUP in other ways. He persuaded Paisley to ditch the *Protestant Telegraph* and replaced it with a much more secular paper called *The Voice of Ulster*. Out went the Popish plots and in came a well-written political paper, geared to the rational dissemination of DUP views on a wide range of constitutional, security, economic and social issues. It even included a page of cookery tips for busy DUP wives.

Robinson also encouraged an influx of educated and talented activists, many of them graduates who had been active in the party's branch at Queen's University. The contrast between these new members and the older, traditional DUP member was striking. Most of the old guard had only the most basic education, a simple unquestioning faith in fundamental Protestantism and an equal faith in the infallibility of Ian Paisley. Invariably their route into the DUP was via the Free Presbyterian Church.

The new breed, people like barristers Jim Allister and Alan Kane and economics graduate Sammy Wilson, were different. Some were Free Presbyterians but many were not. They had been attracted to the DUP principally because it was so much more assertive than the rival Official Unionists. "We were regarded by the rest of the party as suspect," recalled Wallace Thompson. "There was a feeling in the DUP that anything intellectual was not good, that we couldn't be trusted completely. Their attitude was 'We'll have to watch these fellows in case their education goes to their head and they become compromising or soft'. It was part of the anti-intellectualism that's within fundamentalism and Ulster Protestantism in general."

Paisley, perhaps feeling his own lack of formal education, encouraged the Queen's members for sound pragmatic reasons. "Paisley knew he needed to broaden the base of the party, otherwise it would have become stagnant, and he wasn't capable of holding it all together. He also felt embarrassed by some of his older people who didn't have the brains to scratch themselves with. He was afraid they'd destroy the party," commented another member of the branch.

It was Robinson, though, the party's General Secretary at this time, who had the freedom and time to cultivate the Queen's branch and it was Robinson who became their leader, as one contemporary recalled:

> Robinson gained all of the Queen's branch because they couldn't go through university politics on a fundamentalist evangelical platform. You've got to rationalise, consider your argument, be articulate and think. Don't forget we weren't insulated like the rest of the DUP, we had to argue with SDLP and Alliance Party students. Those who do that will obviously end up in the same wing of the party as Peter Robinson, because that's what he does.

> Anyone who goes through Queen's gets his mind broadened from the religious and academic point of view, not broadened in that you change your views, but you learn to articulate them. You're always looking for answers, reasoning out, which is not the basis for Paisley's power with the rest of the DUP. The transition from Queen's to Peter Robinson was automatic.

By the mid-1980s the DUP was developing in ways that would eventually make the deal of May 2007 possible. It was beginning to shed its Free Presbyterian outer layers and soften its fundamentalist Protestant character and by so doing widen its appeal so that non-evangelicals could quite happily vote for it. While Unionists regularly voted in huge numbers for Ian Paisley in European elections, that was a cost-free exercise and also sent a warning message to Nationalists, the British government and, increasingly, the Dublin government not to push them too far. But in Northern Ireland itself the Ulster Unionists were still the natural party of government. If the DUP was ever going to replace their rivals, it would have to show Unionist voters that the DUP had become a broad party. The DUP was also becoming equipped with talented, young activists and in Peter Robinson, Ian Paisley had a deputy leader who was both a threat to his dominance of the party and the source of the modernising ideas and strategies that were necessary if the DUP was ever to grow. All that was missing was a willingness to embrace one other characteristic of a normal political party: a readiness to entertain compromise, to bargain and negotiate and to acknowledge that the business of politics was about attaining power or it was about nothing at all. That process would soon begin too.

The grand old Duke of York,
He had ten thousand men.
He marched them up to the top of the hill
And he marched them down again.

CHILDREN'S NURSERY RHYME

❧

"What strikes you about Ian is that he's like the Grand Old
Duke of York – there's a point at which he will always retreat.
He'll huff and puff to bring about a situation and then he'll come
back from the edge. People are in jail for going over the
top because they thought he was leading them there.
You can do that sort of thing too often."

FORMER SENIOR DUP MEMBER

❧

"Ian will fight till the last drop of everyone else's blood."

FORMER FREE PRESBYTERIAN CHURCH OFFICIAL

CHAPTER TEN

The Grand Old Duke of York

In 1973, after two years of bloody violence, the British government launched the most ambitious political initiative in Ireland since 1921. The initiative was a victory for Nationalists and a defeat for traditional Unionism but Loyalists responded in time-honoured fashion. They organised to defy the will of the British as their forefathers had in 1912 and as Paisley had so often warned they would need to do again to preserve their way of life.

The initiative was a product of British frustration. The year 1972 had been the most violent in Northern Ireland's short history: 457 people had been killed – 103 of them British soldiers – and there were nearly 1,400 explosions. The unprecedented ferocity of the Provisional IRA's shooting and bombing campaign had littered the North's streets with mutilated bodies and had provoked an equally murderous Protestant backlash. Loyalist paramilitaries mushroomed and, led by the Ulster Defence Association, struck back with a series of random assassinations of Catholics.

The year 1973 had been little better – a thousand bombs and 250 deaths. Internment and harsh security policies had failed to undermine support for the IRA. The Direct Rule Secretary of State, William Whitelaw, turned to politics as a solution.

In October 1972 he announced proposals for a power-sharing government, in which Nationalists would serve, and said that an "Irish dimension" would have to be included. A subsequent White Paper endorsed the plan and the SDLP, the main constitutional Nationalist party, gave it a warm welcome, as did the new Fine Gael–Labour coalition government in Dublin.

In December 1973, the British and Irish governments together with the new power-sharing Executive, which included Brian Faulkner's Unionist Party, the SDLP and the Alliance Party, met at Sunningdale in southern England and after three days of negotiations announced agreement on the "Irish dimension".

The Sunningdale Agreement, as it became known, provided for the establishment of a Council of Ireland, drawn from the Northern and Southern cabinets which would have a wide range of economic and cultural functions in both parts of Ireland. Arrangements were also made to try to harmonise cross-Border police work and anti-terrorist laws.

They were radical proposals which were sure to attract Loyalist fury – a similar body had been envisaged in 1921 and at the time the British made no secret of their hopes that it would lead eventually to a united Ireland. But the British had reason to believe that they might be able to finesse the deal.

The Unionists were deeply divided and absorbed in mutual recriminations. Paisley was still in the political wilderness after two years of toying with integration and he and Craig, his main rival for hardline Loyalist support, were at daggers drawn. Craig had set up Vanguard, an umbrella for Unionist right-wingers which included the largest paramilitary group, the UDA, and workers from the Belfast shipyard and Protestant-dominated factories grouped together in the Loyalist Association of Workers (LAW), to oppose direct rule. At Nazi-type rallies Craig made blood-curdling threats of violence and hinted at a campaign to achieve independence if Loyalist demands for the restoration of Stormont were not met.

In February 1973 an attempt at a one-day Loyalist strike, supported by Craig's Vanguard movement, had ended in an orgy of violence. It had been called by the paramilitaries to protest at the extension of internment to Loyalists. By the end of the day, five people had been killed in gun-battles between Loyalists and the British Army and there had been rampant intimidation of Protestant workers. Paisley joined in the widespread Protestant condemnations which were reflected in the next day's banner headline in the Unionist daily, the *Belfast News Letter*: "Ulster's day of shame."

Brian Faulkner, meanwhile, still led the largest Unionist bloc and his ambition was undiminished. Whitelaw and his advisers reckoned that, with other Loyalists divided, Faulkner would be ready and able to make a deal.

Although Loyalists reunited to oppose their proposals, the British could still afford to be optimistic. There were signs before and during the Assembly election campaign in June 1973 of uncertainty and tensions in their ranks. Although Craig and Paisley sank their differences to form an electoral pact, it was an alliance that existed only on paper. When the campaigning started, Paisley abandoned his partners and poured all his party's energies into his own party's effort. His DUP ended up with one more seat than Vanguard.

It was the first evidence of what later became an accepted part of Unionist wisdom – that Paisley's ruthlessness gains him more advantage than anyone else when he joins in coalition with other Loyalists. Paisley also made the most gains when the Loyalists escalated their opposition inside and outside the Assembly following agreement in November to set up the Executive and to take office the following 1 January.

In the Assembly, the Loyalist tactics were to disrupt debates with noisy protests and DUP members were to the fore each time. The protests were intensified after the Sunningdale negotiations. During the first Assembly meeting after the agreement, in January 1974, Paisley was forcibly removed from the chamber by the RUC – it took eight policemen to carry him out. The protests earned Paisley and the DUP considerable publicity and the admiration of militants outside.

He was reaping so much benefit from the protests that his allies in the other two Unionist blocs had difficulty persuading him to drop them. Craig complained that Paisley had broken an agreement to boycott the Assembly after the Executive took office: "I think if he'd had his way we would have stayed in the Assembly quite a while; he needed an arena," he said later.

Paisley also had one other major advantage over Craig and West. He was much more forceful and articulate on TV and radio and as a result the media regularly sought him out for comment. This helped to enhance the impression that he was leading the Loyalist campaign and uniting its previously divided factions. Faulkner also helped by singling him out for attack, on one occasion dubbing him, much to Paisley's annoyance, "the Demon Doctor".

Paisley's skills with the media heightened his profile further when the Loyalists launched a "Save Ulster" campaign in the closing weeks of 1973 in protest at Britain's refusal to invite them to the Sunningdale conference and when, at the same time, Harry West's Unionist dissidents broke off from the Official Unionist Party and joined with

Paisley and Craig in the United Ulster Unionist Coalition (UUUC). Much of the media saw the UUUC and the "Save Ulster" campaign as Paisley creations.

The UUUC was from the start an uneasy alliance and, thanks to Paisley's opportunism, it very nearly broke up at the first hurdle. That came in February 1974 when Ted Heath called a Westminster general election in the wake of a successful coalminers' strike in Britain. The UUUC agreed that only one Loyalist candidate should go forward in each constituency but, inevitably, the three parties squabbled about the share-out.

In the end West's party got seven nominations, Vanguard three and the DUP only two. But behind Craig and West's backs, Paisley had afterwards attempted to increase the DUP total by one when he secretly approached the North Belfast Official Unionist nominee, John Carson, with an invitation to join the DUP. Carson refused but Paisley's effort, as a contemporary DUP colleague, Clifford Smyth noted, "could have been sufficient to wreck the UUUC" and with it the anti-Sunningdale campaign.

The Westminster poll gave the Loyalists a huge propaganda and political victory. UUUC candidates won eleven of the twelve Northern Ireland seats and just under 51 per cent of the total vote. The Executive and Sunningdale were at a stroke deprived of much moral and political credibility. The election was also a personal triumph for Paisley, who increased his own North Antrim majority to a massive 25,000 votes and underlined his growing claim to be included in the first line of Loyalist leadership.

Despite their victory, however, neither Harold Wilson's new Labour government, which appointed a former schoolmaster, Merlyn Rees, as NI Secretary, nor the Faulkner Unionists showed any sign of giving way. While Faulkner had lost the support of the Ulster Unionist Council and resigned as Official Unionist leader, he nevertheless retained the support of his Assembly party. The Executive continued to function and plans were made to ratify Sunningdale at Stormont and to implement its provisions. The Westminster results were seen as a temporary setback which could be reversed when Protestants saw the arrangements bringing Catholic rejection of the IRA.

Other Loyalists, however, were working on plans to force Faulkner and the British to yield. The Ulster Workers Council (UWC), the successor to the LAW which broke up in early 1973, had been making plans for a general strike since the summer of 1973 and had held discussions with Craig about its timing and scope. Like many grassroots Loyalists, they were angry and frustrated with the politicians' failure and were eager to take their own action.

The UWC had members, many of them trade unionists, in most major Protestant-dominated factories in Belfast and County Antrim but, more crucially, had supporters in the North's two major electricity plants: Ballylumford, near Larne, County Antrim; and Coolkeeragh, outside Derry. Between them they generated most of the North's electricity and, deprived of it, Northern Ireland would literally grind to a halt.

The UWC wanted to launch a strike in December but West talked them out of it on the grounds that the cold weather would cause suffering to their supporters. Another date was set but that was postponed when the British miners' strike started. Finally the UWC and the UUUC chose Tuesday 14 May, the day when the Assembly was due to ratify Sunningdale, as the trigger for the strike. That evening the UWC chairman, shipyard shop steward Harry Murray, told journalists at Stormont that the strike would start immediately; the only thing that could stop it would be fresh Assembly elections.

The strike was slow to take effect. On the first day, 80 per cent of the Northern Ireland workforce turned up. The UWC panicked and turned to the UDA leader, Andy Tyrie, for help. Loyalist paramilitary groups, including the illegal UVF, Down Orange Welfare, a doomsday outfit led by a former British Army Colonel, Peter "Basil" Brush, the Orange Volunteers and the Ulster Volunteer Service Corps, had joined Craig, West and Paisley in the UWC's co-ordinating committee to run the strike. But Tyrie, the most important paramilitary leader, had been excluded from the strike planning by the UWC.

A portly, bespectacled and mustachioed figure with a genial, friendly manner, Tyrie's appearance disguised a shrewd, calculating mind. He had started his paramilitary life with the UVF back in the late 1960s where he had been active on the fringes of Paisley's UPV and had risen through the UDA's tough ranks to become its commander in 1973. He agreed to help, and that, together with the increasing impact of power cuts, was the turning point in the strike. During the next few days Tyrie's UDA men were out in force, intimidating workers, forcibly closing factories and shops and placing barricades across major roads.

Those four or five days at the start proved vital to the strike's success but they were nervous ones for Loyalist paramilitaries and politicians alike. Both were worried that the intimidation wouldn't work and they expected the British to strike back – memories of the disastrous 1973 strike were still fresh.

The British response was in fact timid. Attempts to take down barricades were delayed for a fatal week and there were few efforts to confront the strikers. The British Army also signalled, in no uncertain fashion, its reluctance to switch resources from its war against the IRA and its inability or unwillingness to run the power stations. Rees proved to be indecisive and baulked at ordering the Army to take action.

The government also surrendered the propaganda initiative to the strike leaders – after the strike, UWC leaders acknowledged their debt to the BBC in particular for co-operating with the UWC publicity machine. Power cuts eventually reduced electricity output to a mere 30 per cent of normal, closing virtually every major factory and imposing widespread and lengthy blackouts. Fine weather cushioned the hardship and, thanks to a generous gesture by the SDLP Minister for Health and Social Services, Paddy Devlin, the strikers were allowed to collect unemployment benefit.

More significantly, though, the strike gathered popular support among Protestants. Nearly everyone had underestimated the strength and solidarity of Protestant hostility towards Sunningdale – even those opposed to the strikers' methods showed no willingness to undermine them.

By the end of the first week the UWC had almost acquired the status of an alternative government. Its leaders co-ordinated the distribution of essential supplies to farmers and hospitals – some UWC leaders were jokingly called "ministers" – and middle-class Protestants, some of them civil servants in the government under siege, queued patiently at the UWC offices in Craig's Vanguard headquarters for travel passes and petrol coupons.

The strains inside the power-sharing Executive were by then beginning to show. The Unionist members were under intense pressure from their constituents to negotiate with the UWC while the SDLP contemplated resignation in protest at British inaction. Harold Wilson made sure of a UWC victory when, in a TV broadcast, he called Northern Ireland's Protestants "spongers", an insult which solidified their hostility to the British and their support for the strike.

On 28 May, thirteen days after the strike had started and as

Northern Ireland was about to face a complete power shutdown and the grim prospect of sewage seeping onto the streets, Faulkner and his ministers resigned and the Executive collapsed. The most concerted challenge to Westminster from Ulster Loyalism since 1912 had brought victory and it had been ordinary Protestants who had delivered it.

Paisley had not been around to see the UWC strike turn from uncertainty to success. On Friday 17 May, two days after the strike started, he flew to Toronto, Canada to attend a funeral. There were conflicting versions at the time of whose funeral it was. Some were told an aunt, others an old fundamentalist family friend. The reason for his sudden trip was never fully explained.

Paisley could not have chosen a more crucial time to leave Northern Ireland. The paramilitary bully boys were out on the streets intimidating Protestants into joining the strike and there was every chance that even if they didn't resist, the British would. The strike's success hung in the balance.

Within the UWC co-ordinating committee the interpretation of Paisley's absence was virtually unanimous. One of their members recalled: "His decision to go to Canada was noted by all and sundry and most of them believed he'd gone just in case the strike turned out to be a flop." Another commented: "We just accepted that it was Paisley doing his usual thing. When things got hot, Paisley got offside until he saw which way the land was lying."

Few were surprised either because Paisley, like the other two Unionist leaders, had been unsure of the strike's success long before the final decision to launch it was given the go-ahead. When the strike did start, the UUUC leaders didn't give it their approval until the third day. "Paisley thought that the strike wouldn't work and I think he, like the others, had bad memories from the 1973 strike," recalled a strike leader. "It wasn't that he was opposed to the strike in principle; he just had to be convinced that it was worthwhile. Paisley had his doubts, as did Craig and West."

Of the three political leaders, West was most nervous about the strike – "he stayed well clear of us until Paisley came back," commented one UWC member – while Craig was the most committed. "Craig said to us at the start, 'It's not going to work but I'll stay here and help you out.' To his credit, he did and he was the only politician to do so. He let us use Vanguard headquarters and his people helped as well," remembered a paramilitary leader.

Paisley was, in the eyes of the strike organisers, "bouncing about" somewhere between West and Craig but edging more towards West. Two days before the strike he and other UUUC politicians met the UWC and UDA at a hotel in Larne, County Antrim where they were told that the strike was going to go ahead as soon as the Assembly ratified Sunningdale. Paisley, according to the *Times* journalist Robert Fisk's account of the strike, "voiced his disapproval immediately, questioning once again whether the timing was right".

Some in the UWC suspected that Paisley had more pragmatic reasons for questioning the strike tactic. The UWC and the UDA were both close to Craig's Vanguard party and had co-operated closely in the past. The link was symbolised by Glen Barr, the chairman of the co-ordinating committee, who was both a member of the UDA and a Vanguard Assembly member for Derry. If successful, the strike would probably benefit Craig most.

That would hold whichever way the strike turned out, as one of the more astute UWC leaders appreciated:

> Paisley, at that time, was just switching off from integration and didn't know where he was going. The strike would though kill off integration as an option because it was more than just opposition to Sunningdale, it was a challenge to Westminster's authority. Craig, on the other hand, was in a different position. Vanguard's policies came close to demanding dominion status and if the worst came to the worst and Britain washed its hands of Northern Ireland, he would see no dilemma in that. But if the strike was successful, then Craig's strong stand from the beginning would be to his benefit.

When Paisley returned from Canada at around the end of the first week of the strike his prevarication had gone. "From the distance of Canada he could perceive that something massive was taking place, that the strike was biting, and when he came back, I have to admit, he came in with his batteries charged," recalled a UWC leader.

From then on Paisley attended every meeting of the UWC coordinating committee and was given the task of "stomping the country", whipping up support at Loyalist rallies and meetings. This followed a UWC decision to mobilise rural areas behind greater Belfast, which until then had taken the brunt of the strike.

He is credited in particular with mobilising the farmers and making a dynamic impact in the media – "He really sold the strike to the grassroots and to the world's press", commented the same UWC leader. He also drafted key DUP personnel into the strike headquarters – up to then the DUP, like the Official Unionists, had been noticeably absent – and one of them, Peter Robinson, made a vital contribution.

"Paisley's view on communicating the strike was that it had to be communicated right on down the line to the grassroots," a strike leader remembered. Robinson was given the task of compiling the co-ordinating committee's daily brief – outlining strike plans, dispensation for essential services, plans for the distribution of petrol, feedstuffs and so on – copying it and sending thousands of copies down to the people on the ground. "That whole communication system was down to Robinson," said the same leader.

Paisley's relations with the paramilitaries on the co-ordinating committee were acrimonious, however. Since the 1969 bombings Paisley had steered well clear of any paramilitary associations and groups like the UDA suspected he was resentful of their links with Craig. According to one strike leader, the paramilitaries had no love for him either: "They didn't like his fundamentalist views and were pretty contemptuous because of his Canadian trip. They had nicknames for him in those days like 'God' and 'Papa Doc'."

The hostility, according to one account, showed when Paisley returned from Canada. By that stage UWC morning meetings were so busy that the chairman, Barr, had ordered two tough UDA men to stand guard at the door to prevent interruptions:

. . . I remember very distinctly looking out the window and seeing Paisley arrive at about 9.30 but he never appeared in the room. We went out for a cup of tea at about 11 and when I came back there was Paisley sitting in Barr's chair, the chairman's chair. Barr said, "Ian, that's my chair, would you move round a bit?" "No," he says, "I'm just disgusted. I came here to lend my support and I couldn't get in." So Barr said "What do you mean?" "Those two big fellas outside wouldn't let me in." Apparently they'd stopped him and he'd said, "Do you know who I am? I'm going into this office." But they wouldn't budge. He was extremely annoyed, I can tell you. Anyway Barr insisted that he get his chair back, he was the chairman and Paisley would have to move. "Well, I've got a sore back, my back's not well," said Paisley. So Barr said, "I'll tell you what we'll do. You take my chair and move to the end of the table. You're sitting in the chairman's place. You know the position, you're not as big a man here as you are outside." So reluctantly he took the chair and moved.

There were more jibes later:

We'd knocked off all the public transport and there were no buses moving at all but Paisley wanted special dispensation for his buses on Wednesday nights which took people from behind the City Hall to the Martyrs' Memorial. Andy Tyrie said to him jokingly that he'd let him have the buses if Paisley would let Andy lift the collection.

Then the boys from the airport approached us and said they wanted to join the strike and shut the planes down. Paisley raised such a furore that day: "We've got to get to Westminster to present the case on behalf of our people and that's the way we travel." So Tommy Lyttle looked at him and said: "It's not true then?" Paisley says, "What do you mean?" and Tommy replies, "You can't walk on water." Thirty seconds later Paisley joined in the laughter.

The chair incident convinced Barr that Paisley would try to take control of UWC meetings and the two became intense rivals. Relations reached a low point when Barr ordered the UWC switchboard to stop any outgoing calls made by Paisley or West, who started attending meetings when Paisley returned from Canada.

We discovered that decisions we were taking in the morning, particularly about releasing feedstuffs to the farmers, were being credited to Paisley and West. They were running out of meetings and phoning up people in their constituencies and telling them: "I've got you that load of feed now." They were trying to give the impression that they were running the committee. So Barr told them they weren't allowed to use the phones until all the regional commanders had been told what the committee had decided.

Paisley's most significant contribution inside the co-ordinating committee came at the end when the Executive collapsed. The UWC and many rank-and-file paramilitaries wanted the strike to continue, either to press on for the demand for new elections or to take advantage of their power by establishing a provisional government. Tyrie and some other paramilitary leaders were under considerable pressure from their members but realised that the strike was a lost cause. Yet it was left to Paisley to argue successfully that Protestant workers were already voting with their feet to end the strike. Paisley proposed the motion to call off the strike and Tyrie seconded it.

Former DUP colleagues like Clifford Smyth now reckon that Paisley was shocked by the UWC's success and, like other Unionists, was worried that, by mobilising working-class Loyalist strength, the UWC might have developed into a serious threat to established politicians.

That threat never materialised and the politicians survived. But of the three UUUC leaders, Paisley probably came out ahead. During the strike his media profile was much higher than either Craig's or West's. At the end, as one paramilitary leader bitterly noted, "He even managed to push us into the background at the Stormont victory rally." His initial caution was noticed only by the strike leaders. To the mass of Loyalists he was once more the familiar forthright Protestant leader, his brief liaison with moderation forgotten. Any residual doubts about his Loyalist credentials were gone.

Paisley's return to the first line of Loyalist leadership had been noted with mounting concern by an old discarded ally from the 1960s, Major Bunting. About a week after the strike ended, he turned up at the UWC offices, determined to warn them against further involvement with Paisley. The UWC was in conference but he insisted that he speak to somebody important. He was shown into an adjoining room and asked to wait. A UWC member took up the story:

> We had our meeting and then three of us went to speak to him. There he was sitting, a shell of a man, nervous and almost demented. He explained who he was and begged us, quite literally begged us, to make sure that under no circumstances would we allow Ian Paisley to benefit from the strike.

> He was totally obsessed and was quite prepared to damn Paisley with stories of what had happened to him – how he had jeopardised his health and career for Paisley, how he had been made to look ridiculous in public and how, when the activities he'd embraced on Paisley's behalf had brought him into conflict

with the authorities, he'd been dropped and left high and dry. We sympathised but we had to explain that there wasn't anything we could do. What happened to Ian Paisley was out of our hands.

◄○►

The 1974 UWC strike not only rehabilitated Ian Paisley, it convinced him that the strike tactic could be used again to advance his own and the Loyalist cause. Three years after the fall of Sunningdale, that conviction led him into the greatest political miscalculation of his career and brought him to the verge of quitting politics altogether.

The Loyalist strike of 1977 – "Paisley's strike", as the public saw it – was an ignominious failure which many thought would help to strengthen Paisley's moderate Official Unionist rivals and thus pave the way for a political settlement between Nationalists and Unionists. The strike in fact had the opposite effect. Although an operational disaster, the strike touched a Protestant nerve, an achievement that was given eloquent expression by substantial DUP gains in the local council elections which immediately followed it.

The gains made by Paisley's DUP in that election were all at the expense of the Official Unionists. They killed off any hope of moderation from that quarter and renewed Paisley's faith in his political instincts. But they also destroyed his last Loyalist political rival – the remnants of Bill Craig's once powerful Vanguard party. From then on Unionist politics would be dominated by a titanic struggle between the DUP and the Official Unionists – the only survivors from a decade of Protestant political turbulence and fractures.

In 1977, Paisley snatched survival from impending obliteration and it was ruthlessness which did it – not his this time, but that of his able and devoted lieutenant, Peter Robinson. As Paisley, for the first time in his career, reeled directionless in the face of defeat, Robinson took charge and rescued him and his party.

A political vacuum and a cynical change in British security policy provided the backcloth to the 1977 strike. On the political front, the realignment of what remained of Bill Craig's Vanguard into the United Ulster Unionist Movement (UUUM), led by Ernie Baird, a right-wing East Belfast Presbyterian and the prosperous owner of a chain of chemist shops, went hand-in-hand with the reimposition of Direct Rule by the British. Policy-makers in London and Belfast also began refocusing on the war against the Provisional IRA. The IRA was lured into a *faux* ceasefire in 1975, and the deliberately protracted and unsuccessful contacts with British intelligence that followed gave the government sufficient breathing space for the crafting of an ingenious new security policy.

It had many names – "Ulsterisation", "Normalisation", "Criminalisation", "the primacy of the police" and "the Castlereagh conveyor belt" among them. What it amounted to was this. Internment and all its trappings would be phased out and all terrorist-type cases would be dealt with by the courts. The Long Kesh internment complex would be replaced by a modern prison and its H Block-shaped wings and blocks renamed the Maze prison. Special Category status – effectively prisoner-of-war status – granted to IRA and Loyalist prisoners would also be phased out. All prisoners would be treated like ordinary criminals, with no special privileges.

The most significant change, though, was in the field. The British Army's leading role in the struggle against the IRA would be reduced and their duties would be gradually taken over by local security forces: the 90 per cent Protestant RUC and the 98 per cent Protestant Ulster Defence Regiment.

This new security policy would have long lasting effects. Catholic criticism of RUC interrogation methods and of the judiciary intensified but in the jails the effort to criminalise prisoners was resisted by Republicans, at first by refusing to wear prison uniform but eventually by a hunger strike that cost the lives of ten republican inmates and 61 civilians and security personnel outside. It also gave the IRA's political wing, Sinn Féin, a springboard to mount a successful entry into electoral politics.

The first and most immediate effect of the new British security policy, however, was felt by the Protestant community. As the RUC and the UDR took over more and more of the British Army's role, so the IRA turned its guns increasingly on them.

In the early years of the "Troubles", from 1970 to 1974, the British Army had borne the brunt of IRA attacks – deaths of British soldiers accounted for nearly 20 per cent of the 1,380 death toll during that period. "Ulsterisation" of security meant that it was increasingly UDR and RUC men, the vast majority of them Protestants, who were dying in their place. In 1976, the first year of "Ulsterisation", they suffered 42 deaths, a fatality rate four times greater than the British Army, the worst year for these local forces since the murderous slaughter of 1972, and nearly all the dead were Protestants. The British had reduced the cost of staying in Northern Ireland and released battalions to serve in NATO but at considerable cost in Northern Ireland.

The immediate effect was to intensify Protestant demands for tougher security measures, particularly in rural and Border areas where most of the killings had taken place. In the long term it meant that sectarian antagonisms would be heightened throughout the whole community – Loyalist allegations of an IRA campaign of "genocide" dated from this period. The cynicism of the British move was noted by the Orange Order in a wide-ranging review of British policy in early 1977: "the 'Ulsterisation' of the security battle represents nothing more than the 'Ulsterisation' of the victims."

The political vacuum and the new emphasis on security were given physical shape by Merlyn Rees's replacement as Northern Ireland Secretary in August 1976. The new man was Roy Mason, a blunt, pipe-smoking former coalminer from Barnsley in Yorkshire. He came to Northern Ireland, much to the dismay of Nationalists, with a name for being an "Army man", a reputation earned during a spell in the Ministry of Defence. It wasn't long before he signalled his intentions. In his first speech he spoke of the IRA "reeling" under the weight of security pressure. A few months later he candidly told the political parties that he had no plans for a political initiative unless they had.

Mason was popular with the Official Unionists. They liked his commitment to the war against the IRA and they were happy with his reluctance to launch political experiments. Direct Rule was preferable to the uncharted waters of protest and the uncomfortable prospect of alliances with paramilitants and Paisleyites which would inevitably follow another British attempt at partnership government.

Mason also secured extra financial help for Northern Ireland from the Labour cabinet and at Westminster Harold Wilson's successor, James Callaghan, negotiated a deal with the Official Unionist parliamentary leader, James Molyneaux, under which support for his minority government would be exchanged for extra House of Commons seats – most of which would inevitably go to the Official Unionists. In the respectable, cautious, middle-class eyes of Official Unionists, the Union was more secure, Northern Ireland more prosperous and the IRA more resolutely pursued than at any time since the "Troubles" started.

268

To Loyalists of Paisley's ilk, for whom a state of permanent insecurity was part of the natural order, the relative tranquillity of the Mason era was, by sharp contrast, deeply unsettling. It was this, as much as the rising death toll of RUC and UDR men, which led to the 1977 strike. As one of its leaders put it: "Things were slipping and flagging and people were getting into the way of Direct Rule. We thought we'd give it a wee bit of a jab."

Loyalist political dislocation was shown in various ways. The UDA and Loyalists like John McKeague began espousing the idea of Ulster independence. They were spurred in this direction by the belief, shared by Loyalist politicians like Ernie Baird, that Britain was secretly withdrawing. The NIO's talks with the IRA had planted this seed and it was nourished when decisions were made in 1976 to close factories like Rolls-Royce in East Belfast and the Royal Navy's refitting yard in Belfast. The pro-independence lobby was not confined to Loyalists – some in the SDLP flirted with it, as did elements in the IRA.

The Loyalist mainstream, however, including Paisley, stayed with the traditional and familiar demand to have the old majority-rule Stormont parliament returned. The only problem was that there was no chance that any British government would grant it.

Many in the Official Unionist Party appeared to give only token support to that demand while others were, under Enoch Powell's influence, beginning a cautious move towards integration. Loyalists, however, wanted action. On the urging of Baird, a Loyalist Action Council, later given the unwieldy title of the United Unionist Action Council (UUAC), technically a sub-committee of the UUUC, was set up to agitate for devolution and better security. The Official Unionists quickly made their disapproval of the Action Council known.

The Action Council soon acquired a semi-paramilitary wing. Loyalists in Counties Tyrone and Armagh, many of them former "B" Specials, set up an organisation called the Ulster Service Corps (USC). In May, following a declaration from Paisley and Baird that they were not prepared "to sit idly by and watch our province being destroyed" by the IRA, the USC announced plans to mount overt and covert patrols, some armed with legal weapons. Their action was also a calculated defiance of the authorities, a challenge to the State's monopoly of security powers.

That autumn, as local security force deaths multiplied, the lobby for more direct action intensified. The USC staged more roadblocks and in

September the authorities moved against them. Five USC men from County Armagh were arrested – one of them was Robert Murdock, the Portadown Free Presbyterian who in 1966 and 1969 had faced UVF explosives charges. The Action Council stuck up posters in Loyalist areas which read: "How long before you join the Direct Rule death toll?" In November, Paisley told MPs at Westminster that he had been out on patrol with the USC in Portadown. The patrols were necessary, he said, "because of the continuing apparent lack of will on behalf of our Government to defeat the terrorists in our midst".

The Action Council, which included the DUP, Baird's party, the UWC, the Apprentice Boys of Derry, the Royal Black Preceptory and the Independent Orange Order began in October and November to seriously discuss plans for a repeat of the 1974 strike. The aims this time were to be radically different. In 1974 the goal was to bring down Sunningdale; this time the strike's objectives were to bring back a majority-rule Stormont and to force the British to introduce a new tougher security policy.

Paisley for one was convinced that the tactic could work again. Significantly the Official Unionist leader, Harry West, and the Orange Order chief, Martin Smyth, disagreed. They both attended some early Action Council meetings but pulled out as the strike plans were laid, leaving Paisley isolated. The Action Council included some of the paramilitary groups involved in the 1974 strike – the UDA, the Orange Volunteers and Down Orange Welfare – but the absence of the Official Unionists badly weakened it.

These moves were paralleled by signs of increased militancy within Paisley's DUP. According to Clifford Smyth, who was then secretary of the UUUC, Peter Robinson approached him in June 1976 with the suggestion that the party should set up a paramilitary wing. According to a senior UDA figure, his organisation was also approached later that year by a leading DUP member with a request for assistance in setting up the force – in particular the DUP man wanted drawings of home-made rocket launchers. The ideas came to naught and the DUP, and Paisley in particular, was forced to go to the UDA, still the largest paramilitary group, to ask for help.

Relations between the three UUUC leaders and the paramilitaries had deteriorated since the 1974 strike. The paramilitaries wanted their crucial role in the strike officially recognised by being given a seat on the UUUC executive but the politicians refused, citing the illegality of some groups. Paramilitary resentment at being dropped after they had outlived their usefulness boiled over on occasions. During one meeting of UUUC politicians in Craig's Vanguard headquarters in 1975, two armed UDA leaders from North Belfast burst in, threatening to shoot them. Fortunately for the politicians, a senior UUUC figure managed to calm them down.

Paisley played a prominent role in negotiations with paramilitaries during this period. One senior paramilitant recalled an important and secret meeting in the Martyrs' Memorial between Paisley and a group of paramilitary leaders which included two representatives of the illegal UVF – Billy Mitchell and Ken Gibson, both of whom, ironically, were former Free Presbyterians. At the meeting, according to this man, "Paisley gave an undertaking that he would try to get us recognised within the UUUC".

When a few weeks later the UUUC decided to exclude both the UWC and the paramilitaries from membership, the paramilitaries, in particular the UVF, turned against Paisley. "Shortly after that all the groups held a conference to work out our strategy for independence and one group under Mitchell had the job of looking at the military implications. I remember some of them talking about bumping Paisley off because of the way we had been treated."

Paisley's relations with the UDA leader Andy Tyrie had also soured. The UDA had initially supported Craig's Voluntary Coalition proposal and strongly criticised Paisley and West for their opposition. Paisley replied to the criticism in swingeing terms:

The brazen effrontery and confounded cheek of Mr Tyrie baffles description. He is a man who leads an organisation whose members in the past months have been tried in the courts and have been pleaded guilty or have been found guilty of the most diabolical of crimes.

They have murdered Protestants as well as Roman Catholics in the most sadistic and inhuman ways and have sought to intimidate decent people who seek to carry out their business in a proper manner.

Stung by his attack, the UDA considered releasing a dossier to the press containing details of "talks Mr Paisley has had with Loyalist paramilitary groups and also the use of Loyalist funds", but it stayed its hand.

During 1976, as the plans for strike action hardened, Paisley was forced to eat humble pie and apologise to Tyrie. Unable to create its own paramilitary wing, the DUP needed the UDA's skills in intimidating "decent people who seek to carry out their business in a proper manner" to enforce the strike. Lengthy talks took place between Tyrie and Paisley and Tyrie extracted a price for the UDA's co-operation. "We deliberately put Paisley and Baird into the front line; it wasn't going to be another case of the UDA carrying the whole can," recalled a UDA member.

During the last half of 1976 and the spring of 1977 – as the strike plans took firmer shape – Paisley made the first of several mistakes. He alienated the Official Unionists and the Orange Order. Their support for a strike would have made a crucial difference but since they had both already signalled an unwillingness to be involved, Paisley should have ensured that they stayed on the sidelines – but he didn't. In June 1976 he leaked details of secret meetings between the Orange leader, Martin Smyth, and the SDLP. As a result, Smyth, whose intense dislike for Paisley dated back to the 1950s, was heckled during Orange demonstrations in July – it was hardly calculated to make him sympathetic to Paisley's plans.

In April 1977, only three weeks away from the start of the strike, Paisley used the DUP conference to launch a vitriolic attack on a whole litany of past Official Unionist traitors from O'Neill to Craig. They included members of Harry West's party, who had been tempted during the Convention, he claimed, to make a deal with the SDLP by the bait of "a Government car, a Ministerial office, and so many thousands a year". When the strike started, the active opposition of both the Orange Order and the OUP was a significant factor in its failure.

As 1976 turned into 1977, a decision in principle to launch the strike had been taken – Paisley signalled it by announcing that he was thinking of boycotting Westminster in protest at British security failures. By that stage not only had the UDA committed itself to the strike but the Ulster Workers Council, the people who had organised factory closures and the critical pulling of the plugs in the power stations in 1974, were on board.

The UWC leadership had changed in the intervening years. Some leaders had gone "moderate" and had been sacked while others just drifted away. Loyalist paramilitary leaders suspected that Paisley had had a hand in most of the changes and was trying to take over the UWC. The two most important 1974 veterans left were Jim Smyth, the eloquent former Rolls-Royce shop steward, and Billy Kelly, the small, shy, bespectacled union convenor in one of the small Belfast power stations who, in 1974, had won over the power workers in the key Ballylumford power station. That alone had ensured the strike's success.

Kelly was a strong Paisley supporter and a passionate believer in British-Israelism, a bizarre claim that the Protestants of Northern Ireland were the descendants of the lost tribe of Israel. After the 1977 strike he joined the Free Presbyterian Church in Omagh, County Tyrone, and was involved in a bitter split there when the minister opposed the growing influence of Kelly's élitist and extreme British-Israeli supporters. During the run-up to the 1977 strike, he assured the Action Council that he had talked to the Ballylumford power workers and had secured their support for industrial action.

The second and most important mistake made by Paisley and the strike leaders was to believe him. Kelly, in fact, had barely consulted the Ballylumford workers – when the strike started their resentment over this denied Paisley and the Action Council the support of the one group of workers who could have made the strike a success.

When the Action Council discovered that Kelly had misled them and that the promised co-operation of other key sectors, like the petrol tanker drivers, was also non-existent, it was too late to stop.

The bearer of the bad news was Jim Smyth, who had doubted Kelly's assurances from the start and had decided to check up for himself. "Smyth discovered that Kelly's key man at Ballylumford turned out to be the man who worked at the gate. Smyth met him with Kelly and asked him about the workers' support and he was saying things like, 'I haven't asked so-and-so because I don't work on the same shift but I hope to see him before the strike.' This was only four weeks before it was due to start and none of the 1974 people had been talked to. Smyth couldn't believe it," recalled an Action Council member.

The UDA and the other paramilitaries didn't believe Smyth and neither, to begin with, did Paisley. Smyth also saw Baird and spent six hours trying to talk him out of the strike. According to an Action Council member, Baird was unmoved: "He said, 'No, we're too committed – we've said too much in statements and have committed our people.'"

A week before the strike, Smyth again checked around Ballylumford, the Coolkeeragh power station, the Harland and Wolff shipyard and Shorts aircraft factory and discovered that most of their workers were either opposed to the strike or were deeply confused.

"They just couldn't see how a strike would achieve the aims we were after," said one strike organiser.

The UDA insisted that their own intelligence indicated that there was support for the strike and they urged that it should go ahead – but in reality the organisation was divided, with some key areas like West Belfast opposed to the strike. Paisley was, however, "shaken" by the news. "He kept insisting that we have support in the grassroots, our people expect us to do something and so do the relatives of the security forces. He knew there was a risk that, if he lost, the DUP would be pilloried, but if he won, he knew that the Official Unionists would lose badly," remembered one Action Council member.

Paisley's doubts did, though, surface at the Action Council meeting which decided to launch the strike, held in the DUP's Ava Avenue headquarters in South Belfast on 23 April. He voted against the strike and only one other significant group, the Belfast UWC, supported him. Everyone else, including the UWC's rural members, voted for it. There were also differences about the strike demands. Paisley was alone in advocating that the demand for majority rule should not be included, while everyone else wanted tougher security to head the list of demands.

The trigger for the strike came on 19 April when the five Portadown Ulster Service Corps members arrested the previous September appeared in court charged with operating illegal roadblocks. The centre of Portadown was brought to a standstill by hundreds of Loyalists as Paisley, flanked by Baird and Tyrie, told them they were beginning a campaign that would lead to the restoration of Stormont, the return of security to local hands and the "extermination" of the IRA.

On 26 April, the Action Council delivered an ultimatum to Roy Mason. He had seven days in which to show a new determination to defeat the IRA and willingness to implement the Convention report. Otherwise there would be an indefinite strike. The Official Unionists retorted with an appeal to Protestants to ignore the strike and to go on working normally.

As the Action Council well knew, Mason would never grant their demands. So at midnight on Monday 2 May, with the Official Unionists and Orange Order actively hostile, the Action Council itself divided on major issues, the key power workers unconsulted and workers in major Belfast factories confused or in outright opposition, Paisley and his Loyalist allies began the second major challenge to Westminster's authority in three years.

There were other important differences between this strike and 1974. Roy Mason's decisiveness was one. Before the strike started he promised firm action against the strikers, ruled out the possibility of negotiating with them and committed the British Army to underpinning essential services. An extra 1,200 troops were flown in on the eve of the strike. Mason also ensured that government policy was consistent and well-informed throughout. A three-man committee, composed of the NIO's Permanent Secretary, Sir Brian Cubbon, the NIO's Chief Information Officer, David Gilliland, and a member of the British Security Services, was set up to advise him. It met every morning at 8 a.m. to review overnight events and that day's policy options, and met Mason at 9 a.m. when final decisions were taken. Any Protestants who imagined they might be dealing with another Merlyn Rees were quickly disabused. The British had also learned important lessons from their 1974 mistakes. One of these was on the crucial question of propaganda and public relations, which in 1974 had been virtually surrendered to the UWC. During the 1977 strike, in contrast, the NIO's press office operated 24 hours a day, pumping out hourly statements from 5 a.m. onwards and holding frequent Ministerial press conferences to disseminate the government's view. Nor was there any repeat of Harold Wilson's disastrous "spongers" jibe. The unemployment problem, which had worsened considerably since 1974, was skilfully exploited. Mason and his Ministers constantly emphasised the threat to inward investment posed by the strike, and other groups, the trade unions, business organisations and some Protestant churches echoed it. The British thus had a PR edge on the strikers throughout the protest and this became particularly evident in disputes with the Action Council over the numbers of people at work.

Paisley's high media profile, which had been his great asset in 1974, inflicted a mortal wound on the Action Council. He dominated its press conferences and pushed all the other participants into the background. On the eve of the strike, in an extraordinarily careless and completely uncharacteristic move, he also staked his political career on the strike's success, declaring: "I am only remaining in public life to see the thing through, and if it fails then my voice will no longer be heard."

The combined effect was to personalise the strike, making it appear as "Paisley's strike". In contrast, the 1974 strike had been successful partly because it was viewed as a united and general Protestant protest dominated by no single person. Paisley's dominance succeeded only in highlighting Official Unionist and Orange opposition. This discouraged support from Protestants who might have been sympathetic to the strike's aims but were loath to identify so closely with a strike leader who had built his career by attacking and dividing Protestant institutions. Paisley was incapable by himself of uniting and leading all the disparate sections of Unionism.

On 3 May, the first day of the strike, it became clear that intimidation would be the organisers' principal weapon. Gangs of up to 100 UDA men roamed the streets "persuading" factories and shops to close. Shipyard workers, who had voted against the strike at a mass meeting, were told their cars would be burned if they stayed at work, and a bomb damaged the Bangor-to-Belfast railway line, the main commuter line from East Belfast and the dormitory suburbs.

The next day there was more of the same. The UDA was again out on the streets and the RUC reported 400 complaints of intimidation in Belfast. The UDA was, however, anxious to avoid direct confrontation with the police or Army and no roadblocks were set up. Nevertheless the strike appeared to be biting. A lot of large factories in Belfast closed and commercial life in towns like Ballymena, Coleraine, Lurgan and Portadown came to a standstill. The strikers had also scored a major achievement when the important cross-channel port of Larne closed down.

The turning point in the strike came early in the morning of the third day, Wednesday 4 May, outside the UDA's headquarters on the Newtownards Road in East Belfast when the paramilitaries, frustrated at their lack of success, erected their first road block to prevent shipyard workers from getting into work. There at 8 a.m., gangs of UDA men clashed for an hour with the RUC's anti-riot, Special Patrol Group in what appeared to be a confrontation deliberately engineered by the authorities. The riot started when the police moved in to remove a makeshift barricade constructed of beer barrels and ended with the successful clearing of the road of both rioters and obstructions. During the riot the UDA Commander, Andy Tyrie, appeared on the scene shouting angrily at the police and threatening "aggravation" everywhere.

He had, as he later admitted, "fallen into the trap" of confronting the very security forces whose safety the strike was aiming to improve. Furthermore, the RUC had signalled right on the UDA's doorstep its determination to deal firmly with Loyalist roadblocks, one of the most effective weapons of the 1974 strike. By the end of the strike they had taken down a further 700.

Political pressure on the Action Council increased after that. Harry West called for an end to the strike but protected his Loyalist flanks with a parallel demand for better security. Craig also joined in, calling the strike a "debacle". His Vanguard party had summed up Loyalist confusion over the strike tactic with a statement on its eve: "A strike can only bring something down – like the Assembly in 1974 – it cannot build anything up."

Intimidation, though, increased, much to Paisley's embarrassment. In some areas Loyalists stoned police land rovers and in North Belfast a police station was bombed. By Thursday, the RUC had logged 1,000 complaints of intimidation.

Confronted with the allegations and his own association with bully boy tactics and violence, Paisley hopped between bald denials, disassociation and ingenious and extravagant counter-allegations. On the first day of the strike he said: "Whatever happens out there is no responsibility of mine. If the British Army and Mr Mason bring about circumstances in which this [intimidation] happens, that is their business."

On the second day he accused the authorities of intimidating the strikers and maintained, to the astonishment of observers, that if the strikers were engaged in intimidation, then that was "an indictment of the RUC", which had utterly failed in its duty. When Mason pointed out that all the Westminster parties had condemned intimidation, Paisley lost his temper: "When I consider the drunkenness, lewdness, immorality and filthy language of many of its [the House of Commons] members, I care absolutely nothing for their opinions." In contrast, Paisley condemned the UDA after the Newtownards Road riot, promised it would never happen again and pledged an end to roadblocks.

Paisley's attitude towards intimidation irritated UDA leaders. They felt that he was distancing himself from it in public while inside the privacy of the Action Council's meetings his DUP members had sanctioned its use.

By the fifth day, Friday 6 May, it was clear that the strike was fast losing ground. More and more people were getting into work, buses and trains were operating normally, petrol was freely available and the RUC was dealing firmly with roadblocks. All this was possible because the 450 workers at Ballylumford, where two-thirds of Northern Ireland's electricity is generated, had not joined the strike. By refusing to join, the power workers had ensured sufficient power for industry and had forced the organisers to rely more and more on physical intimidation. Billy Kelly had promised that electricity output would be reduced to 30 per cent of normal within three days – not only had that failed to materialise but Kelly himself took ill and was hospitalised two days after the strike started.

At Ballylumford, Paisley was outmanoeuvred by old-fashioned trade union wheeling and dealing. One sparsely attended meeting during the first two days had voted for the strike but when it was clear that a majority of the other workers would still be opposed, a delegation, led by some shop stewards, decided to meet Mason and relay the results back to a mass meeting which would take the final decision.

On Thursday 5 May, they travelled up to Stormont Castle where Mason unveiled a security package which he had been working on before the strike started. The RUC's strength would be increased to 6,500 and they would have modern weapons and vehicles, he said. The full-time UDR complement would also be raised to 1,800; there would be ten new RUC Divisional Mobile Support Units (DMSUs) – an updated version of the Special Patrol Groups – a review of anti-terrorist laws with a view to increasing prison sentences and a greater emphasis on SAS covert operations by the British Army. Mason signed a statement to that effect in the presence of the delegation.

It did the trick. The next day, much to Paisley's chagrin, the Ballylumford workers voted against joining the strike by nearly a three-to-two majority. Paisley tried to put a brave face on the reversal by claiming that the mass meeting at Ballylumford had been unrepresentative of the key electricity workers who, he maintained, were in favour of the strike. The managing director, senior executives and canteen staff had all been included in the vote, he said. He went on to maintain that the strike had in fact been a success, pointing to Mason's security package as evidence, and he accused the media of "lying propaganda" in their claims that industry and commerce were working normally.

More ominously, he said that the people of Larne were "very sore" with the power workers. Privately, the Action Council let it be known that intimidation of the Ballylumford workforce would be stepped up.

Defeat now stared Paisley in the face. On the Saturday he decided to have one more try at talking the power workers round. If that failed, it looked as if his political career was over. He drove down to Larne with Baird and a delegation from the Action Council to speak to the workers for the last time.

It was a grim, depressing journey full of foreboding for Paisley. One of those with him recalled:

> On the way down, and I can remember it clearly, he was at a crisis point and he and everyone else knew it. "I'm finished if this doesn't work," he said, and then he started to tell us that he didn't need to be in politics and that he wanted to spend more time in his church work. As we arrived he confided to me that he felt he was on his last legs and had completely lost the will to win. He was at the lowest ebb I've ever seen him.

Paisley's forebodings were well-founded. The workers listened politely and then gave him an ultimatum – full power or no power at all. They would only come out en bloc – not in support of the strike but because of intimidation and fears of violence – and furthermore it would have to be a total walk-out which would result in a complete blackout. There would be no power for essential services; hospitals, old people's homes and the like would be without any heat or electricity and, inevitably, there would be deaths.

Paisley backed down and to all intents and purposes the strike was over. In the middle of the next week he and Baird were arrested at a roadblock in Ballymena in a last desperate attempt to boost the strike by their martyrdom but whatever slim chance of success that had was undermined by the paramilitaries.

Their reaction to Paisley caving into the Ballylumford ultimatum was furious. The UDA said it would have called the power workers' bluff and lived with the consequences. Paisley got the blame: "The rank and file didn't like it at all. We were being led by a man with no balls and from then he was the Grand Old Duke of York to us," recalled one UDA member.

In desperation the paramilitaries intensified the violence and intimidation the following week, with disastrous, self-mutilating results. On 10 May, the UVF shot dead a Protestant busman in North Belfast and the UDR son of one of the strike leaders was killed when a massive bomb destroyed a petrol station in the same area. Another man was killed as he assembled a fire bomb. Intimidation had failed to stop Ballylumford, fewer and fewer businesses were affected and by this stage even Larne was operating normally.

On 12 May, after a brief meeting of the Action Council, the strike was called off "to give Mr Mason the opportunity to turn the additional security forces onto the IRA". Paisley moved fast and ingeniously to limit the damage. He withdrew his promise to leave politics, he announced, on the pretext that the strike had been a success in his North Antrim constituency. He also claimed a wider victory, maintaining that Mason's security package would not have materialised without the strike.

The strike's failure was, however, widely seen as a victory for Paisley's rivals in the Official Unionist Party. That was expected to be reflected in the local council elections on 18 May, days after the end of the strike. Ironically the strike date had been chosen with the council elections in mind; but instead of having their triumph confirmed at the polls, the DUP was now apparently facing the prospect of a severe bruising.

The results startled everyone. The DUP more than doubled its total of councillors to 74, won outright control of its first council, Ballymena, and gained seats in all the 23 councils contested by the party. The Official Unionists lost 35 seats, nearly all to the DUP, while Baird's party was all but obliterated. The results were seen as a vindication of the strike and evidence of support for Paisley's forthrightness. More significantly, the election had left only two Unionist parties to contend for the Protestant vote. The stage was set for the professionalisation of the DUP in preparation for the destruction of the Official Unionists. The DUP had been hauled back from the edge of defeat.

The truth was that the DUP had been saved by Paisley's young deputy, Peter Robinson. On 8 May, the day after the ultimatum from the Ballylumford workers, he and Jim Smyth met to discuss the next step. "Smyth told him the strike was all but finished and that the DUP should try to salvage what they could," recalled a strike leader. "Robinson agreed and together with some DUP councillors they decided to use the second week of the strike for the election by switching all their energies to the council campaign and to attack the Official Unionists for undermining the strike. Robinson went to see Paisley and he was so grateful for any ideas by this stage that he immediately agreed."

The DUP took that decision unilaterally, leaving their allies, particularly Baird's party, to fend for themselves. The destruction of Baird's party had been in senior DUP minds long before the strike, as Clifford Smyth, purged from the party in late 1976, could testify: "I remember walking in to headquarters one day and there they were talking about how Ernie Baird's people would be destroyed." The strike headquarters were abandoned by all but the UWC, a few of Baird's people and the odd paramilitary. Apart from an occasional appearance by Paisley, the DUP had discarded the strike for the hustings.

During the second week, Robinson "went out with a great deal of guts on the basis that there were two ways to go – down the plughole or out campaigning. And it worked. Paisley was completely rudderless and Robinson rescued him," said an Action Council leader.

Baird's party was not the only casualty. The UDA was also severely damaged by the strike's failure. In the months following the strike the RUC took advantage of its new initiative and cut swathes into UDA membership by arresting and charging many of its most active middle-level leaders. Morale dipped badly and for the next four years the UDA was hard-pressed keeping its organisation intact. Of the principal participants in the 1977 strike, only the DUP, by ruthless concentration on its self-interest, had prospered.

◄O►

If there was one thing Margaret Thatcher would not tolerate, it was being threatened. If there was one thing Ian Paisley cannot stand, it is being contradicted. In December 1980, just six days before Christmas, the British Prime Minister received the DUP leader in her office at the House of Commons to discuss her summit meeting with the Taoiseach, Charles Haughey, in Dublin 11 days before. Northern Ireland Secretary Humphrey Atkins had told Thatcher that if Paisley appeared in a collar and tie he would probably behave reasonably, but if he had donned his dog collar, he would bang the table and shout at her.

On that occasion Paisley was wearing a tie, but it was the dog collar man who was doing the talking. He was not interested in an exchange of views. He read her a prepared statement in a loud and hectoring voice and accused her of having given Dublin a "direct involvement" in Northern Ireland's affairs through her joint pledge with Haughey to consider "the totality of relationships in these islands". He alleged that the "joint studies" of Anglo-Irish and cross-border matters of common interest would inevitably threaten the Union. He quoted Lord Carson, threatening that if the British government created "a situation that it is impossible for men in Ulster to bear", then the responsibility for any resulting confrontation would be the government's.

Thatcher was coldly furious. She interrupted him continuously with the retort: "I stand by the guarantee." As Paisley's tirade climaxed, she became angrier. She repeated again and again, hitting the side of her chair, "I stand by the guarantee." She said very little else. Colleagues said she was repelled by his tone, unconvinced by his arguments. That meeting was to form her opinion of the DUP leader in all future dealings with him. He was a bully, and as a bully herself, she took a deep dislike to him.

For Paisley it was the end of a year of conciliatory chats over cups of tea with Humphrey Atkins. It was time to launch another campaign to whip up the fears of the North's Protestants into a menacing street-marching fever that would, he hoped, scare the British out of their dealings with Dublin. Such a campaign would serve the added purpose of throwing his Official Unionist rivals on to the defensive in the run-up to the following spring's local elections.

"No British government could resist the passive disobedience of the Protestant people. It would bring this province to a complete and total standstill," he told one TV interviewer. "Under Lord Carson, our founding father, and Craigavon, the Protestants of Ulster armed themselves and said, 'We will resist to the death' . . . I would resist to the death any attempt to subvert the democratic wishes of the Ulster people."[1]

It was an almost Pavlovian response, and one his Loyalist followers understood only too well, for Paisley to appeal for legitimacy to the great 1912–14 Home Rule crisis that had led to the foundation of the Northern Ireland state. "It was only fitting," he wrote, "that in 1981, when Ulster again was called to face a serious effort by a British government to edge us out of the United Kingdom, that Ulstermen should revert to the ways of their fathers."[2]

The exaggerated claims of Haughey and his foreign minister Brian Lenihan – the latter said he foresaw a united Ireland within ten years as a result of the new relationship – had certainly set alarm bells ringing among ordinary Unionists, especially in the countryside. Rural Official Unionists reported larger attendances at political meetings, while previously defunct paramilitary groupings in Tyrone and south Derry started talking about re-forming.

As usual it was Paisley who cashed in most effectively on the popular mood with a piece of paramilitary theatre that was flamboyant even by his standards. On a bitterly cold night in early February 1981 he brought five journalists to a hillside outside Ballymena, where 500 men, some of them dressed in combat jackets and balaclava helmets, were lined up in the dark in military formation. At a command from

Paisley they held above their heads pieces of paper which he said were certificates for legally held firearms. They were not armed.

The midnight parade, it was learned later, included members of the Ulster Defence Regiment and the RUC reserve. One man who had been approached to join the new force said the men involved were "all solid country types". The UDA and UVF were not involved. For the moment Paisley was steering clear of any involvement with the hard young men of such existing paramilitary groups, and they were equally wary of him after his performance during the abortive 1977 strike. Instead, he was launching his first serious attempt since the late 1960s to organise his own paramilitary unit: later that year it would re-emerge under the title the "Third Force".

First, though, he had some more conventional showmanship in mind to raise the sectarian temperature. The following Sunday he preached one of his classic political and anti-Catholic sermons at the Martyrs' Memorial church. He told his attentive congregation that in this "hour of crisis", they faced a double threat from the Irish Republic and the IRA's campaign of "Protestant genocide". Roman Catholics had a peculiar advantage when it came to terrorism, he went on – "All they have to do is to go to their priest and get a pardon. Isn't it remarkable that all the worst crimes of republican violence have been committed immediately after Mass?"3

Having appealed to his followers' fear of Catholicism, he turned to one of the most potent of their historical symbols: the signing by nearly half a million Unionists of the anti-Home Rule Ulster Covenant in 1912. He now produced an "Ulster Declaration", which he invited Loyalists to sign in protest against the Thatcher–Haughey initiative. It was a bizarre document, an ill-spelt attempt to adapt the archaic language of 1912 to the circumstances of the 1980s, and clearly intended to invite comparisons with the most heroic era of Ulster Unionism.

Next he turned to the kind of politics he loved best: he announced a series of eleven rallies around Northern Ireland, again copying Carson's 1912 campaign, to culminate in a mass demonstration of Loyalist solidarity at the foot of Carson's statue outside Stormont.

The "Carson Trail" rallies were typical Paisley affairs. His speeches were aimed at evoking all the gut-fears of rural loyalism. In his attacks on Charles Haughey, he used "language which the crowd understood and loved", noted the chronicler of the rallies, Sammy Wilson, later the first DUP Mayor of Belfast and an MP. At Omagh, County Tyrone, he boasted that "our ancestors cut a civilisation out of the bogs and meadows of this country while Mr Haughey's ancestors were wearing pig-skins and living in caves. . . .When our forefathers donned the British uniform and fought for their King and Country, Mr Haughey's fellow countrymen used their lights to guide enemy bombers to their targets in Northern Ireland."[4]

At Newtownards, County Down, it was Margaret Thatcher's turn to feel Paisley's wrath as he played the role that came most naturally to him – not the leader of, but the spokesman for the inarticulate Loyalist masses. "The wee woman washing the dishes is saying the same things about Margaret Thatcher as I'm saying – 'Let them have it, because that's what I would do.' All I am is your representative – if you want me to say these things I will say them and no-one will stop me, inside or outside of Parliament, even should it bring an even greater volume of abuse, hatred, spite, even physical violence," he told the wildly cheering crowd.[5]

Former colleagues have frequently observed that large crowds have a peculiar effect on Ian Paisley, or rather on his rhetoric, which can sometimes become violent and even menacing. During the "Carson Trail" he excelled himself. At Newtownards the applause was so ecstatic that he produced an astonishing new claim in response to it. He accused no less a party than the Official Unionists of plotting to assassinate him, a claim based on an anonymous phone call to the *Belfast News Letter*.

At rally after rally he fed the faithful with what they wanted to hear. At Newtownards he conjured up a picture of Haughey with "a green baton dripping with blood" in one hand and "a noose specially prepared for the Protestants of Ulster in the other". At Banbridge the crowd spontaneously burst into the DUP anthem – "Paisley is our leader". He told the crowd in Cookstown that "we will have the last word – there will be no structures in our province or no control exercised by anyone of which we do not approve".

After the rally at Enniskillen, County Fermanagh, Paisley and four colleagues drove to Hillsborough Castle to deliver a protest note to Margaret Thatcher, who had flown into Northern Ireland on a hurriedly arranged mission of reassurance. As they handed it in at the gate of the sleeping castle at 3.45 in the morning, they bawled together at the top of their voices, "No surrender". It was a symbolic act of defiance which had no effect on Thatcher but was calculated to warm the hearts of the Loyalist faithful.

There were two other elements without which no Paisley extravaganza would be complete. One was a tantalising hint of mysterious and threatening events to come. Peter Robinson told the crowds that after the rallies there would be third, fourth and fifth phases of the campaign still to come, if necessary, "and no-one but a few know the timing and the details". All they had to do was put their "trust in Dr Paisley. Times past have proved his advice and warnings to be true. Give him your trust and he, with God's help, will give this country the leadership it needs."[6]

And, with the May local elections in mind, there were the constant attacks on the vacillations of the Official Unionists and "the pathetic spectacle" of their leader, Jim Molyneaux, "falling over himself to excuse the Prime Minister as he blames the civil servants and everyone but the lady who did the dirty deal with Dublin".

There were, of course, no third, fourth or fifth phases. The crowds at the rallies became ever smaller as it became apparent that Thatcher's dialogue with Haughey carried no immediate threat to Northern Ireland's Britishness. To make up the numbers, devout Paisleyites were bussed in from all over the province. Fewer than 10,000, including two and a half thousand bandsmen, turned up for what was billed as the final triumphant rally at Stormont at the end of March, although Paisley kept doggedly insisting that 100,000 were present.

The faithful waited in the drizzle to be told what to do in the "third phase" of the now cold and mucky Carson Trail. They were to be disappointed. For the moment their only instruction was to go out and vote for the DUP in the May local government elections. These, Paisley said, had a significance far greater than electing councillors and aldermen. They would be the thermometer which measured the temperature of the Loyalist people. Votes cast for the DUP were votes for resistance to Haughey and Thatcher.

And that was exactly what they and tens of thousands like them did. Few showed any disappointment at the unfulfilled promises, the unrealised threats of action, the clear evidence of a crisis manufactured and exaggerated by a master manipulator for his own electoral advantage. It seemed to be enough that Paisley was once again seen to be doing something, seen to be eternally vigilant against the ever-present menace of Dublin. In the May 1981 local elections, with the community more polarised than ever by the Republican hunger strike in the Maze prison, Unionist voters pushed the DUP's vote for the first time above that of their Official Unionist rivals. The "Carson Trail", despite its abortive finale, and despite the fact that the Anglo-Irish dialogue was still going strong, had served Paisley well.

—◦—

It did not serve him so well six months later, when a real crisis blew up in the wake of the IRA's assassination of the Official Unionist MP Rev Robert Bradford, shot dead in one of his advice centres in South Belfast on 15 November 1981. While the "Carson Trail" bluster had disillusioned many, nonetheless the immediate reaction of many ordinary Unionists was that Bradford's murder had proved Paisley right. For months his had been the lone voice warning against the hidden dangers of the dialogue with Dublin. Now Official Unionists like Harold McCusker – a bitter critic of the "Carson Trail" – rushed to join Paisley in condemning the Anglo-Irish process as the "the spur the terrorists needed" to step up the push for a united Ireland.

The killing of Robert Bradford came in the middle of a wave of murderous IRA attacks on UDR and RUC men in Border areas. The killing affected the Unionist community like almost no other atrocity since the beginning of the "Troubles". Unionist politicians were inundated with phone calls from their constituents demanding extreme measures, ranging from laying waste to the Falls Road and the Bogside to the setting up of a Protestant provisional government. UDA leader Andy Tyrie spoke of a black mood in the Protestant community, a feeling that a civil war was inevitable. "They were saying to us, let's get it over with," he recalled.

Bradford's murder had a deep personal impact on Paisley. The slain MP was a close friend and ally who personified the contradictions at the heart of Unionism: he was an ultra-right-winger with identical views to the DUP leader, yet was in the Official Unionist Party. Three years previously he and Paisley had staged a joint protest at Westminster, walking out of a religious service because a Catholic priest was taking part. Known as a British-Israelite sympathiser, whose ranks included a surprising number of senior Unionists, Bradford was a fierce campaigner against homosexuality, child pornography and the employment of alleged IRA sympathisers in Belfast's Royal Victoria Hospital.

Paisley had been caught unprepared by events. The Official Unionists had been meeting in their Glengall Street headquarters to discuss the Border killings when the news of Bradford's assassination came through, and they took the initiative. It was the Official Unionist MPs and councillors from Border areas, led by McCusker, who made the running in calling for a one-hour work stoppage on the day of Bradford's funeral, and who set in motion a boycott of local councils in pursuit of tougher security measures. Again it was Official Unionists who drew up tentative plans to establish their own alternative government and security structures if their demands were not met.

Paisley's immediate response was a typical piece of one-upmanship: he called for people to come out in mourning for Bradford an hour before the Official Unionist-called work stoppage was due to begin.

At Westminster his antics were even more calculated to grab centre-stage. The previous week he was reported to have called Mrs Thatcher "a traitor and a liar" from an upstairs gallery of the Commons. On 16 November he appeared there again, apparently attracted by its theatrical possibilities, together with Peter Robinson and Johnny McQuade. MPs said they had seen him laughing and joking with his colleagues beforehand.

Halfway through a lengthy and sombre statement on the assassination by the recently appointed Northern Ireland Secretary Jim Prior, Paisley shouted "nonsense", and Robinson and McQuade, as if on cue, also started barracking. When they refused to stop, the Speaker stopped the debate, and then suspended them. They refused to leave. Both Labour and Conservative MPs shouted, "Out! Get out!" The speaker threatened to suspend them for the session. Paisley rose contemptuously to his feet with the words "Amen, there is no use coming here anyway", pulled a reluctant Johnny McQuade after him, and stalked out.

If Paisley was alienating the politicians in Britain, he was dividing the Unionists back in Belfast. He was once again spouting unspecified threats about making Northern Ireland "ungovernable". When asked what concrete measures he had in mind to achieve this, all he could come up with was a threat of more demonstrations and the non-cooperation of already virtually powerless local councillors, with mayors refusing to "wine and dine" government ministers.

The problem was that his party controlled only two councils out of 26, so he needed the Official Unionists to join him to make any protest action effective. His next move, a call for a half-day work stoppage on

23 November, did receive a positive response from ordinary grass-roots Unionists. The DUP leader also promised the first show of strength of his newly created "Third Force", the fruit of the seed planted on the County Antrim hillside the previous February.

Most of the Official Unionist leadership, though, dismissed all this as a typical piece of bluster and political opportunism. They called a rival demonstration at Belfast's City Hall on the same day and, just to make matters even more chaotic, the UDA refused to have anything to do with Paisley's "Third Force", and called their own rally outside the Belfast shipyard. Little wonder that the maverick Unionist MP Jim Kilfedder raised a cheer at this last rally when he deplored the previous week's "confusion and disarray" among Unionists.

However, Paisley still had one card to play: his putative Loyalist army. That night, in pouring rain, the 6,000 men of the "Third Force" marched through the streets of Newtownards, County Down, to a rally outside the town's handsome eighteenth-century courthouse, where nearly two centuries before the Presbyterian United Irishmen had been despatched to the gallows and the convict ships. The town square was full of foreign journalists and television crews, lured back to Northern Ireland by hysterical rumours of impending civil war.

There was no civil war: instead, Paisley was offering them a piece of paramilitary melodrama, a private army complete with masks and cudgels. The theatre was more impressive than the threat. Peter Robinson asked for two minutes' silence "and you'll hear something that will bring joy to your hearts". The crowd hushed in the dreadful hope of hearing gunfire. Nothing happened. Paisley, looking like Lord Carson in a heavy overcoat and homburg hat, strode across the square. There was a tense pause, perfectly stage-managed, followed by a chorus of wild cheers as the first ranks of the "Third Force" spilled into the square.

They were a motley crew. The leading squad wore paramilitary uniforms and carried swagger sticks. Most of the rest were clothed in a mixture of masks, flak jackets and forage caps; a few carried heavy sticks. Others were still in their work clothes; some had donned their Sunday best. There were sallow-faced teenagers and plump, prosperous farmers. They stood awkwardly in lines under the harsh television lights. The crowd revelled in the spectacle but was disappointed by the absence of one vital ingredient – there was not a gun to be seen anywhere.

From the platform Paisley thundered that he wanted to see a force of 100,000 men "on the march in Ulster". He said that recruiting officers would soon be visiting every community, and there would be a women's corps as well. Cedric Wilson was then starting his career in the DUP and that night had the job of organising matters for the media. "We gathered in the Albertbridge Road office afterwards to listen to the radio reports," he recalled, "and Paisley said 'Did you see all those men? Where did they come from? Maybe there were angels there.' Robinson was behind him out of his view and he just rolled his eyes to heaven."[7]

The "Third Force" never marched again. Little more was heard about it apart from a few desultory gatherings of men in Loyalist housing estates and on country roads in the following few weeks. Once again, Paisley had brought his people to the edge of the abyss of civil war, and then led them away from it. In a pointless last gesture he offered the "Third Force" as a back-up to the existing security forces. But Loyalists brought up in the tougher school of Belfast's sectarian ghettoes were already sneering at what they called the "Third Farce", and at the calibre of its self-styled "county commanders" – Rev Ivan Foster in his dark sunglasses, and Rev William McCrea with his gospel recordings.

Some key actors in future Northern Ireland scenarios would never again take the threat of a Paisleyite backlash quite so seriously. Members of the Thatcher government, for example, were known to share the view of the *Daily Telegraph* editorial on the day of Robert Bradford's funeral: "The posturing of Mr Paisley . . . continues to do much to persuade the British people that Ulster is a strange and alien land which tends to inspire not terror, but ridicule."

Nearer home, the Official Unionists were more suspicious than ever of any efforts to include Paisley in a broad Unionist front against the Anglo-Irish dialogue. The UDA, whose central role in the 1974 UWC strike had shown that any long drawn-out campaign of loyalist disruption required their muscle to be successful, had also refused to become involved in Paisley-organised protests. The UVF and the Red Hand Commandos had followed suit.

A leading UDA man, Freddy Parkinson, issued a statement from his cell in a Dublin jail, where he was serving a sentence for a firebomb attack in that city, which summed up the feelings of many former paramilitary activists about Paisley. Appealing to "Third Force" members not to become involved in violence, Parkinson wrote: "I remember vividly the parliamentary megalomaniacs of the late 1960s and early 1970s who beckoned us to follow them but who later left us abandoned to be scorned as common criminals."

Paisley, he went on, "the tarantula who spreads the venom of further conflict around us, has been a major contributor to our prolonged tragedy". He concluded with the words of Major Ronald Bunting about his former master: "He uses words to create violent situations, but never follows the violence through himself." Was the master showman of the "Carson Trail" and the "Third Force" beginning belatedly to be seen as an empty vessel? It would take another constitutional crisis, a real constitutional crisis this time, to find out.

—◄o►—

His unceasing vigilance – almost to the point of paranoia – about the possibility of a "sell-out" by Britain, often made Paisley sound like a prophet. And sometimes he was. He foresaw the form the first serious weakening of the constitutional link with Britain would take nearly ten years before it happened. "It is eventually going to be a confrontation between the Protestants of Ulster and Westminster," he told a Loyalist rally in Omagh in January 1976. Nearly five years later, on the day after Margaret Thatcher first met Charles Haughey at Downing Street, he warned the British Prime Minister that should she dare to give the Republic a say in Northern Ireland, he would "lead the Ulster Protestant people in whatever actions are necessary to thwart and destroy such machinery".

He may have been engaging in his well-tried tactic of scaring governments out of new Northern Ireland policies by threatening murder and mayhem against them. It was a gambit with diminishing returns. By the mid-1980s the British government had a more pressing concern than Paisley's endless threats of violent Protestant backlashes. Worried by the growth in electoral support for the Provisional IRA's political wing, Sinn Féin, Margaret Thatcher and her ministers were feeling their way towards the first major political initiative in Northern Ireland for more than a decade.

First and foremost Thatcher wanted to put the IRA out of business. The Taoiseach, Garret FitzGerald, with John Hume in support, was as concerned about Sinn Féin's electoral threat to the SDLP, and began arguing that the way to tackle both the IRA and Sinn Féin was to give the Dublin government an input into the North's affairs. This, they argued, would reduce long-standing Nationalist "alienation" from the police and judicial system in particular, and would lead to a falling off in support for the "men of violence". Dublin's input to security matters and their collective awareness of Nationalist sensitivities might also smooth the rough edges of a British security approach to the IRA which was often counterproductive.

The two Unionist parties, already working together to boycott newly elected Sinn Féin councillors on local councils, desperately tried to pre-empt a deal. In August 1985 a joint Official Unionist–DUP working party was set up to co-ordinate opposition to any agreement which might give the Irish government a say in the North's affairs. Later that month Jim Molyneaux and Ian Paisley wrote to Margaret Thatcher. "The people of Ulster" – which in Unionism's exclusivist language meant the North's Protestants – were "profoundly anxious" about the secret Anglo-Irish talks, they wrote. Their leaders, they went on, were "fearful for the future of constitutional politics" – a coded threat of a Loyalist paramilitary backlash – if Dublin was given any say in the North.

A second letter a month later contained a uniquely Unionist mixture of wild anti-Catholic paranoia and a claim that for once was unerringly accurate. It alleged that "a cardinal from the Vatican" had been briefed by the Irish government on the talks – "the Pope is to know more about your deliberations than Unionist members of the British Parliament", the two leaders complained. But they also claimed that any Anglo-Irish agreement would result in a secretariat, staffed by Irish as well as British civil servants, being set up in Belfast.

That, as it turned out, was exactly what was at the centre of the agreement signed on 15 November between Thatcher and FitzGerald in the old governor's residence at Hillsborough, one of Northern Ireland's most picturesque Georgian villages. A permanent Anglo-Irish Conference was to be set up, serviced by a joint secretariat which, it later emerged, would be situated beside a British Army complex on the edge of East Belfast. This physical symbol of Dublin's input, the Maryfield "bunker", became the focus of Unionist fury.

The most striking image on that cold but historic autumn day was Paisley, his face bloated with suppressed rage, towering over his grim little band of disciples outside the gates of Hillsborough Castle. His words, though, were unremarkable. After two decades of blustering and threatening, there was little new he could say now that a real deal had been struck with the detested traditional enemy.

Strangely, in the weeks following the Anglo-Irish Agreement, his level of rhetoric continued to be noticeably lower than in earlier "crises" largely manufactured by him for his own ends. Even at the enormous "Ulster Says No" protest rally outside Belfast's City Hall on 23 November, he kept his fearsome tongue under control, mindful perhaps of the warning in Jim Molyneaux's opening speech that this time the crisis was too serious for fever-pitch oratory.

It was all too clear from the array of faces in that huge crowd that the Unionist people in their hour of need were demanding a united stand from their long-divided leaders. Civil servants and their smartly dressed wives, tweed-capped farmers and venerable sash-wearing Orangemen mixed with the "boot boys", "Kick the Pope" bandsmen, punks and the pinched-faced men and women of the Belfast ghettoes. Paisley, sensitive as always to the feelings of the Loyalist masses, would not disappoint them.

He had his own reasons for his anxiety to maintain Unionist unity. The fiasco of the 1977 Loyalist strike was a reminder of the impotence of a divided Unionism. He knew too that in the past he had dominated any Unionist coalition, particularly at a time of crisis, through his powerful personality, huge personal appeal to the Loyalist public, and unimpeachable position at the hardest, purest end of the Unionist spectrum.

However, he left to his deputy leader, Peter Robinson, the hard job of starting to spell out what every intelligent Unionist was thinking, that the Agreement was the beginning of the end of the union with Britain as they knew it. "The Union I was taught at my father's knee was nothing like the Union we have today. The Union then was a protection to the people in Northern Ireland who wanted to remain out of a united Ireland. Now the Union forces us towards a united Ireland," was Robinson's verdict. "The Anglo-Irish Agreement has pushed us onto the window ledge of the Union."

Robinson and his following of "Young Turks" in the DUP were by this stage talking increasingly about independence. But they knew that the only man who could sell such a radical prescription to grassroots Loyalists was the man those people had come to worship almost as their messiah, "God's man for the hour", Ian Paisley.

When the House of Commons endorsed the Anglo-Irish Agreement by one of the largest majorities in living memory, the logic of the extreme Unionist position became inescapable. However, Paisley refused to face up to it. At post-agreement strategy meetings Unionist politicians of both parties asked the inevitable question: what would a militant campaign of civil disobedience, political strikes and violent street protests lead to if not a serious weakening of the link with Britain?

Paisley, however, was the first to throw up his hands in horror at any suggestion of independence, said Unionist colleagues. He would often say that the leaders of Unionism had to face up to swallowing "a dose of unpleasant medicine", but would recoil when it was suggested to him that there were only two kinds of medicine – to deal with the British on their terms in order to stay inside the United Kingdom, meaning some role in government for the SDLP and some relationship with Dublin; or to go it alone in an independent Ulster.

Many Official Unionists believed they had finally found out Paisley. The deep contradiction which had been at the heart of his politics for most of his career was now a crucial factor in the confusion in the Unionist camp. As long before as 1973, senior Northern Ireland Office officials had pointed out that the DUP leader could not have it both ways: he could either go along with Brian Faulkner and remain inside the United Kingdom on the terms dictated by the British government and parliament, or he could follow the logic of William Craig's arguments and go for independence.[8]

Thirteen years later, in the middle of the most serious constitutional crisis of the "Troubles'", he was still trying to have it both ways. He seemed incapable of telling his blinkered supporters the plain truth: that the relationship with Britain would never be the same again. He was still clinging to the vain hope that another bout of sabre-rattling, this time in concert with the Official Unionists, would force the British to renege on their deal with Dublin.

"He has the leadership ability to take Northern Ireland out of this crisis – he could save the province from absolute mayhem if he used his tremendous abilities for good", said one leading Official Unionist. "But I don't think he will. At the end of the day he's a weak man, and a scared man – he's always scared of losing his support – it's the weakness of the politician."

Another colleague put it even more bluntly. "It's a case," he said, "of 'I am the leader, there is the mob, I must follow'." Paisley was now the prisoner of the "no surrender" instincts of that mob – instincts to which he had done so much over the previous 20 years to give expression and credibility.

The two pressures on Paisley – one to maintain Unionist unity, the second the absence of a workable alternative to the Agreement –

worked together to force him into a huge blunder and one of the most humiliating episodes in his career.

The occasion was the long-requested meeting at Downing Street between the two Unionist leaders and Margaret Thatcher on 25 February 1986. They went with two messages from the joint DUP–Official Unionist working party: firstly, an offer of a two-tier conference on devolution and a new relationship with Dublin if the Anglo-Irish Agreement was put into cold storage; and secondly, a threat that if the Prime Minister was not interested in this, a one-day strike would be mounted, and the protest campaign would be stepped up, increasing the likelihood of confrontation with the RUC.

Neither message was delivered. Instead Paisley proposed a conference on devolution, a suggestion seized upon by Mrs Thatcher and Northern Ireland Secretary Tom King. At an impromptu press conference in the House of Commons afterwards, Molyneaux said they had got away from "a deadlock situation", and he hoped that the organisers of the threatened one-day strike would now not put their plans into action.

Paisley sat beside him leaning backwards and smiling approvingly. In the corner of the crowded room Peter Robinson shook his head after every statement. "That sounds all right," someone said to him as the journalists filed out. "It's all right till we get them home to Belfast," Robinson replied.

Back in Belfast even Paisley's most loyal lieutenants were shouting about a sell-out. Significantly it was his fellow clerics, William McCrea and Ivan Foster, who issued the most angry denunciatory statements. There was an only half-joking proposal to send a DUP delegation to give the two leaders a hot reception when they arrived at Aldergrove airport. One wag suggested they carry placards demanding "Paisley must go".

However, for once Paisley knew when to backtrack. Robinson had quickly convinced him that there would be hell to pay back home. Within an hour of the press conference he was already on the phone to Belfast contradicting Molyneaux and insisting to colleagues that nothing acceptable had come out of the meeting with Thatcher. He finally conceded defeat at a stormy session with senior DUP men early that evening.

When the joint working party met that night at the Official Unionist headquarters in Glengall Street, Paisley went on to the offensive, denying that the government statement issued after the Downing Street meeting had been approved by him and describing it as having been a "very angry" affair. Molyneaux, also under pressure from his lieutenants, reluctantly went along with his version. Both men then put their names to a statement rejecting further talks with the government and announcing an intensification of the protest campaign. It was Peter Robinson's finest hour.

All that was left was for Paisley and Molyneaux to meet representatives of the "1986 Workers Committee", a group of factory and power station workers brought together largely at Robinson's instigation to co-ordinate strike action against the agreement. The two leaders assured them that the "day of action" could go ahead the following Monday, 3 March.

Suddenly Robinson was the man to watch. British journalists, well briefed by a Northern Ireland Office only too anxious to split Paisley's party, started to speculate about a bid for the DUP leadership and the end of the Paisley era. They were right about Robinson but wrong about Paisley.

PART TWO

Peace

"We are playing a game of constitutional chicken where we both run headlong at each other and the Government of the United Kingdom know they are going to have to give way eventually."

PETER ROBINSON, 4 JANUARY 1986

"Better to languish in jail . . . than to forsake principle and betray future generations."

PETER ROBINSON, 11 FEBRUARY 1986

"Ulster Resistance is not for the faint or half-hearted and we will use all means which are deemed necessary to defeat the [Anglo-Irish] Agreement"

IAN PAISLEY, ULSTER RESISTANCE RALLY, ULSTER HALL, BELFAST, 10 NOVEMBER 1986

"Two men will visit you in your home. If there is one bit of green or yellow in you, you won't get in."

IAN PAISLEY ON RECRUITING TO ULSTER RESISTANCE, 19 NOVEMBER 1986

CHAPTER ELEVEN

The Rise, Fall and Rebirth of Peter Robinson

Clontibret in County Monaghan is one of those villages in rural Ireland that most tourists, even in these days of peace, would decide to give a miss. Effectively a one-street affair with a few shops, a couple of schools, a police station and a surfeit of pubs, there's not much to tempt the passing visitor to stop and stay a while. Situated almost halfway between Castleblayney and Monaghan town, with a mixed Catholic and Protestant community, it is both small – the population was around the 300 mark in 2006 – and poor. Villagers can probably blame the Troubles in adjoining Northern Ireland for both deficiencies.

Clontibret's misfortune was to be situated midway along the eastern flank of the Monaghan salient, the phallic-shaped tip of County Monaghan that juts into Northern Ireland and adjoins three of the North's most restive counties, Armagh and Tyrone on the east and Fermanagh on the west. Although Monaghan had shared a place in the historic province of Ulster with the three adjoining counties, the partition settlement of 1921 had imposed separation from them, and when the Troubles erupted, hostility between Unionists and Nationalists in this strategically important part of the Border area was sharpened by the area's geography. The salient afforded ready access to the North and, just as conveniently, a safe retreat and refuge, and so it became an IRA base and hotbed for Republican activity during some of the worst and most violent years of the recent conflict. Using an unapproved road, a favoured option for locals and the IRA alike during the height of the violence, the

Border is less than two miles away and a short drive away from there are towns and villages in the North that became synonymous with the death and despair of the Troubles, places like Darkley, Keady, Markethill, Crossmaglen and Armagh. If this part of County Monaghan was to become a launch pad for IRA bombings and ambushes, it also attracted the IRA's enemies. British intelligence activity and undercover RUC operations abounded, especially in the 1970s, prompting one local historian to describe Monaghan as "a county of intrigue".[1] And Loyalist paramilitaries, some with dark links to the security forces, repeatedly targeted this part of Monaghan with no-warning car bombs, indiscriminate bursts of automatic gunfire and the well-aimed assassin's bullet. Clontibret was at the edge of a nasty and violent battleground.

This was not the first time that history had placed Clontibret at the centre of Irish politics. Four centuries or so before the world had heard of people like Ian Paisley or Gerry Adams, the fields around the village were the scene of a victory by Irish rebels over the English Crown that is remembered and celebrated to this day. The Battle of Clontibret in 1595 was one of the opening shots in what became known as the Nine Years' War, the conflict Queen Elizabeth I and her successor, King James I, waged against the Gaelic chieftains of Ulster, then the part of Ireland most resistant to English influence. The victory was short-lived. In 1602 the Ulster chieftains, led by Hugh O'Neill, 3rd Earl of Tyrone, were obliged to surrender and five years later they fled Ireland in an effort to win Spanish support for a second rebellion. But the Flight of the Earls, as their exodus was called, was a doomed mission and the chieftains never returned to Ireland. The era of Gaelic Ireland had ended and England's control over the country strengthened. The Crown then confiscated the Earls' lands and upon it settled thousands of English and Scottish Protestants, whose loyalty to the Crown could be assured. Native Catholic Irish tenants were evicted and the loss of their land created a resentment that can be felt to this day. The plantation of Ulster was designed to pacify Ireland, which it did, but at the cost of sowing sectarian hatred and establishing conditions which led to partition, the creation of the Northern Ireland state and ultimately the modern-day Troubles.

So in a very profound way it was entirely fitting that the latter-day descendants of those Protestant planters chose Clontibret in which to demonstrate their readiness to resist another native Irish rebellion, this one more subtle and intangible than that faced by Elizabeth's generals, to be sure, but designed, in their minds at least, to achieve the same objective of ending the Crown's writ in the one part of Ireland which had remained loyal to Britain, Northern Ireland.

◄○►

Garda Frank Gallagher, who lived in married quarters at the rear of Clontibret police station, later recalled during subsequent court hearings that the first he knew about events in the early hours of 7 August 1986 was being roused by noise in the street outside at about 1.35 a.m. He went to the back window overlooking the street and peered outside. He could see the headlights of numerous cars and a large group of people walking along both sides of the road. Realising something was amiss, he radioed Monaghan Garda station for reinforcements and shortly afterwards heard the door of the police station being kicked in and the sound of splintering glass. Not long after that he heard what he thought was the sound of a single gunshot and then the barking voice of a man issuing marching orders: "Left, left, left, right, left."[2]

Local man Charles Shalvey told the court that as he was driving towards Gallagh Cross outside the village he could see that the road had been blocked completely by a crowd numbering between 50 and 60. He attempted to reverse but as he did so his car was attacked on both sides by the crowd, who used iron bars and sticks. Someone hammered on the roof and then an iron bar came flying through the windscreen. The left passenger window shattered and someone tried to open the door. He could distinctly recall, he told the court, someone saying something like "turn over the car" and at that stage he felt as if his life was in danger. Mrs Bernadette McCaugue, travelling in the family car with her husband, was also stopped by the crowd, one of whom said to her: "The North is taking over the South tonight." Dr Theresa Golden was also stopped and told to turn back. Her car was surrounded by men with cudgels and they broke the front headlights. She told the court she was very frightened.[3] Other witnesses, speaking to reporters on the morning after the invasion, claimed some of the mob carried guns, fired rockets as signals and paraded in military formation three times through the village before setting up a roadblock on the Dublin road.[4]

Senior Counsel Kevin Haugh, representing the prosecution, told the no-jury, anti-terrorist court in Dublin that in the early hours of that morning Clontibret was taken over by a large number of people who had driven over the Border and had then marched into the village, armed with sticks and cudgels. The crowd, later estimated by Garda witnesses to be 150 strong, had set up a human barrier to turn back cars. They wore balaclavas, masks or motorcycle helmets and were dressed in anoraks and paramilitary-style clothing. They daubed slogans on the walls of the Garda station and other buildings, including the words "Ulster has awoken". Shots had been fired by some in the crowd at an early stage, suggesting that firearms had been brought along. The aim was to provoke a reaction, Haugh said. "It was to test the reaction of our own security forces to see how they would react to the taking over of the village in this manner. It was designed to excite fear and alarm in the inhabitants of the village."5

Reinforcements from Monaghan town arrived at about 2.00 am, in the form of three Special Branch officers. Detective Sergeant Peter Hunt headed the group and was armed with a .38 calibre revolver, while his junior colleagues carried Uzi submachine guns, the hallmark of the paramilitary-style and much-feared Garda unit known as the Task Force. When they arrived in their unmarked patrol car, there was a line of men blocking the full width of the village's main street. They reversed the car and withdrew to about 150 yards distant and slowly approached the line of men. As they did so they were joined by two members of a uniformed police patrol who drove their marked car ahead of the Special Branch men. As they neared the mob Garda Leo O'Hara got out of the car and approached a car parked near the human barrier. Within moments the crowd moved forward, shouting and roaring. As he turned to run, O'Hara was struck in the back. He managed to make it to his own vehicle but the crowd prevented him getting into the vehicle and he was savagely attacked, as he later recalled: "The crowd then grabbed me and pulled me on the road. I struck out with my fists but was overwhelmed by the numbers of the crowd. I was thrown to the ground, kicked and beaten repeatedly with an iron bar. I heard shouts of 'Get the bastard, kill him' and I screamed and screamed."6

The Garda Special Branch officers raced to the rescue of their comrades. Sergeant Hunt fired five shots from his revolver over the heads of the crowd while his two colleagues discharged bursts from their Uzis. The crowd turned tail and fled for their parked cars. Hunt ran after them and grabbed a man who was fleeing with them. There was no selection in the man he arrested, he later insisted. It was just random. The man was dressed in a dark blue rubber suit. Fragments of glass recovered later from his clothing matched that from the windscreen and headlamp of the attacked Garda car. He was arrested under the Republic of Ireland's anti-terrorist law, the Offences Against the State Act, and taken to Monaghan for questioning. When they arrived, Garda suspicions about the identity of their prisoner were confirmed: they had just arrested Peter Robinson, deputy leader of the Rev Ian Paisley's Democratic Unionist Party. It was the start of a saga that was to have enormous implications for the outcome of the Northern Troubles and the way Ian Paisley would end his political career. Once again Clontibret had played its part in Irish history.

—◄◦►—

In the months following the November 1985 signing of the Anglo-Irish Agreement at Hillsborough the pendulum of popularity within the world of hardline Loyalism swung away from Ian Paisley towards his 38-year-old deputy. The most iconic image of the Unionist protest campaign against the Hillsborough deal was also its most misleading, that of Paisley roaring "Never! Never! Never!" to a huge crowd gathered outside Belfast City Hall. The image signalled determination and decisiveness, whereas the reality was that the agreement between Margaret Thatcher and Garret FitzGerald to give Dublin a role in the government of Northern Ireland had found Ian Paisley unsure how to respond and unwilling to take to street politics unless all of Unionism was with him, a difficult and unlikely prospect. For Peter Robinson, though, the Anglo-Irish Agreement was a call to action, even a call to arms.

In reaction to this perceived act of treachery by the British, Robinson and his allies flirted with Ulster independence, an idea rooted deeply in the Covenanter strain that defines the political DNA of the DUP's style of Unionism, in which loyalty to the Crown is dependent upon the Crown's loyalty to the religion and culture of Ulster Protestantism. But that was an option that implied the use of violence. Everyone knew, not least Loyalists, that there would be fierce resistance from Nationalists and it was even likely to pitch Northern Ireland into a full-blown civil war if it ever became a serious possibility. It signalled a growing ambiguity by Robinson and his followers to the use of violence which was evident in other ways. While mainstream Unionists condemned rioters who had battled with the RUC outside Maryfield, the joint British–Irish secretariat on the eastern outskirts of Belfast which was at the heart of the deal, Robinson refused to join them. When Loyalist paramilitaries began firebombing and intimidating RUC families out of Protestant areas, he stayed silent. Instead he set up the 1986 Workers Committee, with power station workers amongst its membership. Peter Robinson was, it appeared, moving towards an attempted repeat of the 1974 UWC general strike whose success had been achieved through control of the North's power stations. To even contemplate using such a weapon without the backing of Loyalist paramilitaries like the UDA and UVF would render the idea meaningless. But Robinson had the hard men of Protestantism on his side.

That had initially become apparent when he first became an MP, winning the East Belfast seat at Westminster from Bill Craig in the general election of 1979. In those days he looked and sounded the part as well; invariably unsmiling and grimly oozing acrimony, he sported blue-tinted eyeglasses, inspiring one wag to make the comparison with Robespierre: "True-blue and incorruptible." The UDA, which had been impressed by his performance in the 1974 UWC strike, threw its weight behind his campaign and Robinson won by a mere 64 votes, a victory that put him in debt to the group. But, as one contemporary colleague recalled, that was not a burden to the UDA for Robinson could be a precious ally if events demanded: "There was always this view in paramilitary circles that while Paisley was the 'Grand Old Duke of York' and had become something of a joke because of it, Robinson was made of different stuff, that he would go over the top."[7]

Robinson's analysis of the Anglo-Irish Agreement and especially his ideas on how to frustrate it suggested a readiness for conflict. In a lengthy *Irish Times* interview in January 1986, he accused the British Foreign Office of surrendering to the IRA's violence. The British had contrived the Hillsborough deal, he claimed, so as to advance a larger strategy of gradual withdrawal and disengagement from Northern Ireland, a view he shared, much to their delight apparently, with Enoch Powell and the Official Unionist leader, James Molyneaux. And, of course, the British, having caved in to IRA violence and given a foothold in Northern Ireland's affairs to the Dublin government would, he went on, give more if pressured to do so. The IRA, Robinson believed, had more reason than ever to intensify its campaign.

Both London and Dublin had tried to present the Agreement as a measure to enhance Garda–RUC co-operation or to undermine Catholic support for the IRA and Sinn Féin, but such claims were unsustainable, he insisted, given the evidence on the ground of tougher police handling of Orange marches and the like. The theory behind the Agreement was that Nationalist support for the IRA was in no small measure a reaction to heavy-handed security policies and a Unionist bias in their execution.

Dublin saw its role as ameliorating this flaw, both through the Maryfield Secretariat and the permanent intergovernmental conference that discussed security policy. Loyalists, however, could only see Orangemen being prevented from marching through Catholic districts. The RUC Chief Constable, Sir John Hermon, who had the job of implementing this new approach, had, Robinson taunted, become "a lap dog" of the Irish government and should "find a boarding kennel in the South", while it was imperative that Unionists should "wreck" the intergovernmental conference. Further and more intense conflict with Britain was almost inevitable, and worse could happen, he hinted, if politicians like himself were undermined. "We are playing a game of constitutional chicken where we both run headlong at each other and the Government of the United Kingdom know they are going to have to give way eventually," he declared. "But they are hoping that by running down the road full pace towards us, as if they are going to take us head on, that they will scare us off. There isn't the remotest chance of Unionists stopping. We're going down that road. . . . Of course, the worst of all alternatives is if the political leadership in Northern Ireland loses control. In those circumstances, as I have said before, Dublin knows that – what was the expression? – that GB is 22 miles away by sea, whereas the Republic is only an isolated unapproved road away."[8] Translated into simpler words, this was Robinson parading his big black dog and saying, "This animal is safe as long as I hold on to its leash, but should my hand slip, which would be a terrible thing to happen, I couldn't be responsible for what happens."

In February 1986 Robinson announced that he was ready to go to prison to kill the Agreement: "Better to languish in jail . . . than to forsake principle and betray future generations," he told reporters in Belfast as he urged Unionist councillors to withdraw from local government. As Paisley condemned Loyalist rioters and those who intimidated RUC officers, Robinson stayed silent, implicitly condoning what was going on and enhancing the image of a principled and resolute leader, the Loyalist who would do what his leader dare not and take his troops over the hill and into battle. As Robinson hardened his profile, speculation grew that he was, in effect, preparing to challenge Paisley's leadership by occupying ground that had once been Paisley's. The differences between them were significant. While Paisley favoured a political approach and placed his pact with the Official Unionists above all else, Robinson's direct methods appealed to the instincts of the grassroots. Nonetheless, Robinson denied there was any split or leadership pretensions on his part, albeit not very convincingly, with a declaration of fealty to his divinely inspired leader: "I believe that Ian Paisley was raised for this day," he said. ". . . No matter how much you try, Ian Paisley and I know there is no difference in our attitude to this agreement or in the tactics needed to defeat it."[9] That persuaded no-one and it seemed only a matter of time before Paisley would be forced to rise to the challenge. It appears to have been the British government's decision to prorogue the decaying Prior Assembly in June 1986, finally admitting that its bid to achieve voluntary power-sharing had failed, and perhaps more pointedly the experience of being carted struggling and shouting out of the Stormont chamber by the RUC as he and other Unionists protested the decision, that jolted Ian Paisley back to a more hardline stance. Either that or the knowledge that his deputy was outflanking him and he had better react before it was too late.

Paisley's opportunity to tack back towards his Loyalist base came a few weeks after Stormont was suspended when Portadown Orangemen geared up to defy a ban imposed twelve months earlier on their annual traditional Twelfth of July parade through the Catholic Obins Street section of the town, an occasion that always inflamed Nationalists and was a routine source of violence. Charging that the ban was really Dublin's work, Paisley rallied thousands of Loyalists to Portadown to force the Orangemen through. The threat of conflict worked and the RUC backed down and sought a deal. The proposal accepted by the Orangemen was to abandon the Obins Street parade in return for the right to march through another equally contentious and Catholic part of Portadown, a district that would a few years later be known throughout Ireland as a byword for the North's sectarian politics: Garvaghy Road.

This was a significant victory for the tactic of confrontation and, by implication, for Robinson's approach. The RUC had backed down in the face of hardline Unionist resistance; the British government's first line of defence had been breached. If the RUC could be moved, then so could others. Peter Robinson had identified the next weakest link in the Anglo-Irish chain some time before: "[Garret] FitzGerald is in a weak position," he had declared at the start of 1986. "Perhaps at the moment he is being supported and held up slightly by the agreement but, again, when it brings the Republic of Ireland closer to the problems of Northern Ireland, I don't think he'll be thanked too much by the people in the Republic who'll be looking for someone to blame for having brought catastrophe on them."[10]

It was in the context of this analytical framework that the invaders of Clontibret, a motley crew of DUP and Free Presbyterian Church faithful and members of the Ulster Clubs, a new broader-based protest group spawned by the Hillsborough deal, made their way that August night in 1986 to Clontibret by way of "an isolated unapproved Border road", with the aim of bringing a "catastrophe" of some sort to the sleeping villagers. Later there were claims, from Robinson and others, that the exercise was intended to test the Republic's security response and to expose the myth of improved cross-Border co-operation. But if that had been the case, then surely the invaders would have brought along cameras to record the security lapses or media witnesses to support their case? But they hadn't. Instead they had brought cudgels and iron bars and, if some witnesses were to be believed, also firearms. The invasion of Clontibret had all the hallmarks of an act of provocation intended to drive the Irish government and Loyalism into a conflict that could inflame Northern Protestants and awake awful fears in the South that the no-warning bombs in Dublin and Monaghan of 1974 might be repeated. If that happened, then, as Peter Robinson had foretold, the South's affection for the Anglo-Irish Agreement might indeed weaken. For a while it looked as if it could work. But only for a while.

—◁◦▷—

To this day there are people in Loyalist circles who firmly believe that Peter Robinson deliberately got himself arrested in Clontibret. After all, what better way was there, they will ask, to catapult over Ian Paisley in the pantheon of Protestant leadership than by doing jail time deep in the heart of the enemy's territory, an ordeal that would have put Paisley's stints in Crumlin Road prison during the 1960s in the ha'penny place? Robinson and his friends have always denied it, while Garda evidence at his trial claimed that he had been arrested at random and had been running away when caught. Nonetheless there is no doubt that the DUP deputy leader would have been a most unwelcome prisoner in the Republic, not least because of the real possibility of violence by fellow Loyalists attempting to secure his release, as well as the risk that the experience could well transform him into a Protestant martyr. Nor was there any doubt that other, more moderate, Unionists viewed the prospect of Robinson rising to such heights with utter dismay. "He'd be Paisley, but with balls," said one at the time. Another Official Unionist can remember running to the radio every half hour on the day of his arrest hoping against hope to hear that he had been released.

Whatever the truth, Robinson's demeanour in the hours following his arrest was not dissimilar to that of the martyr-in-waiting. He refused food and water while being held at Monaghan Garda station, apparently for fear of being poisoned, and protested his innocence. His wife, Iris, travelled from Belfast with the necessary provisions: "country produce, good wholesome food, from home," said his lawyer Alan Kane, the DUP General Secretary. Robinson told a Belfast radio station that he could have run away but decided not to. "I was there to observe security," he claimed. He also was refusing to talk to the police. The minister of Monaghan Free Presbyterian Church, the Rev Maurice Baxter, visited him and reported that he had requested a Bible to read. Alan Kane said the prisoner had kept up his spirits by "singing hymns and Orange songs".[11] A myth was being created that had the potential to make Peter Robinson a new Protestant hero, one who could even overshadow Ian Paisley.

The following day he appeared at Ballybay District Court and was charged with four offences: unlawful assembly, causing malicious damage to a police car and two charges of assaulting gardaí causing actual bodily harm. Bail was set at IR£10,000, twice the sum anticipated by Robinson's lawyers, so money had to be fetched from across the Border. The Rev William McCrea arrived with the balance of IR£5,000 in a bag, made up of sterling, punts and travellers' cheques. Peter Robinson was released on bail and driven away at speed.

He was due to appear next at a court in Dundalk on the Louth Border with the North and for a while it seemed as if the town's reputation as an IRA version of "El Paso" might deter him from making an appearance. If that had happened, the Irish government would almost certainly have sought his extradition from the North and, however that resolved itself, one certain result would be an even more enhanced status for the East Belfast MP. If Britain refused his extradition, that could drive a wedge into the intergovernmental alliance and into the heart of the Hillsborough Agreement; if the British did extradite him, then Loyalists would have final proof of Albion's perfidy and a just cause to rally around. It was a win–win situation for Peter Robinson.

But there was one person whose interests were to ensure that Peter Robinson was never elevated to such a stature and when Paisley arrived back from a trip to the United States nearly a week after the Clontibret incursion, he settled the matter of whether or not the DUP deputy leader should keep his court date. Claiming that if he had been in Northern Ireland at the time, he would have gone along with Peter

Robinson to Clontibret as an observer, Ian Paisley said his inclination was that his deputy should turn up at court and so should as many Loyalists as possible to show their support. Whether intended by Paisley or not, this was a clever move. Forcing an extradition crisis was surely the most politically astute route to take if he had really been interested in a confrontation with Dublin – but if it was the growing challenge from his deputy that was more on his mind, then Peter Robinson had to go to Dundalk. By this stage the chatter and rumours linking Robinson to a leadership bid against Paisley were rampant and at the press conference called to outline DUP plans for the court hearing, Paisley, who was flanked by Peter and Iris Robinson, was closely questioned about his leadership. One report said he "sternly" rejected suggestions that he would stand down, either because of his age or because of his deputy's actions.

As the date of the hearing approached, Dundalk shopkeepers and residents hunkered down for the inevitable trouble. Yet only a dozen or so cars loaded with Loyalists arrived in the town to support the DUP deputy leader on the day of his appearance, a week to the day after his arrest. Of the thousands of protesters talked about there was no sign, evidence of much common sense at least. The Robinson supporters parked their cars on the outskirts of Dundalk and marched into town, over a bridge spanning the Castletown River. It was locals who began the violence, although the Loyalists were undoubtedly intent on causing offence, shouting insults at "Fenians and papists" in the deserted town centre and singing Orange songs. Stones flew in the Loyalists' direction, followed by petrol bombs. A mob of local Nationalists gathered and soon they were chasing Robinson's supporters out of town and back towards their parked cars, many of which had had their windows broken. Peter Robinson was remanded to appear again in October.

When he next appeared in court, it was to receive bad news, so bad that it changed the way the Clontibret saga would end. At Ballybay District Court Robinson was served with seven further charges, most of them variations on malicious damage. The last one was the most serious. He was charged with assaulting a garda officer in the lawful execution of his duty. What made this serious was the penalty, if he was found guilty: up to two years' imprisonment. That sentence would trigger another law whose consequences could be much more severe for Robinson. In 1981, after the election and then death of IRA hunger striker Bobby Sands, the British government took measures to ensure that it would never again be possible for a convicted prisoner like Sands to become an MP. The

Representation of the People Act 1981 said that if any person was convicted and sentenced to more than one year in jail, either in Britain or the Republic of Ireland, he or she would be prevented from standing for election to Westminster. Any sitting MP so convicted would immediately lose their seat, as Robinson would if he was sent to jail for twelve months or more. Peter Robinson now faced the prospect of ending up in a Southern jail and losing his Westminster seat by virtue of a law created to strike at the IRA, not at Loyalists like him. Martyrdom was still on offer, for sure, but with a very big price tag attached.

There was more bad news later in October when the authorities decided that his case should be heard in front of the Special Criminal Court, the no-jury tribunal for political offences that sat in Dublin in front of three High Court judges. The court had been created out of fear that juries in cases dealing with IRA activists could be intimidated but here it was about to deal with one of the most prominent Loyalist politicians in Northern Ireland. The Clontibret incursion had its fill of ironic consequences.

Robinson's trial began on 13 January 1987 and lasted for two days. Representing him was Paisley's old friend, colleague and sometime adviser, Desmond Boal QC, who was specially called to the Southern Bar on the day of the trial so that he could appear for the DUP deputy leader. On the first day the courtroom was packed. Paisley was there and so was Iris Robinson and other DUP stalwarts. By the end of the second day, it was clear the prosecution had built a strong case. Peter Robinson was undoubtedly present at the fracas, forensic evidence linked him to the injured garda's car and the court had heard unsettling evidence about the mob's violent intent. The risk of conviction and a sentence that would disqualify him from parliament was clearly very high. At one stage, however, one of the presiding judges referred to Robinson as "an extremist politician", a remark that Boal seized upon, calling it "most disturbing". After the judge withdrew the comment, Boal made it clear that nonetheless, what the judge had said would form the basis of an appeal if Robinson was convicted. To prevent that happening, with all the attendant delay and embarrassment, a deal was offered by the prosecution that saved Peter Robinson's political career while denying him the martyr's scaffold and the chance to overtake Paisley as the leader of Northern Loyalism. Desmond Boal's legal dexterity had done another great service for his friend but it also kept in play a politician who would play a key role in strategising the political deal that would help end the Troubles.

The deal was straightforward. In return for the most serious charges being dropped, including the assault on the garda, Robinson agreed to plead guilty to an unlawful assembly charge. On 17 January, after a night spent in Limerick jail, he appeared again for sentencing at the Special Criminal Court. Boal pleaded for leniency – arguing *inter alia* that his client was unaware that the Loyalist crowd would be armed and masked – and Robinson was fined IR£17,500 and set free. The court called the invasion of Clontibret "grossly offensive, provocative, cowardly and terrifying" and the presiding judge, Mr Justice Barr, told the East Belfast MP that, but for his status as an MP, he could have been sent to jail. Newspaper reports describe Robinson as appearing "relieved" when he received a non-custodial sentence.

Unaware how big a part the threat of disqualification from parliament had played in bringing the Clontibret saga to this end, most people, including fellow Loyalists, assumed that Robinson had struck a deal out of fear of ending up in a Southern jail. That suited Paisley well, for his deputy's image as a hard, determined loyalist had been badly dented, perhaps for good. Although Paisley organised a "welcome home" party for his deputy and a fund was set up to repay the IR£17,500 borrowed to pay his fine – earning Robinson the soubriquet in Loyalist circles of "Peter the Punt" – Paisley knew he had less to fear from his deputy, at least for now. He had seen off a potentially serious challenge to his authority and status and Robinson had emerged from the story a diminished figure in hardline eyes.

That was one consequence of the Clontibret incident but another was that a new paradigm in DUP politics had been established. Rivalry and distrust between Ian Paisley and Peter Robinson would increasingly shape the way the DUP would conduct its politics in the coming years and this would have profound implications for the outcome of the Troubles. As for Robinson, he had successfully, if briefly, opened up clear blue water between himself and his leader, displayed considerable independence and had shorn the image of the devoted, unquestioning disciple. He had risen but now he had fallen. The question was, would he come back and if so, how?

◄○►

As the summer of 1986 turned into autumn, it became clear that the Clontibret incursion was just part of a wider move by hardline opponents of the Anglo-Irish Agreement into paramilitary-style street politics. One key feature of the period was the willingness of senior

DUP figures like Peter Robinson to associate more or less openly with the real Loyalist paramilitaries, especially the UDA. In March, Robinson's 1986 Workers Committee called a one-day strike which was supported by the UDA and UVF and by the Ulster Clubs. A Loyalist Co-ordinating Committee had been set up in April and amongst those attending were the DUP's Sammy Wilson and Alan Wright, the leader of the Ulster Clubs. Wright, a volunteer in the Salvation Army, was a fierce opponent of the Agreement and hinted broadly that he would be ready to fight the RUC and British Army to overthrow it. He had reason to be extreme: his father, an officer in the Royal Ulster Constabulary, had been killed in an INLA bombing. Also present was John McMichael, the UDA's capable deputy leader. His presence confirmed a growing relationship between some in the DUP and the more violent elements of Loyalism. The first signs of what was underway came on a July night just before the RUC climb-down in Portadown, when some 4,000 Loyalists, led by Paisley and Robinson, occupied the centre of Hillsborough, the village south of Belfast which is second home to the British Secretary of State and the venue for the signing of the hated Anglo-Irish Agreement. The occupation was given a code name: "Operation Mobilisation".

Then came the Clontibret incursion, after which the decision was made to form a proper paramilitary force. As the first anniversary of the Hillsborough deal approached, the new secret army finally emerged in public for the first time. The chosen location was fitting: the Ulster Hall, the venue of Edward Carson's anti-Home Rule meetings in 1912. On 10 November 1986, five days short of twelve months since the Hillsborough deal was signed, the army paraded before its founders and supporters and the paramilitary overtones were unavoidable. On the platform in the Ulster Hall were the main organisers, Paisley, Robinson and Alan Wright, and in the chair sat Sammy Wilson, then Lord Mayor of Belfast, who wore his chain of office. Suddenly the skirl of bagpipes plunged the hall into silence as a lone piper led an honour guard of eleven men, each dressed in khaki shirts and trousers with white Sam Browne belts. Nine of them carried standards showing the Red Hand of Ulster on a purple background and stitched on each were the names of towns in every district where the army had members. On their heads sat the distinctive headgear that would soon make Ulster Resistance a household name: a red beret. There were some 3,000 supporters in the audience, all of them male, who had each been invited in person to attend. One report said the audience was dressed as if they were going to church and it seemed both rural as well as urban Loyalists were represented.[12] The honour guard marched up the hall and onto the stage where they flanked Wilson and the scheduled speakers. Hymns were then sung, including the classic Ulster battle anthem "O God, Our Help in Ages Past". The press was barred but one enterprising reporter from the Belfast nationalist paper, the *Irish News,* managed to smuggle himself in and gave his readers an eye-witness account.[13]

Noel Russell wrote that the flags were handed up to clergymen who solemnly dedicated them before the speeches began. Paisley's speech was unambiguous and no-one listening to it could have concluded anything less than that this time the "Grand Old Duke of York" really was preparing to do battle on the other side of the hill. He was ready, he told the audience, to give Ulster Resistance "his undivided support" and, to rapturous applause, promised that he would provide "whatever political cover it needed". Political methods had failed to move Mrs Thatcher, he went on, and it was time to take other action. But some in the audience, he warned, "would not see the end of the campaign which was just beginning", a clear hint that ahead lay conflict and even death. He was aware, he said, of the seriousness of the course of action they were embarking upon and warned that the new force was not "a bluff". That last pledge drew more applause. There was even a suggestion that after destroying the Anglo-Irish Agreement the new force would turn its attention to the IRA and what he called the forces of "militant nationalism". An Ulster Resistance pledge was distributed and signed by most in the audience, but that did not mean automatic membership. Potential recruits would be vetted, as Paisley explained at a later recruiting rally: "Two men will visit you in your home. If there is one bit of green or yellow in you, you won't get in."[14] Peter Robinson also spoke. All the constitutional methods had been tried, he said, but they had failed so there was no option but to take other action, adding "it is better to be prepared and not needed than be needed and not prepared". Robinson's words were somewhat more guarded than Paisley's. While Paisley hinted at a coming, even imminent, battle, Robinson seemed to regard Resistance more as a doomsday outfit which would be deployed only if the worst came to the worst.

As more information leaked out about Ulster Resistance, it was difficult not to see it as the paramilitary arm of the DUP. Two of its most active leaders, Peter Robinson and the Rev Ivan Foster, were prominent in the party and Free Presbyterian Church respectively, while its titular head was Ian Paisley. Only Alan Wright had no history with the DUP. Resistance, as it became known in Loyalist circles, gave expression to a common view held by hardliners in DUP circles, which was that the Anglo-Irish Agreement would never be brought down by the polite political pact Ian Paisley had forged with Jim Molyneaux but by more direct methods. And there was a strong suggestion from some of those around Resistance that Peter Robinson had been the moving force behind the creation of the group. And then there were the links to the hard men of Loyalism. The UDA had negotiated an alliance with Resistance, as had the UVF, and UDA Chairman Andy Tyrie was explicit about Robinson's influence: "His intentions are to go all the way. Dr Paisley wants power without responsibility. Peter Robinson wants power and to accept the responsibility along with a lot of other people. He feels there's a need for an army . . . a new army . . . and that's what he's intent on bringing together."15 Tyrie forecast friction between Paisley and Robinson over the use of force. Paisley's followers, he said, ". . . are determined that he'll not be able to dismiss it like he had dismissed all his armies in the past 17 years. He has opened a Pandora's Box this time and he'll have great difficulty controlling it."16 Alan Wright said of Robinson, simply: "[He] will go the whole way."17 Any attempt to compare this group to Paisley's Third Force was wide of the mark, he insisted. "The people who are organising this are different," he said, "I can guarantee. I just wanted to ensure that if they were calling me into an organisation for controlled, disciplined action that they were prepared to use legitimate force . . . that when the time comes to return force with force they wouldn't chicken out."

Talk of guns was commonplace. Alan Wright said that he had been given assurances by the organisers that resources would be available for arms. Ivan Foster added that there was any amount of guns available to Resistance – legal guns that is – and the group's greater difficulty was to put together a disciplined force of men. A Resistance source told the author back in 1989: "People in the DUP knew this was to be an armed organisation and that we were seeking guns."18 All this, and the alliance with the UDA and UVF, made Resistance a distinctly non-Paisley type of group. Forces that he had raised in the past, from the UPV to the Third Force, were his creation, were tightly under his control and loyal to him. This one was none of those.

In the following weeks eight more Ulster Resistance rallies were held, in Kilkeel, Larne, Portadown, Derry, Enniskillen, Bangor, Ballymena and

Coleraine. Each saw the same format, the colour party leading Orange bands, speeches from the DUP leaders and appeals for recruits. By the end of November, Resistance sources were claiming a 12,500 membership. At Larne, Paisley warned Mrs Thatcher that if she would not listen to 300,000 protesters outside Belfast City Hall, maybe she would listen if "the 300,000 had guns in their hands".[19] The largest gathering was in the citadel of Orangeism, Portadown. One sign that some of those present expected conflict was that booklets were available setting out people's rights if they were arrested; but they were for sale only.

The RUC began paying Resistance more attention. Crack units, like the Divisional Mobile Support Units, were assigned to police the rallies, and the British Army sent in reinforcements just in case of trouble. On a number of occasions the colour party was detained at police roadblocks before parades. Then the police issued a warning that civilians wearing uniforms in public could be prosecuted and followed this up by threatening to charge a member of the colour party. At the next rally in Portadown, Robinson appeared in a red beret, as did Alan Wright; each carrying a blackthorn stick to reinforce the message. When Paisley arrived, Alan Wright placed a beret on his head and challenged RUC Chief Constable, Sir John Hermon, to arrest the DUP leader. Paisley said: "I made it clear to police that I would be wearing a red beret for one reason. All during my political career I have never asked any Ulsterman to do anything I wouldn't do myself. . . . When the hour of crisis comes, I will not be leading from the rear but from the front."[20] In Ballymena the red berets were donned again and many of the marchers were clothed in paramilitary outfits and some wore masks.

Paisley's language throughout the period of the Resistance rallies was characteristically extravagant and provocative but there was a nuanced caution in some of Peter Robinson's comments. Although in the main supportive of what Resistance was doing, occasionally there seemed indications in his words of a wish to distance himself somewhat from what was happening, minimise his own role and to paint Resistance in less threatening colours. Interviewed on RTÉ radio, for instance, he said: "Let me make it very clear. I believe that they are 100 per cent justified and I give them 100 per cent support in what they are doing. [But] I can't take credit for the Ulster Resistance for I am not a commander or an organiser of it."[21] At the rally in Larne he said: "There are many like myself who would like to see the Agreement brought down by democratic means but wouldn't we all be fools if we weren't prepared?"[22]

The Ballymena rally was the last outing and effectively that is where the story of Ulster Resistance appeared to come to an end. There were no more military manifestations in public, no incursions across "isolated, unapproved Border roads", no attempt to confront the RUC, the British Army or Margaret Thatcher. It seemed that Ulster Resistance had just faded away, seemingly vindicating those like Peter Robinson who claimed it to be a doomsday organisation only, ready, waiting but inactive until the right moment.

Nothing more was heard of Resistance until November 1988 when police uncovered an arsenal in Markethill, County Armagh, containing RPG-7 rocket launchers and rockets, Czech-made AK47 automatic rifles, pistols and 11,000 rounds of ammunition. Also in the dump were parts of a Javelin missile system which had been stolen from a sensitive section of the Shorts Missiles factory in Belfast and a number of the distinctive red berets which Ulster Resistance had sported at their founding rallies. Police investigators were able forensically to link the berets to the weaponry.

Faced with such incriminating evidence of a link to their party, the DUP moved swiftly to distance itself. A statement was issued to the press: "While not members of the organisation, we openly and publicly encouraged recruitment and canvassed support for the organisation and its aims. Sometime later we were informed the organisation was put on ice, and our association and contact was terminated. At no time during our association was anything done outside the law and no member was ever charged with any offence." The assurance which Alan Wright insisted he had been given, that those who had set up Resistance would "not chicken out" when the going got tough, had turned out to be worthless.

But that was only the beginning of what proved to be an extraordinary tale of intrigue. The next twist in the story came on 21 April 1989 when French police swooped on a group of five men meeting in the Hilton Hotel in downtown Paris and arrested them. One was a South African diplomat, Daniel Storm, another was an American arms dealer, Douglas Bernhart, while the other three were all Northern Loyalists. Their leader was Noel Little (40), from Markethill. He was a Free Presbyterian and a former DUP council candidate. His link with Resistance had been caught on camera. At the Portadown rally he had been photographed alongside Peter Robinson and Alan Wright wearing the group's red beret in defiance of police warnings not to. Also arrested was a fellow County Armagh Loyalist, James King (52), whose association with Paisley stretched way back to the 1960s when he had been arrested and jailed with Paisley after clashes at a civil rights march in Armagh city. The third Loyalist was Samuel Quinn (42) from Newtownards, County Down, who, it later emerged, was a junior officer in a Territorial Army missile battery. His presence explained why French police had intercepted the three Loyalists trying to hand over a demonstration model of a Blowpipe missile system. They had foiled an ambitious plan that involved the apartheid South African government facilitating arms supplies to Ulster Resistance in return for missile secrets.

More details of what lay behind all this emerged in the following weeks. The plot hatched by Resistance, in tandem with the UVF and UDA, began in July 1987, when gunmen posing as policemen robbed the Northern Bank in Portadown, County Armagh, of stg£300,000, half of which was spent on buying weapons: ten RPG-7 launchers and 150 rockets, 200 AK47 rifles, 90 Browning pistols and 450 fragmentation grenades.23 The operation had been started by the UDA, which had the initial contacts in South Africa. The government there, banned by UN sanctions from legitimate arms-dealing, was eager to acquire the Javelin and Starstreak missile systems manufactured by Shorts in Belfast. The Pretoria government offered the Loyalists millions of pounds in return for blueprints or working models and, as a gesture of goodwill, facilitated the arms deal in the meantime.

It seems that British intelligence were on to the plot almost from the beginning. One of the first emissaries the UDA sent to South Africa was Brian Nelson, the UDA intelligence chief who, it emerged a few years later, worked secretly for the British Army's principal intelligence-gathering outfit in Northern Ireland, known as the Force Research Unit. The weapons were smuggled into Portadown in January 1988 and the UDA and UVF were called by Resistance to an isolated farmyard where the weapons were shared among the three groups. The UDA lost its part of the arsenal on the journey back to Belfast when they were intercepted by RUC officers clearly acting on a tip-off. One of those arrested had Noel Little's phone number scrawled on his forearm but Resistance and the UVF had a lucky escape. UDA men in a second car saw the RUC stop their colleagues and quickly phoned the farmyard where the remaining conspirators fled with their weapons, escaping only minutes before the police arrived.24 Although the UVF soon lost most of its share of the haul and Resistance lost much the following November, enough of the weaponry got into circulation to cause death and mayhem. Michael Stone, the lone Loyalist who attacked an IRA funeral in 1988, used the South African-supplied grenades and a Browning pistol to kill his three victims. The UVF used AK47 rifles from the deal to riddle a Catholic bar the same year, killing three customers.

Following the loss of weapons in 1988, both the UDA and UVF withdrew from the arrangement with Resistance but it was apparent from the Paris arrests that Noel Little and his associates believed the more ambitious deal with South Africa could be revived. It was a foolish decision for it was now obvious the police had sources inside the ranks of the conspirators, including Resistance, and since at least January 1988 also definitively knew of Little's role in the plot. Indeed he had been arrested and quizzed about the deal but released for lack of evidence. He had to assume that he and his Resistance colleagues would be under the most intense surveillance. But despite that, he persisted and was caught.

There was another reason why the Paris expedition was foolish and that was because it was unnecessary. Resistance had its own home-grown supply of weapons – guns that were being manufactured at more than one location by engineers who had the requisite lathes, skills and supplies of metal. In September 1988, the police discovered one such "factory" near Ballynahinch, County Down, but there were others. An arsenal of home-made weaponry was discovered a year later on the Ards peninsula but the lathe that made them was never traced. One DUP source told the author in 1989:

> Resistance were stupid to continue after Portadown [the bank robbery], they were stupid to start it to begin with because there was no need for so many guns if they were serious about being a doomsday organisation. And I told them so. They were making their own guns, everyone was, and they could have had plenty for their needs. They should have been stockpiling material to manufacture more rather than deal with South Africans. But it was the Carson thing deep in Protestantism, the need to smuggle guns.[25]

–◦–

The Ulster Resistance episode demonstrated that both Ian Paisley and now Peter Robinson were unwilling to finish what they had started, which was to lead into battle the organisation they had created. It was not in Paisley's nature to do so and as for Robinson he had, as one colleague recalled, been affected by his narrow escape after Clontibret: "He had been the hard man before that but shortly after came the change in Peter; he went into a negotiating mode."[26] For different reasons it suited both men that Resistance should truly become a doomsday organisation, waiting for the day that in all probability would never come. Rather than doing anything to give all the threats and menace real meaning, it was better to turn Resistance into yet another harmless, if colourful, side-show. Others, Noel Little included, had evidently disagreed.

Clontibret and Resistance effectively brought Peter Robinson's days of flirting with paramilitary extremism and street politics to an end and with it the reason for his procrustean image. But Paisley was probably the greater casualty. At a press conference a few days after the Paris arrests he disowned Ulster Resistance almost entirely, blaming the group for its own misfortunes. He had offered to give them political cover, he admitted, but "they did not carry out what they were [supposed] to carry out and we have made a statement and have said we have no connection with them. If Ulster Resistance had kept the principles that were enunciated they would not have been in the position they are at the moment."[27] One veteran of Paisley's paramilitary adventures described the DUP leader's approach more cynically: "The way [Resistance] was being operated was 'If you are successful we will lead you, but if you get caught we don't want to know you'."[28] What Paisley had done, in a way, was to deny his own history and values, as another colleague explained: "He had modelled himself all his life on Carson, yet disowned modern-day Carsons." He went on: "Paisley should have said that the Paris arrests were the fault of the British, driving people to such lengths, etc., but he wouldn't do that. The Resistance people would have accepted that quite happily."[29] Instead, the DUP rank-and-file grumbled that once more they had been let down and abandoned by Paisley when it suited him; once more they had been marched to the top of the hill and then marched down again. In the aftermath of Resistance, one activist complained to a friend: "I joined so many armies all the years. I never fought once and all I have to show for it are a bunch of badges."[30]

There was another more profound consequence from all this. Paisley's disavowal of Resistance angered and alienated many of the rural grassroots Loyalists who could always be guaranteed in the past to rally round the flag for Paisley. But now, after the Resistance letdown, few of them would wish to make the same mistake again. And in the urban world of Loyalist paramilitarism, the experience was one more reminder that in Ian Paisley they would always have an inconstant ally, full of bluster and angry words but little else. The "Grand Old Duke of York" had marched up his last hill.

—◦—

By his own account Peter Robinson's Damascene conversion from the politics of protest to more conventional methods happened one day in April 1987, some three months after his appearance at the Special Criminal Court in Dublin, and once again it was a brush with the law that brought it about. The Anglo-Irish Agreement had set up a permanent Ministerial Conference which met monthly to discuss and decide policy issues of common interest, alternating between Dublin and Belfast. Every time one of the meetings took place in Belfast, Unionists would mount a picket as near to the venue as possible and, as Irish politicians and officials scrambled out of the helicopter that had landed them a short walking distance from the British Secretary of State's offices in Stormont Castle, the wailing, angry cries of protesters could always be heard in the distance. Those making the noise were invariably DUP politicians or Loyalist sympathisers whose protests took on a ritual quality. A phalanx of politicians would charge at police lines and attempt to break through coils of barbed wire to get at the Irish politicians disembarking from the helicopter. Invariably the police would overwhelm them but they would shout and scream, there would be wrestling matches with burly policemen and it always made good television, for it showed the DUP men to be as resolute and determined as ever in their opposition to the Anglo-Irish Agreement, which presumably was one reason they did it.

The Anglo-Irish Conference set for April 1997 was at Stormont Castle and so it was that on 22 April a group of DUP politicians made their ritual charge at the wire. This time Peter Robinson found a way through, a gap wide enough for him and others to clear. There was a chance to get close to the Irish government's helicopter, so Robinson broke through but ran straight into a pack of policemen who brought him to a sudden halt. As he turned round, he could see that he was alone; none of his DUP colleagues had followed him. Had even one or two braved the gap in the wire with him, then maybe they could have evaded the police long enough to embarrass the British and Irish governments– but it was not to be. Arrested but released some time later, Robinson was left to reflect on another reality – Ian Paisley's unwillingness to march over the top of the hill was widely shared in the DUP.[31]

The event was a watershed in Robinson's political life, or at least that is how he saw it at the time. In a way, the barbed wire incident, coming so soon after Clontibret and the Ulster Resistance fiasco, was also a metaphor for a closing chapter in Loyalist politics, the final episode in an annal of street politics, noisy rallies, sabre-rattling and private armies. Robinson told the story to many people in the months afterwards, including the author, to explain why he now preferred politics to protests. Cedric Wilson was once one of Peter Robinson's closest colleagues in the DUP and when Wilson complained about his new unwillingness to confront the Anglo-Irish Agreement, Robinson evoked the memory of that day outside Stormont Castle: "Peter said . . . that he was prepared to go over the top but whenever he looked back no-one was with him."[32]

Peter Robinson's journey away from the politics of street protest had actually started some two months before when, at the insistence of others in their parties, the two Unionist leaders, James Molyneaux and Ian Paisley, announced that a joint Task Force would be set up to examine strategies to oppose and replace the Agreement. Three people made up the Task Force team: Harold McCusker, the Upper Bann Official Unionist MP; Frank Millar, General Secretary of the Official Unionist Party, who had conceived of the idea; and Peter Robinson. His decision to join the group is the point at which one can say his formal break with the past happened. After consulting a wide spectrum of Unionist opinion, including the churches, the Loyal Orders and other politicians, the three would write a report and submit it to Molyneaux and Paisley.

The establishment of the Task Force was in itself an implied criticism of the Unionist *status quo*. Eighteen months of protests, strikes, secret armies, council boycotts, border incursions and even concerted attacks on RUC families had not even dented Mrs Thatcher's resolve to protect the Anglo-Irish Agreement. Unionists refused to talk to anyone else in the Irish political world until the Agreement was scrapped but their problem was that no-one seemed to care – certainly not the British and Irish governments. In fact, the flirtation with violence that characterised early Unionist opposition to the Agreement had, if anything, strengthened British resolve. Unionism was both isolated and under assault, but powerless to change either.

In the background was a barely concealed dissatisfaction with the two Unionist leaders; they had no road map worth talking about and were offering little direction. Part of the rationale of those behind the Task Force proposal was that Paisley and Molyneaux were so bereft of ideas that they would surely welcome assistance. After all, their record was dismal. Their one major initiative, conceived after the British refused to hold a referendum on the Agreement, was to contrive the mass resignation of Unionist MPs so that in the resulting by-elections Unionist discontent with the Agreement could be measured. But that backfired badly when Seamus Mallon of the SDLP captured one of the Unionist seats and by so doing helped to vindicate the Agreement, one of whose prime aims was to bolster the SDLP against Sinn Féin's electoral threat. The creation of the Task Force not only implied criticism of the current Unionist leadership but also a demand for change. That would mean abandoning street politics and softening the terms for entering talks – as well as overcoming resistance from Paisley and Molyneaux.

The Task Force report was presented to the Unionist leadership on 16 June 1987 but it was not made public until 2 July, over two weeks later, a sign that, as expected, both Paisley and Molyneaux intensely disliked its contents. In May, Paisley had publicly opposed ever making its contents public. "It is a private report to the leaders and it's not for publication," he said. But with the report likely to be leaked anyhow, common sense prevailed and it was finally published.[33] Tellingly entitled "An End to Drift", it unmistakably rejected the politics of protest in favour of dialogue and compromise. A Unionist Convention should meet to endorse the campaign against the Agreement, said the report, and to approve "without prejudice" discussions with Mrs Thatcher's government to discover whether or not the basis for wider negotiations existed. Unionist leaders, it said, should signal that "no matter" (the phrase was printed in bold type in the report) should be excluded from the agenda, a concession that opened up the likelihood that Unionists would have to accept power-sharing with Nationalists and cross-Border links to Dublin, ideas previously considered heretical, especially in the DUP.[34] Reading between the lines, it was clear that the Task Force authors favoured toning down previous demands that the Hillsborough deal had to be suspended before talks could take place. For Peter Robinson, the report represented a major break with the past but it was a bridge too far for Paisley and others in the DUP. Hardliners were already lining up behind the likes of the Rev William McCrea, who had labelled the report "a sell-out".[35]

It was no secret that Ian Paisley regarded the Task Force report as a thinly veiled attack on himself, which it clearly was. One withering sentence was clearly aimed at him. "Reliance on other people to undertake a campaign of violence which can be disowned, but from which can be extracted political advantage, would be disreputable and dishonest in the extreme," the report declared.[36] In a single sentence, Paisley's entire career had been devastatingly critiqued. Others believed that Paisley hated the report because his deputy and rival, Peter Robinson, had co-authored it. James Molyneaux, meanwhile, disliked the report because it advocated devolution, which he opposed, and by August a whispering campaign was underway against both Frank Millar and Peter Robinson and articles critical of them started appearing in the Unionist press. In September, Millar quit the Unionist Party and politics for a television job in London. Peter Robinson lasted just a few days longer. At the end of September he told Paisley he was resigning as DUP deputy leader and the news leaked out in early October. The resignation came before the DUP Executive for approval but his supporters put down a motion asking him to reconsider; it was passed only by the casting vote of the chairman, Denny Vitty, a fellow Castlereagh councillor. The DUP was exactly split down the middle, for and against their deputy leader.

Some two-and-a-half months later, Robinson was back. Paisley had been forced to reconcile with his deputy. Robinson was the only real strategist in the DUP and his managerial skills, which were largely responsible for building up the party beyond its narrow Free Presbyterian base, were sorely missed. Paisley and Molyneaux had also failed to move the British and with no viable alternative policy for dealing with the Anglo-Irish Agreement they had been forced, reluctantly, to return to the Task Force and the ideas contained in the report. Paisley also knew widespread rumours that Robinson might defect to the rival Official Unionists were based on more than gossip. There was a risk that Robinson, who knew more about the internal workings of the DUP than anyone, would take his knowledge and skills to Paisley's rivals. So he agreed to Robinson's demand.

A ten-strong joint DUP–Official Unionist policy group was set up with a brief to formulate proposals to take to the British government aimed at replacing the Anglo-Irish Agreement. Implicit in all this was a softening of the terms for starting negotiations. One way or another, Unionism would have to abandon demands that the Hillsborough deal be scrapped. Harold McCusker, the remaining Official Unionist member of the Task Force, was appointed to the group, as was Robinson. Paisley and Willie McCrea represented the Free Presbyterian wing in the DUP team and Robinson was joined by his ally Sammy Wilson. In the middle, politically, was Nigel Dodds, a Cambridge-educated barrister and a rising star in the party. By May, the group had put together power-sharing proposals and submitted them in talks started with the Northern Ireland Secretary, Tom King.

The direction of the policy group was plotted and its journey steered by Robinson, with Paisley very much in second place. In March 1988 Robinson declared his readiness to accept some form of power-sharing with Nationalists in a devolved system of government that would have control over security and a constructive relationship with the Irish government, provided the territorial claim enshrined in the Republic's constitution was abandoned. In April he repeated this theme and a day later Paisley endorsed his deputy's proposal.

Although Unionism was still divided about the way forward, as a secret report on a conference involving Unionist and Nationalist politicians later in 1988 showed, Robinson had emerged as the dominating influence in the inter-party discussions:

> . . . in the group of ten, five representing each of the DUP and OUP, exactly half were wholeheartedly in favour of the partnership proposals which had been put to government. Four went along with them but would be quite happy to see them fall and one constantly sat on the fence. . . . Peter Robinson was the principal author of those proposals and was totally committed. It was Paisley's refusal to put those proposals to the Government in the first instance that led to his resignation as Deputy Leader of the DUP and it was only after Paisley did agree, after much delay, to put the partnership proposals to the British Government that he agreed to return as Deputy Leader. He had in that period contemplated joining the Official Unionist Party but recognised the problems that that would have presented during the period of the Unionist pact. That option remains open but the present circumstances make it impossible.[37]

—◁○▷—

Robinson began his journey by challenging Paisley from the fundamentalist and hardline wing of the DUP but failed. Then he executed a 180 degree political turnabout and now confronted him from the pragmatic, moderate end of the Unionist spectrum, with much more success. In the process he had demonstrated that the DUP really couldn't do without him. For the first time in his political life, Ian Paisley was faced with a deputy who was his match in all the important ways and was intent on pushing the DUP in a direction that sometimes unnerved Paisley, even though privately it may have been where he wanted to go or knew he should go. The DUP leader had discarded earlier rivals with ease but neutralising Robinson would be a much more difficult task. While Paisley distrusted Robinson, he also needed him both to formulate new policies and strategies and to take the heat for himself. Whenever the DUP lurched in a direction that alarmed the Free Presbyterian base of the party, as it did quite dramatically in the years of the peace process, Robinson was always there for Paisley to blame, a readily available whipping boy who would carry the can. And by scapegoating him, Paisley had to undermine him.

One incident captures all this perfectly. In October 1988, as Unionists desperately sought an acceptable way of entering all-party talks, ecumenical clergymen in Germany and Ireland invited the four main parties – Official Unionists, SDLP, DUP and Alliance – to a weekend conference at a hotel in Duisburg, Germany. The invitation was sent to each party leader, who was asked to nominate a representative, preferably the party's deputy leader, to send to the meeting. Peter Robinson was Paisley's choice. The Duisburg gathering wrestled with the question of how the Anglo-Irish Agreement and the Maryfield Secretariat could be suspended in a way that would be credible to Unionist supporters, acceptable to Nationalists and sufficiently compelling to allow talks to begin with London. Discussions continued for weeks in the wake of Duisburg but eventually the story was leaked to the BBC and a full-scale political row followed, with both the SDLP and Unionists downplaying the significance of events at Duisburg.

The political panic that followed disclosure of Duisburg was out of all proportion to the event itself and it was not until many years later that the real reason for the fuss became clear. Also invited to the conference was a Redemptorist priest called Fr Alec Reid who, unknown to the outside world, was in the midst of secret discussions with the president of Sinn Féin, Gerry Adams, and the British and Irish governments which later took more formal shape as the peace process. He was there, as the report described it, "in the capacity of someone who was familiar with the Sinn Féin view".[38] There was so much panic after the BBC revelation about Duisburg because the Unionist politicians who had attended were terrified that Reid's presence would become public. Back in 1988, speaking to anyone associated with the Provisional IRA or its political wing was unthinkable, almost an act of political suicide, especially to Unionists.

In no party was the reaction to Duisburg as bad as in the DUP. Had the party's grassroots known that a Catholic priest was also there, speaking, no matter how obliquely, on behalf of Sinn Féin, there would have been an explosion of anger inside the DUP. As the participants in the Duisburg conference prepared to travel to Germany, Ian Paisley was, by happy coincidence, strengthening his fundamentalist credentials elsewhere. Pope John Paul II had been invited to address the European Parliament in Strasbourg and as he appeared in front of the ranks of Euro-MPs, Paisley interrupted him. Holding up a poster saying "JOHN PAUL II ANTICHRIST", he shouted "I renounce you as the Antichrist" several times before being escorted from the chamber. Respectable Unionists shuddered with embarrassment but in the Free Presbyterian heartlands they smiled with pleasure and pride. So when news of Duisburg leaked, Paisley was easily able to disown it and blame Robinson. Cedric Wilson remembers the incident well:

> When Duisburg became public I told Peter that he had been wrong to go, that it sent the wrong message. I also told him that Paisley was saying that he was very upset and that he hadn't known anything about the conference beforehand. But Peter replied, "If he tries to hang me out to dry on this I'll finish him." The implication was that Paisley had known beforehand about Duisburg, was fine with it but had disowned Robinson when it all became public.[39]

From this time onwards it would become harder and harder to disentangle the two men; the story of Paisley became the story of Paisley and Robinson, each man distrusting, perhaps even disliking but needing the other, one to provide the DUP with ideas and direction and the other to give cover to the departures from orthodoxy that followed.

The story of the "local option" is an example. For years the DUP's stand on Sunday observance mirrored that of the Free Presbyterian Church, which was that public facilities, such as parks, leisure centres and the like, should be closed on the Sabbath. But that was a minority view within Northern Protestantism, especially amongst working-class Protestants in Belfast, the DUP's target constituency for growth. The Free Presbyterian policy would inhibit the DUP's ability to expand and had to go. So in 1986 the idea of the "local option" was born. Each local council could decide for itself if it wanted to impose or abandon strict Sunday observance. The issue came to a meeting of the DUP Executive but a motion proposing it should become party policy was defeated by one vote. Paisley intervened and angrily demanded a recount. He wanted the policy changed because he knew that removing the sabbatarian ban would help the DUP grow. The vote was retaken and this time Paisley won by one vote. In Free Presbyterian circles, though, Paisley acted as if he still supported the ban. When Castlereagh council, by then firmly under Peter Robinson's control, opened an ice rink in September 1986 and decreed that it should open on Sundays, Paisley and a group of Free Presbyterian clerics and lay members mounted a noisy protest and picket outside. In such a way could responsibility for the change be shifted on to Peter Robinson's shoulders and Paisley exonerated.

It is no surprise that, over the years, the relationship between the two men soured. At one point, Cedric Wilson complained to Paisley about Robinson's growing willingness to accept the Anglo-Irish Agreement:

> I expressed my reservations to Paisley about where Peter was taking us and Paisley said to me – and, remember, he was always reluctant to discuss such things – that "I have great difficulty walking with that man", which if you know your Bible is a statement full of significance. He had also referred to him, to my knowledge, as being too clever by half, building up a power base in Castlereagh. Unlike [Nigel] Dodds and [Willie] McCrea, with whom Paisley would socialise, Peter never fell into the category of a close colleague. Remember as well that he was Pentecostalist, never a Free Presbyterian.[40]

Paisley may well have had great difficulty walking with Robinson but nonetheless he continued to do so.

*"You have sold Ulster to buy off the fiendish
Republican scum."*

IAN PAISLEY TO PRIME MINISTER JOHN MAJOR, OUTSIDE 10 DOWNING STREET ON
THE DAY THE DOWNING STREET DECLARATION WAS PUBLISHED

*"Some of Ulster's maimed have no eyes. Some have no ears.
Some have no hands. Some have no arms. Some have no legs.
Some are imprisoned in a wheelchair for their life's duration.
They are the limbless, the eyeless, the earless and the faceless,
the ones who took the shock of IRA bombing. But what do
these unionists care? They go into talks with Bertie Ahern,
who took an oath to destroy Ulster."*

IAN PAISLEY ATTACKING DAVID TRIMBLE AT DUP ANNUAL CONFERENCE, 1997

CHAPTER TWELVE

The Assembly of the Wicked

Peter Robinson and those others in Unionism eager to oppose the Anglo-Irish Agreement with more conventional, constitutional tactics would soon get their way, although ultimately they would be disappointed. A more ambitious initiative aimed at bringing the Republican men of violence into the political fold while securing a stable and long-lasting peace would replace and eclipse their efforts and give Ian Paisley a chance to once more play all the roles he had perfected in over thirty years in politics: the fearless, heroic defender of Ulster Protestant rights, the clear-sighted prophet, the forthright and outspoken scourge of Unionist traitors. But while the peace process, as the strategy was soon christened, was excoriated by Ian Paisley and his disciples as a dastardly appeasement of the IRA and a plot against the Union, it brought him undreamed-of opportunity. It enabled him first to achieve a great prize, whose attainment had driven him for years: the undisputed hegemony of Northern Irish Unionism. And that feat would propel Paisley towards the second, even greater triumph, one that nobody could have foreseen, not even a prophet raised by God. It would send him on a determined mission for political power which would end in the First Minister's office at Stormont Castle where he would bask in the approval and gratitude of those in the British and Irish establishments who had, in the past, always condemned him. And that would make Ian Paisley's journey one of the strangest and most fascinating in Irish history. But that was to come later; in the meantime there was treason and perfidy to expose to the light.

―◇―

It was not until three years after the Duisburg Conference that a satisfactory formula was crafted to allow Unionists to enter talks. During a managed gap in meetings of the Anglo-Irish Intergovernmental Conference, all-party talks began in April 1991 and lasted, with an eight-month break, until November 1992. Although no agreement was reached, the Brooke-Mayhew Talks, so-named after the two British Secretaries of State who oversaw them, did establish new political benchmarks that would become more important later. The talks were divided into three separate strands which became a template for the future: agreement was sought on government institutions within Northern Ireland; between North and South; and between Ireland and Britain, the so-called East–West strand. As that structure implied, Unionists had made two concessions, although these were made more grudgingly and deniably by the DUP than by the Ulster Unionists.[1] The two elements of a settlement which had always been fiercely resisted in the past were conceded: the principle of sharing power with Nationalists and the idea that there should be all-Ireland institutions of some sort linking policies on a range of issues between Dublin and Belfast. During the negotiations, Ulster Unionists talked to ministers in the Dublin government and even travelled south to Dublin Castle for sessions with the Irish government, the first time this had ever happened. The DUP refused to take part in these meetings, saying it would not do so until Dublin abandoned its claim on the North, but even so the party did interact with the Dublin delegation, another first in Irish politics. By the standards of Northern Ireland's politics at that time, this was real movement.

Nonetheless the talks ran into difficulties. The SDLP, which had pioneered the three-strand approach, appeared to have lost interest in it and the party leader, John Hume, proposed a mostly powerless Assembly and a partly appointed Executive or cabinet, neither of which were of any interest to the two Unionist parties. There was also a long-running dispute with the Irish government, at this point led by Taoiseach Albert Reynolds, over when and in what circumstances the Republic would remove the territorial claim to the North contained in the Irish constitution. Big differences had also emerged over the extent and powers of any cross-Border arrangement. Eventually, in November 1992, the talks collapsed.

During the talks Albert Reynolds had insisted that if the Irish constitutional claim to the North was to be on the agenda, then so should Britain's 1920 Government of Ireland Act, which expressed

British sovereignty over Northern Ireland. This and Hume's curious departure from SDLP orthodoxy were vital, but missed clues that the two leaders of Irish Nationalism had other, bigger things on their mind. Five months after the talks ended, on 10 April 1993, the President of Sinn Féin, Gerry Adams, was spotted entering John Hume's house in Derry and the reason for Hume and Reynolds's preoccupation became public. The Derry journalist Eamon McCann was told about the visit and immediately phoned the news desk of the *Sunday Tribune* in Dublin, for which he then wrote, explaining that while his source would be compromised if he followed up on the story, someone else definitely should. The story was passed on and in due course John Hume was phoned by the paper. Initially Hume denied the sighting but then rang back a few minutes later to admit that it was true and to apologise for attempting to mislead the journalist. What Hume had to say was the first evidence of what would become known, in some circles notoriously, as the Hume-Adams talks.

Unionists reacted with predictable suspicion. Ian Paisley threatened to boycott any future talks if Hume persisted in the dialogue with Adams, while Peter Robinson said it was an attempt by Sinn Féin to acquire respectability prior to trying to enter resumed all-party talks that had stalled the previous November. The DUP leader presented the meeting as part of a strategy to pressurise Unionists by threatening a separate settlement with Sinn Féin. Later, when Hume and Adams issued their first joint statement – on the same day as an IRA truck bomb devastated the City of London, killing one person and causing stg£1 billion of damage – Paisley characterised the talks in a phrase that would stick, at least as far as most Unionists were concerned. The words of Hume and Adams proved, he said, that there was a "pan-Nationalist league" at work against Unionists, involving the Catholic Church, the IRA, Sinn Féin and the SDLP.[2] Paisley's phrase would soon become "the pan-Nationalist Front" in everyday usage.

He could have added the Irish government to that list, and the British for that matter. The truth about the Hume–Adams dialogue is that it was only the most recent manifestation of a process that had been in gestation for at least a decade and which had already involved secret diplomacy between Gerry Adams on the one hand and the Catholic Church and the two governments on the other. Thoroughly soaked in ambiguity, the initiative, which had been started by Adams and a Belfast-based Redemptorist priest, Fr Alec Reid, back in 1982, was all things to all men. To Adams's colleagues on the Army Council and to the IRA and Sinn Féin rank-and-file, it was a clever and innovative effort to achieve their goal of obtaining British withdrawal. To the two governments, it was a signal from Sinn Féin that it wished to abandon violence and leave the IRA behind in return for an influential seat at the negotiating table. Of the two, the governments were nearer the mark. Privately, Adams had let it be known that he was prepared to accept a new definition of British withdrawal in which Britain agreed to abide by the outcome of all-party talks, as long as they involved Sinn Féin, and would not try to impose her will.[3] Implied in that approach was that Sinn Féin would accept the principle of consent and Northern Ireland's constitutional status in return for a share of power.

Unaware of all this and seeing only that which was before their eyes, many Unionists immediately sensed treachery and, as he had always done in the past, Ian Paisley had put the right words together to describe their fears and suspicions. And, not for the first time in Northern Ireland's recent troubled history, there would be others in the Unionist community for whom words were insufficient but who would nonetheless find inspiration and direction from them. Throughout the rest of 1993, the largest Loyalist paramilitary group, the Ulster Defence Association made a series of attacks on the homes and cars of SDLP politicians and party members. It was a clear attempt to intimidate and punish the party for the actions of their leader, to strike out at the pan-Nationalist Front that was conspiring against Ulster. But in February 1994, the UDA ratcheted up its campaign. An attempt was made to assassinate two SDLP figures, and the UDA warned of an escalating murder campaign against the party. Peter Robinson commented in response that it was "probably logical that people in the loyalist community have seen that terrorism has worked for the IRA and feel that they can make it work for themselves".[4] He added that the DUP would not attempt to talk to the UDA to try to persuade it to end this violence since that would only legitimise John Hume's talks with Gerry Adams. If there was such a thing as pan-Nationalism, then its mirror image was being created on the Unionist side – and these were the circumstances in which Ian Paisley's politics had always thrived.

–◄o►–

The DUP's annual conference in November 1993 gathered in a fever pitch of excitement generated by the certain knowledge that treachery was everywhere and, with it, the need for resolution and courage in the difficult but rousing days that lay ahead. Since the Hume–Adams dialogue had been exposed, evidence of a wider and deeper plot had surfaced. Against a background of large and destructive IRA bombs in Protestant towns like Portadown and Newtownards and the wrecking of the newly renovated Grand Opera House opposite Ulster Unionist Party headquarters in central Belfast, Irish President Mary Robinson had met Gerry Adams in West Belfast. Although Robinson refused permission for a photograph of her handshake with the Provisional leader, it was an act that symbolically began Adams's rehabilitation by the Irish establishment. Since this was happening while Adams's colleagues in the IRA were bombing Protestant shopping areas, it could have only one effect on Unionist thinking. A delegation of weighty Irish-Americans which included corporate leaders, people who in the past would never have come near the Provisionals, had travelled to meet Sinn Féin leaders and it emerged that a seven-day IRA ccasefire had been arranged at their request and for their benefit. Hume and Adams sent a report on their talks to the Irish government, saying that they had put together an agreed joint statement and there were leaks to the media that an IRA ceasefire had been offered in return for British recognition of the Irish people's right as a whole to national self-determination. That phrase had taken on a new ambiguity in the light of Adams's secret redefinition of the concept, although Unionists didn't yet know that. As Ulster Unionists like James Molyneaux joined British Premier John Major in hinting that Sinn Féin might be able to join talks in the right circumstances, there were leaks in Dublin to the press suggesting that Irish unity would be on the agenda if talks began. Meanwhile the British and Irish prime ministers met to agree a common approach to the Northern Ireland problem. Taken together, these were all signs to Loyalists of a conspiracy to sell them out.

And as had happened so often in the past, these were the circumstances in which the first Loyalist paramilitary instinct was to reach for the gun. Indiscriminate killings of Catholics rose dramatically and the UVF, in a not very subtle message, officially admitted for the first time that it had bombed Dublin and Monaghan during the 1974 Sunningdale experiment and was responsible for the thirty-three deaths and scores of injuries. Between the lines, the UVF was saying ". . . and we can do it again". In response to a surge in UDA killings, the IRA attempted to wipe out the group's Inner Council but the effort was badly botched and nine Protestant civilians were killed as a powerful bomb reduced a Shankill Road fishmonger's shop to rubble. A tenth victim was one of the IRA bombers and at his funeral Gerry Adams shouldered his casket, provoking more anger in the Unionist community. The DUP met as the North slid towards a precipice.

DUP annual conferences were invariably among the most colourful and ritualised pieces of theatre in British and Irish politics, although some would say that "circus" would be a more fitting word. The ringmaster was, as always, Ian Paisley, who ran the show without ever having to crack his whip; and then there were the performers, the second rank stars who each year would have to put on a show that would have the rank-and-file cheering or laughing. A politician's standing in the DUP was to no small extent determined by how well he performed at conference. The unchallenged star was always Sammy Wilson, the leftish former Belfast Lord Mayor, who invariably had the best lines and stage presence. No performance was complete without colourful, sometimes wounding and always personal insults being hurled at the DUP's many enemies in Ireland – Catholics and Nationalists, who were by definition the traditional enemy; and the Ulster Unionists who were the real enemy, not least because their votes were coveted by DUP leaders. If imitation is indeed the sincerest form of flattery, then DUP conferences were really love-ins dedicated to Ian Paisley, who, by common consent, was master of the well-worded barb.

The 1993 conference saw a veritable competition in insults. The Catholic primate, Cardinal Cahal Daly, was described as "the little hump from Armagh – Hell will never be full until he's in it"; Irish Taoiseach Albert Reynolds was "The green gnome of Irish politics"; Ulster Unionist MP, Ken Maginnis, was "the great Walrus from the lakes of Enniskillen". Ulster Unionist leader Jim Molyneaux was a "market trader" who sold his vote at Westminster for prime ministerial favour. Other Unionists were selling tickets to Sinn Féin for seats at the negotiating table. And so on. Paisley himself was at his best. He spoke for 75 minutes and won a standing ovation and the usual chorus of "For He's a Jolly Good Fellow!" His speech, as one report noted, "took the audience on a journey from 'the rivers of blood in 1641, when a murderous scheme to exterminate Protestants forever' was hatched, through to the Second World War, when the Republic was 'a hyena to the fascist wild beast, happy and ready to pick the bones of its victims'". Invoking the memory of Carson, and by implication himself, he described what was happening as "the greatest threat to the Union since the Home Rule crisis". Prime Minister Major, the Taoiseach, Albert Reynolds and Cardinal Daly were all doing deals behind Protestant backs and their plan was simple: "Sell out loyal Ulster to those who have already committed genocide amongst us. Destroy our democracy. Dislodge the union. Turn your back on your friends. Embrace our enemies. Enter into the assembly of the wicked. Stain your hands in the congregation of the murderers, but remember that the Almighty God of justice still rules. That truth can never yield the throne. That the lie is bound to perish. That wickedness cannot prosper."[5]

Willie McCrea, who always opened DUP conferences with a lengthy prayer and at other DUP occasions like the annual dinner would regale diners with gospel songs, was another conference favourite. To wild cheering, he said he could find a place for Gerry Adams but not at the talks table: "in a cell in Crumlin Road jail, C-Wing, hanging by the neck until he's dead!"[6] Part of the reason for the excitement at conference was that those in the know were aware that, thanks to Willie McCrea, the following day would see undeniable proof of British perfidy. McCrea had acquired a document which later turned out to be an extract from a written record of secret talks between the IRA and British officials. He had passed it on to a local reporter, Eamon Mallie, who was a stringer for the Sunday *Observer* in London – "[You] slid it to a journalist", hissed an angry British Secretary, Sir Patrick Mayhew, to McCrea in the House of Commons a few days later. The story confirming that secret talks had been underway and had started in 1990 was duly published.[7] During his annual *tour de force* Ian Paisley had demanded that John Hume publish the full details of the agreement hatched with Gerry Adams and after the report was published, it looked as if once again he had asked the right question, although the finger of suspicion for the leak to McCrea pointed to an unknown sympathiser in the RUC Special Branch.

Nothing was more calculated to cause alarm and heighten insecurity in the collective Unionist psyche than the revelation of secret contacts between the IRA and the British, since, in their minds, it could only mean they were being sold out. During previous IRA ceasefires and periods of contact with the British, in 1972 and between 1974 and 1975, Loyalist paramilitaries had gone on the rampage, killing scores of uninvolved Catholics in random, often savage, murders. That was always a reliable barometer of feelings in the wider Unionist community, a clue that distrust of the British was deeply embedded in the genetic makeup of Unionist politics. It did not take much to stir the suspicion that the British would betray them, that efforts would be made to appease the IRA so as to end its bombings and shootings. Rumours of the secret diplomacy had been circulating for months, each time being met with indignant British denials. So when the talks were confirmed, British assurances that they were really about persuading the IRA to abandon violence consequently cut little ice with Protestants. In July, Jim Molyneaux and fellow MP John Taylor had alleged there had been secret contact in the previous twelve months but the Northern Ireland Office had denied this, saying: "The policy of the British government is not to talk to Sinn Féin or the IRA until they renounce violence." That now looked like a barefaced lie, and Willie McCrea drew a conclusion shared by most of his co-religionists: "If they have told us untruths about this, then it is fact that they could tell you untruths about the final sell-out of the Province."[8]

It was left to Ian Paisley to give dramatic shape to Unionist misgivings, as he would do throughout the early years of the peace process. The day after the *Observer* revelations, he stood up in the House of Commons and called Sir Patrick Mayhew a liar. Only the week before, Paisley claimed, Mayhew and Major had rubbished rumours of such contacts in a meeting with him. "I stand by what I said. It was a falsehood. It was worse. It was a lie."[9] The Speaker intervened, admonished Paisley for making such an allegation against a fellow member and suspended him from the chamber for five days. Ever the master of political showmanship, Paisley had signalled to the folks back home that, as long as he was around, British treachery would be exposed and confronted.

◄○►

When the Anglo-Irish Agreement had been signed back in 1985, Paisley had responded by seeking a political alliance with the Ulster Unionist leader, Jim Molyneaux. The pair met often to plot strategy and so did members of their parties. The arrangement was called the Unionist Pact and, although cynics would maintain that Paisley had sought the arrangement because he was unsure how else to respond to the deal and was nervous about adopting more direct tactics, the instinct to band together for better protection was deeply embedded in Unionist culture, and the Hillsborough deal had brought that instinct to the surface. The huge anti-Agreement rally outside Belfast City Hall in November 1985, which brought tens of thousands of Protestants of all classes on to the streets, from the tatooed toughs of the Shankill Road to the north Down swanks, was evidence of that and it would have been a mistake on Paisley's part to ignore it. But the pact with their rivals came at a heavy cost to the DUP, as such arrangements always do when a smaller party links up with a larger one. Invariably the smaller group's identity is blurred and with it a reason to motivate voters is lost and the DUP was no exception to this rule. The DUP vote had fallen by over six points in a local government election in 1989, some three years after the pact was agreed, and later in the year Ian Paisley's vote in the European election dipped badly from the 230,000 he had won in 1984 to 160,000. This was alarmingly short of the 200,000 target set privately by the party leadership and evidence that apathy had kept voters at home – one survey of a Bangor housing estate, where usually 1,000 votes went to the DUP, showed that only 40 supporters had stirred themselves. If there was one saving grace, it was that the same malaise had affected the rival Ulster Unionists. Only in Peter Robinson's Castlereagh council had the vote risen and this was because the pact had broken down there and the two parties "were fighting with [the local Ulster Unionist leader] John Taylor like cats", as one local source put it. The conclusion was clear: "Paisley now accepts that the pact was at fault for the drop in our vote," a senior party source told the author at the time.[10]

There would be no Unionist pact in the wake of Hume–Adams and all that followed, for sure, and if there were efforts from time to time to construct one, these were mostly half-hearted and for the optics or to highlight the unreliability of putative Ulster Unionist allies. Ian Paisley would, from 1993 onwards, target the Ulster Unionists as enthusiastically and bitterly as he did the IRA, Sinn Féin, John Hume and the British. His argument was simple: without weak-kneed compromisers inside the Unionist camp, none of the Republican plotting and deception could succeed. So the compromisers must be exposed and rooted out. This was the Ian Paisley of the 1960s doing what he did best, revealing and reviling traitors and Lundies in the Protestant camp. The approach had served him well back then and it would serve him well now.

John Hume and Gerry Adams had put together a document that they wished to be published by the two governments as a definitive statement of British policy towards Northern Ireland. Nowhere in the peace process was the inherent ambiguity of the strategy more evident than in the version of the Hume–Adams statement that the two governments eventually did publish. Adams had secured the IRA Army Council's authority to negotiate with Hume on the basis that their joint statement would commit the British to withdraw from Northern Ireland. The IRA agreed, as an incentive for agreement, to drop its customary demand for speedy withdrawal, saying instead it would be content if the process took even 20 or more years. What mattered to the IRA was the public commitment to withdraw. In the Hume–Adams document there was actually a space left blank to be filled in eventually with the date for British withdrawal. It was to remain blank.

None of this squared with the secret commitment that Gerry Adams had made in his dealings with government. At the core of these was a redefinition of Irish national self-determination. As long as Britain promised not to dictate or interfere with negotiations, Sinn Féin would abide by the outcome of all-party talks which would become the forum for the self-determining process. Since such talks would certainly not set aside the principle of consent, the one sure outcome was that Northern Ireland's constitutional position inside the United Kingdom would remain untouched. Sinn Féin would thus accept the consent principle and with it the existence of Northern Ireland. The core of the Sinn Féin approach was spelled out in a secret letter to Charles Haughey, sent in 1987 by Fr Reid, which outlined Adams's proposal. Far from seeking British withdrawal, it read, Sinn Féin would "accept, and would even insist on the need for a continuing British presence" to implement and oversee the new dispensation agreed at the all-party talks.[11] In other words, Sinn Féin would exchange the goal of expelling the British for a place in a new settlement based on the constitutional status quo. As for the IRA Army Council, it was between a rock and a hard place. It had entered the process on the basis of securing British withdrawal but such was the expectation of peace generated by the Hume–Adams talks that it risked censure and blame if the outcome of those talks caused it to withdraw from them and the peace process collapsed.

─◄○►─

The Downing Street Declaration, unveiled on 15 December 1993, was the result of weeks of negotiations and wrangling between the British and Irish governments but in its final form it more resembled the private commitments given by Gerry Adams than the outcome set and anticipated by the Army Council. There was no date for British withdrawal, nor anything remotely resembling it. An "agreed Ireland" replaced a "united Ireland" in the lexicon of Anglo-Irish diplomacy. But there was enough green language in the document to unsettle Unionists. Britain declared once again that she had no selfish strategic or economic interests for staying in Northern Ireland and then came the sentence that had some Unionists up in arms: "The British Government agree that it is for the people of the island of Ireland alone, by agreement between the two parts respectively, to exercise their right of self-determination on the basis of consent, freely and concurrently given, North and South, to bring about a united Ireland, if that is their wish." Translated from the dense language of Whitehall, this was actually a restatement of the principle that Northern Ireland would stay British as long as most of its citizens wished. Nor was it new. The Heath government back in the early 1970s had first set out this idea. Many Unionists, though, just focused on words like "self-determination" and "a united Ireland". Even though the Irish government also pledged that such self-determination, "must be achieved and exercised with and subject to the agreement and consent of a majority of the people of Northern Ireland", Unionists of the Ian Paisley variety remained unconvinced.

Knowing that the Declaration would have to be written in such a way as to give Republicans a reason not to walk out of the process, the John Major government had been careful to keep key figures in the Unionist community on board. Ulster Unionist leader, Jim Molyneaux, who had been tipped off by the British about the *Observer* story on the secret IRA talks for the same reason, had been allowed to contribute to the text and was regularly consulted throughout. The Church of Ireland primate, Dr Robin Eames, also had helped to write it, as did Loyalist paramilitary politicians who were offered a hand in its composition by Taoiseach Albert Reynolds.[12] On the day of publication, Molyneaux gave a cautious response to the document, saying it would be dangerous only if its implementation was not properly scrutinised. But Paisley, sensing both double-dealing and opportunity, took a more direct approach and wrote his own letter to John Major, which he delivered to 10 Downing Street within minutes of the publication of the Declaration. Denouncing Major's part in "this dark hour of treachery", he read his letter aloud, refusing the aid of a microphone, to bewildered Fleet Street journalists: "It is a tripartite agreement between Reynolds, the IRA and you. You have sold Ulster to buy off the fiendish Republican scum and you are prepared to do this notorious deed with such speed that time is not even given for the Christian burial of their latest victim, a gallant member of the RUC." This was a reference to two RUC detectives shot dead by the IRA in County Tyrone three days before. "You will learn in a bitter school that all appeasement of these monsters is self-destructive. The hand which reaches for your blood money will never be satisfied until it destroys you."[13] Asked by reporters what he would do now, Paisley replied: "Actions speak louder than words."

—◄○►—

Northern Ireland was now headed towards an IRA ceasefire. The Army Council had rejected the Declaration but Adams had persuaded his colleagues to keep this a secret. The Council agreed and by so doing effectively made the cessation possible. The Irish government repealed legislation that had kept Sinn Féin off the airwaves and Adams was granted a three-day visa to visit New York to address a foreign policy conference, where he was feted by the American media and courted by a new generation of wealthy Irish-American business leaders. Paisley was also invited to speak but declined to share a platform with Adams. Later that year he did give an address to the group but such was the lack of interest that the organisers, who included Bill Flynn, chairman of the insurance giant Mutual of America, were obliged to conscript Mutual employees to make up a decent-sized audience. One can only imagine what they made of Ian Paisley. As the IRA floated on a sea of Sinn Féin concessions towards the August 1994 ceasefire, many Unionists felt even more reason to be suspicious. Molyneaux swung between calling the Declaration "a comparatively safe document" to saying "it has the makings of a betrayal", but Paisley was forthright and unambiguous. He accused Molyneaux of misleading his community. "How could a plea to the IRA that wants to destroy Northern Ireland be anything but a sell-out?" he asked. "You cannot appease the IRA." Peter Robinson said that the Declaration was "sustained by the acquiescence and support of Ulster Unionist MPs and the terrible consequences that will flow from it will be the responsibility of Ulster Unionist MPs".

As the 1994 European election poll neared, Paisley's language drew more and more from the Paisley of the 1960s. "Save Ulster" rallies were launched and at one in Newtownards, he pointed out that everyone responsible for Ulster's present travails was "a practising Roman Catholic, a Son of the Church". There was the Sinn Féin president Gerry Adams, "who once had met the Pope; and the SDLP leader, Mr John

Hume, who was reportedly overjoyed that Sunday Mass could be attended on Saturdays. This pair had held their meetings in Belfast's Clonard Monastery. And who had presided over them? None other than a priest of Rome." Language used to attack Ulster Unionists grew more extreme. Molyneaux he described first as "a Judas Iscariot" and then as "a Lundy", the worst insult in the Unionist dictionary. The only way to prevent the sell-out was to vote for him, he said. In the June Euro-election, Paisley topped the poll but his 163,000 votes were a disappointment, not much better than the result in 1989. Nonetheless he claimed the victory as an endorsement of his view of the Declaration.

Just before the ceasefire, he reverted to Paisley the prophet of doom. The British had opened up another channel to the IRA, he claimed in mid-August. When the ceasefire came a few days later, this was proof to more than just the DUP faithful that he had got it right once again. Molyneaux responded to the ceasefire by tacking in a wholly different direction. Seeking to reassure the Unionist community, he said: "I am now in a position to advise that, contrary to wild speculation . . . there has been no shift in the attitude of Her Majesty's Government in regard to the future constitutional position of Northern Ireland." Paisley knew that many grassroots Unionists would see things very differently. A week or so after the ceasefire announcement, as Gerry Adams was photographed outside Government Buildings in Dublin with Albert Reynolds and John Hume, the principal partners in the hated "pan-Nationalist Front", Ian Paisley was ejected from Downing Street by the Prime Minister. During a meeting with the Prime Minister, he had refused four times to accept John Major's assurance that there had been no secret deals with the IRA and Major threw him out. According to Paisley, he had said, "Get out of this room, and never come back until you accept that I speak the truth."[14]

As the British and Sinn Féin leaders bickered over whether or not the ceasefire was permanent, two events occurred that would shape the future direction of the peace process. In November 1994 armed IRA robbers shot dead a postal worker during a raid and, despite IRA protestations of innocence, the incident placed decommissioning at the top of the agenda. If IRA words about the permanence of the peace were ambiguous, then the British, and the Unionists, would need independent, transparent evidence and what better proof could there be of peaceful intent than scrapping redundant weapons?

The process also lumbered uneasily and uncertainly towards the political talks that everyone knew had to happen to place the ceasefire beyond breakdown. Major first made "a working assumption" that the ceasefire was permanent and announced that the media ban on Sinn Féin in Britain would be dropped. There would also be talks between Northern Ireland Office officials and Sinn Féin. Members of the Provisional delegation wore two hats. The leader of the team, Martin McGuinness, was called Sinn Féin's chief negotiator but Republicans also knew that he was chairman of the Army Council, in which capacity he was the IRA's traditional representative in contacts outside the organisation and in negotiations with other parties. The number two, Gerry Kelly, was IRA Adjutant-General, the Chief of Staff's deputy. The British were really talking to the IRA as much as to Sinn Féin. When the talks began, Paisley called it "the darkest day in Ulster's history" and thousands of Unionists nodded in agreement.

The second thing Major did was to work with Dublin on a settlement plan and, in February 1995, the British government published a putative agenda for substantive talks, once more based on the three-strand approach. There would be an Assembly, an Executive of sorts and a North–South body with "dynamic", i.e. evolving executive, harmonising and consultative functions over a range of all-Ireland issues. To win over Unionists, the Irish government pledged to modify its territorial claim by inserting a consent clause for Irish unity in the constitution. Although Major told Unionists that nothing could happen without the approval of Unionist politicians and a referendum vote, the Framework documents, as the British proposal was called, threw Unionism into a tizzy. Suddenly the warnings from Paisley looked prescient, while the assurances of Molyneaux appeared naive and even foolish. The process was moving, it seemed, in an all-Ireland direction just as the DUP leader had forecast. "A one-way street to Dublin," he had called it.

The first casualty was Jim Molyneaux. The Frameworks documents had caught the Ulster Unionists entirely by surprise and this immediately cast doubt on Molyneaux's claim to have an inside track to John Major, a relationship that had grown out of Major's thin parliamentary majority and his need for Unionist votes. It looked as if Molyneaux had been gypped. That was bad enough but this was the second time this had happened to the Ulster Unionist leader. In 1985, he claimed to have had a similar close relationship with Margaret Thatcher but was wrong-footed when she put her name to the Anglo-Irish Agreement. "Fool me once, shame on you. Fool me twice, shame on me" became the catch-cry of Unionism and by September 1995

Molyneaux had been overthrown and replaced by David Trimble, the MP for Upper Bann, whose elevation was greeted with a groan throughout Nationalist Ireland. As one report put it, "He rarely laughs. . . . He's the OUP's answer to Peter Robinson."[15]

There can be little doubt that Trimble's name for being a hardliner was one reason party delegates had voted for him; they wanted someone with backbone, whose judgement they could trust and who wouldn't be conned by the Prime Minister. An academic lawyer, Trimble had backed the tough former Unionist Home Affairs Minister, Bill Craig, when he split from the Unionist Party way back at the start of the Troubles and in 1974 he had played a role in organising the Ulster Workers Council strike that brought down the Sunningdale power-sharing deal. When Harold McCusker, the Unionist MP for Upper Bann, suddenly died of cancer, Trimble made a bid for nomination as his successor. A week or so before the selection meeting, he played the Paisley card. The occasion was a visit in April 1990 to Belfast by the Irish Taoiseach Charles Haughey, who had agreed to attend a business conference at the Europa Hotel in the centre of the city. As his car drove into the hotel's underground car park in Glengall Street, there was a sudden commotion from the roof of the Unionist Party headquarters opposite. Three figures could be seen on the roof — Ian Paisley, Peter Robinson and David Trimble — waving Union Jacks and hurling insults at Haughey. One of the DUP men later explained that Trimble had let them into the building and led them up to the roof. A week or so later Trimble won the nomination and romped home in the by-election.

Nationalists had more recent cause to distrust Trimble and Unionists to see in him the sort of leader the impending crisis demanded. In July 1995 he had joined Paisley in supporting Orangemen who wanted to march through the Catholic Garvaghy Road area of Portadown, despite the vehement opposition of locals and government fear that if the Orangemen got their way, the resulting violence could derail the peace camp in the IRA. The RUC had blocked the Orangemen's path and the pair mediated on their behalf in an attempt to get the police to lift their roadblock. But the confrontation had turned violent. The police and Orangemen were fighting running battles through the fields surrounding the roadblock; stones were hurled at the police, who replied with plastic bullets. In the face of more serious threats of violence from the thousands of Loyalists who had flocked to Portadown and from extremists elsewhere in the North, the RUC capitulated and, after talks led by Trimble, allowed about 800 local Orangemen to march through the area, without bands but in full regalia. After the march had passed by, victorious Orangemen in the centre of Portadown called for Paisley and Trimble and the pair raised clasped hands and walked through a tunnel of clapping and cheering Loyalists. On television it looked like a jig of triumph and although Trimble would later say he joined Paisley only to avoid being upstaged, the image was glued into the Nationalist consciousness forever and confirmed their doubts about the new Unionist leader. Trimble had twice hitched his wagon to Paisley's train and had come out ahead as a result. As they saw it, Paisley had helped Trimble become an MP and then leader of the Ulster Unionists. After all, when Unionist delegates gathered to elect a successor to Molyneaux two months later, the scenes in Portadown were still fresh in their minds.

That is how Paisley saw it as well. Trimble's election, he said, was a result of the hardline stance the pair had taken at Drumcree and it was clear that Trimble's identification with himself had done him "a lot of good". He went on: "Instead of painting Ian Paisley as the king-breaker, it seems I had a role to play as the king-maker." He also claimed that Trimble's election was a vindication of his tough stand on the peace process and noted that liberal candidates in the Unionist leadership election had fared poorly.[16]

Paisley wasn't the only maverick Unionist to welcome Trimble's elevation. The Belfast barrister Bob McCartney said Trimble was the sort of man who was sound on the Union "but could engender such trust on that score that he would be able to make the right concessions elsewhere". He wouldn't be "a de Klerk figure", he added. A former leading figure in the Ulster Unionists, McCartney had broken with the party and had then embraced the idea of Northern Ireland fully integrating with Britain. The peace process had brought him back into politics and he had joined Paisley in criticising the Downing Street Declaration. He had also played a part in bringing down Molyneaux. In June 1995, he stood in a by-election in the prosperous constituency of North Down, where he lived, and was supported by the DUP, whose analysis of the peace process mirrored much of McCartney's, including the claim that British appeasement of the IRA was due to the threat of large bombs in London. He easily defeated the Ulster Unionist candidate and his victory was seen as evidence that anxiety about where the peace process was going had spread to the Protestant professional classes and thus made Molyneaux's position even more difficult. McCartney later founded his own party, the United Kingdom Unionists, which enjoyed modest but brief electoral success and even had Conor Cruise O'Brien as an adviser. His election also forged a working alliance with the DUP which lasted for a decade but ended unhappily for McCartney, as similar arrangements had for other leaders of small Unionist parties who had tied themselves to the DUP leader. Invariably they would be used, discarded when drained of political nutrition and then see their supporters desert to Paisley. It was also a highly unlikely partnership. McCartney, who was a very successful barrister specialising in civil litigation, was a working-class Protestant from the Shankill and, although he was a firm Unionist, he abhorred sectarianism. He also reflected the schizoid view of Paisley shared by many in the Unionist middle class; while they were ashamed and embarrassed by his crude bigotry, they were still rather glad he was around.

McCartney had entered politics in 1979 following a horrific botched killing by the IRA in West Belfast. Members of the IRA had spotted a motorcyclist entering Andersonstown RUC station and assumed he was a member of the security forces. They lay in wait for him and when he emerged they machine gunned him to death from the back of a van. In fact the motorcyclist was a law clerk, John Donaldson (23), who had gone to the police station to serve a summons on a policeman in a civil case. A horrified and unsettled McCartney decided that to change things for the better he should join the political world. His very first outing saw him clash with Paisley outside Belfast City Hall at a Unionist rally during the day of action called in protest at the IRA's murder of South Belfast Unionist MP, Robert Bradford. The next day he called Paisley "a fascist" in a newspaper interview, adding that Paisley was "more interested in an independent Ulster, a mini-Geneva run by a fifth-rate Calvin". After this McCartney was feted in Dublin and the new Taoiseach, Garret FitzGerald, dubbed him "the authentic voice of Unionism". His alliance with Paisley during the early years of the peace process was therefore difficult for a lot of people to understand and McCartney himself would bridle at the suggestion that he had become a Paisley supporter: "I was not. We were both anti-Agreement and it would be like saying that because Churchill supported Stalin he was a Communist."[17]

There was another reason that people thought the relationship an odd one and that is because they were both men who were used to having their own way. How could two such headstrong politicians get along, people wondered. In fact, according to one former member of McCartney's party, the answer was rather well:

> They would go to meetings as a team, Bob and his deputy Cedric [Wilson] and Peter and Paisley. There was a great feeling of comradeship in those days. Paisley and Bob got on famously, especially when you remember what he had called him at the city hall. They used to sit and swap stories about the old days in Belfast when there were horse-drawn carts going through the streets and how the sparks would fly off their hoofs on the cobbled streets.

During party talks and after the 1998 Assembly was up and running, members of the two parties would eat together in the Stormont canteen and Paisley would regale McCartney with the latest gossip. "I remember one story he told about meeting Mo Mowlam [the Blair government's first NI Secretary]", recalled the same source.

> "I was sitting in my room at Westminster," says Paisley, "when there's a knock at the door and it's a messenger from Mowlam asking to meet me in her room, our first meeting. So I went along and she's sitting there with her feet up on the desk. It was disgusting, Bob; you could see everything." So Bob asked, "What happened next?" "It was embarrassing," said Paisley. "I didn't know where to look, she was a real slut. So I made an excuse to leave as soon as I could and as I was stepping out the door what does she say to me but 'Would you like a kiss, Ian?'"[18]

The honeymoon with David Trimble didn't last long. As his biographer Dean Godson put it: ". . . unlike Robert McCartney, [Trimble] did not regard the peace process as a fraud designed to deliver a united Ireland by stealth; rather, it was something which, if the terms were right, was worth studying and could yield fruit."[19] Immediately after his election as leader, Trimble sent that message out to Nationalism when he met Proinsias De Rossa, a junior minister in the new Rainbow Coalition government in Dublin. De Rossa had been a member of the Workers Party, the Marxist-leaning political wing of the Official IRA, from whose ranks in 1969, following a bitter quarrel and split over Republican strategy, the Provisional IRA had sprung. The Provisionals were wedded to the gun, while the Officials preferred politics and took a gradualist approach to achieving Irish unity. In 1972 they had forsaken the use of violence, at least against the institutions of the Northern Irish State. Following the collapse of the Soviet Union, the Workers Party split and a reformist wing, Democratic Left, was formed which De Rossa joined and led. After their meeting Trimble commented: ". . . some Unionists at the moment would have difficulty envisaging Gerry Adams coming to Glengall Street, but that's because they see Adams as he is today. But if we have a situation where people have proved a commitment to exclusively peaceful methods and have shown that they abide by the democratic process, that will put them in the same position as Proinsias De Rossa is today."[20] This hint that one day he might treat Adams like any other politician was all Paisley needed. By the time the DUP conference met in November 1995, Trimble was on the hit-list for the mandatory insults. "Was he David Trimble or David Tremble?" asked Sammy Wilson, to hoots of derision from the audience.

—◄○►—

The formal break between Trimble and Paisley/McCartney would not come for nearly a year, by which time the situation in the North had once more undergone dramatic change. Not least of the reasons for that was that the angst created in the ranks of Unionism by the peace process was also to be found inside the IRA. While Unionists suspected the British of selling them out, some Republicans suspected that Adams was doing the same to them. Although Adams had cleverly manoeuvred the IRA towards a ceasefire, it was called on the basis that it would be ended if the British refused to admit Sinn Féin into talks which the Army Council hoped would be about eventual withdrawal and Irish unity. A four-month limit was set but when that elapsed there was still no sign of the British granting full participation in all-party dialogue. To complicate matters, the British had imposed tough preconditions, effectively saying that the IRA would have to start decommissioning its weapons before that could happen. By the end of 1995, members of the IRA leadership were so unhappy that they demanded the convening of an IRA Convention to reconsider the Adams strategy. To forestall further rebellion, Adams and his allies on the Council supported a motion to end the ceasefire and in February 1996 the cessation evaporated in a huge lorry bomb explosion at Canary Wharf in London. The next eighteen months were to be nerve-wrecking for Gerry Adams and his allies, but they survived. A putsch against Adams, organised by the

IRA's Quarter-Master General, Michael McKevitt, narrowly failed and by the summer of 1997, when, happily for Adams, general elections in Britain and Ireland brought into power new political leaderships sympathetic to his strategy, another IRA ceasefire was called. This one was arranged after a promise of early Sinn Féin entry into talks was given by the new British Prime Minister, Tony Blair.

The prospect of talks involving Sinn Féin brought the differences between Trimble and Paisley/McCartney to a head. They did so over the choice of chairman of the talks, the former US Democratic Majority leader, Senator George Mitchell, a move that infuriated Paisley. Mitchell's substantive involvement in the process, effectively as a White House envoy, began in late 1995 and signalled, much to Unionist alarm, not just a departure from the view that the Northern Ireland problem was primarily a British concern and not the business of foreigners, but also the growing influence of the Clinton administration in Washington, which Unionists viewed as unashamedly sympathetic to Sinn Féin and in the pockets of the equally malign Irish-American lobby. It had not gone unnoticed in the DUP that when the US President visited Belfast in December 1995, he had praised every single local party leader for their contribution to the peace process, even the leaders of the tiny Loyalist paramilitary parties, but omitted Paisley's name. Earlier that year, Mitchell had agreed to head an international body charged with examining how to tackle the issue of paramilitary decommissioning and his report recommended diluting the hard line previously taken by the British. Instead of groups like the IRA being asked to disarm before entry to talks, they should agree instead to disarm during talks. His report also drew up six principles of non-violence which participants in negotiations should be required to sign up to and recommended the setting up of an international body to oversee and regulate any decommissioning process. He warned that if there was no flexibility on the matter of weapons, there could be a split in the IRA; a week later the Canary Wharf bomb exploded.

Mitchell was asked to return to Belfast in the summer of 1996 to chair all-party talks, at this stage minus Sinn Féin of course, and he agreed without much enthusiasm. At least twice during the next two years he asked Clinton to relieve him so he could return to his new wife and mainstream American public life but he was persuaded each time to stay. An enraged Paisley claimed that "the Clinton crony, George Mitchell" had got the job because the British had caved in to Dublin, while Peter Robinson asked: "What degree of impartiality can Unionists expect from a Catholic Irish-American from the same stable as the Kennedys?" Mitchell's religion became part of the quarrel. His father was from Maine but his mother, Mary Saad, was a Maronite Christian from the Lebanon who had emigrated to the United States at the age of 18. One DUP member can remember Paisley and Trimble arguing for the best part of an afternoon about whether this Maronite association made Mitchell a Roman Catholic. Paisley insisted it did, and that was another black mark against the American intermediary.

Both Paisley and McCartney, who had told Mitchell he had no personal objections to him but rather objected to the way he had been imposed on the local parties, opposed Mitchell's chairmanship, but Trimble did not. As Mitchell later noted, had Trimble joined them against him the peace process would have ended there and then; but the Ulster Unionist leader had realised that this would have meant Unionists shouldering the blame for the breakdown.[21] When Trimble signalled his support for Mitchell, Paisley and McCartney angrily stormed out of the talks. McCartney said of the Ulster Unionists, "They are gutless, unprincipled and a disgrace," while Paisley complained, "They have sold this country tonight as they have never sold it before." In a TV studio later, Willie McCrea interrupted an interview with Trimble and accused him of "lying to the people of Ulster".[22] Notwithstanding their histrionics, Paisley and McCartney returned the next day to sign the Mitchell Principles and to rejoin the talks process.

Paisley was not quite done with Senator Mitchell, though. At the end of November, he announced, "I want to . . . put on record . . . that I believe that certain people in Mr Mitchell's office are talking to the IRA."[23] A day later, on 30 November, at the DUP conference he had returned to the theme with a warning that "people in Senator Mitchell's office are not to be trusted for they're friends of leading members of the IRA".[24] The Senator himself, he added, "was no friend of Ulster". The next day, the meaning of Paisley's words became clear. One British and two Irish Sunday newspapers – the *Mail on Sunday*, the *Sunday World* and the *Sunday Tribune* – reported that a senior member of Mitchell's staff, Martha Pope, was having an affair with Sinn Féin's Gerry Kelly, who doubled as the IRA's deputy Chief of Staff, and that British intelligence had monitored their trysts. The story was clearly ludicrous but it was too salacious for some editors to ignore. The author was phoned about the story by his news desk in the *Sunday Tribune* on the

Saturday evening and strongly advised against using it. But the new editor, Matt Cooper, showing more confidence in his *Sunday World* sources, overruled his man in Belfast and the report appeared the next day. It looked like a great story but in reality it was nonsense.

Martha Pope successfully sued most of the papers, winning damages and retractions. Pope was a sophisticated and experienced political operator who had spent years in Washington and at one time had headed the Capitol police force. Kelly was a convicted IRA bomber and prison escaper. He did, however, have a name as a rake and this was widely enough known to make the story more believable. Nonetheless, the notion that these two very different people had enjoyed romantic weekends together during which Kelly had written Pope love poems, as one report alleged, was beyond belief.

Suspicion about where the story had come from were sharpened the day after the reports appeared when Paisley called for Pope's dismissal and Peter Robinson disclosed that he and Paisley had discussed the allegations with NI Secretary Sir Patrick Mayhew and British Prime Minister, John Major, the previous week. "We have received information," he said, "that indicated that an MI5 report had been submitted to Sir Patrick. We raised the matter at a meeting with the Prime Minister and Sir Patrick and we are still looking at it." Mayhew refused to confirm to George Mitchell whether or not such a report existed but did tell him he didn't think there was anything to the allegation. Paisley persisted, though, and when he was told that Mitchell had dismissed the assertion as false and scurrilous, he replied: "He better be careful when the MI5 paper appears. I am suggesting that papers have a habit of turning up."[25] It never did. John Steele, the head of the Security Division at the NIO, later told the *Boston Globe* that he routinely read all intelligence reports in Northern Ireland and nothing like that had ever come across his desk. The story was "bogus", he added. Responsibility for the slur was never established with confidence. While the DUP's hand was certainly suspected, there was no doubt either that the British government's media handlers in Belfast had done little to discourage the story. Whoever was responsible, it was beyond question that the story had been fashioned to undermine George Mitchell.

The year 1997 opened with what soon became an eagerly anticipated annual peek at British and Irish government archives released under the thirty-year confidentiality rule. Only a small fraction of government documentation was released each year by the notoriously secretive bureaucracies of both jurisdictions (there are still unreleased documents from the 1920s in the files of the North's Public Records Office) but since those papers that were allowed to make their way into circulation were now beginning to deal with the early years of the Troubles, their contents were enthusiastically scanned by journalists and historians. The 1966 papers released by Dublin contained one gem. A briefing from the Secretary of the Department of Justice in the Irish government, Peter Berry, to the Taoiseach of the day, Jack Lynch, was evidence that Paisley was considered an important player in the North even back then. Berry's report assessed the potential for political instability arising from the approaching fiftieth anniversary of the Easter Rising in Dublin. While concerned at the growth in IRA membership, by then estimated at around the 1,000 mark, it was Paisley who was on the Secretary's mind. Paisley's activities, he wrote, like the setting up of the Ulster Protestant Volunteers, the launch of the weekly *Protestant Telegraph*, and his courtship of Sir Edward Carson's son, whom he brought to Belfast in an effort to undermine the moderate Prime Minister, Captain Terence O'Neill, meant that Paisley had dominated the year's news. Berry told the Irish Prime Minister that if the IRA was to start violence in 1966 it might use either of two excuses – the Easter Rising commemoration ceremonies or what he called "the Paisley riots". Implicit in the analysis offered by Berry was the view that the IRA and Paisley were politically dependent upon each other, that they fed off each other's success. He was correct both then and later. The relationship was one reason why the IRA never contemplated assassinating Paisley when the Troubles did break out. As the outward symbol to the world of what Nationalists had to endure in Northern Ireland, he was much more useful alive. Equally, IRA violence and the threat it represented to Unionists' political security provided the nourishment that sustained Paisley's political and religious outlook and recruited his supporters in their droves. That symbiotic relationship between Paisley and the Provisionals was to flower in the years of the peace process and would, arguably, even enable its final resolution.

While 1966 had been dominated by the threat of an outbreak of violence, 1996 ended with peace still tantalisingly in the balance. As it would turn out, the subsequent twelve months would come to an end with the IRA having fired its last angry shot at the British and a fresh bid would be made to bring the peace process towards the point of no return. A ceasefire called in July 1997 – decided by the Army Council before the annual Drumcree stand-off but only announced after Orangemen had once more been allowed to parade – had been facilitated by a British climb-down on decommissioning fashioned by the new Prime Minister Tony Blair. It was to be the first of many.

Sinn Féin could enter all-party talks without the IRA having decommissioned first, a British letter to Sinn Féin said, as long as its delegates subscribed to the Mitchell Principles. These moves also signalled the restoration of Gerry Adams's control over the IRA, although a subsequent split from the organisation led by McKevitt and other figures in the Southern section of the IRA over signing the Mitchell Principles would enable Adams to argue that fear of further internal dissension meant that he had to move slowly and carefully. Both the British and Irish governments took notice and the indulgence they granted the Sinn Féin leadership was to last well beyond the sell-by date attached to Adams's argument. To Unionists, it seemed as if preserving Gerry Adams was more important to the governments than recognising their fears and interests. And that was all grist to Ian Paisley's mill.

The British U-turn on IRA weapons, which had been endorsed by Dublin, made the division between Trimble and Paisley/McCartney permanent and irreparable. A month before, the IRA had shot dead two policemen in Lurgan, County Armagh, in a particularly cold-blooded way and the scarcely interrupted British and Irish search for a formula suitable for Sinn Féin's entry to talks had enraged many Unionists and deepened suspicions of British treachery. It made Unionist co-operation with the talks process a risky endeavour. While Trimble responded by sending out conflicting messages, Paisley and McCartney left the talks process, first temporarily and then, when Sinn Féin officials arrived at the venue at Castle Buildings in the Stormont complex to prepare office suites, permanently. Trimble clung on to the hope that decommissioning would happen in the course of the talks, as Mitchell had recommended, but it never did. Paisley warned him that he would be ousted by his party if he accepted the British compromise but, after a one-day walk-out protest in September when Sinn Féin signed the Mitchell Principles and joined the talks, Trimble ignored that advice and stayed inside the negotiations. Paisley said he was "aghast" at Trimble's decision while McCartney accused the Ulster Unionists of breaking every promise made on decommissioning.

Who exactly first had the idea of leaving the talks, why and what impact the decision had, is now a matter of considerable dispute, not least between the DUP and the remnants of McCartney's UKUP. But everyone agrees it was a significant moment in the peace process. A decade on, Bob McCartney insisted the idea was his and that the DUP was obliged to follow:

It was clear from events that there was going to be a stream of concessions. Mitchell had compromised first by saying decommissioning would happen in tandem with the talks but after the shooting of the two policemen, it became clear that Blair was going to let Sinn Féin into talks without any decommissioning at all. At that point it was clear that to continue talks with Sinn Féin or to admit them in such circumstances was a breach of the spirit of the whole thing. Also it had been accepted that decisions [in the talks process] would be taken on the basis of 51 per cent of each designation [either Unionist or Nationalist] and along with the Loyalist paramilitary parties, Trimble had that majority. So we told the DUP we weren't staying and they followed. They were worried. Remember we went on to get five members elected [to the 1998 Assembly] and we could outflank them.[26]

McCartney's former deputy leader, Cedric Wilson, who along with three other Assembly members of the UKUP would eventually break with McCartney, put it even more strongly:

Bob was the moving force. Bob and I were sitting in his office in Castle Buildings and we discussed it all in detail. He said the only way to stop the negotiations would be to walk out. If we took a stronger line than the DUP, then we would force their hand while leaving Trimble exposed, and with the level of disquiet that there was inside his own party that would bring him down. I remember going into the press cabin to make the announcement and the DUP were running around like headless chickens but they quickly followed suit. There was no way that Robinson and the others, left to themselves, would have been of a mind to walk away. I believe that if we hadn't walked away they would have stayed, huffing and puffing from the sidelines.[27]

Not surprisingly these are versions of history that find no echo within the DUP. "No, that's nonsense," insisted one party member who was unwilling to be named. "This was the result of, and was all about the core values of the DUP. You had the whole background of the Shinners being up to their necks in murder and they wanted to be able to say they have shot us, they have bombed us and now they have made them talk to us. If we had stayed in the talks, we would have given them the legitimacy they craved and that was never going to happen."28 Another said: "We had a manifesto commitment not to negotiate with Sinn Féin so we did not need a tiny group to be our prompt."29 Whatever the truth, even David Trimble, now committed to hammering out a settlement in the talks process, was sensitive about contact with Sinn Féin. He refused to talk to the Republicans directly during the talks, spurned eye contact with Adams and communicated with Sinn Féin via intermediaries. Embarrassing efforts by Sinn Féin figures, including Adams, to socialise with Unionists, which invariably happened in the vicinity of Castle Buildings' Gents urinals, were always rebuffed. Trimble didn't speak directly to Adams until September 1998 and it would be nearly five years after that before he shook the Sinn Féin leader's hand.

Notwithstanding these and many other difficulties, agreement in the negotiations was reached on 10 April 1998, a Good Friday, just after the deadline set by the two governments. The Belfast Agreement, as the deal was officially called, sat quite happily within the parameters for a settlement outlined secretly on Adams's behalf to the Irish government eleven years earlier.30 The principle of consent was enshrined in the deal which meant that the Republicans had abandoned the idea that Unionists could be forced into a United Ireland. It was a huge concession, which struck at the heart of the reason for the IRA and its violence, but in return the British agreed, as Adams had requested, to scrap the 1920 Government of Ireland Act while Dublin agreed to incorporate the consent principle into its territorial claim. In exchange, Unionists were obliged to accept a 108-member legislative Assembly, a power-sharing Executive and a North–South Ministerial Council which would direct cross-Border co-operation in a number of areas. Its powers were to be determined by a weighted vote in the Assembly, as was the law-making process, or by a majority in each designation, an arrangement that gave both communities a veto. Executive membership would be shared amongst parties elected to the Assembly, which meant there would be Sinn Féin ministers running government departments. Decommissioning was again long-fingered;

parties repeated their commitment to achieving it and a target date of two years was set for completion. Paramilitary prisoners were to be released within two years, a commission established to examine the future of the RUC and an equality agenda, embracing the Irish language and Ulster-Scots, was agreed.

With the Agreement finalised, one question had not been answered. Had the decision by Paisley and McCartney to leave the negotiations assisted the deal-making process or had it made no difference to the outcome? Would Unionism have got a better deal if they had stayed in? Sir Kenneth Bloomfield, who was head of the NI Civil Service for many years and an adviser to successive British Secretaries of State, indicts Paisley for his absence. He wrote: "[He] must bear a not inconsiderable share of the blame for an appalling period in Northern Ireland's history. By the refusal of the DUP to participate in the talks process culminating in the Good Friday Agreement, he ensured that the true strength of Unionism was underrepresented at the negotiating table, leaving the heat and burden of the day to David Trimble's UUP . . ."[31] It was an accusation that would be often repeated when Paisley replaced Trimble as the dominant force in Unionism some years later, a charge that Trimble had done the heavy lifting while Paisley took over only when the most disagreeable part of the work was finished.

From his vantage-point as chairman of the talks, Senator Mitchell disagreed. "No one can ever know for certain what might have been, but I believe that had Paisley and McCartney stayed and fought from within, there would have been no agreement. Their absence freed the UUP from daily attacks, and gave the party room to negotiate that otherwise it might not have had."[32] David Trimble agrees: "I would have found it much more difficult to manage the party. Had Paisley been there I couldn't have kept free of commitments to tell opponents in the party what was going on and critics would have insisted that we define our positions much more clearly. We would have been forced to raise our terms too high for Sinn Féin or either government to accept. As it was we got to the last week without any hostages and with my opponents in the dark."[33] It may not have been Paisley's intention but, if Trimble and Mitchell are right, the DUP leader had made a huge contribution to the search for a final settlement.

Whatever the truth, the Good Friday Agreement, as many people preferred to call the deal, was now part of the political landscape and it caused heartache in both camps. Republicans had not been prepared for the deal, which had effectively abandoned or at least long-fingered the goal of Irish unity. It required two Sinn Féin conferences before it was accepted by the party's rank and file. The second *ard-fheis* was an exercise in emotional blackmail. Long-term IRA prisoners were specially released on a one-day furlough to attend the meeting and to remind delegates that they would linger in jail if the deal was rejected. That and assurances from party leaders that the Good Friday deal was not a final settlement but rather a transitional stage on the way to a 32-county Republic clinched the matter. Unionists were upset about a number of aspects and there is little doubt that the significant gains they had made, especially the removal of the IRA's *raison d'être*, were badly undersold by the Trimble leadership, then and later. Unionist concern dwelt less on the institutional arrangements and more on parts of the deal that had been designed to make the whole thing more palatable to Sinn Féin and the IRA. It was the deal's musical score, not its lyrics, that upset them. The prospect of IRA killers roaming the streets as free men, the awful possibility that those who had directed them would soon sit at the cabinet table and the threat to their beloved Royal Ulster Constabulary, which Sinn Féin had demanded be disbanded and replaced, sent a chill down Unionist spines. The absence of IRA decommissioning, which had unexpectedly been decoupled from prisoner releases during the negotiations, was another bitter pill. It looked as if a still-armed IRA might get into the government of Northern Ireland. Trimble sought and obtained side letters from Blair giving what turned out to be worthless assurances about disarming the IRA. Blair's handling of decommissioning and Sinn Féin's skilled exploitation of it in subsequent years would prove to be Trimble's downfall and the route by which Paisley would scale the heights.

—◁○▷—

The night before the Agreement was finalised, Ian Paisley led several hundred of his supporters into the Stormont estate and, after being blocked from the Castle Buildings talks venue, they made their way to Carson's statue where they chanted anti-Trimble slogans and waved Union flags. Some were masked and it seemed there might be trouble. However, Paisley agreed with British officials to disperse the crowd if he could hold a press conference outside Castle Buildings. In the press cabin, Paisley tried to speak but he was shouted down by members of the Loyalist paramilitary parties, the Ulster Democratic Party (UDP), which represented the UDA, and the Progressive Unionist Party (PUP), political arm of the UVF. The heckling was loud and rude. One shouted, "We fought for our country while you were living in a big house!" Another told him, "Your days of telling people to shut up are gone. You're finished." Eventually a chant went up, "Go home! Go home!" An astonished Senator Mitchell watched the scenes on television and a British official with him commented: "'Once he would have brought thousands, tens of thousands, with him. Now he has a few hundred. And look at those Loyalists. Many of them thought him a God. They went out and killed, thinking they were saving the Union. Now they've turned against him. It's the end of an era.' Paisley left the press conference. The negotiations ground on."[34]

The final breakdown of relations between Ian Paisley and the North's Loyalist paramilitaries was one of the more significant but least commented-upon features of the peace process. It meant that no longer could the DUP leader call upon the Loyalist black dog to back up his warnings of disaster or to enforce his sabre-rattling. Both the UDP and the PUP had backed David Trimble and had stayed in the talks. They favoured the peace process for one reason above all, although briefly it seemed that both might also enjoy a Sinn Féin-type electoral surge. The peace process offered the possibility that their prisoners might be released, while Paisley and other anti-Agreement Unionists, having set their faces against IRA releases, also opposed the freeing of Loyalist prisoners. Relations with the UVF and the PUP were particularly bad. The UVF leader in Mid-Ulster, Billy Wright, had broken with his Belfast leadership and came out against the peace process. He and his supporters had provided the muscle at Orange confrontations with the RUC at the annual Drumcree stand-off. In 1996, Trimble actually met him, drawing Nationalist charges of hypocrisy, while a sectarian murder carried out near Drumcree by Wright's gang just before the stand-off was played down by Paisley: "I don't think the murder has anything to do with Drumcree whatsoever . . ." he declared.

Wright was expelled from the UVF shortly after this and set up his own paramilitary outfit, the Loyalist Volunteer Force (LVF) which soon acquired a name for sectarian murder. He was given 72 hours to leave Northern Ireland or face assassination. Mainstream Loyalist suspicion that the DUP favoured the LVF were confirmed when Paisley's son, Ian Junior, condemned the threat as "contemptible, repugnant" and Willie McCrea shared a platform with Wright at an anti-peace process rally in

Portadown. The PUP's Billy Hutchinson, a former UVF prisoner who was no great fan of the Good Friday Agreement, believed the DUP saw the LVF as being more compliant: "When I went down to Drumcree in 1995 to order Billy Wright not to have anything to do with talks that Paisley was having with the cops, Wright told me Paisley was saying to the police that if you don't deal with me you'll have to deal with the UVF. Paisley's people were ready to share a platform with him after the split because they could control him."[35] The DUP and the PUP never met once during the peace process and the loathing between them was almost tangible. Relations with the UDA's political wing were hardly any better. A month before the Belfast Agreement was signed, the police had to be called to a DUP rally in a Lisburn Orange Hall following angry clashes and exchanges between UDP members and DUP supporters.

The view that the Paisley era had come to an end was strengthened when in May, six weeks after the talks had ended, the Belfast Agreement was endorsed by 71 per cent of the North's electorate in an 81 per cent turnout, a huge disappointment to anti-Agreement Unionists who had been hoping for a "yes" vote around the sixty per cent mark, a result that would have meant that a solid majority of Unionists had voted against. At the count in the King's Hall in south Belfast, Paisley, McCartney and their supporters were barracked by Loyalists once again. "You're yesterday's men! Go home, dinosaurs! Ulster says Yes!" chanted PUP supporters.

It looked as if Paisley's day had indeed come to an end, but as always in Northern Ireland, first impressions could be deceptive. The Belfast Agreement had brought to the surface deep divisions inside the Ulster Unionists, especially amongst those who had been kept in the dark about the detail of the talks by Trimble. A talks colleague, Jeffrey Donaldson, walked away from the negotiating team on Good Friday itself, saying that the decommissioning arrangements had allowed the IRA off the hook. Four of Trimble's MPs, Roy Beggs, Martin Smyth, Willie Thompson and Willie Ross, later came out against the deal and three of them turned up at one of Paisley's largest "Vote No" rallies during the referendum campaign. David Trimble had lost the backing of half his parliamentary party.

But there was worse. Conventional wisdom had suggested that 55 per cent of Protestant voters had backed the deal, a narrow margin to be sure but one that could be built upon. But Trimble, for one, believed otherwise: "I sat down after the referendum and calculated that the pro-Good Friday Agreement vote in terms of the Unionist community was only a few hundred ahead of the antis."[36] A widespread suspicion that many of those who had come out to vote "yes" in the referendum normally stayed at home during other elections was confirmed in the contest to the new Assembly a month later. Turnout fell by some 13 points and pro-Agreement Unionists were the main casualties. The Ulster Unionists actually polled fewer votes than the SDLP and were just three points ahead of the DUP. In terms of seats, Trimble's party won 28 but the anti-Agreement bloc, 20 DUP, five UKUP and three anti-Agreement independent Unionists, exactly matched them. The two pro-Agreement PUP seats gave Trimble a slim majority of the Unionist designation as a whole, but the result meant that a couple of defections from his Assembly team could make life for Trimble very difficult indeed. At the very best the new Assembly would have a fragile existence. For Paisley and the DUP, that meant there was everything to play for. Predictions of an end to the Paisley era were premature.

"He is a liar, a cheat, a hypocrite, a knave, a thief, a loathsome reptile which needs to be scotched. I will let the people of Ulster detect for themselves the traitor and then pass their own verdict."

IAN PAISLEY ON DAVID TRIMBLE, DUP ANNUAL CONFERENCE, NOVEMBER 1998

"The only cabinet the Provos should be in has brass handles on it."

PETER ROBINSON TO THE DUP ANNUAL CONFERENCE, NOVEMBER 1998

"No deal in Northern Ireland will be stable until it is supported by the DUP"

DUP ASSEMBLY ELECTION MANIFESTO, NOVEMBER 2003

CHAPTER THIRTEEN

"Custodianship of Our Province"

David Trimble was not alone in concluding that a majority of Unionist electors, albeit a slim one, had voted in the referendum against the Good Friday deal. The DUP had come to the same conclusion. But still, the deal had been endorsed by a thumping majority and the DUP could hardly oppose the will of the greater number without debasing the core of Unionist politics, which was that the Union existed because most of the North's people wished it so. Referenda had taken place on both sides of the Border on the same day and the use of this device restricted the freedom of movement of both extremes in Northern Irish politics; the vote had also cost the IRA its traditional justification for violence – the 1921 all-Ireland vote for Sinn Féin and an all-Ireland Republic.

In the past the DUP's instinct would have been to take its opposition to a deal like the Good Friday Agreement on to the streets but that option was now not available, even if there had been the stomach for it. The Resistance experience had disillusioned so many of Paisley's hardline supporters that a repeat attempt would likely be an embarrassing flop, while their traditional allies in such endeavours, the mainstream Loyalist paramilitaries, all championed the Belfast Agreement, so their muscle would be damagingly absent from any campaign. And experience – the successful UWC strike of 1974 and the failed attempted repeat of 1977 – demonstrated that such efforts were doomed in the absence of Unionist unity. When Unionism was divided, as in 1977 and now, such campaigns would likely fail. There was another, no less telling difference from 1974 and 1977. Like nearly everyone else in Northern Ireland's political life, Paisley and his colleagues were some

25 years older and the seemingly endless Troubles had sapped their enthusiasm, optimism and energy as much as anyone's.

With direct methods ruled out, the DUP had little choice but to accept the new dispensation and, once that realisation had sunk in, to work within the institutions rather than outside. But it was also clear that this avenue provided ample opportunity to make trouble for Trimble while prospering electorally at his expense. After all, not only had at least half the Unionist electorate rejected the new deal but there was a host of contentious matters outstanding from the Good Friday negotiations, whose implementation would surely add to Unionist alienation and bring votes the DUP's way. IRA prisoners would soon be released; the issue of IRA decommissioning was still to be resolved; the RUC would be reformed; and eventually Sinn Féiners would assume ministerial office. The DUP was not alone in suspecting that the way each one of those issues would be played out could be to their advantage. Added to all this were the divisions within Ulster Unionism and David Trimble's growing political isolation. If Paisley could win this battle for the middle ground between the DUP and the Ulster Unionists, then the future for him and his party boded well. As one DUP source close to all these events put it, admittedly with the benefit of a decade's hindsight: "We had developed the conditions that made the '98 deal unacceptable and half the Unionist community agreed. We knew that time would be our friend and we set the conditions for a new deal knowing that traffic would come our way. We were not against devolution. We were against the nature and surrounding aspects of it."[1]

Whether Ian Paisley and others in the DUP were quite so clear-sighted back then may be a matter for debate but there was little doubt that in the next few years the actions of both the IRA and Sinn Féin were to be of huge assistance to the DUP. By the way that the IRA and its political leadership in Sinn Féin handled weapons decommissioning, firstly by refusing to begin it or to accept that it was linked to Executive membership, and then later on, when it was begun, to carry it out in a niggardly and less than transparent fashion, all helped to gnaw away at Trimble's support. The IRA always moved too late and insufficiently far for the Unionist middle ground, even when the Adams leadership had achieved full and virtually total control over the organisation and could do what it liked.[2]

To make matters worse for the Trimbleistas, as the putative First Minister and his followers were dubbed, the IRA continued to do many of the things the IRA had always done, Good Friday Agreement or not. There were murders committed by IRA front groups or done anonymously or deniably, robberies, paramilitary policing with punishment shootings and beatings that sometimes ended very badly, arms smuggling, target surveillance and other activities that pointed to a still active IRA. Although both London and Dublin were inclined to turn a blind eye to all but the most excessive activity, most Unionists regarded them as breaches of the ceasefire, and evidence that the IRA's word was not to be trusted. The British and Irish governments' contrary view – that the Adams camp was weaker than it seemed and was obliged to allow their "harder" colleagues some leeway in order to survive – cut about as much ice within Unionism as the governments' conclusion from all this, which was that, with the passage of time, Adams's control would tighten and gradually these activities would disappear. The fact that the governments were even making these arguments, which essentially echoed advice from Adams and his colleagues – and to discount converse advice from the RUC Special Branch and intelligence agencies in both Britain and Ireland[3] – was a sign that Unionism's new sense of isolation was not entirely unfounded.

The result was that slowly but surely Trimble's hold on the Unionist electorate loosened and more and more voters drifted away in the direction of the DUP. Trimble's predicament was even worse within the ranks of his party, where now a clear majority of his MPs opposed him and had been joined by his predecessor, Jim Molyneaux, now elevated to the House of Lords. When this process had fully worked its way through the electorate and Ian Paisley and his team became masters of the Unionist house, it was in no small measure thanks to the IRA that it happened. It worked the other way round as well, of course. As the DUP came to dominate Unionism, more Catholics were inclined to vote for Sinn Féin in defensive response, evidence that once again the extremes were sustaining each other. But there can be little doubt that ultimately the IRA, as much as anyone or anything else, helped propel Ian Paisley into the First Minister's office.

‹○›

A week after the referendum votes had been counted, and as politicians geared up for an election to the new Assembly, Paisley and Robinson, the latter by now the DUP's chief strategist, unveiled the new approach. The DUP would not set out to wreck the Assembly, they promised, but would resist either Sinn Féin joining the planned Executive or IRA prisoners being released prior to some paramilitary decommissioning. Robinson explained: "An imposed Assembly we would be entitled to destroy, but an agreement endorsed by the electorate – even though not with the politically efficacious majority that it needed from the Unionist community – no democrat is entitled to overthrow." Paisley put it more colourfully: "We are not wreckers, we are savers. Our 'No' vote has put the bit and curb upon the governments' rash run down the hill."[4] Trimble's adviser from the world of academe, Professor Paul Bew of Queen's University, was one of the first to record the change in DUP strategy. Noting that Paisley had played a minimal role in DUP television election broadcasts – a sign the party's handlers did not wish to antagonise moderate Unionists – he suggested that the "new DUP" would henceforth appeal to a much broader Unionist audience by presenting itself as "the guarantors of the Trimble/Blair pledges on paramilitary violence. . . ." He went on: "This new DUP was a party of the respectable middle class alarmed by the prospects for investment if terrorists entered government; a party of mothers worried about the public morality of releasing paramilitary prisoners; a party, in other words, which shared concerns which are widespread within the Unionist community."[5] Frank Millar, now the London editor of *The Irish Times*, went one further and speculated about a split inside the Ulster Unionists and the eventual realignment of Unionism. Peter Robinson and Jeffrey Donaldson, soon to be a thorn in Trimble's flesh, would be in competition, he wrote, for leadership of the new bloc.[6]

As the DUP strategy had anticipated, "the traffic" did come the party's way in the months and years after the Good Friday Agreement. With Paisley and McCartney piling on pressure from the sidelines and his own party seething with discontent, Trimble was obliged to conjoin IRA decommissioning and Sinn Féin's membership of the new, but still putative power-sharing Executive. But it proved to be a task beyond Trimble's capabilities. Bit by bit he was forced to dilute his stance, to give ground to Sinn Féin and the two governments and, each time that happened, more Unionist votes leaked in the direction of Ian Paisley and the DUP.

The negotiating phase of the peace process had begun in 1994 with Unionists, and later the British government, demanding that the IRA would have to begin destroying its weapons before Sinn Féin could be admitted to all-party talks. But in 1996 the IRA ceasefire broke down and, while there was more than one reason for that, the failure of the Adams leadership to gain entry to all-party talks was undoubtedly a major contributing factor. Eighteen months later the Adams camp re-established control of the IRA and the ceasefire was restored. Although Adams's opponents soon defected to form a rival IRA and gradually ceased to be a threat, these events were the source of the conventional wisdom that the Sinn Féin leader and his supporters had to move slowly and carefully. Accordingly, the hardline government stance on decommissioning was abandoned. In the next stage, devised with the blessing of President Clinton via his envoy, George Mitchell, decommissioning ceased to be a precondition to talks and instead was supposed to happen alongside the negotiations – so-called parallel decommissioning.

But the Good Friday Agreement emerged from that phase without a single IRA bullet being destroyed and with the linkage between disarmament and ministerial office fatally weakened. Decommissioning was treated almost as an aspiration rather than an obligation. The Agreement merely committed parties like Sinn Féin "to use any influence they may have, to achieve the decommissioning of all paramilitary arms within two years" of endorsement of the deal by the twin referenda. In this context Trimble's insistence that decommissioning would have to begin before the establishment of the new Executive and other institutions such as the North–South Ministerial Council was like swimming against a powerful tide.

In the ensuing battle between himself and the forces of Irish nationalism, Trimble could rarely count on the support of British Premier Tony Blair. Invariably it seemed that Blair would put preserving the IRA's ceasefire above all else while his public pledges and private promises, such as those he made to Trimble about IRA decommissioning in the wake of the 1998 Agreement, proved to be worthless. For its part, the Irish government seemed unaware or uncaring about his deflating support base; Sinn Féin's complaints about Trimble – that decommissioning was just an excuse not to share power or that he had failed to sell the Good Friday Agreement to the larger Unionist community – found a ready echo in Dublin's Department of Foreign Affairs. Nor could he find much comfort from the SDLP, his principal government partner, which was itself under pressure over decommissioning from Sinn Féin. It didn't help that personal relations with Trimble's Deputy First Minister, Seamus Mallon, were disastrously bad. Shy and reserved almost to the point of rudeness, Trimble just could not get on with Mallon nor Mallon, in his own way just as difficult a personality, with him. Sometimes they argued over the most petty of matters, once when Mallon discovered that Trimble's office in Stormont Castle had a private bathroom while his didn't. Eventually, to facilitate their mutual aversion, their offices were situated almost as far apart as the building's architecture allowed.

Trimble had few friends and sometimes undependable allies and in such circumstances it was perhaps inevitable that he would take his eye off the ball, as he did over the renaming of the RUC, and hand the DUP ammunition to use against him. Dean Godson's definitive biographical study of the doomed First Minister and the peace process, *Himself Alone*, was well named. Eventually Trimble was worn down. Sinn Féin would get into government without any IRA weapons being put beyond use and in return for gestures that qualified as signals of a future intention to decommission only to those who hoped or wished it was so. And so to anti-Agreement Unionists of a DUP bent of mind, David Trimble became the new Captain Terence O'Neill, the new Brian Faulkner, the new Lundy whose machinations against Ulster, God had sent Ian Paisley to confound.

—◄○►—

The tone for the next few years would be set at the very first DUP annual conference held some seven months after the closing of the Good Friday Agreement, in November 1998. The party had chosen Omagh as the venue for their get-together quite deliberately. For many years the DUP had occasionally chosen to take its conference to locations that had a notorious connection with IRA atrocities, so as to remind its supporters of their enemy's evil ways and intent and the DUP's mission to confound them. One of the DUP's favourite venues was the La Mon hotel in the Castlereagh hills east of Belfast where in 1978 twelve Protestant revellers had been incinerated to death by a clumsily executed IRA blast incendiary attack. This year it was Omagh's turn, thanks to the botched dissident Republican bombing of August 1998, the joint work of the Real IRA, Continuity IRA and the INLA, which had devastated Omagh and had killed 29 people, the worst death toll in any single incident during the Troubles. Choosing Omagh to stage the conference sent a message about the perfidious peace process: David Trimble had entered into a deal with the IRA but, despite his treachery, there was still terrible violence.

Both Ian Paisley and Peter Robinson zeroed in on David Trimble in their conference speeches, Robinson singling out the Ulster Unionist leader for critical mention no less than fifteen times and Paisley excoriating him in particularly violent terms: "The worst and most loathsome person in society is the traitor – the Judas, the Iscariot," he thundered.

> Who dares to excuse and whitewash treachery but he who is a party to that treachery? Who dares to sustain the treachery but he who has helped the traitor to bring it about and remains to see the vile deed through, eager to enjoy the payoff? Of him who professes to be a dedicated ally but who goes over to the enemy because of personal advantages, no words in any language are adequate to describe. He is a liar, a cheat, a hypocrite, a knave, a thief, a loathsome reptile which needs to be scotched. I will let the people of Ulster detect for themselves the traitor and then pass their own verdict.

Paisley pressed all the right buttons during the rest of his speech, instinctively recognising those issues which had most alarmed and unsettled the broader Unionist community in the weeks since the Agreement. 421 terrorist incidents since Good Friday; Adams and McGuinness feted by Prime Minister Tony Blair; Orangemen barred from walking their own streets; the Union Jack insulted, and the Queen reduced to the same level as President Mary McAleese. And there was more perfidy, all of it enabled by Trimble's treachery:

> Today the worst murdering scoundrels ever put behind bars are being set free. Today those scoundrels are being paid compensation by the Government. Today those they have maimed for life, the injured and bereaved, have to suffer in silence, a deaf ear having been turned to their cries for help. Today Protestants are being discriminated against in the workplace. Today those who should be in the front line defending the Union are in cahoots with the enemy and surrendering in an unholy partnership the very principles that they swore to uphold. Today is the eve of the abolishing of the RUC. This is Trimble's legacy to our province. The Ulster Unionist people themselves must make their own judgements and pass their own verdicts. The facts stare them in the face and those facts need no arguing.[7]

The deadline for setting up the power-sharing Executive, like so many other peace process deadlines, was repeatedly extended: from October 1998 to 10 March 1999, to 2 April and then to 13 April and then finally to what Tony Blair called, without a blush, "an absolute deadline" of 30 June 1999, which quickly became July, then November, before settling on the end of January 2000. Throughout these tortuous months and the bafflingly complex negotiations which accompanied them, signs of some of the enduring and defining features of the post-Good Friday Agreement phase of the peace process became visible. The first was Tony Blair's addiction to what he would call "hothousing" – lengthy, chaotic, unstructured and nebulous gatherings of political parties and government leaders usually held at a castle or grand home which would last for several days, see most invited politicians wander corridors aimlessly while a few key individuals from one or two parties did the talking. These events invariably ended in confused uncertainty with a communiqué that more often than not reflected the hopes of the British and Irish governments rather than any agreement reached between them and the parties. "We hated them," admitted one Irish government source, "but Blair just loved them."[8]

The other characteristic was a growing willingness to bend in Sinn Féin's direction and what some would come to regard as a virtual addiction to granting the Republicans concessions in the absence of cast-iron commitments, what one frustrated American government official would later call "giving candy to the kids before they misbehaved".[9] Responsibility for the hothouse format was Tony Blair's but both he and Bertie Ahern, the Irish Taoiseach, agreed on the tactic of giving concessions to Sinn Féin. To the extent that all this contributed to Trimble's eventual downfall and to the rise of both the DUP and Sinn Féin, the prime ministers have a shared culpability for it happening. Trimble was himself also partly at fault. Dean Godson's biography of the Ulster Unionist leader makes it clear that in his eagerness to tie the Provos into a deal that would negate the IRA's traditional agenda of Irish unity, Trimble would sometimes move too far, too fast for his own constituency. He was also prone to hold Tony Blair in too much awe, and to bend in the face of the Prime Minister's blandishments.[10] Seamus Mallon put this point more bluntly: "[Blair's] tactics and approach was as a master of flattery. He loved nothing better than getting you on your own and worked on the assumption that because the Prime Minister was talking to you alone you were a very important person. Trimble fell for it. Trimble loved the trappings. He liked to be in Chequers at the weekend, as any normal person would. And the little *tête-à-têtes*."[11]

The first few months of 1999 were to see ample evidence of all these traits as efforts were made to get the Good Friday institutions into place. In early April 1999, after a four-day "hothouse" at Hillsborough Castle, Blair and Ahern issued a statement outlining a scenario for getting the institutions up and running. First, Ministers in the power-sharing Executive would be nominated under the d'Hondt procedure, which allocated posts in line with party support, but they would be shadow, powerless Ministers until the IRA kept its side of the deal. Sometime later – a month was suggested – a voluntary act of decommissioning by the IRA would take place, part of a "collective act of reconciliation" which would precede further moves towards British demilitarisation. "Around" this time, but presumably after decommissioning had commenced, powers would be devolved to the Executive and Assembly, followed by the other institutions such as the North–South Ministerial Council. While there were a lot of blank spaces in the prime ministerial plan, it looked like a sensible compromise. But the problem was that it wasn't an agreed compromise, certainly not by the Provos. Within days, Army Council member Brian Keenan, a west Belfast veteran who would play the role of the IRA's pre-eminent black dog for some time to come, called the proposal an attempt to force the IRA's surrender, while Army Council chairman and Mid-Ulster MP, Martin McGuinness, said the IRA would reject any effort to extract decommissioning as a precondition for entry to the Executive.

These barks and growls from the IRA's hard men had the desired effect. In mid-May another Blair "hothouse" was held, this time on home ground in 10 Downing Street, involving the Irish government, the SDLP, Sinn Féin and the Ulster Unionists, led by David Trimble, who, fatally, conducted the final negotiating session alone. That produced a scenario in which the terms of March's deal would be almost totally reversed and Sinn Féin's entry into the Executive would precede IRA decommissioning. Under this plan, Ministers would be nominated almost immediately and, following a report from the head of the decommissioning body, General John de Chastelain, devolution would be activated by 30 June. The IRA wouldn't be pressed to dispose of any weapons for all this to happen; no "product", as it was called, would be necessary. The only condition was a commitment from Sinn Féin to do all it could to achieve full decommissioning by the Good Friday

369

deadline of May 2000, a formula that was little different in substance from the April 1998 deal.

Astonishingly, Trimble accepted the deal but then, in the face of a revolt from his Assembly members and amid anger in the ranks of his Westminster party and talk of a plot to depose him as leader, he rejected it. Although it seems that Blair, more than Bertie Ahern, regarded the proposal as something that Trimble could deliver to his party and had urged the Unionist leader to accept it, the significance of it all was that the terms for decommissioning had changed decisively in Sinn Féin's favour. That much was confirmed by the next "hothouse" session in Castle Buildings at Stormont towards the end of June 1999. The "deal" that was unveiled then was preceded by a typical piece of Blairite spin. There had been, he claimed, "seismic shifts in the political landscape" during the talks. Under the new plan, Ministers would be nominated by 18 July, and powers would be devolved to the Executive three days later and "shortly after" this, IRA decommissioning would begin and be completed by May the next year. If the IRA reneged, promised the premiers, fail-safe legislation would suspend the operation. Outside the conference rooms, Ian Paisley Junior was praying for failure while his father, or "Da" as he called him, was certain that God was on his side. "I am confident there will be no deal . . . I don't think at this late hour they can sell the pass," he predicted. Bitten once in May, Unionists were now shy and in no mood to repeat the experience. Realisation that the IRA would get Sinn Féin into government without any disarming and suspicious that Tony Blair would never suspend the institutions once they were up and running, no matter how badly the IRA behaved, doomed it to failure. The Ulster Unionist Executive rejected the proposal while Trimble said he would not co-operate in the selection of Ministers. There had been no "seismic shift", merely a slight shiver.

The significance of these events was that once again the two governments had decided that Sinn Féin's interests came before those of David Trimble, who was now cast permanently as the party leader of least resistance. Prior decommissioning as a precondition for entry to all-party talks had been abandoned and now the same had happened with Sinn Féin's admittance to government. It merely remained for this new position to win the endorsement of the Clinton administration for it to become, in government eyes, the only available way forward. So when the latest deal stalled in mid-July, Clinton's envoy, Senator George

Mitchell, was sent for to do for Sinn Féin's entry into government what he had done for its passage into negotiations.

The deal that Mitchell brokered at the end of November 1999 was essentially the same as that put together in June and July. Nominations to the new Executive would happen immediately, as would full devolution of powers, while the IRA would be expected to begin decommissioning its weapons by the end of January 2000, some two months later. Trimble got the deal through a fractious meeting of his Ulster Unionist Council (UUC) by virtue of lodging a post-dated letter of resignation with the Speaker of the Assembly which would become active if the IRA defaulted on its promise to begin disarming. The UUC would reconvene in February 2000 to make "a final decision", i.e. to endorse Trimble's resignation in the event of the IRA's failure to deliver. After years of demanding that the IRA make the first move in the choreography of entering government, Trimble was now reduced to telling Gerry Adams and his colleagues after the UUC meeting, "We've jumped, now you follow."

On 29 November 1999 the d'Hondt procedure was triggered in the Assembly and the ten-member Executive appointed. At midnight on 1 December 1999 devolution went live, David Trimble and Séamus Mallon entered office and Northern Ireland had the first taste of self-government since 1974. That bit of the plan, at least, went smoothly, but not the IRA's part of the deal. By the end of February 2000, General John de Chastelain could report only that there was no sign at all of the IRA following David Trimble anywhere. At one press conference, Gerry Adams had waved a copy of the Good Friday Agreement at journalists and indignantly demanded to know where in the text there was any commitment to IRA disarming. In mid-February, with no signs of the Provos changing their minds and to forestall Trimble's probably irreversible resignation, the new Northern Ireland Secretary Peter Mandelson stepped in to suspend the power-sharing Executive and restore direct rule from London.

—◇—

By this point, the damage to David Trimble was such that Mandelson's move could do him little good. Not only had Unionists seen Trimble admit Sinn Féin into government without any IRA decommissioning at all, but their anger turned to horror on the day the Executive was chosen. Sinn Féin plumped for two high-profile portfolios – Martin

McGuinness as Minister of Education and Bairbre de Brún in charge of Health. McGuinness's elevation was particularly galling. Most Unionists knew that he was a former IRA Chief of Staff and in that capacity had directed the IRA's violence; the notion that he would be charged with overseeing their children's education filled them with dismay. McGuinness's selection was due in no small part to clumsy oversight on Trimble's part but the intensity of the reaction within the Unionist community was nonetheless marked and could be measured by the number of walk-outs staged by pupils in the mostly Protestant State school sector in the following days. Predictably, the DUP was accused of organising some of the walk-outs.

To add to Trimble's woes, the IRA had continued much of its paramilitary activity throughout the months of post-Good Friday negotiations, some of which took place in the shadow of one or other damaging revelation about IRA excesses. In July 1998, just three months after the Good Friday talks, the IRA killed Belfast teenager Andrew Kearney in a punishment shooting that had gone wrong. In early 1999, a former IRA intelligence officer turned fierce critic of the organisation, Eamon Collins, was butchered to death near the south Armagh border. It was widely known that he had angered the IRA's south Armagh-based Chief of Staff, Tom "Slab" Murphy, after testifying against him in a libel hearing – but despite certain suspicion of IRA responsibility there were no negative consequences for Sinn Féin.

Unionist anger turned to rage in September 1999 when then NI Secretary, Mo Mowlam, whose sympathy for Irish Nationalism was often barely concealed, declared the IRA ceasefire intact despite the death of a Belfast teenager, Charles Bennett, shot dead by the IRA for stealing a gun from the organisation. This and other punishment shootings and beatings, as well as some 384 expulsions from Northern Ireland ordered by the IRA since April 1998, fell into the category of "internal IRA housekeeping", Mowlam declared, and thus did not qualify as reasons for Sinn Féin's expulsion from the process. In July 1999, FBI agents in Florida intercepted weapons en route to addresses in the UK and Ireland and their inquiry uncovered an ambitious plot by the IRA to smuggle scores of modern handguns from America. In this instance the Clinton administration leaned on Ulster Television in an effort to spike a documentary on the operation which quoted an FBI agent saying that the IRA leadership, which included Gerry Adams and Martin McGuinness, had authorised the operation. The DUP alleged that the White House had intervened on David Trimble's urging and, although this was denied, for some Unionists the implications were clear-cut – even if the IRA did decommission, it could soon replace lost weapons, and the governments would seek to excuse them.

Even the IRA's most rancorous critics will now concede that winning the British and Irish governments and most of the media to their side in the context of all this, remains the single most stunning achievement of any party involved in the peace process. The Adams leadership could make one very powerful argument to win outsiders over. No Republican group in the history of the conflict with Britain had ever disarmed before, no matter how complete their defeat, and the demand that the Provos do so now, as David Trimble insisted, was unprecedented. To many it seemed that Trimble and other Unionists were intent on humiliating the IRA and Sinn Féin or, by seeking what amounted to their public surrender, to provoke another split. The Provos had already split in 1997 and the rival Real IRA, other dissident groups like the Continuity IRA and the INLA, were still around despite suffering a series of setbacks in the wake of the 1998 Omagh bombing, including the collapse of a paramilitary pact between them. Privately, Sinn Féin spin doctors, who were every bit as skilled as their government opposite numbers, warned British and Irish officials, as well as journalists, that up to a third of the IRA's membership would defect to these dissidents unless the decommissioning issue was handled with extreme sensitivity. The governments believed what Sinn Féin told them and while that was understandable in the immediate aftermath of the Good Friday Agreement, London and Dublin behaved as if it were still the case long after the Sinn Féin claim had been devalued, both by the passage of time and by Gerry Adams's tightened control of the IRA.

While the Republicans argued that they had much to lose if decommissioning was mishandled, the truth is that Sinn Féin also had much to gain out of the issue. Participating in Blair's endless "hothouse" decommissioning diplomacy placed Sinn Féin at the centre of the political stage and enabled the party to overshadow its Nationalist rivals in the SDLP. Much of Nationalist Ireland sympathised with Sinn Féin's resistance to IRA disarming and was receptive to the argument that Trimble was using the issue as an excuse to avoid having to share power with Republicans. Evidence that this found an echo way beyond the confines of Irish Nationalism is to be found in the diary kept by Blair's chief spin doctor during these years, Alastair Campbell, which was published after Blair's departure from Downing Street. During the June 1999 "hothouse" session, Campbell wrote of Trimble and his colleagues: "TB [Tony Blair] was getting close to the view that deep down they just didn't want to share power with Catholics."[12] As many Nationalists saw it, Sinn Féin had already made enough of a compromise by accepting the Good Friday Agreement with its recognition of the constitutional status quo. The SDLP had little choice but to fall in behind Sinn Féin and the more Trimble made decommissioning an issue, the more Nationalist voters felt obliged to show their opposition to him by supporting Sinn Féin. As this tribal drumbeat intensified, so did Sinn Féin's domination of Nationalist politics until eventually the party was able to overtake the SDLP. In this sense the peace process was as much an electoral strategy for Sinn Féin as it was anything else.

The reality of Trimble's position – that his support was leaching dangerously away to Paisley and the DUP – did not register with Downing Street until months later, even though the warning signs were there to see. The June 1999 European election gave anti-Agreement Unionists a chance to present the poll as a re-run of the 1998 referendum and to inflict electoral damage to Trimble at the same time. The stratagem worked. Ian Paisley topped the poll for the fifth successive time, while his vote, added to Bob McCartney's, enabled their camp to claim that the two men's share of the vote, at some 31.5 per cent, meant that most Unionists had turned against the Good Friday deal. The vote for Trimble's candidate, Jim Nicholson, plummeted by 6.5 points to 17.6 per cent, only a fraction ahead of Sinn Féin. At the start of July 1999, on the same day as Blair and Ahern were unveiling another ill-fated decommissioning deal, the DUP won a by-election to Lisburn council whose significance lay in the fact that the DUP's vote had doubled in what was normally a safe Ulster Unionist constituency.

In September 1999, Trimble suffered another grievous blow. The Patten Commission on policing published its report and recommended, inter alia, that the RUC should be renamed the Police Service of Northern Ireland (PSNI), that a determined and mandatory effort be made to recruit Catholics to the new force, and that a new "cross-community" crest and badge be adopted. Patten also recommended that local policing boards be set up, drawing their membership from local communities and that a new, locally recruited reserve force should be set up. These suggestions opened the way for Sinn Féin and IRA involvement in grassroots policing – or as Unionists preferred to see it, to help them subvert and corrupt it.

Such was the shock to Unionism at this assault on the beloved RUC that Trimble was forced to reject the report as "a gratuitous insult" to the police. Paisley joined in, although there was little need for him to do so as the report said it all for him. The Patten report was worse than he had feared, he said, and amounted to "the disbandment of the RUC". He and Bob McCartney's party announced plans to campaign against the Patten report and Paisley helped to place crosses in the grounds of Stormont in memory of the 302 RUC officers killed during the Troubles, most by the IRA.

Trimble's internal difficulties multiplied. A leading ally, John Taylor, quit George Mitchell's devolution talks in protest while others, including one MP, called for Trimble's resignation. One of his Assembly members, Peter Weir from North Down, had lost the party whip in early 1999 when he voted with the DUP against the devolution scheme agreed by Trimble and the SDLP. The First Minister's subsequent reluctance to deal decisively with Weir became an index of his weakness. When the Mitchell deal collapsed in February 2000, the South Belfast MP and former Orange leader, the Rev Martin Smyth, mounted a leadership challenge to Trimble and won 43 per cent of the UUC votes, many more than had forced Jim Molyneaux's resignation back in 1996.

By May 2000, Blair had returned to a "hothouse" mode and produced a deal that represented, as Frank Millar in *The Irish Times* noted, "a clear shift away from the original decommissioning concept".[13] Under the terms of the deal, devolution would be restored if the IRA placed an unspecified amount of its weaponry in dumps which would be inspected at regular intervals by two international figures who would be able to say whether or not any of the arms had been tampered with. Although this confidence-building measure, as it was termed, was a move forward, it was still far from being an act of decommissioning. There were other difficulties. The inspection process was shrouded in secrecy, the first indication of a problem that would bedevil the decommissioning process when it did get going later on. A number of unanswered questions surrounded the proposal. Where were these dumps and how many were there? What weapons were in them, what proportion of the IRA's total arsenal did they represent and how would the inspectors know whether or not they had been moved? The deal's credibility was not assisted by the choice of the inspectors: the colourless ex-Finnish President Martti

Ahtisaari and South African Cyril Ramaphosa, the former general secretary of the African National Congress. During their respective conflicts, the ANC and the IRA were allies and the two groups had helped each other out, on one occasion in an operation in which Gerry Adams had personally participated. Since the start of the peace process, Sinn Féin had reached out to the ANC, in particular to Nelson Mandela, as fellow seekers of peace and justice and liked to present the Irish peace process as a mirror image of the ANC's victory against apartheid in South Africa. Unionist trust in the word of Cyril Ramaphosa was not something that could be taken to the bank.

Nonetheless, Trimble supported the deal and tried to argue that the IRA's move signalled the end to its 30-year war. But the ensuing Ulster Unionist Council meeting was more sceptical; there was more slippage in Trimble's support, this time down to 53 per cent from the 58 per cent registered just a few months before. A measure of Trimble's increasingly perilous position was that his support had fallen from a high of 71 per cent just two years earlier when the UUC had endorsed the Good Friday deal. With Trimble squeaking through, devolution was restored on 30 May 2000. The event was a triumph for Sinn Féin since it meant that not only had the party re-entered government without any IRA weapons being put out of action, it had done so without even any real commitment to that happening.

The backlash came not long afterwards, at a Westminster by-election in South Antrim in September 2000, caused by the death of the sitting Unionist MP, Clifford Forsythe. South Antrim was the second safest Ulster Unionist seat in the House of Commons, with a majority in the 1997 general election of over 16,000. As it turned out, David Trimble was fated to lose no matter what the result, the only question being how badly. The Ulster Unionists chose to run David Burnside, the abrasive and ambitious former head of PR at British Airways. A controversial figure, who had been accused of running a dirty tricks campaign against Virgin Airways founder, Richard Branson, Burnside came from the same Vanguard stable as David Trimble but had remained a hardliner. He was a stringent critic from the sidelines of Trimble's handling of the peace process and his victory would mean that Trimble had lost a mild critic at Westminster only to gain a tougher and more ruthless one.

Burnside's opponent was the DUP's Rev William McCrea, who had lost his Mid-Ulster seat at Westminster to Martin McGuinness in the 1997 general election. The only result worse for Trimble than Burnside winning would be a DUP victory, since this would be a signal to other MPs and Assembly members that unless they moved against him, they might be the next to lose their seats. Knowing this, the DUP threw its entire weight behind McCrea's campaign, although once again, as if not to alienate more secular voters, Paisley stayed in the background. By this stage, the last IRA prisoner had been released from jail and the Unionist electorate were now fully aware of the implications for the RUC of the Patten report. The DUP campaigned on the slogan, "Your chance to put things right". McCrea told the media that the South Antrim electorate had "seen IRA prisoners released, the RUC destroyed, Martin McGuinness in government and still no guns handed over". David Trimble, he added, was out of touch with the ordinary Unionist voter, who was angry and frustrated. That was the message he hammered home at every opportunity.

On the day of the poll it appeared that a large number of Unionists, unable to bring themselves to vote for a Paisleyite, had decided to stay at home and it was this silent protest that dealt a stunning blow to the First Minister. An Ulster Unionist majority of some 16,000 was turned into a DUP majority of 822. In the wake of the result, Trimble's internal critics moved in, if not for the kill, then to badly wound. David Burnside blamed Trimble for taking part in "a drip-by-drip appeasement process" of Sinn Féin. Jeffrey Donaldson, who had broken with Trimble in 1998 and then returned briefly to his fold, called on Unionists to quit the Executive. "Time to draw the line," he said. Martin Smyth warned Trimble he would have to either change tack or resign. The DUP Westminster team, now a third larger, urged Trimble to heed the voters' message that he should go. "The voters of South Antrim were loud and clear on that last night," crowed Paisley. Peter Robinson said that the DUP had its eye on eight other vulnerable seats, including Upper Bann, Trimble's constituency. "Unionism is now being led by this party, the DUP," he declared. "The Ulster Unionist Party is today in tatters . . . Even the removal of David Trimble won't save them. Half the UUP believes that Sinn Féin/IRA should be in government even though they haven't given up their weapons. That is a fault line that cannot be papered over."[14] The writing was on the wall and those who could see it, in London, Dublin and at leadership level in Sinn Féin, would have to adjust their expectations accordingly.

Remarkably, the one place where the message from South Antrim took longest to register was in 10 Downing Street. According to

Alastair Campbell, it wasn't until January 2001, during a meeting with the DUP held some four months after the by-election, that Tony Blair finally began to appreciate how much difficulty Trimble really was in:

> TB said he was really worried, that he had not quite realised how much ordinary Unionist opinion had moved away from us. He had been alarmed by the meeting with the DUP. Even without Paisley there, they had been very chipper, cocky even, and he sensed that they sensed things were moving their way. They told him straight out that Trimble was going down the pan and he'd better get used to dealing with them. I didn't like the tone or feel of it one little bit. TB now feels that unless there was decommissioning – and that meant product not words – then he feared Trimble was dead and without him there was no peace process as things stood. . . . He really was worried, more worried that I had heard or seen him in ages.[15]

One important aspect of the South Antrim by-election result is that it suggested that Trimble's downward slide was probably irreversible and that even if decommissioning happened the following week, it couldn't repair the damage done by the release of IRA prisoners, the presence of two Sinn Féiners in government and especially by the perceived bad treatment of the RUC at the hands of the British. Had the IRA disposed of some of its weapons before these blows, their impact might have been softened – but not any more.

Like it or not, everyone involved in the peace process, the two governments and the Provos especially, now had to seriously contemplate the possibility of the DUP replacing Trimble's Ulster Unionists as the voice of the Protestant community and to consider the implications for the Good Friday Agreement. The conventional view was that this would be a mortal blow for the Agreement since the DUP would never share power in a government of which Sinn Féin was an important constituent. How could they, it was asked, given Paisley's many years of bitter opposition to Irish Republicanism, and the scourging David Trimble had received at his hands for doing so? And hadn't he repeatedly said publicly that he would never do such a thing? Take for example, a 1997 interview Paisley gave to Robert Fisk of the *Independent*, who had cut his reporting teeth in Belfast back in the

1970s and had returned from his Middle East beat to interview Paisley and Gerry Adams about the peace process. Paisley had changed little in the intervening 25 years, Fisk reported, and was as ready as ever to clothe his views in divine justification: "'I will never sit down with Gerry Adams.' But he's just told me he'd sit down with you, I said to Paisley. 'He'd sit with anyone. He'd sit down with the devil. In fact, Adams does sit down with the devil.' And if there is a devil, there must, of course, be a God. 'I believe,' said Paisley, his voice rising, 'that I will see God, as the scriptures make it clear, because I'm a sinner saved by grace.'" Adams, he appeared to be saying, was a sinner beyond salvation and would never see God. The thought of Paisley and Sinn Féin sitting together at the same cabinet table seemed an impossible one but a closer scrutiny of the available evidence suggested that maybe this was not quite such an outlandish thought as it seemed at first blush.

Way back at the time of the Good Friday referendum, the DUP's public line matched the mood of the anti-Agreement Loyalist grassroots, which was that no matter what the result the party would not participate in any of the institutions. Asked if he was not tempted by the prospect and lure of office that the Agreement dangled in front of him, Peter Robinson had, for instance, replied: "Anyone involved in politics would welcome the opportunity to exercise power and realise their political philosophy. But I won't sell my principles in order to get that position."[16] Paisley put it in somewhat blunter terms: ". . . it can't be a real Assembly except everything is working, including the cross-border bodies with executive powers, and we will not work those bodies at all. We will not have anything to do with them. We will enter the Assembly to destroy the attempt to put us into a united Ireland." That included, it seemed, entering the planned Executive: "I am opposed personally to power-sharing with nationalists because Nationalists are only power-sharing to destroy Northern Ireland and you don't put people into a government to destroy a country, you put them into the government to protect a country and defend it and do the best for the country."[17]

Two months later, after the Assembly election had placed the anti-Agreement bloc – the DUP's members plus Bob McCartney's – within a tantalising four seats of overtaking the Ulster Unionists, the DUP switched horses. Initially committed to subverting the Agreement by recruiting disaffected Ulster Unionist Assembly Members – a strategy designed ultimately to rob Trimble of his working majority – the DUP suddenly decided that it would be better to take up the ministerial jobs they were entitled to under the terms of the Agreement. When the Executive went live in late November 1999, the DUP took its two seats but, to deflect hardline criticism, announced that its ministers would not sit in the same Executive meetings with Sinn Féin and would have nothing to do with the North–South Ministerial Council. Peter Robinson became Minister of Regional Development while Nigel Dodds took the Social Development portfolio. Robinson represented the party's more pragmatic wing while the Cambridge-educated Dodds – a better "people person" than Robinson, as one colleague put it – was on the rational side of the DUP's Free Presbyterian arm. To broaden support for the tactic, the two men quit between July 2000 and November 2001 to allow allies to have a taste of governing. Fellow pragmatist Gregory Campbell took over from Robinson while the Paisley loyalist, Maurice Morrow, replaced Dodds. Robinson and Dodds returned for the last year of the Executive's life before the October 2002 suspension. By all accounts the two men were regarded as among the Executive's most efficient and accomplished ministers.

The DUP's decision to take up office signalled the break between Paisley and Bob McCartney and their respective parties, although by this stage McCartney's influence had diminished following a split in his UKUP which had seen four of its five Assembly Members leaving to form a new bloc, the Northern Ireland Unionists. Divisions in the ranks of their former Loyalist allies doubtless made the DUP's decision to accept office easier. Nonetheless both McCartney and his former colleagues were incensed by the DUP's move and saw in it unmistakable clues that the DUP's real game plan was to supplant Trimble and to work the Agreement in his stead.

Bob McCartney recalled his falling-out with the DUP over the issue:

> I met Paisley, Robinson and Dodds and I advised them not to take seats. If they were truly opposed to the Good Friday Agreement, then by taking up posts they were giving it recognition. Their true role is that they should have formed an opposition along with the UKUP and other smaller Unionists. I said that if you don't, you will be part and parcel of the

Executive and even if you don't sit in the same room with Sinn Féin you will be answerable as Ministers on the floor of the Assembly. Not only that but because the responsibilities of ministers overlap, civil servants from ministries where Sinn Féin has power will be talking to your officials; therefore you will be in indirect contact with the Provos.

Later he tackled the DUP Ministers in person:

In 2000 I had a conversation with Robinson and Dodds in the corridor up at Stormont. I said most people would argue that you are the most able and efficient ministers and managers – Robinson in particular is a technocrat par excellence – but there's a paradox here, and aren't you aware of it, which is that the more efficient and capable you are the greater stability and legitimacy you're giving the whole thing?[18]

His former deputy, Cedric Wilson, who had walked out of the Assembly chamber in disgust when Martin McGuinness was nominated as Education Minister, remembers a more ill-tempered exchange with the DUP:

The oath of office, paragraph one, requires that you pledge to agree a programme of work and then implement it. Whenever the DUP took the oath I criticised them from the floor; rather than smashing Sinn Féin they were now effectively in partnership with them. Robinson called me a detestable man, the most hateful man in politics. When Gregory Campbell took over from Robinson he said that he had taken the pledge in the Speaker's office and implied that it was a different pledge, so I checked with the Speaker and it was the same oath everyone else had taken in the chamber. I knew then where this was going and it was just a matter of preparing their people.[19]

Both Bob McCartney and his former colleagues also refused to take seats on any of the Assembly committees, since to do so would mean treating Sinn Féin members as equals and would bestow more credibility on the institutions. Not only did the DUP participate fully in the committee system but some, like Ian Paisley, became committee chairmen, a decision McCartney once challenged:

Now my conversations with Paisley and other DUP types consisted of social contacts in the cafeteria and I would shout over points to them. So I sat down one day and I said to Paisley, "You're chairman of the agriculture committee and you have Sinn Féin members on it, like Francie Molloy, and you'll have to interact with them. How does that square with your non-involvement in the Good Friday Agreement?" He took his pen out and flourished it and said, "I just point the pen at them when they want to talk and wave it." So I said, "What's the difference between that and speaking to them?"[20]

Nearly a decade on, the DUP justifies the move on two grounds, firstly, because it was the right thing to do in the circumstances and, secondly, because of self-interest. One of those who helped formulate the approach put it this way:

It depends on how you analyse the basis of DUP opposition. If our opposition was in principle to the idea of partnership government, then we should have refused ministerial jobs but if it was based on opposition to the mechanisms and the unsavoury aspects of the deal, then it was okay to take the jobs. Our objections were that Sinn Féin had been allowed into talks and then into government without decommissioning and there was an accent on North–Southery as opposed to East–West.

He went on:

The decision to take ministerial posts was a big one. We had a couple of away days to discuss it, in hotels in Portrush and Craigavon. On the one hand the logic of opposition to the Good Friday Agreement extends to not taking seats but the problem is that if we had taken that route and the Good Friday Agreement hadn't collapsed we would have become isolated and we would become marginalised. Then we realised that we could become Ministers in opposition and that won the argument.[21]

Put another way, the DUP's days of principled and instinctive opposition to power-sharing were over, replaced by the sort of ambition to be found in any normal political party, and if Sinn Féin could be persuaded to behave like other non-violent, constitutional parties, then the DUP, presumably, could even share power with them.

Whatever the truth about DUP motives, the move was undoubtedly full of significance. Although the party was only half-in the Good Friday Agreement, the fact of the matter is that the DUP had never been half-in anything even remotely resembling the 1998 deal before. It had always stayed outside such experiments, shouting "traitor" as it strove to bring the arrangement crashing down. Being half-in also indicated the direction that the party really wished to travel and it meant that the Good Friday institutions were in no peril from the DUP, as former First Minister David Trimble recalled:

> When they took seats in the Executive, that was a key moment. Their unwillingness to wreck the thing soon became clear and was exemplified by a budget crisis we had in late 1999. To keep the budget in line we had a procedural motion pushed through the Assembly and if even one voice had been raised against us in the chamber, the budget would have gone belly up and the deal would have been pitched into crisis. But no-one said no, least of all the DUP.[22]

The PUP's Billy Hutchinson, elected to the 1998 Assembly alongside fellow UVF veteran, David Ervine, remembers a DUP Assembly team content with its position in life:

> When I went up there [to the Assembly], the DUP were very comfortable about the place and it was clear that they wanted to do the business. They were very capable. The 1998 decision to take Executive seats was the clue that the DUP would be going into government, it was just a matter of when they became the largest party.[23]

It had escaped no-one's notice that the date of the weapons inspection deal, in May 2000, coincided with the deadline set for the completion of decommissioning in the Good Friday Agreement. It was a bad omen. Any hope that the new agreement would quickly resolve the arms crisis was soon dashed and for the next twelve months and more the Good Friday Agreement stumbled from one crisis to another, each one sapping what remained of David Trimble's political strength.

Events outside Northern Ireland – in South America and on Manhattan island – would eventually precipitate a decisive move by the IRA, but before that happened the DUP would make another giant stride towards government.

The small print of the May 2000 deal included a broad hint that Blair and Ahern expected IRA decommissioning to be completed by June 2001. For its part the IRA had said it would resume contact with de Chastelain's decommissioning body and called this the start of a process "that will completely and verifiably put IRA arms beyond use", language that generated considerable excitement in London and Dublin, if not in Belfast.[24] The first weapons inspection happened in June 2000, and another followed in October, but the promised contact with de Chastelain never materialised, much less any beginning to the disarming process. Unionist scepticism about the IRA's real intentions deepened not long after the second weapons inspection when the Provisional IRA gunned down and killed Joe O'Connor, the Belfast commander of the rival, dissident Real IRA. O'Connor was shot in broad daylight as he sat in a car outside his home in Ballymurphy, a Republican stronghold in West Belfast. He was shot seven times in the head by two gunmen who were recognised by members of O'Connor's family and by neighbours. Although most of West Belfast knew that the Provos had killed him and by so doing had breached their ceasefire, the IRA denied it and the two governments took their word.

There was another tilt at Trimble's leadership at yet one more meeting of the Ulster Unionist Council in November 2000, this time orchestrated and led by Jeffrey Donaldson, who demanded Sinn Féin's expulsion from the Executive by 30 November if the IRA had not by then commenced decommissioning. Trimble survived by pushing through a motion to exclude Sinn Féin from the cross-Border ministerial council instead but the margin of his victory, 54 per cent to 46 per cent, showed that he was running out of wriggle room. Donaldson's role was an intriguing one. Although he wielded the dagger against Trimble, he could never, for some unexplained reason, bring himself to plunge it between his shoulder blades. For some time Frank Millar had been speculating in the columns of *The Irish Times* about the roles Donaldson and Peter Robinson might together play in the event of an Ulster Unionist split and a realignment of Unionism. Cedric Wilson believes the Donaldson-

Robinson relationship was actually much closer at this time: "I once told Jeffrey about something the DUP were up to and the next thing Peter Robinson was challenging me about it. I can only think that he'd gone straight to tell him what I had said. I remember talking to Martin Smyth about it and he was in no doubt that Jeffrey was a Fifth Columnist."[25] If this was true, that Donaldson and Robinson enjoyed this sort of relationship, then the former's reluctance to finish off David Trimble made sense for Trimble was more use to the DUP staying on as Ulster Unionist leader, a figure who could be blamed and castigated for problems in the peace process, a contrast to the DUP leader's forthright resolve.

Three weeks after the UUC meeting, the DUP held its annual conference in Enniskillen, Trimble's value to the DUP as a sort of political Aunt Sally was again evident when Paisley rounded on the beleaguered Unionist First Minister:

> David Trimble, I indict you. In the name of Ulster's honoured dead, I indict you. In the name of the majority of Unionists, I indict you. In the name of the anguished bereaved, I indict you. In the name of those who trusted you and discovered, after the Referendum, your hellish treachery, I indict you. This day I say: David Trimble, in God's name go before you bring any more sacrifice, sorrow and shame to the people of this province.[26]

And so it went on throughout the first half of 2001. In February, Brian Keenan warned that the IRA ceasefire could break down unless the pressure over decommissioning was eased but the following month the IRA finally agreed to talk to General de Chastelain. Suddenly in early May, the process was pitched into another crisis with an announcement from David Trimble, made only hours after Tony Blair had called a general election, that he would resign as First Minister on 1 July if the IRA had not by then started disarming. The prospect of a Westminster poll had changed the game. In the wake of the November UUC meeting, one leading Trimble critic had expressed the hope that a general election would achieve what they couldn't and permanently knock their leader out of the ring: "We have taken the fight as far as we can. It's up to the DUP to do the rest now."[27] Trimble's resignation threat was a desperate attempt to stave off the inevitable.

Trimble's Ulster Unionists went into the election with nine seats at Westminster, a 32.7 per cent share of the vote and a leadership role in the Unionist community that seemed beyond challenge. By the time the last vote had been counted on 9 June, all had been changed. The DUP, which had again campaigned on the intriguingly ambiguous slogan, "Put Things Right!", now had five seats in the House of Commons to the UUP's six and the party's share of the vote rose nearly 9 per cent while the Ulster Unionists' had dropped by six points. The Ulster Unionists were still ahead, but only just – the two parties were now separated by a mere 35,000 votes or so. Council elections held on the same day produced an even narrower gap of just 12,000 votes. Ian Paisley and Peter Robinson were joined at Westminster by Robinson's wife, Iris, who captured Strangford on the County Down coast, Gregory Campbell, who won in East Derry, and Nigel Dodds in North Belfast. The one consolation for Trimble, if such it could be called, was that David Burnside had recaptured South Antrim from Willie McCrea. Trimble himself had survived a challenge from David Simpson of the DUP by just 2,000 votes and narrowly escaped physical harm when he and his wife Daphne were mauled at the count by a vicious and ugly mob of DUP supporters. In East Antrim, Sammy Wilson had been denied victory by 128 votes, while the result in North Down was also good for Paisley; Bob McCartney was soundly beaten by Sylvia Hermon, wife of the former RUC chief, Sir John Hermon, leaving Paisley the unchallenged leader of anti-Agreement Unionism. Sylvia Hermon was the only member of his parliamentary party whose support David Trimble could count on; the other four, Jeffrey Donaldson, Roy Beggs, Martin Smyth and David Burnside wanted him out. Whichever way he looked at it, the result of the 2001 election was a disaster for the First Minister.

The election had produced an even more significant realignment in Nationalist politics. After several years of gradual but inexorable encroachment, Sinn Féin had finally triumphed over the SDLP in the battle for the leadership of anti-Unionism. The Republicans won four seats, a gain of two – Pat Doherty in West Tyrone, who defeated UUP dissident Willie Thompson, and Michelle Gildernew, who squeaked past Ulster Unionist James Cooper, a Trimble supporter. The SDLP kept its three seats but Sinn Féin increased its share of the vote by six-and-a-half points to lead the SDLP by just 0.75 per cent. It was a narrow but decisive victory and a testament to the success of the decommissioning issue in blurring the difference between the two Nationalist parties. If Trimble could be said to be forever looking over his shoulder at the DUP, then the SDLP was continually chasing after Sinn Féin for fear that Nationalist voters would write them off as political wimps.

In July, Trimble duly resigned as First Minister as he had threatened. The election result had left him little alternative and once again Tony Blair moved into "hothouse" mode in response, this time convening a gathering at Weston Park, a stately home in Shropshire in the English Midlands. But if friends of the Ulster Unionist leader expected or hoped that the result would galvanise Blair into shoring up the besieged David Trimble, they were to be sorely disappointed. Trimble came a poor second on Blair's "to do list" behind Sinn Féin, whose demands for concessions in advance of IRA decommissioning had grown in proportion to the expectation of their being granted. The list of goodies given by Blair to Gerry Adams and his colleagues at Weston Park made impressive reading, especially since many would be implemented no matter how the IRA responded. They included: a renewed pledge to set up the part-time PSNI Reserve, which the IRA would surely infiltrate; the closure of a major police interrogation centre in County Armagh; the restructuring of the Special Branch; the phasing out of plastic bullets; a promise to accelerate British troop withdrawals; the demolition of four British Army bases and spy towers, three of them in south Armagh; judicial inquiries into a number of controversial killings in which security force collusion was alleged by Nationalists; an increased Garda role in the PSNI; and, crucially, an amnesty for IRA fugitives, the so-called "on-the-runs". For his part, Trimble received a dish filled with the thinnest of gruel: one essentially meaningless paragraph on decommissioning buried in the middle of a five-and-a-half-page statement; a fund to assist the families of RUC officers killed by the IRA; and a review of the Parades Commission which policed Orange marches. It was beginning to look as if Tony Blair had written off David Trimble.

It wasn't just friends of David Trimble who accused the British Prime Minister of appeasing Sinn Féin. Peter Mandelson, Blair's New Labour ally and NI Secretary until a political scandal drove him from office, provided a revealing insight into Blair's management of the peace process in March 2007, some six years after he had left Belfast.

Although he later tried to disown it, Mandelson's account was full of credible detail. To begin with, he said, Ministers like himself were obliged to maintain the fiction that when they met figures like Gerry Adams and Martin McGuinness, they were not talking to the IRA but to Sinn Féin. No serious student of the Troubles could ever believe that, but since Adams had made a career out of insisting he had never been in the IRA, Blair was doing him a huge but unnecessary favour.

Mandelson had also quarrelled with Blair, he revealed, over the Prime Minister's habit of making concessions to Sinn Féin. Not long after he had taken over from Mo Mowlam as NI Secretary in late 1999, he had refused Blair's request to send a secret "side letter" to Sinn Féin offering an amnesty to IRA on-the-run fugitives. Mandelson recalled:

> I was at a performance of the Royal Ballet visiting Belfast and I was taken out three times during the performance to talk to No. 10 about this. I said . . . I am not prepared to do it because I have my own standing to think of and a secret side letter is not how I want to do business. They came back and said that the Prime Minister takes a different view, that you do need to make these offers to the Republicans and he wants you to write this letter. I said if the Prime Minister wants to make these offers I am afraid he will have to write his own letter.

The concession was eventually made at Weston Park by Mandelson's more obliging successor, John Reid. "Weston Park," added Mandelson, "was basically about conceding and capitulating in a whole number of different ways to Republican demands, their shopping list. It was a disaster because it was too much for them. . . . That was a casualty of my departure, I would say."[28]

Perhaps the most scathing assessment of Tony Blair's handling of the peace process during these years came, however, not from one of his New Labour colleagues, but from Seamus Mallon, Deputy First Minister to David Trimble until the winter of 2001 and deputy SDLP leader under John Hume. No friend of Trimble's, Mallon blames Blair for the SDLP's electoral demise during the peace process, a victim of a cynical decision by Blair and his adviser Jonathan Powell to dispense with what he called "middle nationalism". Both Mallon and Hume retired from the SDLP leadership in the wake of Sinn Féin's 2001 electoral triumph and when Mallon quit Westminster in 2005, his Newry-Armagh seat, once regarded as one of the safest held by the SDLP, was captured by Sinn Féin. Interviewed two years later, he said of Blair:

> Here was a guy with a moral dimension to everything. And I'm not sure at what point I began to realise that in his political dealings he was amoral and didn't know the meaning of the word "honesty" . . . I don't know whether that came all in one go, how quickly it came. At a point I came more and more to the view that this man's word was worth nothing. In reality his whole strategy in terms of resolution of the Northern Ireland problem – I don't use the term peace process – was "Who do I buy and who do I sell?"

Mallon wasn't just speaking metaphorically. One of the secret side deals struck between Blair and Adams at Weston Park allowed Sinn Féin to take up offices in the House of Commons for their four MPs, even though Sinn Féin refused to take its seats at Westminster because of the required oath of allegiance to the British Crown. Allowances and office expenses for the MPs amounted to over stg£400,000 per annum.

In return for all his generosity at Weston Park, Blair was rewarded with an agreement between the IRA and General de Chastelain on a scheme ". . . which will put IRA arms completely and verifiably beyond use". In other words the IRA had finally indicated an acceptable method by which arms could, theoretically, be destroyed. It had taken three years for the IRA to move just this minimal distance but there was still no date or commitment to actually begin the disarming process. This agreement was announced in an IRA statement issued on 9 August 2001 but it was withdrawn just five days later, making it possibly the most short-lived agreement in the history of the peace process and one of the poorest trades in the history of political bargaining. The IRA blamed the Ulster Unionists for withdrawing the deal after Trimble had rejected its statement as inadequate.

But it was surely no coincidence that this all occurred just a day after an ambitious IRA operation in Colombia had been brought to light with the arrest of three Republicans, two with IRA records, at

Bogotá airport as they boarded a plane to Paris. The three were in Colombia participating in an exchange deal between the IRA and left-wing FARC guerrillas, in which IRA mortar technology and know-how was swapped for millions of dollars generated by FARC's cocaine trade. The truly astonishing, even mind-boggling, aspect of these events was that Tony Blair had been told about the IRA's expedition to Colombia by his own intelligence agencies as he sat down with Sinn Féin at Weston Park to grant the party's "shopping list" of concessions.[29] It was difficult not to conclude that there was almost nothing that Blair would not do to preserve the IRA ceasefire, no concession too costly to keep the Adams leadership in place. In such an endeavour, Trimble's fate and the benefits that would accrue to Ian Paisley were but afterthoughts. As Mallon put it: "Anyone who knows the north of Ireland would not have contemplated actions which sold middle unionism to Paisley [in this way]."[30]

◄O►

Within a month the twin towers at New York's World Trade Center had been reduced to rubble and ashes by Islamic jihadists under the direction of Osama bin Laden and six weeks later the IRA finally began to decommission its weapons. Two factors led to this move. One was the influence of Irish-America. Already unsettled by the IRA's flirtation with Colombian Marxists, Irish-Americans had been traumatised and enraged by the September 11th attacks. Had the IRA refused to decommission in these circumstances, then Sinn Féin would have risked losing their dollars and the political leverage they could wield. It was no coincidence that one of the first people made aware of the IRA's intentions was Bill Flynn, then the powerful former CEO of Mutual of America, who had eased Sinn Féin's foray into the powerful and wealthy Irish-American establishment. The second was the Sinn Féin leadership's fear that if the IRA did not decommission, then the White House would isolate the party and international public opinion would shun them. Years of indulgence on the part of Tony Blair and repeated crises in the peace process had failed to move the IRA but dread of being classed alongside suicide bombers and mass murderers, and the potential loss of Irish-America's dollars did. In late October, less than two months after the hijacked jet aircraft had slammed into the twin towers, an unspecified amount of IRA weaponry was put beyond use. The event was endorsed and verified by General de Chastelain but crucial details were withheld, thanks to a secrecy agreement between him and the IRA.

The Good Friday institutions were restored but the secrecy surrounding the decommissioning act, along with the manner in which Trimble was reappointed First Minister, diminished the impact. Two of Trimble's Assembly members, Peter Weir and Pauline Armitage, were sceptical about the decommissioning move and announced they wouldn't vote for his re-election. Robbed of his majority, it seemed it might not be possible to restore Trimble as First Minister. The Assembly was suspended by the ever-helpful John Reid to facilitate the search for a solution, while the DUP sued unsuccessfully in the High Court in an attempt to force a new election. Finally the Alliance Party redesignated three of its members as Unionists and the Women's Coalition restyled one, and their votes helped Trimble scramble back into office, the leader of Unionism now rendered reliant on the support of non-Unionists. The IRA had finally started to disarm but the great irony was that by doing so it had further weakened David Trimble.

Afterwards in the Great Hall of the Stormont parliament building, at the foot of a staircase dominated by a statue of Northern Ireland's first Unionist Prime Minister, Sir James Craig, later Lord Craigavon, David Trimble and his new deputy, Mark Durkan of the SDLP, struggled to hold their first joint press conference as all around them DUP Assemblymen, infuriated by Trimble's manoeuvres, scuffled with Ulster Unionists and members of the SDLP and Sinn Féin. As Trimble and Durkan arrived in front of the microphones, Ian Paisley Junior shouted, "Here come the First Cheat and the Deputy First Cheat." Punches and kicks were exchanged and scores of civil servants packed the balconies above to watch the "Brawl in the Hall", as the free-for-all was soon dubbed. Finally PSNI officers and security guards separated the quarrelsome politicians and restored order.

Much of the DUP rage was an act though. Before Trimble's election, the party had quietly reappointed Peter Robinson and Nigel Dodds to their ministerial posts in the Executive and soon it was back to business as usual, boycotting cross-Border gatherings and meetings with Sinn Féin Ministers for sure but content, nonetheless, to be in government and knowing that even more "traffic" would come their way.

Just over two weeks later a triumphant DUP held its annual conference in Newcastle, County Down – "more like the Nuremberg rally," admitted one delegate, Jim Wells – and Paisley was led into the hall by a bagpiper, to the approving roars of the party faithful, a conquering hero among his grateful people. If there was more than the usual touch of arrogance about the DUP at the 2001 conference, it was because the party, having already feasted on David Trimble's vital fluids, could now smell Ulster Unionism's life blood. The DUP was poised to become the dominant force in Unionism, Peter Robinson predicted. Just look at the difference between the DUP's conference, "the largest and most successful ever", and the Ulster Unionists' affair a week before, he declared: "Their numbers had thinned. Delegates were in sombre mood. Their grey faces, furrowed brows and slumped shoulders told the story. The whiff of embalming fluid hung in the air." Paisley was in an exultant mood, defying the media consensus that with the new deal at Stormont, his day would soon be over. "I was treated like a creature that should have died before Noah's flood," he told one reporter. "But this dinosaur is still sailing on and things have never been better for him or his party." As for the Ulster Unionists, they were finished. Those who were dissatisfied with David Trimble's leadership should follow the example of his assistant, and he pointed to Timothy Johnston, a young accountant who had quit the UUP in June, "in protest at its pro-agreement stance and leadership lies" and joined the DUP.[31]

Thanks to Osama bin Laden and al Qaeda, the Good Friday Agreement was up and running again.

–◁○▷–

If Tony Blair's behaviour at Weston Park suggested that, as far as the Unionist part of the peace process equation was concerned, he had written off David Trimble and had decided instead, in Seamus Mallon's words, "to sell middle Unionism" to Ian Paisley and the DUP, he wasn't the only one to realise that the 2001 election result had fundamentally altered Northern Ireland's political map and to speculate, and even plan, for the consequences.

The election had changed everything for the Republicans as well. Thanks in no small measure to the IRA and Sinn Féin, the main Unionist prop holding up the deal looked as if it was fated to collapse.

In fact it appeared that neither Trimble nor any replacement chosen from his party could survive as long as the DUP was sniping away at them. It would have been strange if Sinn Féin, like Tony Blair, had not wondered if a more stable Unionist partner could be found in the DUP. According to one Irish government source who was never very far from the centre of events during these years, it was after this that Sinn Féin's interest in the DUP noticeably perked up: "They were always coming to us to ask, 'What is Paisley up to, what is the DUP saying?'" he recalled.[32]

The other change had taken place in Sinn Féin's own backyard. Victory over the SDLP in the Westminster poll meant that the goal of out-polling their Nationalist rivals in the next Assembly poll seemed easily within reach. By a quirk, Trimble's Deputy First Minister was Mark Durkan, who took over when Seamus Mallon retired. He had been Hume's parliamentary assistant for many years and was elected SDLP leader when Hume stepped down. Durkan held the post by virtue of the SDLP's success in the 1998 Assembly election but, because of the recent general election result, Sinn Féin could now be forgiven for regarding the post as really and properly theirs, and that Martin McGuinness, not Mark Durkan, ought to be Deputy First Minister. The next election was scheduled for May 2003, some seventeen months ahead, and only an SDLP revival could deny Sinn Féin their expected domination of Nationalist politics, both in the power-sharing Executive and at the polls.

If the SDLP was to have any chance of holding back or reversing the Sinn Féin tide, then the new power-sharing Executive and Assembly had to work smoothly and efficiently, free of the battles between Trimble and Sinn Féin which in the past had disrupted its workings and driven Nationalist voters into the welcoming arms of Sinn Féin. For the SDLP to win back Nationalist voters, they needed to be able to show that they were the real party of government, not Sinn Féin – and for that they required time and stability. But that was a forlorn hope; the IRA and Sinn Féin would deny them both. Like every year since the signing of the Good Friday Agreement, 2002 would be wracked by disputes, this time provoked by high-profile IRA operations. There was one difference though: 2002 would set the scene for the final defeats of both the SDLP and the Ulster Unionist leader. There would be one other consequence: the crowning of Ian Paisley as the leader of Northern Unionism. Once again the Provos and the DUP would prosper together.

Unionists were, of course, well aware that Sinn Féin could become the top Nationalist dog and that some time in the not-too-distant future a Unionist First Minister might have to share the post with someone like Martin McGuinness, whose IRA credentials and paramilitary record were well known. The prospect added to the unease that grew in the following months. Although the IRA carried out a second act of decommissioning in April 2002, this was outweighed by suspicion that it had been timed to coincide with the Republic's general election and the launch of Sinn Féin's bid to gain a real foothold in the Dáil. The IRA's hand was suspected in the killing of a Catholic man, an alleged drug dealer, in County Down. Then on St Patrick's night, the Special Branch offices at Castlereagh police station in East Belfast were broken into, a policeman tied up and sensitive files on informers and their handlers stolen. It was clearly an operation based on inside information and, because of that, initial suspicion was directed towards dissident members of the security forces, rather than the IRA. PSNI chief constable, Sir Ronnie Flanagan, said he would be "most surprised" if paramilitaries were involved but within two weeks the PSNI decided that it had been the IRA's work after all. If so, it was a perfect operation for Sinn Féin from a public relations point of view, completely deniable yet calculated nonetheless to anger and deepen Unionist suspicion.

In late April there was another killing, this time in County Tyrone, which some laid at the IRA's feet. Then Gerry Adams refused to attend a US Congressional hearing on the IRA's links to Colombia, which heard evidence of a five-year relationship between the IRA and the FARC, involving as many as 15 IRA members who had trained Colombian guerrillas in IRA bomb technology. In June there were gun battles between the UVF and the IRA in the sensitive Catholic enclave of Short Strand in East Belfast accompanied by hand-to-hand fighting between Protestants and Catholics. In July, the NI Affairs Committee at Westminster claimed that the Provisional IRA was raising between stg£5 million and stg£8 million each year through smuggling, counterfeiting, extortion and armed robbery.

By early July, unease within the Unionist grassroots had reached a dangerous level and David Trimble warned that within a month he would impose sanctions on Sinn Féin or even withdraw from the

Executive if IRA activity did not cease. In September, the First Minister ratcheted up his threats; he brought leading dissident Jeffrey Donaldson into his tent and between them they agreed on an immediate boycott of the North–South Ministerial Council and signalled an intention to withdraw from the Executive by 18 January 2003 if by then the IRA had not disbanded and decommissioned.

Two weeks later Trimble's threat was rendered unnecessary. On 4 October 2002, PSNI land rovers arrived at the Stormont parliament building and, to the fury of Nationalists throughout Ireland, raided Sinn Féin's offices and took away computer disks. Two days later, Denis Donaldson, the party's head of administration at the Assembly, was charged with participating in an IRA intelligence-gathering plot in the Stormont complex. A bag stuffed with government documents, including transcripts of phone calls between President Bush and Tony Blair and sensitive briefing papers, had been discovered at his home. Detectives would later allege that the documents were being copied by low-level IRA sympathisers in the civil service and passed on to the IRA. They also let it be known that "Stormontgate" was the brainchild of the same figure who had been behind the Castlereagh operation, Bobby Storey, the IRA's Director of Intelligence and a close ally of Gerry Adams. A week later, the scandal was spiralling out of control and NI Secretary John Reid suspended the Good Friday Agreement and reimposed direct rule from London. The scandal had a bizarre sequel when three years later Donaldson was exposed as a long-term British spy; not long afterwards he was shot dead by still unknown assailants.

The key question that jumps out from all this is how much of the IRA's activity during this time happened because the IRA was still an organisation not yet fully under the control of its political leadership, or because the Adams leadership fully intended it to happen, knowing that some operations, such as the very visible Castlereagh raid, would keep the power-sharing deal unstable.

Whatever the answer to that question, IRA activity in 2002 kept the political pot boiling. The key event of the following year was the Assembly election scheduled for May 2003. Without it, neither Sinn Féin nor the DUP would be able to attain political mastery of their respective communities and for a while it looked as if the election might not happen. Tony Blair, for once playing something like hardball with the Provos, postponed the election, first to the end of May and then indefinitely, on the grounds that the IRA had rejected demands that it completely rule out paramilitary activity. But Blair was careful to apply some generous sugar-coating to the pill. The Joint Declaration of April 2003, crafted by Blair and Ahern, offered Sinn Féin another host of concessions, including curbing the British government's ability to suspend the Assembly, further moves to demilitarise the North, proposals to devolve policing and justice to the Executive – which raised the extraordinary possibility of a Sinn Féin minister being in charge of the PSNI and courts system – and generous arrangements to permit IRA "on-the-runs" to return home. The one concession to Trimble was a new ceasefire monitoring body to adjudicate on IRA activity.

In response, the IRA and Sinn Féin dropped enough hints about their willingness to participate in a final, all-encompassing deal that David Trimble agreed to another push in October 2003. The deal that transpired was, in the words of one participant, "a debacle, the greatest nightmare" but in hindsight it was a deal that was damned almost from the start. As speculation about a fresh bid to restore the Good Friday Agreement intensified, three of Trimble's most determined critics, Jeffrey Donaldson, Martin Smyth and David Burnside, resigned the party whip at Westminster and demanded that before anything could happen the IRA had to carry out "acts of completion". In a counter-move, Martin McGuinness warned that Sinn Féin would go nowhere near the IRA with such a demand unless and until a date was set for the Assembly election. Irish Premier, Bertie Ahern, and the White House envoy, Richard Haass, backed McGuinness and by the end of the first week in October, Tony Blair caved in. Soon Downing Street's spin doctors were telling the media that a date, 13 November, had been set for the poll.

That effectively doomed the initiative. Conceding the Assembly election meant that Blair had given away his strongest leverage over the Provos and that promises made in the course of negotiations needn't be kept. The deal was to be unveiled on 21 October 2003 in a choreographed sequence of events, beginning with the formal announcement of the Assembly election and ending with Trimble agreeing to the restoration of the Executive. In between, the IRA was supposed to announce the end of its war against the British and to indicate that it would soon begin to dismantle its military structures.

The centrepiece of the day's proceedings was supposed to be a major piece of IRA decommissioning and a more comprehensive description of what had happened from General de Chastelain, containing the sort of detail about what had taken place that had been so damagingly absent in the first two decommissioning events. The assumption and general understanding – and on Trimble's part, expectation – was that this time the IRA would relax its insistence on secrecy and that what General de Chastelain would be able to say would be enough to win over even sceptical Unionists. In the days leading up to 21 October, Martin McGuinness gave a public assurance that previous credibility problems associated with IRA decommissioning would be addressed. The third act of arms destruction, he said, "would prove more convincing for Unionists". Disastrously, no-one, neither Trimble nor either of the governments, had bothered to check with de Chastelain whether or not McGuinness and his Army Council colleagues were actually going to deliver on this understanding and, if so, what it would mean.

On the night of 20 October, the eve of the deal going live, Bertie Ahern sensed that something was amiss and ordered his officials to contact de Chastelain to get an answer to these questions. But the decommissioning supremo was already "in the field" with the IRA and his cell phone was switched off. The next morning at 6.30 a.m. there was still no sign of the General. At 7.00 a.m. the sequence kicked in with a statement from Blair's office confirming that the Assembly election would indeed happen and that it would take place on 26 November, five weeks hence. Astonishingly, those who had scripted the choreography had agreed that the election announcement would be the very first item in the sequenced events, meaning that, no matter what happened afterwards, the public commitment would stick.

It was one of the best examples of "giving the kids candy before they misbehaved", the Americans' perennial complaint about Blair's handling of the IRA and Sinn Féin. When General de Chastelain finally emerged from the IRA's safekeeping, it was to confirm Ahern's worst suspicion. Dishevelled, inarticulate and clearly exhausted by his experience, the head of the decommissioning body could say little more about what had happened than he had after the first two decommissioning events – which was essentially nothing. The IRA had refused to relax its secrecy arrangement with the decommissioning body. Realising that the game was up, David Trimble halted the sequence. The deal remained frozen in the state precipitated by the Stormontgate crisis of autumn 2002, but with one key difference: Sinn Féin had secured their Assembly election and with it the chance to kill off the SDLP. So, had the Provos reneged on their part of the deal to make this possible? "Let's put it this way," answered one Irish government source; "there were some very strong feelings expressed about Sinn Féin afterwards."[33]

In David Trimble's view the damage had been done by Blair's early concession of an Assembly election date, which had railroaded him into a deal he might otherwise not have contemplated. "It was obvious there was going to be an election," he recalled, "and unless Stormont was up and running beforehand, I knew we would get beaten, because I would have nothing otherwise to show to our voters. So I needed a deal." As for the Provos, he now believes they knew exactly what they were doing on the day they traipsed General de Chastelain around the Irish countryside. "The fact that the Provos denied me the transparency [on decommissioning] that I required meant that effectively they had plumped for a deal with Paisley."[34] In that, at least, it seems Trimble was dead right.

◄○►

The Assembly election campaign, which began almost immediately provided the first public glimpse of the strategy that had been driving DUP policy since just after the referendum on the Good Friday Agreement in 1998, and which, just over three years later, would propel it into government with Sinn Féin. The party's slogan was, "It's Time for a Fair Deal" and it was accompanied by a personal message to the voters from Ian Paisley: "This election is Ulster's date with destiny," he wrote. "It is the chance to put things right, to give a mandate to a strong and united Democratic Unionist team and to negotiate a new agreement."[35]

The strategy, which had in the main been devised by Paisley's deputy, Peter Robinson, showed that both the DUP and Sinn Féin viewed the peace process in the much same way, as an electoral opportunity. While Sinn Féin's aim was to displace the SDLP by mobilising Nationalists in opposition to Trimble's incessant and unreasonable decommissioning demands, the DUP's goal was to overtake Trimble and his Ulster Unionists by highlighting their failure to achieve credible and transparent IRA decommissioning. And both parties wanted to end up running the power-sharing executive together – even though it was an ambition they were careful not to highlight publicly.

To achieve its goal, the DUP had completed two stages of a three-part plan. Firstly, it had shown that DUP leaders were willing to enter government and could do the job – hence the decision to become "Ministers in opposition". Secondly, it had undermined the DUP's principal rival, the Ulster Unionists, by contrasting Paisley's resolution and firmness with Trimble's alleged weakness which had only succeeded in obtaining concessions for Sinn Féin. The third part of the plan was to insist that once the DUP became the majority Unionist party it would press for "a new agreement" that would deliver a genuine, unambiguous peace, secure the Union and end the ceaseless indulgence of the Provos. An opinion poll carried out for the *Belfast Telegraph* two weeks before the vote suggested the third part of the strategy echoed the mood of the Unionist electorate pretty accurately: 61 per cent of Unionists, the poll found, wanted the Agreement renegotiated. Even if the IRA did all that was required of it, 55 per cent of Unionists would still want a recast deal.

At the hustings, the DUP's campaign stressed three themes: Peter Robinson and Nigel Dodd's "flawless" record as Ministers: "The best in office," the party claimed; the DUP's veto over any arrangement: "No deal in Northern Ireland will be stable until it is supported by the DUP," said the manifesto; and the looming, ever-present threat of a rampant Sinn Féin whose leaders, either Gerry Adams or Martin McGuinness, would probably become Deputy First Minister in a new Executive and who might, unless challenged, fill the post of Minister for Policing and Justice with Gerry Kelly, whom most Unionists knew as the man who had bombed London for the IRA in 1973.

At the launch of the DUP manifesto, Paisley rounded on the Ulster Unionist leader for going into government with Sinn Féin. "Only a vote for the DUP," he declared, "can stop the nightmare of David Trimble partnering Gerry Adams in the running of our province." But elsewhere there was evidence, well-hidden for sure but nonetheless available to the persistent researcher, that the DUP was willing to consider exactly the same partnership in the right circumstances. Absent from the manifesto was an explicit, unconditional commitment never to go into government with Sinn Féin and, at the launching of the manifesto, Peter Robinson outlined seven tests for any new deal, the third of which said that "only those committed to exclusively peaceful and democratic means"[36] could get into power. In other words, if Sinn Féin could pass that test, then the DUP would go into government with them.

One fascinating and telling aspect of the campaign was the relatively low profile of Ian Paisley. It was of course in the DUP's interests to minimise Paisley's influence since success in the election depended on appealing to Unionist voters who in the past had shunned the DUP precisely because of Paisley's divisive and embarrassing image. But there was another possible reason he was assigned a low profile. The 77-year-old leader was in ailing health, both physical and mental, and there was a suspicion that the DUP's handlers were terrified that "a senior moment" during a television interview or public performance could be deeply damaging. Ulster Unionists accused Paisley of avoiding a radio or TV debate with Trimble and dropped hints to the media about the reasons. Paisley himself was obliged to respond to the rumours and questions, insisting that they were groundless. "They say I've cancer," he told one reporter. "They say I'm dying, but I'm taking a long time to die. I rise at 3.00 a.m. I have breakfast and read the Bible. I'm on the bus from morning until evening. I attend nightly campaign meetings. I love elections."[37] Questions about Paisley's mental agility gave rise to the election campaign's most charged moment, a toe-to-toe confrontation between Paisley and Trimble and their respective teams outside the Ulster Unionist's East Belfast headquarters. "When are we going to have a debate, Ian? When are you going to stop running?" a laughing David Trimble taunted. Paisley replied: "I choose what radio programmes I go on. I made my choice. I knew I was needed in the sticks." That was the cue for an angry finger-pointing, abusive maul between their respective acolytes, all of it captured for the evening television news.

Vastly entertaining though it was, the slanging match made no appreciable difference to the outcome of the election, which turned out more or less exactly as Peter Robinson and the DUP's strategists had anticipated. The DUP increased its tally of seats by a third, from 20 won in the 1998 Assembly to 30, and secured an impressive 25.7 per cent of the vote, three points ahead of the Ulster Unionists. Trimble's party lost only one seat, though, and that was evidence that the DUP performance had been made possible by the collapse of the smaller Unionist parties, whose vote had just folded into the DUP. Bob McCartney's divided party lost four of its five seats – the North Down barrister getting in on the fourteenth count to win a single seat – while all five independent Unionists lost their seats to the DUP. The Ulster Unionists hadn't quite been routed but the psychological damage from finally losing the forty-year-long electoral battle with Ian Paisley was huge. The rout would come later. At the DUP's annual conference a few months after the election result, Ian Paisley was triumphant. "The majority of Ulster's unionists have given the Ulster Democratic Unionist Party the custodianship of our Province," he declared. "They have charged us with the trust deeds of our future."

The Nationalist result was also as expected. In the 1998 Assembly election, the SDLP had won twenty four seats to Sinn Féin's 18; now their positions were exactly reversed with Sinn Féin securing 23.5 per cent of the vote to the SDLP's 17 per cent. Five years of attrition had finally worked for both the DUP and Sinn Féin. For those who believed that the only stable, long-term deal would come not from the centre ground of Northern Irish politics but from its extremes, their day had come.

"The IRA needs to be humiliated. And they need to wear their sackcloth and ashes, not in a back room but openly. And we have no apology to make for the stand we are taking."

IAN PAISLEY, 27 NOVEMBER 2004

❧

"Inclusive, mandatory coalition government which includes Sinn Féin under d'Hondt or any other system is out of the question."

DUP MANIFESTO, MAY 2005 GENERAL ELECTION

❧

"No unionist who is a unionist will go into partnership with IRA-Sinn Féin. They are not fit to be in partnership with decent people. They are not fit to be in the government of Northern Ireland. And it will be over our dead bodies that they will ever get there."

IAN PAISLEY, 12 JULY 2006

❧

"I and my party will not be found wanting in our search to get it right."

IAN PAISLEY, ON THE EVE OF THE ST ANDREWS TALKS, 28 SEPTEMBER 2006

CHAPTER FOURTEEN

A Narrow Escape

The Reform Club in London's Pall Mall, between Trafalgar Square and St James Park, has played a long and venerable role in British and Irish politics. Established in the wake of the Great Reform Bill of 1832 by radical Whigs, as a centre for progressive ideas, it became the unofficial headquarters of the Liberal Party before evolving in the 1920s into an exclusively – and exclusive – gentlemen's social club which, despite its enlightened origins, refused to accept women members until 1981. In the latter half of the nineteenth century, the Club was witness to many of the great dramas of British politics, few of which reverberated as strongly or for as long as the quarrel between two of its most distinguished members, Liberal leader William Gladstone and his predecessor Lord Hartington. In the 1885 general election, Parnell's Irish Parliamentary Party had secured the balance of power in the House of Commons and, driven by pragmatism if nothing else, Gladstone became a convert to the cause of Home Rule. In the following years he tried, but failed, to push two Home Rule Bills through parliament and succeeded only in dividing his party. Hartington and others in the Liberal Party feared that Home Rule for Ireland would begin the disintegration of the United Kingdom and they broke off to form the Liberal Unionist Party. In 1912, as the third and last Home Rule Bill was being fiercely opposed by Edward Carson, whose Ulster Volunteer Force was drilling openly in Belfast, the Liberal Unionists merged with the Conservatives to form the Conservative and Unionist Party, the modern Tories.

It was perhaps fitting then that the Reform Club was chosen, in the last days of 2003 and just after the DUP had established hegemony of

Unionist politics in Northern Ireland, as the venue for a meeting that, in the view of many, would lead to the most determined effort to end the long divisions between Irish Nationalism and Unionism. The meeting had been sought by the Irish government, which was represented that evening by Michael Collins, the most senior official in the Department of the Taoiseach, Bertie Ahern, and Dáithí Ó Ceallaigh, Ireland's ambassador to Britain. Their guests were Peter Robinson, the deputy leader of the DUP, and Nigel Dodds, Paisley's former European adviser and now a member of the DUP front bench. Between them, the two men represented the two wings of the party, pragmatic and conservative, whose joint approval would be required for any political deal. The two officials had only one question on their minds as they sat down with Robinson and Dodds: was the DUP ready to talk?

The Assembly election was on its face a disaster for Bertie Ahern. At the urging of Sinn Féin, Ahern, more than anyone, had pressured Tony Blair to agree to the election and then had seen the Provos renege on the understanding that this time IRA decommissioning would be more transparent and convincing. In the early hours of 21 October, when General de Chastelain was still wandering the Irish countryside in the company of the IRA, Ahern's instincts told him that the deal was dead. He was supposed to travel to Hillsborough Castle that morning to join Blair and celebrate their success in restoring the Good Friday deal but now he decided it would be more prudent to stay in Dublin. Only after urgent phone calls from Jonathan Powell and then Tony Blair did he change his mind. When Ahern's plane was hit by lightning on the way to Belfast, it was a grim omen. The result of the subsequent Assembly poll appeared a portent of more calamity. David Trimble and the SDLP had received a drubbing, the centre ground upon which the Good Friday Agreement had been constructed had collapsed, leaving the two extremes, the DUP and Sinn Féin, triumphant. While many, if not most of those involved in the peace process diplomacy were plunged into bleak depression by the outcome, there was a contrary, more optimistic, view. This said that if somehow a deal between the two extremes, between Sinn Féin and the DUP, could be crafted and made to stick, it would certainly be more viable and less vulnerable than anything David Trimble had so far put his name to. But was Ian Paisley the man to do it?

Paisley's initial comments in the wake of his victory were discouraging. "No, I'm not talking to Sinn Féin," he replied to questions about how he planned to deal with his putative partners in government.

"And my party's not talking to Sinn Féin, and anybody that talks to Sinn Féin will be out of my party. I think I'm entitled to ignore murderers. I don't see Mr Bush and Mr Blair talking to terrorists." The Good Friday Agreement was dead, he added, and the DUP was now committed to going "back to the drawing board and get a system of democracy that both Nationalists and unionists . . . can buy into".[1]

The problem for Dublin was that there was no ready way of judging whether this was all typical Paisley bluster or if the DUP leader's private stance was just as hardline, and that the idea that Gerry Adams and Ian Paisley could be coaxed into government together was just a wild, impossible pipe dream. "We had never really met the Paisleyites," said one Irish government source. "We had had very limited contact and that was true of the Travellers as well."[2] The Travellers were officials from the Department of Foreign Affairs whose job entailed moving around the North talking to politicians and passing the resulting gossip cum intelligence back to Dublin. Hence the request to meet Robinson and Dodds. To Dublin's surprise, not only were the two DUP men quite happy to meet but it was clear from the exchange that they and Paisley were prepared to engage with the Irish government. "They wanted to do business," said the Irish source. And so, at the Reform Club, the decision was made to set up a meeting between Ahern and Paisley, the respective leaders of Irish Nationalism and Unionism.

Paisley's only previous political interaction with an Irish prime minister had been back in 1967 when the then Protestant Unionist leader had tossed snowballs at Jack Lynch's car after he had met Captain O'Neill at Stormont. Paisley had met Ahern before, in September 1999, but that was in his capacity as Moderator of the Free Presbyterian Church. He had asked to see Ahern after one of his churches in County Monaghan had been burned down in an arson attack. Paisley had signed the official visitors' book in Government Buildings and the two men had sipped a cup of tea but they "did not exchange the normal pleasantries", as one report put it. A political meeting between Paisley and Ahern would be the first ever such contact and the historical significance of the event would be enormous.

But there were sensitivities to cater for. It was agreed that the two men would not meet either in Belfast or Dublin but at the Irish embassy in London, in the United Kingdom's capital to be sure, but in a small bit of it over which the Irish had sovereignty. Then there was the question of a handshake. Paisley had not shaken Ahern's hand in 1999 and he wouldn't do so now. The handshake had come to play a hugely symbolic role in the Irish peace process; culturally it signified that the person extending his or her hand carried no weapon and thus presented no threat, while a positive response from the other party meant that the assurance was accepted. Since Sinn Féin's partners in the IRA still had weapons, there was a refusal on the part of Unionists to shake Sinn Féin hands. There had been no handshake with Ahern in 1999 because, as Paisley explained then, "I will not shake hands with a prime minister of a country which still has a claim over my country." In fact, by this time the Irish claim to the North had been amended to encompass the consent principle and the probable real reason was because his grassroots would have been appalled and suspicious.

Nonetheless a choreography for the embassy meeting was agreed. The two parties were to meet in the embassy dining room on the evening of 30 January but when Paisley and his DUP colleagues were ushered in, Ahern and the Irish delegation would remain seated, since to stand up was a natural prelude to a handshake. The rest of Paisley's team, MPs Peter and Iris Robinson, Nigel Dodds and Gregory Campbell, had no problems shaking hands with the Irish government contingent who, aside from the Taoiseach, included Foreign Affairs Minister Brian Cowen, Justice Minister Michael McDowell, the latter a stringent critic of Sinn Féin, and various officials. Paisley brought two of his own officials along. One, Richard Bullick, was a "baby barrister", one of the young lawyers who had defected from the Ulster Unionists in exasperation with David Trimble and was now an adviser to Peter Robinson. The other was Paisley's aide, Tim Johnston, another Ulster Unionist defector who was to play a key role in subsequent events, as an Irish source explained: "Timmy was a real hero in all of this; he was our guide to the DUP. He guided us through and told us what would work with Paisley and what wouldn't and what sentiment in the party was. Our problem was that we and the DUP genuinely did not know each other and we needed him."[3]

Paisley had paraded Tim Johnston to the media before this as an example that other discontented Ulster Unionists should follow. Fellowship and relief from David Trimble's infuriating stand on the peace process, he had suggested, could be found under the DUP's ever-expanding umbrella. Six days into the New Year, Jeffrey Donaldson took Paisley's advice and finally quit the Ulster Unionists to defect to the DUP. He brought two Assembly colleagues with him, Arlene Foster from

Fermanagh and Norah Beare, Donaldson's Assembly colleague from Lagan Valley. When Paisley turned up at the Irish embassy in London, Donaldson came along with the other MPs. Thanks to Donaldson's defection, the DUP now had six MPs at Westminster, to the Ulster Unionists' five, while the party Assembly team had overnight increased to 33. Trimble's Assembly team fell to twenty four, the same as Sinn Féin.

Donaldson would later claim that his resignation from the UUP had been precipitated by the Trimble camp: ". . . the Party Executive opted to deliver an ultimatum to me, that if I did not endorse the failed agreement and support David Trimble's leadership, I would be expelled from the Party," he claimed. Donaldson, Arlene Foster and Norah Beare had published their own "mini-manifesto" before the Assembly poll, stating that they would "promote greater co-operation between Unionists to more effectively represent the Unionist case in the negotiations that will follow the election". With Sinn Féin now aiming to become the largest single party in Northern Ireland, their defection to the DUP was not only consistent with that pledge but, Donaldson would claim, necessary also. "The realignment of Unionism," he wrote, "is well underway . . ."[4] Some of his new DUP colleagues believe that it was Peter Robinson, not Ian Paisley, who was responsible for bringing him into the DUP. "Jeffrey's just in awe of Peter," said one DUP man.[5] Ulster Unionists suspected that Donaldson and Robinson had already been in secret alliance against Trimble for some time and in the coming years the same double act would work to edge the DUP towards government, with Robinson playing the role of Gerry Adams to Donaldson's Martin McGuinness.

David Trimble has a more cynical explanation for the departure of Donaldson, Foster and Beare: "They moved at a point when the Robinson wing needed them. In the run-up to the Assembly election there were constituency fights in the DUP between the church wing and Robinson's wing and Robinson lost out. So bringing Jeffrey and Arlene in was a boost to him."[6] Whatever the truth, there is little doubt that the influx of Ulster Unionists would change the DUP and over time smooth the party's harder, fundamentalist, Free Presbyterian edges and push it towards the politics of compromise and power.

It is, perhaps, no coincidence that Sinn Féin had undergone a similar change. During and after the 1981 hunger strikes, an influx of more politically motivated activists diluted IRA influence inside the republican movement and helped Gerry Adams steer the party into electoral politics and towards the peace process. This was yet another characteristic that the DUP and the IRA's political wing had in common.

—◄○►—

The embassy meeting lasted just an hour and again confirmed to the Irish government what Collins and Ó Ceallaigh had heard at the Reform Club – the DUP was ready to do business. Standing under a fluttering Irish tricolour outside the embassy, Paisley said as much publicly. Nonetheless, Bertie Ahern, he added, would have to face "the big issue" which had not changed despite other altered circumstances: "getting rid of the guns of the terrorists". Events moved with remarkable speed after that, dispersing the pessimism that had settled like a dark cloud immediately after the Assembly elections and underlining emphatically that Paisley and the DUP were ready, even eager for government.

Peter Robinson and others had generated some 400 pages of documents outlining their critique of the Good Friday Agreement during the campaign and it soon became clear that as much care and planning had gone into preparing the DUP's post-election strategy. Soon it was possible to isolate and identify the main strands of the DUP's approach. The first was that, while the DUP talked of "burying" the Good Friday Agreement and of negotiating a new deal, in reality Paisley, Robinson and their colleagues would be content with recasting aspects of the 1998 settlement – or at least enough of them to bestow credibility on the claim that they had delivered a new deal to Unionists. Secondly, although the DUP would not talk to or deal directly with the Provos, the party would, as they had told the Taoiseach in London, take part in a process in which there would be, via the two governments, indirect and substantive contact with Sinn Féin. Thirdly, the Provos would have to disarm and end IRA activity, to accept what Robinson called "the Blair necessities" before progress could be made – that was a reference to Tony Blair's call for acts of completion by the IRA in the weeks before the ill-fated October 2003 decommissioning deal.

In essence it would have been difficult to slip a cigarette paper between that programme and David Trimble's, except that the DUP insisted it would accept no half-measures when it came to the required IRA acts of completion. The Paisleyites were pushing at open government doors – as long as the fundamentals of the 1998 deal, inclusive power-sharing and North–South co-operation, were untouched, both Dublin and London were ready to accommodate them. By happy coincidence a five-year review of the Good Friday Agreement was due to begin in February 2004 and that gave Bertie Ahern the opportunity to send a signal to the DUP that amendments to the 1998 agreement were possible and acceptable to him. "I accept fully that the review is going to mean change," he said.[7] These included making Executive Ministers accountable to the Assembly, an important item on the DUP's list.

Both London and Dublin were eager to see the DUP participate in the review, not least because it would give the party a sense of ownership of whatever emerged at the other end. The opening session of the review was structured in such a way that all the parties and their leaders would be seated around the same table and the meeting would be chaired by Paul Murphy, the new NI Secretary, and Brian Cowen, the Republic's Foreign Minister, before breaking into smaller groups dealing with aspects of the Good Friday Agreement. On 3 February, in the Stormont parliament building, the plenary session of the review was duly opened and signalled another first in the DUP's evolution, this time the presence of Ian Paisley and Gerry Adams in the same room for the same political purpose. But it was clear afterwards that the experience, or rather the anticipated response from a disconcerted DUP grassroots, had unsettled Paisley. "I made it clear we are not negotiating with IRA/Sinn Féin," he thundered. "Today was the farce of everyone making a statement. It was only to please the Governments, to let them say they got everyone in the same room."[8]

Perhaps, but that was indeed the significance of the event. The sight of Paisley and Adams sitting at the same table would have been unthinkable just a couple of years before, and only three days later there came the most compelling sign yet that Paisley would oversee a process that one day would mean the DUP joining Sinn Féin in government. Accompanied by the entire DUP Assembly team, Paisley called a press conference to unveil what had been trailed in the media as "radical" devolution proposals. Three plans were suggested. The first was called a Corporate Assembly in which the parliament would behave rather like a large county council, taking decisions on the basis of the consent of a majority of both Unionist and Nationalist members. The second was Voluntary Coalition, a variant on the idea which Paisley had rejected, to his party's electoral profit, way back in the mid-1970s. The third was called a Mandated Coalition, which was essentially the Good Friday system with changes in the detail. There was provision for the two Executive models to develop out of a re-established Assembly but for either to come into existence the IRA would have to "wind up and pack up as a paramilitary organisation" first, as a DUP source put it.

The "Devolution Now" proposals, as the DUP scheme was called, had been presented to Tony Blair at a meeting at Downing Street the day before, where Peter Robinson had put on a PowerPoint show to illustrate the plan, a speciality of Paisley's technologically accomplished deputy. The Prime Minister was reportedly impressed, both by the content and the presentation. While some in Sinn Féin, led by Martin McGuinness, dismissed the proposals as an attempt by the DUP to wriggle out of the Good Friday Agreement, both London and Dublin, the former more explicitly, correctly recognised the significance of the DUP move: Paisley would, in the right circumstances, share power with the Provos. And having signalled that, the DUP had put the onus on Sinn Féin, or more accurately the IRA, to make the next move.

That move came two weeks later but it was not the one that anyone wanted to see. In the early evening of 20 February 2004, as former INLA member Bobby Tohill sat sipping a pint of beer in Kelly's Cellars, one of Belfast's oldest bars where leaders of the United Irishmen rebellion of 1798 had met to plot their insurgency, four men rushed in and set upon him. The four wore balaclavas and boilersuits – and that was the first clue as to his assailants' identity. Their clothing was the customary garb of an IRA active service unit, a balaclava to hide their faces and a boilersuit that afterwards could be burned to destroy forensic evidence. The IRA men beat Tohill with US police-style expandable batons and then dragged him outside and into a car which drove off at high speed. There were aspects to Tohill's kidnapping that made the suspicion of IRA responsibility inevitable. Kelly's Cellars is situated just off Royal Avenue in central Belfast and is adjacent to the newly opened Castlecourt shopping centre. Dozens of people, drinkers in the bar as well as shoppers on the streets outside, would have seen Tohill's abduction. The Provos had accused Tohill of being a member of the dissident Real IRA and six months before he had complained to the media about IRA threats against him. So it was well known that he and the IRA were in conflict. But rather than abduct Tohill from his home or grab him later that night as he made his way home from the bar, the IRA had chosen to kidnap him in circumstances that almost suggested they wanted to flaunt their involvement. Predictably, the kidnappers didn't get very far, perhaps half a mile, before a PSNI patrol forced them to a halt and rescued Tohill, who later needed 80 stitches to his head, and arrested the four IRA men.

By this stage the IRA had been on its second ceasefire for the best part of six years and Gerry Adams and his colleagues had consolidated their hold on the organisation. Michael McKevitt, the leader of the dissident splinter, the Real IRA, was in jail, convicted on the word of an FBI informer who had infiltrated the RIRA with embarrassing ease. The Real IRA was in the process of itself splitting and now presented a minimal threat to the Provisional leadership. It is difficult not to make two conclusions from all this: one, that even if Tohill's kidnapping had been warranted, it could have been carried out in a more discreet, even secretive, fashion; and secondly, that the operation was sanctioned by an IRA whose operational leadership was by this stage firmly under political control. As the late Sinn Féin Assembly member John Kelly once put it, when asked about this issue: "I go back to what the Bible said, that not a sparrow falls from the sky but that the man above does not know about it and Gerry Adams in terms of the Republican movement is the man above. He is God, so he knows and would want to know, and would be disappointed if he didn't know everything that happens within the Republican movement and nothing will be hidden from him."9

Whatever the motive for the Tohill kidnapping, its effect was to test both the new ceasefire watchdog, the Independent Monitoring Commission (IMC), and the DUP. In April, the IMC issued a tough report, blaming the IRA for the abduction and saying that if Sinn Féin had been in the Executive it would have recommended its expulsion. It also threatened to name Sinn Féin members who were in the IRA leadership, a possibility that enraged Gerry Adams, while the British slapped a stg£120,000 fine on Sinn Féin. The incident demonstrated the value of the IMC – the integrity of the IRA's ceasefire would now be judged independently, relieving both Unionist politicians and the British of the onerous and divisive burden. The IMC had been created to make David Trimble's life easier but, ironically, it would be the DUP which in the longer term would derive most benefit from it. Even so, in the days after Tohill's abduction, Paisley and Trimble reversed the roles they had played before the 2003 election. Trimble withdrew from the Good Friday review in protest when both London and Dublin refused to expel Sinn Féin, while the DUP remained stubbornly immoveable. Peter Robinson even managed to turn the incident against the Ulster Unionist leader. "We will continue to talk to legitimate politicians about how to deal with Sinn Féin," he declared. "He [Trimble] can run away if he wants to. Our renegotiation of the Agreement goes on."

An incident which, prior to 2003, would have pitched the process into crisis and put the DUP at David Trimble's throat with cries of "Judas", proved to be just a rumble strip in Paisley's journey to power. To be sure, the DUP's strategists toughened up the demand for "acts of completion" by the IRA and began to talk of a necessary testing period of weeks or months to verify what Peter Robinson, in Washington for the St Patrick's Day celebrations – the first such trip by the DUP – called "the durability" of any IRA decision to end its activity. But it is likely this would have happened anyway. By the end of June, following a mini-"hothouse" at Lancaster House in London, the governments set mid-September 2004 as the date for the first major negotiation involving the DUP and Sinn Féin. Within days the DUP was quietly briefing reporters that a political deal then could see Paisley in government with Sinn Féin by the spring of 2005, just 18 months after the party had seen off David Trimble. The agenda or wish-list for the talks contained no surprises: a definitive end to IRA activity along with "convincing" and complete IRA decommissioning; Sinn Féin's support for the PSNI and the devolution of policing powers; a commitment to ensure the new deal's stability; and, finally, the changes to the Good Friday Agreement agreed in the course of the review. It was largely a DUP agenda and it was no surprise that Paisley called the session at Lancaster House, where Margaret Thatcher's intelligence services had allegedly bugged the Zimbabwe independence talks in 1980, "a very useful exchange of views". He could detect, he added, "the faint outline and context of a way forward that would be agreeable".[10]

–◦–

The venue for the weekend "hothouse" session in mid-September was a place calculated to make every "B" movie director in Hollywood go weak at the knees. Set on two small islands on the River Len near Maidstone in the heart of Kent, Leeds Castle has moats, turrets, battlements, banqueting halls and splendid grounds, a perfect location for one of those quaintly clichéd movies about jousting knights and comely maidens that Americans so love. Built in 1119, it passed into royal hands in 1278 and became part of the Queen of England's dower, the settlement she would receive if widowed. Henry VIII took his court there in 1520 en route to the Field of the Cloth of Gold where a pact of friendship was made with the French monarch, King Francis I. After that, Leeds Castle was gifted to one of Henry's courtiers and became home to a string of noble and wealthy families. In the nineteenth century it was used as a prison and a convalescent home before becoming in modern times a conference centre and tourist attraction. In July 1978, Egyptian President Anwar Sadat and Israeli Foreign Minister Moshe Dayan met there to prepare for the Camp David Accords which two months later sealed peace between their two countries.

It was a mission to end a conflict almost as long and as intractable as that in the Middle East which brought Sinn Féin and the DUP to Leeds Castle, along with the British and Irish premiers and their relevant cabinet colleagues, the new White House envoy, Mitchell Reiss, and scores of officials. The other parties – the SDLP, the UUP, Alliance and the UKUP – came along as well, but as during most other "hothouse" gatherings, they would spend much of their time wandering the castle gardens as the real talking took place elsewhere.

The DUP sent a huge delegation to Kent, 16 in all, and that suggested the party's leadership had calculated that if a deal did emerge, then it would be wise to have as many fingerprints on it as possible. Party leader Ian Paisley, now in his seventy-eighth year, did not travel with the rest of the DUP delegation. They had flown from Belfast to London and then continued by road down to Kent but Paisley, barred from flying on doctor's orders, came by ferry across the Irish Sea and then by car. The DUP leader was seriously ill at this time, so ill that he nearly died, according to his son Kyle, who had followed his father into the Free Presbyterian ministry. Ian Paisley would recover his health in the months after Leeds Castle, but it was a close-run thing. Introducing his father to his congregation in Lowestoft, Suffolk, in August 2005, Kyle Paisley told them: "This is a special service for me inasmuch as last year my father was very, very ill. He said he was at death's door and it was a very trying and testing time for him and my Mum and all our family."[11]

In early August 2004, Ian Paisley had been admitted to hospital for what the Paisley family insisted were "routine" tests which were "nothing to get worried about" but it soon became evident that he was more seriously ill than anyone wished to admit. He stayed in hospital for more than a week and, when he was released, he raved angrily and in classic Paisley fashion at journalists, and threatened to sue papers that had carried reports about his illness. "Look at me, look at me!" he challenged the reporters who had wondered aloud whether or not he would make it to Leeds Castle. "I hope to take a few thousand pounds off some newspapers who lied about me. And I would say it is just because I happen to be a Protestant and journalists happen to be Romanists that they think they can take it out on me."12

But his illness was serious enough to force him to reduce his workload. Earlier in the year he had decided that the burden of remaining a Euro MP was too much to bear and he announced he would not stand in the 2004 election. Political and church colleagues had noticed that he was not the forceful, extemporising public speaker that he had once been and now relied on notes to help him through a speech or sermon. Some were even planning for a post-Paisley era. The Paisley family have consistently refused to reveal what was ailing him but many, including the Irish government, believe he was suffering from a heart condition. As a child Paisley had thrombosis, which can sometimes have long-term effects, and this along with the medical advice not to fly to Leeds Castle both point to a cardiac problem of some sort. Following the Leeds Castle talks his health improved after he sought a second medical opinion and changed his drug regimen, but those who met him at the weekend "hothouse" session were shocked at his appearance. "The eyes were staring, the flesh had fallen off his face; he was a living corpse," recalled one participant.13 One DUP source agreed: "He was possibly suffering from an enlarged heart and there was a problem with his medication. He was falling asleep all the time, there was no doubt he was very ill; he looked like a walking corpse."14

Paisley was ill for sure, but he was also angry, and not just because newspapers had allegedly exaggerated his sickness. Since the turn of the year, when the DUP began showing signs of seriously wanting to negotiate a deal, there had been intense speculation about divisions in the DUP, primarily between Paisley and "the never, never brigade" on one side, and Robinson and the party's modernisers on the other. Not only was the media full of such stories but elements in the Northern Ireland Office joined in, expressing private doubts that Paisley was fully signed up to the notion of sharing power with Sinn Féin. There was much talk, for instance, of progress not being possible until Paisley had left the scene and been replaced by Peter Robinson. The speculation got so intense that, after Leeds Castle, Robinson felt obliged to address the matter publicly, to dismiss what he called "the media fantasy stakes" about DUP splits. "Let me make it clear," he told East Belfast party workers, "at least to those who allow facts to intrude into their lives, the DUP went into this process united and will come out the other end united. There is but one camp in the DUP – it is the fair deal camp."[15] Whatever about the truth of that, Paisley arrived at Leeds Castle in a foul temper. "He felt that people were conspiring against him. He was in a very angry mood," recalled an Irish government source.[16] And there was little doubt in government minds that the object of Paisley's suspicious ire was his deputy, Peter Robinson.

For Tony Blair and Bertie Ahern and their officials, Leeds Castle was the moment when they realised for the first time that Paisley really wanted to do a deal. As an Irish government source recalled:

> I remember two meetings the DUP had with Bertie and Blair at Leeds Castle. First in came Robinson and Dodds, who stressed how difficult things were and how hard it would be to sell the deal to their people. Then Paisley and Ian Junior came in and their message was that it wasn't nearly as bad as they were painting it. At this point both governments became convinced that Paisley wanted to be First Minister before he died and at Leeds Castle he was at death's door, so the question was quite urgent.[17]

Dublin Ministers and officials suspected that Robinson and Dodds were worried that Paisley was so sick, he would make a concession too far in his eagerness to clinch the deal.

The severity of Paisley's illness and his apparent distrust of close colleagues at Leeds Castle combined to produce a variant on that theory, which says that it wasn't just his own fate that concerned him but also his succession. "The Paisley dynasty idea is very strong with him," explained one DUP source. "He tried to get Kyle into Martyrs' Memorial as his deputy and successor, and would have succeeded but the congregation voted against him, and he would have the same ambition in politics for Junior."[18] In other words, Paisley arrived at Leeds Castle in a very ill state, close to death if Kyle Paisley is to be believed, suspecting that others in the party were plotting against him and so, to thwart them, he would do the deal now while he was able to, before his rivals took his crown, and use his remaining time in this world to ensure that Ian Junior took over as DUP leader when finally he departed.

It is an enticing, compelling and credible theory but it doesn't tell the full story. The evidence suggests that Paisley was ready for a deal long before Leeds Castle, before his illness became a factor. He had, for example, supported the policy of taking Ministerial posts back in 1998;

he had resisted opportunities to undermine the Assembly in its early, vulnerable days; he had agreed to engage with Bertie Ahern; he had stayed inside the Good Friday review despite the Tohill kidnapping; and he had put his name to the various policy documents produced by Robinson and others along the way, each one of which pointed decisively in the direction of doing a deal and edged the DUP ever closer towards that goal. One DUP source said:

> My view is that Ian Paisley had been of a mind to do a deal for five or six years, as far back as 2001. Logically that had to be going through his mind. There were the increasing votes for the DUP and in 2001 there was the Westminster breakthrough. At that point he had to start thinking, what is the inevitable conclusion of this? He is 75 years old, he's shrewd, he's been around in politics here for 40 years, he has to say to himself, "I'm going to become the leader of the largest Unionist party either by a whisker or significantly ahead and what do I do, what is the end result? Do I adopt a holding position or do I sit tight? Do I hold on and refuse to do the deal, knowing that I will hand on the baton to someone who will, or do I do it?"[19]

Nearly all the signs beforehand suggested that while there would probably not be a final deal at Leeds Castle, there would almost certainly be enough progress made to facilitate a deal a little farther down the road. As one member of the DUP delegation put it: "Everyone knew there would have to be another Leeds Castle."[20] Nonetheless things looked good. Back in August, Gerry Adams had dropped a broad hint that the IRA would have to disband if there was a deal. Along with the issue of arms, Republicans needed to recognise, he said, that if Unionists were using these as excuses not to share power, then the excuses should be removed. His remarks were welcomed by the DUP.

Nor was there much difference between the two parties on the issue of Ministerial accountability, which the DUP had put at the top of its list of required changes to the 1998 deal. Once the Executive was up and running in 1999, it became clear that individual Ministers could do more or less what they wanted; the approval of their Executive colleagues was not necessary nor was there any way other Executive Ministers could sanction them afterwards. The issue had gained prominence when Sinn Féin Health Minister, Bairbre de Brún, had given preferential treatment to a hospital in her West Belfast constituency, to the detriment of a hospital in a Unionist area of the city. While that incident had worked to Sinn Féin's benefit, the Republicans knew it could just as easily work against them. The DUP wanted to make Ministers accountable and while there had been some disagreements with Sinn Féin on the matter, these were not so great as to block a deal. Sinn Féin had no problems recognising the PSNI as long as policing and justice powers were devolved to the Executive, while the DUP only quarrelled with the "when, how and to whom" of the proposal, not the "if". The DUP did not want to see Gerry Kelly, Sinn Féin's Justice spokesman, getting the job, for instance. Nor was the DUP in a hurry to have Sinn Féin sign up to policing and justice. Unionist trust in the Provos was still thin on the ground and the idea of Republicans having any say over how Northern Ireland would be policed was still an anathema. The DUP was ready to devolve policing powers but was happy to long-finger the whole question of Sinn Féin and the PSNI, an approach that suited the Provos as well. That much was all well-known before the weekend "hothouse" began. As they set off for Leeds Castle, Peter Robinson talked of the "tantalising" possibility of agreement, while Gregory Campbell told reporters the DUP was "up for a deal". At the end of the first day of deliberations, Paisley emerged to proclaim to the media his commitment to secure "the best possible, fairest deal for all people in Northern Ireland". Things were looking good – but not for long.

One issue dogged the Leeds Castle conference and the weeks of tortuous diplomacy that followed back in Ireland. Sinn Féin had told the governments at Leeds Castle that the IRA was ready to completely decommission all its arsenals by Christmas, thus setting the scene for a power-sharing Executive being in place by spring 2005. A verbal account of this pledge, along with a promise from the IRA to end all its activity, was passed on to the DUP at Leeds Castle and afterwards. But for two reasons the DUP wanted more than that. David Trimble had accepted the IRA's word on such matters and had been misled. The reason that happened was that the IRA's word alone, the DUP believed, could not be trusted.

On the last day of the Leeds Castle "hothouse", Paisley flagged up the crucial significance of this. At midnight, he had a final meeting with Tony Blair and Bertie Ahern to tell them that a deal would be possible if Sinn Féin and the IRA allowed decommissioning to be verified. To emphasise the significance of what he had said, eight members of the DUP delegation came along with him to witness the exchange. "They [Blair and Ahern] were given an ultimatum," recalled a DUP source.

"Paisley told them we were leaving, going home and we'd be out for good unless they could move the situation along with Sinn Féin. If they did that, then we'd be back."[21] Moving "the situation along" meant allowing photographs of the IRA decommissioning its weapons to be published.

The effort to disarm the IRA had been bedevilled from the outset by the secrecy deal struck by the IRA with General de Chastelain, itself a product of Senator Mitchell's advice back in 1996 that the decommissioning process should avoid the impression of surrender or humiliation. When IRA decommissioning did begin, the secrecy bargain prevented de Chastelain from revealing anything about his work. Nothing that happened – neither how decommissioning was done nor which or how many weapons were put beyond use – could be revealed unless the IRA agreed, which it never did. It was this absence of transparency which really undermined the credibility of the exercise within the broader Unionist community and which eventually brought down David Trimble. Not only did the DUP want to avoid Trimble's fate but, having presented itself to Unionist voters as tougher negotiators, Paisley and his colleagues were obliged to demand more exacting preconditions from the IRA.

What happened next depends entirely upon who is telling the story. The parties returned to Ireland to continue negotiations, and by early November 2004, three out of the four issues on the agenda at Leeds Castle had been satisfactorily resolved. But there was no sign that the Provos would allow cameras to record the decommissioning of IRA weapons. On 8 November, Bertie Ahern appealed to the DUP to soften its demand:

> I recognise that – on account of the deficits of mistrust from the past – some additional elements of transparency may be required to close the gap on this most sensitive issue. If the will is there to make an accommodation, it ought to be possible to agree such reasonable steps, which maximise public confidence in the process of putting arms beyond use. On the other hand, if people make unreasonable demands that carry a resonance of humiliation for any side, these will be entirely counterproductive and will not work.[22]

At around this time Mitchell Reiss, George W. Bush's envoy to the peace process, proposed a compromise on the issue and Paisley's agreement convinced the Americans that the DUP leader was ready to go into government with Sinn Féin. As one former official recalled:

For us, the first indication [that Paisley would do a deal] was right in the endgame after Leeds Castle. Paisley called Mitchell to complain about something and they talked. Mitchell's grandmother had just died and Paisley offered his condolences and then they started talking about the deal. So Mitchell said to him, "I understand you're still concerned about photos," and he said, "Yes." Then Mitchell said, "If that issue is solved, are there any other issues?" He asked that question because in negotiations you need to know when all the issues have been dealt with. Nobody ever likes to say they're done and that's why that question is so important. So again he asked Paisley, "If we solve this issue, are we done?" and once more he replied, "Yes." On the photographs Mitchell suggested a new idea. He, Paisley could see the photographs immediately but they wouldn't be released to the public until three months, six months or even a year later. "Would that be acceptable to you?" he asked and Paisley said, "Yes." And once more he asked, just to be sure, "If that's the case, then we're done?" And Paisley said, "Yes."[23]

Reiss took the idea to Jonathan Powell, who was enthusiastic, and the proposal was refined; Paisley and other key figures in the DUP would have immediate sight of the photos but only when the Executive was in place would they be published. By that time, it was reckoned, a different photograph, one of First Minister Ian Paisley sitting beside his new Deputy, Martin McGuinness, would get larger headlines, thus minimising Sinn Féin's difficulties. The DUP were so keen on the proposal that Peter Robinson prepared a list of fifty questions for British and Irish officials to address, many dealing with technicalities of the planned photo shoot. "They were looking for certainty and wanted details such as the pixel count of the photos, clarity of detail, lighting, who would take the photos and so on," remembered an Irish source.[24] If those details could be fixed, then the DUP would go with the proposal. But what of the Provos? Would they accept it?

The Americans say that Gerry Adams rejected the proposal almost immediately, but Dublin differs, and puts the blame not on Adams but on Ian Paisley. According to Irish government sources, while Sinn Féin had signalled "all along" that there were difficulties with the idea, the idea wasn't formally rejected until 6 December 2004, very late on in the negotiations. The tipping point came, they insist, with a speech given by

Ian Paisley – but written, Dublin suspected, by Ian Junior – on 27 November, to the annual dinner of the North Antrim DUP Association.[25] Responding to assertions made by Bertie Ahern, Gerry Adams and by Sinn Féin's Northern chairman, Mitchel McLaughlin, that the DUP seemed interested only in humiliating the IRA, Paisley appeared to confirm their suspicions, using language that would resonate long after:

> On the vital matter of decommissioning of the IRA's illegal arms, I said at Leeds Castle "seeing is believing". This is the vital matter. Unionists will not settle for another disingenuous and valueless decommissioning event. They are going to see before they believe. Seeing is believing. Decommissioning must be credible and it must build the confidence of the Unionist people. Sinn Féin's leader Gerry Adams says we want to humiliate the IRA. There's nothing wrong with that. I think it's a very noble thing. The IRA needs to be humiliated. And they need to wear their sackcloth and ashes, not in a back room but openly. And we have no apology to make for the stand we are taking.[26]

Gerry Adams's version of events chimes more with that provided by the Americans. Speaking after the Leeds Castle initiative had collapsed, he claimed that Sinn Féin first heard about the demand for photos a week before the Leeds Castle "hothouse" and straightaway told both London and Dublin that it was not achievable. "We made it clear from the beginning that this was not a runner," he said.[27] On 8 December though, as each party strove to puts its version of events on record, the IRA cited Paisley's demand for its humiliation as the principal reason for rejecting the photo shoot idea and complained: "For his part, Ian Paisley demanded that our contribution be photographed, and reduced to an act of humiliation . . . we will not submit to a process of humiliation."[28]

London and Dublin decided, nonetheless, to publish the full text of the near-agreement, complete with drafts of statements that each party would have made. The document showed that, aside from the disputed photographs, there was agreement on every issue, and included in all this was the crucial commitment by the IRA to conclude the decommissioning process. Alongside the draft agreement, London and Dublin published a proposed timetable which would have seen the Executive in place by March 2005, just three months later.[29]

The two governments had set 7 December as the date for publishing the papers, aptly called "A Comprehensive Agreement", but someone in the DUP remembered that was Lundy Day in Derry, when Loyalists commemorated the treachery and cowardice of the city's governor who had tried to surrender to the besieging army of Catholic King James II in 1689 by burning his effigy. The incident was the origin of the Loyalist slogan "No Surrender!" and the insulting epithet "Lundy", Paisley's favourite word for weak and compromising Unionists. It would have been difficult to have chosen a less auspicious day upon which to reveal the DUP's near settlement with Sinn Féin. So the following day, 8 December, the Feast of the Immaculate Conception, was chosen instead.

Very soon it began to look as if only a miracle on the scale of the virgin birth could rescue the peace process. A full and final settlement had come tantalisingly close, to be sure, but in the days following the end of the negotiations the chances of overcoming the one remaining and outstanding issue, the verification of IRA decommissioning, receded as the conflicting positions of Paisley and the Provos became damagingly and irreversibly public.

With Paisley continuing to insist that only visual evidence could satisfy his supporters, Bertie Ahern met Sinn Féin leaders Gerry Adams and Martin McGuinness at his constituency offices at St Luke's, Drumcondra, for a talks post-mortem and emerged to declare that in essence he was of the same mind as the Provo leadership. The photographs proposal was "unworkable", he said, and another way forward would have to be found. Paisley responded with fury, as an Irish source recalled: "All hell broke loose with the DUP. Timmy [Johnston] came on the phone and said Paisley was going through the roof, he was berserk, saying he would never speak to the Taoiseach ever again. He said the Taoiseach is going to have to speak to Paisley and apologise, so we said to him [Ahern], just do it. So Bertie lifted the phone and apologised to Paisley."[30]

The year 2004 had begun with the government in Dublin making a historic breakthrough to establish normal, even friendly, relations with Ian Paisley and it ended with their new comity very nearly in ruins. Although Paisley would refuse to meet Ahern for some months, the rift was repaired. But still, nobody could imagine how the deadlock over decommissioning would be broken. There seemed to be only way out – either Paisley or the IRA would have to back down and by so doing lose face. The rules of Northern Ireland's sectarian politics dictated that. But then, suddenly, everything changed.

—◄o►—

At Christmas time 2004, the cash centre at the headquarters of the Northern Bank in Donegall Square West in central Belfast, just across from the City Hall, was overflowing with money, in anticipation of the customary seasonal shopping spree, which this year, the seventh since the last IRA ceasefire, was expected to be a good one for the North's retailers. The Northern Bank's 95 branches would need plentiful supplies of cash for ATMs and one reliable source estimated that the vault held some stg£50 million in the days running up to Christmas.

Twelve days after the collapse of the Leeds Castle negotiations, the IRA emptied stg£26.5 million out of the vault and pitched the peace process into its most serious crisis yet. The drama began in the early evening of 19 December when armed men invaded a house in the Poleglass estate in West Belfast, took away a young bank employee and held his family hostage. At around the same time other armed men, this time disguised as policemen, went to the home of a second Northern Bank official in Loughinisland, County Down, and abducted his wife. Other members of the gang held the two bank workers in the Loughinisland house and the following morning they were forced to go to work as usual. With their families' safety and well-being at stake, the two men had little choice but to assist the IRA, from inside the bank, to cart away the cash. It was wheeled out to a side alleyway disguised as rubbish and loaded on to a van which made two runs, each time with millions of pounds on board. It seemed clear from the circumstances of the raid, especially the manpower and resources devoted to it, that the IRA had spent a considerable time planning the robbery, certainly weeks and perhaps months. It was also apparent that the gang knew a great deal about the bank's inner workings, in particular that the cash centre would be overflowing with money.

It took the best part of three weeks before the authorities acknowledged publicly and officially what everyone else in Ireland had guessed, which was that the IRA was responsible. But there was no doubt of the severity of the consequences. In the short term the robbery killed off all talk inside the DUP of cutting a deal with Sinn Féin and it weakened those in the party, like Peter Robinson, who were most in favour of one. The DUP had just had a narrow escape and everyone knew it. Few doubted that the IRA had been planning the robbery even as their political leaders were smiling sweetly at Leeds Castle and making hand-on-heart affirmations of their commitment to peaceful methods. An even more dreadful thought haunted the DUP, which was that the robbery might have happened even if a deal with Sinn Féin had been struck. Trimble's downfall would then be child's play compared to the DUP's probable fate. While moderate voices in the DUP were silenced, Ian Paisley looked on the bright side and claimed to have seen the hand of the almighty at work, scuppering the talks before catastrophe struck. "He felt he had been saved by God," one DUP source recalled. The raid deepened already profound distrust in the Provos and in the longer term meant that if the process was ever revived, then the DUP would sup with Sinn Féin only with a very long spoon.

The robbery also changed the relationship between Sinn Féin and the two prime ministers, especially Taoiseach Bertie Ahern – at least for a while. A blind eye had been turned in London and Dublin to previous IRA excesses on the usual basis, which was that the Adams leadership needed to indulge the Provos' hard men to keep them on board the peace train. In fact, the IRA had been staging robberies on both sides of the Border for some time before the Northern Bank, with scarcely a whimper of protest from London or Dublin. Three weeks after the Leeds Castle "hothouse", for instance, a gang had held hostage the family of a man who worked in the Gallaher's tobacco warehouse in Belfast, then forced him to go to work as usual before driving a lorry to the plant where it was loaded with stg£2 million worth of cigarettes. With hindsight, the robbery – known as a "tiger kidnapping" by the police because the choice of a hostage is usually preceded by predatory stalking – was a trial run for the Northern Bank raid. The IRA was also active in the Republic in the early months of 2004 and had organised a major warehouse robbery in the Dublin Port complex, in which the IRA provided intelligence to local criminal gangs who staged the robbery for a share of the take. Garda Special Branch officers believed that the IRA figure behind the Dublin robbery was Bobby Storey, the IRA's Director of Intelligence, later identified by the PSNI as the brains behind the Northern Bank robbery. His involvement was significant. He was a close ally of Gerry Adams and that pointed to prior Sinn Féin knowledge and approval of such activity.

Bertie Ahern's priority was to discover whether the Sinn Féin leadership, especially Gerry Adams and Martin McGuinness, had known the raid was going to happen as they sat down for talks with him at Leeds Castle and afterwards. British intelligence and the PSNI provided the answer to that question and it was funnelled to Dublin through Jonathan Powell in Downing Street and later endorsed by the Garda Special Branch. In a radio interview with RTÉ shortly afterwards, Ahern's anger at what he had learned was palpable:

> This was an IRA job. This was a Provisional IRA job. This was a job that would have been known to the leadership. This was a job that would have been known to the political leadership. That is my understanding. I am upset, quite frankly, that in a period when we were in intensive talks, trying to get a comprehensive agreement, that my information is now that people in very senior positions would have known what was going on.[31]

While Ahern was careful not to name Adams and McGuinness as part of that "political leadership", Michael McDowell, his Justice Minister, had no such inhibitions and a month later he named both men as Army Council members. One of the unwritten rules of the peace process negotiations had been broken, which was that the governments would uphold the myth that Adams and McGuinness wore only Sinn Féin hats. The two Republican leaders were summoned to Ahern's constituency office at St Luke's in north Dublin to be confronted by the Taoiseach, the new Foreign Affairs Minister, Dermot Ahern, and Michael McDowell. By all accounts it was a brutal encounter. "A vicious meeting, no quarter spared," said one source.[32] "Bertie had composed in his own mind what he was going to say and he gave them a long and sustained lecture, telling them they had misled the government, that the basis of their dealings had been utterly undermined and confidence had broken down," recalled another.[33]

There was one tangible consequence of real significance that flowed from the meeting. The Sinn Féin leaders were told that, thanks to the deception surrounding the Northern Bank robbery, the Irish government was breaking off contact with Sinn Féin at every level. From that point onwards, no Minister or official from Bertie Ahern's administration would talk to or have any dealings with the party. It would be up to the Provos to alter objective conditions on the ground so as to remove that bar and, if they failed to do so, then the embargo on talking to Sinn Féin would be permanent. The British continued speaking to Sinn Féin and Tony Blair soon had Adams as a guest at Chequers but it was the loss of Bertie Ahern's patronage that really hurt. For much of the peace process, especially since the first IRA ceasefire in 1994, successive Irish governments had sponsored Sinn Féin and argued on its behalf during negotiations – a stance that some Unionists maintained had assisted David Trimble's fall. The alliance – some saw it more as a partnership – with Dublin had enabled Sinn Féin to boast to their supporters that they had fashioned a new and powerful political weapon, a pan-Nationalist alliance which could be more effective than IRA violence in leveraging the British. But now, at a crucial point in the peace process, the Northern Bank raid had robbed Sinn Féin of that sustenance, possibly for good, and pushed the party out into the cold. But conscious that they had weakened the basis of the Adams peace strategy and strengthened potential opponents, Ministers in Dublin decided to keep Sinn Féin's punishment a secret. The fear that Adams's control over the IRA was weaker than it appeared still permeated Dublin's thinking.

The row over the bank raid was still raging when IRA members assaulted and then stabbed to death 34-year-old Robert McCartney after an altercation in Magennis's Bar, a pub that was adjacent to the Republican Markets area of central Belfast. The IRA men had just returned from the annual Bloody Sunday march and commemoration in Derry and were drinking along with scores of Sinn Féin colleagues when the fight began. A quarrel between McCartney's companion, Brendan Devine, and the senior IRA figure present, Gerard "Jock" Davison, deteriorated and Devine was slashed with a knife. He and McCartney fled but they were pursued by several IRA figures, who stabbed McCartney repeatedly. He was later found by a passing police patrol but died in hospital. The IRA sent in a team to forensically cleanse the bar and CCTV footage taken inside Magennis's Bar was confiscated. The killing was not an authorised IRA operation but the cover-up was. And when McCartney's five sisters and his fiancée began to campaign for his murderers' arrest, Sinn Féin leader Gerry Adams was widely accused of assisting the cover-up by failing to encourage the many Sinn Féin eyewitnesses to the murder to co-operate with the PSNI.

The McCartney murder, together with the bank robbery, pushed the issue of IRA criminality to the top of the agenda. It had been raised in the Leeds Castle negotiations but the Sinn Féin leadership had resisted efforts to get the IRA to abjure future criminality, since to do so, they argued, would have amounted to an admission of such behaviour in the past. The Provos had rejected wording in the putative IRA statement put together by London and Dublin but in the end a compromise was reached which was contained in the draft IRA statement included in the Comprehensive Agreement. This read: ". . . recognising the need to uphold and not to endanger anyone's personal rights and safety, all IRA volunteers have been given specific instructions not to engage in any activity which might thereby endanger the new agreement."[34] However, when the IRA's actual post-Leeds Castle statement was published on 8 December 2004, rejecting Paisley's demand for decommissioning photographs but outlining what it had agreed to, it omitted the commitment not to endanger "anyone's personal rights and safety". This was another clue that Sinn Féin was aware of and had approved the planned robbery during the post-Leeds Castle period and wished to keep open the option of further criminal activity.

The Northern Bank raid and the McCartney murder had three important consequences for the stalled effort to get the DUP and Sinn Féin into government together. The two incidents had, firstly, created circumstances which made unilateral IRA decommissioning more possible. Adams and McGuinness could now argue that such a move was needed to get back into the good graces of Dublin and that it offered an opportunity to remove an obstacle in the way of Sinn Féin's entry into government without having to publish "humiliating" photographs of the event. Indeed some would argue that the provocative aspect of the Northern Bank raid was one reason why the robbery was endorsed by the Sinn Féin leadership in the first place. The second outcome was that the two incidents, along with Stormontgate and the Castlereagh raid, had demonstrated that the IRA didn't have to use guns or bombs to exercise a destabilising influence in Northern Irish politics – kidnappings, robberies, espionage and knives could do that just as easily. At Leeds Castle and its aftermath, the DUP had focused on the decommissioning issue, to the exclusion of IRA criminality, and had missed the significant omission in the IRA's 8 December statement. Michael McDowell's Progressive Democrats had picked up on it, however, and so had the White House envoy, Mitchell Reiss. Gradually their influence would persuade the DUP to make acceptance of the policing and justice systems a more telling index of IRA and Sinn Féin intentions than decommissioning. The third piece of fallout raised the price the DUP would charge Sinn Féin for any partnership deal, as one party source explained: ". . . at the very time when they were negotiating to end paramilitary and criminal activity, they were involved in making the arrangements for the cover-up of the McCartney killing and the robbing of the Northern Bank – so it upped the ante in terms of our requirements."[35]

The United States had played a crucial role in the peace process almost from the outset. It is arguable, for instance, that the Clinton White House had made the 1994 IRA ceasefire possible by granting Gerry Adams an entry visa to the US in the early part of that year. Adams was feted in New York and was provided access to a layer of Irish-American society – politicians and corporate leaders especially – that was denied to him in the past due to IRA violence. This enabled the Sinn Féin leader to persuade his Army Council colleagues that a political alliance with Irish-America and domestic Irish Nationalist parties could achieve more than the IRA. The fact that the then British administration, led by John Major, had violently opposed his visa helped Adams make his point. There were other ways in which Clinton had assisted the process. His personal envoy, former Senate Democratic leader George Mitchell, had chaired a crucial commission on paramilitary disarming as well as the Good Friday negotiations – and had returned to help get the Executive up and running. During the Good Friday talks, Clinton had happily agreed to make personal phone calls to Trimble and Adams to urge them to go the final mile. The White House under Clinton was more deeply involved in Irish politics than any previous administration and, although officially neutral, the Unionist perception, going back to the Adams visa, was that Clinton was more sympathetic to the Irish Nationalist side.

The election of George W. Bush in November 2000 brought into power an administration whose foreign policy attitudes would be shaped in significant measure by neoconservative hawks whose deep-seated opposition to terrorism – and distrust of would-be reformed terrorist leaders like Gerry Adams – lay at the core of their ideology. But if David Trimble and his Ulster Unionists hoped that the changes in Washington would redound to their benefit, they were to be mistaken. To begin with, the Bush administration signalled its intention to deprioritise Northern Ireland by taking responsibility for the peace process away from the National Security Council, which had handled the matter in Clinton's time, and handed it to the State Department where the Director of Policy Planning, Richard Haass, became the new

ED MOLONEY

envoy. The White House's lack of interest in Northern Ireland meant that Haass, and his successor Mitchell Reiss, would have a relatively free and unsupervised hand in their dealings in Belfast and that they would come to the issue unburdened by any dogma.

At the beginning of his term, Haass took a tough line with the Provos. When the IRA was found to be active in Colombia in the summer of 2001, Haass travelled to Ireland to warn Adams and McGuinness of the consequences of unhampered IRA activity, a message dramatically amplified by the 9/11 attacks that took place a few hours before their meeting. The IRA's first act of decommissioning happened, not by coincidence, six weeks later. But with the passage of time, Haass's hostility to Adams softened and he became especially vulnerable to the Sinn Féin leader's pleadings that too much pressure on the Provos could destroy the peace process by causing "a mass exodus to the Real IRA".[36] Haass's conversion to the idea of easing pressure on Sinn Féin coincided with his disenchantment with David Trimble, both because of differences in personal chemistry and impatience with the Ulster Unionist leader's demands for concessions from Adams. By the end of his tenure, following the October 2003 decommissioning debacle and the DUP's triumph in the subsequent Assembly poll, Haass had been converted to a deal of the extremes involving Sinn Féin and the DUP.

Haass's successor, Mitchell Reiss, was an academic and expert on North Korean nuclear issues, who would bring a very different style and approach to Northern Ireland. More affable than Haass, Reiss had much less patience with the Sinn Féin leadership and would advocate a tough approach to the Provos when necessary. While sympathetic to the view that Tony Blair had to avoid another breakdown of the IRA ceasefire, he and his staffers in the State Department and in the US Consulate in Belfast were often frustrated to the point of distraction by the indulgence shown to Adams by Blair and his chief of staff, Jonathan Powell. David Trimble remembers that Reiss's opening question during their first meeting was about why Blair made so many concessions to Sinn Féin.[37] Understandably, Reiss and Michael McDowell would eventually become soulmates. The other issue that would define Mitchell Reiss's time as envoy was his belief in the centrality of policing and the necessity of the Provos signing up to the justice system to underpin the stability of any settlement with the DUP.

Reiss was also more proactive than Haass. After Leeds Castle he had authored the proposal to sequence the release of the IRA

428

decommissioning photographs, and that very nearly sealed the deal. In the wake of the Northern Bank raid and McCartney cover-up, he made another intervention which would significantly influence the course of events in 2005. On his advice, the White House invited the sisters of Robert McCartney to the White House to meet George Bush during the annual St Patrick's Day celebrations while banning Gerry Adams. The exclusion of the Sinn Féin leader was accomplished by barring all politicians from the event since to single out Adams would have been to bestow on him the status of victim and that might have obliged the SDLP to take its side. While all the North's politicians would miss out on their annual junket to Washington, everyone knew that the Sinn Féin leader valued his yearly excursion to the White House most.

Not only was Adams excluded from the festivities but he was soon to learn that the bank robbery and the McCartney killing had appalled the Irish-American political establishment. He was snubbed by Senator Ted Kennedy and was forced to listen to a string of powerful and once-friendly politicians criticise the IRA and, in the case of long-time Provo supporter, Long Island Congressman Peter King, even call for its disbandment. Perhaps the worst moment for Adams came on the eve of St Patrick's Day when he was a guest at the American-Ireland Fund dinner which that year was addressed by Senator John McCain. Interrupted by sustained bursts of applause from a largely Irish-American audience, McCain tore into the IRA, saying that it was nothing better "than a criminal syndicate that steals and murders to serve its members' personal interests". Only Richard Haass, now heading up the Council on Foreign Relations, showed an open door to Adams, giving him the opportunity to make a speech in New York, but even then Haass felt obliged to warn Adams not to become another Yasser Arafat.

Reiss's decision to keep Adams away from the White House was intended to signal that behaviour like the Northern Bank robbery and the cover-up of the McCartney killing would and should not go unpunished. But it ran contrary to the conventional wisdom in Downing Street and in Dublin, where the practice before the Northern Bank raid was to turn a blind eye to IRA misbehaviour for fear that Adams and the peace camp would be undermined. Even after the robbery, there was a reluctance to bring Sinn Féin fully to heel. Dublin had, for instance, ended diplomatic contact with Sinn Féin but the impact was blunted when the decision was kept secret. On the basis that Adams should never be undermined, both London and Dublin criticised Reiss for denying Adams access to the White House, even though arguably this added to the pressure on the Provos to make amends. Despite the objections of Tony Blair and Bertie Ahern, the Provos duly bent to the prevailing winds not long after St Patrick's Day.

On 6 April 2005, just nineteen days after his uncomfortable trip to Washington, Adams called a press conference in Belfast and, surrounded by elected and prospective Sinn Féin election candidates, urged the IRA to fully embrace exclusively political methods. On 28 July the IRA leadership responded by announcing that its 35-year war with Britain was at an end. The IRA's volunteers were ordered to dump arms and to pursue Republican goals only by peaceful means. The Army Council also revealed that decommissioning would be concluded later in the year and would be witnessed by two clerical figures, one Catholic, the other Protestant. Towards the end of September, that duly happened and General de Chastelain spent a week touring Ireland to oversee the destruction or disabling of IRA weapons, a process that was witnessed by Redemptorist priest Fr Alec Reid, and Methodist minister the Rev Harold Good.

The presence of clerical witnesses added considerably to the credibility of the exercise but if it had been left to Tony Blair and Bertie Ahern, this vital ingredient might have been damagingly absent. The idea of having clerics along to witness decommissioning and to testify publicly afterwards first emerged at the Leeds Castle "hothouse" alongside the DUP demand for photographs – it was a sort of "belt and braces" approach to the verification problem. The DUP wanted to nominate the Protestant witness and chose a former conservative Presbyterian moderator, the Rev David McGaughey, whose anti-Catholic Church credentials – he had once called the church's teachings "unbiblical" – would make him a credible witness in Unionist eyes. But not only was the IRA unwilling to allow the DUP to nominate a witness, a lengthy dispute followed over how much the witnesses could say about what they had seen. Technically they were bound by the same secrecy agreement as de Chastelain but Blair shocked the DUP by suggesting that the witnesses could afterwards cut their ties to the decommissioning body and talk freely. The DUP pointed out that this would still mean the witnesses would be breaking their word and as Christian ministers they could never countenance that. Blair seemed unconcerned.

On the eve of the IRA's historic 28 July statement, the proposal to have witnesses present during decommissioning was very nearly killed off. If that had happened the integrity of the event, and with it the chances of a settlement between Sinn Féin and the DUP, could have been fatally damaged. One source with intimate knowledge of what took place described the sequence of events:

> On the evening before the [IRA] statement was issued, Gerry Adams phoned Blair to say that the statement was ready to go but the boys wouldn't sign it if the British and Irish went along with the demand for independent witnesses to decommissioning. Blair decided he could live with that and the witnesses would be dropped but it's a joint agreement, so he talked to Dublin and Bertie agreed. But Bertie had to put it to his coalition partners and Michael McDowell said no. For hours McDowell had to field calls from the British and from his colleagues trying to persuade him to capitulate but around 2.00 a.m. he says that's it, no more talking, I'm not moving. So Blair has to call Adams to say, sorry Gerry, I couldn't get it done. So what does Adams say? That's OK, it's not a problem.[38]

Adams had tried to bluff Blair and but for McDowell – "Horatio at the bridge", one source christened him afterwards – he would have succeeded. The episode left some of those involved in the peace process wondering how many other times Blair had made needless concessions to Sinn Féin.

By the time of the July statement from the IRA, Bertie Ahern had re-established normal relations with Sinn Féin and Ministers and officials resumed talking to Gerry Adams, Martin McGuinness and others in the party. In both London and Dublin there was a huge welcome for the ending of the IRA's war, but from Ian Paisley and his DUP colleagues there came a more cautious response, one influenced in large measure by the narrow escape the DUP had in December 2004. "We will judge the IRA's bona fides over the next months and years based on its behaviour and activity," said Paisley.[39]

The DUP leader would find support for his caution in the Bush White House. Like Bill Clinton, George Bush had agreed to phone the party leaders at crucial points during talks to encourage agreement between them. He had phoned both Paisley and Adams during the Leeds Castle negotiations, for example, and he did the same when the IRA statement was issued. When the IRA announced that its war was over, Bush phoned Paisley to urge him not to close off any options and, calling the DUP leader "a man of integrity and faith", agreed with Paisley that the IRA's intentions sounded fine but had to be tested.[40] American sources say that Paisley was "enormously flattered"[41] to be on the receiving end of phone calls from the Oval Office and that is something that Adams savoured too. The evident pleasure caused by presidential attention was testament to a feature of both Paisley's and Adams's journey in the peace process that has attracted less comment than it deserves. The fact is that both of them relished the new-found respectability and status that the process conferred upon them. Both men, after all, had spent their political lives prior to the peace process on the cold and sometimes lonely fringes of decent society, reviled, condemned and even shunned by the mainstream.

The Bush–Paisley relationship was remarkable for another reason and that was the role they both believed, or at least claimed, God had played in their lives. If accounts of Bush's life are to be believed, he became a born-again Christian in 1986 after a youth spent drinking and indulging worldly pleasures and later became convinced that God had selected him to seek the presidency. He was chosen to be, in the words of a senior White House aide not long after the start of the war in Iraq and the battle against Islamic terrorism, "God's man at this hour" in America.[42] Paisley, who was "born again" at just six years old, was regarded by many of his supporters as "God's Man for Ulster", divinely sent to deliver Northern Ireland from IRA terrorism. Both men had paid homage at the ultra-fundamentalist and notoriously anti-Catholic Bob Jones University in South Carolina, Bush to seek the votes of the Christian Right during the 2000 presidential campaign and Paisley to gain academic respectability. Gerry Adams also eagerly sought George Bush's political friendship – he would keep the president on the phone for ages talking about the weather and their dogs – but of the two men, Paisley had the better claim.

The United States was to play another part in the drama about to unfold. While the DUP accepted the need for Sinn Féin to accept normal policing, in practice the party shied away from the issue, paying it lip service more than anything else. As conventionally framed, Sinn Féin support for policing would in the main entail the party joining the new Policing Board, which oversaw the workings of the PSNI. The DUP regarded this as a meaningless act since it involved no real commitment to policing, while the likelihood that Sinn Féin would choose well-known IRA figures to represent the party on the Board could only alarm and alienate their supporters. The draft Leeds Castle agreement had envisaged Sinn Féin accepting the PSNI but the timing was vague and the commitment uncertain, reflecting the DUP's own lack of conviction on the issue. It was perfectly possible, for instance, that had the Leeds Castle deal succeeded, the DUP would have accepted Sinn Féin into government without signing up to the PSNI.

To Mitchell Reiss and his advisers, however, support for the police and justice system was central and gradually, in the wake of the Northern Bank raid and the McCartney killing, the DUP began to see it that way too. The removal of the decommissioning piece from the chess board also meant that another way had to be found to test Sinn Féin's post-Northern Bank *bona fides*. As one former American official recalled:

> We would ask them what Sinn Féin had to do and they would say they have to do more on policing and justice. We would then say, "Well, what do you want them to do specifically?" and they would say "We will know it when we see it." We said to them that we needed more than that; we needed benchmarks to take to the British and Sinn Féin and we suggested some, not just joining the Policing Board but co-operating with the PSNI and encouraging their children to join the force. The change from the DUP wanting them not to do bad things to doing good things – that was the tipping point.[43]

Reiss also set out to pressurise Sinn Féin on policing. "Adams would say, 'I need more time,'" recalled one source. "'I need to bring my people with me. You have no idea how hard it is.' And Mitchell would reply, 'I have no idea how hard it is, I just know you have to do it.'" In late 2005, Sinn Féin began hardening its line on policing. During a trip to Toronto in November, Gerry Adams confirmed what others in Sinn Féin had been saying for some time, which was that only when policing and justice powers had been devolved back to the Assembly and were under the control of the Executive would Sinn Féin accept the PSNI. In other words, just as Sinn Féin had got into government with Trimble without decommissioning, it was aiming to get into government with the DUP without accepting policing. It might even be possible, the Americans thought, for Sinn Féin to entirely avoid signing up to the PSNI, or at the least to delay it for months or longer.

Back in March, during the St Patrick's Day celebrations, the US envoy had warned Adams and McGuinness not to apply for a fund-raising visa since it would be turned down. This was another punishment for the Northern Bank and McCartney scandals. By 2005, Sinn Féin was raising millions of dollars from Irish-America, and figures like Adams and McGuinness drew the largest crowds and the biggest donations. The ban had been kept secret so as not to embarrass Sinn Féin and both Adams and McGuinness decided not to force Reiss's hand by asking permission to raise money. But in September 2005, as the IRA was preparing to finally decommission its arsenals, Adams signalled his intention to come to the US to raise money for Sinn Féin. He and Reiss met for a bad-tempered meeting during which the Sinn Féin leader was told that if he applied again for a visa to raise funds he would be refused – this time because of the party's stand on the PSNI. If, on the other hand, Adams made a "positive, unequivocal statement . . . that all Republicans can and should support the police",[44] the ban would be lifted.

Not long afterwards, Reiss received a phone call from a Downing Street official informing him that Tony Blair was about to phone George Bush to ask that Adams be given a fund-raising visa. Since Bush owed Blair for his support during the war in Iraq, it was unlikely the British Prime Minister would be refused. The envoy immediately complained to the National Security Council and senior figures in the NSC complained in turn to Downing Street. Attempting to change US policy in this way, by going behind the back of a senior official like Reiss, was contrary to diplomatic practice and would undermine America's freedom to construct its own policy on the peace process, let alone the probability that Reiss would feel obliged to resign. The ploy angered the Americans and it didn't help the British that the Sinn Féin leader had few friends in the Bush National Security Council. "There were people there who thought Gerry should never come into the US except in manacles," remembered one former official. The calls worked and Downing Street phoned back to apologise to Reiss: there had been a misunderstanding and the Prime Minister would not now be calling the President. The incident was, in its way, the Clinton visa episode in reverse. The Americans assumed that Adams had called Downing Street to ask for Blair's intervention but Jonathan Powell denied this. Three weeks later the new NI Secretary, Peter Hain, was in Washington and was asked about the affair. "Oh yeah," he replied, "I was in the office when the call [from Adams] came through."[45]

Both London and Dublin would wobble again on the policing issue. In May 2006, Irish Foreign Affairs Minister Dermot Ahern declared

Paisley and an admirer during the final "Carson Trail" march
to Stormont in March 1981. © *Belfast Telegraph*

Paisley, William McCrea and colleagues during the gospel meeting
at Dublin's Mansion House in September 1978. © *Irish Times*

From left: DUP chairman James McClure, UDA leader John McMichael and Peter Robinson marching in front of a Loyalist paramilitary banner in Ballymena in 1984. Third from right is George Seawright, later expelled from the DUP. © *Ballymena Guardian*

Paisley's brother-in-law, Rev Jim Beggs, leads the singing at Portglenone, Co. Antrim.
© *Ballymena Guardian*

Paisley and Official Unionist leader Jim Molyneaux united in Ballymena, Co. Antrim, during a campaign against the November 1985 Anglo-Irish Agreement. © *Ballymena Guardian*

Peter Robinson is bailed at Ballybay courthourse after his arrest at Clontibret. The cross-Border incursion nearly cost him his Westminster seat. © *Pacemaker*

Observe the Sons of Ulster Marching – Robinson dons the
red beret of the DUP's paramiltary wing, Ulster Resistance.
© Pacemaker

Paisley offered Resistance his full support but disowned it when the
South African arms deal was exposed. It was the last time he ever
led his troops up the hill. *© Pacemaker*

Paisley *en famille*: Ian and Eileen with *(left to right)* Kyle, Cherith, Rhonda and Ian Junior.

© *Pacemaker*

When Ian Paisley finally quits, the battle for the DUP leadership will be between
the family's pick, Ian Junior *(left)* and the party's choice, Peter Robinson.

© *Press Eye*

Currently a minister at Oulton Broad in Suffolk, England, Kyle Paisley's decision to follow his father's clerical footsteps means the Paisley name will live on in the Free Presbyterian Church. © *Pacemaker*

His Father's Son? Ian Junior's ambition to lead the DUP may be frustrated by his unpopularity amongst activists and controversy surrounding dealings with a property developer. © *Press Eye*

Ian Paisley leads Portadown Loyalists to the annual confrontation at Drumcree with police and troops. © *Press Eye*

Ian Paisley and David Trimble celebrate after the RUC allowed Drumcree Orangemen to march on the Garvaghy Road, July 1995. When Trimble afterwards became Ulster Unionist leader, Paisley called himself "the king-maker". He bitterly opposed Trimble's subsequent decision to accept the Good Friday Agreement although it paved the way for Paisley to become First Minister. © *Pacemaker*

A Busy Man – Ian Paisley at a book launch to celebrate fifty years of preaching.
© *Press Eye*

Bob McCartney *(far left foreground)* gives Ian Paisley a hard time during the 2007 Assembly
election campaign. McCartney and Paisley forged an alliance against the Good Friday deal
that could not survive the DUP's ambition for power. © *Press Eye*

Ian Paisley tells Independent Orange Order marchers in July 2006 that Sinn Féin/IRA would get into government "over our dead bodies". © *Press Eye*

Ian Paisley said Sinn Féin would not get into government unless the IRA returned the stg£26.5 million it had stolen from the Northern Bank in December 2004 – but the money was never returned and the threat proved to be an empty one. © *Press Eye*

With Eileen in the family kitchen, a favoured venue for family discussions of issues like sharing power with Sinn Féin. Hardliners blamed Eileen for the deal with Sinn Féin but others say that Ian was never pushed where he didn't already want to go. © *Press Eye*

A shudder of horror convulsed the Paisleyite grassroots at the sight of Gerry Adams seated beside Ian Paisley confirming their power-sharing deal on 26 March 2007. © *Pacemaker*

Gerry Adams and Peter Robinson – cunning, clever and ruthless strategists who were more alike than either would care to admit. © *Pacemaker*

As Eileen looks on, Ian Paisley has a final word with the media at the start of Devolution Day, 8 May 2007. Eileen's elevation to the House of Lords marked the Paisley family's acceptance by the British establishment. © *Pacemaker*

"The Chuckle Brothers": to the delight of the British and Irish governments, the anger of hardline Loyalists and dismay of many of Paisley's colleagues, this iconic photo shows Ian Paisley and Martin McGuinness revelling in their first day of shared power.
© *Getty Images*

British premier Tony Blair *(centre)* spent his entire tenure of Downing Street striving for a final peace settlement. He succeeded just before he retired from British politics but his negotiating approach destroyed Northern Ireland's meagre centre ground and rewarded the extremes. © *Getty Images*

The DUP front bench at Stormont: *(left to right)* Nigel Dodds (Enterprise Minister), Peter Robinson (Finance Minister), Ian Paisley (First Minister), Arlene Foster (Environment Minister), Edwin Poots (Culture & Arts Minister), Ian Paisley Jnr (Junior Minister). © *Press Eye*

Will his day ever come? As the architect of the DUP's growth and chief strategist of the party's bid for power, Peter Robinson is the natural choice to succeed Ian Paisley. But the question is, does Ian Paisley also see it that way? © *Press Eye*

The Rev Ivan Foster at his home in south Tyrone. An early convert to the Free Presbyterian ministry and a long-time political colleague and friend, Foster led the campaign to oust Paisley from the moderatorship of the church after the deal with Sinn Féin, ending almost 56 uninterrupted years of Paisley's leadership.

© *Pacemaker*

Ian R. K. Paisley
Eph 6: 19+20

Bertie Ahern

Sinn Féin hoped that the peace deal would boost its performance in the Republic's general election in May 2007 but it was Irish Taoiseach Bertie Ahern who benefited most. Ahern's friends credit Paisley for reaching out to him. Here Paisley and Ahern have their first public handshake outside Farmleigh House, Dublin, April 2007. The two men signed copies of the photo for their colleagues. The Biblical reference, Ephesians 6: 19 & 20 reads ". . . *and also for me, that words may be given to me in opening my mouth boldly to proclaim the mystery of the gospel, for which I am an ambassador in chains, that I may declare it boldly, as I ought to speak.*"

President George W. Bush entertains the First and Deputy First Ministers in the White House in December 2007.
© Getty Images

that policing would not be a precondition for a deal, prompting an American request for clarification. Later that summer, Peter Hain sent out similar signals, again to Washington's great dismay. In the end, though, Sinn Féin's support for policing and justice proved to be the crucial factor in securing DUP agreement to a deal. But for the Americans, that might not have happened.

—◄○►—

The effect of the Northern Bank raid and the McCartney killing and cover-up on the DUP was predictable. Pragmatists in the DUP, like Peter Robinson, or modernisers as the media preferred to call them, were "at their wit's end", as one government source described them, at the faded prospects for a deal. Hardliners were delighted but it was the response of people like Nigel Dodds, who occupied the ground between the party's Free Presbyterian core and the more ambitious centrists, that indicated real DUP sentiment. In February 2005, two months after the Northern Bank robbery, Dodds announced the DUP's unwillingness to join any negotiation "that is going to lead to them [Sinn Féin] coming into the government of Northern Ireland". It's time, he added, "to move on without them. It's over."[46] For a while, Ian Paisley appeared to be the most moderate member of his party, as he had been at Leeds Castle, and conceded that if the Provos abandoned criminality and won a mandate, "I'll have to face up to the fact that I've got to do business with them."[47] Within weeks, however, he was back on the same wavelength as Dodds, demanding the IRA's disbandment as the price for engagement with Sinn Féin. One way or another, it appeared that sentiment in the DUP had turned decisively against power-sharing. Peter Robinson underlined that in April when he said that he could not foresee a time when Sinn Féin could be part of a power-sharing government.

There was little doubt that while much of this reflected a genuine disillusionment within the DUP, even shock at the Provos' behaviour, there was another crucial factor at work. The hardening against Sinn Féin also reflected concern about how the Unionist electorate would react to everything that had happened. As Bob McCartney put it when he confronted Peter Robinson about the IRA's misbehaviour: "I said to him that they'd had a narrow escape with the Northern Bank and all, but he claimed there had been no deal. I replied maybe, but the perception out there was that a deal had been all but done and dusted – and he had no answer to that."[48] There was indeed a widespread

belief that the DUP had come close to going into government with Sinn
Féin but how would that perception work its way out at the polls, the
DUP wondered, when Tony Blair called a general election, expected to
take place in early summer 2005, with memories of the bank robbery
and the McCartney murder still fresh in voters' minds? Would they do
to Ian Paisley what they had done to David Trimble and punish him for
his foolish naivety?

The DUP went into the May 2005 Westminster poll armed with a
strategy designed to minimise the post-Northern Bank damage. On the
one hand, the spectre was raised of an all-conquering Sinn Féin, whose
ambition to become the largest political party in Northern Ireland could
be frustrated only if enough Unionists voted for the DUP. On the other,
the DUP took pains to assure Unionists that events after Leeds Castle
were an illusion and there was no chance that it would enter a power-
sharing government with the Republicans.

The first part of the strategy was based upon the widely held
expectation that the 2005 election would witness Sinn Féin's final and
complete triumph over the faltering and declining SDLP. Both John
Hume and Seamus Mallon, the SDLP's two best vote-gatherers, had
retired from Westminster and Sinn Féin was confident of capturing both
seats, leaving the SDLP with only one seat in the House of Commons,
South Down, which was held by the ageing Eddie McGrady. Very few
observers believed that the election would result in anything less than
Sinn Féin's unchallenged domination of Nationalist politics. If the
election went really well for the Provos, it was even possible that Sinn
Féin could emerge at the top of the electoral heap.

The other part of the strategy, the promise not to share power with
Sinn Féin, came courtesy of a deal the DUP struck with Bob McCartney
on the eve of the election. The DUP wanted to stand Peter Weir, another
Ulster Unionist defector, in McCartney's old seat of North Down,
which he had lost in 2001 to the UUP's Sylvia Hermon. In that and
previous elections, the DUP had backed McCartney but now they were
worried that he would stand in the 2005 poll and by so doing split the
anti-Agreement vote to Weir's disadvantage. About a week after Weir's
nomination was announced, he and Tim Johnston came to see
McCartney to ask him what he planned to do. McCartney recalled:

> I told them I was not happy about the way they had done this;
> this is a *fait accompli*. I said to Weir that unless I got a clear and

unequivocal answer to the question of what is the DUP's position on d'Hondt then I will run and make the DUP's position on d'Hondt and power-sharing with Sinn Féin an issue in my campaign. So Weir went off and about a week or ten days later a meeting was arranged with Robinson, Paisley and Richard Bullick [Robinson's aide]. I said that unless there was a categoric assurance that after this election the DUP won't go into government on the basis of d'Hondt then I would stand. Robinson assured me they wouldn't and sent Bullick to get a copy of their draft manifesto which essentially said that power-sharing was out of the question. That went into the final draft and so I didn't run.[49]

The d'Hondt voting procedure allocated Executive seats according to party strength, thus assuring Sinn Féin of a place in government.

The DUP manifesto was, in this regard at least, quite explicit and not in the slightest way ambiguous. "Inclusive, mandatory coalition government which includes Sinn Féin under d'Hondt or any other system is out of the question," it declared. Voluntary coalition, supported by "democratic parties" was the best way forward, the DUP said, while adding: "It is clear from recent events that Republicans have proven themselves to be incapable of making the move to exclusively democratic means. It is time to move on. Send a clear message to the Government that it must proceed without Sinn Féin."[50] Elsewhere though, the manifesto was ambiguous and it was difficult to read it and not conclude that the DUP had not quite shut the door on Sinn Féin.

The manifesto pledge would later be cleverly reinterpreted to actually allow for power-sharing with Sinn Féin. "They wiped Bob's eye over that. It was all very Machiavellian," recalled a former DUP member. While the pledge failed to do Peter Weir much good in North Down, where he was easily defeated by Sylvia Hermon, it helped the DUP present a tough and uncompromising face to the Unionist electorate which paid off handsomely. Sylvia Hermon's victory in North Down turned out be the sole Ulster Unionist success. Elsewhere the election was a disaster for her party. David Trimble was overpowered by DUP hardliner David Simpson in Upper Bann and soon after resigned as leader. The Ulster Unionists lost four seats, one to the SDLP thanks to a split Unionist vote in South Belfast, and three to the DUP. The DUP now had nine seats at Westminster to the Ulster Unionists' one, while its share of the vote rose by over 11 per cent. Paisley had literally crushed Trimble's party. Sinn Féin turned out to be less of a contender for the position as the North's largest party than suggested in the DUP manifesto and came nearly ten points behind the Paisleyites. Nonetheless, the DUP's scare tactic had worked wonderfully well. As predicted, the Republicans captured Seamus Mallon's seat in Newry-Armagh but in Foyle the new SDLP leader, Mark Durkan, easily saw off Mitchel McLaughlin to retain John Hume's seat. Sinn Féin ended up with five seats to the SDLP's three, a less than comprehensive and convincing victory and a sobering disappointment to the party's strategists.

The election result restored the DUP's confidence and banished worries about an Ulster Unionist comeback. That and the IRA's end-of-war statement in July followed by the completion of decommissioning in September put the effort to get Sinn Féin and the DUP into government back on the rails. Interestingly, Paisley complained about flaws in the decommissioning event but after a private meeting with the two clerical witnesses, Fr Alec Reid and the Rev Harold Good, he went quiet.

The signs of movement were there to see. In June 2005, East Derry DUP MP, Gregory Campbell, wrote to the Catholic Primate, Archbishop Seán Brady, to begin an exchange of views between his party and the archbishop. Ian Paisley "would not shy away" from meeting the Catholic cleric, Campbell declared, and sure enough the following October the two church leaders met at Stormont. That October, Paisley accompanied Peter Hain on a visit to a Catholic school in Ballymena which had been firebombed by Loyalists and condemned both the violence and threats to damage Catholic graves in a disputed part of a cemetery in North Belfast. Also in October, Paisley resumed cordial relations with Bertie Ahern when he, Ian Junior, Robinson and Dodds travelled to Dublin for a meeting in Government Buildings. A witness recalled: "They had a big Ulster Fry in the Merrion Hotel and then a long meeting with the Taoiseach who gave them a plate of sandwiches which Paisley wolfed down. They had a great time together."[51] One result was that the following February, the DUP invited the Dublin government to send an observer to the party conference. Although his presence was not announced to the rank-and-file and there were not a few averted gazes from those sitting at the top table whenever he strode through the conference hall, this was another significant first for the DUP and Paisley.

In the same month, the British began to induct Paisley into the establishment when Blair appointed him to the Privy Council, a largely symbolic but significant token of his new acceptability. While that meant the DUP leader could receive secret briefings on the IRA from British intelligence, another more flattering consequence was that he would henceforth be addressed as "the Right Honourable" Dr Paisley. The 2005 general election result now meant that the DUP was the fourth largest party at Westminster and that qualified it to nominate three members to the House of Lords. Paisley chose his wife, Eileen, as one of them and she took up her seat in 2006 choosing the title "Baroness Paisley of St George's" after the ward she represented on Belfast City Council in 1967, when she successfully tested the political waters on behalf of her ambitious but cautious husband. The Paisleys now joined a select group of four married couples with one spouse in each chamber of the British parliament. Prime Minister Blair would soon catch on that generous doses of soft soap would grease the way to Ian Paisley's political heart.

The DUP had also discovered that the British did not discriminate when it came to dispensing unconditional political favours to important players in the peace process and that if Sinn Féin could get juicy side deals with no obligation to reciprocate, then so could they. In early October 2005 – October was turning out to be a very good month for the DUP and its leader – Peter Hain allowed the DUP to nominate the new Victims Commissioner and the head of the Ulster Scots Agency while lifting real estate tax on Orange Halls, awarded the soon-to-be-disbanded local units of the Royal Irish Regiment generous redundancy payments and giving the DUP extra seats on the Policing Board. When asked what the DUP would have to do in return, Hain told his interrogator: "I'm not expecting them to do anything. I just expect that in the event of a good IMC report they'll talk to Sinn Féin."[52] Hain would have to wait well over a year for any payback.

Slowly and cautiously the DUP moved back into negotiating mode. In February 2006, the party published new proposals for devolved government which Blair bought into, much to Sinn Féin's annoyance. The DUP suggestion of a shadow Assembly that could evolve into something more substantial if Sinn Féin agreed to change the IRA's ways, became part of the new Blair–Ahern blueprint for progress, which was agreed in a series of prime ministerial summits in the early part of 2006. In late January, Blair and Ahern met at Farmleigh House, the Dublin government's splendidly restored official mansion in Phoenix Park, to set a deadline for political talks on a final settlement.

They announced the date, 24 November, at a second meeting at Navan Fort, near Armagh, in April along with plans to revive the long-dormant Assembly at Stormont. In April, the DUP attended, for the first time, a meeting of the British–Irish Inter-Parliamentary Body in Killarney, County Kerry. The decision was significant not least because the BIIPB had been set up under the terms of the hated 1985 Anglo-Irish Agreement.

In May 2006, the Assembly met and predictably failed to agree on the nomination of a First and Deputy First Minister, although Gerry Adams did rise to his feet in an unsuccessful effort to propose Ian Paisley for the top job. The moves were now being choreographed and that indicated a willingness to cut a deal, even an expectation of one. Hain told Dublin and Washington that the DUP and Sinn Féin had privately assured him that they would go through the nomination ritual quickly. Under the British–Irish plan another 12 weeks would be allowed after the summer recess, until the end of November, for agreement on setting up the Executive. The DUP also asked Hain to arrange for the early release of the IMC report on IRA activity so they could consult with their members about its contents. A report on Hain's dealings with the DUP noted that "He saw this as a signal that the party is for real about forming an Executive".[53] Later that month, Paisley let it be known that Sinn Féin had to support the PSNI before there could be a deal. In an interview with Frank Millar, he declared: "The talks have no future until everyone who's going to be in the government of Northern Ireland is a complete and total supporter of the police."[54] That year's Twelfth demonstrations were the quietest in memory and for the first time since the start of the Troubles in 1970, there were no British troops on the streets as Orangemen and their flute bands paraded through Belfast and other towns.

The politicians of Northern Ireland, the DUP included, were moving inexorably towards a deal and with the IRA's decommissioning out of the way and a series of IMC reports that indicated a significant diminution of all forms of IRA activity, the chances of success were widely regarded as good. It was at just this point that Ian Paisley chose to return briefly to his adamantine roots – as he would do again several times before the final settlement was sealed – and at the Independent Orange Order's Twelfth gathering in Portrush, County Antrim, sought to reassure his anxious followers there would be no sell-out from him. During a speech otherwise devoted to the sacrifices made by Ulstermen at the Battle of the Somme in 1916, he departed from his script to declare: "No unionist who is a Unionist will go into partnership with IRA-Sinn Féin. They are not fit to be in partnership with decent people. They are not fit to be in the government of Northern Ireland. And it will be over our dead bodies that they will ever get there."[55] Surprisingly his remarks caused scarcely a flutter of anxiety in government circles. This was the sort of thing Paisley had to say to his followers, it was said, and soon the incident was forgotten by all but the DUP grassroots.

In early August 2006, the governments briefed the media to prepare for another "hothouse", this time at St Andrews in Fife, on the east coast of Scotland. With Tony Blair's retirement from Downing Street pending, this would be, they warned, the last, best chance for a deal. Just before he and his DUP colleagues set off for Scotland, Paisley addressed a fringe meeting at the British Labour Party conference in Bournemouth. "I and my party," he promised, "will not be found wanting in our search to get it right."

"We've been working hard for three days and I think we have seen the first sign of a new light and I hope that this light shines not just on those in this room but on our children and grandchildren."

IAN PAISLEY, AFTER RECEIVING A WEDDING ANNIVERSARY GIFT FROM BERTIE AHERN, ST ANDREWS TALKS, 13 OCTOBER 2006

⚜

"I am not on some selfish climb up the ladder of ambition, as some have said. At nearly 81 years I do not need the spoils of office to satisfy me."

IAN PAISLEY, 2 APRIL 2007

⚜

"From the depths of my heart I can say to you today that I believe Northern Ireland has come to a time of peace. A time when hate will no longer rule. How good it will be to be part of a wonderful healing in this province."

IAN PAISLEY, ON THE RESUMPTION OF DEVOLVED GOVERNMENT, STORMONT, 8 MAY 2007

⚜

"I have not changed my Unionism."

IAN PAISLEY AT STORMONT, 8 MAY 2007

CHAPTER FIFTEEN

"A Great Day for Ireland, A Great Day for Ulster!"

By the time Northern Ireland's politicians gathered at the Fairmont Hotel, St Andrews, on Wednesday, 11 October 2006, only one thing was really certain. Their host, Tony Blair, would not be Prime Minister for much longer. In early September, just a week or so after he and Bertie Ahern had announced plans to have one last go at fostering a deal between the DUP and Sinn Féin, he made formal what everyone had been expecting for more than a year. "The next party conference in the next couple of weeks will be my last party conference as party leader," he had announced during a visit to a school in north London. "The next TUC [conference] will be my last TUC – probably to the relief of both of us." He might have added that the next "hothouse" on the Northern Ireland peace process would quite likely also be his last, and that the TUC's relief would be shared by many of the North's weary politicians. If the Prime Minister had been reluctant to announce his resignation, as the Westminster gossip suggested, one possible reason was that he couldn't be sure what his legacy on the peace process would be. Tony Blair had spent his entire premiership wrestling with its complexities, yet here he was, after a decade in Downing Street and within months of his departure from British politics, and he still didn't know if there would be a final settlement.

History had yet to make a judgement on his performance but already some tentative conclusions about his stewardship of the peace process could be made. In sharp contrast to his Tory predecessor, John Major, he had made preservation of the IRA ceasefire and the survival of the pro-peace Sinn Féin leadership headed by Gerry Adams his priority

443

and had offered them nourishment in two ways. He had indulged Sinn Féin with concessions, an endless stream of them it sometimes seemed, and invariably resisted putting pressure on the IRA when asked – and justified both by the perceived need to keep the IRA from going back to war, as it had done during Major's watch. If there was a flaw in his approach, however, it was that he had continued to cosset Sinn Féin long after it was necessary to do so and failed to lean on the IRA when he could and should have, when the IRA's ceasefire had become irreversible and Sinn Féin's leadership was entirely secure. One consequence was that the peace process dragged on endlessly and for too long would last twice as long as the Second World War. The other was that Tony Blair's approach had helped to bring about the collapse of the centre ground of Northern Ireland politics, allowing Sinn Féin to replace the SDLP as the voice of Nationalism and Ian Paisley to supplant David Trimble as the leader of Unionism. Not everyone, though, thought that this was a bad thing. As Blair prepared for the St Andrews conference, it was in the knowledge that if there was a settlement between these two extremes, it would certainly be more stable and the resulting peace more secure than any deal involving the centre parties. Neither Ian Paisley nor Gerry Adams would need to look over their shoulders. But he would also know that the peace process would end with the two parties who were arguably most responsible for the Troubles being rewarded with a glittering prize. To most, not least in the international community, such a settlement would represent a triumph for the Prime Minister's skill and perseverance but to others, a minority for sure, it would be a testament to his cynicism.

The last two or three years of Blair's premiership saw speculation intensify that when he did leave Downing Street, he would finally and officially convert to Catholicism, which he eventually did just before Christmas 2007. A High Church Anglican whose mother's family were County Donegal Protestants, Blair had been flirting with the Catholic faith for years. His wife Cherie, of Merseyside Irish stock, was a Catholic, and their four children, Euan, Nicky, Kathryn and Leo, were raised Catholics and went to Catholic schools. Blair himself regularly attended Mass at St Joan of Arc church in Islington when he was opposition leader in the 1990s and occasionally took communion until he became Prime Minister and was asked to stop by Cardinal Basil Hume. He had private audiences with Pope John Paul II and his successor Pope Benedict XVI in Rome and attended services at the Church of the Immaculate Heart of Mary at Great Missenden, the nearest Catholic church to Chequers, his official country residence. The rector there, Canon Timothy Russ, often discussed religion with him and in 2004 had predicted that eventually the Prime Minister would become a Catholic. It was widely thought that Tony Blair had stayed a closet Catholic, as one Fleet Street newspaper called him, because of British sensitivities about the place of Catholics in public life and a history beset with suspicion that Catholics had often shown more loyalty to the Vatican and foreign Catholic powers than the Crown. There had never been a Catholic prime minister in Britain and some lawyers argued that there was a constitutional bar on a Catholic becoming adviser to the Queen, who is officially the head of the Church of England. Nonetheless Blair was known to have had discussions about religion with a number of Catholic priests celebrated for their success in "shepherding" high-profile figures into the Church. One was Fr Michael Seed of Westminster Cathedral who claimed to have paid regular backdoor visits to Downing Street.[1]

For much of 2006, Tony Blair entertained another clerical visitor to Downing Street who also engaged the Prime Minister in discussions about religion and theology, except this cleric was not a Catholic priest but Ian Paisley, Moderator of the Free Presbyterian Church of Ulster and perhaps the most notorious anti-Catholic prelate in Europe. It would be difficult to find a more unlikely and unsuitable counsel for a would-be convert to the Church of Rome and regular Mass-goer like Blair than Paisley. Just a small sampling of Paisley's record showed that: in 1988, for instance, he had denounced the same Pope John Paul II to whom Blair and his family had paid homage as "the Antichrist" during a visit to the European parliament; he had made a career out of calling the church that Blair wished to join "the Whore of Babylon, the mother of abominations" and in the 1950s he had sponsored trips to Northern Ireland by an apostate Spanish priest whose speciality was to celebrate "mock Masses" during an anti-Catholic road show. And that was only a part of the story. Yet this was the man with whom Blair chose to discuss his views on Catholicism.

Exactly how many times Blair and Paisley met during 2006 is a matter of some speculation. One DUP source estimated it was "dozens of times",[2] although Irish government sources say this is an exaggeration. The consensus, though, is that they did meet on many occasions. Their encounters were also very private, as the Irish government learned. "We asked Jonathan Powell what they talked about and he said he didn't know," said one source. "They were one-to-one meetings, which was a very unusual thing in the British system."[3] Downing Street refused to comment on the meetings but on one occasion Paisley did, and confirmed that he had indeed helped Blair study theology. "We shared books that I thought would be good for him to read and I'm sure he read them. He always takes books away with him."[4] The former Deputy First Minister, Seamus Mallon, had once described how Blair's flattery, his ability to make others believe that because he was talking to them they were so important, had beguiled David Trimble. Blair's charm had worked then, but had Ian Paisley also fallen for the same trick? Some in the DUP believed he had. "Given what we were dealing with, the significance of the one-to-one meetings is that the Prime Minister's advisers were bound to have sussed him out psychologically and they stroked his ego," said one source. "I am sure Blair played Ian along to impress him. On one occasion he came back from meeting Blair and told us: 'The Prime Minister is a very troubled spirit. I had a long talk with him and he asked me for a Bible.' As if the Prime Minister of Britain would have to go to Ian Paisley for a Bible!"[5]

The view that Tony Blair's real interest in the dialogue was not God but to sweet-talk Ian Paisley into political compromise is strengthened by the fact that many of their discussions were about the peace process and the efforts to cut a deal with Sinn Féin, so much so that others in the DUP grew angry and frustrated at the frequency with which Paisley made significant and potentially damaging concessions to the Prime Minister. As one DUP figure complained: "Ian would never bring a note-taker with him. He would go to a meeting with Blair and then some time later Peter Hain's office in the NIO would ring and say, 'Ian's saying this – is this really the position?' and Peter [Robinson] would have to put them right. It became a big issue for Peter; it used to drive him up the wall."[6] Another party source agreed: "He was making commitments [to Blair] and giving away things. We would hear back from him and then we would hear from the British and the two accounts would never match. We would have to make corrections all the time."[7]

Paisley was undoubtedly one of the North's most successful and able politicians and had been for over four decades but his forte was the politics of confrontation and negativity. The art or skill of deal-making, to put it mildly, was not one of his specialities. Inside the DUP he was regarded, in the words of one figure who had spent years working alongside him, as "the worst negotiator you could imagine". He went on:

I remember the party was fighting for a redundancy package for the Royal Irish Regiment (RIR) battalions that were going to be stood down and, on foot of working alongside the RIR people, we had settled on a gratuity of stg£30,000 for each soldier, not a penny less. The government was offering just stg£20,000 and Paisley, Robinson and Donaldson went along to Blair but beforehand they had agreed that they would not move from stg£30,000. Paisley no sooner had settled his bum on the chair when he's saying, "Now, Prime Minister, I know you can't give us all we want but if you could manage stg£25,000 then I think we could sort this out." Peter and Jeffrey were horrified. And stg£25,000 is what we ended up with.[8]

Nor, surprisingly, is Paisley a figure who relishes the sort of personal confrontation and hardballing that negotiations can often necessitate, despite his many years spent publicly flailing Unionist and ecumenical opponents. "He is a lion in the pulpit but a lamb outside," said another DUP figure. "He tries to avoid conflict all the time. If there is a dispute for instance between two members of his church, say between elders or ministers, he'll never take sides but he'll get them together and say, 'Embrace, we don't want division among us.'"[9] By contrast, Blair was a veteran and able negotiator who had clawed his way to the top of the Labour Party's greasy pole and conducted years of sometimes vicious political warfare with his principal rival, Gordon Brown. In a one-to-one negotiating context, the smart money would have to be on Blair outfoxing Paisley.

At Leeds Castle, his illness and "the glimpse of his own mortality" that it brought, as a colleague put it, had persuaded Paisley that it was time to do a deal. As he got better, he stretched things out – assisted by the Northern Bank robbery and Robert McCartney's killing – but then, after the IRA's final decommissioning act and its end-of-war statement, Paisley began his dialogue with Blair and recovered his enthusiasm for a deal. In the view of one DUP activist, it was Blair who put another crucial notion in Paisley's mind. "Blair gave him the line about the hand of history at work, that it was Ian's destiny to do this deal," he recalled.[10] At the 12 July Independent Orange Order demonstration in 2006, Paisley had ruled out power-sharing with Sinn Féin, declaring that the Republicans would have to clamber "over our dead bodies", as he put it, before it could happen. But the truth was very different, as the same DUP figure remembered: "From the end of the summer of '06, from that point on, he seemed determined that, come what may, he would be First Minister."[11]

When Ian Paisley arrived at St Andrews, beside him was his wife, Eileen, or "Mammy" as she is known in the Paisley household, and when the parties gathered together for the opening plenary session of the talks, Eileen was present as part of the DUP delegation. The couple were just a few days away from their fiftieth wedding anniversary – the last time, one wag quipped predictably, that Ian Paisley had said "Yes" – but her presence was not just because of their imminent celebration. There is remarkable unanimity about the extent and direction of Eileen Paisley's influence over events before, at, and after St Andrews. Both governments and the two wings of the DUP, those in favour of the deal and those with less enthusiasm for it, all say the same thing: that "Mammy" played a crucial role in persuading Ian Paisley to go into power with Sinn Féin.

Eileen Paisley had always been Ian Paisley's closest confidante and adviser but since his illness, party sources say, her influence over him grew. "In a way she saw this as something that he deserved, that it was his due," said a DUP member who knows the family well. "She also has this sense of Ian having a responsibility to deliver peace for the children of the country, and you'll notice how later, children and grandchildren figured so often in his statements about the deal. Then don't forget, after forty years of being spurned by the establishment, they had now become part of it."[12] Ian Paisley has only spoken once about "Mammy's" influence during this period and what he had to say confirmed the assumptions. Asked if it was true that her views had a profound impact, he replied:

> Well my wife and I are very close, and I discuss everything with my wife, and we pray together, read the Bible together every morning before I go out, and we are very, very close. I am well advised by my wife and I don't always agree with her, but on the main things that she has talked with me about, she has been a great help and that is very true . . . on this particular occasion, well it was something that was with us night and day. There was no one else that I could really take confidence with. In our house nothing leaks beyond the walls. So we were absolutely at one on that.[13]

Eileen Paisley had taken her seat in the House of Lords in July 2006, three months before St Andrews, and one of her sponsors was Baroness Boothroyd, the former Labour Party activist and the first woman Speaker of the House of Commons. Some saw Blair's hand in that move, a sign that Downing Street recognised the importance of welcoming Eileen Paisley and making her feel at home and among people well disposed towards her and her husband. Others in the DUP detected an element of revenge against all those who had lined up against Paisley for years: "The key issue was his ego. He had been kicked by the establishment for forty years and this is his revenge. Eileen was very strong on that line: 'You've been kicked for so long and now this is your chance, your turn.'"14

There is also a conviction amongst some that the dynasty factor which had figured so strongly at Leeds Castle, returned to feature in family deliberations in the months before St Andrews. Ian Junior, his destructive role at the time of the "sackcloth and ashes" speech now a thing of the past, joined his mother in urging his father towards a deal and later he would be given a post in the Executive which suggested he was being groomed as the heir apparent. "Look at it from their viewpoint," suggested another DUP figure. "It's all about the succession and wanting to ensure that Junior takes over. They do, after all, regard it as a Paisley family business. The other thing is that he distrusts and dislikes Peter Robinson and so does Eileen."15 Clifford Smyth, who in the 1970s had been as close to Paisley as Peter Robinson became in the 1980s, puts it more colourfully, if somewhat cynically: "The Paisley family acts like a Chinese dynasty – him, her and Junior. All we need to complete the picture is a Pekinese dog on the Baroness's sleeve!"16

—◦—

The talks at St Andrews began with many in the DUP front bench distinctly nervous about Ian Paisley's over-readiness to make concessions. It had been the same at Leeds Castle three years earlier when Peter Robinson and Nigel Dodds had fretted that Paisley would give away too much in his eagerness to seal the deal. The history of the one-to-one meetings with Blair was a bad omen. There had already been a near-disaster when, just days before St Andrews, Paisley had reached agreement with NI Secretary Peter Hain about an election to a new Assembly that would take place in either December 2006 or in January 2007, a concession made in the absence of a detailed settlement with Sinn Féin. "Paisley told the parliamentary party and they were incredulous," recalled one of the front bench. "Nigel and Peter said there were a whole series of things that needed to be hammered out before we could take a decision like that. We needed changes [to the 1998 deal] to be agreed and to discover and test whether the Shinners would do what was necessary. Only then could there be a deal."17 The Hain–Paisley deal was quietly killed off.

Paisley had arrived at St Andrews breathing fire and brimstone. As gusts of wind blew in from the North Sea and showers of rain threatened to overwhelm the party's delegates, Paisley stood in front of a battery of microphones to tell the media that there would be no deal unless Sinn Féin signed up to policing and signified that by handing back "its ill-gotten gains", a not too subtle reference to the stg£26.5 million stolen by the IRA from the Northern Bank. It was not, as one member of the delegation noted, a good start: "If you want to have a deal with people, then you have to be circumspect." It was another index of Paisley's schizophrenic approach to such matters, in public suggesting toughness but in private sending quite the opposite signals. It was just like July 2006 when he had told the Independent Orange Order that a deal with Sinn Féin would happen only "over their dead bodies" while resolving privately in the bosom of the family that he should go down the road towards a deal. The next few hours would illustrate dramatically just how keen Ian Paisley really was to get into government.

The DUP came to St Andrews with a deal more or less teed up. A basis for an agreement had been established during and after Leeds Castle and it was a question of updating "The Proposals for Comprehensive Agreement" and if necessary, adding to them. But two crucial and potentially divisive issues remained unresolved, both legacies of a distrust of the Provos that had deepened after the Northern Bank robbery. One was the timescale for the deal, or more accurately what length of time the DUP required to test Sinn Féin's commitment to the new putative dispensation. How long, in other words, should Sinn Féin's "decontamination period" be, as the Republicans' opponents liked to call it? "There was always going to be a deal, we had signalled that," recalled one DUP figure. "It was all about timetables."18

At Leeds Castle, the consensus was that at least six months should elapse between a deal being agreed and the date when the deal went live with the election of the First and Deputy First Ministers, the selection of Executive Ministers and the formal devolution of powers. Six months, strategists in the party argued, would be sufficient to test the Provos' bona fides. A week or so before the St Andrews talks began, an IMC report claimed that the IRA leadership was committed to following a political path and was dismantling some of its GHQ Departments, such as engineering. While individual IRA members remained involved in criminal activity, the IMC said, this was not sanctioned by the leadership. Ian Paisley claimed credit, saying that the DUP's pressure on Sinn Féin had worked. Nonetheless, the Northern Bank raid and the DUP's narrow escape from entering a power-sharing deal with bank robbers had hardened some attitudes. For example, according to one Irish government source, Nigel Dodds, whose support for a deal would be vital, was talking at St Andrews about the deal becoming active in the late summer of 2007, some nine months ahead.[19] Others in the DUP were even more uncompromising and wanted a testing period of more than a year.[20]

The second issue on the St Andrews' agenda was Sinn Féin's acceptance of the PSNI, the courts and the prison systems. With the help of the Americans, the DUP had come to recognise the centrality of the matter, realising that nothing else would better symbolise Sinn Féin's acceptance of the constitutional status quo and the shelving of the republican demand for Irish unity. It was "the new decommissioning" demand but it was potentially as problematic. The argument, as with decommissioning, would revolve around who should move first. The DUP wanted Sinn Féin to sign up to law and order before agreeing to share power, while the Provos insisted that law and order powers must first be devolved.

It was against this background and a history of one-to-one meetings, in which the Prime Minister had invariably bested the DUP leader, that Tony Blair began the negotiations by attempting to separate Ian Paisley from the rest of his party and by so doing nearly ensured that St Andrews would be a failure. The conference was organised in such a way that, after the opening plenary session, each party was to have an initial meeting with Blair so that their needs and problems could be aired. As the DUP delegation sat waiting to be called into Blair's bedroom, which became the location for all the meetings between the parties and the British Prime Minister at St Andrews, a girl messenger arrived and announced to the DUP leader: "The Prime Minister is ready to see you now, Dr Paisley." As Paisley rose to his feet, Peter Robinson intervened and told the messenger to inform Blair that he was sorry, but the DUP would meet the Prime Minister only as a delegation and not on an individual basis. The messenger returned to the Prime Minister, Blair agreed and the DUP team was eventually ushered into his bedroom where for the next twenty minutes or so, Robinson outlined the party's requirements and the main issues as the DUP saw them.

But Blair had not given up his effort to strike a separate deal with Paisley. As the meeting ended, he turned to Paisley and asked: "Ian, can

I speak to you alone?" Paisley agreed, although the rest of the delegation was unhappy and hung around outside to see what would happen. Paisley was with Blair for some time and when he emerged he was delighted. The Prime Minister, he told his colleagues, had agreed to an election in January. But the delegation was horrified; their leader had effectively put his name to a deal and a deadline before Blair had even begun to address the DUP's wish list, from the changes in the 1998 deal they wanted through to Sinn Féin signing up to law and order.[21] Paisley had come to a similar understanding with Peter Hain before St Andrews, which others in the party had managed to torpedo, and here he was doing the same with Blair. Another DUP figure, who had just missed the delegation's session with Blair, arrived on the scene just after Paisley had emerged from his one-to-one meeting with the Prime Minister.

> He came out to announce, "I got the Prime Minister to agree an election." "To what?" the boys asked him. "To an Assembly," he replied. "And then what?" they demanded. "An Executive would be set up," came his answer. They ate him alive and he stormed out in a huff and went off to his hotel. A lot of our time thereafter was spent trying to claw the date back. He really is a bad negotiator but he was busting to be First Minister.[22]

The following day, Thursday 12 October, Jonathan Powell asked to see the DUP and so Robinson, Dodds, Tim Johnston and Richard Bullick trooped into his room to hear the Prime Minister's chief of staff outline a scenario for an agreement, based upon the understanding reached between Paisley and Blair the evening before. What Powell had to say appalled Robinson and Dodds, who let him know that the proposal was just unsellable to the DUP delegation. They returned to their colleagues, told them what was in Powell's mind and secured agreement to reject the plan. To general astonishment, Paisley sat through their meeting with the rest of the delegation and agreed indignantly with everything they said. "He was saying things about Blair and Powell like 'Who do these people think they are?'" remembered one party figure.[23] Another added: "So now you had a situation where the government just knew they had the leader of the party where they wanted him. We knew that unless we stopped them, they would produce a document saying what they wanted to happen and that would be based on the deal Paisley had made with Blair and so what we agreed to do was to send a delegation along to Powell to tell him this was just not on. And

Paisley was brought along so they would know he was party to this."[24] Another member of the DUP's team at St Andrews chimed in: "It was an attempt by the Prime Minister to pull one over Ian Paisley and our response to the government was that if there was any more silly nonsense like that, they could just forget it."[25]

One consequence of all this was that the DUP dug its heels in on the issue of a testing period for Sinn Féin. The governments had set 24 November as the date for acceptance of any deal way back in April 2006 and since Paisley had agreed with Blair to hold an Assembly election in January, this meant that the power-sharing Executive could theoretically be in place just three months or so after that deadline – and that was in the absence of agreement on such potentially deal-breaking items as Sinn Féin's support for law and order. In an effort to undo the damage, party negotiators insisted on the need for a much longer testing time. It was at this point that Nigel Dodds, for instance, talked of a date some time in the late summer or autumn of 2007, which was sure to be rejected by Sinn Féin. Some so distrusted Tony Blair that they favoured waiting until he had retired to see if they could extract a better deal from his expected successor, Gordon Brown. All this, along with the uncompromising meeting between the DUP and Jonathan Powell, plunged the governments into gloom, a mood that was reflected in pessimistic media reports that night and the following morning. So bleak did the prospects for an agreement seem that one of the principal DUP hardliners, the Rev William McCrea, whose preference for a Sinn Féin decontamination period was said to be well over a year, left St Andrews on the Thursday happy and content that his presence was no longer needed. NI Secretary Peter Hain stopped by the DUP's rooms on the Thursday night to tell the party, "We're going to pull stumps tomorrow", and that night British and Irish officials began preparing a statement for the following day that would couch St Andrews "in terms of it being a failure", as one official recalled.[26]

That Thursday night, though, the Irish government stepped into the story to rescue St Andrews. At around 7.00 p.m., Taoiseach Bertie Ahern asked his senior official Michael Collins to see if Michael McDowell would meet the DUP, find out what was ailing them and to impress upon them the need to do a deal. "The DUP were very reticent, watchful and suspicious," remembered one member of the Irish team. McDowell was chosen because he was a figure the DUP trusted. As Justice Minister, McDowell had led the rhetorical assaults on Sinn Féin and the

IRA in the wake of the Northern Bank and McCartney cover-up and had named Adams and McGuinness as Army Council members. He hated the Provos almost as much as the DUP and he carried weight in Bertie Ahern's cabinet. He was leader of the small Progressive Democrats party, Fianna Fail's coalition partner, and effectively had a veto on the government's policy on the peace process. He had also kept in friendly contact with DUP leaders and would seek them out for a chat if they happened to be at the same meeting or event. McDowell readily agreed and, along with his Departmental Secretary, Seán Aylward, contacted the DUP, who agreed, as long as the meeting was so arranged not to appear conspiratorial but casual and almost accidental.

So they agreed to meet near the hotel's bar area, at a table in one of its many balconies: Peter Robinson, Nigel Dodds, Jim Allister and Tim Johnston for the DUP; and McDowell, Aylward and Dermot Ahern, the Irish Foreign Minister, representing the Irish government. Other members of the DUP delegation milled around, adding to the contrived impression that the encounter with the Irish delegation was a chance happening. The Irish team had been drinking wine but, out of respect for the DUP's sensibilities, switched to orange juice when a drinks waiter arrived to take their orders. After a while, McDowell and Robinson went off to a separate table, just a few feet away, and there the Irish Justice Minister set out his stall.

Like the British, the Irish government favoured a short testing period for Sinn Féin, perhaps two months at most, but it was not the fear that anything longer would be rejected by the Provos that was uppermost in Taoiseach Bertie Ahern's mind. In the same way as the end of Tony Blair's period as Prime Minister was just over the horizon at St Andrews, so Ahern knew that he would have to call a general election in the summer of 2007. And over that decision loomed the electoral threat Sinn Féin presented to Ahern's Fianna Fáil party. Sinn Féin had done well at the 2002 poll, winning five seats to the Dáil, and the conventional political wisdom in Dublin was that the party would perform much better at the next outing. Some predicted that Sinn Féin could even win twelve or more seats, a result that might well happen at Fianna Fáil's expense and which could make the party a candidate for coalition partnership. Sinn Féin had eaten up the SDLP in the North and the question was, could they do the same to Fianna Fáil in the South? The worst scenario for the Taoiseach was an election campaign running in tandem with an unresolved impasse in the peace process, with all the attendant publicity that would bring to

Gerry Adams and Sinn Féin. "Ahern wanted a deal before March," one Irish figure recalled. "He was worried about the Provos and he wanted the deal out of the way by March so he could call an election. He wanted it out of the way during the election campaign so that Adams wouldn't be in the spotlight. One way or the other, the business at St Andrews had to be out of the way."[27]

Persuading the DUP to do a deal with Sinn Féin now fed in to Southern politics in a very profound way and shaped what McDowell had to say to Robinson and the DUP that Thursday night. One source familiar with the exchange remembered:

> Michael said, "There's nobody who dislikes the Provos more than I do, so take what I am about to say in that light. If you walk away in circumstances that allow them to blame you, then you will be the big losers, they'll have a huge propaganda win." He impressed upon them that this was make or break time, that progress was needed before a general election and if there was no deal, then Plan B would come into operation and probably be hostile to them. Plan B was being worked on and while it would fall short of joint authority, it would be a form of inter-governmentalism that was tweakable to make it hurt most the party seen at fault for not delivering.[28]

The existence and nature of "Plan B" was later to become a matter of huge controversy within the DUP after Ian Paisley cited it as one major reason for agreeing to go into government with Sinn Féin. "How would I have faced my people," he asked in the aftermath of the deal, "if I had allowed this country to have the union destroyed and the setting up of a joint government by the south of Ireland?"[29] A "Plan B" did exist but it was not the joint authority described by Paisley or anything close to it. Tony Blair and Bertie Ahern had met in Armagh, in April 2006, to jointly approve the plan – "a full, detailed document that was ready to go," said one source familiar with events – which would restore many powers to the inter-governmental conference set up by the 1985 Anglo-Irish Agreement. The Anglo-Irish Conference was the body under whose aegis meetings still took place between the NI Secretary and the Irish Foreign Minister but it had been substantially superseded by the Good Friday deal.

There were other consequences which would flow from the failure to restore power-sharing but whether or not these could be regarded as being part of "Plan B" is debatable. Nonetheless, without devolved government at Stormont, the DUP would be unable to stop a number of controversial measures that were in the pipeline. These included a plan to create seven new super-councils that would almost certainly give Nationalists control of the area of Northern Ireland that lay west of the Bann. Scheduled increases in water charges and property rates would go ahead and it would become impossible to restore the principle of academic selection and rescue Northern Ireland's much-vaunted grammar school system. It was far from clear if the governments' version of "Plan B" was as "tweakable" as Michael McDowell had suggested to the DUP but, even so, all this, along with threats from Peter Hain to close down the Assembly and throw the 108 well-paid and hardly overburdened Assembly Members out of work, is what would come into effect if the 24 November deadline passed without agreement on power-sharing. But "Plan B" was far from being the full-fledged joint rule by London and Dublin it was later portrayed to be. Joint rule was an option that had the potential to alienate moderate Unionists and drive others to violence, and it would have been at the bottom of the governments' list. And had such a plan really existed, it is likely that Paisley and others in the DUP would have made much more of it long before this.

Michael McDowell got a dusty response from Robinson and other DUP figures and he returned to the Irish camp with bad news for Bertie Ahern. The DUP was immovable and seemed to be further away from a deal than ever. "He came back and said, 'It's Plan B!'," remembered a witness.

Two things then happened which changed matters entirely. That night two senior DUP figures, both MPs, met Martin McGuinness to discuss the impasse. The meeting was not sanctioned by Ian Paisley, nor would he have approved had he known. In fact, he would probably have been furious, judging by his reaction to the first public contacts between his party and Sinn Féin. In October 2002, the DUP had ended its TV boycott of Sinn Féin and agreed to be interviewed together in the same studio, firstly on the BBC, where Jeffrey Donaldson debated with Martin McGuinness, and then on UTV, where an argument between Peter Robinson and McGuinness deteriorated into a shouting match. The sight of their MPs exchanging any kind of words, even angry ones, in the same studio as Sinn Féin had clearly unsettled the grassroots, so Ian Paisley, moving to calm nerves and suspicions, there might be a secret dialogue going on, told the DUP conference in November 2002 that anyone caught talking to Sinn Féin would be expelled from the party. So the secret encounter in Scotland was not something that Paisley would have sanctioned, at least in any attributable way. Neither government was aware of the meeting at St Andrews until later and neither the DUP nor Sinn Féin has ever made it public. What transpired between the parties also remains a matter of speculation but since London and Dublin were at this time only drafting the final proposals they planned to submit to the parties, it is unlikely these were on the agenda. "We suspect," said one source, "that their exchange was along the lines of 'If we do A, will you do B?'" Whatever the truth, the next morning found the DUP in a more flexible frame of mind.

By early the next morning the British–Irish plan was being readied and a senior Irish official, Niall Burgess, then the Director of Political Affairs of the Anglo-Irish Division in the Department of Foreign Affairs, "tested" it out on the DUP and the response was not negative. The two prime ministers had agreed to meet, along with officials and ministers, in Tony Blair's bedroom at 7.45 a.m. Blair was still in his pyjamas when he, Bertie Ahern, Michael McDowell, Jonathan Powell, Michael Collins, Seán Aylward and Robert Hannigan, a Downing Street official, sat down for breakfast amid the expectation that the DUP was still not up for a deal, notwithstanding the fact that, as one source put it, "the DUP had not thrown the draft deal" back in their faces when shown it earlier that morning. Peter Hain had not been invited in case there had to be a meeting with the DUP. The NI Secretary had angered Paisley by publicising how much in salaries and expenses DUP MLAs would lose if the Assembly was wound up, so it was decided to keep him away so as not to cause a row. To avoid offending him, Dermot Ahern was asked to invite Hain for breakfast elsewhere in the hotel. One source took up the story:

> Tom Kelly [Blair's press secretary] and Powell were putting the final touches to a failure package, a statement that would fudge failure by saying work would go on. We had the bones of the statement with us at the meeting and in the middle of all this Hannigan's cell phone went and it was the DUP saying they wanted to meet Blair to talk about a deal.[30]

Blair had finished negotiating with the DUP by 1.30 p.m. and a press conference was pencilled in for 3.00 p.m., preceded by a concluding plenary session, at which the governments would present the final document to all the parties outlining how best they thought devolution could be restored. Paisley was anxious to leave for Ballymena where he and Eileen expected to celebrate their fiftieth wedding anniversary but the plenary had to be put back several times. Gerry Adams was unhappy with the final document and he walked on the beach with Sinn Féin colleagues mulling it over and returning several times for sessions with Blair and Ahern. Both prime ministers had brought along gifts for the Paisleys' wedding anniversary. The night before, Blair had asked Jonathan Powell what gift they had brought to present to Ian and Eileen and was told a leather-bound photo album. Then he turned to Ahern and asked what the Irish government had chosen. "Bertie explained that a 300-year-old walnut tree on the site of the Battle of the Boyne had recently fallen over and they had got a bowl carved out of it," remembered one person present. "Blair went berserk at Jonathan, saying, 'We have to get something better than a photo album!' – but it was too late, they couldn't."[31]

By 4.00 p.m. Paisley was getting restive, anxious both to get to Ballymena with his wife and also about the reception the events at St Andrews would get back home. Adams finally turned up and the plenary began. The text of the document was still being cleaned up and Blair explained that the document would be distributed shortly but in the meantime there was business of greater importance that he and Bertie Ahern had to address. Another person present took up the story:

> Blair made a short speech, saying not many married couples make it this far in life as Ian and Eileen, and he handed over his gift and then said the Taoiseach now wants to give you something. Bertie took the bowl in his hands and without saying anything made his way round the room to Paisley. It took him ages, the room was packed and he had to pick his way over outstretched feet and briefcases. Eventually Paisley rose and moved towards Bertie and they met at the back of the room. You could have heard a pin drop; there was total silence. Bertie whispered to him, no-one could hear what was being said and he gave the bowl to Paisley who took it and sat down. Bertie returned to his seat and just as he did, Paisley got back to his feet and said, "The Taoiseach has just explained that this bowl came from a walnut tree that stood on the site of the Battle of the Boyne. Today this bowl has come home. We've been working hard for three days

and I think we have seen the first sign of a new light and I hope that this light shines not just on those in this room but on our children and grandchildren." At that the room broke into applause with everyone clapping. Paisley's words affected everyone but I don't think he would have said them if the Taoiseach hadn't handled it in the way he did.[32]

Ian and Eileen Paisley did manage to make it to Ballymena that night for their anniversary celebrations. Tony Blair arranged for a small private jet to whisk the couple back to Northern Ireland and with them, stowed safely on board the plane, went the bowl from the Boyne.

The St Andrews conference had not ended with an agreement but cleverly the British pretended it had. At the opening session technicians had strung a big banner over the dais in the conference hall proclaiming "St Andrews Conference" but at the press conference after the final plenary, this had been replaced with a sign that read "St Andrews Agreement". The media took its cue and used the term "Agreement" to describe the conclusion and in this way the perception took root that there had indeed been a deal and that any party who reneged would be walking away from it. In fact, as one government participant admitted, "No-one from either the DUP or the Provos ever said to us that they would run with this. There was still a lot of doubt."[33]

What had been outlined in Scotland were the bones of an agreement, an indicative deal which depended for its success on Sinn Féin and the DUP adhering to a timetable of events and implementing commitments. The "to do" list was a long one. The first item would have the parties consulting with their grassroots and responding positively by 10 November. A new "Programme for Government Committee" at the Assembly would then start meetings to agree the details of devolution and parties would be represented at leadership level – that is by Ian Paisley for the DUP and Gerry Adams for Sinn Féin. On 24 November the Assembly would meet to nominate the First and Deputy First Ministers. In March 2007, the deal was supposed to be endorsed by the electorate either via an Assembly election or referenda in both parts of Ireland. Predictably, both the DUP and Sinn Féin wanted an election but Ahern, with an eye perhaps on the Sinn Féin threat during his upcoming general election, preferred a referendum. Astonishingly, the SDLP, rather like turkeys wishing for Christmas, also wanted an election. On 14 March, the rest of the Executive would be nominated and on

26 March, power would be formally devolved and the Executive posts filled. Implicit in this timetable was an understanding that, early on, Sinn Féin would hold an *ard-fheis* to express support for the PSNI and the criminal justice system, a commitment reinforced by a pledge of office that Executive ministers would have to swear or affirm. Failure to agree "at any stage" would cause the immediate dissolution of the Assembly and the implementation of "Plan B". There were plenty of opportunities for that to happen, as would soon become clear.

◄○►

The St Andrews conference had concluded on a Friday the 13th, a bad omen for those of a superstitious bent of mind. By the next Tuesday those fears seemed to be borne out when Ian Paisley pulled out of the first meeting of the Preparation for Government Committee where he was supposed to have sat down with Gerry Adams and Martin McGuinness to begin the journey towards power-sharing. Paisley and the two Sinn Féin leaders had been in the same room before several times but on this occasion they were expected to speak to each other for the first time ever, an event that would have symbolised the new, positive post-St Andrews climate. But that morning *The Irish Times* had quoted Gerry Adams retreating from a commitment the DUP claimed he had made at St Andrews. This was that the Sinn Féin nominee for Deputy First Minister, Martin McGuinness, would swear an oath pledging support for the criminal justice system when he was nominated to the post on 24 November. Adams told the paper's London Editor, Frank Millar, that this had not been agreed at St Andrews and that McGuinness could not take the pledge until Sinn Féin as a party had agreed to support the PSNI. The implication of this was that Sinn Féin would not hold their special *ard-fheis* on policing until after 24 November, which in turn meant that Ian Paisley would have to agree to become First Minister before Sinn Féin had accepted policing. Once more a squabble over who would jump first threatened to halt the peace process.

The Northern Ireland Office chimed in and supported Sinn Féin's version of what had happened in Scotland and, in response, the DUP, which had been ready to send along Paisley, Peter Robinson and Nigel Dodds to head their team, pulled out of the meeting in protest. The incident illustrated that of all the threads left untied after St Andrews, none was looser than the issue which St Andrews had really been convened to settle: the matter of Sinn Féin supporting the PSNI. St

Andrews had created an illusion of agreement and the reality was that the issue was still unresolved: before St Andrews, the DUP had required Sinn Féin to sign up to policing before it went into government, while Sinn Féin insisted power-sharing had to be up and running and a commitment made to devolve justice powers first. After St Andrews those positions were substantially unchanged.

But all this was only part of the story. The prospect of the DUP and Sinn Féin going into government as partners horrified elements in both parties but arguably the DUP grassroots were the more bewildered and dismayed. If anything, the party's rank-and-file had been prepared for failure at St Andrews, not the success it was presented as, and clung like shipwrecked sailors to the belief that while "modernisers" like Peter Robinson were undoubtedly manoeuvring towards a deal with Sinn Féin, Ian Paisley would in the end put a stop to it all, as he had with every other attempt at compromise. Paisley, after all, had assured Loyalists in July 2006, just a few months before, that a deal with Sinn Féin would happen "over our dead bodies" and in 2004 he had insisted that the IRA would have to repent and "wear sackcloth and ashes" before Sinn Féin could be considered fit for government. That hadn't happened and probably wouldn't. Not only that, but Paisley had made other demands which the Provos would certainly reject, like returning the Northern Bank cash and dismantling the ruling Army Council. And then there was the 2005 manifesto pledge to reject "inclusive mandatory coalition government" with Sinn Féin created under d'Hondt or any other system.

A substantial section of the DUP rank-and-file did not believe a deal with Sinn Féin was either possible or desirable and viewed what had happened at St Andrews with outright hostility and suspicion. Nonetheless, the DUP was committed by the St Andrews timetable to consult its supporters and report back on 10 November to say whether the party would or would not proceed down the path outlined in Scotland. A consultation process confined to party activists would almost certainly reveal a deeply divided party, too divided perhaps to risk accepting the St Andrews blueprint. That was the problem facing DUP managers and strategists as they sought how best to test the waters.

The consultation process they decided upon was so designed as to bypass and minimise the opposition of hardline members and supporters. There were two parts to the approach and, in the first, a four-page glossy document was prepared setting out what the St Andrews deal would mean. This included a detachable coupon that the reader was asked to fill in and return to DUP headquarters to indicate whether he or she wished to accept it or not. The same could be done by accessing the DUP's website. The pamphlet was distributed to the public in an untargeted, largely indiscriminate way, principally through an insert in the *Belfast Telegraph*, Northern Ireland's only evening paper. The *Telegraph* was the largest circulating newspaper in Northern Ireland but it was also the only local paper with a cross-community readership. It was read as avidly on the Falls Road as it was on the Shankill Road and it meant that the inserted DUP pamphlet would be getting to DUP voters and non-voters, Unionists and Nationalists, hardliners and moderates alike. There was nothing in the pamphlet that said only Unionists or Protestants could or should respond. Had the DUP wished to canvass only Unionist opinion, it could have slipped the insert inside the *Belfast News Letter* instead. But the approach taken meant that even if you were a Sinn Féin supporter you could fill in the coupon and send it to the DUP and no-one would know the difference; your vote would count as much as an Orangeman from Ballymena or a Free Presbyterian from Fermanagh. It was a clever move by those in the DUP who wanted to accept the St Andrews deal because it meant that the party was appealing to a constituency way beyond its own base in a way no-one could really object to.

There was one ironic aspect to the stratagem and if anyone noticed they kept silent. When the *Telegraph* had printed coupons back in 1969 headlined "I'm Backing O'Neill" and asked their readers to fill them out and return them, Paisley was outraged and began a campaign to boycott the paper. The *Belfast Telegraph* had decided to print the coupons after the then Unionist Prime Minister, Captain Terence O'Neill, appealing for peace following a series of confrontations between Paisley and the civil rights movement, had gone on television to declare, "Ulster stands at a crossroads", and to ask: "What kind of Ulster do you want? A happy, respected province . . . or a place continually torn apart by riots and demonstrations?" Paisley had used remarkably similar language at the press conference that had concluded the St Andrews talks: "Today we stand at a crossroads," he said. "We stand at a place where there is a road to democracy and there is a road to anarchy. I trust that we will see in the coming days the vast majority of people taking the road to democracy." History was repeating itself in a quite astonishing and ironic fashion.

Even so, the DUP pamphlet was careful to put some distance between the party and St Andrews. "The St Andrews Agreement," it said, "is the document of the two Governments. It is not the Agreement of the DUP or any other political party." At the same time the party could not resist the temptation to claim credit for the positive elements in the Agreement: "If you want to save the Union and have a devolved democratic government then the changes which the DUP fought for and obtained in this new Agreement, to safeguard your British and democratic rights, must be made."[34] Just like the 2005 manifesto, the consultation pamphlet was ambiguous in the places where it mattered.

The second part of the consultation exercise was an internal one, confined to DUP party members. Four meetings were held, in Belfast, Ballymena, Lurgan and Newtownstewart, in late October. Here the evidence is that the party leaders and strategists were given a pretty hard ride. The following is an extract from an account of the meeting at Lurgan which vividly portrays some of the concerns shared at rank-and-file level which were directed at Paisley himself. (See Appendix I for full text.) It is by no means a dispassionate, neutral report. It was compiled by a DUP dissident deeply opposed to the direction his party was taking. But it is authentic and the picture it paints of an unhappy grassroots, at least at this meeting, is accurate, according to one pro-Agreement DUP source who was present that night. On the platform were Ian and Eileen Paisley, Lord Morrow, Peter and Iris Robinson, David Simpson and Jeffrey Donaldson. Portions in italics are comments made by the dissident author. Dr P is Ian Paisley and JD is Jeffrey Donaldson.

> Dr P. commenced his address [by] going on to stress his own credentials. He would not be surrendering and would not be for turning. He had the wording for a pledge for SF to sign up to which would entail them naming the PSNI as the only legitimate policing service in NI and once SF had signed up to this, SF and Republicanism would be destroyed.

> *A lot of heckling and disbelief at what had just been said.*

> Dr P went on to reiterate that the pledge would tear SF asunder and the IRA he would be in Government with would not be the SF of today. *Much more heckling, asking why he was even considering going into gov. after stating he wouldn't? Dr. P. found it difficult to be heard due to the level of heckling at this stage, it continued for quite a while and he refrained from even trying to speak. A dose of his own medicine!*

Being the brilliant orator that he is, Dr P. responded to the heckling by stating that of the meetings that had already taken place, when the forms had been counted, 92 per cent of the party had given their support to his leadership and that he could be trusted.

He agreed and reiterated that Tony Blair had assured him that there would definitely be an election and not a referendum and that he had the final say on whether it would be an election or referendum! . . .

There would be no deal until the IRA had *delivered*. Any new assembly would not be a "love in" for the DUP and SF unlike the situation with the UUP, there would be supping of tea and no liquor, but then you know I would not be supping liquor anyway. The relationship with tomorrow's SF would be honest and straightforward. There would be a barrier between them. I am confident that a good day is coming for NI.

Q.&A.

Q. how long does it take for an unrepentant terrorist to become a democrat? Q. was not answered. Person left after being unable to induce a response.

Much heckling and questions why DUP was even considering gov. with SF?

Dr P. again stated that SF would have to specifically mention PSNI in pledge and this would bring SF republicanism to an end because SF was built on opposition to the police. Then there would be an election, and it would be an election and it would soon be in legislation that it would be an election and not a referendum. *Dr P. again severely heckled and unable to continue speaking.*

Alan Mitchell from Armagh asked whatever happened to the no guns, no government stance? He was laughed at and reminded that that was a UUP slogan. Someone shouted well what have SF to do, the answer, to deliver.

Many people shouting and demanding to know what had happened to decommissioning, transparent and verifiable decommissioning and pictures of same.

J.D. retorted that if we insisted on seeing pictures, then the DUP would be handing a veto on democracy to the Army Council. *Much more heckling.*

Dr P. – when IRA accepts the PSNI pledge the IRA will cease to exist, therefore he will not be in Gov. with IRA. The IRA that he will be going into Gov. with will be stripped of its power. Now we could see our way through the Red Sea with this pledge. PEOPLE CANNOT CONTINUE VOTING FOR THE STATUS QUO. When you are in opposition you can say anything you like, but when you are in a position of power like the DUP now is, then things are different. *In blackmailing tones he shouted* that we either support the St A's A. or we get ready for worse, outlining the seven super-councils, ability of Rep. of Ireland to control affairs in NI etc.

The hall echoed with shouts of blackmail.

J.D. who was very riled, responded that it was not blackmail, but what would happen. He also reminded the meeting that the status quo was not a viable proposition.

If the Lurgan meeting was at all typical, then it was clear that not insignificant opposition or at least unease existed in the ranks of the DUP's activists, those who knocked at the doors and erected the posters at election times. But the tactic of appealing to a wider public worked. When the consultation period ended on 8 November, the DUP reported that between the internal meetings and the coupon campaign, some 90 per cent of respondents were in favour of the party accepting St Andrews. There was no breakdown of the figures, so it was impossible to tell whether or not the feelings of party activists differed at all from the wider poll. This more-than-comfortable endorsement of the St Andrews Agreement, however, sat uneasily beside an opinion poll commissioned by the BBC in Belfast which was published at the same time. This indicated that less than half the DUP's voters backed the deal and that a significant minority, some 32 per cent, were against it.[35] But thanks to the coupon campaign in the *Belfast Telegraph*, the DUP had met the first deadline in the St Andrews timetable. The party's Executive met and gave its conditional and cautious agreement to moving on to the next stage. It wasn't quite a "yes" but neither was it a "no", and that was enough for Tony Blair and Bertie Ahern.

—◦—

By the time the Lurgan DUP gathering had taken place, the names of the party's more prominent doubters and dissidents were pretty well known. One was David Simpson, who had defeated David Trimble to capture the Upper Bann seat and whose contribution at Lurgan showed that he swung between opposing the deal and sitting on the fence. The Rev Willie McCrea was another sceptic and so were Gregory Campbell and Nigel Dodds, three MPs with a following in the party who all favoured, in varying degrees of toughness, a longer testing period for Sinn Féin than had been envisaged in the St Andrews timetable.

Without a doubt the most stringent opponent of St Andrews was the party's Euro-MP, Jim Allister, whose quarrel with Ian Paisley was one of the highlights of the Lurgan meeting. Allister was a blue-diaper baby. His parents were Free Presbyterians from Crossgar, where Paisley had founded the church way back in 1951, and he was brought up in the faith. A trained lawyer and unbending in much of his politics, Allister had been one of the young DUP stars of the 1980s, whose name had often been linked with Peter Robinson's as a leader-in-waiting. But he had severed links with the party after a row with Paisley every bit as bitter as the one he was having now. He had worked as Paisley's assistant in Europe before Nigel Dodds but then returned to Northern Ireland where he was groomed for electoral office. In 1982 he was elected along with Paisley in North Antrim to a seat in the ill-fated Prior Assembly which saw Sinn Féin's first entry into electoral politics. In 1983 McAllister stood in the general election in East Antrim and came only 350 votes behind the sitting Ulster Unionist MP, Roy Beggs. The seat appeared to be his for the taking at the next general election in 1987, but by then the Anglo-Irish Agreement was in place and Paisley had constructed a pact with the Ulster Unionist leader, Jim Molyneaux, which included a gentleman's agreement not to take each other's Westminster seats. Paisley had promised Allister he would be allowed to run but then changed his mind. Allister angrily quit the DUP in protest and began practising at the bar, where he specialised in criminal cases and, in 2001, was made a QC.

It was Paisley's illness that brought Allister back into the DUP. Paisley had been obliged to cut back his workload and decided he would not run for Europe in the 2004 election. That was the signal for an intense internal struggle to choose his successor. One of those seeking the seat, and a favourite to get the nomination, was the Rev William McCrea, who by this stage had lost Westminster seats in both South Antrim and Mid-Ulster and was in search of a new political role in life. But the prospect of McCrea winning the seat, and thus becoming a leadership candidate when Paisley retired, alarmed Peter Robinson and Nigel Dodds and so Allister was approached to see if he was interested in returning to stand. By this stage his career at the bar had given him financial freedom and that, along with Paisley's poor health, decided the matter. "The way Jim tells it," said one source close to him, "is that he wouldn't have done it if he didn't think Paisley was on the way out." The truth was that the 1987 fallout between the two men still rankled. At the selection meeting Allister won fifty six votes, McCrea got forty, Maurice Morrow, who had the backing of the Paisley clan, got just six votes, as did Paul Berry, who a year later would be embroiled in a gay sex scandal. Allister easily retained Paisley's seat at Strasbourg, not quite achieving the same number of votes, but he topped the poll and for every vote secured by his UUP rival, Jim Nicholson, Allister won two. As for Paisley, he never made any attempt to make it up with his successor at the European parliament.

The DUP brought Jim Allister along to the Leeds Castle "hothouse" in September 2004 and it was there that the other parties discovered that he was every bit as uncompromising and hardline as he had been back in the 1980s. The British in particular took a dislike to him. "Allister was very, very negative at Leeds Castle," remembered an Irish government source. "Blair was incensed with him and said, 'If he's where it's at in the DUP, then this thing is never going to happen.'"[36]

Relations between Downing Street and Allister worsened when the parties resumed contact back in Belfast. In early December 2004 negotiations with the DUP, Sinn Féin and the governments were ratcheted up. Proximity talks were held at Hillsborough Castle, and the DUP team, based at the party's offices in nearby Lisburn, liaised with Jonathan Powell, Blair's chief of staff. At one stage, Powell presented a draft of an IRA statement to the DUP for consideration and Allister dissected it, cross-examining the British Prime Minister's adviser as if he was a witness for the other side in a court case. Powell was furious and told the DUP leadership afterwards that he would have no more dealings with the party if Allister was present. From that day onwards, Allister was excluded from the DUP's inner councils and never again attended any high-level meetings with the British, although he was never officially informed of the decision. That the DUP leadership was ready to accommodate Powell in preference to their own European MP was, in retrospect, another highly significant clue as to the party's final intentions.

Allister would have a serious fall-out with Paisley after St Andrews but the two men were already on collision course over Paisley's decision to give his wife, Eileen, one of the peerages awarded to the DUP. The DUP was due at least one peerage after the 2001 general election and more after the 2005 sweep of the Ulster Unionists. Initially Downing Street wanted to give the party just two seats in the House of Lords but this was later increased to three. For some time there had been an understanding with the former Conservative MP Andrew Hunter, an Orangeman and fierce right-winger, that he would get one of the nominations. Hunter had left the Tories to join the DUP's parliamentary team in 2004 but, realising he had no chance of re-election in his Basingstoke constituency in southern England as a DUP candidate and wishing anyhow to move to Northern Ireland to get more involved in DUP politics, he decided to quit Westminster at the 2005 election. His presumption, shared by others in the party, was that he would represent the DUP in the House of Lords. But when it came time to select who would get the peerages, Paisley kept the decision entirely to himself. "He wouldn't tell anyone what was in his mind, not even Peter, who didn't know for months," explained a party source.[37] When he did make up his mind, it was to nominate his wife, Eileen, as one, and party chairman, Maurice Morrow, and Wallace Browne as the other two. At a meeting of party officers held shortly afterwards, Allister complained about the choice of Eileen Paisley, saying this was another example of Paisley family nepotism, perhaps the most sensitive charge one could make in the DUP. Paisley angrily retorted that it was none of his business. There was already bad blood between the two men, but now they were at daggers drawn.

Jim Allister wasn't of course the only elected DUP figure to have reservations about the St Andrews deal and the opportunity for them to show their hand came on Friday, 24 November, the date when the St Andrews' timetable decreed that Ian Paisley and Martin McGuinness should be designated as First and Deputy First Ministers respectively. The week had begun well with the first post-St Andrews meeting of the Preparation for Government Committee, where the DUP was represented by Peter Robinson. The day before, Jonathan Powell had arrived in Belfast and, after talking with Paisley, the DUP leader had phoned Blair to assure him that he would tell the Assembly he was prepared to become First Minister provided Sinn Féin delivered its pledge to support law and order. Later the same day, however, a leading Free Presbyterian Minister and former DUP colleague, Ivan Foster, complained that the prospect of

Paisley sharing power with Martin McGuinness was "heart-breaking" to church members and that was a foretaste of a brewing revolt in the DUP's Free Presbyterian heartland. Another big problem was that Sinn Féin was no nearer calling an *ard-fheis* to express support for the PSNI than it had been at St Andrews. In fact, remarks in a Swiss newspaper by one Sinn Féin Assembly member suggested that approval of the PSNI might not happen until the summer of 2008. A warning of what was to come had come at Westminster early that week when Nigel Dodds said that asking Ian Paisley to designate on the Friday was asking people to jump before Sinn Féin had moved on policing. Once again, the real issue was about who would move first.

The following morning Paisley retreated to the more uncompromising position favoured by his Executive earlier that month. When he rose to his feet in the Assembly it was to say: "Clearly as Sinn Féin is not yet ready to take the decisive step forward on policing, the DUP is not required to commit to any aspect of power-sharing in advance of such certainty. Circumstances have not been reached that there can be a nomination or a designation this day." The first of those sentences was taken word for word from the DUP Executive statement issued just before the first St Andrews' deadline on 10 November but the second was a little more explicit. If he had said instead, "But once that step is taken by Sinn Féin I will be ready to become First Minister", all would have been well; but he didn't. The conditional acceptance agreed the day before was missing, although, astonishingly, the Speaker, Eileen Bell, welcomed the statement as an indication that Paisley would accept the post.

Some thirty minutes after Gerry Adams had nominated Martin McGuinness as Deputy First Minister, events took an extraordinary turn. The former Loyalist assassin Michael Stone was intercepted at the revolving doors that lead into the parliament buildings, carrying a replica pistol and several pipe bombs. After a struggle with two members of the Stormont staff, one of them a woman, he was disarmed, but the building was evacuated and stayed empty for the next four hours. Stone had once been a fearsome character who had come to notorious attention in 1988 when he attacked a triple IRA funeral in West Belfast with grenades that, ironically, had come to Northern Ireland via South Africa, thanks to the deal brokered by the DUP's one-time paramilitary arm, Ulster Resistance. But these days he cut a more pathetic figure. Severe arthritis had crippled him and it took him the best part of an hour to make it up the steps to the parliament building where his physical deterioration had made it easy for the Stormont staff to overpower him. He later claimed that he had gone to Stormont to kill Gerry Adams and, while his intention was to disrupt and even derail the journey to devolution, the irony of his intervention was that it actually assisted it.

As the refugees from the parliament gathered in the nearby Stormont Hotel, a group of DUP Assembly members issued a statement challenging the Speaker's claim that Paisley had been designated as First Minister. The statement was signed by 12 of the DUP's 33 Assembly members, including four MPs, Nigel Dodds, David Simpson, Willie McCrea and Gregory Campbell. Not surprisingly, this move by the "Twelve Apostles", as the group became known, sparked speculation of a serious split in the DUP's ranks but its immediate import was that it was now impossible for prime ministers Blair and Ahern to ignore the meaning of Paisley's speech at Stormont or to fudge it. Michael Stone's aborted attack had, however, given everyone a breathing space long enough to make things right and accordingly the British, apparently with threats to close down the Assembly, persuaded Ian Paisley to moderate his earlier remarks. Early in the afternoon he issued a second statement outside the Stormont chamber saying: "If policing and all of the other outstanding issues that are before us are settled . . . [I] would accept the first minister's nomination provided the election results are favourable." That satisfied Blair and Ahern, and so the St Andrews timetable trundled on to the next deadline. But no-one should have been surprised at what had happened, since the contents of Paisley's Assembly speech had been well advertised in the DUP Executive statement before the 10 November deadline. It was the words with which he chose to express himself that caused the fuss, not their meaning.

The talk of a split in the DUP was somewhat exaggerated, or at least premature. What existed in the party was an incipient split that could open up if there was a significant deviation from the pledge of "no devolution without delivery". There were three groups in the party. The first was a small group, which included figures like Jim Allister and Willie McCrea, whose conditions for accepting Sinn Féin into government were so stringent as to amount to a rejection of the idea altogether. The next group, of which most of the "Twelve Apostles" were part, was amenable to sharing power but only if tough preconditions were met, such as a "credible testing period" for Sinn Féin's acceptance of law and order. They also strongly opposed any early devolution of security powers, especially if Sinn Féin was allowed to nominate the minister. The third group, represented by Paisley and Robinson, was less dogmatic – and in Paisley's case eager to take office – but no less aware that it was necessary to forge an alliance with the second group and bring them along if the deal was to be delivered. Such an arrangement would ensure that the bulk of the party would follow, leaving Allister and McCrea isolated and having to choose between remaining isolated or joining the rest. That meant, though, that the line would have to be held on policing and also that the DUP would have to break through the 26 March deadline. All this also made Nigel Dodds, the unofficial leader of the "Twelve Apostles", a key figure.

Towards the end of December the DUP and Sinn Féin had agreed a procedure for selecting a Minister of Justice which would give both parties a veto. But the question of when such devolution would happen was still unresolved. Just before the New Year the Sinn Féin executive or *ard comhairle* agreed to hold a special *ard-fheis* on policing in January but made this contingent on devolution of Justice happening by May 2007 and the start of power-sharing at Stormont. Paisley would have to signal his agreement first but he issued a distinctly ambiguous response and there were threats from Sinn Féin to call off the *ard-fheis*. Tony Blair had flown with his family for a post-Christmas break in Miami, Florida, to stay at the waterfront home of lead Bee Gees singer, Robin Gibb. Blair's fondness for celebrity vacations was by now legendary but this one was interrupted by a series of phone calls from Paisley – one source estimated around 20 – before he abandoned Miami's winter sunshine to return in an effort to resolve a growing crisis.

By this stage Paisley had almost literally retreated to the family kitchen where for the next two months or so all decisions were made after consultation with Eileen, Ian Junior and Tim Johnston, by now the family *consiglieri*. Others in the party leadership, notably Peter Robinson, were excluded as the Paisley family took charge. After a tortuous, complex and often conflicting series of exchanges between Blair, Paisley and Adams, the policing issue was fudged but with Paisley's apparent agreement that 26 March would see the start of devolution. Sinn Féin duly staged an *ard-fheis* on 28 January 2007 which overwhelmingly passed a motion supporting the policing and criminal justice institutions but making this contingent on the beginning of power-sharing and agreement on the devolution of Justice.

Every 13 July, the day following the Twelfth parades, Orangemen gather at the County Down village of Scarva to re-enact the Battle of the Boyne in 1690 between the Protestant hero, King Billy, and his Catholic rival, King James II. Scarva was chosen because this is where King Billy's army had rested and trained before the battle. The two ersatz monarchs would each year dismount from their horses and with "James" dressed in green and "Billy" in orange, they would battle with wooden swords. No-one ever got hurt and the sword fight would always end the same way, with "Billy" vanquishing his opponent. Fittingly it was called the "sham fight in Scarva". If there was an element of a sham fight between the DUP and Sinn Féin over the policing issue, it was because both parties were eager to proceed to the next stage in the St Andrews' timetable, the Assembly election. The poll was looming, a date of 7 March 2007 had been chosen, and both wanted it to happen for their own reasons. Sinn Féin saw a good election result as a springboard into the Republic's general election, which was expected to happen in the early summer. The DUP wanted it to consolidate their dominance of Unionism and to reunite the party. And both knew that an election would bring devolution inescapably nearer.

One compelling piece of evidence that the two parties shared the same interests in regard to devolution had emerged quietly and out of public view in the weeks after the St Andrews conference, when Sinn Féin and the DUP had sent teams over to London to negotiate with the British the final shape of the Bill that would put the St Andrews accord into legislative effect. Out of that came a proposal to change the way the First and Deputy First Ministers would be chosen which would predetermine the result of the Assembly election and ensure that the two parties would rule the roost in the Executive. Months after the power-sharing arrangement had been put in place, the smaller parties in the Executive began to complain of a Sinn Féin–DUP carve up. This is where the carve-up began.

Under the terms of the 1998 Good Friday Agreement, the First and Deputy First Ministers were elected jointly on a cross-community basis, meaning that a majority of the Assembly and a majority of Unionists and Nationalists in the Assembly were needed to put them into office. It was called the 50–50–50 rule. In practice this meant that the Ulster Unionists, as the largest party in the Unionist bloc, would always provide the First Minister, and the SDLP the Deputy First Minister. There were no difficulties with that until Sinn Féin overtook the SDLP and became the largest Nationalist party. With Martin McGuinness as the new Deputy First Minister-in-waiting, Unionists began to have second thoughts about the procedure. First David Trimble and then Ian Paisley pressed to have the selection of the two posts separated, since neither wanted to stand on the same ticket as a former IRA Chief of Staff. When the DUP replaced the Ulster Unionists, Sinn Féin similarly baulked at having to stand on the same ticket as Ian Paisley. So when the St Andrews Bill was first drafted by officials, the process was changed. From now on the First and Deputy First Ministers would be nominated, not elected, and they would be chosen separately. The First Minister would come from the largest party in the largest designation, that is the Unionists' bloc, while the Deputy First Minister would come from the largest party in the next largest designation, the Nationalists'. In such a way was Northern Ireland's sectarian politics to be set in political concrete; Unionists would always be guaranteed the First Minister's post and Nationalists the Deputy First Minister's job. But the story didn't end there.

The DUP sent over to London its pro-St Andrews MPs, headed by Peter Robinson and Jeffrey Donaldson, along with party officials Tim Johnston and Richard Bullick, to agree changes in the Bill. Members of what were called "the awkward squad", Nigel Dodds, Willie McCrea, David Simpson, Gregory Campbell and Jim Allister, were not told about the negotiations and were therefore unable to influence their outcome. One obvious reason was that they might well have opposed the principal change that was negotiated. This was a second change made to the way the two top jobs in the Executive were to be allocated, but this time a more fundamental and far-reaching one – the First Minister would now be nominated from the largest party in the Assembly and the Deputy from the second largest. Their designations as Unionist or Nationalist were now rendered irrelevant. The effect of this revision was to open, at lest theoretically, the possibility that Martin McGuinness could be the next First Minister of Northern Ireland. That would happen if Sinn Féin topped the poll and it wouldn't matter if the Assembly still had an overall majority of pro-Union members. Sinn Féin's team in London happily backed the change for obvious reasons. In fact, Gerry Adams had raised the matter in the closing stages of St Andrews, as one Irish government figure recalled: "Adams came to us when it was too late and said he'd just bollocked his people for missing out on this as there was a chance Sinn Féin could be the largest party but still be in the second largest designation."[38]

Jim Allister was the only member of "the awkward squad" to publicly protest at the change, calling it "monstrous and a gross affront to democracy".[39] Others in the DUP realised that it could actually work to the party's benefit. By transforming the coming Assembly election into a contest between Paisley and McGuinness, the DUP was now able to tell Unionist voters that if they didn't plump for Paisley, then McGuinness could be First Minister. The move carried the stamp of the DUP's principal strategist. "There was no doubt in my mind," said one DUP figure, "that this was a Robinson ploy."[40]

Equally, Sinn Féin could make the same sort of pitch to the Nationalist electorate to the detriment of the SDLP, urging Catholic voters to vote Sinn Féin to keep Paisley out of the top job. Once again it was a case of the two extremes in Northern Irish politics nurturing and sustaining each other, but this time quite deliberately.

The St Andrews timetable said that the Agreement had to receive the "endorsement of the electorate" but the Assembly election that took place on 7 March 2007 was "a vote for a deal that hadn't been made, for a deal that the electorate hadn't been give a chance to judge", in the words of Queen's University psephologist Dr Sidney Elliott.[41]

By the time voters went to the polls, the DUP and Sinn Féin had still not officially exchanged a single word in public and were still a long way from any agreement to go into government together. Not only was Sinn Féin's support for the PSNI insufficiently untested by time for many in the DUP, it was still far from clear that the DUP would keep to the 26 March deadline, even though that had been implicitly promised by Ian Paisley. As one Irish participant at St Andrews put it, speaking about both Sinn Féin and the DUP, "neither of them ever said to us at any stage, then or afterwards, that they would run with this".[42] The DUP manifesto, an astonishing sixty four pages long, in fact made a virtue out the conditional nature of the putative deal and gave prominence to a key quote taken from the 9 November Executive statement: ". . . there can only be an agreement involving Sinn Féin when there has been delivery by the republican movement, tested and proved over a credible period, in terms of support for the PSNI, the Courts and rule of law, a complete end to paramilitary and criminal activity and the removal of terrorist structures."

The election was called on 30 January, which gave only five weeks for the campaign; that suited the DUP since there was limited time for scrutiny of their policies. When the need for devolution was mentioned on the doorsteps, it was more because matters like water charges, rates and the survival of grammar schools required it. On the vital question of sealing a deal with Sinn Féin, DUP candidates prevaricated and at times denied the possibility. David Trimble experienced it at first hand. Although he had stepped down from the Ulster Unionist leadership, he returned to canvass for the party in his native Lisburn during that election and recalled: "I went into a Housing Executive estate which had a lot of DUP supporters and I tried to tell them Paisley would do a deal after the election but they would not accept that; they were convinced there would be no deal."[43] His successor, Reg Empey, agreed:

> They were specifically unclear about their intentions. Some candidates were saying on the doorsteps they wouldn't do it, others like Robinson were saying that either there was a big economic package from the British or we won't do it. They didn't make it clear, they were very ambiguous. Some people felt that they should vote for the DUP to push them over the line, some were out-and-out anti-Sinn Féin and others were voting for them because they were less likely to do a deal.[44]

Ian Paisley himself fuelled the doubts surrounding the chances of a deal. On a walkabout in the seaside town of Bangor, County Down, he told reporters:

> I think 26 March is a date too early. . . . That deadline is a dream that the Secretary of State has had. It's a nightmare now because he'll never have that. But, of course, let me just add, if the IRA delivers we could have anything.[45]

The DUP's trump card was ordinary Unionists' fear of Martin McGuinness, the IRA's hard man as many saw him, becoming First Minister. As the manifesto put it:

> After the election, in the context of restoration of devolution, the largest political party in Northern Ireland will nominate a First Minister. It is vital that a unionist holds this position. At the last Assembly election, partly due to splitting of the unionist vote, the DUP was just 15,000 votes ahead of Sinn Féin. The UUP was far behind. Only the DUP can beat Sinn Féin.[46]

It all turned out perfectly – for both the DUP and Sinn Féin. The DUP won thirty six seats in the Assembly, a gain of six, twice as many as the Ulster Unionists, who lost nine seats and were outpolled by the DUP by two to one. Sinn Féin gained four seats to win 28 while the SDLP lost two and ended up with 16 seats. Sinn Féin polled 63 per cent of the Nationalist vote, just below what the SDLP had secured in 1982 when Sinn Féin made its first excursion as a party into electoral politics. Between them the two parties, the extremes of Unionism and Nationalism, held a commanding majority of the new Assembly.

The touted threat of a Sinn Féin First Minister had turned out to be a mirage – the gap between the two parties had actually widened – but it had worked to the DUP leader's advantage. Ian Paisley was now guaranteed the job of First Minister of Northern Ireland. The one-time rabble-rousing, street corner preacher and political demagogue stood on the cusp of glory, respectability and sweet retribution against all those who had despised and reviled him for so long. But would he and his party take that last fateful step on 26 March and make the unthinkable a reality?

—◁○▷—

When the counting of votes had been completed, things had changed and they hadn't changed. The DUP's leadership of Unionism was now beyond challenge and its freedom to manoeuvre greatly enhanced. Ian Paisley could now claim a mandate, at the very least, for his party's approach towards devolution and its handling of Sinn Féin, if not for an actual deal with the Provos. Notwithstanding the ambiguity of its election campaigning and the conditional content of much of its manifesto, the DUP had clearly not gone to the voters on a platform of implacable opposition to an agreement with the Provos. There was now a widespread expectation, not least in London and Dublin, that a settlement could and should be reached.

The election had left a number of issues still unresolved, however, not least of which was the difficult and potentially divisive issue of how long the testing period for Sinn Féin should be. There had been some uncertainty as to when this should start. Initially, 24 November 2006, when Ian Paisley and Martin McGuinness were supposed to have indicated their willingness to take up the First and Deputy First Minister's posts, was regarded as the starting point. But once Sinn Féin's *ard-fheis* met on 28 January to give the party's support to the PSNI and the judicial system, that was considered by the bulk of the DUP as the moment from which the republican *bona fides* should be measured. If devolution was restored on 26 March, then less than two months would have elapsed, much less than the six months that had been in most DUP minds since the Leeds Castle conference.

There had been positive and negative developments since Sinn Féin's *ard-fheis*. Two days after the conference, the IMC issued a report, its thirteenth since 2004, which concluded: ". . . we are clear that the leadership of Sinn Féin and the Republican movement as a whole remains firm in its commitment to the political strategy and continues to give appropriate instructions to the membership of the movement."[47] The IRA, the IMC reported, was still committed to dismantling its structures but what these were it didn't say. At the same time, the IMC had implied that the ruling Army Council was still in place and many in the DUP wanted to see that go before committing themselves to a deal. The Provos had, to be sure, agreed to support law and order but this was conditional, both on the beginning of power-sharing and a date for the devolution of Justice powers. Since then, Sinn Féin leaders had drawn a distinction between "civic" policing, which they could support, and "political" policing, i.e. the work done by the PSNI Special Branch and MI5, which they couldn't. On a BBC radio phone-in programme, the Sinn Féin MP for Fermanagh–South Tyrone, Michelle Gildernew, echoed the ambivalence that still existed in the Provos' ranks about policing. She was asked what a citizen should do if he or she spotted dissident Republicans with guns. Should they contact the PSNI? "I personally wouldn't," she replied, "but I am working very hard to ensure those guns are never used again. . . ."[48] It was evident that many in Sinn Féin were still struggling to accommodate a pro-policing mindset, and that had an unsettling effect on the DUP.

Another problem was that Ian Paisley had boxed himself into a corner over the 26 March deadline during that period before and after the New Year when he, Eileen and Ian Junior had made all the party's important decisions. At the conclusion of a three-way exchange with Tony Blair and Gerry Adams over the devolution of policing powers and the deadline for power-sharing, Paisley had issued a tortured form of words in mid-January 2007 which Downing Street chose to interpret in the most positive way. "If a government cannot be formed on 26 March," the DUP leader declared, "because Sinn Féin fails to deliver, it will be clear that Sinn Féin alone is to blame." Blair's spokesman chose to believe that the converse must also be true: that if Sinn Féin delivered on policing, then Paisley would go into government. "Dr Paisley's comments . . . confirm the Prime Minister in his view that it is possible to arrive at a situation where there will be full support for the police and a power-sharing Executive by 26 March," he said.[49] Significantly, the DUP leader chose not to dispute that interpretation.

The truth was that Ian Paisley was ready to meet the 26 March deadline because he was eager to become First Minister, even though this might well appear to be knuckling under increasingly belligerent threats from NI Secretary Peter Hain that he would close down the Assembly and throw its members out of work if the deadline was missed. Others in the party noted ruefully that the Provos had been allowed to ignore one deadline after another at earlier stages of the peace process without any sanctions.

It would be true to say that outside the Paisley family circle, no other major DUP figure was so keen to get into bed with Sinn Féin. Some like Willie McCrea and David Simpson wanted a testing period much longer than six months, perhaps as long as a year. By this stage, Jim Allister was repeatedly opposing the March deadline in public, the only party figure to be so explicitly defiant. Nigel Dodds and Gregory Campbell, the other two MPs who had put their names to the "Twelve Apostles" statement on 24 November, would be happy with a six- to eight-month testing period but were adamantly opposed to one that ended as early as 26 March. Peter Robinson also preferred a longer lead-in and nearly everyone believed that party morale and unity would be strengthened if they could successfully defy the governments' deadline. There was no doubt that, had Ian Paisley insisted, the DUP would have linked up with Sinn Féin on 26 March, but equally the chances of a damaging split would have been that much greater. Paisley had just celebrated his eighty-first birthday and was a figure whose failing powers had been evident for some time. He was still enormously respected but more for his past bravado than his present disposition. The disastrous one-to-one meetings with Blair and his performance at St Andrews were by now well known throughout the party and it was now possible to envision a post-Paisley DUP, one that was not far away. Many would certainly have followed him into government on 26 March – but not all.

It was at this stage that Peter Robinson retook possession of the centre stage and crafted a proposal in the week or so before 26 March that both minimised the DUP's internal difficulties and ensured that devolution would be restored – while still crashing through the British-Irish deadline. The key person to get on board was Nigel Dodds, whose preference was to delay the power-sharing Executive until early September. If Dodds agreed to Robinson's proposal, then so would Gregory Campbell and other would-be rebels would follow. Robinson proposed a compromise between the 26 March date that Paisley had signed up to and Dodds' preference for September and settled on 8 May. One factor that convinced sceptics to go with 8 May was the knowledge that Tony Blair would retire from Downing Street not long afterwards. His replacement was to be Gordon Brown, whose commitment to Northern Ireland was an unknown. Blair, however, needed to complete his legacy and was amenable to another side deal. This one encompassed a financial package to sweeten the pill and "Plan C", an assurance that if the Provos defaulted, Unionists would not share the punishment. "Plan C" was duly negotiated and approved at cabinet level. But what it consisted of has never been made clear, a little like "Plan B".

The drama unfolded during the week beginning Monday, 19 March. That Tuesday evening, Queen Elizabeth held a reception for MPs and MEPs at Buckingham Palace and afterwards three of the leading dissidents-cum-doubters, Nigel Dodds, Willie McCrea and Jim Allister, had dinner together. The 8 May compromise proposal was in circulation by that stage but all three were against it, or at least said they were, agreeing that there still hadn't been enough delivery from the Provos nor a sufficiently long testing time. The following day, Robinson and Paisley met Tony Blair and Peter Hain at Westminster to warn them that there could be a split in the DUP unless the deadline was extended. Blair and Hain refused to budge. Hain later said that he told the DUP duo that an extension to the deadline was impossible "unless the DUP could persuade the other parties that there was a credible reason to do so". The next evening the DUP party officers met at the party's Dundela Avenue headquarters in East Belfast to vote on the Robinson 8 May compromise. The party officers, consisting of the nine Westminster MPs, MEP Jim Allister, party chairman Lord Morrow, Ian Paisley Junior, Nigel Dodds's wife, Diane, and MLAs Edwin Poots and David Hilditch, agreed by 14 votes to one to recommend Robinson's compromise to the much larger Executive. In the space of 48 hours, Dodds had switched over to the Robinson camp, bringing Campbell, Simpson and McCrea with him. Of the three who had dined in London earlier in the week and discussed their opposition to a May deadline, only Jim Allister voted against.

The next day, Paisley and Robinson flew to London for another meeting with Blair and Hain, now armed with the party officers' resolution as evidence of party sentiment. This time, according to Hain, "Again we said no – unless the DUP managed to get other parties, including Sinn Féin, to agree."[50] By this stage in the peace process senior DUP figures had met secretly with Sinn Féin at St Andrews and they had been in face-to-face contact with senior Provos for some months at meetings of the Committee on the Programme for Government at Stormont. There had also been persistent suggestions of secret contacts stretching back some time at locations as diverse as Quaker House in London and the Linenhall Library in Belfast. One way or another, relations were such that communication between the two was not impossible. By that Friday evening and Saturday morning, Sinn Féin had agreed to the 8 May date provided the two parties opened official, face-to-face contact, a development that would also convince Downing Street that they were agreed on the new devolution deadline.

On the Saturday afternoon, the DUP's Executive met in Castlereagh Council's grand new offices in the Knock area of Belfast, Peter Robinson's home ground, for three hours and approved the party officers' motion by 102 votes to ten, a margin of 90 per cent. At this meeting Nigel Dodds's contribution proved to be crucial. After Allister had told the meeting that with only six weeks left until 8 May, there couldn't be any more delivery from the Provos and there wouldn't be, Dodds – his dinner with Allister four days earlier now a faint memory – rose to his feet to insist there would be. As one of the leading sceptics heretofore, Dodds swayed the meeting towards Robinson's compromise. "He was vital," said one Executive member. "He was the one man who could have stopped this and he didn't."[51] Afterwards the choreography continued. The party officers reconvened at Dundela Ave at 5.00 p.m. and voted, this time by fifteen to one, to open talks with Sinn Féin. By that evening, Robinson, Nigel Dodds, Jeffrey Donaldson, Ian Paisley Junior and the two ubiquitous party apparatchiks, Tim Johnston and Richard Bullick, were in conference with a Sinn Féin delegation that included Martin McGuinness, Gerry Kelly, Conor Murphy, Alex Maskey and Aidan McAteer. Their number included one former IRA Chief of Staff, the son of a Chief of Staff and an ex-Adjutant-General. They met at Stormont Castle, since 1972 the British government's operational headquarters in Northern Ireland where hundreds of orders to intern IRA suspects had been signed and security operations approved.

The meetings lasted most of that night and, controversially for the DUP's sabbatarian wing, during the Sunday as well, with the main item on the agenda being a joint press appearance on the mid-morning of Monday, 26 March by Ian Paisley and Gerry Adams to seal their agreement. Every aspect of the two leaders' encounter was discussed and agreed, from the shape of the tables where they would sit, the statements each would make and who else would be in the room. To call what was about to happen a press conference would be well wide of the mark because the media would not be allowed to ask the two men any questions. This was an event, after all, organised by the two most controlling political parties in Ireland.

It took little more than fifteen minutes for Paisley and Adams to read their statements announcing the agreement to begin sharing power but it was less what they had to say than the sight of the two men sitting almost within touching distance that had such a powerful impact. Between them Paisley and Adams had for so long symbolised the intractability of the conflict and the sectarian hatreds that defined it, that no-one had ever imagined that such a spectacle could be possible. There was no handshake between the men, to be sure, and things had been so arranged that Paisley and Adams sat together but not beside each other. After all, the encounter may have been historic but it would also be controversial, especially in the DUP heartlands, and so great care was taken to suggest a businesslike distance between the two men. Nonetheless, it was still an astonishing tableau.

With Peter Robinson and Nigel Dodds to his right, both with set, serious faces, Ian Paisley sat at the apex of two tables that made one corner of a square of tables adorned with a white ruffled tablecloth placed in the centre of the Assembly members' dining room in the parliament building. Behind them sat members of the DUP's Assembly team. To Paisley's left, seated on the other side of the apex, was Gerry Adams, a paper Easter lily commemorating the 1916 Rising pinned to his jacket lapel, in classic Provo style, flanked by Mary Lou McDonald, the Sinn Féin European MP from Dublin, and Catriona Ruane, an Assembly member from South Down. McDonald's presence helped to explain why Sinn Féin had gone along with the 8 May devolution date. It would mean that the accession to government in Belfast, and all the publicity surrounding it, would probably take place at around the same time as the general election campaign in the Republic. By going into government with Paisley on that day, Sinn Féin hoped to get an election bounce that could help propel it into coalition government with Fianna Fáil. The Adams strategy aimed to have seats at the cabinet table in both jurisdictions and going along with the DUP plan would, it seemed, edge them appreciably closer to that goal. Sinn Féin had hopes of winning a dozen or more Dáil seats and Mary Lou McDonald, their most prominent Southern standard bearer, was to stand in a key Dublin constituency. Sitting beside Adams ensured that her face would be beamed by television into the living rooms of thousands of Dublin households. The Provos never missed a trick.

The day had been made possible by Peter Robinson, of that there was little doubt. "Peter was just brilliant," gushed one colleague and ally. "It was he who crafted the settlement in the last seven days, working with people, talking to them and winning them over. Paisley is the titular head of the DUP and while his standing in the community is significant, the key strategist, the real leader is Peter Robinson."[52]

There was, though, another reality about the day's events and it was that the people who had really made the day possible were the Sinn Féin leadership, especially its leader Gerry Adams. They were the people who had ended the IRA's war, who had decommissioned its vast arsenals and dismantled its organisational structures. It was they who abandoned swathes of Republican ideology, who had accepted the principle of consent and the reality of British jurisdiction and had taken their seats in the Stormont parliament. And it was they who had helped to cause the downfall of David Trimble, without which Ian Paisley's presence that day at the same table as Gerry Adams would have been impossible. In contrast, Ian Paisley was obliged to sacrifice only his pride to complete the journey to peace. The core of his Unionist politics had been left untouched and largely unmodified and he had been able to make the journey from demagogue to democrat, from political outcast to political respectability, without altering anything except his standing in the eyes of his more recalcitrant supporters.

While the two governments, the international community and the media welcomed the announcement at Stormont, much of the DUP rank-and-file sat watching their television sets in a state of stunned horror and disbelief, unable to take in what had happened. Even those near the centre of events were overwhelmed. Jim Wells, an Assembly member from South Down who had voted "no" at the Saturday Executive meeting, told the *Sunday Times*, "Every time I look at that picture of the two of them, I keep thinking I will wake up and it will all have been a bad dream."[53] At lower levels of the DUP, there had been no effort to prepare activists for what was coming and the shock was greater. "Within the party," explained one grassroots activist, "so many were convinced the Doc would never do it, that he was really playing a clever game, so that when it happened, when they saw those pictures on TV, they just took refuge in denial."[54] Clifford Smyth, who had battled alongside Paisley in the 1970s and then had been expelled from the party, said "a tremendous sense of shock rattled its way through the DUP" that day. Like so many others, he added, "I had always thought that Robinson would want to do the deal but that Paisley would hold the line against him. I never thought I would see such a day."[55]

Retreating into denial and disbelief was something the Provo grassroots had done in the wake of the 1994 ceasefire but most of them resisted the temptation to defect to dissident groups or to join battle against their former leaders. To do so would be to suffer community isolation or worse and the loss of fellowship that came with being part of a large and successful organisation. Much the same happened in the DUP. Of the prominent sceptics and opponents of the deal, only Jim Allister resigned. No Assembly members defected to join him and just thirteen councillors, the majority in Ballymena, quit in protest. Two MPs, David Simpson and Willie McCrea, did express their dismay but no more than that, and while other figures grumbled, none left the party. Just like the Provos, the DUP had made the transition to a new mode with the minimum of internal damage.

─◁○▷─

By the time 8 May came around, the power-sharing arrangements had effectively been in place for some weeks and just required the formality of the day's events to invest them with power. Each party had chosen its shadow team of Ministers. In the DUP's case the hated d'Hondt mechanism had given the party the greatest number of ministers in the new Executive, five to Sinn Féin's four, while their rivals, the Ulster Unionists, got two and the SDLP just a single post. Peter Robinson and Nigel Dodds were given the Finance and Trade portfolios respectively and there were two other DUP ministers, Edwin Poots and Arlene Foster, while Ian Paisley Junior was made a junior Minister in his father's office. He became the gatekeeper for his father, attended Executive meetings in a non-voting capacity and had the task of co-ordinating work between the First Minister's office and the other departments. His job gave him a lot of power and reignited speculation that he was being groomed to succeed his father. Tim Johnston, the faithful aide to Ian Paisley, and Richard Bullick, Peter Robinson's assistant, were rewarded with special adviser's jobs, reportedly at an annual salary of stg£50,000. The former doubters,

Gregory Campbell and Willie McCrea, were given the chairmanships of Assembly committees, while Jeffrey Donaldson, along with Robinson, was elevated to the Privy Council. Just before the deal had been struck, Peter Hain increased the Assembly members' office allowance from stg£49,000 a year to stg£70,000, a not inconsiderable incentive to accept the new dispensation, especially to the DUP's Assemblymen, many of whom employed family members in their offices. Historians will doubtless unearth many motives to explain why the 2007 deal was accepted by the North's politicians but it would be a mistake if they overlooked or understated the part that the lure of the Stormont gravy train had in deciding many minds.

Ian Paisley arrived at the Stormont parliament building that morning with his black fedora hat perched on his head, chosen, some said, in conscious imitation of the Unionist icon, Lord Carson. Baroness Paisley was resplendent in mauve but it was noticeable that Paisley moved slowly as he made his way into the building. Before that he spoke a few words to the media, who had turned up in huge numbers from around the world to record the occasion, and it seemed as if he had been tutored to keep the atmosphere serious and restrained, befitting his entry into an alliance with a party his grassroots still reviled as a detestable enemy. "While this is a sad day," he said, "a sad day for those who were the innocent victims of all the troubles we've had, yet it is a special day because we are making a new beginning."

The forbearance did not last too long. After taking the pledge of office along with Martin McGuinness and following the nomination of the Executive, Paisley, McGuinness, Tony Blair, Bertie Ahern and Peter Hain settled on leather couches in the First Minister's office to chat and drink a cup of tea, one of those occasions staged for the TV cameras. What followed was the first piece of evidence that Ian Paisley was enjoying himself – revelling, it seemed, in his new role. The five men were all smiles and hilarity, especially when Paisley cracked a joke. "You're going out as a young man," he said to Blair who, two days later, would announce the date for his long-awaited retirement, "and I'm coming in as an old one." "Maybe I should have learned a lesson from you," Blair quipped back to general laughter. Later, after speeches and a performance from a musical group made up of adults with special needs, Paisley and McGuinness posed for pictures on the staircase, both men grinning broadly. Paisley looked as if he was about to throw his head back in a fit of laughter. It was a scene that became the icon for the day, the former IRA commander and the once bitter preacher united in peace and merriment.

The two scenes between them gave birth to the name that soon everyone would call Paisley and McGuinness: the Chuckle Brothers. For those who supported the Agreement, at least those outside the DUP, it was a happy choice, but inside Paisley's party the photograph and the scenes of joviality at Stormont were dismaying and damaging, both to those who backed the deal and those who disliked it. According to one:

People have been appalled at the Chuckle Brothers stuff. Paisley's end of the party was most appalled and even more moderate voters were upset. We were supposed to be the ones who know how to deal with Sinn Féin and the image he gave of "How happy I am to be here" was contrary to the message and contrary to the decisions that had been forced out of the Provos, like backing the police.[56]

Another added: "The Chuckle Brothers thing has been devastating. I have heard so many people say, 'Okay, we know there had to be a deal but don't look as if you're enjoying it so much!'"[57]

There was another reaction to the day's events, perhaps one felt by most people. The St Andrews Agreement is, in its defining elements, indistinguishable from the 1974 Sunningdale Agreement. While some details are different, both embraced mandatory power-sharing at Executive level and both featured institutionalised cross-Border links with Dublin. Both Ian Paisley and the Provisional IRA had set out to destroy Sunningdale, Paisley by throwing his party's weight behind a Loyalist campaign that culminated in the Ulster Workers Council strike and the IRA by significantly intensifying its violence. Between them they brought Sunningdale down and condemned Northern Ireland to some thirty more years of violence. Over 2,400 people died violently in the years between 1975 and 2006, just over 65 per cent of all deaths in the Troubles. Yet here they were, the "architects, perpetrators and perpetuators" of the conflict in many eyes, as Frank Millar aptly described them, putting their names to a deal that was really no different in substance.[58] By so doing, they both trivialised the conflict and raised troubling questions about their motives. In Paisley's case, the questions also concern his recent and often virulent campaign against David Trimble. Clifford Smyth says, that since 8 May 2007, he is routinely asked three questions by ordinary Unionists:

The first is: why did so many people have to die to get us to this position? The second is: what is the difference between the deal that Trimble got and the one Paisley has accepted? And the last one is: if there is no difference between them, then why did Paisley destroy Trimble?[59]

—◄○►—

In the nearly forty years that the Troubles lasted, it was always possible to discern where in the North the Irish government's interests lay by the party with which it chose to forge the closest relationship. During the early years, Dublin courted the SDLP and its leader John Hume for the reason that they offered the best bulwark against the Provisional IRA, whose campaign of violence not only kept the North permanently unstable but often threatened the Republic as well. When the Adams leadership steered the Provos into the peace process, Dublin switched horses and gave Adams and his colleagues all the assistance they could, leaving the SDLP to fend for itself. Once the IRA was safely defanged and Sinn Féin converted to constitutional politics, Dublin's Northern party of choice became the DUP. The survival and stability of the St Andrews' deal, after all, depends heavily on the DUP remaining a happy and politically healthy party. Dublin's interests dictate that everything than can be done should be done to ensure that. That was one reason, for example, why such care and thought had gone into the choice of a wedding anniversary gift to present to Ian and Eileen at St Andrews.

The joint appearance of Paisley and Adams on 26 March was the first concrete sign from the DUP since St Andrews that it was ready to do the deal; so when Paisley afterwards expressed an interest in travelling south to meet and thank Bertie Ahern, the Taoiseach responded positively and enthusiastically. It was decided that the two men should meet at Farmleigh House, recently renovated and now the preferred location for official engagements, on 3 April, a month or so before the North's new Executive would go live. Ahern's officials were not sure if Paisley was ready for their first public handshake. The two men had become political friends and allies but there was still some distance between them; Tony Blair, for instance, was on first-name terms with the DUP leader but the Taoiseach still called him "Dr Paisley".

And so a contingency plan was drawn up. "We choreographed it," said one Irish government figure. "The car carrying Paisley was to stop twenty feet away from the door to Farmleigh, Bertie would walk up and if there was no handshake, then he would give Paisley a hug of some sort." The plan wasn't necessary. Paisley strode from his car and thrust his hand into Ahern's. "I better shake the hands of this man," he quipped. "I'll give him a firm handshake." The two retired inside to hold what one source called "a crackerjack meeting" and then in remarks to the waiting media, announced that Paisley had accepted an invitation to meet again at the site of the Battle of the Boyne. "Not to refight," joked Paisley, "because that would be unfair for he would have the home advantage."

The Boyne meeting took place on 11 May, three days after the celebrations at Stormont, and this time it was Paisley who arrived bearing a gift in the form of a musket, said to have been carried by one of King James's officers at the Boyne and during the siege of Derry a year earlier. If both men had an added reason for meeting again so soon, it was because in less than two weeks' time, Ahern would face what could be the toughest election of his decade as Taoiseach. He was facing allegations that he had received money from a millionaire businessman when he was Minister for Finance in 1993, while Sinn Féin were gearing up for what they and others believed would be a breakthrough electoral success that, if it came, would be at the expense of Ahern's party. The Taoiseach's future in Irish politics was at stake and Paisley was lending him a hand. The conventional wisdom was that Sinn Féin would get an election bounce out of the events of 8 May but, as it turned out, if anyone derived electoral advantage out of the restoration of devolution in Belfast it was Bertie Ahern, aided in no small way by the DUP leader's decision to grasp his outstretched hand so firmly, an act that became a metaphor for the Taoiseach's role in bringing peace to the North. "Paisley turned out to be an election asset for Bertie, no doubt of that," said a source close to him.[60]

As the results started to flow in, it soon became clear that Bertie Ahern and Fianna Fáil were heading for an election triumph and a third term in office. Sinn Féin had performed disastrously, losing a seat in Dublin and failing to make gains anywhere else. Mary Lou McDonald, promoted so brazenly by Gerry Adams on 26 March, flopped miserably in Dublin Central. As the Taoiseach watched the live feed on television, the phone in his office in Government Buildings rang. It was Ian Paisley, overflowing with excitement, delighted that Ahern had survived and ecstatic at Sinn Féin's failure. "I just want to tell the Taoiseach," he roared down the line, "that this is a great day for Ireland, a great day for Ulster!"[61]

"Do not be unequally yoked up with unbelievers. Do not make mis-mated alliances with them, or come under a different yoke with them. For what partnership have right living and right standing with God with iniquity and lawlessness? How can light have fellowship with darkness? . . . So come out from among them and separate yourselves from them, says the Lord . . ."

PAUL'S SECOND EPISTLE TO THE CORINTHIANS, 6: 14-18

꩜

"It is the ploy of Satan to attack those whom God has signally appointed and specially anointed as leaders in His work."

REV IAN PAISLEY, MODERATOR OF THE FREE PRESBYTERIAN CHURCH, WRITING IN *The Revivalist*, MAY 2007

꩜

"Today there are those in church and state whose vision is so distorted by self-righteousness they are of the opinion that they couldn't possibly be wrong and so they go around criticising those to whom under God they owe their very salvation, their positions, their churches. Like the Israelites of old treated Moses so they treat today's God-anointed leader."

EILEEN PAISLEY, WRITING IN *The Revivalist*, MAY 2007

CHAPTER SIXTEEN

An Unequal Yoke

It was easy to forget during the years of political turbulence leading to the DUP's entry into government alongside Sinn Féin, that Ian Paisley headed up another organisation that he had also founded, the Free Presbyterian Church of Ulster, that was, in its way, every bit as important to him as his political party. Apart from a brief period when he was in jail during the 1960s, he had served as Moderator of the Church every year since 1951 and his authority over the church, as all-embracing and strictly enforced as was the Papacy's, had never been challenged in all that time. The Church's Ministers, Elders and congregations had happily endorsed practices that were frowned upon in other evangelical denominations or were theologically questionable, such as Paisley's foray into politics and his pursuit of a seat in the European parliament. They did so because, well, it was Ian Paisley's church. He had founded it, he had built it up and it was almost his to do with as he wished. Until, that is, he came to sit around the cabinet table with Sinn Féin. As that option moved from a possibility to a reality, members of his church, quoting the Scriptures against him, rose up in revolt and under threat of public humiliation forced an end to his career as Moderator. It was an astonishing rebuke to a man whom many of them had long regarded as "God's Man", divinely sent to save the Protestants of Ulster from theological and political compromise. In an important way, Paisley's ouster from the leadership of his church also provided a metaphor for the wider change happening in Northern Ireland and for the transformation that was beginning to overtake Paisley himself. Until 8 May 2007, many of those who had studied Ian

489

Paisley's life would have believed that if faced with a choice between his Church and politics – between God and Mammon – he would always have plumped for the Church. They were wrong.

―◦―

The story of the Free Presbyterian Church and the DUP in the 1990s and during the first few years of the new millennium is a study in contrasts. While the DUP grew in strength and electoral popularity to ultimately become the dominant force in Unionism, the Church experienced slowing growth, then stagnation and now shows the first signs of going into decline. The unspoken but nonetheless motivating ambition to challenge and replace the compromisers in the two main aspects of Ulster's Protestant world had been successful only in the political sphere. The figures speak for themselves. By 2001, according to the official census, there were 11,902 Free Presbyterians in Northern Ireland, 450 fewer than there had been in 1991, the first decade to see a drop in worshippers since Ian Paisley founded the Church in 1951. If the Free Presbyterian Church was a business, it would have just gone into the red and its Board of Directors would be starting to get anxious. The Church's good years were behind it, that was also clear. The best of all years had been in the 1960s, when a young and vibrant Ian Paisley led campaigns against the civil rights movement and the liberal Unionist Premier, Captain Terence O'Neill, and launched an onslaught against ecumenical Protestant churches. In those years the number of new churches opening their doors tripled. In the 1970s, the worst years for IRA violence, new congregations had grown by 70 per cent. In the 1980s there was a 10 per cent growth and again in the 1990s, both decades which witnessed a decrease in IRA violence and the beginnings of the peace process.[1] Free Presbyterian Church membership, it appeared, was directly influenced by the level of threat to the Unionist and Protestant community coming either from their own "weak" leadership or from outside forces. By the dawn of the new millennium there were just over sixty congregations throughout Northern Ireland, only a dozen or so more than there were in 1980.

It must also be the case, in a Church which was so dominated by one man for most of its history, that its health and vitality would reflect the well-being of that man. In Ian Paisley's case his deteriorating health and advancing years appeared to have gone hand-in-hand with the Church's waning fortunes. That is especially evident in Belfast, where the Church's administrative headquarters and Paisley's own ministry are based in the Martyrs' Memorial on the city's Ravenhill Road. Nowhere has the decline of the Church been so consistent or dramatic as in Belfast where, between 1971 and 2001, membership fell in each decade, from 1,360 to 714, a drop of over 47 per cent in thirty years.[2] If the Free Presbyterian Church was faring badly in Northern Ireland's first city, then it could not prosper in general. Free Presbyterian sources say that the slide in the city has been particularly marked in Ian Paisley's own church, "Martyrs" as most Church members call it. As one explained:

> He is at the stage now where he's not as sharp as he used to be. That's obvious in his preaching. The fire and fluency have gone and the sermons are a lot shorter these days. It's reflected in the Martyrs where the congregation has dipped and it has also aged noticeably. The days of 1,200 people seated in the pews are gone; he's now lucky to attract 100 on a Sunday.[3]

Officially the Church claims there are 500 communicant members at Martyrs' Memorial, or at least that was the figure given to author Steve Bruce for membership in 2002, but that figure is disputed by another Church activist. "They announced to us that they had 300 communicants and while that would have been the case ten years ago it is not now."[4] That figure was cited by Paisley's supporters to justify the size of the Martyrs' voting delegation that was dispatched to a crucial Presbytery meeting to decide Paisley's Moderatorship, but even so it represents a 40 per cent drop since 2002, if the figure supplied to Bruce was accurate.

—◄○►—

In decline or not, the Free Presbyterian Church during the years of the peace process still made up a significant part of the DUP's activists and election workers. For example, of the twenty-strong DUP Assembly team elected in the wake of the Good Friday Agreement, four out of five of them were Church members and at the 2005 local council elections, 47 per cent of the 171 successful DUP candidates were Free Presbyterians.[5] The DUP began almost as the political wing of the Church and, while its sway in these years was not what it used to be back in the 1970s, the party's dependence on its members for finance and election muscle in no small way shaped Paisley's response to the Good Friday Agreement and the efforts to craft a deal with Sinn Féin.

At first, Paisley invoked fears of an anti-Protestant conspiracy to mobilise the Church against the Good Friday deal. As 1998 began, he wrote in *The Revivalist*, the Church's monthly magazine, of which he was editor:

> This year will be a crisis year for our Province. The British Government, in cahoots with Dublin, Washington, the Vatican and the IRA, are intent to destroy the Province. The so-called talks process is but a front. Behind it the scene is set and the programme in position to demolish the Province as the last bastion of Protestantism in Europe.[6]

But such language was more appropriate to the 1960s; in the late 1990s it was calculated to embarrass and deter potential Protestant and Unionists allies. Would Bob McCartney, for instance, be entirely comfortable with an ally who espoused such a view of the world?

As the referendum campaign on the Good Friday Agreement got underway in May 1998, Paisley looked to Biblical scriptures instead for an argument that could mobilise and unite evangelicals against the deal, one that would also find an echo in mainstream Protestantism. After the four main church leaders – Catholic, Presbyterian, Church of Ireland and Methodist – urged people to vote "Yes", Paisley organised Free Presbyterians and other evangelicals to call for a "No" vote. The ruling Presbytery of his own Church issued a press statement which cited the Bible in condemnation of the deal. It said:

> The Free Presbyterian Church, recognising the Bible as our sole rule of faith and practice, vehemently opposes the recent April Agreement [the Good Friday Agreement]. Our opposition to the Agreement stems from the fact that it is unscriptural, unethical and immoral.

Paisley then persuaded leaders and members of other conservative and evangelical sects, like the Elim and the Reformed Presbyterians, to join with his ministers, 158 in all, to sign a petition opposing the Agreement, again on Biblical grounds, which was published in the *Belfast News Letter*. Their argument, he knew, would be well received by other conservative Protestants, especially in the much larger Presbyterian Church.

The anti-Agreement Fundamentalists believed that because the Good Friday deal opened up government office to Sinn Féin, and through them to the IRA, then that made the agreement immoral and contrary to the teachings of those parts of the Bible which deal with the nature and authority of government. Bible-believing Christians take the view that governments ultimately derive their authority from God and citizens therefore have a duty to obey government and to pay taxes in the same way as they obey God. But a government which consists of unpunished or unrepentant sinners cannot claim any divine authority and thus has no legitimacy. Since Sinn Féin acted as apologists for the IRA (or in some cases its spokesmen were IRA members), then the power-sharing government of which they were part, or due to be part, was full of sinners and thus illegitimate. This meant that until Sinn Féin and the IRA either admitted their past crimes and gave themselves up to the police for punishment or repented, no member of the Free Presbyterian Church could go into government with them and remain in the Church.

It was at Paisley's insistence that the Church took this stand. It was endorsed unanimously at the Presbytery and was binding on all members. In practice it meant that when Peter Robinson and Nigel Dodds took up ministerial posts in 1999 they could not have sat at the same Executive table as Sinn Féin, even if they had wanted to, without the DUP incurring the displeasure of the Church. A communicant member of the Church, one who has voting rights at Presbytery meetings, would have been expelled for doing this. Although Peter Robinson, at that stage a member of the Pentecostalist Whitewell Metropolitan Tabernacle, and Nigel Dodds, a non-communicant Free Presbyterian, would both have escaped such a fate, going fully into government at this time was not just a political impossibility, it had also been forbidden by the Church.

This stand also explains why Paisley called for the IRA to "wear their sackcloth and ashes" in November 2004, just as the post-Leeds Castle negotiations were reaching a climax. What he was really doing was sending a reassuring message to his Church that he would not go into government with Sinn Féin until the IRA had repented of its sins. The idea of wearing sackcloth and ashes is another Biblical precedent that has its origin in a Jewish custom of wearing a cloth made out of coarse black goat-hair as a sign of repentance and humility, while ashes, often dusted over the cloth, were included as a symbol of personal chagrin or shame. At the time, Paisley's comments were widely interpreted, by the media and both governments, as a calculated effort to secure the IRA's humiliation. There may well have been an element of that present but, if so, it was only part of the story. It was no coincidence that Paisley made these remarks at the North Antrim DUP Association annual dinner, whose councillors in Ballymena were some of the most fervent Free Presbyterians in the party and among those with the greatest reservations about going into government with Sinn Féin. Ian Paisley was talking their language and they understood exactly what he was saying, even if the rest of Ireland didn't.

This Biblical doctrine about the unacceptability of unrepentant sinners holding government office accounts in part for other hardline DUP demands made on the IRA and Sinn Féin in the lead-up to 8 May 2007. Genuine repentance in many Free Presbyterian eyes would have to include the dismantling of IRA structures, the Army Council included, full support for the police and the law-and-order system and the return of money stolen from the Northern Bank. By this stage in the peace process, these were also political necessities for the DUP but when Ian Paisley stood outside St Andrews on the opening day of the conference and called on the IRA to return "its ill-gotten gains", he was really addressing his Free Presbyterian constituency and trying to reassure it. This and the "sackcloth and ashes" episode have their counterpart in American electioneering as practised by George W. Bush, who is an expert at sending messages to his base in the US evangelical community which the media usually misses. In America it is called "dog whistle" politics and no-one does it better than Ian Paisley.

The third, and in its way most significant, implication of the Church's ruling is that it helps to explain why the DUP tried so hard to present talks with the British and Irish governments after 2003 as an effort to "renegotiate" the Good Friday Agreement and to present the St Andrews deal as an entirely new and different document. To have done otherwise or to have admitted the truth, which was that St Andrews was an adjustment to the 1998 agreement, not a replacement, would have meant that the deal negotiated by the DUP fell under the same Free Presbyterian condemnation, that it was "unscriptural, unethical and immoral". In which case Paisley's collision with his own Church might well have been more immediate and decisive.

As it was, the St Andrews Agreement did stir doubt and suspicion in the Church and, in early November 2006, some three weeks after the gathering in Scotland, a delegation of Free Presbyterian Ministers, sent from the General Presbytery, met Paisley at Stormont to register their concerns. A leading figure in the delegation was the Rev Ivan Foster, one of Paisley's oldest political and religious colleagues. Foster had once been prominent in the DUP, at one stage becoming the party's deputy leader. He had represented the DUP in the 1982 Assembly and was prominent in the party's two paramilitary wings, the Third Force in 1981 and Ulster Resistance in 1986, which he co-founded. But he was also a leading figure in the Church. "Saved" by Ian Paisley's preaching, he was ordained in 1967, and he has been Minister of Kilskeery Free Presbyterian Church in south Tyrone since 1978. In the wake of St Andrews, he would become Paisley's most scathing and persistent clerical critic.

Bob McCartney had also arranged to meet Paisley and the DUP leadership to question them about St Andrews but the day before his appointment he was in the canteen at Stormont when he saw a dozen or so Free Presbyterian Ministers, led by Foster, having a bite to eat.

> They all had glum faces and I said to Foster that it looks like a protest delegation and he told me they had a meeting with Paisley and Co. at 2.00 p.m. During my own meeting with Paisley the next day, I warned Paisley there would be a split of some sort or size in his party and he replied, "I had a delegation of Ministers in to see me yesterday and they gave me their full support." So that night I rang Foster to check and he said, "That is just quite untrue."[7]

In fact the meeting had been a precursor to the dissension that would later convulse the Church. Foster told Paisley that if he became First Minister he should not stay as Moderator of the Church and two weeks later he went public with his concerns. On the eve of Paisley and McGuinness being nominated as First and Deputy First Ministers, he told a BBC interviewer that such a prospect would be "heartbreaking to most, if not every, Free Presbyterian".[8]

Many Free Presbyterians harboured the same theological objections to the St Andrews deal as they had to the 1998 Good Friday Agreement, but there was one major difference which made their opposition this time much more intense. In 1998 there was no possibility of the DUP taking charge of government alongside Sinn Féin but the premise of the 2007 deal was that Ian Paisley would become First Minister and Sinn Féin's Martin McGuinness would be the Deputy First Minister, government offices that were legally defined as co-equal and joint. This was an arrangement that went to the core of Free Presbyterianism's being for it would mean their Moderator offending a piece of Biblical teaching that actually defines the

Church and what it stands for in Protestantism. The teaching is called the doctrine of separation and is popularly known as "the unequal yoke". The imagery behind the doctrine is of two entirely different animals, like an ox and a mule, being put in harness together and creating only confusion and disharmony. The doctrine is based upon the belief, supported by passages in the Bible credited to the missionary Apostle Paul, that true Christians should never associate with non-believers in their most important relationships and should keep separate from them. It is this doctrine which helps to explain the intense Free Presbyterian hostility towards ecumenical Protestant Churches and clergymen who interact with the Catholic Church. This and the Westminster Confession of Faith, which designated the Pope as "the Antichrist" and condemns the Mass as idolatry, are the two theological pillars upon which Free Presbyterianism rests.

But the doctrine also applies in other aspects of life, as one member of the Church explained:

> There is an understanding in our circles that while we meet, associate and interact with non-Christians on a regular, even daily basis, our most intimate associations must be with Christians. So that in marriage, business or worship the other parties must be Christians. The power-sharing deal between the DUP and Sinn Féin is very much a business relationship, so Paisley should not be associating with Sinn Féin on the grounds that they are not Christians.[9]

While all this was bad enough for Paisley, the doctrine does not end there. Fundamentalists usually interpret it to mean that Christians who are associated with the person offending this doctrine, such as a clergyman, are as guilty themselves if they do not call for the transgressor's removal or, having failed to achieve that, if they do not end their relationship. So in Paisley's case, the orthodox Free Presbyterian view would be that unless they succeeded in removing Paisley as Moderator, then they would have to quit the Church – to separate from it. That is what was at stake in the Free Presbyterian Church as the DUP prepared to enter and then did enter government with Sinn Féin. Either Paisley would go or the Church would split, the latter being a consequence full of irony, given the large part played in Free Presbyterianism's early growth by schisms in other congregations and churches rooted in the doctrine of separation.

—◄○►—

There was, though, another issue that exercised Free Presbyterians, one that in the words of one source, "nearly overshadows everything else for a lot of Church people". In July 2006, Northern Ireland Secretary Peter Hain approved a package of financial aid to gay, lesbian, bisexual and transgendered groups in Northern Ireland to promote sexual equality. The move was in line with the demands of the equality agenda agreed at the time of the Good Friday Agreement and the time had come to implement reforms in the realm of sexual minorities. Some stg£50,000 was earmarked in 2006 and given to the Coalition on Sexual Orientation (CSO) which represented the various groups. Funding was increased for 2007/2008 to stg£180,000 and, once devolution was restored, responsibility for administering this sum would pass from Peter Hain's office to the First and Deputy First Ministers' offices. This would mean that Ian Paisley, who had founded the "Save Ulster from Sodomy" campaign in 1977 in the face of what was eventually a successful effort to decriminalise homosexual acts in Northern Ireland, would be responsible for the funding of groups dedicated to advancing gay rights. To say that this scandalised the Free Presbyterian rank-and-file would be a huge understatement. Of all the evangelical churches in Northern Ireland, the Free Presbyterians were the most aggressively homophobic, taking their opposition to gay rights from a literal interpretation of the Book of Leviticus in the Old Testament which calls homosexual acts "an abomination".

The news that Ian Paisley would soon be funding gay groups broke just a few days before he and Martin McGuinness took office. The juncture of these events and knowledge that the Church would be outraged helps explain why Ian Paisley Junior took such a public stand against homosexuality soon after. In an interview carried in the May issue of the Dublin magazine *Hot Press*, he was asked for his views on same-sex partnerships which had been legalised in Northern Ireland in December 2005 and replied: "I am pretty repulsed by gay [*sic*] and lesbianism. I think it is wrong. I think that those people harm themselves – and without car[ing] about it – harm society . . . I mean, I hate what they do. I think they should just free them[selves] from being gay."[10] This was not the first time he had made such comments. In February 2005 he had called homosexual relationships "immoral, offensive and obnoxious" in reaction to a report that one of David Trimble's advisers, Steven King, had recently married his gay partner in Canada. The difference now was that Ian Paisley Junior was a junior Minister in his father's office which had responsibility for equality issues, including those affecting sexual minorities like gays and lesbians. SDLP and Sinn Féin Assembly members called for his censure, and that served to highlight the fact that his father was sharing government office with people who approved of homosexuality and deepened Free Presbyterian unease. When Martin McGuinness officially opened Derry's Gay Pride festival in August with a statement condemning discrimination, intimidation or violence against members of the gay community, the controversy worsened for Ian Paisley.

But there was more to come. Later that month, Belfast witnessed its fifteenth Gay Pride march, replete with coloured balloons, bands, outrageous costumes and floats, which travelled through Royal Avenue to end outside the City Hall where it was greeted by the ubiquitous Christian protest. This year the anti-gay protesters were particularly agitated. Partly that was due to a placard carried by one transvestite which declared "Jesus is a Fag", but what had really made them angry was that the parade had been made possible by a stg£5,110 grant from the Department of Culture, whose Minister since 8 May 2007 was Edwin Poots, a DUP stalwart and Free Presbyterian whose church's teaching forbade such support of "abomination". Both Edwin Poots and Ian Paisley argued back that they had inherited situations not of their making and were powerless to change matters. In response, the orthodox wing, people like Ivan Foster, replied that the men could make one of two choices: "One way is the way of political ambition and the other is the way of obedience to God's Word."[11]

The Free Presbyterians were not the only evangelicals in Northern Ireland dismayed at these advances in gay rights. When Peter Hain allocated funds for the CSO, he also announced new legislation outlawing sex discrimination and harassment against gays, with fines of up to stg£25,000 for repeat offenders, which would come into effect in January 2007. A group of fundamentalist churches, ranging from Baptists to the Free Presbyterians sponsored the Christian Institute, an English-based group with offices in Belfast, to challenge the law in the Belfast courts. When devolution went live that May 2007, responsibility for defending the suit fell to the First and Deputy First Minister's office because of its responsibility for equality matters. It was lawyers hired by Ian Paisley's office who defended the new law in court while the lawyers for the Christian Institute, who were seeking to overthrow the gay equality legislation, were paid in part with funds donated by the Free Presbyterian Church, whose Moderator was Ian Paisley. At one and the same time, Paisley was defending the law and trying to have it overturned. It would have been difficult to find a more perfect example of the conflict between his roles as First Minister and leader of his Church. As the campaign inside the Church against power-sharing with Sinn Féin gathered momentum, Paisley's opponents had been gifted a powerful argument that this incompatibility had to end.

―◁○▷―

The gay issue did not become a major matter of contention within Paisley's Church until he took office but before that, as it became increasingly clearer in the weeks and months prior to and after the March Assembly election that the DUP was heading into government with Sinn Féin, the theological and scriptural objections to the power-sharing deal fuelled ever-louder protests within the Church. At one time a figure beyond censure who had spent much of his career denouncing others, Ian Paisley was now increasingly on the receiving end of unprecedented and unwelcome vitriol.

In January 2007, Ivan Foster stepped up his criticism of Paisley and delivered a seventy-minute-long sermon which expressed outright opposition to the DUP leader's increasingly apparent willingness to embrace a coalition arrangement with the Provos. "We do pray for Dr Paisley," he preached, "and I never thought I would see the day that I would stand in this pulpit and say I think him wrong entirely and say I could never support what he is doing, but that day has come."

Soon others would be saying much the same thing. Each month except for July and August, the Free Presbyterian Church holds General Presbyteries, meetings of some 180 to 200 Ministers and Elders, which debate and vote on issues of concern to the Church. Each Minister in the Church can attend and vote and every Elder is entitled to be present but not all can vote; the number of Elders with voting rights is determined by the size of their congregation. The meetings, which usually take place on the first Friday of every month, move around Northern Ireland, taking in different churches. In previous years Presbytery meetings have been sedate, uncontroversial events but the prospect of a DUP–Sinn Féin coalition would make them arenas for ever-more bitter battles between Ian Paisley and his opponents. Everyone knew that the likely climax would come in September, the highlight of the Free Presbyterian calendar, when the Presbytery traditionally assembled at the Martyrs' Memorial, Paisley's church, for the annual election of the Moderator. Until 2007 the outcome of that election was always utterly predictable.

The first sound of dissent came at the March Presbytery which was held in Hillsborough, County Down, where the Minister, Stanley Barnes, was a devoted supporter of Ian Paisley. It was at this Presbytery meeting that Ivan Foster proposed a motion calling on Paisley to step down from the Moderatorship when or if he became First Minister "in the interests of the well-being and unity of the church". Explaining the motion, Foster said that the Church would be linked through its Moderator to a "political regime" which was "utterly rejected by many in this Presbytery and by many within the ranks of general church membership" because the new government would have "unrepentant murderers" in its ranks. The Free Presbyterian Church, he said, "must at all costs be yoked to none but Christ and His Word".[12] This was the doctrine of separation taken to its logical conclusion and underneath Foster's words lay the prospect, even threat, of a split, and the likelihood of church members leaving in protest if Paisley continued on his present course. It was a very confrontational motion that had within it the potential to create an immediate schism in church ranks. After heated discussion, Foster was persuaded not to press for a vote but during the exchanges Paisley made a promise not to sit down with Gerry Adams in any Executive until Sinn Féin had delivered the demands made on it by the DUP. As he spoke, the Assembly election campaign was reaching its climax and the government-imposed deadline for devolution was just three weeks away.

The April Presbytery meeting was held in Portadown and actually took place on 30 March because the first Friday in April was Good Friday, a busy and inappropriate day for such business. The meeting took place just days after Paisley and Gerry Adams had made their joint press appearance at Stormont to announce the formation of a coalition government on 8 May. Going into government with the Provos was no longer just a theoretical possibility and still there were no signs of the promised Sinn Féin repentance. The IRA's Army Council was still in place, the stolen Northern Bank cash was in IRA bank accounts somewhere and Sinn Féin support for the PSNI still untested. After the minutes from the previous meeting were read out, Foster got to his feet to ask whether or not, in the light of the decision to go into government with Sinn Féin, Paisley would now step down as Moderator. He had raised the issue under "business arising from the minutes", which had included a reference to the debate at the March Presbytery. Ian Paisley was in the chair and ruled Foster out of order, saying that he should have given notice beforehand. Normally when such a conflict of interest arises during a meeting, in this case Paisley ruling a motion about himself out of order, the chair steps aside until the matter has been resolved, but the Free Presbyterian Moderator didn't budge or make any offer to. The exchanges between him and Foster grew increasingly angry until finally Paisley declared, "No! I will not step down."[13] At that Foster said he could no longer stay in a meeting under Paisley's chairmanship and walked out, taking about a dozen supporters with him. "This was absolutely unprecedented," said a Church source; "such a thing had never happened before in the history of the Church."[14]

The May Presbytery meeting was no less fractious. It began with an attempt to discipline Ivan Foster and the others who had walked out of the April meeting with him. Disciplinary action could have entailed Foster's trial by a specially appointed Church Commission but it was equally possible that he and other dissidents could have demanded and secured a hearing in front of a full Presbytery. A guilty verdict would have meant Foster having to publicly repent by seeking the Presbytery's forgiveness – an unlikely possibility, given that he would effectively be admitting that he had been wrong to pursue Ian Paisley in the way he had. His refusal would have barred him from future Presbytery meetings and the wider effect would be to end his campaign against the Moderator, at least inside the Presbytery. Silencing Foster in such a way was undoubtedly an attractive prospect to the Paisley camp but it was a risky course to take. Foster's trial could well become a *cause celebre* and it would not be difficult to turn it into a crusade for free speech which the Church leadership might well lose. Foster told the Presbytery that he would welcome the charges as it would enable him to raise issues about the power-sharing government that so far he had been prevented from raising at Church meetings. This appears to have clinched the matter and the discipline charge was quietly dropped, replaced by a warning that if such a thing happened again, then action would be taken. The May Presbytery brought the first sign that sentiment was moving away from Paisley, as one present at the meeting described:

> Ivan was up in the balcony of the church and gave a speech
> from there and addressed Paisley directly, saying that this whole

501

division has come about as a result of the course of action on which he, Paisley, had launched himself and that it was breaking Free Presbyterian hearts to see Paisley going back on his word and making an alliance with a cold-blooded murderer. "No-one," he said, pointing to Paisley, "is to blame for the troubles in this church other than you."[15]

When Foster and his fellow dissidents had walked out of the April Presbytery, the meeting had barracked him, showing clear disapproval. But this time Foster received applause and a burst of foot-stamping. "It visibly shook the Big Man," recalled a witness. The meeting was again a turbulent one but a full-blown confrontation had been avoided. Summer was not far away, and there would soon be a two-month break in Presbytery meetings and time to prepare for what everyone knew was bound to be the crunch meeting in September.

It was not just the big issues – whether it was scripturally offensive to enter government with unrepentant Sinn Féin and IRA members, for instance – that influenced the Church's rank-and-file in these months, but also the small things which can sometimes be more revealing about motives and intentions. In late April, for instance, about two weeks before he and Martin McGuinness were to take up office, he was asked by an Ulster Television interviewer how long he planned to stay on as First Minister. "I am pleased you asked me that question," he replied. "I will serve the full four years. I will not be resigning."[16] The orthodox Christian view was that making such a confident statement about the future was wrong, that such matters were always in God's hands, not man's. They took their guidance on such issues from the Bible and the Book of Revelations which taught "Thou shalt not know what hour I will come upon thee." One Paisley critic observed: "A Christian would usually say, God willing, I will do this or that. The absence of that in Paisley's words was noted on a widespread basis."[17]

Another example came in the May edition of *The Revivalist*. In an editorial Paisley rounded on his critics, claiming that they were doing Satan's work, and he singled out Ivan Foster without naming him, claiming that he had failed to raise his concerns to his face and suggesting that Foster and others were really conspiring to take over the leadership of the Church. The editorial also made the astonishing claim that he, Ian Paisley, was God's "specially anointed" leader. Now it was not unusual for others, both in the Church and in the DUP, to say that

Ian Paisley was "God's man". His followers had been doing that for forty years but for Paisley himself to make the claim disturbed not a few, as one long-time associate noted:

> He would certainly have made the claim that he was speaking with the authority of the Word of God but that's not unusual, every preacher does that. But what he said runs so contrary to the spirit of Biblical Christianity that it made people cringe and tremble that he could speak about himself in such a way. I have never heard him speak in that fashion ever before.[18]

It was an extraordinary outburst by Paisley but it was also something of a missed opportunity. "It showed a lack of judgement," observed a Church insider. "He could have spoken words of peace, he could have reached out to his critics and disarmed his opponents, but he didn't."[19]

Ian Paisley's editorial went down badly but not as badly as an article written in the same issue of *The Revivalist* by Eileen Paisley, who for some years had been contributing a column entitled "Woman to Women" to the magazine. In another veiled attack on Ivan Foster, she criticised people who owed their conversion to Christianity and even their churches to Ian Paisley, and, taking up the theme that he was God's anointed leader, she went on to compare her husband to Moses:

> Like the Israelites of old treated Moses so they treat today's God-anointed leader. They refuse to believe that God is already working in the most unexpected places and in the hearts of some of the most unexpected people. Again, like the Israelites, they prefer to remain in the wilderness of the past than move into the promised land of a better and happier future.[20]

While the reaction of many in the church was along the lines of, as one put it, "Who does she think she is?", the real effect of the column was to convince people that it was "Mammy" who had led Ian Paisley astray and into power with Sinn Féin. Not everyone shares that view, however. "People blame Mammy," said one opponent of the power-sharing deal, "because they refuse to admit that it is really him, in the same way as they blamed Peter [Robinson] in the past."[21]

Whatever the truth, the two pieces in *The Revivalist* indicated that the Paisley wing of the Church was ready to go on the offensive. Ivan Foster had determined that the June Presbytery meeting would be showdown time but the wind was taken out of his sails when Paisley used the meeting to propose the establishment of a commission to investigate the issue of his dual mandate, which would sound out church opinion and report back to the Presbytery. If the purpose of the proposal was to long-finger the issue of his Moderatorship, "to fudge it", as his critics claimed, then it did not work.

The Stormont Commission, as the body was called, was headed by one of the Church's most respected clerics, the Rev John Greer of Ballymena, and consisted of sixteen members, half of them Ministers and the other half Elders, who framed their own terms of reference in conjunction with Church officers, Ron Johnston, the deputy Moderator, and Ian Brown of Derry. The Commission met in June and August and nearly every week there was one full day of hearings, with written and oral submissions from Ministers and lay members of the Church. Some Church sources say that the submissions came only from those who had been present at the June Presbytery, possibly because the constraints of time ruled out a wider canvass of opinion. A Church source took up the story:

> Basically the terms of reference were pared down to one crucial issue: take out the business of the unequal yoke, the unrepentant terrorists, take out the gay stuff and deal solely with the incongruity of one person being Moderator of the Free Presbyterian Church and chief magistrate [First Minister].[22]

Near the end of the summer the Commission met Paisley and told him the potential outcome of their deliberations. While they couldn't reach a consensus and there was a split amongst them, the majority opinion, by nine to seven, was that Paisley couldn't hold both offices. The Commission would be advising the Presbytery that the majority felt Paisley would have to choose between one and the other. He left them saying he would think about it.

July was a fallow month for the Church, as first the Orange marching season came to its annual climax, a busy period for many Free Presbyterian Ministers, and then vacations began. On Sunday, 8 July, Paisley went, as he did every year, to the pre-Twelfth open-air rally at The Diamond, Loughgall, where in 1795 the Orange Order was founded. Normally it was an occasion where he could be guaranteed a warm reception but this year he was heckled with cries of "Traitor" and "Lundy" by some in the crowd while others loudly demanded to know why, after everything he had said, he had gone into government with "murderers". The evening ended with the First Minister and Free Presbyterian Moderator being whisked away from the unruly crowd by his police escort. One of the protesters told a local reporter:

> Watching Dr Paisley being bundled into his car by the PSNI minders was reminiscent of watching David Trimble making his exit, hounded by DUP supporters. In fact, you can go back a lot further than that, for some of us were there when the same thing happened to Brian Faulkner and, before him, Terence O'Neill.[23]

As he did every year, Paisley then addressed the Twelfth of July celebrations held by members of the Independent Orange Order, a more religious, anti-political offshoot of the mainstream Orange Order. In 2006 he had assured the Independent Orangemen there would be power-sharing with Sinn Féin only over "our dead bodies" but this year it was religion, not politics, that dominated his speech. Criticism of Pope Benedict XVI for declaring Protestant churches as not churches in the proper sense but "ecclesial communities" in a recent Vatican paper was followed by an appeal to Protestants to turn back to the Holy Scriptures for truth.

The crunch Presbytery meeting gathered in Martyrs' Memorial on the evening of Friday, 7 September, with the Paisley lobby seemingly confident that their leader would make it through the night. The weeks before had seen intense lobbying by the Moderator's supporters, seeking to sway Elders who might be undecided. According to one source, they had tested the waters and concluded that Paisley would easily see off his critics. "One of the Doc's friends said that they had looked at every congregation in detail, worked out the numbers and reckoned that the 'No' camp would get at most 25 per cent of the vote."[24] Paisley's body language at the start of the meeting suggested that is what he believed as well for he came in full of gusto and exuding confidence. "Himself and Ron Johnston kept repeating the mantra, whatever we decide here tonight we must leave united and to me that suggested they were confident of winning," observed one source with knowledge of the evening's events.[25] The Martyrs' Memorial was packed that night in a way it rarely was for Paisley's Sunday services. Over 200 people had crowded in, most of whom were Ministers and Elders entitled to vote – even Kyle Paisley had travelled over from

Suffolk for the event. The remainder were non-voting Elders, spectators at the most dramatic night in the church's fifty-six-year history.

The proceedings began with the reading of the minutes of the last Presbytery meeting, followed by normal Church business, which took up a lot of time. Eventually it came time to discuss the Stormont Commission's report, which was first formally explained and then debated. The Commission had no recommendation to make to the Presbytery because it had not been able to achieve a consensus. But it set out the minority view and the conflicting majority opinion which members, led by the chairman of the Commission, the Rev John Greer, described. Motions arising out of the report were then duly constructed and proposed, some saying Paisley should stay and others that he should leave in his own time. Ivan Foster's motion said that the Presbytery should adopt the majority view in the Commission report and that Ian Paisley's name should not go forward as a Moderator candidate. But the next move left the meeting "flabbergasted", according to one source. The Rev Alan Smylie stood and proposed that the meeting move on to the next business, which was the election of the Moderator and the other church officers. Taking that route would mean effectively bypassing the other motions and taking no view on the Commission report. But the issue could not be avoided and Smylie's procedural ploy became the surrogate for the real issue: Paisley's continuing tenure as Moderator. To vote "Yes" meant Paisley would stay but "No" signified he was out. By all accounts the debate was an even-tempered affair in contrast to some of the previous Presbytery gatherings. "People spoke frankly but voices were not raised nor tempers lost," said one source. In the end, Smylie's motion was defeated by 112 votes to ninety six, a result that was by no means a comprehensive victory for the anti-agreement lobby but one that showed how closely divided the Church was and how damaging a split could be if the matter was pushed to a conclusion. Nonetheless, the vote demonstrated that Paisley had lost the battle.

Ivan Foster then rose to propose that there should be a vote on his motion. As a source with knowledge of the evening's events disclosed:

At this stage, Paisley turned to Johnston who was chairing the meeting and, knowing he was going to lose, asked for a short adjournment. He retired to the Minister's room and consulted with Johnston and Stanley Barnes, both of them allies, and then asked to meet the Commission. It was a very emotional meeting. Ian said that he would step down but wanted to stay on until January. He didn't want the world to know that he had been rebuked in such a way by his own Church, that he'd been told, "You're out!" It was very heart-moving. No-one in that room wanted to see him humiliated and they readily acceded to his request. Later people were told he needed to stay to see out bookings like Church openings but that was to cover the real reason.

Ivan Foster wasn't on the Commission but since he had just proposed the motion seeking Paisley's ouster, he was asked to join the meeting and was told what Paisley had asked for.

Ivan readily agreed but then said he wanted to say two things to the Doc. One was that if he had been strong on him and had used strong language then that was Paisley's fault since it was he who had taught Foster to fight in this way. The second thing was that he wanted to meet Paisley, have dinner with him and discuss it all.[26]

The two men, who had been colleagues and friends for so long but had ended up as foes, then embraced in the Minister's room.

Paisley, Foster and the Commission members returned to the meeting, where Foster formally withdrew his motion and Paisley announced he would be stepping down at the January Presbytery meeting. Paisley's humiliation had been avoided but it would never have been risked had he and his supporters judged the Church's mood better. The Commission Chairman, John Greer, then spoke and commended Paisley for his gracious behaviour and for avoiding a split, remarks that drew a round of applause, if not for Paisley himself then out of relief that the affair had finally been settled. At 1.00 a.m., after five hours of debate, the meeting ended with the singing of the Doxology:

> Praise God, from Whom all blessings flow;
> Praise Him, all creatures here below;
> Praise Him above, ye Heavenly Host;
> Praise Father, Son, and Holy Ghost. Amen.

An era had come to an end but, astonishingly, its coming had passed largely unnoticed over the heads of much of Northern Ireland's media.

While Ivan Foster's public assaults on Paisley had been covered, the existence of the Stormont Commission and the depth of divisions had gone undetected. Spin from the Paisley camp in the days before the Presbytery suggesting that Paisley would easily survive the meeting was accepted by many in the media and most journalists decided the night's events weren't worth covering. An enterprising reporter from the BBC, Martina Purdy, was one of the very few journalists to realise how significant the meeting could be and was there to record Ian Paisley's reaction as he left Martyrs' Memorial. "Wonderful!" he shouted, to a question about his feelings at the ending of his fifty-six-year reign as head of the Church he had founded.

That was, of course, not the end of the matter. By the following Monday, history was being revised, if not rewritten. "No, I did not make any offer" to stand aside, he told the *Belfast News Letter*. His explanation for the night's dramatic conclusion? "By what I can only describe as Christ's intervention, the atmosphere of that meeting suddenly changed . . . we wept and we rejoiced."[27] Within two weeks, he was hinting that he might not go in January after all. At a fringe meeting at the British Labour Party's annual conference at Bournemouth, an appearance that in the past both he and Labour would have avoided like the plague, Paisley was asked if he was still planning to step down, and replied: "You'll have to wait and see." Suspicious minds in the Church once again began to see the hidden hand of "Mammy" at work but there was other compelling evidence to suggest that Ian Paisley had indeed finally decided against a fight back. An attempt by his allies to pass a motion delaying the Moderator's election from January 2008 to the following September was ruled out of order and, since that traumatic meeting in September up to the time of writing, in December 2007, Paisley himself has not returned to any Presbytery meetings, behaving almost as if that chapter in his life had come to an end. Free Presbyterian sources say that as his role and position in the Church have faded, so sentiment against him coming back and the conviction that the right decision was made in September has hardened.

In the wake of Ian Paisley's departure, the Free Presbyterian Church faces more changes, according to some sources, that could fundamentally alter the part it has played in Northern Ireland's political life heretofore. There is talk of another Commission being set up – January 2008 is mentioned as the likely date – which will draw up a Book of Common Order, effectively a constitution that would set out rules and regulations and describe the government of the Church. The Church never had such a document before and matters like this were often decided at Presbytery meetings, an aspect of its administration that made it vulnerable to the whims and fancies of its leadership. Such a change would make it difficult for the Church to be dominated in the future by one man, in the way it was by Ian Paisley. The ability of Ministers to become politicians could also end or be severely curtailed, meaning that an Ian Paisley figure could never again rise from the ranks of Free Presbyterianism – although it is unlikely such a move would be backdated, leaving Ian Paisley and William McCrea secure in their political careers. Nonetheless, having ditched Ian Paisley as their leader, it now seems possible that the Free Presbyterian Church may be intent on clearing out the vestiges of Paisleyism.

Ian Paisley was not the only Free Presbyterian cleric damaged by the DUP's decision to go into government with Sinn Féin. The Rev William McCrea has also emerged from the episode a diminished figure, at least in the eyes of many in the Church. During the negotiations leading up to 8 May 2007, McCrea was seen as one of the most stringent opponents of power-sharing with Republicans. At St Andrews he held out for a lengthy testing time for Sinn Féin and at the famous dinner in London with Jim Allister and Nigel Dodds in March 2007, came out against Peter Robinson's compromise proposal for a May start to devolution. Those in the Free Presbyterian Church opposed to power-sharing with Sinn Féin who looked to Willie McCrea for leadership and support were heartened when he stood up in the House of Commons on the day after the Paisley–Adams press appearance and declared:

> As far as I am concerned, the idea of Sinn Féin in a Government is obnoxious. It makes me sick to the pit of my stomach. . . . Last week, I believed that Martin McGuinness was a terrorist with blood on his hands. I believed that he had been a murderer. I have to tell the House that I believe that this week, because he is the same person.[28]

Rumours persisted that McCrea was so opposed to the deal that he would publicly turn against it but in July he came out for the agreement, saying that critics of power-sharing with Sinn Féin were playing into the hands of Republican propagandists. Instead, he said, Unionists should celebrate a victory over the IRA. He declared:

> The Provos did not carry out 35 years of slaughter against the Unionist people of Northern Ireland to sit in a British Assembly

at Stormont, a partitionist Assembly, under the Crown and the Union flag. Every time [they] . . . pass through the gates of Stormont, they acknowledge their United Ireland ideas have gone up in smoke.[29]

McCrea's U-turn, from opponent to supporter of the deal, caused huge dissension in both church and party in Magherafelt and Cookstown, his main areas of support. An Elder in his church in Magherafelt was suspended for publicly opposing him, while the DUP branch in the town is so divided that, according to local sources, it stopped meeting after May while the branch in Cookstown met only fitfully. "Willie's favourite song at DUP annual dinners was 'The Preacher on the Fence' and that's what folk around here call him now, the preacher on the fence," said a local source.[30]

Beneath all these swirling currents lay two realities. As the Free Presbyterian Church was shedding itself of Paisley, the DUP is in a process of discarding the Church's influence, becoming more secular and, in terms of Unionist politics, more centrist. As more refugees from the Ulster Unionists have defected to the party, so the influence of evangelical fundamentalists has started to decline. The percentage of Free Presbyterians in the DUP's Assembly team in 2003, for instance, was 52 per cent, the lowest since 1975, and while precise figures for the 2007 team are not available, that proportion seems likely to have fallen even more.[31]

The more subtle, less computable changes provide more convincing evidence of this trend, such as the fact that at the DUP's annual dinner these days, wine is now offered where once only orange juice or water would have been available, or that at Ian Paisley's or Peter Robinson's table, one or two Catholics can be found, seated as welcome guests. As one former, admittedly disillusioned, DUP activist put it:

The new DUP is not made for street politics. It's full of special advisers, people who never had to look under their cars for IRA booby traps. They are people who are happy now that the Church has moved away from the party. The annual dinner used to be Willie McCrea singing "The Preacher on the Fence" but at the last one you had the guy from the "Folks on the Hill", Seán Crummey is his name, who gave a party piece based on a horse race for the leadership if Paisley went. Now ten years ago the concept of a horse race, with all the associations with gambling, someone called Seán compering it and making fun out of the leadership, well, that would have been so scandalous it never would have happened. The DUP dinner of today is an event to which guests are invited, businessmen, non-DUP voters, the whole ethos has changed, and that's all to make them appear as the party of government. That's all happened in the last three years or so.[32]

He might have added that none of this would have taken place, nor could have been possible, without Ian Paisley's say-so.

"*As I saw those tricolours around the City Hall, as I saw that evil man, the godfather of terrors galore, Gerry Adams, and the other murderous godfather, McGuinness, when I saw both of them I said, 'God deal(s) with evil men.' Yes, bloody and deceitful men will not live out half their days, that is what the Book says, and I am praying for funerals, that is what I am praying for.*"

IAN PAISLEY IN *The Revivalist*, MAY–JUNE 1997

"*We have had agreement at the end of the day after perhaps a fair bit of argument and stating our views but it has been courteous, it has been honest, it has been straight . . .*"

IAN PAISLEY ON HIS DEALINGS WITH MARTIN MCGUINNESS,
9 JUNE 2007, *Belfast Telegraph*

"*I think I can say, without fear of contradiction, that he and I have not exchanged one angry word between the two of us and I think the public will be pleased to hear that.*"

MARTIN MCGUINNESS ON HIS DEALINGS WITH IAN PAISLEY,
9 NOVEMBER 2007, *Derry Journal*

"*I sometimes laugh when I come into this room* [First Minister's office, Stormont Castle], *for I remember being in this room when there was some very hard words said by leading politicians from time to time. Here I am, sitting in peace in this room looking out three windows at the same time and looking over this beautiful place that Stormont is based in, and I have said: 'Well, one never knows what happens in one's life.' I never thought I would sit here, I never thought I would be in a place where I could really influence governments the way I wanted to influence them.*"

IAN PAISLEY, 11 JUNE 2007, *Belfast Telegraph*

CONCLUSION

The Self-fulfilling Prophet

It is the question everyone asks. Why did Ian Paisley do it? After all, he had spent a lifetime denouncing compromise and assailing every Unionist leader who came near to making peace with Irish Nationalism, even its mildest and least demanding elements; so why did he end up in government with those who had once been at Nationalism's most inflexible and violent edge, those he said he detested the most for their bloodstained ways?

If that question is put to those who were his colleagues in politics and religion over the years, who saw him up close the longest, the answers are varied but also remarkably similar for what they don't say about his motivation. There are those who credit, or blame, Eileen his wife – "Mammy" – for pushing him down this road, who believe that otherwise he would never have done it; but still others who insistently add that he needed very little pushing. Yet more suggest that his illness and the glimpse it gave of his own mortality played a part, at least in the timing of events. Some say it was his revenge, his way of getting back at the Unionist and Protestant establishment which had reviled and denigrated him for so long. And then there are those who claim it was his sense of history that drove him to this end or that it was done to satisfy an inner, hidden craving for respectability.

What is striking are the number of his past and present disciples who have come to believe there always was a concealed ambition in Ian Paisley, a part of his ego that yearned for power and was just waiting for the right time and conditions, and the presence alongside him of enablers with the required strategic skills to allow it to be realised and satisfied. What absolutely none of them say is that he did this because

513

he had finally recognised the errors of his past and wished to make amends before the end; that this was Ian Paisley's redemption.

Whatever the truth, in the end the answer to that question may be the simplest one of all: that he went into government with Sinn Féin because he could, and because the Provos made it possible. And since it was Ian Paisley more than any other single individual who had brought the Provos into being, it may be that ending up in power with Sinn Féin qualifies as one of the greatest self-fulfilling prophecies in modern politics.

Paisley's renown as a prophet, for being the political Moses of Northern Ireland Unionism, was earned at the very dawn of the Troubles when he helped bring about the fall of Captain Terence O'Neill, the modest reformer of Unionism, whose agenda involved nothing more threatening to Northern Ireland's place in the United Kingdom than friendly conversations with Dublin, some less than earth-shaking cross-Border co-operation and a commitment to be nicer, if not necessarily fairer, to Northern Catholics.

Paisley greeted O'Neillism with a blood-curdling prediction that the Prime Minister's compromising policies were the thin end of an apocalyptic wedge that could end in the destruction of the Unionist citadel and its absorption into the confessional Catholic state south of the Border. And so he set out to incite and agitate for O'Neill's overthrow and by so doing helped set in motion the very forces that made his prophecies seem so accurate and prescient to many rank-and-file Unionists.

Paisley was the self-fulfilling prophet from the start. Left alone, O'Neill's milk-and-water reformism would probably have satisfied the bulk of Nationalists and Northern Ireland would have been spared four decades and more of bloodshed and suffering. It was not Paisley alone who destabilised O'Neill and Northern Ireland, to be sure, but neither would have happened so completely or quickly without him. His gospel succeeded not just because there were so many receptive ears in the Unionist community but because he had special qualities – the oratory, the showman's skills and the ability to imitate and evoke Unionist icons – which in combination made his message so powerfully effective.

There were two consequences of Paisley's campaign against O'Neill and then his fall. As O'Neill retreated from Paisley's assaults, impatient Catholics rallied around the civil rights banner and, in the heightened sectarian climate, created in no small way by Paisley's protests against marches for political and economic equality, Northern Ireland was pitched into a summer of mostly anti-Catholic violence in 1969. With the IRA unable or unwilling to defend Catholic communities, the year ended with a split in Republican ranks and the creation of a new Provisional IRA dedicated to the destruction through physical force of the state seen responsible for its community's misfortunes.

Even though he had been its midwife, the birth of the Provos was seen by his followers as testament to Paisley's God-given powers of prophecy and, from that day on, the IRA's fortunes and those of Ian Paisley would go hand-in-hand. Since the IRA was, in important ways, Paisley's creation, it was fitting that when the IRA prospered or later its political wing Sinn Féin, then invariably so did Paisley. Each time the Republicans made advances, Paisley's renown as a clear-sighted prophet was confirmed and consolidated in the eyes of many rank-and-file Unionists, and more votes went his way. The truth about Paisley and the Provos is that they were yoked together from the very beginning.

The other consequence of O'Neill's downfall was that the Protestant middle class, embarrassed or intimidated by Paisley and dismayed by the downward spiral to chaos, deserted politics and left it to others, inevitably Unionists of a more rigid mindset, who were most susceptible to Paisley's charges of treachery and weakness. In such a way Paisley was given a veto over the programmes of other Unionist leaders who learned that to incur Paisley's wrath was to court disaster. The only Unionist politician unhampered by a veto was Paisley himself.

It was no accident surely that when the dust settled after the collapse of the Sunningdale power-sharing Executive and the humiliation of Brian Faulkner, the mainstream Ulster Unionist Party that he had led chose, as his successor for the next sixteen years, James Molyneaux, a figure who became a byword for caution and inactivity and whose political preference was for an alliance with Paisley rather than conflict or competition.

When the peace process brought another opportunity and David Trimble decided to try where Faulkner had failed, to craft a settlement with Irish Nationalism, Paisley was there to shout "Lundy" from the sidelines, as he had done in O'Neill's and Faulkner's day, and to pick up the votes of disillusioned and deserting Trimble supporters. And once again the iron law of Northern Ireland's political extremes ensured that in the era of the peace process, as before, Sinn Féin's rising fortunes went hand-in-hand with Ian Paisley's.

The means by which Sinn Féin overwhelmed the SDLP was also the route through which Paisley saw off David Trimble to emerge the leader and voice of Unionism. By delaying and then drip-feeding IRA decommissioning, Sinn Féin deepened a conflict with David Trimble that only the Provos and Paisley could win – Sinn Féin by rendering the SDLP irrelevant and Paisley by playing the role of trusted Protestant defender steadfastly opposing a compromising Unionist leader and a growing Republican threat.

And so the peace process ended with Paisley and the Provos, having fed off each other for nearly four decades, now the unchallenged masters of Unionism and Nationalism respectively. All that remained was to go into government with each other.

Again it was the Provos who had facilitated that option. In the decade or so since the IRA first declared a ceasefire in 1994, Ian Paisley was perhaps the most prominent Unionist sceptic, arguing that the IRA and Sinn Féin were engaged in trickery and deceit. He was of course wrong. The Provos' decision to make IRA violence a thing of the past was genuine, done not because they had turned against violence but because they realised the IRA could never win its war. Instead, like Collins and de Valera before them, Provo leaders decided to join the system they had tried to destroy and instead to try to dominate it using the ballot box instead of the armalite. This meant that defining elements of traditional Republicanism would have to be discarded and Northern Ireland's constitutional status quo accepted, a process they began to undertake during the talks that led to the Good Friday Agreement. Once Sinn Féin completed this journey and finally did for Paisley what they refused to do for Trimble and shed the last of their Republican garments, the final objection to joining with the Provos around the cabinet table dissolved. In the end, Ian Paisley went into government with Sinn Féin because he could and because the Provos made it possible.

—◄o►—

Paisley and the Provos, the DUP and Sinn Féin, approach their first anniversary in power together confident in the knowledge that as long as they maintain electoral dominance of their particular communities and do not fall out with each other, they can be sure that control of the government of Northern Ireland will be in their hands for the foreseeable future. The stability of the deal was further strengthened by Sinn Féin's disastrous general election performance in the Republic in May 2007. With a place in Dublin's coalition government denied to them for the foreseeable future and nothing else to show for their leadership's peace process strategy, Sinn Féin dare not risk losing what they have at Stormont.

The DUP has demonstrated its determination to stay in power and its unwillingness to fall out with Sinn Féin on at least three occasions in the months since Ian Paisley sat beside Gerry Adams at Stormont to announce their impending deal. In different ways, each compellingly demonstrated either the DUP's readiness not to press their partners on matters affecting IRA misbehaviour or a willingness to turn a blind eye to the activities of an organisation that has still not entirely gone away.

On 27 March 2007, the day after his appearance with Adams, Ian Paisley stood up in the midst of a House of Commons debate on a piece of emergency legislation introduced as a result of his deal with the Sinn Féin leader that would extend the devolution deadline to May, and told his colleagues that during his discussions the day before with Gerry Adams, he had raised the case of Robert McCartney whose unauthorised murder by leading IRA figures in 2005 had been covered up by Sinn Féin. "We raised that issue again," he declared, "and we said that we felt that it would be a great opportunity for Sinn Féin to do something about Mr McCartney's death. We got a promise that something would be done, and we look forward to something being done."[1]

The unresolved murder of Robert McCartney was a running sore in Northern politics. Sinn Féin's reluctance to endorse full co-operation with PSNI investigating detectives on the part of its members who had witnessed the killing was a metaphor for the party's unsuitability for government, and not just in the eyes of the DUP. Ian Paisley's remarks at Westminster suggested that a significant change in the Republican mindset had occurred.

Three weeks later, Robert McCartney's sisters trooped up to Stormont to meet Ian Paisley to discover what this promise had been and what, if anything, had been done. They were to be sadly disappointed, however, and emerged from Paisley's office after a mere thirty-minute encounter with the First Minister-in-waiting empty-handed. "Dr Paisley," Catherine McCartney told waiting reporters, "said that there were difficulties with the Republican organisation. Very senior members would have difficulties."[2] In other words, Gerry Adams couldn't deliver up Robert McCartney's killers because this would anger their friends in the IRA. This was a variation of the reason given by Adams and others in the Sinn Féin leadership for the slow and less than transparent process of IRA decommissioning not so long before and the principal cause of David Trimble's political ruin at the hands of Paisley and the DUP. Had the Ulster Unionist leader been the First Minister-in-waiting and had offered such an excuse a few days before he was due to enter government with Sinn Féin, Ian Paisley would have eaten him alive.

On 20 October 2007, Paul Quinn, a 21-year-old lorry driver from Cullyhanna in south Armagh, was lured to a farm near the Border town of Oram, County Monaghan, less than three miles from the Border, where he and a friend were set upon and separated. Paul Quinn was taken to a shed where a group of men, wearing boilersuits and surgical gloves, the IRA's customary active service garb, savagely beat him with iron bars and nail-studded clubs. The beating continued for half an hour and by the end nearly every major bone in his body had been broken. At around 6.00 p.m. the Irish police were called to the farmhouse where Quinn was found, barely conscious, and taken to hospital in Drogheda where he died.

Paul Quinn's family immediately blamed the Provisional IRA, and detailed accounts provided to the media by them, former Sinn Féin councillor Jim McAllister, and other local people, suggested that the young man had been killed in revenge after he had clashed, verbally and physically, with relatives of senior and influential IRA members in the area. "Paul Quinn had run-ins with the Provos, that's why he's dead," said McAllister. "To claim otherwise is lies."[3] Sinn Féin leader Gerry Adams and other party figures responded with a counter-claim that there had been no IRA involvement in the murder and that Quinn was killed because of a dispute between fuel smugglers, an assertion Quinn's family angrily rejected. The family, Sinn Féin figures maintained, was being manipulated to blacken the party's name.

The question of responsibility was clearly crucial, since if the IRA had carried out the killing, then the basis for the DUP's Executive partnership with Sinn Féin would have evaporated. It was the sort of issue that the DUP and Ian Paisley would have used to crucify David Trimble, had he still been the dominant Unionist political leader and in government with Sinn Féin. So how did the DUP respond? Three days after the murder, Jeffrey Donaldson told the media that "If the IRA were corporately involved in this murder, that may mean that the Executive is finished in its current form".[4] The use of the word "corporately" suggested that only if the IRA's Army Council had ordered the killing would the DUP be forced to act. Otherwise the killing would not disturb life at Stormont.

Under pressure from DUP dissidents, Donaldson modified his stand and then said that if any IRA member was involved, then he would consider Quinn's killing an IRA action. Four days later, however, Peter Robinson told the BBC that, on the basis of information he had, the killing had not followed "a decision taken at some central command". The incident emphasised nonetheless, he added, the need for the IRA's structures "to be closed down completely".[5]

Some two weeks later, confirmation of IRA involvement was given by the Independent Monitoring Commission, one of whose members, John Grieve, the former head of the anti-terrorist squad in London, told the media that although the killing was the result of a local dispute, ". . . we do believe that those who were involved in the attack on him – in his brutal murder – included people who are members or former members or have associations with members or former members of the Provisional IRA".[6] On the same day a detailed claim of "corporate" IRA participation in the killing was made under parliamentary privilege in the House of Lords by the former Ulster Unionist politician, Lord Laird, who named nine south Armagh IRA figures involved in the decision to "execute" Paul Quinn, as he described it. Altogether some twenty members or former members of the IRA took part in various phases of the assault and the killing had been sanctioned, he said, by the south Armagh IRA commander and by the IRA's Chief of Staff, a local smuggler and military commander of the IRA since 1996. The Chief of Staff traditionally has considerable latitude in making operational decisions, in which capacity he stands in for the full Army Council. His decisions are about as "corporate" as it is possible to get. When it became clear that local people were up in arms about Quinn's death, the Chief of Staff offered to pump money into the Cullyhanna area and warned local people, through an emissary, not to talk to the PSNI or the gardaí. Laird concluded: "The involvement of the Republican leadership in south Armagh in the planning, commission and now cover-up of this murder means that it is directly implicated."[7]

With individual IRA participation in Paul Quinn's murder confirmed by the IMC and detailed, credible allegations made about "corporate" IRA involvement, the DUP's response was to ask for a meeting with PSNI Chief Constable, Sir Hugh Orde, to discuss the matter. That was, of course, the same Sir Hugh Orde who told the DUP on 23 October that there was no evidence of IRA involvement in the Quinn killing and whose Assistant Chief Constable, Peter Sheridan, had assured the NI Policing Board that Sinn Féin was co-operating in the investigation into the murder of Robert McCartney, a claim made not long after the senior detective in charge of the inquiry had told the murdered man's sisters ". . . that there had been no useful co-operation, nothing had changed, those connected to Sinn Féin . . . [had] maintained their wall of silence". The McCartney sisters Catherine and Paula, already disappointed by Ian Paisley's inability to move Gerry Adams on their brother's case, went on to allege that since Sinn Féin had joined the Policing Board, there had been political interference in the PSNI inquiry.[8] The McCartney sisters' campaign to obtain justice for their murdered brother centred on the demand that those responsible should be made amenable in law and put on trial and that Sinn Féin should oblige eye-witnesses under their influence to give evidence in court. It is a demand that Sinn Féin leaders like Gerry Adams have either stonewalled or evaded. In the case of Paul Quinn, the DUP has not made a similar priority out of the search for justice for his killers. A cynic might say that the demand has not been made because its refusal would pose a fundamental challenge to the integrity of the DUP–Sinn Féin partnership.

Not long after the IRA announced that its war with Britain was over, the three IRA fugitives who had been arrested in Colombia in 2001 and charged with giving left-wing FARC guerrillas training in home-made mortar technology, returned to Ireland. The three had been found guilty in Bogotá of passport offences and were given bail but then went on the run. Their reappearance in Ireland just a few days after the IRA's July 2005 end-of-war statement was presumably no coincidence.

After their arrest in Colombia, an embarrassed Sinn Féin claimed that the three men had been in the country to study the local equivalent of the peace process, an assertion that only the most credulous took seriously. Undeterred by the widespread scepticism that greeted their explanation for being in Colombia, the most senior of the trio, James Monaghan, decided to write a book about the affair, which was published by Brandon in County Kerry, Gerry Adams's publisher.

The book, *Colombia Jail Journal*, appeared in the bookstores in November 2007, but the head of Brandon Books, Steve MacDonogh, announced that Monaghan, who was allegedly the IRA's engineering chief at the time of his arrest and rejoiced in the nickname "Mortar Monaghan", had pulled out of publicity interviews on the orders of the IRA. In response, MacDonogh angrily withdrew from the promotional campaign himself, saying: "That isn't the way Brandon does business."[9]

The significance of this episode, which was in itself inconsequential except to Brandon, is that it was compelling evidence that a high-level IRA command architecture was still in place, in spite of the understanding between the DUP and Sinn Féin that IRA structures, including the Army Council, would be folded up. The Colombian operation, which allegedly would have seen the IRA being paid millions of dollars for its mortar expertise, was devised, approved and controlled by the Army Council. It is difficult not to believe that the Army Council feared that Monaghan might reveal the truth about the IRA's Colombia expedition in television interviews and so moved to suppress them. If the Army Council interfered at this level, were there other areas of greater relevance to the government of Northern Ireland where it was exerting similar influence? Was Martin McGuinness subject to the same level of Army Council control as Jim Monaghan? If so, just when would the IRA leadership's meddling end? Judging by its silence on the matter, the DUP seemed less than eager to discover the answers to these questions.

The stark contrast between the DUP's disposition during these incidents and the party's indignant fury whenever David Trimble had been similarly exposed by IRA activity, leaves Paisley and his colleagues open to the charge that their campaign against the Ulster Unionist leader was disingenuous and mendacious, merely a ploy to exact political advantage and not, as they implicitly claimed, a principled effort to expose and correct failings in the peace process. Was it fear that double standards like this would be publicly aired, some asked, that explained why the DUP's annual conference in 2007 was postponed?

Others, like former DUP stalwart Clifford Smyth, point at this and other issues to raise a larger question about the meaning of Ian Paisley's long life and career as a Loyalist politician and church leader and come to a conclusion that, while undoubtedly cynical, is nonetheless shared and expressed by more than himself. "I now believe," said Smyth, "that his only consideration was to get to the top of the heap and that he used religion and politics as a route to power. He has become and maybe always was the consummate post-modern politician."[10]

Whether or not Ian Paisley's entire political career, or just the tactics he employed during the peace process, smacked of insincerity, the polling evidence suggests that for the moment the voters of Northern Ireland, Unionist and Nationalist, were happy with the DUP's decision to enter government with Sinn Féin. A survey carried out for the *Belfast*

Telegraph by MORI, published to mark the first 100 days of the power-sharing Executive, showed that 58 per cent of DUP voters now backed the deal, compared to 46 per cent just after the St Andrews Agreement. More significantly, 54 per cent of Sinn Féin voters felt that Paisley was doing a good job, while 48 per cent of DUP supporters felt the same way about Martin McGuinness.[11] There is also compelling evidence to show that, after a decade or so of gloom and pessimism, the Paisley-McGuinness deal gave a considerable boost to Protestant confidence about their future in Northern Ireland. Survey evidence put together by Northern Ireland's leading advertising agency LyleBailie and based on opinion polls conducted by Millward Brown between February 1995 and August 2007 pointed to a 42 point jump in Protestant self-assurance between the end of IRA decommissioning in September 2005 and the restoration of the Assembly in 2007. Pollsters had asked the question "How confident are you about your own personal future in Northern Ireland?" and the results showed that after a high point around the time of President Bill Clinton's visit to Northern Ireland in November 1995, Protestant self-confidence was consistently in negative territory for the ensuing ten years, in sharp contrast to Catholics, whose confidence levels were just as consistently positive. Only when the final power-sharing deal was clinched did Protestant confidence rise, from a low of minus thirteen to a positive twenty-nine. (See Appendix II.) As long as figures like these hold and show Protestant approval for what Paisley has done, the DUP has little reason to worry about IRA misbehaviour.

—◦—

From all the available evidence, especially the photographs of a smiling and laughing Ian Paisley at Stormont, there seems little doubt that the DUP leader and former Free Presbyterian Moderator is thoroughly enjoying life as Northern Ireland's First Minister. He and McGuinness appear to have struck up a genuine rapport and so far the Sinn Féin leader has not noticeably complained about Paisley's habit of regarding himself as the Prime Minister of Northern Ireland and McGuinness as his junior assistant. There is, though, judging by the record so far, one part of his duties that Ian Paisley must not relish, and that is First Minister's question time in the Northern Ireland Assembly.

During such occasions Ian Paisley Senior is usually seated beside his son, Ian Junior, who can be relied upon to prompt his father and pass appropriate documents his way. Paisley's first Assembly question time as First Minister on 11 June 2007 did not go well. The SDLP's Thomas Burns asked him about the appointment of junior Ministers in the office of First and Deputy First Minister, one of them Ian Paisley Junior. Was it not the case, he asked, that this was done to prevent proper scrutiny of the First Minister's office?

To which Ian Paisley replied:

> The Deputy First Minister and I have made it clear that the Office of the First Minister and the Deputy First Minister is totally committed to promoting equality and human rights. The First Minister and the Deputy First Minister are completely opposed to any form of discrimination and harassment against any citizen.[12]

He had answered a question about an entirely different topic, his son's controversial comments on gays, and hadn't noticed his mistake.

Three months later, something very similar happened. DUP Assembly member Ian McCrea, son of the Rev Willie, asked Paisley what progress there had been in efforts to recognise driving disqualifications on each side of the Border. Paisley replied:

> I would like to see a good relationship between both parts of this island without any political claims of jurisdiction by either one. We are not claiming that the South of Ireland should be part of the United Kingdom, and they should not claim that we should be part of the Irish Republic. That should be borne in mind. This is not a place for arguing constitutional positions: it is a place for arguing for the best arrangements for the ordinary people who can benefit from them.[13]

Once again it was the answer to a very different question.

Now, it may well have been that Ian Paisley Junior handed his father the wrong papers and a genuine, understandable mistake had been made. But Ian Paisley nevertheless continued to read the answers even though it was plain that they were the wrong ones. And he did so twice. There have been other mistakes. The DUP is opposed as a party to a new Single Equality Act, a Nationalist initiative to bring together all the separate existing pieces of equality legislation, on the grounds that Sinn Féin and the SDLP would probably want to add to them. The matter is a contentious one inside the power-sharing Executive but one thing the DUP wished to avoid was making any public commitment to a new

Single Act. At First Minister's question time in early September 2007, Paisley was asked if he would now commit himself to a timescale to introduce a new, unified Act. To the dismay of his colleagues, he replied: ". . . I wish that I could. I would like to do it tomorrow, but that is not possible. We must take time."[14]

DUP colleagues have other complaints, such as his tendency to behave as if he were the Prime Minister of Northern Ireland, rather than a co-equal First Minister with Martin McGuinness, and difficulties he has had both with his officials and in coping with the sheer complexity and scale of the office. The complaint is delicately phrased: "He's come to office just a little late in life," is the way one DUP source put it.[15]

At one point, in the autumn of 2007 when speculation that the new British Prime Minister, Gordon Brown, might call a snap general election was particularly intense, things got to the stage where a substantial body of opinion in the DUP, according to interviews conducted with elected members, believed that Ian Paisley should quit as First Minister and as party leader. One source at the time said that eight of the nine DUP MPs thought he should go, as did thirty three of the thirty six Assembly members. Another DUP figure put that number a little lower and estimated that around three-quarters of the Assembly party wanted a new leader.

He described the DUP's mood at the time in this way:

> We have this difficulty where a large body of opinion wants him removed and people like myself are saying you owe this man respect and loyalty, let him get his own way out. Some want him to stay because of fears about their future otherwise. Some want him to stay because letting him go would harm the process. Others want him to go because him staying would harm them politically and others want him to go because that would harm the process. So it's when the group wanting to avoid political harm to the process decide that he must go, that he will go.[16]

Another said simply: "The feeling that he should go is quite widespread but at this stage it is being said quietly." The conspiracy against Paisley was fuelled by the prospect of an early Westminster election and appeared to have been rooted in fears that internal DUP divisions would impact negatively on the party's likely performance. It would have been an extraordinary twist in the story of the peace process, but the plotting faded as the chances of an early election dissipated. The drama, however, has by no means come to a conclusion.

In November 2007, Ian Paisley repeated the pledge he gave before taking up office as First Minister, that he would serve the full four-year term, meaning that he will be 85 years old when he finally retires.[17] There is a strong view in the party that one reason he wants to stay on is to ensure that Ian Junior succeeds him and that the Paisley dynasty will be secure. But Ian Junior is far from being a popular figure in the DUP and he would make an unlikely contender. The controversy over his association with a County Antrim property developer, Seymour Sweeney, and allegations that he may have acted improperly when lobbying for a visitors' centre at the Giants Causeway planned by Sweeney would also make him a contentious candidate.

Until recently the succession was thought to have been Peter Robinson's for the asking. As the figure who strategised the DUP into power, he also has the support of Nigel Dodds who, at ten years younger, would be well placed to succeed him when he retires in turn. The prospect of Ian Paisley staying as First Minister until 2011, with the accompanying possibility that Ian Paisley Junior might succeed him, is not something either man would welcome.

The story of Ian Paisley's journey from street-corner preacher and political demagogue to power and respectability is one of the most extraordinary in Irish history. And it may yet have a Shakespearean ending.

—◦—

These days, Ian Paisley rarely sees his old friend Desmond Boal. Like Paisley, Boal is getting on in years and has been in poor health. Now retired from the Belfast Bar, he spends summers in Ireland but his winters in Florida, on the gulf coast where the skies are blue, the sun shines nearly every day and temperatures rarely fall below the mid-70s. Although the two men's association went back almost exactly fifty years, to the Fethard boycott, and Boal was at Paisley's side when the DUP was founded and has been an adviser and confidant in the years since, the DUP leader made his journey into government with Sinn Féin without the counsel or approval of his old friend. As was always his way, Desmond Boal has refused to talk to the media about his views on Paisley's partnership with the Provos and did not return phone calls from the author. When he meets old friends in and around Belfast though, it is a different matter and he leaves them in no doubt about his feelings, as one recounted:

Desmond is so angry he can hardly talk about it. A while back he bumped into Rhonda [Paisley's daughter] and said to her that he wanted to speak to her father but that what he had to say, he'd rather say under his own roof. Eventually Paisley came to see him and Desmond spent well over an hour berating him, saying he had lied, that he had betrayed everything he stood for. Paisley just sat there, not saying a word, with his head hanging. Eventually he got up to leave and said, "Well it would have been different, Desmond, if you hadn't left."

APPENDIX I

The following is the exact text of the notes taken by a DUP dissident at an internal DUP meeting held in Lurgan in late October 2006, to discuss the St Andrew's Agreement. (*Comments by the dissident are in italics.* Square brackets are mine and indicate an explanation. St A A is St Andrews Agreement.)

Democratic Unionist Party Consultation meeting for members of South Down, Lagan Valley, Upper Bann and Newry & Armagh Associations, held in Lurgan Town Hall on Thursday 26th October 2006 at 8 pm.

Meeting commenced at 8.20 pm'ish.

Town Hall and balcony were packed, with some folks standing at rear.

Lord Morrow, Party Chairman operated as meeting Chairman and after a Scripture reading and prayer from Dr Paisley, Maurice Morrow outlined the meeting's format:– we had to vacate the building by 11 pm, Peter Robinson would outline the path leading to the St Andrews agreement, Dr Paisley would offer an address which would be followed by a Q & A time. Following this, forms would be handed out asking people to indicate whether the leadership had the support of the members and also the form would have space for comments to be made.

Peter Robinson made light hearted jests on trivial matters before introducing a Power Point presentation with the following issues:–

Plus points of the St Andrews Agreement –

- Changes to the Belfast Agreement
- Fundamental changes to the B.A. – *accountability was stressed*
- DUP Veto, no decisions taken without Unionist approval
- DUP Veto on North–South decisions
- Significant DUP influence on all Government decisions (*not specified how they would influence or where this "promise" is in legislation!*)
- Retention of Academic Selection (*P.R. made reference to a letter he thought that Dr P. had regarding this and asked Dr P if it was from the P.M. Dr P. nodded in acknowledgement*)
- Cap on Rates (*no details!*)
- Local control on issues such as water charges (*really licking the bottom of the barrel for + points!*)
- Ability to stymie the RPA [Review of Public Administration] and its all-Ireland agenda (*no details on how this would happen*)

527

- SF must give full support to Police and Courts *(some time spent expounding this)*

Constant heckling and questions relating to the vagueness of much of these issues, response to questions and heckling consisted entirely of sarcasm.

- An end to all IRA paramilitary and criminal activity *(despite questions as to how this would be measured, no answer was forthcoming, just more sarcasm)*

- A testing period to ensure republicans have delivered (Spring – March 2007)

- An end to Unionists jumping first *(why jump at all? More sarcasm)*

- An election for the community to pass its verdict (PR – Dr P had an assurance that it would be an election and not a referendum. *(Pressed for evidence – more sarcasm)*

- End to 50/50 recruitment when 30 per cent of PSNI is R.C. *(PR thought this would be in 12 to 18 months)*

- DUP veto on devolution of Policing & Justice powers *(PR didn't know why the press were giving May 2008 as the date for this – as the DUP had secured a veto on the devolution of these powers)*

- Significant financial package for Northern Ireland

- Policing devolved – agreed by First Minister

Went on to illustrate very quickly, too quickly to actually read on screen, the B.A. [Belfast Agreement] versus St Andrews A. as per points in "Your Verdict – What Is It To Be?" document.

Continued heckling and a point made – you have agreed to put soldiers out of work and IRA men and ex-prisoners into jobs! More sarcasm.

Irish language – would have to be issued for consultation putting forward four options *(didn't elaborate)*

It was pointed out that it was part of the St A. A. with no mention of a consultation, he insisted it could not be actioned until or if it was agreed by the assembly!

Matter of Irish Republic citizens entering the NI Civil Service was on screen as "EU Nationals" and not commented on.

No private understandings, all undertakings had to be made available before any decision was made.

As SF would not be in a position to offer support to PSNI by Nov. 10th, the DUP executive would meet to determine on what basis the DUP will move forward.

PR left to attend his council meeting amid jovial remarks about the best council in NI.

Dr P. commenced his address on the same jovial theme before going on to stress his own credentials. He would not be surrendering and would not be for turning. He had the wording for a pledge for SF to sign up to which would entail them naming the PSNI as the only legitimate policing service in NI and once SF had signed up to this, SF and republicanism would be destroyed.

A lot of heckling and disbelief at what had just been said.

Dr P went on to reiterate that the pledge would tear SF asunder and the IRA he would be in Government with would not be the SF of today. *Much more heckling, asking why he was even considering going into gov. after stating he wouldn't? Dr. P. found it difficult to be heard due to the level of heckling at this stage, it continued for quite a while and he refrained from even trying to speak. A dose of his own medicine!*

Being the brilliant orator that he is, Dr P. responded to the heckling by stating that of the meetings that had already taken place, when the forms had been counted, 92 per cent of the party had given their support to his leadership and that he could be trusted.

He agreed and reiterated that Tony Blair had assured him that there would definitely be an election and not a referendum and that he had the final say on whether it would be an election or referendum!

He then went on to berate Bob McCartney, mocking his claim that the DUP would not be the largest party in any new assembly if he put forward candidates in Unionist constituencies. The DUP had trounced Bob McCartney before and would do it again.

There would be no deal until the IRA had *delivered*. Any new assembly would not be a "love in" for the DUP and SF unlike the situation with the UUP, there would be supping of tea and no liquor, but then you know I would not be supping liquor anyway. The relationship with tomorrow's SF would be honest and straightforward. There would be a barrier between them. I am confident that a good day is coming for NI.

Q.&A.

Some questions were difficult to hear. They were taken in batches of four or five at a time. One of the first was what was required for SF to enter Gov.?

A. To deliver.

J. Donaldson answered most of the questions with Dr P. putting his penny worth in now and again. Without exception, all questions were answered with a heavy presence of sarcasm. One Q. from the balcony appeared to be from a DUP councillor who announced his disapproval over the party's stance on the section 75 regarding homosexuality. He said he was told something by Dr P. A pantomime pursued [sic]. Oh yes you did, oh no I didn't, etc. J.D. said he would be surprised if he had have been told what he claimed and went on to the next answer.

While Maurice Morrow had asked those posing the Qs to keep them structured and short, he addressed remarks to J.D. that he expected the As to be equally structured and short without engaging in making statements.

Another Q. asked about the legislation on consenting adults and "toilet sex" etc. J.D. responded by implying that if the assembly was back, this issue could be addressed more.

Q. how long does it take for an unrepentant terrorist to become a democrat? Q. was not answered. Person left after being unable to induce a response.

Much heckling and questions why DUP was even considering gov. with SF?

Dr P. again stated that SF would have to specifically mention PSNI in pledge and this would bring SF Republicanism to an end because SF was built on opposition to the police. Then there would be an election, and it would be an election and it would soon be in legislation that it would be an election and not a referendum. *Dr P. again severely heckled and unable to continue speaking.*

Alan Mitchell from Armagh asked whatever happened to the no guns, no government stance? He was laughed at and reminded that that was a UUP slogan. Someone shouted well what have SF to do, the answer, to deliver.

Many people shouting and demanding to know what had happened to decommissioning, transparent and verifiable decommissioning and pictures of same.

J.D. retorted that if we insisted on seeing pictures, then the DUP would be handing a veto on democracy to the Army Council.

Much more heckling.

Dr P. – when IRA accepts the PSNI pledge the IRA will cease to exist, therefore he will not be in Gov. with IRA. The IRA that he will be going into Gov. with will be stripped of its power. Now we could see our way through the Red Sea with this pledge. PEOPLE CANNOT CONTINUE VOTING FOR THE STATUS QUO. When you are in opposition you can say anything you like, but when you are in a position of power like the DUP now is, then things are different. *In blackmailing tones he shouted* that we either support the St A's A. or we get ready for worse, outlining the seven super-councils, ability of Rep. of Ireland to control affairs in NI etc.

The hall echoed with shouts of blackmail.

J.D. who was very riled, responded that it was not blackmail, but what would happen. He also reminded the meeting that the status quo was not a viable proposition.

Jim Allister rose to speak. Having listened to his party colleagues expound the St A. A. he said he would not be putting any spin on his position. It was true that the party stood at a crossroads. It had to decide if it was going to enter gov.

with SF's blood brothers in the IRA on March 26th. Under the terms already discussed, there was no test for SF/IRA. St A. A made no compulsion for SF to commit to policing and rule of law. J.D. was condemned for his current stance on decommissioning. His stance offered incomplete decommissioning, the issue of the Army Council as expressed in the Seven Principles (no. 4) [disbandment of Army Council] was not addressed, the IRA was no longer required to go out of business, nor was the issue of ill-gotten gains even mentioned.

St A only amends the BA, it does not replace it. When St A. A. mentions the BA it refers to it as a capital A, while reference to the St A. A. gets a small a. The fundamental structures of the BA were still in place. The presentation showing the BA versus the St A. A. was very misleading. The party had failed to address the issue of mandatory coalition. Claiming that it was in "the matters in progress" was misleading, they knew what the outcome would be, the nationalist parties were not going to agree a voluntary coalition arrangement.

More cross-border bodies were being established, this was not addressed either, and more importantly, the issue over the new assembly having to recognise the joint nature of the office of the First and Deputy First Minister! In fact the situation regarding this matter was actually worse as every single member of the assembly would have to acknowledge the joint nature of the office.

Arguing with Dr P. took place for a few moments.

J.A. continued and finished his address with a quotation from Gerry Adams after reminding us that Dr P. had earlier quoted from Young SF. Adams had reassured Republicans that what was on offer, perfectly fitted in with the current phase of the Republican aim of a united Ireland.

Dr P. then stated that he would not stand for J.A. issuing libel and slander against leading members of his party. He said J.A. needed to remember that he was not the leader of the DUP, I am. *A loud cheer.*

There were lots of exchanges between J.A. and Dr P. but they couldn't be heard.

Maurice Morrow attempted to gain control of the chaos when David Simpson indicated he wished to speak.

D.S. said he would not speak for long and he merely said he fought the last election on the basis of a fair deal for Unionist people, we still haven't got a fair deal. If the St A. is all there is, I will not agree to it. But we need to remember that much of it is still work in progress.

More people indicated that they had questions to ask, M.M. pointed out the time and the voting forms were handed out to members only. As they were being collected, the glossy "Your Verdict" document was distributed.

National Anthem

531

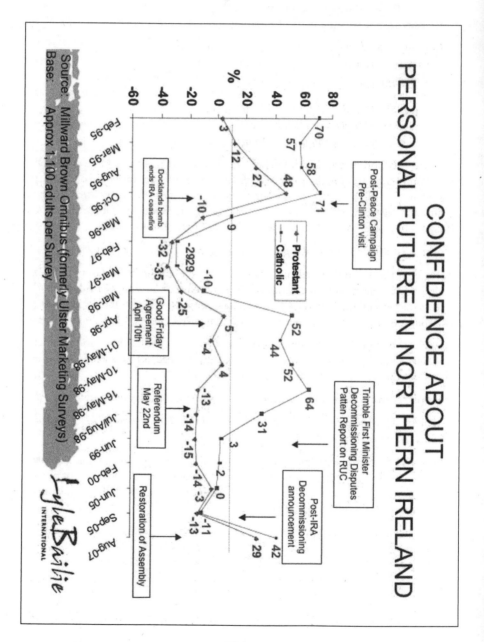

CONFIDENCE ABOUT
PERSONAL FUTURE IN NORTHERN IRELAND

NOTES

INTRODUCTION

1 *Irish Times*, 17 December 1994.

2 *New York Sun*, 22 June 2005.

3 *New York Times*, 20 March 1983.

4 *Irish Times*, 17 December 1994.

5 BBC NI News, 27 May 2005.

6 *Washington Post*, 5 May 2005.

7 *The Greenville News*, 16 January 2007.

CHAPTER ONE

1 In 1926 the make-up of Armagh City Council was: Catholic Labour 8 seats; Nationalist Combine 4 seats; Unionists 6 seats.

2 According to local historian Oliver Gibson, himself an Omagh DUP councillor, the Republicans had been in two minds about the attempt anyway, believing mistakenly that the barracks was too heavily guarded.

3 *The Baptist Magazine*, 1923.

4 "My Father and Mother" – two sermons preached by Paisley on 22 August 1973 and 9 April 1972.

5 David Taylor, "The Lord's Battle: An ethnographic and social study of Paisleyism in Northern Ireland." PhD, thesis, Queen's University Belfast, 1983. pp. 123-27.

6 Rev R.J. Beggs, "Great is Thy Faithfulness: an account of the ministry of Pastor Kyle Paisley and a history of the separatist testimony in Ballymena".

7 "The Four Windows of Life" – two sermons preached by Paisley; summer 1983.

8 "This is my Life" – taped series of sermons by Paisley, Part 1, 1979.

9 Michael Farrell, *The Orange State*, London, 1976, pp. 85–86.

10 *Belfast Telegraph*, 22 June 1946, church notices.

11 "The Four Windows of Life".

12 Paul Blanshard, *The Irish and Catholic Power*, Connecticut, 1953, p. 234.

13 *Irish News,* 1 June 1948.

14 All examples from John Whyte, *Church and State in Modern Ireland*, Dublin, 1971, pp. 163–93.

15 Interview with "The Voice of Ulster", December 1982.

16 Conversation with Lord Fitt, April 1986.

17 He also had his first writ served on him, to prevent him from abusing a Labour election agent whom he was accusing of having tricked a loyalist worker into signing Downey's nomination papers – Conversation with Jack Myers, May 1986.

18 *Belfast Telegraph and Northern Whig*, 14 August 1950, and conversation with Rev John Brown, former County Antrim Grand Master.

19 Conversation with Jim Welsh, May 1986.

20 *Woman's Own*, 24 May 1986, and conversations with former members of Ravenhill Free Presbyterian Church.

21 Reprinted in *The Revivalist*, December 1967.

22 *Northern Whig*, 21 March 1951.

CHAPTER TWO

1 Interview with Orange Order member.

2 *The Revivalist*, April 1955.

3 *The Revivalist*, August 1955.

4 *Belfast Telegraph*, 15 October 1953.

5 *Belfast Telegraph*, 19 April 1952.

6 *Northern Whig*, 9 June 1954.

7 Paul Blanshard, p. 226.

8 *The Irish and Catholic Power*, p. 233.

9 *The Revivalist*, January 1957.

10 *Belfast Telegraph*, 21 December 1956.

11 *Irish News*, 21 December 1956.

12 *Belfast Telegraph*, 11 May 1957.

13 *Belfast News Letter*, 13 July 1957.

CHAPTER THREE

1 *Belfast Telegraph*, 18 March 1958.

2 *Irish Times*, 13 August 1959.

3 *Belfast News Letter*, 12 April 1954.

4 *Belfast News Letter*, 8 October 1959.

CHAPTER EIGHT

1 Ian Paisley, *The "Fifty Nine" Revival*, Belfast, 1958.

2 "This is My Life" – series of taped sermons by Paisley, part 2.

3 *The Revivalist*, June 1955.

4 *The Revivalist*, October 1955.

5 *The Revivalist*, November 1961.

6 Apostasy is one of Paisley's favourite charges against other Protestant churches and the World Council of Churches. He explains to his congregation that it is derived from the Greek word for "falling away" and thus means the abandonment of the true Christian faith.

7 *The Revivalist*, February 1959.

8 *The Revivalist*, June–July 1962.

9 *The Revivalist*, July–August 1957.

10 *The Revivalist*, April 1962.

11 *The Revivalist*, September 1959.

12 Alan Bestic, *Praise the Lord and Pass the Contribution*, London, 1971, pp. 85–9. Bestic visited Rockford and talked to Robert Hansen's ex-wife, who said he had been a minister in the Church of Christ, a fundamentalist Baptist sect, but had left to start his own church. She said he was a great preacher but mentally deranged. Also *Christianity Today* (Washington, USA), 9 May 1960: "The Scandal of Bogus Degrees".

CHAPTER NINE

1 Clifford Smyth, "The Ulster Democratic Unionist Party: A case study in political and religious convergence", PhD. thesis, Queen's University Belfast, 1983, p. 27.

2 *The Times*, 3 August 1971.

3 *Irish Press*, 15 March 1971.

4 *Irish Times*, 29 November 1971.

5 *Irish Press*, 29 November 1971.

6 *Irish Times*, 29 November 1971.

7 *Sunday Independent*, 12 December 1971.

8 Interview with David Trimble, September 2007.

9 David Boulton, *The UVF 1966–73: An Anatomy of Loyalist Rebellion*, Dublin, 1973, p. 149; *Belfast News Letter*, 1 December 1971; *Sunday Times*, 12 December 1971.

CHAPTER TEN

1 LWT Weekend World, 14 December 1980.

2 *The Carson Trail,* Foreword, Belfast, 1981.

3 *Irish Times,* 9 February 1981.

4 *The Carson Trail,* p. 35.

5 *Irish Times,* 20 February 1981.

6 *The Carson Trail,* p. 36.

7 Interview with Cedric Wilson, September 2007.

8 Simon Hoggart, *The Guardian* – "A stone's throw away from independence?" 4 June 1973.

CHAPTER ELEVEN

1 "Monaghan, County of Intrigue: An insight into the political, legal and religious intrigues in this Border area during the period 1968–1979", M. Ó Cuinneaghain, unknown binding, 1979.

2 *Irish Times,* 14 January 1987.

3 *Irish Times,* 15 January 1987.

4 *Irish Times,* 8 August 1986.

5 *Irish Times,* 14 January 1987.

6 *Irish Times,* 14 January 1987.

7 Interview with Cedric Wilson, September 2007.

8 *Irish Times,* 4 January 1986.

9 *Irish Times,* 24 April 1986.

10 *Irish Times,* 4 January 1986.

11 *Irish Times,* 9 August 1986.

12 *Irish Independent,* 19 November 1986.

13 *Irish News,* 11 November 1986.

14 *Belfast Telegraph,* 18 November 1986.

15 Ibid.

16 Ibid.

17 *Irish Independent,* 19 November 1986.

18 *Sunday Tribune,* 30 April 1989.

19 *Belfast Telegraph,* 18 November 1986.

20 *Belfast Telegraph,* 20 November 1986.

21 *Belfast News Letter,* 15 November 1986.

22 *Belfast Telegraph,* 18 November 1986.

23 *The Independent,* 24 April 1989.

24 Confidential information, UDA source, 1989.

25 Conversation with DUP source, June 1989.

26 Interview with former DUP member, September 2007.

27 *Belfast Telegraph*, 24 April 1989.

28 Interview with former DUP member, September 2007.

29 Conversation with DUP source, June 1989.

30 Interview with DUP member, September 2007.

31 *Irish Times*, 23 April 1987.

32 Interview with Cedric Wilson, September 2007.

33 *Irish Times*, 13 May 1997.

34 "An End to Drift", Task Force report, 16 June 1987.

35 *Irish Times*, 7 July 1987.

36 "An End to Drift", p. 7.

37 Report on Duisburg Conference, October 1988. Author's copy.

38 Report on Duisburg Conference, October 1988. Author's copy.

39 Interview with Cedric Wilson, September 2007.

40 Interview with Cedric Wilson, September 2007.

CHAPTER TWELVE

1 By the time the peace process began, the Official Unionist Party was more widely called by its proper title, the Ulster Unionist Party.

2 *Irish Times*, 26 April 1993.

3 See Appendix 8, Ed Moloney, *A Secret History of the IRA*, Penguin, July 2007, London.

4 *Irish Times*, 15 February 1994.

5 *Irish Times*, 29 November 1993.

6 *Irish Times*, 29 November 1993.

7 *The Observer*, 28 November 1993.

8 *The Observer*, 28 November 1993.

9 *The Irish Times*, 30 November 1993.

10 Conversation with DUP source, 8 June 1989.

11 Appendix 7, Ed Moloney, *A Secret History of the IRA*, Penguin, July 2007, London.

12 Paul Bew and Gordon Gillespie, *Northern Ireland – A Chronology of the Troubles, 1968–1999*, Gill and Macmillan, Dublin, 1999, p. 285.

13 *Irish Times*, 16 December 1993.

14 *Irish Times*, 8 September 1994.

15 *Irish Times*, 9 September 1995.

16 *Irish Times*, 11 September 1995.

17 Interview with author, September 2007.

18 Interview with ex-UKUP member, September 2007.

19 Dean Godson, *Himself Alone – David Trimble and the Ordeal of Unionism*, Harper Collins, London, 2004, pp. 116–117.

20 Godson, p. 160.

21 George J. Mitchell, *Making Peace*, University of California Press, London, 2000, p. 47.

22 *Irish Times*, 13 June 1996.

23 Mitchell, p. 90.

24 *Irish Times*, 2 December, 1996.

25 Mitchell, p. 93.

26 Interview with Bob McCartney, September 2007.

27 Interview with Cedric Wilson, September 2007.

28 Interview with DUP member, September 2007.

29 E-mail from DUP source, October 2007.

30 See Appendix 7, *A Secret History of the IRA*.

31 Sir Kenneth Bloomfield, *A Tragedy of Errors: The Government and Misgovernment of Northern Ireland*, Liverpool University Press, Liverpool, 2007, p. 209.

32 Mitchell, p. 110.

33 Interview with David Trimble, September 2007.

34 Mitchell, p. 177.

35 Interview with Billy Hutchinson, September 2007.

36 Interview with David Trimble, September 2007.

CHAPTER THIRTEEN

1 Interview with DUP source, October 2007.

2 Ed Moloney, *A Secret History of the IRA*, Penguin, 2007, pp. 520–21.

3 Confidential information from sources in NI, Republic of Ireland and US.

4 *Irish Times*, 27 May 1998.

5 *Irish Times*, 8 June 1998.

6 *Irish Times*, 16 May 1998.

7 Speech to DUP conference by Ian Paisley, 28 November 1998.

8 Interview with Irish government source, October 2007.

9 Interview with former US government official, August 2007.

10 Dean Godson, *Himself Alone: David Trimble and the Ordeal of Unionism*, HarperCollins, London, 2004, Chapter 27.

11 *Guardian Special Reports*, 14 March 2007.

12 *The Blair Years: The Alastair Campbell Diaries*, Alfred A. Knopf, New York, 2007, p. 412.

13 *Irish Times*, 5 May 2000.

14 *Irish Times*, 23 September 2000.

15 *Campbell*, p. 489.

16 *Irish Times*, 19 May 1998.

17 *Belfast News Letter*, 16 May 1998.

18 Interview with Bob McCartney, September 2007.

19 Interview with Cedric Wilson, September 2007.

20 Interview with Bob McCartney, September 2007.

21 Interview with DUP member, September 2007.

22 Interview with David Trimble, September 2007.

23 Interview with Billy Hutchinson, September 2007.

24 IRA statement, 6 May 2000.

25 Interview with Cedric Wilson, September 2007.

26 Speech to DUP conference, Enniskillen, 18 November 2000.

27 *Irish Times*, 28 October 2000.

28 *The Guardian*, 13 March 2007.

29 Godson, p. 686.

30 *Guardian Special Report*, 14 March 2007.

31 *Irish Times*, 24 November 2001.

32 Interview with Irish government source, October 2007.

33 Interview with Irish government source, October 2007.

34 Interview with David Trimble, September 2007.

35 DUP manifesto, 2003.

36 DUP manifesto, 2003.

37 *Irish Times*, 30 November 2003.

CHAPTER FOURTEEN

1 *Irish Times*, 28 November 2003.

2 Interview with Irish government source, October 2007.

3 Interview with Irish government source, October 2007.

4 http://www.jeffreydonaldson.org/Why.asp

5 Interview with DUP source, September 2007.

6 Interview with David Trimble, September 2007.

7 *Irish Times*, 1 December 2003.

8 *Irish Times*, 3 February 2004.

9 Channel Four television, *The Big Heist*, 22 September 2005.

10 *Belfast News Letter*, 26 June 2004.

11 *Irish Times*, 24 August 2005.

12 *Irish Times*, 2 September 2004.

13 Interview with Irish government source, September 2007.

14 Interview with a DUP source, September 2007.

15 Peter Robinson, speech marking his reselection as East Belfast DUP Westminster candidate, 12 November 2004 in http://cain.ulst.ac.uk/events/peace/soc.htm

16 Interview with Irish government source, October 2007.

17 Interview with Irish government source, September 2007.

18 Interview with DUP source, September 2007.

19 Interview with DUP source, September 2007.

20 Interview with DUP source, September 2007.

21 Interview with DUP source, September 2007.

22 Speech by Bertie Ahern to the Philosophical Society, TCD, 8 November 2004.

23 Interview with former US Government official, August 2007.

24 Interview with Irish government source, October 2007.

25 Interview with Irish government source, November 2004.

26 Ian Paisley, speech to North Antrim DUP Association, 27 November 2004 in http://cain.ulst.ac.uk/events/peace/soc.htm

27 Statement by Gerry Adams, 8 December 2004.

28 IRA statement, 9 December 2004.

29 Proposals by the British and Irish Governments for a Comprehensive Agreement, 8 December 2004.

30 Interview with Irish government source, October 2007.

31 RTE Radio, *This Week*, 9 January 2005.

32 Interview with Irish government source, October 2007.

33 Interview with Irish government source, November 2007.

34 Proposals by the British and Irish Governments for a Comprehensive Agreement, 8 December 2004.

35 E-mail from DUP source, November 2007.

36 Mary Alice C. Clancy, "The United States and Post-Agreement Northern Ireland, 2001–2006", *Irish Studies in International Affairs*, Vol. 18, p. 165.

37 Interview with David Trimble, September 2007.

38 Interviews with Irish government and US sources, August/September 2007.

39 *Irish Times*, 29 July 2005.

40 Interview with DUP source, September 2007.

41 Interview with former US official.

42 *New York Observer*, 19 August 2003.

43 Interview with former US official, August 2007.

44 Interview with former US official, August 2007.

45 Interview with former US official, August 2007.

46 *Irish Times*, 24 February 2005.

47 *Irish Times*, 28 February 2005.

48 Interview with Bob McCartney, September 2007.

49 Interview with Bob McCartney, September 2007.

50 DUP manifesto, May 2005.

51 Interview with Irish government source, November 2007.

52 Confidential information, August 2007.

53 Confidential information, August 2007.

54 *Irish Times*, 13 May 2006.

55 "Making History or History Made", speech by Ian Paisley, Portrush, 12 July 2006, in http://cain.ulst.ac.uk/issues/politics/docs/dup/ip120706.htm

CHAPTER FIFTEEN

1 *The Guardian*, 22 June 2007.

2 Interview with DUP source, September 2007.

3 Interview with Irish government source, October 2007.

4 *The Guardian*, 14 March 2007.

5 Interview with DUP source, September 2007.

6 Interview with DUP source, September 2007.

7 Interview with DUP source, September 2007.

8 Interview with DUP source, September 2007.

9 Interview with DUP source, September 2007.

10 Interview with DUP source, September 2007.

11 Interview with DUP source, September 2007.

12 Interview with DUP source, September 2007.

13 *Belfast Telegraph*, 9 June 2007.

14 Interview with DUP source, September 2007.

15 Interview with DUP source, September 2007.

16 Interview with Clifford Smyth, September 2007.

17 Interview with DUP source, September 2007.

18 Interview with DUP source, September 2007.

19 Interview with Irish government source, November 2007.

20 Interview with Irish government source, September 2007.

21 Interview with DUP source, September 2007.

22 Interview with DUP source, September 2007.

23 Interview with DUP source, September 2007.

24 Interview with DUP source, September 2007.

25 Interview with DUP source, September 2007.

26 Interview with Irish government source, October 2007.

27 Interview with Irish government source, September 2007.

28 Interview with Irish government source, September 2007.

29 *Belfast Telegraph*, 5 April 2007.

30 Interview with Irish government source, September 2007.

31 Interview with Irish government source, October 2007.

32 Interview with Irish government source, November 2007.

33 Interview with Irish government source, November 2007.

34 *Your Verdict – What Is It To Be?* DUP, October 2006.

35 BBC, *Hearts and Minds*, 9 November 2006.

36 Interview with Irish government source, October 2007.

37 Interview with DUP source, September 2007.

38 Interview with Irish government source, October 2007.

39 Jim Allister Press Release, 17 November 2006.

40 Interview with DUP source, September 2007.

41 Interview with Dr Sidney Elliott, September 2007.

42 Interview with Irish government source, October 2007.

43 Interview with David Trimble, September 2007.

44 Interview with Sir Reg Empey, September 2007.

45 *The Guardian*, 1 March 2007.

46 DUP Manifesto, 2007 Assembly election.

47 Thirteenth Report of the Independent Monitoring Commission, 30 January 2007.

48 *Irish Times*, 21 February 2007.

49 *Irish Times*, 16 January 2007.

50 *Hansard (House of Commons Daily Debates)*, 27 March 2007, http://www.publications.parliament.uk/pa/cm/cmhansrd.htm

51 Interview with DUP source, September 2007.

52 Interview with DUP source, September 2007.

53 *Sunday Times*, 1 April 2007.

54 Interview with DUP source, September 2007.

55 Interview with Clifford Smyth, September 2007.

56 Interview with DUP source, September 2007.

57 Interview with DUP source, September 2007.

58 *The Irish Times*, 31 March 2007.

59 Interview with Clifford Smyth, September 2007.

60 Interview with Irish Government source, October 2007.

61 Interview with Irish Government source, October 2007.

CHAPTER SIXTEEN

1 Steve Bruce, *Paisley: Religion and Politics in Northern Ireland*, OUP, Oxford, 2007, *Appendix*.

2 Steve Bruce.

3 Interview with Free Presbyterian source, September 2007.

4 Interview with Free Presbyterian source, September 2007.

5 Steve Bruce.

6 *The Revivalist*, January 1998.

7 Interview with Bob McCartney, September 2007.

8 BBC NI Newsline, 23 November 2006.

9 Interview with Free Presbyterian source, September 2007.

10 *Irish Times*, 31 May 2007.

11 *The Burning Bush*, May 2007.

12 *The Burning Bush*, June 2007.

13 Interview with Free Presbyterian Church source, November 2007.

14 Interview with Free Presbyterian Church source, September 2007.

15 Interview with Free Presbyterian Church source, November 2007.

16 UTV Live, 18 April 2007.

17 Interview with Free Presbyterian Church source, November 2007.

18 Interview with Free Presbyterian Church source, November 2007.

19 Interview with Free Presbyterian Church source, September 2007.

20 *The Revivalist*, May 2007.

21 Interview with former DUP member, September 2007.

22 Interview with Free Presbyterian Church source, September 2007.

23 *Portadown Times*, 13 July 2007.

24 Interview with Free Presbyterian Church source, September 2007.

25 Interview with Free Presbyterian Church source, September 2007.

26 Interview with Free Presbyterian Church source, November 2007.

27 *Belfast News Letter*, 10 September 2007.

28 Hansard, 27 March 2007.

29 *Belfast News Letter*, 18 July 2007.

30 Interview with DUP/Free Presbyterian source, September 2007.

31 Steve Bruce.

32 Interview with former DUP source, September 2007.

CONCLUSION

1 Hansard, 27 March 2007.

2 Ulster Television, 17 April 2007.

3 *The Sunday Tribune*, 28 October 2007.

4 *The Times*, 23 October 2007.

5 BBC NI News, 27 October 2007.

6 *Irish Times*, 13 November 2007.

7 House of Lords Hansard, 12 November 2007.

8 *Observer*, 7 October 2007.

9 *Belfast Telegraph*, 21 November 2007.

10 Interview with Clifford Smyth, September 2007.

11 *Belfast Telegraph*, 9 August 2007.

12 Official report of the NI Assembly, 11 June 2007.

13 Official report of the NI Assembly, 18 September 2007.

14 Official report of the NI Assembly, 10 September 2007.

15 Interview with DUP source, September 2007.

16 Interview with DUP source, September 2007.

17 Ulster Television, 6 November 2007.

BIBLIOGRAPHY

Akenson, D.H., *Education and Enmity: The Control of Schooling in Northern Ireland 1920–1950*, David & Charles, 1973.

Bardon, Jonathan, *Belfast: An Illustrated History,* Blackstaff Press, 1982.

Barkley, John M., *A Short History of the Presbyterian Church in Ireland*, Presbyterian Church in Ireland, 1959.

Barrington, Ruth and Cooney, John, *Inside the EEC*, O'Brien Press, 1984.

Bell, J. Bowyer, *The Secret Army: the IRA, 1916-1979*, The Academy Press, 1970.

Bestic, Alan, *Praise the Lord and Pass the Contribution*, Cassell, 1971.

Bew, Paul and Gillespie, Gordon, *Northern Ireland: A Chronology of the Troubles, 1968–1999*, Gill and Macmillan, 1999.

Bew, Paul, *The Making and Remaking of the Good Friday Agreement*, The Liffey Press, 2007.

Bew, Paul, *Ireland: The Politics of Enmity, 1789–2006*, Oxford University Press, 2007.

Blanshard, Paul, *The Irish and Catholic Power*, Greenwood Press, 1953.

Bloomfield, Kenneth, *A Tragedy of Errors: The Government and Misgovernment of Northern Ireland*, Liverpool University Press, 2007.

Boulton, David, *The UVF: 1966–1973*, Torc Books, 1973.

Boyd, Andrew, *Holy War in Belfast: A History of the Troubles in Northern Ireland*, Grove Press, 1969.

Brown, Terence, *Ireland: A Social and Cultural History, 1922–2002*, Harper Perennial, 2004.

Browne, Vincent (ed.), *The Magill Book of Irish Politics*, Magill Publications Ltd., 1981.

Bruce, Steve, *Paisley: Religion and Politics in Northern Ireland*, Oxford University Press, 2007.

Buckland, Patrick, *A History of Northern Ireland*, Gill and Macmillan, 1981.

Buckland, Patrick, *The Factory of Grievances: Devolved Government in Northern Ireland 1921–1939*, Gill and Macmillan, 1979.

Budge, Ian and O'Leary, Cornelius, *Belfast: Approach to Crisis, A Study of Belfast Politics 1613–1970*, Macmillan, 1973.

Campbell, Alastair, *The Blair Years: The Alastair Campbell Diaries*, Alfred A. Knopf, 2007.

Coogan, Tim Pat, *Ireland Since the Rising*, Pall Mall, 1966.

Coogan, Tim Pat, *The Irish: A Personal View*, Phaidon, 1975.

de Paor, Liam, *Divided Ulster*, Penguin, 1970.

de Paor, Liam, *Portrait of Ireland*, Rainbow, 1986.

Deutsch, Richard and Magowan, Vivien, *Northern Ireland 1968–73: A Chronology of Events*, Blackstaff Press, 1974.

Devlin, Bernadette, *The Price of My Soul*, Pan, 1969.

Dillon, Martin and Lehane, Denis, *Political Murder in Northern Ireland*, Penguin, 1973.

Elliott, Sidney and Flackes, W.D., *Northern Ireland: A Political Directory, 1968-1999*, Blackstaff Press, 1999.

Farrell, Michael, *Arming the Protestants: The Formation of the Ulster Special Constabulary and the Royal Ulster Constabulary 1920–1927*, Brandon, 1983.

Farrell, Michael, *Northern Ireland: The Orange State*, Pluto, 1976.

Fisk, Robert, *The Point of No Return: The Strike Which Broke the British in Ulster*, André Deutsch, 1975.

FitzGerald, Garret, *All in a Life: An Autobiography*, Gill and Macmillan, 1992.

Flackes, W.D., *Northern Ireland: A Political Directory 1968–1983*, BBC, 1980.

Fulton, Austin, *Biography of J. Ernest Davey*, Presbyterian Church in Ireland, 1970.

Godson, Dean, *Himself Alone: David Trimble and the Ordeal of Unionism*, HarperCollins, 2004.

Gray, Tony, *The Orange Order*, The Bodley Head, 1972.

Harbinson, John F., *The Ulster Unionist Party 1882–1973*, Blackstaff Press, 1973.

Heskin, Ken, *Northern Ireland: A Psychological Analysis*, Gill and Macmillan, 1980.

Holmes, Finlay, *Our Irish Presbyterian Heritage*, Presbyterian Church in Ireland, 1985.

Jones, Bob, *Cornbread and Caviar*, Bob Jones University Press, 1985.

Kelly, Henry, *How Stormont Fell*, Gill and Macmillan, 1972.

King, Cecil, *The Cecil King Diary 1970–1974*, Jonathan Cape, 1975.

Knight, Derrick, *Beyond the Pale: The Christian Political Fringe*, Kegan Paul, 1981.

Mallie, Eamon, and McKittrick, David, *The Fight for Peace: The Secret Story behind the Irish Peace Process*, Heinemann, 1996.

Marrinan, Patrick, *Paisley: Man of Wrath*, Anvil Books, 1973.

McBride, Paula J., *A Geographical Analysis of the Free Presbyterian Church 1951-78*, Unpublished dissertation, Department of Geography, The Queen's University of Belfast, 1978.

McCartney, Catherine, *Walls of Silence*, Gill and Macmillan, 2007.

McKittrick, David et al., *Lost Lives*, Mainstream Publishing, 1999.

Millar, David W., *Queen's Rebels: Ulster Loyalism in Historical Perspective*, Gill and Macmillan, 1978.

Millar, Frank, *David Trimble: Prince of Peace*, The Liffey Press, 2004.

Mitchell, George J., *Making Peace*, University of California Press, 1999.

Moloney, Ed, *A Secret History of the IRA*, Penguin, 2007.

Murphy, Dervla, *A Place Apart*, Penguin, 1978.

Nelson, Sarah, *Ulster's Uncertain Defenders*, Appletree Press, 1984.

O'Clery, Conor, *The Greening of the White House*, Gill and Macmillan, 1997.

O'Malley, Padraig, *The Uncivil Wars: Ireland Today*, Blackstaff Press, 1983.

O'Neill, Terence, *The Autobiography of Terence O'Neill*, Granada Publishing Ltd, 1972.

Patterson, Henry, *Class Conflict and Sectarianism: The Protestant Working Class and the Belfast Labour Movement 1868–1920*, Blackstaff Press, 1980.

Paulin, Tom, *Ireland and the English Crisis*, Bloodaxe Books, 1984.

Rees, Merlyn, *Northern Ireland: A Personal Perspective*, Methuen, 1985.

Smyth, Andrew Clifford, *The Ulster Democratic Unionist Party: A Case Study in Political and Religious Convergence*, Unpublished Ph.D thesis, The Queen's University of Belfast, 1983.

Stewart, A.T.Q., *The Narrow Ground: Aspects of Ulster 1609–1969*, Faber and Faber, 1977.

Stewart, A.T.Q, *The Ulster Crisis: Resistance to Home Rule 1912–1914*, Faber and Faber, 1967.

Sunday Times Insight Team, *Ulster*, Penguin, 1972.

Taylor, David Frank, *The Lord's Battle: An Ethnographic and Social Study of Paisleyism in Northern Ireland*, Unpublished Ph.D thesis, The Queen's University of Belfast, 1983.

Whyte, J.P.H., *Church and State in Modern Ireland*, Gill and Macmillan, 1971.

Winchester, Simon, *The Holy Terror: Reporting on the Ulster Troubles*, Faber and Faber, 1974.

Paisleyite Publications

Beggs, R.J., *Great is Thy Faithfulness*, Ballymena Free Presbyterian Church.

Calvert, David, *A Decade of the DUP*, Crown Publications, 1981.

Cooke, Ronald, *Ian Paisley: Protestant Protagonist Par Excellence*, Manahath Press, 1984.

McCrea, William and Porter, David, *In His Pathway: The Story of Rev William McCrea*, Marshall, Morgan and Scott, 1980.

Paisley, Ian R.K., *These Twenty-eight Years*, Martyrs' Memorial Productions, 1974.

Paisley, Ian R.K., *The Four Windows of My Life*, 1983.

Paisley, Ian R.K., *My Father and Mother*, Martyrs' Memorial Publications, 1973.

Paisley, Ian R.K., *Richard Cameron: The Lion of the Covenant*.

Paisley, Ian R.K., *God's Ultimatum to the Nation: The Ulster Problem* (Spring 1972), Bob Jones University Press, 1972.

Paisley, Ian R.K., *An Exposition of the Epistle to the Romans*, Martyrs' Memorial Free Presbyterian Church, 1968.

Paisley, Ian R.K., *Messages from the Prison Cell*, 1969.

Paisley, Ian R.K., *No Pope Here*, Martyrs' Memorial Publications, 1982.

Paisley, Ian R.K., *The Man and His Message*, Martyrs' Memorial Publications, 1976.

Paisley, Ian R.K., *Northern Ireland: What Is the Real Situation?* Bob Jones University Press, 1970.

Paisley, Ian R.K., *W.P. Nicholson: Tornado of the Pulpit*, Martyrs' Memorial Productions, 1982.

Paisley, Ian R.K., *The "Fifty Nine" Revival*, The Free Presbyterian Church of Ulster, 1958.

Paisley, Ian R.K., *This is My Life*, Tape Recordings, Martyrs' Memorial Productions, 1979.

Wilson, Sam, *The Carson Trail*, Crown Publications, 1981.

Ulster Democratic Unionist Party Yearbooks.

The Protestant Telegraph, 1966–1982 (Protestant Unionist/DUP newspaper).

The Revivalist, 1955–2007 (Free Presbyterian Church Magazine).

Voice of Ulster, 1982–1983 (DUP newspaper).

The Protestant Bluprint (Martyrs' Memorial news sheet).

The Burning Bush (Magazine, now website, produced by Rev Ivan Foster)

Pamphlets and Articles

Belfast Workers Research Unit, *Belfast Bulletin 8: The Churches in Northern Ireland*, Belfast, 1980.

Brown, Terence, *The Whole Protestant Community: The Making of a Historical Myth*, Field Day, 1985.

Clancy, Mary Alice C., "The United States and post-Agreement Northern Ireland, 2001–2006", *Irish Studies in International Affairs*, Vol. 18, p. 165.

Egan, Bowes and McCormack, Vincent, *Burntollet*, LRS Publishers, 1969.

Elliot, Sidney, *Northern Ireland: The First Election to the European Parliament*, The Queen's University of Belfast, 1980.

Smith, Peter, *Why Unionists Say No*, The Joint Unionist Working Party, 1986.

Wallis, Roy, Bruce, Steve and Taylor, David, *"No Surrender!" Paisleyism and the Politics of Ethnic Identity in Northern Ireland*, The Queen's University of Belfast, 1986.

Wright, Frank, "Protestant Ideology and Politics in Ulster", *European Journal of Sociology*, Vol. XIV, 1973, pp. 213–80.

Newspapers and Periodicals

The Belfast Telegraph

The Belfast News Letter

The Northern Whig

The Irish News

The Irish Times

The Irish Press

Irish Independent

The Ballymena Guardian

The Ballymena Observer

The Lurgan Mail

Loyalist News (John McKeague publication of the early 1970s)

The Portadown Times

The Independent

The New York Times

The Washington Post

The Greenville News

The New York Observer

The New York Sun

The Sunday Tribune

The Sunday Times

The Observer

INDEX